Michael Fellman

CITIZEN SHERMAN

A Life of William Tecumseh Sherman

UNIVERSITY PRESS OF KANSAS

MODERN WAR STUDIES

Theodore A. Wilson
General Editor

Raymond A. Callahan
J. Garry Clifford
Jacob W. Kipp
Jay Luvaas
Allan R. Millett
Dennis Showalter
Series Editors

Published by the University Press of Kansas (Lawrence, Kansas 66049), which was
organized by the Kansas Board of Regents and is operated and funded by Emporia State
University, Fort Hays State University, Kansas State University, Pittsburg State University,
the University of Kansas, and Wichita State University

Library of Congress Cataloging-in-Publication Data

Fellman, Michael
Citizen Sherman: a life of William Tecumseh Sherman / Michael Fellman.
p.   cm.
Includes bibliographical references and index.
ISBN 0-7006-0840-0
1. Sherman, William T. (William Tecumseh), 1820–1891.
2. Generals—United States—Biography. 3. United States. Army—
Biography. I. Title.
E467.1.S55F45   355'.0092—dc20   94-41087

Reprinted in 1997 by arrangement with Random House, Inc.

Printed in the United States of America

10   9   8   7   6   5   4   3   2   1

The paper used in this publication meets the minimum requirements of the American
National Standard for Permanence of Paper for Printed Library Materials Z39.48-1984.

For Santa

Preface

This book had its genesis many years ago when I read, in his 1875 memoirs, William T. Sherman describing his motivations for undertaking the "March to the Sea," which ravaged Georgia in the hot summer of 1864. "My aim then was to whip the rebels, to humble their pride, to follow them to their inmost recesses, and make them fear and dread us." For rage, ruthlessness, cold psychological calculation, and clarity of expression, no American military figure has equalled Sherman's statement.

After living with him for many years now, I am more convinced than when I began that Sherman's statement was utterly authentic. This was not merely powerful rhetoric, but deeply felt and intentionally expressed anger. This was a warrior, and his enemies knew it. My primary tasks are to understand the origins and shaping, both personal and cultural, of this man; to set his profoundly important Civil War leadership in emotional as well as in social, intellectual, and ideological contexts; and to place his military activities in the far broader webs of the experience of a long life, one that was tumultuous for all his seventy-one years and not merely for the four years of the Civil War.

As it happens, far more of this life can be recovered than is usually the case for historians. Sherman was voluble; in letters as in speech, he rarely kept his thoughts or feelings hidden. And because he was so famous, nearly everyone kept his letters, while archivists have solicited them eagerly ever since his death in 1891. Particularly rich are the family papers, where one can find the residue of a long and deeply stressful marriage. Sherman lived apart from Ellen Ewing Sherman for at least half of their marriage, and they wrote every three or four days, holding nothing back, particularly their angry feelings. In addition, Sherman corresponded with each of his children, and so one can retrieve the hopes and disappointments of Sherman as husband and as father of a big family. Beyond them, Sherman must have had one of the widest circles of friends and acquaintances of any public man of his time, and here too his letters document not merely his career but his expressive emotional life with a vast array of women as well as men.

Taking these sources together one can reconstruct not just a general but a man, a famous and furious man, in all the stages of an endlessly restless life, from humiliating youth and younger manhood, through personal transformation during the Civil War, to a later life lived in great fame. He was always vivid and dramatic, self-absorbed and gregarious, depressed and elated, opinionated and fearful, searching and bigoted, repellent and charming. And his was a life that made an important impact on American history; his values, both military and social, made a difference.

This book studies the origins of Sherman's rage, its applications and complex moral meanings. It also examines the building of a mid–nineteenth-century man's life, private and public together, personal characteristics expressed in social and antisocial activities, the general in the citizen, the American as a man of war.

WRITING SEEMS a solitary activity, but it is also social, and I wish here to acknowledge many institutions and friends who have helped me along the way. The Social Sciences and Humanities Council of Canada provided a major grant, which speeded completion of the research for this book. For the year 1992–93, I was fortunate to receive a Marta Sutton Weeks Senior Research Fellowship at the Stanford Humanities Center. I am most grateful to Wanda Corn, director of the Center; to Charles Junkerman, associate director; and to Susan Sebbard, Sue Dambrau, and Margaret Seligson, for many acts of thoughtfulness, not the least of which was the use of a beautiful and appropriately Victorian office. The Huntington Library also made me a fellow during my period of research, for which I owe special thanks to Martin Ridge. Deans Robert C. Brown and Evan Alderson of Simon Fraser University provided timely aid in many ways. James Dobbie and Scott Perchall were energetic and attentive research assistants.

My fellow fellows at the Stanford Humanities Center, especially Marleen Rozemond, Stephanie Lysyk, Theodore Andersson, Roland Greene, Colin Palmer, Lyman Van Slyke, and Harry Harootunian, were boon companions who heard far more about General William T. Sherman than they could possibly have anticipated. Much the same can be said of several colleagues in the History Department at Simon Fraser, notably Hannah Gay, Andrea Tone, Paul Dutton, Richard K. Debo, and Ian Dyck.

Several friends generously took the time to read my work. Leon Litwack and Charles Junkerman read portions, while Stephanie Cole, Christopher Morris, Rick Henderson, and Edward C. Coffman read the whole manuscript, much to my edification. As always Robert H. Wiebe gave me the kind of brilliant analysis that first took my breath away and then put me back to work. My persuasive and tactful agent, Bella Pomer, opened the right doors. At Random House, my legendary editor, Robert D. Loomis, gave me the benefit of his good cheer and thoughtfulness as well as that of his very sharp pencil. My two sons, Joshua and Eli, have not read a word of this book yet, but they encouraged me in many more important ways. My father, David Fellman, my late mother, Sara Dinion Fellman, and my sister, Laura Fellman, supported me in this project, as they always have. Finally, my wife, Santa Aloi, listened to the first draft of this book with her artist's eye and ear. For this, and far more for all the caring and loving, I dedicate this book to her.

—Vancouver, British Columbia
March 6, 1995

Contents

Part I

HUMILIATION

1

Rosebud: A Truncated Patrimony

NORMALLY THE MOST GARRULOUS and self-revelatory of men, William Tecumseh Sherman had curiously little to say about his boyhood. Indeed, in his *Memoirs,* published in 1875, the fifty-five-year-old autobiographer opens his story in 1846, when he was already well launched in his career as a first lieutenant of Company G, Third Artillery, United States Army, stationed at Fort Moultrie, South Carolina, from where he soon was to be reassigned to California.[1]

Looking back at his younger self from the perspective of 1875, when he was still commanding general of the army and a man of immense military fame, it was as if it had been the ambitious young officer who had given birth to the triumphant general. In his private correspondence too, Sherman, who reviewed the smallest as well as the largest events of his life over and over, almost never alluded to his boyhood, and when he did so, his habit was simply to insist that he had been a normal, fun-loving, mildly roughhousing sort of boy living comfortably among his mates. Evidence from others suggests that this affirmative boy had existed, but that this was a far-from-complete picture.

In 1887, by then retired from the army, Sherman entered a more reflective and reconciliatory phase of his life. It was at this point that he first commented in print on his childhood, in a chapter added to the second edition of his *Memoirs.* The two interconnected stories he finally told about his past in Lancaster, Ohio, were an intensely con-

densed public testimony to the severe pain he had experienced as a
child. Both stories recalled his early feelings for his father, Charles,
who had been a circuit-riding Ohio State Supreme Court justice.

"My memory extends back to about 1827," the aging Sherman told
his readers, "and I recall him, returning home on horseback, when [my
brothers and I] used to run and contend for the privilege of riding his
horse from the front door back to the stable. On one occasion, I was
the first, and being mounted rode to the stable." To this point, this
is the story of the seven-year-old Tecumseh triumphantly wresting his
father's horse, perhaps for the first time, from the grasp of his two big
brothers, twelve and sixteen years old, and then riding high and proud
on his father's mount. However, Sherman continued, " 'Old Dick' was
impatient because the stable-door was not opened promptly, so he
started for the barn of our neighbor Mr. King; there, also, no one was
waiting to open the gate, and, after a reasonable time, 'Dick' started
back for home somewhat in a hurry, and threw me among a pile of
stones . . . where I was picked up apparently a dead boy; but my time
was not yet, and I recovered, though the scars remain to this day."

"The year 1829 was a sad one to our family," Sherman went on,
skipping silently over the two intervening years of his life and launching immediately into his second childhood story. By then, Sherman's
two older brothers had left home, Charles for university in Athens,
Ohio, and James for a clerking job in a store in Cincinnati. Little
Tecumseh, at nine years old the eldest of eight children remaining at
home, was therefore the "man of the house" when his father was off
riding the judicial circuit, as he was frequently. In these circumstances,
the sad news came. Jane Sturgeon, a neighbor girl, came to school one
day, "called us [Sherman children] out, and when we reached home all
was lamentation," for father was "ill unto death" at Lebanon, a town
one hundred miles distant from Lancaster. Sherman's mother raced off
by carriage, but soon turned back, after she learned en route of her
husband's death, on the sixth day of his illness. Later in life Sherman
had established, he wrote in a detached and scientific manner, that in
1829, as there had been no Asiatic cholera epidemic, typhoid had been
the probable cause of his father's death.

The death of Charles Sherman left the widow and her eleven children "very poor," Sherman wrote in his second *Memoirs,* and "with
the exception of the three youngest children, the rest of us were scat-

tered. I fell to the charge of the Hon. Thomas Ewing, who took me to his family, and ever after treated me as his own son."

Sherman condensed his life from age nine to sixteen even more briefly, and presented it in a flat narrative. He had had excellent teachers at school, and "we made good progress. . . . Time passed with us as with boys generally." In 1834, young Sherman got his first job, as a part-time surveyor for the Ohio Canal. In 1836, at sixteen, he went off to West Point. End of childhood and of youthful recollections.[2]

Losing the continuity of parents and home, the traumatized boy had in no way chosen his subsequent fate. As he recounted to his readers in passive voice, he "fell to the charge" of Thomas Ewing; he was called out of school, told of his father's death, and thrust from home and mother into a neighboring family. His statement that Thomas Ewing took him in and treated him as his own son was, as we shall see, a formulaic insistence of Sherman the adult who thus covered over disturbing memories.

Fear of betrayal and abandonment, bouts of depression, and diffuse and frequently explosive rage characterized the adult Sherman. But when one searches for direct evidence of the wounding caused by his early childhood losses, these two brief, grief-laden stories are all Sherman would ever admit in print. One should not draw automatic conclusions about the effects of even the most frightening of childhood experiences. In this case, given many of the same childhood events, Sherman's younger brother, John, the future senator, turned out to be a deeply reserved, carefully controlled, cold, and conventional adult. But Tecumseh would act with fury, fear, hurt, and longing, which must have been connected to his experience of truncated patrimony.

THOMAS EWING, a huge, somber, and imposing man, was a wealthy and influential lawyer who, in 1831, went to the United States Senate as a conservative Whig. His family lived two houses up Main Street in Lancaster from their close friends, the Shermans. When Charles Sherman died in 1829, leaving his family impoverished, Ewing selected Tecumseh (nicknamed "Cump") to take into his home as his ward, while others of the Sherman children went to various other friends and relatives. Ewing never legally adopted Tecumseh, evidently out of consideration for Sherman's mother, Elizabeth.

In 1865, when General Sherman had attained his enormous fame, Ewing recounted in a letter to his daughter, Ellen, the story, by now a kind of family legend, of the manner in which he had selected little Tecumseh from the Sherman litter. "I want one of them," he wrote Ellen that he had said to Elizabeth in 1829. "You must give me the brightest of the lot, and I will make a man of him." "Take Cump, the red-haired one," Elizabeth supposedly replied, bypassing Charles and James, her older boys, "he's the smartest."³

Soon after the Ewings took in Tecumseh, they baptized him in the Roman Catholic Church, adding what they considered to be a proper Christian first name. (Charles Sherman had named his third son in honor of Tecumseh, a powerful Indian chieftain who had been killed in the war of 1812, and who was remembered with admiration as well as with fear by the white settlers of the Great Lakes region.) In the Ewing family legend, one day in 1827 or 1828, Maria Ewing, Thomas's wife, had had Tecumseh baptized as William Tecumseh, at the insistence of the itinerant priest doing the baptism, who thought it unacceptable for a white boy to be named after a pagan Indian savage. As it was St. William's day, June 25, the priest picked that name.⁴ Nevertheless, the boyhood nickname of "Cump" stuck to the lad, who had never chosen William. Nor, despite the baptism, had he ever chosen to be a Roman Catholic; indeed he resisted such a conversion to the religion of his quasi-adoptive home in a most strenuous manner, one that would have lifelong consequences.

Although Thomas Ewing and William Tecumseh Sherman both insisted, after Sherman had become famous in the Civil War, that the little boy had instantly become integrated into the Ewing household as a son among sons and daughters, letters written by both of them when Cump had been growing up indicate that this had not been the case. In 1831, shortly after he went off to Washington to enter the Senate, Thomas Ewing wrote a paternalistic letter of instruction on child rearing to his wife. Following some general advice concerning development of the reading skills of all the children, Ewing added, "And there is Cumpy too—he is disposed to be bashful, not quite at home. Endeavor to inspire him with confidence and make him feel one of the family."⁵ Two and a half years after the lad had entered the Ewing household, his stepfather sensed he was still not quite at home with the Ewings. In his bashfulness and lack of self-confidence, the little boy appeared to remain at the edge of the family, somewhat silent, lonely, and withdrawn.

In the first letter he ever wrote to his stepfather, whom he addressed as "Dear Sir," nine-year-old Cump confessed he "did not know any news from town [as] I do not go into town very often." He also told Ewing, concerning two of his stepbrothers, "tell Tommy and Boyd that they must not forget me and I will not forget them."[6] This fear of renewed loss should not come as a surprise from a boy who had so recently "lost" his natural brothers and sisters to the four winds, lost his father literally and his mother functionally. In what family could he place basic trust? Was he a Ewing or was he not?

In letters written to Ewing during his adolescence, Sherman expressed considerable ambivalence toward his stepfather and his partially adoptive family. In 1836, Ewing obtained an appointment to West Point for his stepson without consulting him beforehand. In a letter of May 5, 1836, formally signed "your most obedient servant," Sherman responded to Ewing's letter of May 1 in which Ewing had scolded the boy for not reporting on his travel preparations to West Point. "Had I delayed [action] till now," Sherman wrote, "justly would I have deserved your reprobation, but to show that I attended to it faithfully I will state now what I did from the time of the appointment until now."[7] Sherman then narrated all the appropriate and dutiful steps he had taken. But it was clear he did not like being forced to account for himself to his stepfather, who had imposed a career choice on him, about which he remained uncertain.

After he arrived at West Point, Sherman continued to express both esteem and an only partly concealed anger to his stepparents. As the first West Point winter closed in, the sixteen-year-old plebe wrote to his stepmother, whom he addressed as "Mrs. Ewing," "It has been a long while since I wrote to you, but it is still longer since you have written to me. Therefore I expect an immediate answer to this." He went on to ask for money for gloves and earmuffs. "You may think it strange that I should ask for money, but in reality I would be the last person that would ask for it unless it were absolutely necessary, but you yourself know that it would by no means be comfortable to walk post in the open air with a cold gun and thin gloves."[8] Sherman was lonely and cold and broke. He did not know how he stood on money matters with his stepmother, who he feared would find his request inappropriate, but he also had nowhere else to turn. He was also typically adolescent in his assertion of independence even while demonstrating continued dependency. He addressed his tentativeness by appealing to his stepmother not in her maternal role but on grounds of fellow feeling—one sufferer from the cold to another.

Sherman would always find it difficult to cope with these sorts of confused feelings for his stepparents. Writing to his stepsister, Ellen, from West Point in 1839, he paired gratitude with remoteness, warmth with estrangement, in a manner demonstrating the unnaturalness he felt toward his second family. Referring to his stepsister's strictures about what she perceived as his filial ingratitude, Sherman replied, "You certainly misunderstand me with regard to *your* mother. Although I should feel highly honored did she condescend to notice me, still, I am fully aware how slight are my claims to her regard and how many troubles and cares she must experience since you . . . have left home. . . . Very often I feel my insignificance and inability to repay the many kindnesses and favors received at her hands and those of *her* family." Sherman continued to his stepsister, "Time and absence serve to strengthen the claims and to increase my affection and love and gratitude to those who took me early under their care and conferred the same advantages as they did upon their own children." This genuine, if stiff, gratitude, this expression of a love he ought to feel was intended for his stepmother and stepsister's family, not for a family he could simply claim as his own.

Although this distance was natural enough, it did make Sherman feel marginalized and hurt, as well as eager to please. He told his stepsister he was aware that he rarely articulated his loving feelings; he did not admit to her, nor to himself, that he was unsure, if not incapable of those feelings. "Although I have rarely spoken of it still I assure you that I have always felt sincerely and deeply grateful, and hope that some event may occur to test it." Duty and sacrifice would demonstrate his actual loving feelings, Sherman hoped. An outward manifestation would be the best means to demonstrate his feelings to her family and to himself. "Indeed I often feel that your father and mother have usurped the place which nature has allotted to parents alone and that their children those of brothers and sisters."[9] Sherman could not let himself become fully a Ewing son (an unlikely possibility in any event, given what he felt to be the remoteness of the Ewings), at least in part because he feared that to become so would be to betray his natal

Sherman family. The dilemma presented by his double childhood would prove unresolvable. He would always have one foot in and one foot out of the Ewing family, be poised for both flight and return.

In 1844, five years after writing this contradictory letter to his stepsister, the twenty-four-year-old Sherman, now an artillery lieutenant stationed near Charleston, South Carolina, wrote to his stepfather, beginning as he would to a military superior, "Sir," and closing, "I am yr ob sevt, W. T. Sherman." "It has been a very long while since I have addressed you by letter, for the simple reason that I believed I had nothing of interest to send or business to submit." (It had been four years in fact.) After this perfunctory opening, Sherman continued, "now however after reflection I have concluded to trouble you with a little of my experience, and to do so the more readily as it does not concern me personally but one for whom you must feel the greatest interest, *your own son* H[ugh] B. Ewing." Hugh had confided his desire to enter the military to Sherman, who in this letter was passing along the information, telling Thomas Ewing that he would be pleased to smooth Hugh's path at West Point were he to enter, though he thought the army would be a mistake for Hugh.[10] How conscious Sherman was of his hostility in this letter is impossible to determine.

Not that we should blame Thomas Ewing, a formal and cold man, for not accepting Sherman as a son among sons. In fact, he may have been just as aloof to his natural sons, and he did spend rather a lot of effort over the years to support this oddly needy and ever dissatisfied young man with funds and offers of work. What is significant here is that Sherman felt personally shunted aside, personally excluded from what he imagined to be Ewing's stance to *his own* sons. The subjective hurt in this letter is central, whatever a more evenhanded assessment of Sherman's standing among the Ewings might suggest.

Three months later, in a much friendlier letter addressed to "My dear Friend" Hugh, Sherman expressed his relief that Hugh seemed unlikely to obtain an appointment to West Point after all. As for himself, Sherman wrote, although there were few junior officers who had received "more rapid advancement or higher marks of favor" than had he during his first three years of service, "yet believe me, I have often regretted that your father did not actually instead of sending me to West Point, set me at some useful trade or business." Sherman was expressing a feeling he often had, one widely shared in the nineteenth-century American middle class, that the peacetime army was an almost shameful backwater, and that commercial life was the seat of action for real men. Sherman went on to admonish Ewing's "real" son: "Make up your mind to study whatever profession your father may desire you and follow his wishes as near as you can till you are called upon to act for yourself."[11] Not just for Hugh did Sherman express confused understandings of personal autonomy and familial attachment.

Compared to his other personal correspondence, most of Sherman's letters to Thomas Ewing during his young manhood were written from a chilly distance. The nearest approach to warmth with Ewing came in their exchanges about Sherman's debt-ridden mother, Elizabeth. While making their careers, Sherman and his brothers undertook to pay off Elizabeth's debts in Lancaster, and to move her to Mansfield, a task that took fifteen years. Sherman's share of the load was $200 per year, about 15 percent of his salary. To this effort Thomas Ewing contributed his considerable legal talents, his moral support, and perhaps some financial assistance. For this Lieutenant Sherman was grateful. At one point in 1845, he wrote to Ewing, signing the letter, "your sincere and obliged friend." "Again I thank you for your valuable interest in her welfare, and will be a thousand times obliged if you will complete what we have begun—rescue Mother's property from impending danger."[12] In their joint undertaking of rescuing his mother, Sherman felt more on a plane of equality with Ewing than he did in his role as subordinate stepson. To redeem the Sherman name, he was, in concert with his brothers and aided by Thomas Ewing, acting as a rescuer of a weak and dependent woman, a role that gave him a sense of long-term purpose, solidity, and strength.

For the remainder of Ewing's life, Sherman would continue to admire his distant stepfather and to resent him, while he often served him by attending to some of Ewing's far-flung real estate interests, on which he would report to Ewing in great and careful detail, pridefully showing fealty through duty rather than through affection. For many years the only major form of correspondence initiated by Sherman was when he would detail his business and career losses to Ewing, often accompanied by requests for money and expressions of fear that he could not maintain his independence, his distance from Ohio and from the Ewing sphere. Ewing would always send the money, but he would never be able to reassure his stepson, whose emotional needs remained utterly bewildering to him.

Sherman would also continue to express his resentment, at least obliquely, when he repeatedly refused to return to Lancaster or to work directly for Ewing. In Lancaster he was nothing, he would insist repeatedly to his stepsister, Ellen, while in the army, abroad in the world, he was making his own way. However, his army career presented problems of its own, and more generally he frequently failed in his efforts to become his own man, which frustrated him and filled him with self-loathing. And as if his often broken career would not present enough problems for him, on May Day 1850, after a prolonged engagement, he would marry his stepsister, Ellen Ewing, and thus Thomas Ewing, the distant stepfather, whom Ellen adored, would become his father-in-law as well. Coming from a tragically torn family, entering incompletely a second one, Sherman's confusions about marriage and parenthood would be lifelong.

2

In the Army: A Dead-end Career

OVERCOMING his initial homesickness and suppressing his shame that his stepparents seemed not to really care about him, Sherman spread his wings at West Point, discovering that he could both excel and fit into a military society. He proved to be a first-rate student, and he also had a lot of fun.

During the antebellum years, the American Military Academy offered what was probably the most rigorous civil engineering program in the United States, producing many of those bridge builders and railroad builders who proved so successful both fighting the Civil War and during the nineteenth-century peacetime revolution of the transportation network. West Point also inculcated a quasi-aristocratic set of hidebound values about honor—political, religious, and moral—that were quite at variance with the rough-and-tumble ethics current in American political and economic life. Indeed, recognizing and detesting the elitist qualities of West Point, Congress frequently threatened to curtail or destroy it. Only the military model of George Washington, and the knowledge that Americans had twice gone to war to secure the nation and might need to do so again, stopped antigovernmental, antielitist politicians from acting on their bias against West Point. Knowing all this, cadets like Sherman clung to the belief that when needed they would prove to be the detached and superior military leaders who alone could preserve the nation in times of her direst need.[1]

Adept at mathematics and sciences, Sherman was even more delighted that he led his peers in drawing, a talent he had not even known he had. He wrote his stepbrother, Phil Ewing, "I flourish as usual with regard to drawing, which is an entirely new thing."[2] Surviving sketches show that Sherman was taught primarily to copy prints and plaster casts of Greek and Roman martial statuary, but he also drew landscapes in the realistic mode, with more clarity than inspiration. Whatever his limits, his horizons had broadened, and all his life he would enjoy art and artists, and even more, actors and the theater. From late adolescence, he resisted the reductionist image of himself as merely a military man or engineer, though he also frequently asserted that, in addition to his artistic flair, he had a scientific grasp of the material realities that were the building blocks making up the natural world of men and events.

Sherman's teachers recognized his considerable intellectual abilities. Academically, he graduated in 1840 third in his class of forty-three (of those left from the 115 who had entered four years earlier). However, once demerits for misbehavior were calculated into the final standings, Sherman dropped to sixth place. The aging memoir writer of 1887 tells us, with a certain covert pride, that he had failed only in "neatness in dress and form," and in "strict conformity to the rules."[3] He had been a fine student, but no toadying conformist: He had been too high-spirited to become transformed into a systematized cipher.

Intense ebullience marked Sherman's years as a military apprentice. Doubtless the self-confidence that came from doing so well in his studies contributed to this mood. But, in addition, comfortable with his peers, happy in his newfound independence and sense of vocation, Sherman relished good times outside the classroom. Regular studies at West Point were dull rote learning; discipline was often overbearing and arbitrary (Sherman was arrested one night for going to the hospital to get a tooth extracted without permission); the food was monotonous and execrable (boiled potatoes, boiled meat, boiled pudding, bread, and coffee). Therefore, good times consisted in large part of subverting the routines, a speciality of adolescent males then as now, which was especially necessary to this set of young men undergoing a severely disciplined and bounded education, so unlike that experienced by their peers in other colleges or in the world of commerce.[4] Most cadets are "fine fellows up to any kind of devilment or fun which must occasionally be resorted to as the only relief after our arduous duties and studies," the seventeen-year-old Sherman wrote to Phil, the step-brother to whom he was closest.[5] Often the devilment consisted of sneaking off in the evening with one's mates to the nearby tavern, Benny Havens, to eat and drink, the joy of which was multiplied by the risk of expulsion should one be caught.[6]

The most common single form of brotherly subversion consisted of surreptitiously cadging food from the dreaded mess hall and cooking it up in a stew over the fire in one of the cadets' rooms. By all reports, Sherman was a prized chef of these stolen meals. In 1838, William Ewing wrote home to Phil about their stepbrother, "Cump is standing by me with his coat open and his shirt sleeves rolled up, smashing potatoes like a fine fellow, and there is every appearance of our soon having what we consider a glorious hash." These secret meals created a kind of subversive fraternity in which Sherman was the admired leader. "A dozen of us [stood] around the pot," William Ewing wrote, "with one knife which we all used by turn."[7]

To counter the dull routine of the academic year, West Point commandants themselves had long since institutionalized periodic diversions for the cadets. Chief among these was the summer encampment, when the cadets left the classroom, pitched tents, and invited in family and other visitors for an elaborate series of ceremonies. Although some of the cadets considered the encampment an ordeal, Sherman found it highly romantic. He wrote glowingly to his then-stepsister, Ellen, in August 1839, "The Ball was a grand affair, in a large fine [wall tent], the walls decorated with wreaths of laurel and cedar, crossed swords, sabres, and bayonets, and the flags of nearly all the nations of the world. From the ceiling hung a great number of elegant . . . chandeliers, and when with ladies and officers both naval and military in their uniforms it presented the most dazzling and brilliant appearance I ever beheld. The crowd of ladies and gentlemen" visiting were attracted in particular to "what most accorded with my taste," Sherman wrote, "the 'Stag' dance," on the parade ground illuminated by the lighted tents where the cadets "assembled to dance a figure, similar to what we in the West term a country dance, only that each one can shuffle and cut up as much as he pleases, provided he goes through the figures."[8] At West Point, groups of cadets could delight innocently in the dance figures they cut with other men, some as male lead, some in the woman's role, a pre-Freudian practice that lasted as late as the 1940s.

Sherman clearly relished joining such an exhibition, just as in later life he would adore dancing with the ladies.

The second institutionalized break in routine offered cadets was a furlough granted after two years of study and drill. "The third class are feeding on the anticipations of a fine furlough," Sherman wrote Phil Ewing in April of his second year at the academy, "the good dinners they shall enjoy the fine figures they shall cut and a great many of them, upon the balls, dances parties etc they shall attend—in a word they expect all kinds of pleasures and not one of pain." Food, parties, and girls were much on Sherman's mind, as he anticipated his vacation in the world of pleasures denied the cadets at their austere academy. In the same letter he went on to tell Phil, "I have it on good authority that you have become a perfect male coquet," and after naming four girls, asked, "Guilty? or not guilty?" Doubtless, Sherman was anticipating making every effort to duplicate or surpass his stepbrother's record.[9]

During his furlough, Sherman visited relatives in Brooklyn Heights, where, on July 4, he strolled to Castle Gardens for the evening fireworks, "which were quite splendid," Sherman wrote Phil. "But what astonished me most was to meet A[braham] Pitcher formerly of Lancaster with a great big whore (I expect) on his arm. He left her and came up and spoke to me but I left him as soon as common politeness would admit of." Sherman was rather shocked by this accidental meeting with a brazen man who, Sherman knew, had deserted his family back in Ohio. But the incident was also part of the erotic tinge in his letters about his furlough in the urban pleasure dome, both as he anticipated the vacation and as it transpired. He did not report directly, however, on whatever pleasures of the flesh he took himself.[10]

Sherman excelled at West Point, and he believed that his talents were appropriately rewarded. He was independent, away from Lancaster and the Ewings and the painful ambivalence his childhood aroused in him. He had gained focus and direction. He was at the start of a career that he considered significant and that would pay him a regular salary he would use to support not only himself but his destitute mother. It was a career that seemed to promise both order and a certain amount of glitter, and, if there were war, glory and renown.

Sherman even felt a kind of relief that he had avoided the extreme competitiveness of the outside world of business. Learning that his younger brother, John, had decided to study law, and admitting that "it would be rather impertinent for me to object" to John's choice, Lieutenant Sherman added that "for my part, it would be my last choice. Everybody studies law nowadays, and to be a lawyer without being exceedingly eminent—which it is to be hoped you will be some day—is not a sufficient equivalent for their risks and immense study and labor."[11] Sherman, who a few years later would read law books while posted at remote military stations, was expressing to his brother the snobbery of the officer caste to a nonmember, and he was also projecting onto John his own fears of the chaotic marketplace of mid–nineteenth-century America.

The new officer's first military experience came during his initial assignment, to Fort Pierce, Florida, where he participated for nearly two years in the small-scale but dreadful guerrilla war against the Seminole Indians. In this conflict, Sherman found much pain and precious little glory.

Five months after arriving at Fort Pierce, in another letter to John, Sherman wrote a prescient general analysis of the long American war against the Indians, in which he placed the Seminole phase. This fight in particular and the larger struggle over many decades were bound to be inglorious, sporadic, and endlessly repeated. "A treaty for the removal is formed by a few [Indian chiefs] who represent themselves as the whole; the time comes, and none present themselves. The government orders force to be used; the troops in the territory commence, but are so few that they all get massacred. The cowardly [white] inhabitants, instead of rallying, desert their homes and sound the alarm—call for assistance. An army supposed to be strong enough is sent, seeks and encounters the enemy at a place selected by the latter, gets a few hundred killed. The Indians retreat, scatter, and are safe. This may be repeated *ad infinitum*."[12]

During the daily grind of guerrilla war, Sherman most often remained at Fort Pierce while others went into the swamps to attack Indian villages. Sherman reported a typical raid by Lieutenant Ware and sixty men in a letter to Phil Ewing. Ware had captured a lone Indian while he was fishing and forced him to guide the American troops back to his village, where, the next dawn, "the soldiers rushed upon the unconscious Indians—captured 23 and killed 6 women & a baby & a child—here they found a good many rifles." The soldiers then torched the village. At another village, Ware's men captured fifty-five, all but twenty of whom were women and children, and killed eight Indians whose ages and gender Sherman did not mention.[13] These were typical operations.

Sherman reported such raids with no sense of revulsion or censure, in large part because he, like his compatriots, citizens and soldiers alike, assumed Indians were pagans, savages, remnants of an earlier stage of humanity who were to be destroyed in the natural course of events. Given the opportunity, Sherman believed, the savage Indian would always kill the civilized white, and so turnabout was fair play. At one point, Sherman wrote to Phil Ewing about interviewing a captive warrior named Wild Cat [Cooacoochee], who told Sherman "boastfully" that when his war party had captured six white men and a Negro after their ship had been wrecked on Cape Canaveral, they had beaten their brains out, Wild Cat taking the occasion to "initiate his boy" upon a handsome young white youth, urging his young son to finish him off, "as a free lesson in manhood."[14]

A second example of Indian inhumanity was their apparent lack of normal human reactions. Of one party of thirty-four captives, Sherman wrote to John, "I wish you could see the group in its savage state; although many have lost their husbands and fathers and wives and children, yet they show no grief. Several are very badly wounded; one little girl, with a ball through the back and coming out in the cheek, scarce utters a murmur; another woman, a buckshot through and through, bears it with the fortitude of a veteran soldier." Almost despite himself, Sherman evinced a sense that even these "savages," who responded to loss in subhuman silence, had noble human qualities too. In some ways he recognized the courage of these mortally wounded women—they were, he felt, nearly as brave as white soldiers after all. White women who had lost family members or who were painfully wounded would presumably wail and weep, and so these were not properly civilized women, but they still had human capacities. Sherman continued to be fully ambivalent in another letter, when he praised as admirable the Seminole "qualities" that had allowed them "to maintain the country this long," though adding that "these qualities had been chiefly cunning and perfidy." Sherman could also be contradictory—even guilty—about the morality of a militarily superior society attacking such an outnumbered and hapless people. "You doubtless little sympathize with us in hunting and harassing a poor set of people," he wrote John.[15]

Nevertheless, in the same letter that included his remorse about Indian hunting, Sherman added, "I, of course, regretted very much not having been along, but consoled myself with the idea that I'll have a chance yet."[16] Sherman was twenty-one and a soldier. This was his first war, and he wanted to see action. Despite the pathos and brutality that he observed his comrades inflicting mainly on old men, women, and children, Sherman was eager to participate, to experience blooding, to shoot his "man," as had Cooacoochee and his son.

Sherman's moment approximating glory came by luck when he simply rode into Wild Cat's camp, and noting that the Indians' arms were stacked against a tree, clapped the few warriors present in irons. But this task was so easy and unfulfilling that Sherman concluded, "It is absurd any longer to call [this] a war."[17]

Far more typical of such warfare was extreme boredom, discomfort, and feckless pursuit. Most of the time was spent hanging listlessly around Fort Pierce. Taking to the field, that is to say the swamps, was at least as tedious in another way. During 1841, Sherman wrote Phil of two typical scouting missions. On the first he took nineteen men in small boats on a four-day expedition to what was reported to be a main Seminole camp, only to find it and all the others en route deserted. On a second patrol, his party took "six about as disagreeable days as one would wish to spend" rowing thirty miles each day without finding any of the enemy. "The sky would pour down his burning rays" followed by a "tremendous storm wetting everything," and then at night "we have to sleep with swarms of mosquitos ready to eat the very life of one, to avoid which we had to wrap ourselves in our dirty and wet blankets." This was "just about . . . as much as a Christian could well bear."[18]

Sherman's initiation into Indian war was far from what he must have expected. Indians would probably be his enemies throughout his career, and he already had learned that this form of warfare was morally unworthy. The passage of the years allowed Sherman to render memories of his first Indian war more poetically. Writing nearly fifty years later, his recollection was that "Those excursions [against the Seminoles] possessed for us a peculiar charm for the fragrance of the air, the abundance of game and fish, and just enough adventure, gave to life a relish." Fragrant air, fish, and adventure had not appeared in his reports from Florida during the war, while mosquitoes, rain, and frustration were forgotten in the memoirs nearly five decades later.[19]

If the war against the Seminoles proved appalling to the young officer, subsequent peacetime stations nearly crushed him with the boredom of perpetual routine and sloth. For four years, 1842–46, Sherman was posted to Fort Moultrie, near Charleston, South Carolina, where the triviality of army life was compounded for him by the idle lives of the Charleston nabobs among whom he moved socially when he was off duty. In 1843, he wrote to John, "I presume you have heard from home that I am in existence, and to tell the truth that is all I could have said about myself." In retrospect, even the miserable Seminole war had been engaging. His current posting was "almost devoid of interest." He described his entire daily routine to John. "Up at reveille, attend a drill . . . breakfast at 7, have a dress parade at 8 & half an hour after the new guard takes place of the old." The "work" for the day was done at 8:30 A.M. "After that each one kills time to suit himself till reveille commences the new routine—we have nothing to do but amuse ourselves—some read, some write, some loaf and some go to the city." Sherman did all of those, and he also hiked and rode the countryside, hunted deer, and took to painting landscapes with some passion.

He also partied a great deal with Southern bloods for whom he felt basic Yankee contempt. They were a motley collection of the "worthless sons of broke down, proud Carolina families, [who] boast of (they know not what) their state, their aristocracy, their age, their patriarchal chivalry and glory—all trash." Social pretensions concealed shabby realities for these braggarts themselves, but they didn't fool him. "No people in America are so poor in reality, no people so poorly provided with the comforts of life." Sherman never had reason to change his resentful, contemptuous picture of South Carolina's would-be aristocracy; he would attack them with unbridled energy during his tour through the state in 1865, at least in part because of what he concluded about them during his residency among them in the 1840s.[20]

The lower reaches of the Carolinian white populace appeared as strange to Sherman as did the self-styled aristocracy. One day he watched a total immersion baptism such as he had never seen in sedate Lancaster, Ohio. "I have just been out to the suburbs of the village to see a girl dipped," he wrote to Hugh Ewing. "The water was pleasantly cool. She sneezed and coughed as was her bounden duty and looked very much more like a sailors mop than a sensible Christian."[21] Truly this was an odd collection of white folks, doubtlessly incapable of the discipline and attainments of the progressive Yankee culture in which he had been bred.

Sherman barely referred to black slavery, the economic foundation of the South Carolina gentry, and gave no hint that the institution shocked him or that he found it wrong or even questionable morally. On the contrary, he once remarked, in passing, that the general poverty of the state and the premature decay of the pretended aristocracy stemmed from the fact that "many plantations have been wasted and blighted under the care and tillage of lowly irresponsible negros." Turning the land over to Negroes had led to the South's ruination; such a choice both demonstrated and deepened Southern white decadence in Sherman's eyes.[22]

Though bored, at least Sherman was making his own way. After avoiding writing to his stepfather during his first four years of service, a demonstration to them both of his assertion of independence, Sherman finally did write that letter concerning Hugh Ewing's proposed entry at West Point. Thomas Ewing's reply, Sherman wrote to Ellen Ewing in 1844, had been "very kind," but had finished by urging Sherman to study for "Civil Life." Sherman had thought his stepfather had accepted his position as a military officer, which, after all, he had forced upon the young man. "He knows my perfect dependence," Sherman wrote Ellen, "and that were I to resign, I would have to depend upon someone till I could establish myself in the practice of some profession." Any thought of loss of autonomy filled him with anxiety. "I shall never depend upon anybody, nay, not even were he a brother. . . . I have now studied for the military profession and hold a place envied by thousands and for which hundreds of the best young men of their country toil every year. It would be madness at this late date to commence something new."[23] Sherman was protesting very loudly. Four months later, he was reading Blackstone, the English jurist, so his ambivalence about continuing in the service seems clear. Pressured by his brother, John, as well as by his stepfather, to leave the army, bored by the realities of military life, disgusted by his taste of Indian warfare, yet proud of his independence and his professional skills, he was not yet ready to decide on a break with the life he had entered as an adolescent near-orphan boy. And then in 1846, the United States went to war against Mexico, and Sherman believed he would have his chance to demonstrate his profession and his manhood on the field of honor.[24]

After President James K. Polk eagerly maneuvered the United States into the war against Mexico, which was declared in May 1846, expeditionary forces were organized, quickly and chaotically, mostly on the southwestern frontier. Sherman, however, was pulled from his regiment, which soon was sent to Mexico. With a heavy shipload of troops, officers, arms, and equipment, to avoid difficult overland transshipment in Nicaragua, he sailed the long way around Cape Horn to California, leaving New York on July 24, 1846, and arriving at Monterey only the following January 27. Before Sherman's ship even departed, American settlers in California had broken away from Mexico, and so his regiment became an army of occupation and annexation, opposed only by the sullen anger of the few thousand local Mexicans. While victorious action raged in Mexico during 1847 and 1848, while young American officers made their fame and their careers, Sherman was forced to sit out the war in remote garrison duty, tearing out his hair in frustration.

Sherman felt cut off, even exiled, both from home and its comforts—an enormous sea voyage away—and from what he knew ought to have been "his" war. After spending nearly eleven months in what was to him a desperate circumstance, he slipped into the first of what would prove a lifelong series of depressions. On November 10, 1847, he wrote back to Ellen Ewing in Lancaster, "I am so completely banished that I feel I am losing all hope, all elasticity of spirit. I feel ten years older than I did when I sailed, and though my health is good I do not feel the desire for exercise I formerly did." Most likely these symptoms were accompanied, as they were in later episodes, by sleeplessness, loss of appetite, and bouts of recurring asthma. Sherman knew there was no way to arrange a transfer to Mexico, and so now he could only stew and "make the best of a bad bargain," while his only contact with great events would be "to hear of the war . . . and the brilliant deeds of the army, of my own regiment and my own old associates everyone of whom has gained honors, and I am out here in California, banished from fame [and] from everything that is dear."[25]

As the war climaxed in a series of American triumphs, about which Sherman was hearing and reading in melodramatic journalistic detail, his frustration and shame mounted. On February 3, 1848, when the war was nearing its end, he wrote to Ellen Ewing, "there is nothing new here, no stirring events, no hair-breadth escapes, red battles, no storming parties, no nothing, and this war will pass and I will have to blush and say I have not heard a hostile shot." For him there would be no war, no mortal risk, no glory, no proof of manly steel. "This may be a pleasing considering for you, for women," he wrote Ellen, "but we who build our only hopes of distinction and fame upon the chances of war cannot but feel very different." Sherman then tried to call up the stoic spirit to still his unhappiness. "Still it cannot be helped and I must grin and bear it till opportunity may bring about what my own eager desire for action . . . aspires me of."

A part of Sherman, which was both sensible and filled with envy, wanted to believe that this had been an ignoble war, not for the political reasons that had led to so much antiwar sentiment in the United States, but because the enemy was so weak and pathetic. "Since poor Mexico is without an army, it is but little glorious to carry on war against her people, her children, without arms and without subsistence."[26] In this discussion Sherman may have exaggerated somewhat, as the Mexican army was large and some of its best officers were trained in Europe. Yet the ranks were poor, illiterate peasants whose morale tended to fall apart in combat, which gave some credence to Sherman's beliefs.

Sherman's detached military analysis and his stoicism only went a little way to counter the deep anguish he felt in his banishment from the seat of action. Although on an intellectual level he was well aware that circumstances were out of his control and that he just had had bad luck, at a deeper emotional level Sherman blamed himself for missing the war. At the end of the conflict he wrote Ellen Ewing, merging all these confused levels of thought and emotion. "I have felt tempted to send my resignation to Washington as I really feel ashamed to wear epaulettes after having passed through a war without smelling gunpowder, but God knows I couldn't help it and so I'll let things pass."[27] There was no manifest reason for Sherman to feel ashamed, but his missing the war—preparation for which was the whole point of his young career—underlined the worthlessness he had felt both while chasing Indians through the Florida swamps and while twiddling his thumbs in South Carolina. This giant anticlimax, where there ought to have been a glorious reward, was just too unfair. Did God know about that? Could Sherman show his shamed face to those he loved, from whom he was so distant, and to his now-renowned brother officers, when he would meet them one day back home? Such obsessive brooding marked nearly all of Sherman's letters.

Sherman also vented his frustrated martial feelings by expressing an urgent desire to take them out on the local Mexicans he saw every day in California. "The state of feeling of the Mexican people towards the

Yankees is of such a hostile character that peace cannot last long. They want and deserve richly a better whipping than they have got and they will have to receive it before they are content." Sherman, the avenger, did not expect anyone of Ellen Ewing's gender to understand or share in such sentiments. "You of course are horrified at anything like war, but you cannot understand anything like too obstinate pride, egotism and nonsense that characterize them as a people."[28]

Sherman did not lose control of his behavior, whatever were his punishing fantasies. Indeed, though he blurted out that the Mexicans both wanted and deserved a whipping, which they "will have to receive," his demand for their punishment was phrased in a way that guarded against a completely explicit avowal that he, Sherman, would be pleased to whip them, and that he would do it right then and there.[29] Sherman truncated even verbal expressions of anger toward the Mexicans, swallowing them in a way that would compound his self-loathing and depression rather than bring him relief. Although he had no way of knowing it, he would have another chance at war thirteen years later, another opportunity to gain glory by striking out against the foe in licensed anger. But that was not now evident in any way to this banished warrior, and his subsequent life before that as-yet-unimaginable Civil War would be marred by the kind of shame he now was feeling.

Now, much of his frustrating duty consisted of policing Mexicans. In common with members of all armies of occupation, Sherman and his comrades believed themselves forerunners of a superior culture. To Sherman, the core of the inferiority of Mexican culture was located in what he believed to be its indifference to material progress: "the truth is, simply, that all Mexicans attempt to arrive at the state of their forefathers," he wrote Ellen. The paradigmatic example of this cultural lassitude was their failure to make bricks and build fireplaces in the new land of California as they had not needed to do so farther south in Mexico. "Those living in a warm country had no fire-places and thus concluded that none were needed here, and if you were to transplant a Mexican from his native city to Canada he would not think of warming his house by artificial heat."

Sherman took his cultural antipathy out on Mexican men in particular: Their supposed laziness partially accounted for their military losses, losses that demonstrated, in the circularity endemic to racialist contempt, their laziness. "They do not love us, they do not like our ways, our institutions, our restlessness. Our internal taxes, our labors are all too complicated for their brains, and lazy hands. All they want is a *bueno cavallo* (good horse), a lasso, a glazed hat and tassels, a flashy serepa, slashed pantaloons tipped with velvet and corded with bright silk ties, . . . a pair of spurs as big as a plate, [and a] greasy platter of beans and mutton." These were the attributes of greedy, materialistic, exhibitionist, dirty children. Their "greasy" food (and Sherman would have heard other Anglo-Saxons call the Mexicans "greasers"), connoted uncleanness, even self-soiling—a characteristic of subhumans in all racialist imagery, who lack sufficient civilization even to keep themselves clean. This "race" of men clearly was fit for cultural marginalization or even elimination by the new conquerors of the superior race, by American men like Sherman who knew how to heat houses, work hard, apply their intelligence to material progress, dress modestly and eat tidily—the list of "civilized" values he was implying when he constructed his lengthy list of inferior Mexican qualities.

If Mexican men were fit for destruction, Mexican women—treated by their own men as abused "servants" according to Sherman, in yet another proof of the inferiority of Mexican culture—were curiously attractive as well as backward, and were objects for potential rescue and implicit assimilation. Less than completely white or civilized, they were far better than Indian "squaws," who fell beneath the cultural pale altogether and thus were not fit objects for personal or cultural uplift by the American gentleman. Compared to Mexican men, Sherman wrote Ellen Ewing, "the women are better, kinder, and more industrious."[30] Sherman had learned that in their own eyes, whiter was better for Mexican women at least as much as it was for Americans, and at times he dismissed this belief as pretentious vanity on the part of a basically ignorant and illiterate "race" of women. "The women are like all Spanish women, the prouder the more Castillian blood they can boast of. Some are pretty, all dance and walk well, but scorn the vulgar accomplishments of reading and writing."[31] If backward in many ways, these women nevertheless had some fine and ladylike qualities, which would even be recognized as such in the cultural metropolis of Lancaster, Ohio. During the summer of 1848, Sherman lived in the home of Doña Augustias, whom he described to Ellen Ewing as "the very first lady of . . . all of California," and her "pretty little daughter Mannelita." He considered this grand lady to be "very kind and intelligent." Her husband, who must have been a fool, did not live with his family, as should a proper husband, but "passes most of his time on his rancho about forty miles off so that I am a species of guardian to the family. I have not been so comfortably situated for a long time."[32] To Sherman, the picture he was painting was of a worthwhile and respectable woman, and so he felt easy telling his fiancée back home about the situation. While living with Doña Augustias as her "guardian," he was in his own mind demonstrating his superior gentlemanly nature by uplifting her from the limits insensitively imposed on her by Mexican male culture. Anglo-Saxon American gentlemen like Sherman knew how to treat women as ladies. Doña Augustias, who embodied the very best element of Mexican culture, might be worthy of cooptation rather than destruction. Potentially at least there was something in this project for men like Sherman. While he was in Florida, Sherman had never fantasized about rescuing Seminole women, and the most his fellow military officers would do would be to make "squaws" their mistresses, never their wives, a perfectly acceptable solution for sexually inclined conquering males toward any "inferior race."

In 1860, in a letter to Hugh Ewing, the stepbrother who had begun to develop a reputation for wildness that Sherman envied, and in whom he confided some personal longings, Sherman made an oblique reference to his free life in California, which had included traveling about "and fetching up occasionally at Doña Augustias," which suggests that Sherman might have taken care of his more worldly needs at this grand doña's house, despite the care with which he had presented her as utterly respectable in his letters to Ellen. He had admitted only to living with Doña Augustias, but perhaps the cohabitation had not been as incomplete as he had pictured it.[33] Such a love affair or even a subsequent marriage would not have been inconceivable in Sherman's time had the lady been high-born enough, and indeed just such marriages provided the foundation of several elite California families. However, the obverse—marriage of a well-bred Anglo woman to a Mexican male—would have been inconceivable. The potential for "whitening by marriage" of a Mexican woman and a white American man—which sociologists call hypergamy—was the soft edge of cultural contempt.[34]

But then one day gold was discovered near Sacramento, thousands of Americans poured in, the faint possibility of a gradual Mexican-American cultural blending was shoved aside, and Sherman's role shifted from being a member of an army of occupation to being a policeman among the greedy hustlers at the mines. He was appalled at the effects gold fever had on the economy and on morality, but he also was fascinated.

At once gold was discovered, inflation skyrocketed, and men deserted their daily routines to try for their main chance. This panic of migration struck the army directly and immediately. "Every [soldier] can get immediate employment, can go to the mines and can earn more than a Colonel's pay," Sherman wrote a military superior in August 1848. "Our regular soldiers have mostly deserted . . . and as to apprehending deserters, it is now out of the question. We have not the power, and the mines are so wide spread that the devil himself could not find one."[35]

Deserting soldiers were joining men from everywhere in the mad rush. "Monterey is now nearly deserted of male population," Sherman wrote that August, "and the same may be said of San Francisco and other towns. All are gone to the gold fields."[36] Normal urban activities had ceased: "a tailor wont work, nor a shoemaker," Sherman wrote John. "The sailors desert their ships as fast as they come to the coast." Indeed there was insufficient crew left to man ships needed to take the gold back east. The scum of the earth were moving in, in Sherman's opinion, filling the country "with the hardest kind of a population of deserters and foreigners." Common laborers could get $15 per day, as opposed to the normal dollar a day; any man could earn $25 a day at the mines. Coarse shoes went for $10; a blanket costing $1 or $2 in New York would fetch $50. Every worker stole gold from his employer. "No less a personage than the Governor has to cook his own breakfast. . . . Even the ragged Indians are on their knees worshipping the common idol." This social dissolution frightened Sherman. With "no troops and no civil power," California was in a state of incipient breakdown. "A government of some kind must exist here soon, or the devil will be to pay." In this legal vacuum, vigilante justice soon blossomed, a form of self-regulation rather admired by later generations of historians, but abhorred by men like Sherman as mob rule. Thus Sherman viewed in the raw not just ragged Indians or greasy Mexicans but Anglo-Americans of his own ilk, and he shuddered at their violent tendencies toward anarchy.[37]

Despite being shaken by what he observed in others during the gold rush, Sherman also participated in it, to his considerable profit. In October 1848, Sherman and two other junior officers became silent partners in a store near the gold fields, each realizing, within months, a profit of $1,500 on a $500 investment (the profit about equalling Sherman's annual military salary). During the winter and spring of 1848–49, encouraged by their commander, Sherman and the same two colleagues hired themselves out as surveyors, using a skill they had learned at West Point. Sherman earned at least $6,000 for two months of labor. (Sometimes they took their pay in Sacramento city lots, and then quickly turned them over for additional profits.) By late 1849, having seized his main chance, second class, Sherman had accumulated rather a lot of cash, several choice lots in San Francisco, and part of a large ranch on the Cosumnes River in the Sacramento Valley.[38]

Sherman failed to notice the contradiction between his negative moral view of the mad dash speculations of others and how he himself was behaving. To the contrary, he resented others, formerly his peers, who now were capitalizing even more efficiently than he, accumulating far larger fortunes even more quickly. Writing to a military superior, in April 1849, shortly after receiving news that his name had been bypassed in the latest round of army promotions, Sherman moaned that some officers had gained promotion inside the army, and others, even enlisted men who had deserted their posts, had profited enormously, while he, who had stood by his duty, had decayed in place. "I am compelled to remain here to my utter ruin and degradation," Sherman wrote in high self-pity, ignoring his considerable speculative success, "performing duties of a rank higher than my own, upon a subaltern's pay—Therein my pay here would not employ a servant. . . . I can believe you can appreciate the feelings of one, who by bad luck in coming to California, has worked down hill, whilst my former equals and subordinates have leaped over my head."[39]

Sherman seethed with envy, resentment, and grievance, thereby demonstrating yet another form of corruption caused by gold fever. He had made a small fortune, but others had done even better, and this relative impoverishment multiplied the frustrations he had long felt in his career choice, in which he now believed himself unjustly stymied in terms of advancement. Only so many chances came by, and he really was not well positioned, in his opinion, to grab that opportunity when it came. That he had been passed over several times already was a bad omen for his chances in the future.

As did many others in the peacetime army, the frustrated Sherman spent a lot of time and malignant energy in petty feuds with fellow officers. In January 1849, for example, Sherman quarreled with Lieutenant Henry W. Halleck, a young officer with whom he would have a long shared history. On January 27, 1849, Sherman wrote to Colonel R. B. Mason, their commander, asking, "Would you be kind enough to write on this slip of paper—which of the two, Lieut Halleck or Sherman, first communicated to you the fact that they were not on 'speaking terms.'" Below, Mason endorsed the letter, "In a conversation which arose on the 25th inst., Lt. Halleck mentioned that Lt. Sherman and himself had not been on speaking terms for some time; that was the first I ever heard of the existence of any unkind feeling between these gentlemen." Sherman pounced on Mason's reply, and sent it triumphantly to Halleck, as proof that it was Halleck who had first squealed to Mason. "I shall expect you to acknowledge this simple fact," he wrote Halleck, pushing him to fess up to breaking one of the cardinal rules of honor among American boys, against tattling to superiors. Halleck and Sherman appeared to have worked out their quarrel, where many others escalated into duels, but Sherman had demonstrated that prickliness and readiness to take offense, which were so characteristic of young military men. The dark side of honor, which in wartime produced revenge vented on the enemy, was in peacetime the uselessly destructive, and frequently self-destructive, institution of the feud. Martial impulses, trained up and then suppressed, sought outlets.[40]

Sherman bided his time for another year, and then was ordered back east. He left California in January 1850, to marry Ellen Ewing, following their long courtship through the mails. Although he stayed in the army for three more years, fundamentally he had already made his decision to leave it and to strike out directly into the world of commercial riches. He remained fearful of leaving the security of his military career, but he also felt bottled up, angered, and, in some fundamental way, defeated by it. Indian war held no real glory, the peacetime army was an extremely boring career carried out on the whole in cultural backwaters, his salary was meager in comparison to the wealth awaiting entrepreneurs, he resided far from the comforts of home, and, worst of all, he had missed his opportunity at war making, and did not anticipate a second chance.

3

Marriage Triangle

SHERMAN'S ISOLATION in California had been literal as well as psychological. In early March 1849, he received a packet of letters from Ohio and points east. It was the first time he had heard from Ellen or any of the home folks in a full year. Ellen expressed her unhappiness at Sherman's great distance, and this made his feelings that he had to get out of California, the locale of his loneliness and his defeat, all the more urgent. "I cannot describe my feelings at your sad letters," he wrote to Ellen on March 5, 1849. "I must come home to see you this year and will make every sacrifice to accomplish it." Ellen was his talisman of continued home amid the shreds of his career and his shattered self-esteem. "Though my hopes in life are all destroyed, my love for you has never abated, never waned in the least and upon it you may constantly rely."[1]

Sherman was almost never this affirmative and openly loving during his long courtship with Ellen, which dated back to his days in South Carolina in 1843. She was more often warmer than he, but most of her letters were distant and doubting. As would be their marriage, their courtship was marked by longer periods apart than together. Sometimes this served to heighten their romantic feelings, as in this instance, when they had been separated physically for three years, and had shared no correspondence for a year. More often than not, separation gave them both space and time to brood and question, doubt, argue, and blame.

Little eroticism tinges this correspondence—in part reflecting social conventions that led to self-censorship and silent censorship by literary heirs—in part reflecting a lack of physical passion between them. In common with many Victorians when writing their beloved, Sherman was frequently passionate in correspondence to other women later in his life.[2] But this woman was, after all, his stepsister as well as his fiancée, and the erotic confusion that conundrum contained served to limit expressiveness. Sherman had moved into the Ewing home when he was nine and Ellen was four. Ellen had been only eleven when Sherman had left home for West Point at sixteen, and their distance had allowed them to revise their feelings for one another toward that of potential lovers; yet when they were together, particularly in Lancaster, in the Ewing home, older familial issues would reemerge. Still, of course, "near-incest" (or whatever it was between them), upon which they both reflected in their courtship letters, was strange and enticing.

There is one letter, written to Ellen in 1841, when the twenty-one-year-old lieutenant was chasing Seminoles in Florida, two years prior to their marital understanding, that shows him fantasizing about her in a symbolically erotic manner. He wrote her that he had bought a real Indian pony, and added, "if I ever have the pleasure to come home the first thing I will expect of you will be to mount the wildest horse and charge over the hills and plains. Next to drawing it is the most ladylike accomplishment in my mind."[3] In this fantasy, he was playing both with erotic androgyny and with a desire that a real lady, even sweet little Ellen, would possess both the refinement of artistic pleasure and the wildness of a charge over the hills, bareback on a savage Indian's pony. From about this time, Sherman's stance toward Ellen began to shift toward that of an eligible man to a marriageable woman. They saw one another for a considerable period back in Lancaster in 1843, arriving at some kind of understanding as potential romantic partners.

Fewer of Ellen's letters remain than Sherman's from this period, but it is possible to reconstruct some of what she wrote from his replies. There was little overt romance, in a time when the mails were filled with sugar and spice between courting couples.[4] They addressed the issues of contention between them: religion repeatedly, career and money, autonomy and mutuality, the appropriate place to live, Ellen's health, Thomas Ewing, handling separation and living together. From the first tentative days of their courtship in 1842, through their marriage in 1850, and then continuing, often in twisted and transmuted ways, until Ellen's death in 1888, these two willful and contentious partners seemed to feed off animosity far more than affection or esteem.

For example, in a letter he wrote Ellen on November 19, 1845, from Fort Moultrie, South Carolina, Sherman acknowledged that Ellen might have reason to find his letters "cold." What was bothering him was her insistence, and that of her mother, that he ought to leave the army, when he was without other profession or prospects. "I stand well in my present profession, and have done all I can to be respected and esteemed, in that should you join me you should not have cause to regret it—but you seem to feel a prejudice to the army." She had disparaged his army career, and had balked at joining him in it after marriage, urging him to return to Lancaster. "Now Ellen think well about it," he warned her, concerned that she would not cleave to him during their marriage. "Think of the trials we may have to endure and the resolution I have made of never living in Ohio, or accepting ought of anyone there," he continued, meaning her rich father, Thomas Ewing, into whose pocket he could easily be swept, becoming that half-orphan, half-son to the Ewings once more. "I should delight to be near you for a long time yet I do not like to loaf around Lancaster with no one idle but myself and everybody thinking, there is a fellow who has nothing to do but spend his money."[5]

About six weeks later, Sherman drew back from this declaration of dominance, realizing that he may have scared or offended Ellen. "Since writing my last letter I have been really uneasy lest in it I may have used stronger language than necessary," he wrote. "So fearful am I that I may give wrong impressions that our future life may not be fulfilled [that I was] actuated by the most powerful motive so as to place myself that there would be no chance of disappointments." He had exposed his region of dread, which was literally a place—Lancaster ("Ewingville")—hoping that she could leave the confines of that place and come to him. "I trust you received it in that spirit as the evidence of an honest intention and not by way of opposition."[6]

In response, Ellen never agreed to drop everything, to leave Lancaster and security and the father she worshiped for the peripatetic and often rugged life of an army officer's wife. Neither did she refuse unconditionally ever to leave home. Nor did Sherman ever insist un-

equivocally that she do so as a condition of their marriage. These conflicts were deepened rather than eased or eliminated during their long
courtship. After marriage, Ellen Ewing Sherman never did break from
her natal home and Sherman never ceased wandering far away after an
honorable station, anywhere but in Lancaster.

The most powerful issue between them, however, was religion,
which Ellen saw as the core of her identity. Half-Irish, on her mother's
side, she was a pious, intense, and exclusionist Roman Catholic, while
Sherman, despite his Episcopalian family and his Catholic second family, in whose home and church he had been baptized, was a Jeffer-
sonian deist, a believer in ethics and civil religion. Early in 1842, in a
letter in which he again resisted her question, "why don't I leave the
army," he fended off her even stronger admonitions to search his heart
and convert to the true faith. "You speak so liberally and feelingly
upon the subject of religion," he wrote. He professed, "no particular
creed, believing firmly in the main doctrines of the Christian religion,
the purity of morals, the almost absolute necessity for its existence and
practice among all well regulated communities, to assure peace and
good will amongst all." The ethical content of organized Christianity
was fine; churches were not. "I cannot with due reflection, attribute to
minor points of doctrine or form the importance usually attached to
them," he asserted, referring to the highly ritualized forms of the
Roman Catholic service. "I believe in good works rather than faith,"
he continued, rejecting the inner religious spirit as well as its manifest
institutional forms, "and believe them to constitute the basis of true
religion, both as revealed in Scripture and taught by the experience of
all ages and common sense."[7]

Ellen could not accept even an iota of this liberal humanism, yet she
never baldly insisted that he convert to Roman Catholicism as a pre-
condition of marriage. In turn, during their courtship, Sherman never
refused religious dialogue. Just as she did not foreclose the possibility
of leaving Lancaster and joining him, neither did he categorically refuse all potentiality of conversion to her faith. They bargained toward
an equilibrium of approach and rejection, each to the other. In a letter
written in 1844, he expressed his "feelings of delight" that his inability
to convert to her faith did not seal his "doom" as a potential husband,
but rather, that he had, while still unconverted, "the assurance of your
love," and that she would settle for "a desire that I should examine
with an honest heart, and a wish to believe, if possible, the doctrine of

your church."⁸ It was a slender offer, one that matched hers when he asked her to leave her Ewing home for a Sherman tent.

In her first surviving letter to her beloved, written in 1844 at age nineteen, Ellen expressed her longing, her fantasy, that Sherman would accompany her to Rome, where "we will (or I at least) interrogate Catholics," so she could better "defy my protestant friends to taunt me with untruths" about supposed paganism and ignorance in Italy. She lived in an intense Catholic subculture in a society dominated by anti-Catholic Protestants. "But I must not scold you for what they say. . . . You are not one of them.—But yet when you become my protector," she continued, pressing conversion on him immediately after easing off, "how can you be sincere in your defense unless you *have proved* and *can prove* the truth of that which I claim to be true, pure and holy?" Ellen's faith was absolute, which differed in fundamental structure from Sherman's tolerant relativism. It would never be enough for her that he would support her in her faith; his soul would be in perpetual peril, and he would be less than fully her husband, unless he were to leave the heretical world behind and join her in the only true faith. "But . . . I must not tire you with too much upon the subject," she added, not wanting to drive him off but to attract him, "yet I must either write or speak my indignation at times."⁹

In her next surviving letter, written five years later, toward the end of their courtship after Sherman had been away for three years in California, Ellen expressed, rather clinically, her feelings about her shortcomings as a potential wife. She had had "a correct but not flattering likeness taken," which she had thought of sending him. But it showed her "not so young and pretty as I might be," so she had thought to withhold it. Neither did the photo demonstrate that she had "health sufficient to justify me in becoming your wife," she wrote, with allusion to a mysterious heart condition that she would insist she had for the rest of her long life. Her disease rendered her "incapable" of marriage. "You would afterwards reproach me with a want of all those qualities did I not thus betray them now." She was certain that rather than looking at her picture, he would prefer "looking upon some bright-eyed original near you." She, so shabby, was willing to cede his partnership in marriage and to revert to their preromantic bond, and so, in that half-light, she had decided to send on the likeness after all. Even if he were to go elsewhere for a wife, "mine will be to you still the likeness of a sister than whom no one could cherish for you a truer affection."¹⁰

Sisterly love was more spiritual than the carnal love of a wife, Ellen was implying rather broadly, and perhaps ought to displace it, given their original bond of stepbrother and stepsister. She wanted, with timidity and fear, to achieve a fully marital tie with him, but she felt barely qualified for the role. Her insistence on her supposed unattractiveness, on her advanced age (all of twenty-five), and her physical malaise were the means by which she articulated her fears of marriage, sex, and childbearing, and her sense that he—so high-spirited and worldly—and she—so timid and withdrawn—would prove incompatible emotionally.

Often she just wanted to disappear for him, just wanted to be the encouraging sister. "If you think that any of the girls of [California] capable of making a companion for you," meaning one of the Mexican women about whom he had been writing her, "do not let a thought of me prevent your marrying—I have always thought you ought to have a woman much my superior—handsome, of sprightly mind and character and withal of fine principles and strong affections. . . . You might marry a *young* girl and cultivate her mind and mould her character to suit you." Earlier in their courtship, Sherman had indicated his awareness that he was encouraging talk of marriage "with one whom I have so long loved as a sister," implying that they must shift from siblings to lovers.[11] She did not flow with passion, she insisted, nor surge with sexuality; neither was she young and malleable, nor of high spirits attuned to those of her bursting fiancé. Through her realism, which contained self-reproach and even self-pity, there also glimmered, however, broad hints of pride and self-worth—she was no nubile young thing; she had a will and a mental shape and a sense of place; she was a grown woman. Her lack of self-esteem contained the obverse quality. If you really want me, she challenged Sherman, you will have to take me as I am, without girlish illusions about myself, or, inferentially, about *you.*

Such mistrust of romance, searching self-presentation, and questioning of the inner qualities of the other were, in a sense, remnants of Puritanism in these two lovers. However, they also practiced romantic love in a more modern sense, alongside the sensible realism they had learned. After four years of separation, when Sherman strode back into Ellen's life, they merged with eager pleasure. As Sherman family legend has it, early in February 1850, Sherman showed up unexpectedly from California at the Ewing house in Washington, where Ellen was staying with her father, who at that point was the secretary of the interior. "Ellen was in the greenhouse" bathing her canary. "A bright patch of sunlight turned the red of her gown to ruby and whitened the snowy cuffs and collar. [She] caught the sound of his quick step—guessed who it was and sped quickly down the hall to be encircled in Sherman's arms." Right then, at Sherman's urging, the couple set their wedding for May Day.[12]

Before the wedding, Sherman went back to Ohio to visit his mother and his sisters and brothers. From there he wrote his betrothed with unaccustomed tenderness and a touch of gruffness, with some realism as to his own limits, and with paternalism, "I publicly assume the high trust of your Guardian & Master. I will not promise to be the kindest-hearted, loving man in the world, nor will I profess myself a Bluebeard, as there is a wide medium in which the happy world moves on, and so will profess contentment and joy. [Should] that love and mutual confidence which I trust we both deeply feel continue, we stand [a] fair chance for a slight share of worldly contentment and happiness." To her guardian and master, she should play, Sherman added, "my Adjutant & Chief Counsellor, and I'll show you how to steer clear of the real and imaginary troubles of the world. Only be contented, happy and place your proper trust in me."[13] Doubtless Ellen subscribed intellectually to the notion that she ought to be the chief and most valued subordinate to her guardian and master, and she would indeed prove to be his chief counselor. However, the prompting of her heart, and her behavior, would never demonstrate much submission.

In part because Thomas Ewing was in the federal cabinet, Sherman knew that the wedding would be full of pomp and ceremony. Professing to prefer simplicity, he grew quite excited about a major event that was being taken out of his hands and placed in a glittering public forum. For example, he invited his West Point chum, Lieutenant James A. Hardie, to come down from his post in Connecticut and stand up for him in the wedding. Thomas Ewing's fellow cabinet members and a few choice senators would attend, he told Hardie. The wedding "will be as unostentatious as is consistent with the position of the family." After a brief disclaimer that he had not wanted all this flash—"were I to consult my own tastes, I should dress as a Citizen"—nevertheless, "out of respect to the Service . . . I have concluded to its means and dictat as to marry in harness," meaning, "full [dress] uniform . . . with sabre, spurs etc complete."[14] Protestations of modest private values notwithstanding, Sherman was quite eager to don the public dress uniform and be wed before the elected heads of the nation and invited members of the press. If the Ewing family ensconced in Lancaster presented fundamental problems that repelled him, the Ewings of Washington and national standing highly attracted him. Marrying into the Ewing family would lend power and authority to his future career, whatever else it might bring.

President Zachary Taylor and his cabinet, Senators Henry Clay and Daniel Webster, the grand and doddering old men of American politics, and even the English envoy to Washington all showed up that May Day evening. Afterwards, the couple's honeymoon trip took them to New York City, West Point, and Ohio. During the summer, Sherman was posted to St. Louis, where he leased a house for the two of them. Almost immediately, when she was three months pregnant, Ellen returned to her parents' home in Lancaster, where, precisely nine months after her wedding night, she gave birth to her first child.[15]

Left on his own, in a strange new town, so soon after his marriage, Sherman felt bewildered and lonely. He walked frequently through the booming city, marveling at all the "wealth and improvement that would seem miraculous in any country save this," he wrote to Ellen. His fantasy was that he might persuade all the Ewings to relocate in St. Louis. "I cannot help thinking how your father can for one moment hesitate in leaving that insignificant town of Lancaster . . . and obtain [here] a [law] practice worth twenty times any amount of business in Ohio." St. Louis was the gateway to the West, the future, his kind of town; Lancaster was the sleepy small-town past. Even while writing this letter, however, Sherman sensed the faintness of his hopes that such a Ewing family transformation would come to pass. He did not write these reflections directly to Ewing. "I observe your father is easily dissuaded by obligations, and write you merely to use my influence with you."[16] Despite his keen desire to reunite with his wife by bringing her whole family with her to St. Louis, Sherman knew that Ellen would not attempt even to talk her father around, much less to succeed in the effort. The Ewings, who were deeply rooted in Lancaster for all sorts of political, business, and family reasons, had no reason to begin all over in a raw boomtown on the frontier.

In his next letter to Ellen, Sherman tried to entice her back to St. Louis with descriptions of nice quarters and charming companions, but he soon gave up this effort, gave up the rented house, and moved into a boardinghouse. He felt lonely, aimless, and frustrated with

Ellen's absence. He was at sixes and sevens about how to occupy himself. Thus far he had avoided, he wrote Ellen in October 1850, "theatres, billiard rooms, and bar rooms where so many loafers congregate to ask me to take a drink. In this course I know I have your sanction," he wrote Ellen, thus demonstrating that he was keeping clean and loyal by sacrificing pleasures on her behalf, while at the same time hinting at his temptations and his resentments.[17]

In December 1850, Sherman paid a quick visit to Lancaster. He was relieved by what he found, as he wrote in a gentlemanly letter to Ellen's brother, Hugh. Ellen "is detained by a cause common to married ladies and will not probably be able to join me till April. I found her in much better health than even last summer, so that it may be assumed that married life agrees with her."[18] If Ellen was blooming, he had not done her harm by impregnating her, whatever had been the fears for her health she had expressed to him throughout their courtship.

Maria Ewing Sherman, nicknamed Minnie, was born January 28, 1851, and a few weeks later Sherman returned to Lancaster to take mother and child back to St. Louis. All the Ewings seemed "very proud" of Minnie, Sherman wrote Hugh. "I cannot see that it is very different from other babies of the same age, and have come from St. Louis to take it back with me."[19] Sherman had had enough of female gush, but he was also proud as well as possessive. Presumably Ellen too would return with Minnie, but he had come to pick up *his* daughter and to whisk her back to *his* home.

Hearing that Sherman was taking Ellen and Minnie off before he would have a chance to see his granddaughter, Thomas Ewing, who had been held up in Washington by the prolonged congressional session, wrote Ellen, requesting that the Shermans delay their departure. After cooling his heels several days, Sherman insisted that they leave. Having asserted his authority over Ellen and Minnie against the will of her father, Sherman left behind a letter of apology for Thomas Ewing, seeking to explain, he told him, what "might be construed into a disregard for your known wishes. I want Ellen with me in St. Louis," he insisted, "and according to my expectations find her quite well and the baby equally so." The weather was good and the train connections were also far better on the departure day than they would be in later days. On this thin pretext, he was disregarding Ellen's "and her mother's solicitations" that they wait one day more for Ewing's arrival.[20] Ellen submitted to her husband's quite brutal affront to her father; the Shermans entrained for St. Louis. Sherman won this battle in the family struggle, and he may have believed at the time that this would mark a turning point in his relationship with Ellen and in his rivalry with Thomas Ewing, but he would lose many more rounds. Until her father's death in 1873, Ellen would spend more time in her natal home than she would with her husband.

Having succeeded in reuniting his family in St. Louis in another rented house, Captain Sherman (who had finally been promoted in 1850) soon grew restless with his moderate stability. For example, he began looking back at California, which on the whole he had loathed, with nostalgia. He wrote to Hugh, who was out there, that he could not "shake off" longing for "that wild roving life on mule back, sleeping on the ground . . . with wild gold seekers." Such memories were enough to "strip quiet life here of all interest and charms." In reverie, the wild life called him—"my fancy will rove back to Monterey . . . and the wild scenes of Gold Mountain." It was at times such as these that he had "fetched up" at the house of Doña Augustias. On the other hand, "my reason tells me that it is a barren region as compared with the great valley of the Mississippi, and that this country is better suited to one who is head of a family."[21]

Sherman projected his longings for the wild life on Hugh, insisting that Hugh had "seen enough of the Elephant Rampant," and now ought to come back to the Midwest "and try some other means of living." Sherman felt that "I am now fast settling down into an old fogey," and he really wanted Hugh to join him. "You may depend upon a hearty welcome, for it seems you are regarded as the wildest, most prodigal son of the family, and ever since the Bible was written parents and families have leaned toward such youths."[22] Sherman was projecting his yearnings onto his younger stepbrother at the same time that he was censoring those yearnings by urging Hugh to give up the wandering single life and accept the civilizing constraints of family and the settled life as he had done. Ambivalence, not resolution, marked this admonition.

The scene of the stable little family in St. Louis did not last long in any event. In order to maintain the St. Louis home he had been compelled to borrow from both his brother, John, and from Thomas Ewing. After fourteen months, Ellen, pregnant again, hurried back to Lancaster, and Sherman went on alone to his new assignment in New Orleans.

Just before he left St. Louis, he received news of his mother's death. He did not return to Ohio for her funeral. "Poor Mother! She has had hard times," he wrote Ellen, "and nothing but the kindest, most affectionate and simplest heart would have borne her up under her varied fortune." He had recently received a letter from her in fact, filled with her "usual style of childish delight."[23] Under the loving surface, there was something more than a little condescending and even angry in this image of a mother who was too simple and childish ever to have functioned as a real mother should, who had effectively abandoned him way back when. This was far less than a loving portrait of a maternal figure, especially telling for a man who lacked a real paternal figure as well.

It was at this difficult point in his shaky new marital life that Sherman left the army in which he had spent half of his still-young life. If boring, the army had been secure, but now he cast his lot with risky speculative capitalism.

Before quitting altogether, Sherman had taken a six-month leave of absence from the army in order to follow up a business offer he had been negotiating in St. Louis. Approached by Henry S. Turner, an old army colleague who was now the partner of James H. Lucas, reputedly the richest man in St. Louis, Sherman traveled to San Francisco to explore opening a branch of the Lucas & Turner Bank. Liking the prospects out West, Sherman resigned from the service on September 6, 1853, to seek his main chance as a banker. His spirits soared, his sense of adventure reinforced by his starting salary of $7,000, triple his army wages.[24]

During the following eight years, Sherman's public fortunes would frequently rise and fall, mainly fall. He would continue to move about, and Ellen would come to live with him in San Francisco and elsewhere, only to leave him for Lancaster, where she lived most of these years, without her husband, in her paternal home. By 1861, they would add four more children to the two they had, children on whom they both would dote. But the quarrels of their marriage would rigidify into fairly violently expressed rituals of mutual recrimination, punctuated from time to time by protestations of admiration and affection. The wide world that lured Sherman only to cast him down frightened Ellen, who wanted her church and her Lancaster nest. They were hurt and angry to be apart—being together made them angry and hurt as well.

The triangular tensions with Thomas Ewing also continued. Much to his chagrin, Sherman had to borrow heavily from Ewing in 1852. On the other hand, when he prepared to leave for San Francisco in 1853, he protested his independence from Ewing yet again. In his new job he could "provide for [Ellen and the children] handsomely," so why should he not take them with him, he wrote Ewing. But his independence from Ewing was incomplete, as was Ellen's break with her father, and so he felt the need to half supplicate Ewing about going off with his daughter and grandchildren, and at the same time demonstrate his manly competence. "I ask your free and hearty consent to ease the shock of Ellen's leaving home." A word from Ewing would placate Ellen and therefore would relieve Sherman of a burden in her heart by showing her that her father acknowledged Sherman as master of his daughter. Ewing's words with his daughter went unrecorded, so one cannot know how this nuance within the long struggle transpired.[25] In any event, Ellen followed her husband to San Francisco, but not for long.

Furthermore, Sherman wanted Ewing to declare, man to man, that Sherman had to make his way for his little nuclear family. "You will appreciate my position when I add that I would rather be at the head of the Bank in San Francisco, a position attained by my own efforts, than to occupy any place open to me in Ohio."[26] Such an Ohio place would have been, it went without saying, in Ewing's sphere, and Sherman wanted his father-in-law to clearly recognize the inappropriateness of this option.

When his bank in California failed in 1857, Sherman once more felt himself drawn back toward Thomas Ewing's realm, like iron filings to a powerful magnet. "I have my doubts if Ellen will be satisfied anywhere else than Lancaster," he wrote Ewing then, "and for me to be there seems an impossibility—I'd rather take to the woods and try a quarter section in Illinois."[27]

While paying a visit to the hated Lancaster in 1858, Sherman wrote Thomas Ewing, Jr., "your father thinks there is enough work for me hereabouts—It may be so—I think not—I think your father says so because he wants Ellen here." Sherman feared that the father-daughter bond that subconsciously motivated Thomas Ewing was far stronger for both of them than his marital ties with his wife, and that his economic failure, contrasted to the older man's wealthy grandeur, left him little to claim either with Ellen or among the world of men. Yet in this same letter to Thomas, Jr., Sherman wrote that in his current "fit of the

Blues . . . I am very anxious to see your father, very much indeed," because he believed he had no clear alternative to returning to the elder Ewing's orbit. As an independent agent he had "foolishly resigned one of the best posts in the Army" in 1853, tossing over a sound place he had secured by his own long-term efforts, and had taken an ignorant dash at banking "without a knowledge of business or an appreciation of the dangers intendant thereto." Now he had left himself "as poor as a churchmouse, without profession, without confidence, without physical strength." In this weakened state he turned to Thomas Ewing, confessing his utter failure as a businessman.[28]

To his stepfather, Sherman blamed himself for failing. In his despair, he also blamed Ellen for being a spoiled rich girl. Although Ellen "professes great willingness to live in a log house, feed chickens and milk cows," Sherman wrote Thomas Ewing in 1858, "I know better. She can't come down to that. She requires and must have certain comforts which to another would be superfluities and in whatever scheme I embark her wants and those of our children must be first considered." In the last clause of that complaint, Sherman seemingly had assented to Ellen's needs, which an honorable middle-class gentleman should provide his wife. On the one hand, a truly spirited woman ought to be able to tough it out by her husband's side, he told this woman's father; on the other hand, the husband should not expect her willingly to slide down the class scale into rural roughness, he also concluded. Given this situation, and much to his annoyance, Sherman was increasingly resigned to having Ellen live in the Ewing fold. But he could not bring himself to return there himself, as Ellen, often joined by her father, was urging, and he thought Thomas Ewing ought to be able to understand his need to retain at least a thread of independence and honor, adulthood, and self-esteem. "All I stipulate is that I don't want to live in Lancaster. You can understand what Ellen does not—that a man needs consciousness of position among his peers. In the Army I knew my place, and out here [in California] we are of the pioneers, and big chiefs—at Lancaster I can only be Cump Sherman."[29]

Although she wished to support and nurture him, Ellen could neither understand nor sympathize with her husband's familial dilemma, and she never comprehended why she ought to feel the need to break with her family of birth. She never reconceptualized herself as just Mrs. Sherman, not that she was any sort of proto-feminist who felt the need for genuine autonomy, but that she felt comfortable in her Ewing identity and social sphere, one that was pre-Sherman and often despite Sherman. Writing to one of her brothers from California in 1854, Ellen vented her unhappiness, insisting that she was there, "in this outlandish place" on protest, and only for a "reasonable length of time." "The Bible says 'let a *man* leave his Father's house and cleave unto his wife,'" she insisted. She was not "prepared to acknowledge [that a] wifes duty is to act without a will." She is a man's "better half—and not his slave, and due regard to her taste fears & feelings" must be paid. She simply was not going to give up friends or family—defined as "those that have loved me and labored for me since my birth"—even for "all the gold in California. . . . I would rather live near my home poor than to be a millionaire away from it."[30]

Much of her long-term quarrel with her husband stemmed from their differing assumptions about appropriate familial structure. But they also had fundamental unresolved personality conflicts that only festered over the years of their disjointed marriage. He had his list of her failures; she had her list of his; and through the decades they each endlessly repeated the same complaints. One can sample their compilations in turn.

"I will stay here as far into the year as I can keep Mrs S quiet," Sherman wrote his business partner, Henry S. Turner, in 1858, "but she is disposed to be insubordinate."[31] And to Ellen, two years later, Sherman insisted, "Tis your part to follow me without imposing conditions that cripple my actions."[32] Ellen was not submissive, as an ideal wife ought to be.

Ellen did not appreciate her husband's need for manly standing in the world. "You have often misinterpreted my uneasiness and my unhappiness to [mean] annoyance with you. I do not find fault with you for living [in] your old house more than our new one . . . but you know I would be out of my element there. . . . A man must fill a man's place and I know I am better known and appreciated here," in California, in 1855, "than I am in Ohio."[33]

In her husband's opinion, Ellen permitted herself to be dominated by fear of life. To give one of many such examples, after the shipwreck of the *Golden Age,* on which Ellen had sailed to California in the spring of 1855, Sherman, who had survived two shipwrecks on his trip to California in 1853, wrote to Henry Turner about his wife's horrified reaction to the event, beginning sardonically and ending in contempt: "All travellers should experience a wreck once, to know how it feels to expe-

rience that delightful sensation of timbers grinding and crashing . . .
copper cracking and splitting under the ocean's powerful grasp, like
dry leaves in the hands of a strong man. I despair of Mrs Sherman ever
taking a reasonable or practical view of such things, for she will not be
convinced that the Creator made all the world for the use of civilized
beings, or the sea was made for any purpose but to drown people who
are fools enough not to stay at home."[34]

Worst of all, Sherman hated his wife's ceaseless campaign to convert
him to what he found to be an intolerant Catholic faith. "If you really
wish me to settle down you must bear with my impatience and must
not misconstrue my motives or denounce so severely my religious opinions or what you believe my want of religious faith," he warned her in
1860, using language to which he returned frequently over the years.[35]

For her part, Ellen wrote to Hugh, right after arriving in California
in 1855, repeating a theme she evidently shared with her husband
whenever she went to live with him away from Ohio, "I never expect to
get entirely over my home-sickness, until my own health improves."[36]
In general, Sherman failed to understand the needs of a civilized, refined, sickly woman, and of middle-class white children. "I never expect to be capable of living as you have always desired, without
servants," she wrote him furiously in 1859. "My wants are more numerous and expensive than a ploughman's and . . . our children are
more tender and require more care than young squaws."[37]

When they were apart for their long stretches, Ellen keenly felt her
husband's inability to mollify her from a distance with kind words. "If
you are determined not to live with your family very soon you might at
least wish to write to us very frequently. . . . [Y]our letters are very few
and far between [and] unsatisfactory. If [your] rather harsh [reflections]
had been accompanied by a single expression of regret at the separation it would have been less mortifying to me. [T]he absence of all the
evidences of affection is now a great hindrance to my happiness."[38]

Ellen simply could not comprehend what was so terrible about Lancaster for her husband. "You ought to be able to understand why I
should be glad to have you live where we have both grown up, where
we are known and respected (no matter how poor we may be) and
where my Father & Mother are to spend the remnants of their life. You
expected me to live cheerfully in California & you think it unkind that I
should wish you to live in Lancaster [where] you would be happier than
you now imagine." And again, "I hope you come in this summer &

perhaps you will make arrangements to remain here for a year or two."
And again, "We can make some arrangements [here in Lancaster] that
I *know* will please you."[39]

Not only was he indifferent to her fragile constitution, Ellen believed
her husband lacked sympathy for her frequent, painful pregnancies.
Pregnant for the fifth time in nine years, and in her seventh wretched
month, she wrote, "Does it ever occur to you . . . that the pangs of
labor are terrible and that from the oppressive weight of child bearing I
shall find relief only in agony?" And pregnant a sixth time a year later,
she wrote, wondering at his insensitivity for seeking to drag her into
the distant tropical wilderness of Louisiana, "the terrible prostration
of childbirth will be as much as I can bear well in a northern summer
with the comforts of an Ohio home about me." And to top it all off, her
husband seemed uninterested about even the name or sex of one of her
forthcoming children. "Have you ever thought or wondered what the
child might be—have you no preference as to the name it might bear. I
think it is truly, as you often remarked, a 'good thing for children that
they have mothers.' "[40]

When she thought she was going to die, which she feared frequently,
especially during her pregnancies, Ellen would beg her husband to replace her with a good Catholic mother, one who would take over their
children's Catholic education. Although Sherman did not interfere
with their children being raised in the Catholic Church, he did impose
his authority over them, even when he was away from home, by insisting that they go to public rather than parochial schools. Ellen rounded
on him on this issue, telling him lurid tales of immorality at the Lancaster public school. One teacher, the son of a Protestant minister no less,
had been dismissed, "owing to his habits of intimacy & familiarity"
with the older schoolgirls. Nine-year-old Minnie told her one day,
Ellen reported to her distant husband, that the boy who sat next to her
on a bench at school frequently "made the most indecent exposure of
his person," and that a bunch of naughty boys "make holes in the
fence and wet on the girls as they pass to the necessary." This exposure
to gross sin would never be permitted by the nuns and priests of Catholic schools, where the children were appropriately separated by sex.
"Had I known these [public] schools to be . . . schools of immorality I
never would have suffered my children to have gone to them. But now
that they are there by your act, I wait out of deference to you for your
command to take them away."[41]

An unconverted husband could not possibly be a proper father. For this reason, and because she knew he would go to hell if he were to die unredeemed, Ellen continuously returned to this most fundamental of their unresolved issues, the one that made her husband the angriest, which she must have discerned. "My prayer and hope are that you may not only die a Catholic but [live many years] in the enjoyment of the faith." She prayed for his soul in peril, again and again and again. "My prayer [is] that neither of us may leave the other when called away, desolate and uncomforted by the sure hope of a reunion hereafter, where the spirit will be unencumbered by the frail and erring body."[42]

This mutual blaming habit, this failure of basic communication and empathy, provided the leitmotiv of the Sherman/Ewing marriage. In sheer pigheaded willfulness, Ellen and William Tecumseh were just about a perfect match. Whatever the greater role of the man out in the world (a role in which Sherman knew he was failing), in the domestic arena these two warriors circled about each other and delivered about an equal number of brutal verbal blows. Neither sought to be fair in argument, neither pulled any punches or took the time for self-analysis and fellow feeling. Each was quick to be hurt and to lash out in anger. It must be added that from time to time each also apologized, cajoled, took on blame, although on balance these were but patches of warmth in a bad marriage.

Occasionally Sherman would write Ellen that it was not anything she did but his own isolation in a heartless world, and his loneliness caused by their separations, that led him to blurt out angry feelings growing from a frustrated heart. He also admitted that he did not do enough to censor his tongue and his pen, and that he was aware this was a major flaw in his character. In 1852, while Ellen had been in Lancaster during her second pregnancy, he wrote, "I have missed you so much this summer, and I have all along been impressed . . . that you would remain away all winter that you should pardon me for any hasty expressions—I write hastily, as hastily as I think and speak and I know full well that I often write and speak things that should have remained unsaid."[43] In a similar vein, eight years later, in his 1860 Christmas letter, he wrote that it was fate and his own shortcomings rather than Ellen's obstinacy that kept them in a separation that ate at his heart. Immediate reunification still seemed unlikely. "We have been too much separated, and I deeply feel at times the absence of you all, and had looked forward to our all being together . . . that this new disappointment breaks me down. It does seem the whole world conspires against us."[44]

When writing to others, as well as complaining about her, Sherman sometimes expressed admiration for Ellen's considerable well of courage when the stakes were high. In the same letter to Henry Turner in which he criticized Ellen for her overabundance of fear during the shipwreck of the *Golden Age,* Sherman added, "Nevertheless, when there was danger, she was cool and brave and . . . perfectly self-possessed."[45]

Immediately after surviving that shipwreck, Ellen had written Sherman that she had thought of him with love and regret when she believed she was lost. She did recognize that she was difficult and that, underneath it all, he was loving to her. "Your kind heart will forgive my many, many failings which I certainly regret, and believe that my heart is yours." She stressed that she gladly accepted that her primary role was as his wife. "It is of course my first duty to be near you." Yet even in this letter, Ellen added that when she had thought she was to die, it was a Roman Catholic heaven to which she had set her aspirations. "The hope I most cherish is of meeting you in heaven." Right after affirming her wifely duties, freely and gladly, she insisted that she should be with him "unless you can freely assent to my absence as you did when [last] I left. . . . I know your kind heart prompts the desire that I should make as long a visit as I can to please myself and Father." His kind heart willingly assented to her desires to be away from him and with her father, this rather complex formulation went.[46]

Once in 1858, while Sherman was off on the wild prairies of Kansas, and very depressed, Ellen wrote him that she had been filled with a great dread that he had died. "If you had been [dead] I should have lost my reason. I have never loved you as I do now, and I freely confess that even religion could not sustain me were you to die without my seeing you again." This statement seemed to indicate that her love of him was more important to her than the everlasting love of God. Yet, positively loving as she felt at that moment, she could not help appending her usual refrain, that, "were you to die without my seeing you again, and without your coming into the Church," their marriage would be less than the sacrament it ought to be.[47] To truly fulfill their marriage, he too had to unite agape with eros, as she believed in her heart she had done.

Writing two days later, still flooded with her love for him, and responding to his despondency, she wrote that she was willing, even eager, to join him immediately and that she was "willing to live in the plainest—indeed humblest manner & serve myself & children. . . . If the home is ever so small, so mean, so out of the way, never fear but I shall make the best of it . . . wear cheap clothes, put them on the children, eschew society in toto, live far from the church . . . if you will only be cheerful and happy." In this fantasy of a pioneer reunion, which of course did not take place, and which he scoffed at to her father as insincere, Ellen indirectly acknowledged that his complaints about her were not completely wrong, and that she was not always fair in her demands. She had often put her needs above his; she had insisted on servants, material comfort, nice clothes, her girlhood circle of friends and family, daily mass; and now she wished to put all these aside for reunification with her husband. However, she continued, she was willing to create a perfectly self-sufficient domestic sphere if and only if he would be willing to enter it absolutely, dropping all ties to the horrid surrounding society. "If you can concentrate your desire entirely on your family, feeling no desire for the esteem of those beyond, [then] *your unsullied conscience* & your love of *your own* will sustain you." Only this domestic monad, entirely separated from the world, could potentially prepare them all spiritually for the "bright and beautiful day [which] is dawning."[48] The perfect love in heaven could await the Sherman family, if only . . .

Very occasionally, Ellen would refer shyly to the erotic love they shared, which he never returned to her in his letters. "I dreamed of you all night," she wrote Sherman one April day in 1860, when he was far away in Louisiana. Soon after temporarily setting up house on her own, around the corner from her parents in Lancaster, in 1859, during one of her husband's prolonged absences, she described her very own bedroom, in which she had, she believed, transformed her inherited furniture. "I have Mother's old gild bedstead—it looks very pretty— My room is most cozy and comfortable—I only want you to be here satisfied & happy—but that is a sad *want*." She hoped to lure him back to that gilt bed, which, whatever her sexual complaints, she did enjoy sharing with him. "It is a poor house with the Father gone," she quickly continued, altering the meanings of the love she wanted. "The children are constantly expecting you."[49]

At her fondest, Ellen was capable of allowing herself to feel, and of telling her husband, that all in all theirs was a loving union. On May Day 1860, she wrote, "Ten years ago, this evening, dearest Cump, we were married. . . . Looking back, I cannot help feeling that we have been particularly blessed, notwithstanding all our cares & trials & disappointments. Our children are healthy . . . good . . . bright and pretty. . . . We ourselves—I speak from my own heart—are more attached more fondly, love and more truly esteem one another than ever before." This does not read as a hollow formula. Ellen doubtless felt swept with real affection from time to time, although she expressed her anger far more frequently, and with more fervor. At the end even of this unusually loving letter, she included her ritualistic religious appendix—her prayer for their "reunion hereafter, where the spirit will be unencumbered by the frail and erring body." Although such language sent Sherman up and over the wall, in her heart it did not detract from the worldly love she did sometimes feel for him; rather, such spiritualized language expressed those feelings in light of what she considered the only appropriate telos. God the Father alone lent grace to marital union.[50]

This idealized home, which would shut out the greater world of snares and delusions, would lead toward perfectionism in love, and after this preparation, this idealized family would be poised to receive His grant of final grace when they all should die and gather together again in final and perpetual perfection above. This vision of the spiritualization of home—divine domesticity—was in fact impossible to attain on earth, as men and women and children all are mortal—in the appropriate lexicon, all sinners. Thus the life Ellen wished for in her home could not be correlated with the kind of life possible for actual human beings. She was bound to be terribly disappointed in the daily realities of life and husband and home that were available to her. She denied the pleasures offered by what she did have in the name of a spirituality she could not share on this earth. In Lancaster she greatly idealized her own father, Thomas Ewing, and she let her husband know that he could not possibly measure up to him. But even her own father was the palest earthly representation of Him, her true Father, who was Perfection. Her focus on Him was a distant gaze, up at a plane, which meant that real families, real husbands, were mere dust. Nevertheless, the perfect love in heaven would await the redeemed Sherman family, if only her husband took the great first step and joined the true faith. He refused what was to her this simple but all-meaningful step, and thus the spiritual progression to family redemption—to divine domesticity—could not begin. If he had fulfilled this request, she would have had to up the spiritual stakes after discovering that even the converted Sherman remained more or less the man he had always been, and had not been transformed into a Thomas Ewing, much less an angel. But he did not accede, and thus she could focus her disappointments and anger with him on this issue, blame him completely, and exonerate herself, on the true, spiritual level of life, where she was strengthened by her absolute faith, and where he had none. If he were not above her, he would be beneath her: There was no egalitarian, level meeting ground on earth. There were many issues her spiritualized approach did not deal with directly, but she could deny their importance, retreat up into her argument about final things, and gain an extraordinary amount of power over him.

Sherman shared nothing of Ellen's faith in divine domesticity and in final states. All that spirituality, which was simply meaningless to him, deepened the sense of claustrophobia he felt about Lancaster and the Ewings. When he was away from there, which was as often as possible, and away from Ellen, he never gave her much affection and esteem in his letters. He rarely mentioned their anniversary, for example. One time he did was in 1862, shortly after his triumph in the battle of Shiloh. In a passage that someone attempted to erase, either then or years later, he wrote, "This is the anniversary of our marriage—truly it has been as full of change as the moon."[51] As contrasted to Ellen's seasonal effusions, Sherman's rendition of their anniversary was both more accurate and more heartless—and without underlying affection.

In an extraordinary, extended metaphor he wrote to Ellen in 1860, Sherman compared himself to a free and wild animal, while Ellen, Thomas Ewing, and Lancaster were his Fate—the ever-patient hunter—waiting to bring him down. "I feel very much an antelope—not a sheep or goat. . . . The antelope runs off as far as possible but Fate brings him back—again he dashes off in a new direction, but curiosity and his Fate lures him back, and again off he goes but the hunter knows he will return and bides his time. So I have made desperate efforts to escape my doom. . . . Ohio it is—I have made desperate attempts to escape but I see it is inevitable and so might as well surrender."[52]

Sherman never did go back to Lancaster and Thomas Ewing, nor surrender to Ellen and her ideal of divine domesticity. Neither, however, did he ever escape that sphere, for he did not want a conclusive break. He could not share Ellen's absolute faith, nor could he develop a counterfaith, or even a clear image of what he would like a marriage to be, what needs the domestic sphere ought to fulfill, how it ought to operate from day to day. Having no alternatives to present to Ellen, he simply lashed out in blame at her for not being of the world in which he participated. He was unhappy nearly all the time and quite often deeply depressed, in part because of his worldly failures, but at least as much because of his marriage, which he wanted both to escape and to engage in in a warmer manner. He had these feelings both when he was away from Ellen and when he was with her, both when he was fleeing and when he was returning. He had set up an impossible division in his heart. He was wild and free, but so lonely that he was lured by Ellen, family, home, and stability, all of which he deeply resented for constricting his freedom. He was an antelope, but he was also a sheep or goat, a resentful but willing domestic animal. To him, the mystifying and insufferable Ellen was his hunter and his wife for life. To her, this peculiar, wild, cold, and injured vagabond, so unlike her rock-solid father, so disappointing to her, so alienated from her home, her town, and her Father in heaven, and of course from her, was also her kind and wounded husband for life.

4

Failure as a Banker and Debts of Honor

SHERMAN'S SPIRITS bounded high as he left the army and Ohio far behind in pursuit of fortune in San Francisco. He was certain that he would slough off past failures. Backed by the richest merchants in St. Louis, with whom he had built ties during his six-month leave prior to his resignation, he was keen to open the Lucas & Turner bank in California, in order to cash in on the economic boom that had accompanied the gold rush.

Preparing to settle in California, Sherman literally rid himself of his encumbrances with a devil-may-care buoyancy. On March 4, 1853, he wrote his brother, John Sherman, that he had sent Ellen and the children back to Lancaster, and that he was selling off all the family household goods in St. Louis "at auction for whatever they will bring" (which turned out to be $504.35) "and I will again be like a soldier with his camp chest." He took West only his army title—telling John to address his mail to Captain Sherman until advised otherwise.[1] He had stripped for action in his next campaign, and it felt good: He would travel light, travel with hopes of the future, leave behind the burdens of the past. And he went with John's blessings. "The spirit of the age is progressive and commercial," John wrote, implying that the only mystery concerned why his brother had dallied so long in the service. "You ought in a few years to acquire a fortune . . . which will amply compensate you for the loss of the [prospective] title of Colonel."[2]

A booming city greeted Sherman in 1853, where just three years earlier he had left a grubby little town. Before, he had gone a full year without a mail ship bringing letters from back East; now dozens of steamers traveled back and forth from San Francisco, connecting through Nicaragua with ships from the rest of America. "This is the most extraordinary place on earth," he wrote John of his first impressions of San Francisco. "Large brick and granite houses fill the site where stood the poor, contemptible village; wharves extend a mile out, along which lie ships and steamers of the largest class, discharging freight in a day that used to consume with scows a month." American capitalism was parading its energetic, improving face, and he would join in the flow. Even in his excitement, however, Sherman was realist enough to note the dark side of such boom times. "Yet amid all this business and bustle there is more poverty than in New York. Not a day without distressed individuals ask for money."[3] Intending to join in the mainstream of wealth, given his past and his fears, Sherman could not help adding to his soaring expectations the troubling thought that there but for the grace of God . . .

Inklings of anxieties notwithstanding, Sherman's next year was full of activity, building, and hope. He was starting to prosper, augmenting his $7,000 salary with real estate speculation on the side. He was becoming recognized as a gentleman of standing and property among his peers. He had sent for Ellen and all but one of their cheerful children. At times he nearly burst with creative energy, as he demonstrated in a letter to John, on June 3, 1854. "I have a great deal to do nowadays being compelled to give my personal attention to a thousand daily details," wrote the man of business, "and to the construction of a handsome Edifice we are erecting for our Bank," on the northeast corner of Montgomery and Jackson streets. He was planning on building for Ellen a grand house on a big lot where there would be room for a "large garden . . . flowers and everything necessary." Lizzie, the two-year-old whom he adored, was blooming—"The picture of health and as self-willed as a half a dozen ordinary children. She has plenty of friends and a great supply of bouquets, oranges and presents!" And best of all, his first son, Willy, a robust, handsome chap, had been born a week earlier in San Francisco. "The little fellow has a wonderful appetite, and is already beginning to develop on his original birth weight of 9, ¾ pounds, which among those versed in such matters is considered very large. He is much larger than Minnie or Lizzie was, and is perfectly happy." When he was up in spirits, Sherman was intensely up. He was building his bank and his house, he had lovely daughters, and now he had a blessed son.[4]

Even so, there were discouraging notes. Ellen hated California and pined for Lancaster. Sherman's asthma was exacerbated by the fogs and dusty winds of San Francisco, so that he was wheezing and coughing, especially at night, when he often had to sit in a chair and inhale the fumes of burning niter paper. He slept little and, already thin, grew thinner. He believed it was probably "foolish to count on a long life," yet he was not certain of physical doom either.[5] Another bother was that his eldest daughter, Minnie, who was five, had remained behind in Lancaster at her grandparents' insistence and with Ellen's agreement. In 1856, Sherman demonstrated his annoyance at this circumstance in a letter he wrote to Minnie, telling her of the birth of a second Sherman son, Thomas Ewing Sherman, "a fine healthy little fellow." The other children had greeted the birth with open hearts. "Willy [already two] considers himself a large sized fellow and says he is so large now that he cannot stay at home so his Mama had to send yet another little baby in his place. Lizzie is a good little girl and wants to nurse the baby all the time." Only Minnie was missing from this concert of loving siblings. "I am glad to hear such good accounts of you," her father wrote her. "I wish you could be here with us but your Grandma and Grandpa seem to think you very necessary to their happiness and I hope you will continue to be good to them. As soon as you can write you must send me letters."[6] Sherman could scarcely conceal his resentment at the Ewings in a letter that they would read out loud to Minnie. One can only imagine their feelings and those of Minnie when they read this letter to her, and what explanations might have followed. At the least this missive was meant to instruct the Ewings that Minnie was only on loan, and to remind Minnie that she was in the Sherman fold, not in that of the Ewings. Even under what were for him optimum conditions, Sherman could not quite unite his family under his own roof.*

*Sherman was a loving if sometimes exasperated and perplexed father. Of his favorite, two-year-old Willy, for example, he wrote to Turner, "I presume Willy would make a sensation in a fair in the Feegie Islands and would excite the palate of some epicure there, but he is a hard specimen for civilized people—he walks over us all rough shod, and rules his poor sister Lizzie without a particle of charity for her inferior strength of body and purpose." Earlier he had remarked with feigned annoyance at Lizzie's willfulness. She had been displaced by this real little

The most ominous cloud on Sherman's horizon, it quickly became apparent, was the increasing instability of business in the late 1850s. The general crash of 1857 was preceded by an economic tightening on the speculative frontiers of the economy, precisely in places like San Francisco. In retrospect, one can date this downturn from October 1854, when Henry Meiggs, the leading merchant of the city, fled one night for Peru after having bilked local bankers and businessmen of nearly $1 million. In a letter to his partner, Henry S. Turner, back in St. Louis, Sherman described Meiggs's "swindle, forgery and flight" as "forming in all its details a perfect Epic of Circe." Not trusting Meiggs, Sherman had taken little of his paper, and although Lucas & Turner therefore remained "pretty well off," Meiggs's disappearance had produced a negative atmosphere—"now we suspect everybody," was the way Sherman put it—and he began, as did others, to curtail loans.[8] When bankers began restricting new investments, the business cycle tipped from expansion to contraction, a particularly noticeable redirection in a highly speculative, real estate–based local economy like that of San Francisco.

As were most businessmen in this boomtown, Sherman was overextended in his personal investments as well as in his capacity as head of a bank. He was particularly concerned because he and Ellen were living beyond their means, in their grand new house—which he had borrowed $7,000 to build, coincidently equivalent to one year's salary—keeping three servants, a carriage, and two horses, and entertaining as splendidly as would befit the prosperous banker. Perhaps even more worrying to Sherman's conscience was the large sum of money entrusted in him personally by many of his army chums, which he had invested for them in San Francisco municipal bonds.[9]

Although he exercised every reasonable precaution, Sherman was in the business of loaning money to merchants, manufacturers, and real estate investors, and so he watched the passing show with mounting concern. Mighty entrepreneurs tended to climb out on rather fragile limbs. On January 25, 1855, Sherman wrote Turner, "Our first men were too rich, valued their lots too high, flattered themselves they were

---

man, still delectable with baby fat, but already becoming a proper rough customer. Sherman employed the conventional macho picture of manhood and of male dominance in his culture, but he did so with genuine affection toward the girls as well as the boy.[7]

making no end of money, but one by one they have slid down and you would hardly recognize your rich friends of last year, but our financial condition is evidently on the mend." In comparison to the vivid imagery he used to describe failure, the reassurance tacked on at the end seemed pallid indeed.[10]

Less than five weeks following this cautious prognosis that business conditions were likely improving despite the bad augurs in several corners of the financial community, Sherman was confronted by a dramatic run on his bank. On February 17, 1855, the steamship *Oregon* brought the news that Page & Bacon, another St. Louis bank, had gone bankrupt, and this produced a run on the Page & Bacon branch in San Francisco, just up Montgomery Street from Lucas & Turner. Sherman immediately began to refuse new loans and discounts, and to insist on all payments due, in order to build up his liquid reserves. The morning of February 22, Page & Bacon did not open its doors, and went into receivership. The following morning, three other banks, including Wells Fargo, were afraid to open, but along with most of the other banks in the city, Sherman opened, and as did several of the others, experienced an immediate run. By noon he had paid out about $337,000 of his approximately $1 million on hand. "Things looked desperate," at this point, Sherman wrote Turner. He convinced several friends to make deposits, one as large as $10,000, in order to reverse the rumors on the street. "Our clock seemed provokingly slow," Sherman wrote, but at 4:00 P.M. he could close the doors for the evening with $45,000 still on hand, and without pledging his securities. Sherman spent the evening scurrying after help from other bankers, and the key figure at the strongest bank pledged $40,000—"a noble act on his part," Sherman believed, although that banker, fearing a domino effect, was really practicing enlightened self-interest. The next morning, after news of these new deposits circulated, the atmosphere calmed, and by day's end the bank's balance was 75 percent restored. "So the battle is over, and we are not dead by a damn sight," Sherman concluded to Turner in triumph.[11]

Although he had remained cool and organized, this near disaster undercut the thin veneer of optimism of Sherman the banker. Soon he was writing stoically to Hugh Ewing that he was "going to stick it out and do my duty to my partners," but that his thoughts "sometimes turned toward the East." He blamed Ellen for her "persistent hostility" toward California, but he was even more concerned at the time

with the economic "backsliding" of San Francisco, the plunge in property values, the enormous risks he was taking, with rapidly decreasing
rewards.[12]

All during the spring and summer of 1856, the economic slide in San
Francisco continued. "When we began here, the city was at the summit
of prosperity," Sherman wrote Thomas Ewing on August 3. Since then
banks had failed, merchants had failed, "and now the bonds of the city
are dishonored in New York." This latest event destroyed the investments of Sherman's army comrades, who had put their money and
trust in his hands, although Sherman did not tell Thomas Ewing that
part of the story. Lucas & Turner had as of yet continued to maintain
its "high reputation" in San Francisco and elsewhere in the nation, but
the house had made larger loans and smaller profits than anticipated.
In terms of his personal finances, Sherman was tightening his belt, selling his horses and carriage, considering discharging a servant. Just
keeping the family going and putting on the optimistic face for the
world, which was the sine qua non for a banker, were extremely trying
for Sherman, who lacked wells of self-assurance or sangfroid, or put
another way, who had trouble denying his fears. "I would not go
through the same anxiety again for an independence," Sherman confessed to Thomas Ewing, the very man from whom he had hoped to
wrest his independence by his banking gambit.[13]

Like the San Francisco fog, during the summer of 1856 doom
seemed to be gathering, threatening to roll over Sherman once more.
Just when oncoming financial problems so unnerved Sherman's faith
in the financial world, armed citizens took over San Francisco, threatening Sherman's confidence in the political system. There was some
connection between these events, as economic instability heightened
the highly personalized struggle among contending political factions in
San Francisco. Indeed, the Vigilance Committee took over the city in
late May 1856, when one newspaper editor, a corrupt "in," shot another, an equally corrupt "out," and the "outs," screaming public
purification slogans, took to the streets, overwhelmed the police,
lynched the shootist, formed a committee of public safety that was
quickly co-opted by ambitious would-be political bosses, and attempted to purge the city of corrupt gamblers and ward heelers.

Sherman was appalled by what he saw as base mob rule. He was no
bystander to these events. Just before the Vigilance Committee seized
power, he had been named major general in charge of the California

State Militia by Governor J. Neely Johnson. This was a militia only on paper, however, and Sherman's subsequent inability to restore public order proved frustrating, unsuccessful, and finally humiliating to him.

Early in the chain of events, Sherman stood with the governor and the sheriff by the jail in which the editor was being held prior to his trial for murder. The armed mob, which Sherman estimated at twenty-five hundred men, surged toward the prison. To Sherman they were an undifferentiated, ominous mass. As he wrote to Turner right after the events, "All the houses commanding a view were covered with people. Telegraph Hill was black with them, and the street was a complete jam." Fearing that if the sheriff and his handful of deputies were to fire on the mob the ensuing bloodshed "would be terrific," Sherman supported the governor's decision to surrender the prisoner for lynching, under protest. This was "humiliating," Sherman wrote, "but I think he did right."

This popular uprising seemed to Sherman just like the "Paris Committee of Public Safety," which had seized power during the opening days of the recent Revolution of 1848 in France. "Once put in motion, they cannot be stopped," Sherman predicted, drawing on this analogy from recent history. When the prisoner had been surrendered, Sherman turned on his heel and left. "I did not stay long. I came home. San Francisco is now governed by an irresponsible organization claiming to be armed with absolute power by the people. The government is powerless and at an end." What Sherman saw was a conglomerate monster, "vast numbers of desperate men, too lazy to work . . . unable to go away, strong for mischief and powerless for good," led by "some of our worthiest and best men who profess to improve on the law and its administration."[14]

The business elite of San Francisco was badly split by the Vigilance Committee, and Sherman represented a minority faction who defended the elected municipal government. He signed up about eight hundred men for the militia, but felt he was badly outnumbered by up to six thousand opponents—probably a fearsome exaggeration of the enemy force, although there is no doubt he was badly outnumbered and that popular opinion was enthusiastically on the other side. To employ the analogy of the 1848 French Revolution, which Sherman himself applied to these events, he was a Royalist supporter of the previous regime. Soon the Vigilance Committee seized the militia armories in San Francisco, in Sherman's words "a regular *coup d'etat a la*

Louis Napoleon." Subsequently, "the state of California ceased to have any power to protect men here, in defense of her sovereignty."

It was difficult for men like Sherman to leave the mob in unchallenged power. A few days later, in early June, Governor Johnson sent for Sherman and together they formulated a plan to use United States Navy ships to transport federal arms from the army base in Benicia across the bay, arm the militia, and confront the Vigilance Committee. Both Commodore David Farragut and General John E. Wool refused federal assistance of this sort to suppress what they considered a local and internal police matter, and so, after a feeble attempt to support mediation by some moderate businessmen, Sherman resigned his command of the militia and moved to the sidelines. His immediate reaction was annoyance at his disempowerment and disgrace, and disgust with the public, but he tried to put himself in a good light. "I am out of it, and believe I have lost nothing in public estimation for what I did," he concluded rather lamely. "At all events it is a lesson I will never forget—to mind my own business in all time to come."[15]

In the weeks that followed, the Vigilance Committee exercised power both by secret plotting and through democratic street theater. Sherman told John on July 7 that he was "purposely aloof from all parties," and blamed his banking interests for his discomfiting neutrality. "I cannot act with that decision otherwise than would suit me," he admitted, downplaying his recent martial ineffectiveness. He looked at the spectacle with contempt. "I think the community is getting sick and disgusted with their secrecy, their street fools, and parades, and mock trials—worse, far worse, than the prompt, rapid execution of a mob or lynch court."[16]

Sherman could integrate rough justice into his politics, if it were direct and quickly done, thereby reinforcing rather than undermining or revolutionizing general public order. It was the anarchic replacement of regularly elected officials with self-appointed popular rulers that he found so threatening. Writing to John early in August, two months after the Vigilance Committee had grabbed power, Sherman conceded that prior to the Vigilance Committee's seizure of power, San Francisco had suffered from "bad administration of law, and more than a fair share of rowdies." Nevertheless, Sherman insisted that the Committee was no better at governing, and even more important, that "if we are to be governed by the mere opinion of the Committee, and not by officers of our own choice, I would prefer at once to have a Dictator."[17] Ideologically Sherman resembled those French monarchists who willingly joined the Second Empire when Louis Napoleon derailed the Revolution of 1848, and seized dictatorial power.

In his heart, after this event Sherman would always distrust and even despise democracy. The product of elitist West Point, the stepson of an extremely conservative Whig who believed in the rule of the best sort, Sherman mistrusted democracy well before his ineffective opposition to the Vigilance Committee. What he saw there, juxtaposed to the increasingly violent events of the late 1850s across the United States, as exemplified by the nasty guerrilla war under way that summer of 1856 in "Bleeding Kansas," led Sherman to conclude that a surfeit of democracy—popular resistance to law and order—was leading to a terrible political cataclysm. In 1855, Sherman had refused the Democratic nomination for San Francisco city treasurer, declaring a hostility to elective politics that he would maintain throughout his lifetime. Now in October 1856, he made it clear to Henry S. Turner, in opposition to the politics of his own brother, John, who had become a powerful Republican member of the House of Representatives, that he would vote for James Buchanan for president despite his disgust with the Democratic party, in order to suppress public disorder, which John C. Frémont and the Republican Party represented to him. "I would submit to almost anything rather than see the United States in danger of Civil War, but the sample we have here, shows that we have engrafted on our people, all the dangerous elements of anarchy and civil war. Of course dissolution of the union cannot be peaceful."[18] As a purifying Napoleonic dictatorship was implausible to Sherman, the likely outcome was disunion, anarchy, and finally, repression and reconstruction, achieved only through armed force widely and harshly applied.[19]

Disunion and anarchy were not the greatest danger the Vigilance Committee experience had demonstrated for Sherman, although many historians have made just this connection, and stopped there. Rather, democracy itself was the evil phenomenon for him, with disunion and anarchy evil epiphenomena. He rarely put this argument point-blank, because he doubtless knew that this ideological line was taking him toward advocating or at least welcoming the violent overthrow of the Constitution and the whole tradition of American political liberty. Perhaps he was also hesitant to develop this argument for personal reasons. In the current political climate, it would lead to his social ostracism. His rejection of democracy and his semisecret reactionary faith in a military seizure of power deepened through the secession crisis and into the opening stages of his involvement in the Civil War.

As the political and economic stage darkened while the days grew shorter in the fall of 1856, Sherman's fears rose. "Everybody says we will have good [economic] times after the election, some say after the rain falls," he wrote to Turner on November 4, "but I think it will be some years before proper government and men are well enough established here, to make business satisfactory." Furthermore, Sherman expressed to Turner his anxieties over his personal financial overextension, especially that big mortgage. "I am willing to abide my fortune here, and ought to do it, to remedy some of the errors committed, the greatest of which was building that house."[20]

By December 18, the general slump had deepened drastically in San Francisco, Sherman reported. Business was down sharply, and therefore tax revenues had dried up, destroying municipal institutions. "At nights there is but one lamp to a block; the public schools will be closed—the police [sharply] reduced." Among the merchants, "business is awful dull," and Sherman was convinced that the outlook for the future was not promising. In general, "gold does not leave any profits behind," Sherman suggested to Turner, and thus San Franciscan wealth was in reality but an illusion—"this is essentially a poor country." Sherman believed that he had run Lucas & Turner "as strictly as I know how," and that their losses were lighter than any other San Francisco banking house, "and yet we [are] close to short." Despite having "the best and safest of merchants" as borrowers, he was failing to clear any profits, and there were no signs of upturn for the bank. Indeed, if affairs were to continue "downhill, as for the past four years . . . the same amount of money could be used more profitably in St. Louis." Sherman concluded his gloomy prognostication by asking Turner to come out to California to see for himself and to help him consider whether he ought to scale back the bank, perhaps selling their handsome new edifice.[21]

In January 1857, without further consultation with Sherman, Lucas & Turner responded to his negative analysis, and to their other financial problems, by pulling the plug on the San Francisco branch of their bank. Sherman professed surprise to Turner that he and Lucas had taken this decision as opposed to the retrenchment he had advised. However, he refrained from expressing any sense of betrayal he may have felt at either the decision or the manner in which it had been made.[22] Ellen was eager to depart at once for Lancaster, but Sherman was bewildered about the future, being apprehensive as well as mollified by Turner's suggestion that he might pursue the bank's interests as their representative in New York City, the consolation they offered Sherman for closing him down in the West. Even after having been deeply anxious throughout his San Francisco sojourn, which had failed to match his dreams of four years earlier, he feared the loss of station and of self-worth he had achieved so tenuously in San Francisco. "I feel no little regret at looking forward to leaving this place, where I am somebody, and going to be swallowed up in that vast gulf of mankind where I will be small indeed," he wrote to Turner.[23]

Sherman rented out his house, sent Ellen and the children back to Ohio, and left California in early May 1857, with considerable dismay about what had gone wrong and about the moral structure underlying business in San Francisco. Probity, honesty, perseverance—all those good Protestant commercial values he believed he embodied, or at least attempted to embody—seemed to count for nothing there. "My opinion is the very nature of the country begets speculation, extravagance, failure and rascality. Everything is chance, everything is gambling, and I shall be relieved when I am not dependent on the people of California for my repose."[24]

Befuddled by the lack of connection between moral correctness and business success, after a brief visit with his employers in St. Louis, Sherman went on alone in early July to open a branch of the Lucas & Turner bank, at rented offices on 12 Wall Street. So beset was he by doubts and defeat, so aware was he of the deepening general financial emergency, that he could not take up his new post with much cheerfulness. Even more pressing to him than his personal financial crisis or that of his bank were the enormous losses suffered by his fellow army officers, who had trusted him during his San Francisco years to be their sensible investor. In their names he had bought about $136,000 in San Francisco municipal bonds, on which the city had defaulted. Sherman was aware that other bankers would not worry about such losses. Technically and legally speaking he was not liable for the collapse of the bonds, the risk of which the investors had assumed when agreeing to the purchases. Nevertheless, Sherman believed himself honorbound to assume these debts, and to pay them off to the last penny. That was the only path true to the army code of honor that was central to his personal set of values. Therefore, he began to liquidate all the assets he had accumulated in San Francisco, including several lots and the family house, a dozen lots in St. Louis, and 640 acres across the river from St. Louis in Illinois, all at fire-sale prices, and, borrowing the last $13,000, including $837.50 from Thomas Ewing and larger amounts from his brother, John, he paid off his $136,000 debt to his comrades, a dispiriting process that took more than a year. "I am going to quit clean-handed" as he began, he wrote Ellen. "This is not modern banking, but better be honest." His creditors, quite aware both of Sherman's legal position and of his moral fortitude, were terribly impressed with this action. As they knew, his action was highly unusual in the easy-come-easy-go environment of nineteenth-century speculation, and it gave him a long-term reputation for peculiar honesty. But for the foreseeable future all was lost save honor, which gave him scant comfort—and he hated himself for his failure.[25]

During his stay in New York, Sherman felt doomed by gathering financial clouds, as if he were biding his time until the other shoe dropped. Therefore on October 6, he wrote Turner that "I cannot say I was much surprised" when one of Sherman's cousins banged on his bedroom door early that morning to tell him that all the papers had announced the failure of J. H. Lucas & Co., the personal holding company of Lucas & Turner. He was only slightly offended that once again Lucas had not notified him personally, and then he advised St. Louis headquarters to begin immediate liquidation of their Wall Street operation. Within a week "all hell . . . broke loose" on Wall Street, he wrote Turner on October 13. Almost all the banks were failing simultaneously during the worst day of the panic of 1857. "Wall Street is black as a beehive, and nobody pretends to do business."[26]

Throughout that catastrophic summer and fall of 1857, Sherman fundamentally blamed himself for all his troubles. "It seems that I am the Jonah of banking," he wrote John, not really in irony. "Wherever I go, there is a breakdown."[27] He was just a little fish swimming the rough, immense ocean, swallowed by the great economic whale.

But what was the whale? A German contemporary of Sherman would have blamed the unseen monster of Capital, faceless but devouring, developing a kind of analysis foreign to Sherman. Ellen would have blamed the sordid world, or perhaps the machinations of evil men. A few months earlier, Sherman had toyed with another analysis about the shabby trimming in a frontier society of gamblers, speculators, and extravagant rascals, but on further reflection he now wrote that California was a "riddle" rather than an evil entity. "I would no more trust money there than throw candy among a parcel of school boys, and yet I don't believe theoretically that they are more dishonest than here," he wrote to Turner from New York in August 1857.[28] Neither did Sherman blame Lucas & Turner, though they had sent him to New York without full disclosure of what must have been their faltering economic position in St. Louis, on what some might have considered a fool's errand. To the contrary, he expressed guilt about his role in inducing Lucas and Turner to open up the San Francisco bank in the first place—"I feel bad enough about having involved Mr. Lucas in that California venture," he wrote Turner, and the worst he would say about his partners was that they, like he, had marched with naïveté into a business they did not really understand. "We know now, too late, that we ought not to be bankers," he wrote Turner. Turner and Lucas should have stuck to their traditional roles as merchants and real estate operators, he was inferring, just as he should have clung to his army role; all of them should have avoided the lures of fast new venture capitalism. Greed was a sin, no matter how fashionable, that merited punishment.[29]

He, Sherman, had not only misled his good friend, Henry S. Turner, into this banking venture, there was something terrible about his nature that would always infect those around him. Although he knew such brooding was irrational—"[It] is the most consummate folly to suppose it," he wrote Turner—nevertheless he did believe on some deeper level that "I carry misfortune in my train, and I yearn to escape." Bad enough that he repeatedly injured himself, "but to entail it on others makes me half desperate."[30] Feelings of shame and guilt compounded one another. The forthright Sherman, who would not blame others or consider systemic forces, swirled down into another depression as he internalized the blame for his failures. In his code of personal honor, in his assumption of personal responsibility, he was very unfair to himself, exhibiting an innocent individualism that blurred into negative narcissism. Unable to confront others or to make detached analyses, there was only one option, his traditional assertion that he, rather than anything outside himself, was fully the author of his own failure, and so he plunged inward and downward.

In this spirit, Sherman wrote Hugh Ewing, "I am of course used up root and branch." To Ellen he added, "I am afraid of my own shadow." He felt so defeated, he despaired to Ellen, that he almost hoped that his asthma would deepen into consumption and kill him. "If my lungs are actually diseased one winter will finish me off, which would be infinitely more satisfactory than struggling with trials."[31] In a similar, if more jocular vein of wishing himself dead, he would later write to Turner, "The worst mistake I made was in not succeeding in getting drowned on my first arrival [in San Francisco], or not getting knocked in the head in some of the rows of the country."[32] If he had been killed right off in 1853, he would have been spared all this humiliation. What a destructive waste had been the whole of his banking career. On the verge of willing his death, he did not really consider the optimistic conclusion of the Bible story, where God saved Jonah from the belly of the whale and let him live on.

As his foray into banking wound down mercilessly, Sherman revealed his hitherto concealed feeling that, when in charge of Lucas & Turner, he had always felt the perfect imposter. "I know no position in life so unenviable as one . . . of position not merited and . . . I think I occupy that most unenviable post," he wrote Ellen. Only now could he begin to depict in words "what has been a nightmare to me for years," a nightmare he could not articulate very directly. "Of course we did not break. We held high reputations among men, but who can tell the secret sorrows of the most pleased looking man who walks the highway?" Sherman was trying to tell Ellen that he had always felt like a fraud whenever he had assumed his bold banker's face to the world. He had never made a convincing case that he *was* a banker, certainly not to himself. Bankers had to tell lies of self-conviction, and of that he had been barely capable. "Of all lives on earth a banker's is the worst, and no wonder they are specially debarred from all chances of heaven."[33]

Six months later, Sherman would add that he was an army officer and only an army officer, and that he had been destroyed for his presumptuousness in thinking that he had some sort of general set of skills and values with direct applicability to the banking world. He lamented to John, in February 1858, "I suppose I am justly punished for giving up my commission for which I was well qualified for this place for which no amount of natural sagacity would suffice." But as he wrote Ellen a month later, he also lacked natural wisdom. "What I failed to do, and the bad debts that now stare me in the face, must stand forever as a monument of my want of sense and sagacity."[34]

In his breast-beating Sherman could even argue that his honesty, his subscription to his code of honor, demonstrated his lack of sense, his want of moral flexibility among the American men of commerce. "I wish I could, like most men, harden my conscience," he wrote Ellen at his juncture. He ought to be able to externalize the blame, "and say that I could [no more] help the downfall of this country, than to have dodged a cannon ball, or escape an earthquake." Why did he, alone among men, have to forfeit all hope of regaining "what little self-respect or composure I have ever possessed"? He ought to be able to slough off guilt and become a bear who triumphed even in a falling market. As he wrote to Ellen in the reflexive folk anti-Semitism of his era, "Individuals may prosper in a failing community . . . but they must be jews, without pity, soul, heart, or bowels of compassion." He ought to be able to become Shylock.

Of course this rhetorical reimaging was inaccurate and contrived. Sherman was writing this confused and deflating picture of his innermost sense of moral structure out of the delusionary logic of depression. He joined self-hatred for failure with self-inflation for honoring his debts. Perhaps his failure might even be a badge of inward grace for doing the right thing. But if he were good, God ought to have smiled on him rather than punishing him. He felt lost.

After walking away broke from banking late in 1857, Sherman experienced a miserable, restless two years in New York, San Francisco, St. Louis, and Kansas. He was unemployed and brokenhearted, his wife and children were back in Lancaster, being supported completely by Thomas Ewing, and he was not merely looking for another career, but literally scratching for a living. Things had come to such a pass that he was grateful, as a "broken banker," to accept the $20 John sent him three days after his bank failed.[35] Things went from bad to worse. After his four dispiriting months in New York during the financial panic, Sherman spent the ensuing months in St. Louis desperately liquidating his assets to meet those debts of honor. He spent three weeks at Christmastime in Lancaster, returned to New York for three weeks, followed by five months in San Francisco, to sell off remaining assets and those of Lucas & Turner at low depression prices. After a brief visit to Ellen, he went down to Leavenworth, Kansas, where his stepbrother, Thomas Ewing, Jr., practiced law, and subsequently out to Indian Creek, forty miles west of Leavenworth, where Thomas Ewing, Sr., owned tracts of land. Occasionally during this terribly rootless period, which seemed without prospective end, Sherman felt glimmers of hope. He was cheered somewhat when he contrasted San Francisco, where only pitiless Jews could succeed, with "rising, growing, industrious" places like St. Louis, where he thought "all patient, prudent, honest men can thrive."

But joining the world of solid St. Louis prosperity was a pipe dream, he usually believed. More often, Sherman felt miserable. "I look at myself as a dead cock in a pit, not worthy of further notice," he moaned to Ellen. "I am doomed to be a vagabond, and shall no longer struggle against my fate."[36] Sherman was in bondage to his wandering. Without career or home or self-respect, with such a perpetually insecure personal history behind him, he was without the most basic centeredness that anchors a personality; he was without a clear sense of self.

One of his first thoughts was to reenter the military, a nearly impossible task, as Sherman well knew, in the antebellum army, which could not accommodate all its own cadre of junior officers, much less invite back former ones. Acting on the chance that Congress might enlarge the army, he wrote Colonel Samuel Cooper, the adjutant general, in Washington, to register his name as an applicant for a commission above the rank of captain. "Recent events have destroyed all the plans and prospects in life which led to my resignation in 1853," he wrote to Cooper. This was hardly a good job-hunting tactic, but it was a heart-on-sleeve demonstration that Sherman sorely missed the security of camp life, particularly if he repressed memories of the intense boredom and restlessness he had experienced when he had been in the service. Nostalgia tugged, as he indicated to Ellen after a visit to Fort Riley, Kansas, in 1858. "It makes me regret my being out of service thus to meet my old comrades, in the open field, just where I most like to be." To further his attempt to gain a good reenlistment, Sherman wrote to his brother, John, the congressman, telling him whom to visit among the army brass in Washington in order to further his efforts to obtain a colonelcy or lieutenant colonelcy. Sherman did not hesitate to use these political contacts. He was certain, he wrote John, that he was "better qualified than many who will succeed," but realized that he was motivated by desperation, and that realistically speaking, he was unlikely to obtain such office, even with inside help. "I am adrift, and would like such a good commission, but I expect too much." He did. No commission appeared.[37]

The move to Leavenworth was another desperate gambit. Sherman begged work of Thomas Ewing, Jr. "All I want is a start, and I think I would settle down and not budge unless some unexpected good luck should turn up."[38] Responding to this down-and-out letter from his kinsman, Ewing invited Sherman to join him. During his army days, Sherman had read a bit of Blackstone, and following the incredibly casual licensing procedures for lawyers in mid–nineteenth-century America, particularly on the frontier, Sherman, who was neither a felon nor an idiot, but a respectable man who was motivated to practice law, was admitted to the bar. He added his name to Tom Ewing's shingle. If he had been an ersatz banker before, Sherman was an even more ersatz lawyer now.

In the event, almost no clients appeared, and so Sherman was left idle in his office. One day he bumped into Stewart Van Vliet, an old West Point classmate, now a major at Fort Leavenworth. As Sherman reported to Ellen, Van Vliet took one look at Sherman, "asked how I stood and I told him at once the whole fact that I was adrift seeking employment." Van Vliet immediately offered him a month's contract to superintend some federal road repairs and to run an auction of army livestock. Sherman was not too proud to leap at this chance even though he considered the jobs a bit demeaning. He then admitted his fears to Ellen that he was slipping out of the broad American middle class. As for himself, he would be content with "a tent and soldier's rations," and as for Ellen, he "should not like you to feel at all lowered in the social scale," by his taking such employment, "nor do I wish to contemplate our children occupying a lower seat in the synagogue than we do," Sherman wrote, fearing just that loss of social status for his children. He concluded with a homily that "real respectability consists in honorable action and not riches," but between the lines he revealed both that he knew how tenuous was his grasp on the kind of social standing represented by the solid Lancaster Ewings, and that he feared falling all the way down into the chasm of the unrespectable poor, dragging Ellen and his children with him.[39]

The route to the gold rush at Pike's Peak, Colorado, which began in the spring of 1859, ran through Leavenworth, and Sherman hoped to strike it rich supplying this population surge, much as he had done in California a decade earlier. "We are said to have brilliant prospects," he wrote John, but he was now so bruised and wary that what he most strongly anticipated was not so much the boom as the subsequent "collapse, just as San Francisco did when in size and population she got in advance of the wants of the country."[40] Sherman's new effort to seize the main chance was to invest $2,000 of his own money and $3,340 of

Thomas Ewing, Sr.'s, in the purchase of seventy-two hundred bushels of corn to sell to the trekkers heading west. Others had the same idea. There were few buyers, prices fell, and Sherman was left with four thousand unsold bushels and a substantial financial loss for both him and Thomas Ewing. It was another confirmation of his pattern of failure.[41]

Throughout this period of his life, Sherman's self-contempt deepened. To Turner he wrote, "I am utterly disqualified for business. . . . My experiences [have] completely destroyed all confidence in myself." So driven to the wall was he that he would probably have to admit defeat and go back to Ohio to accept "some obscure post," such as managing Thomas Ewing's saltworks. Without a steady career, his family threatened to disintegrate as well. To Ellen he confessed that he could not see how they could reclaim Minnie from the Ewings, who still had her as their own. "As long as we are vagabond, with no home or visible means of livelihood, I suppose we must give her up." Because he felt so inept, Sherman feared recapitulating his stricken childhood. If, in addition to failing to make a real career, he failed as well as a father and husband, then he would lose his daughter to the Ewings. Minnie would repeat little Cump's experience, and Sherman would have no one to blame but himself for this final mortification of abandoning Minnie in a manner so emotionally reminiscent of his own abandonment. Given such devastation, such seemingly endless depression, he just wanted to run for cover. As he frequently told Turner, "I would feel rejoiced to hide myself in any obscure corner."[42]

5

Going South and Leaving: The Ambivalent Unionist

PURSUING HIS seemingly perpetual job hunt in June 1859, Sherman dunned his old friend and army acquaintance, Don Carlos Buell, now assistant adjutant general of the army in Washington. Although Buell could not deliver the paymastership Sherman wanted, he sent along a job notice for the superintendency of the as-yet-unbuilt Louisiana State Military College, together with a letter of recommendation written on Sherman's behalf. Sherman applied immediately, in part because he was aware that he was known to several members of the board of supervisors and to Braxton Bragg, another old army comrade, a North Carolinian who had married into a wealthy Louisiana plantation family and was now a political power in Louisiana. Almost by return post he got the job.[1]

Buell and Bragg were also two of the grateful officers to whom Sherman had repaid those California debts of honor. Oddly, Sherman never seems to have commented in his correspondence that his virtue had been rewarded after all. In common with many white, Anglo-Saxon Protestants of his era and earlier, rewards always lacked the vivid reality associated with punishments: In this case something positive came back to help him.

As were his hosts, Sherman was well aware of the political dangers an Ohio man would face in 1859 by going south into a prominent public position. But Sherman was broke and desperate for a steady income and a respectable position, such as this college presidency and its $3,500 salary offered. These needs led him to overcome his fears of what he knew would be the political minefields of his new job.

Although he did have a history of contempt for the South, dating from his South Carolina days in the 1840s, and although he knew that he could never join in the secession Southerners were threatening with increasing energy, his reservations about the South did not stem from any personal antipathy to slavery, the great underlying issue dividing the sections. Nor did he disagree with the racism that rationalized the institution. Still, one cannot find anything so consistent as an integrated ideology concerning the slavery issue in Sherman's reflections. As in the rest of his intellectual life, he would blurt out his feelings, his prejudices, his ideas, his fears and hopes in often contradictory but personally and culturally revealing ways. He encapsulated many of the internally conflicting attitudes that he shared with a broad range of Americans concerning slavery during the 1850s, highlighted in all cases by fear and confusion.

As early as 1854, when his brother, John, was first elected to Congress, Sherman was warning him "not to be too forward" on the slavery issue. Because of his six years in Florida and South Carolina, Sherman felt he understood the South firsthand as most Northerners, John included, did not. "Having lived a good deal in the South, I think I know practically more of slavery than you do," he asserted. The concrete reality of slavery ought not to be confronted with abstract pleadings about its theoretical moral evil. "It is an old and historical fact that you must take as you find it." Slavery was "chargeable on the past," but could not be abolished in the present without forcing disunion. To this argument stemming from historical practicality, Sherman immediately added a curiously convoluted racist spin. "Negros free won't work tasks, of course," and whereas whites cannot bear labor during the southern summers, "the negro thrives in it," and therefore rice, sugar, and cotton "cannot be produced except by forced negro labor." Negroes would easily endure in the climate, but would work only by being enslaved and beaten.

Sherman did not add for John the caveat, which might have been expected from even the most conservative Northern man, that if a necessity, slavery was a regrettable necessity. Rather he argued that it ought to be allowed to expand along the Gulf of Mexico, "but not in the high salubrious prairies of the West." This was geographical determinism about the natural limits of slavery, a kind of argument Sherman thought ought to be used by Northerners to reassure themselves that slavery would prove self-limiting rather than endlessly expansionist, despite what the most aggressive proslavery ideologues were proclaiming of the infinitely expansive nature of the system. Therefore, both idealistic abolitionist arguments and divisive Republican Party politics, which insisted on an explicit territorial limit to slavery, would not be needed to curtail its spread. As he wrote John in 1856, "time and facts" were limiting the spread of slave territory, and John ought to avoid following the lead of politicians like the Ohio Republican, Congressman Joshua Giddings, or Senator William H. Seward of New York, who were insisting that there was an irreconcilable conflict between slave labor and free labor. John should "avoid the subject [of slavery] as a dirty black one," a formulation that suggested, in racist symbolism, that the whole subject was tainted with the filth of the inferior race.[2] Geography, history, and racism all led Sherman to the conclusion that slavery ought to be quarantined in national political discourse. Clean white men ought to avoid politicizing the dirty black issue. This was classic aversive racism: Slavery, blacks, and social problems should just go away.

Sherman worried, in letters written to others in 1856, that John might ignore the precedents of towering political figures like Henry Clay, Thomas Jefferson, and Thomas Ewing, who though opposed to slavery in principle always dampened down the issue in the political realm in the name of national unity. He feared John might commit some rash and "fatal error" as an antislavery agitator. "The slave states have claims to sympathy," he wrote his equally conservative business associate, Henry S. Turner, "for the institution is fixed on them by by-gone ages and instead of being badgered and irritated they ought to receive the assistance of all national men in regulating their affairs according to their own best judgment." Unlike his rather elaborate argument to John, with whom he was in fundamental disagreement, and whom he was eager to bring around if possible to a more conservative position, this was a simple declaration to a like-minded man that the North ought to leave the slave states alone. This was more accurately Sherman's own position.[3]

Sherman simply was indifferent to any moral dimension of the slavery issue in large part because he did not see Negroes as humans. In moral opacity, he resembled no northern political figure so much as

Stephen A. Douglas. In the political context of the late 1850s, particularly in the militantly antislavery Ohio Republican Party milieu in which John was moving, this moral neutrality was what one might term anti-antislavery, a form of opposition to Republican ideology deriving from what was becoming an extremely conservative perspective for a Northern man, one who knew that by then advanced public opinion in the North was becoming more opposed to slavery than was he. Willy-nilly he was aligning himself with the deeply racist position of the Democratic Party.

On a broader cultural level, especially when placating John, Sherman found some common ground with the antislavery beliefs welling up in Republican circles in the North. He recognized that in a wider European context slavery was fast disappearing—"the whole civilized world is opposed to it," he was willing to concede to John. Obviously he shared the American hubris that his nation was in the vanguard of civilization. Slavery, a system reliant on inferior labor, was retarded economically, and was bound to lose out, he believed, to the more progressive and productive Northern free labor. Given the inevitable decline of slave labor, he failed to feel any need to act politically on this sectional issue; indeed he bragged to John that he did not even vote himself. The backward South was not a powerful threat to the North; it needed to be combated at the polls, but was comparable to a "man having a deformity, like the fox who lost his tail and wanted all the others to cut theirs off." Sherman prescribed "indulging [Southerners] in their delusion with the . . . complacency of a strong man," as they lacked the "physical or political power to oppress the Free States."[4] In this rather passive manner, Sherman did adopt some of the free-soil argument of the Republican Party that the inferiority of slave labor would limit the spread of the regressive system, even if nature did not oppose slavery where it stood. But more generally, in his apolitical stance, one that was more nearly antipolitical, Sherman was implicitly allied to those in the North who would appease proslavery leaders and even secessionists.*

---

*Sherman gave this free-soil ideology its most conservative possible reading, adopting far more the racism of the Democratic Party, which held that slavery, attached as it was to an inferior race, was not an issue that ought to divide white men. Unlike John, Sherman was not a Republican, in fact opposing their basic energy, which was, however diluted, still antislavery in insisting that the institution must not be allowed to spread into any new territory. It is not sufficient to claim, as

Riding southward from Ohio on the steamboat *L. M. Kennett* in October 1859, Sherman was reminded, while listening to the political discussions among his fellow travelers concerning John Brown's recent raid, that Southern men "are as big fools as the abolitionists of the North," he reported to Ellen. The reaction to Brown's raid in Ohio had proved to Sherman's satisfaction that Northerners opposed slavery in the abstract, but that almost none were prepared to act as had Brown. The babble of the Southerners onboard, however, demonstrated that they misconstrued Northern opinion. "Extreme Southerners pretend to think that the northern people have nothing to do but steal niggers and preach sedition." A plague on both their houses, Sherman wrote his wife. "Feelings run so high when a nigger is concerned that, like religious questions, common sense is disregarded."[6]

While in the South, Sherman would remain in a ticklish position on the slavery issue. The gentlemen in his Louisiana circle would be pro-slavery, violently anti-Republican, and finally secessionist. Knowing John Sherman as one of their political enemies, they would as proper gentlemen scrupulously refrain from pushing William T. Sherman on the subject of his brother's politics or about the slavery issue in general. Despite his detestation for his brother's antislavery politics, Sherman did not want to repudiate him; neither would he bring up his feelings on slavery, which in any event were not at great variance with those of his hosts, despite the fact that he remained a loyal Unionist and, after all, a Northern man.

His professed neutrality gave Sherman a certain unmerited feeling of objectivity or even superiority on the slavery issue. While on leave in Lancaster from his job, after a year in the South, he would write to one of his close Louisiana associates that he was "sick of this war of prejudice." Up here in Ohio, the prejudice was that Southern planters had nothing to do but "hang abolitionists and hold lynch courts," while in Louisiana the prejudice was that all Ohioans were rabid abolitionists.

---

some historians have argued, that Sherman was simply an Old Whig, like Thomas Ewing, who opposed raising disruptive issues. Sherman was not such a museum piece as that; neither was he an intellectual. Lacking a coherent ideology, he did have a set of conflicting ideas gathered from across the political spectrum of the 1850s, which he blurted out rather than thinking through. In this he was like the majority of citizens who did not know what to think about dealing with slavery, any discussion of which gave them headaches. Perhaps historians should take such confusion rather than coherence as their organizing principle more often.[5]

Each side was doing the other basic "injustice" and each should "forget [prejudice] and mind their respective interests."[7] This was an increasingly thin wall between the sections on which to perch, when confrontation defined the political activities of the day, undermining any argument for simply maintaining the status quo.

In a curious way, being a Northern man in the South suited Sherman's apolitical politics. When he wrote back home to Northerners with whom he was politically antipathetic, he made pronouncements such as, "I have purposely kept aloof [of] the whole negro question." It is a "dirty subject," not worth contesting. "The freedom or slavery of a single negro is a small matter." This indifference was functional for him in his role in Louisiana, and it gave him a tiny ideological base from which to assault the growing antislavery Republicanism of the North. To Thomas Ewing, Jr., by then a leading Republican in Kansas, one less moderate than John, Sherman wrote in December 1859, "I would not if I could abolish or modify slavery. . . . Negros in the great numbers that exist here must of necessity be slaves." The "commercial fact" of their labor value would not be altered by "theoretical notions of humanity and religion." Northern people should "confine their attention to the interests of their own towns and property, leaving the South to manage slavery." This was in fact a standard proslavery argument, much akin to the defense of their peculiar institution made by the planters with whom he was drinking and breaking bread. Sherman did add, "Still of course I do wish [slavery] had never existed, for it does make mischief." But Sherman could convert even this tincture of antislavery into a racist sentiment, blaming the victims for the political tumult that surrounded their enslavement. In this vein, he wrote to Ellen, "Like Burton in 'Toodles' I say, 'damn the niggers.' I wish they were anywhere [else] or [could] be kept at work." Despite his intellectual notion of the superiority of free labor in the North, on moral, political, and social grounds, Sherman agreed with the planters in the defense of their institution against what they insisted was Northern interference, including that advocated by his politically active siblings.[8]

Sherman seemed at times to relish the slavehound aesthetic of shock he was applying to his antislavery brothers. For example, he made a sick joke about the servant issue. Should the ever-delicate Ellen come South to join him as they planned, early in 1861, Ellen's Northern white servants would all quit, "and then she will have to wait on herself or buy a nigger. What will you think of that?" he goaded his antislavery activist stepbrother, Thomas Ewing, Jr. "Niggers wont work unless they are owned, and white servants are not to be found, [and] everybody owns their own servants."[9] At another level the prospect of personally participating in slavery was unthinkable to him. He was not looking forward to the concrete resolution of Ellen's servant problem, whichever way it fell.

Sherman's new Louisiana career forced him to live a double life, building a new institution in the South, working with the Southern leadership cadre and training their sons, while suppressing, in tandem with his hosts, discussion of the basic issue of secession, which if it came to pass would make impossible his position among them. Even if proslavery, he was not a Southern planter, nor was he expected to become one as a condition of employment. As he wrote to Thomas Ewing in June 1860, "Not a man has said one word about John, or anything at which I could take exception," but this delicate avoidance could not go on forever.[10]

Action provided the best form of sublimation of issues for Superintendent Sherman and his hosts alike, and so, after his arrival at the grounds of the new academy in November 1859, Sherman plunged eagerly into work. He rapidly drew blueprints and then lived amid the carpentry as workers framed the first college buildings. He worked closely and positively with the supervisory board, governor, and legislature; he hired faculty, bought books in New Orleans, interviewed prospective cadets, and with whirlwind energy, opened the doors to the first students on January 2, 1860, a scant two months after his arrival—surely a record for instantaneous higher education!

Throughout 1860, Sherman continued to focus his talents and energy on building a sound college, a task he enjoyed, political undercurrents notwithstanding. He made an excellent impression on the planters who had taken a chance on him, and so, when he was offered a commercial banking position in London, one that would pay him well, but that also frightened him for all sorts of reasons, not the least of which was his personal history as a banker, the board countered with an improved contract and much praise. Gratified, Sherman stayed on. "[I have] the most friendly relations with the Board of Supervisors," he assured John. "I have a good berth here, and all are anxious for me to remain."[11]

Sherman's favorite task was to design and oversee the construction of a breezy and bright house for the superintendent's family. He wrote

Ellen in great detail about their home-to-be. At the end of his first year in the South, on December 16, 1860, he wrote his eldest daughter, Minnie, "the house is all done. . . . It looks beautifully; two front doors and one back one. All the windows open to the floor like doors, so that you could walk out on the porch either up stairs or down stairs. I know you would all like the house so much." Sherman wrote about this house with pride, but only in the conditional voice, for Lincoln had just been elected, South Carolina was on the verge of seceding, and Louisiana was preparing to follow within weeks. Thus the emotionally sustaining project of reunifying his family under a fine roof of his own making was about to vaporize. "My dear little Minnie," he wrote, "man proposes, God disposes. What I have been planning so long and patiently, and thought we were on the point of realizing—the dream and hope of my life, that we could all be together once more in a home of our own, with peace and quiet and plenty around us—all, I fear is about to vanish, and again I fear I must be a wanderer, leaving you all to grow up at Lancaster without your Papa."[12] Minnie was the daughter the Ewings had claimed during the San Francisco years, the daughter to whom he had never functioned as a proper father, the daughter whose early life most nearly resembled his own. The possibility of reunification with her and with the rest of the family was slipping away once again. "We have been too much separated," he wrote Ellen at this point; he had so "looked forward to our all being together . . . that this new disappointment breaks me down. It does seem that the whole world conspires against us."[13]

Just as it seemed that Sherman had built a castle for his family only to watch it vanish, so did it appear that the school he had well and truly built was going to slip from his grasp. He had not just built buildings, but had begun to shape with a firm leading hand, out of the lazy and self-indulgent sons of the Louisiana planter class, a real, disciplined core of serious students. Sherman had obtained his control of the student body through dealing with a two-day campus revolt four weeks into his first term, three months after his arrival in Louisiana. The first day of the uprising, he summarily expelled two sons of rich planters following a knife fight, and the next day expelled three of their friends for possession of tobacco and for back talk to him. "I will see if I am to govern here or to be governed by the cast off boys of rich planters," Sherman wrote Ellen, showing his continuing underlying contempt for the planter aristocracy he also admired and served. One must impose "severe restraint over the boys, who have been indulged at home to an unlimited extent." The Board of Supervisors approved his tough course without hesitation, demonstrating their willingness to deputize discipline over their sons, to support strictures far stronger than many imposed themselves. This discipline reduced the student body from fifty-six to fifty-one, but Sherman had gained the upper hand and had created a solid foundation.

Sherman was now, he boasted to Ellen, rid of five "noisy, insubordinate boys," and he had won "the struggle for mastery." Those boys remaining understood his authority, and were buckling down. "There can be but one master."[14] This was an interesting choice of words for a man living in a slave culture, but boys, even the sons of large slaveholders, were in their youthful rebelliousness rather like slaves, and therefore needed forceful guidance. "They had been so used to delay and procrastination that they could not understand the necessity of time," Sherman wrote several months after the rebellion to Thomas Ewing. He went on to describe the other chief mores of his Southern boys, beyond the tendency to insubordination and violence. "I took things in hand *a la Militaire,* usurped full authority, and began the system *ad initio.* We now have 32 cadets [of the original fifty-six, an acceptable attrition rate by West Point standards] who attend Reveille and all roll calls like soldiers, have their meals with absolute regularity, and are already hard at work at Mathematics, French and Latin. I am the only West Pointer, but they submit to me with the docility of lambs."[15] The authoritarian West Point system worked. Sherman's education and military experience paid off in Louisiana. Doubtless this enabled many of these young men to make the transformation into junior officers in the Confederate army far more smoothly than would have been the case had they not been put through this stern basic training by the man against whom many of them would be fighting in the not-too-distant future.

This masterful suppression of the rebellious sons of Louisiana was a microcosmic paradigm of the well-ruled society for Sherman. Social disorder and reordering in the wider society were much on his mind as the South approached secession, but he knew of course that he would not be able to deal with the larger Southern rebellion personally. Indeed, that larger political world was crashing in upon his fragile seminary, blowing away his ability to create order even in this one small place, this immediate creation of his own hands and will. Slavery had never been the issue for Sherman; "hyper-democracy" leading to disunion was the problem, and that condition would lead on directly to the anarchy of civil war. "My dear General, we are in the midst of sad times," he wrote at Christmas 1860, to G. Mason Graham, who headed the supervisory board at the academy. "It is not slavery—it is a tendency to anarchy everywhere. I have seen it all over America, and our only hope is Uncle Sam. Weak as that government is, it is the only approach to one."[16]

Shortly thereafter, as news of the secession of South Carolina spread through the lower South, Sherman was plunged into gloom. Six more states were also thundering toward secession, Louisiana included. In a fuller exposition of his thesis that an excess of democracy was finally leading to civil war, Sherman wrote to his wife that "our country has become so democratic that the mere popular opinion of any town or village rises above the law." Not "constitution and law books," but "popular opinion," as formulated in "bar rooms and village newspapers," had become the fount of the law. In the North, stupid, unrealistic, and unmanly advocates of the position that the higher natural law supervened the Constitution—"old women and grannies of New England, reasoning from abstract principles"—and in the South, law-defying adventurers intent on spreading slavery by unconstitutional means—people who "favor filibustering expeditions against the solemn treaties of the land"—had joined to foster anarchy. But really, it was a national, not a sectional, degenerative democracy that had led to secession. "Everywhere from California to Maine any man could do murder, robbery or arson if the people's prejudices lay in that direction." He had seen mob rule firsthand in California, and had been powerless to avert it; he had listened to extremist politicians in Congress and read them in the gutter press; he had watched as the gentlemen planters of Louisiana had allowed themselves to be swept by secessionist passions. The American people as a whole had descended into base anarchy. American democracy was rotten to the core.[17]

Secession would prove only the beginning of a general social collapse, Sherman predicted. Liberated from the remaining shreds of federal constraint, state governments, even more democratic, weak, and pusillanimous than the government in Washington, would blow up almost immediately. "These state governments are ridiculous pretences of a government, liable to explode at the call of any mob." Within the South, this disaster would create a situation of "worse wars and tumults than now distinguish Mexico." In his purview, Mexico, to which his thoughts frequently turned at this time, was a Hobbesian land of perpetual war, a bastard land of race mixing. Their form of anarchy was precisely race war, caused when the white power structure had dissolved, leaving the savage inferior races to gain access to white women, to weapons, and to the power to destroy that which they were incapable of ever rebuilding. "Mexico shows the result of general equality and amalgamation." In the United States a parallel example of the access of an inferior race to weapons and a measure of power was provided by "the Indians [who] give a fair illustration of the fate of negros if they are released from the control of the whites." The national government was collapsing, the state governments would soon follow, and then bands of savage Negroes would roam the South, making an endless guerrilla war against whites.[18]

This vision was not merely a hysterical adaptation by Sherman of those powerful subterranean fears Southern planters held of an always incipient slave revolt—although it was in part just that—but was also an expression of Sherman's obsessive, long-term fears that the bottom could always drop out of society, as it had in San Francisco in 1856, as it frequently did for him personally, and that loathsome chaos underlay the always-thin gloss of civilization. This apocryphal vision led Sherman into a reluctant and backward endorsement of national sovereignty over states' rights—the national government might be contemptible, but it is all we have. This was, however, only a weak argument, and Sherman's central expectation was of an imminent collapse at the center. Not for a moment did he accept the Southern argument that secession would be easy and peaceful—its core meaning to him was anarchy and a long, destructive civil war. However, Sherman did buy the argument, made by Southerners and a sizable minority of Northern conservatives, that the central government was corrupt and powerless to sustain the collective social good. If it fell, this was its well-earned fate.

The general government had failed to assert national authority by reinforcing Fort Sumter, "and will wait till [it] is attacked," Sherman noted to Ellen on January 8, 1861. "This disgusts me, and I would not serve such a pusillanimous government. It merits dissolution." As the Civil War began, Sherman was the most conditional of conditional Unionists. He defended slavery, and he hated the American government, the American democratic political system and its leaders, and

American commercial practices—and he despised the American people. He anticipated a political collapse, which he intended to sit out. "I see every chance of long, confused and disorganizing civil war, and I feel no desire to take a hand therein. When the time comes for reorganization, then will be the time."[19]

For at least a year, Sherman had been anticipating the collapse of constitutional democracy in America and its replacement with an authoritarian new order. "If our country falls into anarchy, it will be Mexico, only worse," he had written John early in 1860. "Disunion would be civil war and you politicians would lose all charm—Military men would then step on the tapis, and you would have to retire." Now, in early January 1861, Sherman insisted to G. Mason Graham, his Louisiana supporter, "My only hope for the salvation of the constitution of the country is in the army." He was telling off Graham, whom he considered a secessionist upstart, just as he was telling off his own brother, as an arriviste Northern Republican politician, letting them both know that only men like himself now could save the nation. To Ellen he argued, "This rapid popular change almost makes me a monarchist, and raises the question whether the self interest of one man is not a safer criterion that the wild opinions of ignorant men."[20] Though he qualified his monarchism, he was indeed positing an alternative to American constitutionalism—a military dictatorship.

Disunion, anarchy, purgation, national revitalization through an authoritarian new order—only thus might America be saved from itself, brought about only by harsh application of the thickest of iron rods. To David F. Boyd, his favorite on the Louisiana faculty, who would surely become a Confederate officer, Sherman wrote on May 13, 1861, "I still think in the hurly-burly of strife, order and system must be generated and grow and strengthen till our people come out again a great and purified nation."[21]

Observing onrushing secession with loathing and fear, Sherman knew that he would have to leave Louisiana and return North when the crisis came. He had known before he accepted the superintendency in the summer of 1859 that his stay would be contingent on national unity, and he had made this position clear to his Southern hosts, who accepted him on those terms. (This willingness reflected the beliefs of the Louisiana planters who hired Sherman as late as mid-1859 that somehow disunion would be averted.) As the denouement approached, Sherman was certain of his course. He wrote to John on December 9,

1860, "as long as [Louisiana] is in the Union I will presume she will remain, but the minute she cuts loose . . . I must settle up my affairs and leave." All reservations about the stupidly democratic United States notwithstanding, "still I cannot bear the idea of being opposed to the United States." Because of his deepest fear, he could not and would not "cut [myself] off from the northern states"; he could not abandon his homeland lest he be abandoned.[22]

Sherman's college incorporated a federal military post, with a stock of arms and an armory, over which he had command, and he wanted to avoid being put in the position of collaborating, whether actively or passively, with a military effort against the Union when the state militia would move to seize the post. Sherman's honor would be put to the test on this specific issue in a way he could neither finesse nor rationalize. Though certain of his course of action should these events unfold, as they were certain to do, Sherman was apprehensive about his choice, for material reasons at least as much as for ideological ones. "All patriotism aside," he wrote John on December 29, 1860, "I cannot afford to give up the means of livelihood I now have until others are at my disposal." A few days earlier, writing to Hugh Ewing, he had put the matter of self-interest even more bluntly. "I shall hold on to the last minute solely for the pay." In particular, Sherman was stalling because the state owed him $500, which he reckoned the legislature would not appropriate if they knew for certain that, rather than standing by Louisiana, he would in fact head up to the land of their enemies. To meet the "wants and necessities of my family," he wrote Hugh on January 12, 1861, principle had to be subordinated, and "I am compelled to stay here until I am turned out."[23]

Damned if he stayed, morally besmirched for hesitating, Sherman also felt he would be damned if he left, in the way his whole adult life had been accursed. To John, he wrote that he hated to "start again: the fourth time in the last four years. Each time from calamity." At least he was out of the banking business, that "most disastrous of all vocations." But he was in a financial vise and needed a well-paying career, not just some job. "I feel needy—my family requires money, & that a good deal, as much as I can possibly earn." Sherman pressed his brother to get him "something to do," something well paying, in Ohio or St. Louis, or better yet, in the inspector general's office in Washington. Sherman was again grasping at all career straws as he prepared to leave Louisiana. "I fear I must cut loose again with nothing."[24]

Accompanying his fear of dropping back into the void, however necessary politically that might be, was anger. He could blame the fates, he could blame himself, but he could also blame his wife. Ellen had been urging him to leave Louisiana for several months, and although he had made overtures to do so, like those to John, he was at his wit's end about an alternative livelihood. "If I could hear of anything . . . I could do for a bare maintenance I would forthwith quit here," he wrote Ellen on December 18, 1860, when he was without any such prospects. Two days earlier he had written her, "If you want me to come away you must move to get me something to do." As a rich Ewing, she should be the one to take care of business for a change, he implied. It was hardly manly to voice such a resentment, in Sherman's own vocabulary of values, and so he immediately added, "I know it is ridiculous of me to ask this of you, but on the other hand I could not stay ten days in Ohio without employment."[25]

After resentment, supplication, remorse, and self-abasement came fury. When Louisiana had seceded, he would resign, "and then the trouble begins," Sherman threatened Ellen. "Your necessities are great and you need a deal of money, and where it is to come from I know not." All his anxieties were really her fault. Without her bottomless material demands—a "deal of money" was his resentful mantra in letters about her to others as well as directly to her at this juncture (while not mentioning the five children, and a sixth on the way, whom he had sired)—he would be able to lead the simple life, the one *he* wanted. Well, like a worn-out workhorse, he would "stay in harness," he wrote his wife in ill grace, taking "anything in reason" in the way of work "that will increase your personal comfort. . . . Only be prepared for the hardest kind of times," he renewed his warning to her, immediately after reassuring her. If "worst comes to worst, I will rent your father's farm and pitch in for bread and butter."[26]

If he dropped into the impoverished classes, he was threatening to pull her down with him. It evidently gave Sherman a bitter satisfaction to return to such ritualized old marriage quarrels in times of stress. Although he was also intellectually capable of making the more detached analysis that he had been swept up in the rank politics of secession, on the moral level where he operated most of the time, he put politics aside, and in his heart felt he had failed once more. This gave him all the more reason to unload some of his disappointment onto Ellen, even though he knew that when he was writing this way he was being unfair. He understood that his looming unemployment had depressed his spirits as had the unlikelihood of his finding means to end his separation from his family. However, there was no one else besides himself to blame than Ellen, and given his modes of analysis, he had to blame someone and not just abstract forces. Mostly he fell back into the old grooves—blaming himself, as usual, as well as blaming his wife.

By the time it came, on January 18, 1861, Sherman's resignation was something of an anticlimax. He had held on as long as he could, long enough to collect that $500. His Louisiana planter friends were putting together a convention that would take Louisiana out of the Union on January 26. On January 18, in his official letter of resignation, he simply told the governor that he would maintain his allegiance to the old Union, "as long as a fragment of it survives." After secession, his staying on would be simply "wrong in every sense of the word." In a personal note appended to his official letter, he added that he had only the "kindest feelings to all" in Louisiana and that he was leaving "with much regret. Only in great events we must choose one way or another."[27] His resignation was accepted with equally sincere regret. He had liked them and they had liked him.

Sherman stated to the governor that he had resigned out of principles of honor, and that was true in the sense of the final and necessary cause of his resignation. But he himself sensed that there had been something ignoble in the more material motivations that had led to his long delay in choosing the only right course. He could not deny that in considerable part he had hung on for money and out of fear for his personal future. Less consciously, Sherman also feared political engagement on the irrepressible issue of the day. He was a conservative without anything to conserve. He was not an ideological nationalist in the way in which Northern Republicans, now in power, were beginning to redefine the nation. Neither, of course, was he a Confederate, who would destroy the nation to preserve the local liberty to hold slaves. When push came to shove he was a Northern man rather than a Southern man, however obscure that identity was ideologically.[28] Given all his conflicts—ideological, material, and emotional—it would prove hard for him to engage himself fully in the great civil war that he fully anticipated.

6

Into the Abyss: Collapse in War

IN LIGHT OF THE ferocious warrior he was to become by 1864, it is striking how reluctant Sherman was to take up the sword in 1861. At West Point he had read the Latin classics, but at no time during the Civil War did he indicate that he was Aeneas. Like Virgil's hero, he would hesitate to fight at the start, but then, after a long descent into the underworld, he would emerge as the most bloody-handed and bloody-minded general of them all.

Some of Sherman's reluctance was tactical—at the onset of war, he wished to position himself in just the right place in the army; some was ideological—he continued to abhor the Republican aggressiveness against slavery; some was personal—he liked the Southerners among whom he had been living, and hesitated to attack friends, thus violating bonds of personal loyalty; some was emotional—he was deeply afraid of failing once more, and this time of failing in the public glare and in his first and true vocation. Sherman was not afraid of battle itself, nor of death, but he was mortified with the anticipatory shame failure in war would bring to him.

Following his resignation from his college presidency on January 18, 1861, it took four weeks for him to settle up his administrative affairs, during which time Louisiana seceded from the Union. He parted with mutual sadness from his cadets and his hosts, several of whom he would meet again in battle, though none of them could have foreseen such an event with much clarity at this point. He then steamed up the Mississippi River he soon enough would begin to reconquer for the Union, up toward Ohio. During these last weeks he had put out all his usual job feelers, and, acting on her own, Ellen was pushing John aggressively—"begging," she called it—to obtain for Sherman one of the regular army commissions deserted by the traitorous departing Southern officers. "I am convinced that he will never be satisfied out of the army & I know that you can obtain for him a high position in it," she insisted.[1] Indeed, John's political star was rising. After Lincoln had appointed Ohio senator Salmon P. Chase to his cabinet as secretary of the treasury in early March, the Ohio legislature elevated John to Chase's Senate seat. John went right to work on his brother's behalf. It is ironic, in light of the scorn Sherman would pour on "political generals" during the war, that he was, in terms of political leverage, about the most political general of them all, as many events would prove during the opening year.

Not only was a generalship not in the works in early March, scant weeks before Fort Sumter, but service in the Union army was also not certain. Soon after he arrived back in Lancaster, Sherman received an offer from his old banking partner, Henry S. Turner, of the presidency of the St. Louis Railroad Company, a rather inflated title for the Fifth Street horsecar line. This respectable, if modest, job ($50 per week) was a good entrée into the business community of booming St. Louis and, most important, an opportunity to reunite his family, Minnie included, under his paternal aegis. However, the same mail that brought him Turner's job offer brought him a letter from the new junior senator from Ohio, urging him to come to Washington immediately to discuss a major military role directly with the new president.

There is no trustworthy account of this brief meeting, but even Sherman's self-interested recollection of it, written fifteen years later in his *Memoirs,* indicates that it was a disaster. John introduced his brother as fresh from Louisiana. "Ah, how are they getting along down there?" Sherman recalled Lincoln asking, probably in that bantering manner in which Lincoln handled most stressful situations, much to the discomfort and even anger of his less-than-ironic visitors. Sherman told Lincoln that the Southerners were "getting along swimmingly—they are preparing for war," to which Lincoln had replied, "Oh well, I guess we'll manage to keep house." Sherman recalled that he had been stunned by this jocular dismissal of the national military emergency. "I was silenced, said no more to him, and we soon left." Walking out of the White House, Sherman exploded to John, "damning politicians . . . [saying] you have got things in a hell of a fix and you may get them out as best you can." The national political volcano was soon to erupt, but he was off to St. Louis to take care of his family. John begged him to be patient, but he said he would not do so and would return to the Midwest immediately.[2]

Whatever the harried and temporarily insensitive new president may have intended by his remark about keeping house, Sherman took it to mean that Lincoln believed that politicians could manage the war without the services of professional military men. Judging from his immediately subsequent remarks and actions, Sherman had felt personally insulted and rejected by the leader of what he considered the stupid political caste that had caused the incipient war, the same sort of men who had debased commercial life as well, the same sort of fast operators who had led him to perpetual failure, the very men whose leadership would have to crumble away before they could be replaced by an appropriately ironhanded regime.

Off to St. Louis the Shermans went (this time Ellen and the children came too), where Mr. Sherman almost immediately fired a batch of workers, thus improving the profitability of the trolley line, and where Mrs. Sherman, to her husband's customary irritation, bought expensive furniture and a first-class Brussels carpet to furnish their rented house on Locust Street. During these same springtime weeks, the opening gambits of the war increased in pace, moves that would lead to the explosion at Fort Sumter on April 12. While these momentous events were unfolding, Sherman pushed his brother for the post of federal sub-treasurer in St. Louis, a political plum the powerful Blair family of Maryland and Missouri controlled rather than John. Not even attempting to take on the Blairs on their turf, John worked hard to procure the chief clerkship of the War Department for his brother, not so grand or lucrative a post, but better than a horsecar presidency. Immediately after Fort Sumter, John conveyed a War Department offer to Sherman that he become the major general in charge of all Ohio volunteers, and the much-distrusted Frank Blair offered Sherman the parallel post for Missouri. He turned down these chances, out of a deep funk that was both emotional and ideological. During the next ten weeks, as the war commenced, he gave this sullenness several iterations.

Sherman believed that his having left Louisiana was in itself a unique declaration of loyalty by a professional army man, during a period when so many others had deserted to the South. "I am the only northern man who has declared fidelity to the Union in opposition to the modern anarchist doctrine . . . of secession," he wrote John. "Twice . . . have I sacrificed myself"—in San Francisco, to a "northern mob"—and in Louisiana, to a "southern rebellion . . . and yet this is as nothing as compared to local partisan service." Republican politicians, including the president, "in shameful neglect & pusillanimity," had only wanted Republican hacks, not West Pointers, to defend the Union. While the South "try to attract" the best military men (soldiers just like William T. Sherman), "the north don't care a damn." Lincoln was incompetent. "I have not confidence in the head and advisors." Lincoln had rejected him to his face, rejected him right out of hand. "Had Lincoln intimated to me any word of encouragement, I would have waited" in Washington for a command. He would not be drawn into the "muddle" of the first call for three-month volunteers—"I like not the class from which they are exclusively drawn [i.e. Republicans]"—a class that inevitably "will be defeated and dropped by Lincoln like a hot potato." Nor would he return to Ohio to head the volunteer efforts, for "no man is a prophet in his own land, and in my case it is especially so." The current war effort was unworthy of him, as were the American people, and he would bide his time "until the [political] leaders will be cast aside" and a new set of men will arise to create a real military government, the fantasy of imminent dictatorship he had been polishing for quite some time.[3]

Sherman's litany of resentments climaxed on April 8, when he wrote to Montgomery Blair, the postmaster general, rejecting the War Department chief clerkship, and concluding, "I thank you for the compliment . . . and assure you that I wish the Administration all success in its almost impossible task of governing this distracted and anarchical people."[4] John let his brother know that this letter had given great offense when it was passed around in Washington, and that several of the cabinet had concluded that Sherman would turn traitor, as had so many other Union officers, Northerners included.

Although he was a Unionist in principle, Sherman was refusing to come to the aid of his country in her hour of trial; he was failing to abide by the martial code and his own code of personal honor. His family began to pressure him to cast off his reservations and personal grievances and to do his duty. "I know a good many will be displeased with my apparent apathy," he wrote to Thomas Ewing, Jr., on April 26, and on May 13, he noted to a Louisiana friend, in an image replete with fears of abandonment, "my friends and family are almost cold to me and they feel and say that I have failed at the critical moment of my life. It may be that I am but a chip on the whirling tide of life destined to be cast on the shore as a worthless reed."[5]

Sherman saw himself as a passive victim, spinning downward once more into destruction. He felt personally wronged by his experience of American life, and, paradoxically, he also feared being drawn into a war of potentially endless furor, fought against fellow Americans of the South whom he knew and admired, and fought for a principle, abolitionism, that he rejected. But after several weeks of rapidly escalating public events, and considerable pressure from his family, the shame and isolation of failing to participate became insupportable, and so, on May 9, he volunteered his services to the secretary of war. Fortuitously, at this moment the government created several new regular army regiments in addition to far more numerous volunteer state forces, and on May 14, Sherman was offered the colonelcy of the Thirteenth Infantry. As he was preparing to accept this offer, Sherman wrote to Thomas Ewing, Jr., to say that such a position was "as much as I could ask. . . . Frankly I am not entitled to the Brigadier General's place." Even in a colonel's role, his cold feet told him he might prove inadequate. "I shall occupy it, and when ordered shall do my best." He was prepared to react but not to act, to respond to higher authority rather than to be authoritative.[6] In this spirit he packed his grip, his sash, and his sword and went to Washington to join the war, far more in relief than in exaltation. Joining the army only answered the issue of serving or not serving, pleasing or offending his family and friends. It did not assure Sherman that the war was worth fighting, that it would be fought properly, or that he would do other than fail once more in his new task as a fighter.

The democratic army he was joining in Washington that June was a pell-mell ingathering. Americans had been willing to maintain only a tiny army in peacetime and had no experience in large-scale centralized bureaucracy; and so they had to improvise, equip, train, and send into war an immensely complex social organization starting from scratch. For several weeks in Washington, Sherman was deputized the job of inspecting and organizing raw troops from all over the North. He then was assigned a command of volunteers rather than a regular army unit, which he apparently accepted without protest. He did not join his brigade of one Wisconsin and three New York City regiments until July 5, and had the opportunity to drill them only a handful of times before they marched on July 16, on to Richmond, on to Bull Run.

Sherman despised his untrained troops—"rabble" was the term he applied to them in his correspondence—and they in return hooted and jeered his attempts to discipline them. On the eve of battle, Sherman was still distant from his men, and he was also hesitant about an anti-Southern crusade. At this time, he wrote from Alexandria, Virginia, to little Minnie, of his desire for a limited war. "We must fight and subdue those in arms against us, but we mean them no harm. We have not disturbed a single slave," not even those of Robert E. Lee, on whose plantation he was encamped. Sherman admonished his daughter not to get swept into war hatred, for he was fighting "thousands . . . whom I used to know as kind, good friends," who, moreover, in their own eyes were fighting in self-defense, of "their country, their houses and families against foreign invaders. So my dear child, do not get into the habit of calling [them] hard names of rebels, traitors." Rather, they had become "deceived," which was "easy enough for a people to do."[7] When writing to Minnie, Sherman was also reminding himself about the need to keep his heart open to his all-too-human enemy. An old army man, he had never been in battle, and was far more apprehensive about the moral price relentless killing might exact than he was about the possibility of death.

Bull Run was a Union disaster. After advancing in relatively good order for most of the day, in midafternoon the Union army broke and fled back to Washington. No worse nor better than other Union troops, Sherman's brigade exemplified the tactical errors. His four regiments attacked *ad seriatim* rather than together, each in turn advancing bravely up the same hill, only to fall back in the face of heavy Southern musket fire. Until midafternoon, his troops remained in their place and "seemed perfectly cool," Sherman reported three days later. But when sufficient numbers of Southern infantry approached closely enough to produce intense small-arms fire, his units finally panicked and fled the field. By the next morning, back in the fortifications outside Washington, Sherman wrote to the army authorities that his brigade, "in common with our whole army [had] sustained a terrible defeat, and has degenerated into an armed mob." They may have been little more than a mob, but he was hardly a proper colonel—"I know not if I command."[8]

As for the Unionists in general, "the North is after all pure bluster," he wrote Ellen. "Courage our people have, but no government." As for his own troops, this armed mob had fallen into "shameless flight." He believed that he had stood up to gunfire in terms of personal courage, but that he had failed to lead. "I am absolutely disgraced now," so much so that he wished to "sneak into some quiet corner" following this "mortification of retreat, rout, confusion, and now abandonment by whole regiments." In the privacy of his correspondence with his wife, Sherman demonstrated that he had tasted once more the familiar and bitter acid of defeat.[9]

The military leadership did not agree with Sherman's private self-devaluation, and gave him a de facto promotion to brigadier general, adding four more regiments to the three already under his command. To his way of thinking this affirmation just added to his problems, as he had not received real troops, but "volunteers called by courtesy soldiers," as he wrote to Ellen. To John he added that three of his seven regiments were in a state of mutiny, half of them "clamorous for discharge on the most frivolous pretexts," over one hundred of them prisoners in the hold of a nearby man-of-war, and the one company of regulars among this rabble "all ready with shotted guns to fire on our own troops."[10]

In his *Memoirs,* Sherman later wrote that at this juncture a captain from one of his New York regiments, an Irish lawyer, announced to Sherman, while standing among a crowd of his fellow Irishmen, that his three-month term was up and he was going home, to which Sherman recalled barking, "If you attempt to leave without orders, it will be mutiny, and I will shoot you like a dog!" while reaching his hand into his overcoat as if to draw a pistol. The captain looked at Sherman hard and backed down. Later that day, President Lincoln and Secretary of State Seward came riding by in a carriage and invited Sherman to join them while they rallied the troops. Inside the encampment, the carriage stopped and the mutinous captain approached it, announcing, "Mr. President, I have a cause of grievance. This morning I went to speak to Colonel Sherman, and he threatened to shoot me." After a moment's hesitation, Lincoln leaned down to the captain and said in a stage whisper, "Well, if I were you, and he threatened to shoot, I would not trust him, for I believe he would do it." The men all roared, laughing at the captain, and the carriage drove on, Sherman quickly explaining himself. Lincoln reassured him, "Of course I didn't know anything about it, but I thought you knew your own business best."[11]

Even though Sherman had cleaned up this legend fourteen years after its occurrence, making himself look good and in charge, as all memoir writers do, there remains also in the retelling something of the intense antipathy between Sherman the martinet and his disaffected troops. It took a long while and searing events for raw recruits to be turned into soldiers, and Sherman was hardly alone in these early wartime experiences of near-mutiny. But given his shaky self-confidence, and following the rout at Bull Run, such scenes hit him hard and made him feel increasingly isolated and downcast. While in this condition, in mid-August, Sherman was asked by Robert Anderson, the ailing and aging hero of Fort Sumter, to join him as his second in command in Louisville, where Anderson had been created head of the new Department of Kentucky. Sherman agreed to his new appointment reluctantly, and only after explaining to the president his "extreme desire to serve in a subordinate capacity, and in no event to be left in a superior command." Lincoln readily agreed to this odd request, joking that his usual problem was in finding places for generals who demanded to be heads of armies. To Ellen, Sherman wrote about his new position that "not till I see daylight ahead do I want to lead," thereby expressing his lack of confidence not only in the Union war effort, but also in himself.[12]

Full of anxiety, Sherman soon fell into command of the Department of Kentucky, which was charged with holding Kentucky, the border state that Lincoln, among others, considered key to maintaining the Union at this time. Sherman had gone west in early September. Robert Anderson, who was not up to a major command, either physically or emotionally, resigned on October 5, and Sherman was appointed to replace him three days later. Sherman could neither run a theater of command nor hold himself together. He fell into what we would now consider a clinical depression, and on November 9 was removed from command in disgrace. This catastrophe and its aftermath were the nadir of Sherman's career and of his life.

There is a great deal of evidence on the subject, which has never been thoroughly analyzed, and it is worthwhile to carefully unravel the characteristic negativity of this sort of horrific personal crisis. This deconstruction of self also exemplified the cultural catastrophe of the Civil War.

Shortly after arriving in Kentucky, Sherman took about four thousand men on a reconnaissance in force into Kentucky's interior, to Muldraugh's Hill. Once there, he felt cut off and imperiled. "We can barely supply our wants, and are liable at any moment to have [our] wagons seized," he reported to Anderson. He had come "for effect" but after a week "nobody has rallied to our support," while, "on the contrary," hundreds had gone South to join the Confederate forces. He should have had at least twenty thousand men to counter this popular Confederate rising in the making. The very countryside seethed with hostility.[13]

Back in Louisville to take command of his army of about eighteen thousand men, on October 8 Sherman had further forebodings. "Kentucky looks for some bold stroke," he wrote a fellow general, meaning by this a Confederate assault and not a Union action. The same day he wrote a local Unionist citizen, "I am forced into the command of this department against my will, and it would take 300,000 men to fill half the calls for troops," a truly remarkable inflation of numbers required. Expression of his anxieties would continue unabated in all his letters. "Arms are coming forward very slowly. . . . They have not sent me a single regular. . . . They don't do us justice. . . . We are moving heaven and earth to get the arms, clothing and money necessary in Kentucky [but] the supply is scant. . . ." To Abraham Lincoln, he wrote, "The Kentuckians, instead of assisting, call from every quarter for protection against local secessionists." To army headquarters in Washington, Sherman importuned, "the great center of our field [is] too weak, far too weak, and I have begged and implored till I dare not say more. . . . Our force here is out of all proportion to the importance of our position. Our defeat would be disastrous to the nation, and to expect of new men who never bore arms to do miracles is not right."[14]

By the beginning of November, Sherman was beside himself concerning the military onslaught he anticipated. To Brigadier General George H. Thomas, in the field at Crab Orchard, Sherman wrote, "In the present aspect of affairs it is impossible to say how or where we shall winter. This will depend on our enemies. They will not allow us to choose." Sherman told Thomas, "I can hardly sleep to think [of] your fate." In other letters to Thomas, Sherman warned of a "vast force" of the enemy, who were engaged in an enormous conspiracy, a "Herculean effort," to seize Kentucky, a design he found "impossible to penetrate," though he knew it was huge. For evidence of this conspiracy, he told Thomas that "they have pressed all the wagons from several counties, for they could have no other use other than what I name." Against such rumored forces "it would be madness to contend." Should the Confederates succeed in cutting Thomas's supply lines, "I have never had a force anything approximating the magnitude of the occasion."

To Washington, Sherman warned that the enemy was everywhere. "Our enemies have a terrible advantage in the fact that in our midst, in our camps, and along our avenues of travel they have active partisans, farmers and businessmen, who seemingly pursue their usual calling, but are, in fact, spies. They report all our movements and strength, while we can procure information only by circuitous and unreliable means." Sherman felt on the brink of being "overwhelmed." In response, "we should have here a very large force." Now we are at a "stand-still" and to advance would be "simple madness." All our columns "are in peril, not so much in front as rear." Under these apocalyptic circumstances, Sherman in effect conceded that he could no longer carry on. "Do not conclude . . . that I exaggerate the facts. They are as stated, and the future looks as dark as possible. It would be better if some more sanguine mind were here, for I am forced to order according to my convictions."[15]

On October 17, Simon Cameron, the secretary of war, swung by Kentucky to make his personal assessment of the military situation in Kentucky as well as of the commander's state of mind. The fullest account, in Sherman's postwar *Memoirs,* is retrospectively self-justifying, but revealing enough even so. Cameron, who was a corrupt, incompetent, and vicious opportunist, soon to be cashiered by Lincoln, assured Sherman that everyone in his hotel room with him during the meeting was a friend, and that Sherman should speak out without restraint. In fact, Samuel Wilkerson, a *New York Tribune* reporter, was in the room, and two weeks later he published an account of the meeting. With full gloom and voluble expression, Sherman let loose all the fears that were filling his letters. He expected an enormous Confederate army to march into Louisville any day. Instead of the 18,000 troops at his disposal, he needed, immediately, 60,000 men for the defense of his position and 200,000 to go on the attack. McClellan's chief Union army was 100,000 strong to cover a hundred-mile frontier, while he had to cover over 300 miles. Cameron chimed in, "You astonish me!" and later "Great God, where are the men to come from?"[16] When the *New York Tribune* published its version of the story on October 30, which many papers across the country rushed to reprint, Sherman's mental stress became a national sensation.

Compositely, the fears Sherman expressed to his military peers and superiors amounted to a delusion. Nearly every civilian was a spy, the enemy was omnipresent, invasion of Louisville was imminent, the Union cause was helpless and passive, the army required would have to be twice the size of the Army of the Potomac—and all of this Sherman expressed in the most unguarded, public manner. None of this made much sense; and the package revealed Sherman's mental distress more than a military analysis based on realistic assumptions. In particular, it was unsound to conclude from mere rumors, such as those concerning a great gathering of enemy wagons, rather than from concrete intelligence, evidently missing from Sherman's reasoning, that the enemy was all that powerful, pervasive, and well organized.

One demonstration of the level of unjustified alarm in Sherman's picture is to contrast it with the view of other military commanders in Kentucky at the same time. General George H. Thomas was reserved and calm in expressing his opinions. In early November, General A. McD. McCook, who commanded a division in the field, wrote Sherman to reassure him, out of exasperation or friendship or both, about the actual military situation. "My command is improving each day, and you need have no fears for us. I will be timely apprised of their movements, and will move to please you. Bear in mind also they cannot insult a force of 12,000 with impunity, particularly when my movements can be more rapid than theirs." Judging from later developments, McCook's assessment was astute. Soon after he took over from his old friend Sherman, Don Carlos Buell wrote east to George McClellan, "Sherman still insists that I require 200,000 men. I am quite content to try with a good many less." In contrast to Sherman, Buell wrote that "as for the enemy, I do not find it difficult to ascertain what he is and what he is doing." His reading of military intelligence was that the enemy was fortifying one place strongly, and two weakly, and could concentrate a maximum of twenty-five thousand men. "As for his attacking [Louisville], though I do not intend to be unprepared for him, yet I should almost as soon expect to see the Army of the Potomac marching up the road." Both McCook's gentle rejoinder and Buell's heavy sarcasm simply flattened Sherman for drawing and broadcasting catastrophic conclusions from such modest evidence.[17]

Where McCook and Buell were detached in their manner, Sherman had conveyed an out-of-control quality in his dispatches, the same impression he made on many people whom he came in personal contact with at that time. He forcibly struck two New York journalists, Henry Villard and William G. Shanks, with his strange energy and behavior. He was "a bundle of nerves all strung to their highest tension," Shanks later recalled. Both reporters shared the Louisville telegraph office with Sherman nearly every night, from about 9:00 P.M. often until 3:00 A.M. All would pore over the Associated Press reports as they came in. Sherman unceasingly talked, paced, and smoked cigars. He seemed to smoke, Shanks concluded, "not from pleasure but as if it were a duty to be finished in the shortest imaginable time. . . . Sherman puffs furiously." He would never finish a cigar, and his stumps, as many as ten a night, which would accumulate on the telegrapher's desk, were named by the porter who cleaned the rooms "Sherman's Old Soldiers." Sherman simply never sat still, Shanks wrote. His fingers were always busy, "twitching his red whiskers—his coat buttons—playing a tattoo on the table—or running through his hair." While sitting he would cross and uncross his legs continuously. And on and on he talked, nervously and obsessively. "He *must* talk quick, sharp . . . making his odd gestures which . . . emphasize his language. He never hesitates at interrupting anyone, but he cannot bear to be interrupted himself." Sherman admitted to a bad temper, but "what is worse, he makes no attempt to control or correct it."

Sherman's lack of tact and self-censorship in his conversational monologues, as in his official dispatches and in his letters to friends and family, troubled the newspapermen, not just because he offended them with his rudeness, but because they felt he was giving away too much, in a manner of less-than-appropriate manly reserve. "He expressed himself entirely without any reserve about men and matters," Villard recalled, "trusting entirely to the good faith of the hearer" not to bear tales. He also discussed the political and military situation in Kentucky, "and I could not help thinking that, in doing so, he said more than was wise and proper." Sherman clearly communicated to Villard his certainty of failure should his command be attacked, a "dread" that "took . . . hold of him." When he had talked himself into gloom,

he would "lapse into long silent moods" and would "literally brood
. . . day and night." After returning to the Galt House from the telegraph office, he could not sleep, but would "pace by the hour up and
down the corridor . . . smoking and obviously absorbed in oppressive
thoughts." By spending the nights in such "strange ways," in such public misery, Sherman had almost guaranteed that the hotel guests would
both notice and gossip, "and it soon was whispered about that he was
suffering from mental depression."[18]

During her husband's few weeks in command of the Army of the
Cumberland, Ellen, who knew him best, became increasingly concerned about his mental state. He wrote her extensively and repeatedly
of the imminent military catastrophe he anticipated, and added, in
both intended and unintended ways, descriptions of his emotional condition, which alarmed Ellen.

"We have no weapons to move forward"; the Kentuckians are "unfriendly" and many are spies; the enemy must "design to advance," or
else they are "bigger fools than I take them to be." This he wrote on
October 3 in a letter he signed off with, "for myself I care little but for
those entrusted to my care in a desperate cause I am oversensitive,"
thus indicating to Ellen that he was wound too tight to remain calm
and detached. Each subsequent letter gave more highly colored reports
about the hidden enemy and his sense of an imminent military collapse. On October 6 he wrote, "instead of being wiped out they [the
enemy] propose to wipe us out," and added that he feared the raw
weather would bring on his asthma, and that despite being quartered in
a comfortable house, "I am up all night." He also reported headaches
from smoking too many cigars. In this way, Sherman told his wife
about the aggravated insomnia the reporters and his fellow guests at
the Galt House in Louisville soon would notice. He concluded that he
had never "felt so much a desire to hide myself in an obscure place
. . . to avoid the storm that threatens us," a storm in which he would
"drift to the end [and] what that will be God only knows." The worst
and "most unpleasant of all feelings," he added in several later letters,
was to be "in the midst of people ready to betray," for he was constantly under the "quiet observation of spies." He also hated the feeling that in the South he was now "esteemed a cold-hearted man," as
the pro-Confederate ladies of Louisville often told him. The enemy was
coiled, "and [we] might be surprised and taken any night. This thought
alone disturbs my sleep, and I cannot rest." And so he continued, in a

repetitious, compulsive, downward spiral of brooding, where each fear fed on the others, and where insomnia, loss of appetite, chain-smoking, and most likely, drinking too heavily deepened his depression, carrying him into a delusory worldview.

By the time of his November 1 letter to Ellen, Sherman was in utter panic. "To advance would be madness and to stand still folly." Now he wanted to hide not just himself, but also "you and our dear children . . . in some quiet corner of the world," in order to escape his current locale, where "I find myself riding a whirlwind unable to guide the storm." The minutiae of command absorbed all his time, and he felt swept up in an oceanic guilt toward Ellen that "I have not laid open to you the secret movings of my mind and heart." He was coming hard to the end of his life, and that end would be one of total dishonor, the inevitable culmination to his life of failure and humiliation. "The idea of going down to History with a fame such as threatens me nearly makes me crazy—indeed I may be so now."[19]

As she read these letters, the handwriting and content of which were losing shape and clarity, Ellen's fears for him mushroomed. On September 29 she wrote that she was "sorry to find you still desponding," and assured him that he would "lead [his] army, not to death but to victory." She had become accustomed over the years to black moods and alarmism in her husband's letters, but when these missives grew ever more deeply depressed, her concern grew apace. On October 4, she wrote him that his most recent letter had caused her "greatest anxiety and pain," and had driven her to feel "so nervous and uneasy that I am fit for nothing and cannot even write with a steady hand." By the time of her letter of October 10, she seemed to have realized that she could not be swept up in his fears, nor give in to her own, and so she wrote him a chatty sort of letter, asking him in a jollying way, "Do write me a cheerful letter that I may have it to refer to when the gloomy ones come." At this point there is a gap in the correspondence, and one cannot follow Ellen's mounting alarm.[20]

Given the contents of her husband's letters, it could not have come as a total surprise to her when, on November 8, a captain on Sherman's staff telegraphed to Thomas Ewing, "Send Mrs. Sherman and youngest boy down to relieve General Sherman immediately from the pressures of business. No occasion for alarm." This was an extraordinary request, one that reflected the concern of his staff that he had lost self-control. As Ellen wrote to John from Louisville on November 10, the telegram had appalled her, and she had rushed to Louisville immediately. "Knowing insanity to be in the family," she wrote John, referring to their uncle, Charles Sherman, who was a chronic "melancholic," and "having seen Cump in the seize of it in California," when Lucas & Turner had disintegrated financially, "I assure you I was tortured by fears" when called to his side. These fears "have been only in part relieved since I got here." The crisis had just come, when Sherman had asked McClellan to have him relieved. Ellen arrived on November 9, the same day McClellan had complied with the request, appointing Buell in his stead.

Ellen did not like what she saw during the week she spent at the Galt House with her husband. "His mind had been wrought up to a morbid state of anxiety," she wrote John. She was not discounting the remark in his recent letter that he felt he might be crazy, which was rather more confirmed than refuted by the other evidence she had discovered in Louisville. "He has had little or no sleep or food for some time." His "servant boy" told her he "seldom took a meal lately—that sometimes he would eat nothing all day." Perhaps even more alarming, he seemed to have lost normal human contact with those around him on his staff, who struck her as normal, plausible men concerned in a caring way about their commander. "Several of the army officers are staying at the hotel and all seem deeply interested in him. He however pays no attention to them, or to anyone, and scarcely answers a question unless it be on the all engrossing subject. He thinks the whole country is gone irrevocably & ruin & desolation are at hand."[21]

John, in Ohio when Ellen returned, was mortified by what she told him. However, he decided not to return to Washington to fight his brother's case, and on November 19, wrote rather cold-bloodedly to him why he would not. "You are not only in error" about Kentucky, he wrote Sherman, "but are laboring under some strange delusions. . . . You have been so harassed with the magnitude of your labors & have allowed yourself so little rest . . . that your mind casts a sombre shadow on everything. . . . Your manner is abrupt and almost repulsive . . . so unlike your usual manner." John was writing this way, he insisted, "with the freedom of a Brother," but Sherman hardly could have taken other than discomfort from these words.[22]

Ellen was deeply shaken by Sherman's mental condition, which she assessed both sympathetically and tough-mindedly. She observed obsessiveness, insomnia, loss of appetite, loss of realistic contact with others, and delusional misjudgments, which are characteristic of depression, or melancholy, as it was called more frequently in the nineteenth century. It was a well-understood illness then, one probably as widespread as now. She also noted a prior bout of depression in 1856–57, in California, to which she might have added his bitterly unhappy stay in Kansas in 1858–59, and she commented on the previous history of depression in the Sherman family. As we shall see, Sherman had at least one later episode of depression, in 1878, and one of his sons became a deeply depressive adult. As Ellen understood intuitively, there was an endogenous and recurrent biological element in Sherman's depression, although apparently this was the one time in his life when he collapsed this far, when he believed he had failed at his chosen life task and not just at subsidiary careers, and when his failure was made in public, his shame placed on display across the Union.[23]*

Short of capable officers and eager to occupy his old friend outside of Kentucky after Buell had arrived to relieve Sherman of command, Henry Halleck ordered Sherman to join him in Missouri, another badly divided border state. Immediately after Sherman arrived in St. Louis on November 23, Halleck sent him down on an inspection tour to Sedalia. There Sherman found another imminent popular insurrection of the type only he had discerned in Kentucky. "The country is full of returned secessionists who are driving out all Union men. . . . We must move forward or backward." On his own hook, Sherman ordered the whole Union force to advance from Sedalia. Back in St. Louis, and acting on his own analysis of military intelligence, Halleck immediately reversed Sherman's decision. Halleck was "satisfied, from reports of scouts received [in St. Louis] that no immediate attack on

*Here I disagree with the analysis of John F. Marszalek, in his recent biography, that Sherman never "lost his mind" but "remained whole." I am not sure what either losing one's mind or remaining whole might mean as mental categories. In an earlier book, Marszalek argued that Sherman was not "psychotic" at the time, because if he had been, nothing would have prevented him from taking his own life as he threatened (and as I discuss below). By this standard, only suicide itself could prove psychosis, an analysis I much doubt. But, more significantly, the use of the category of "psychosis" is not helpful in discussing what happened to Sherman in Kentucky late in 1861. Sherman's society recognized melancholy and mental breakdown much as we recognize clinical depression, not as psychosis nor as necessarily fatal but as deeply painful and incapacitating mental stress, a condition surely characteristic of Sherman at this time. Psychosis, which was never Sherman's problem, is another issue.

Sedalia is intended. You will therefore return to the city," he ordered Sherman, "and report your observations on the conditions of the troops you have examined."

Halleck let Sherman know that he looked deluded and foolish. What was worse for Sherman, when the ever-present reporters got hold of this flurry of telegrams, they published them, using them to reaffirm the picture of looniness Sherman had already created in Kentucky. Even before sending him to Sedalia, Halleck had had a physician examine Sherman, and the doctor had reported a condition of "such nervousness that he was unfit for command," an analysis for which Halleck found ample confirmation in Sherman's strange initiative in Sedalia.[24]

Halleck sent for Ellen Sherman, who was waiting in St. Louis for her husband on December 1, when he returned from his ill-fated scout into the interior of Missouri. At the urging of Ellen and Halleck, Sherman took a twenty-day leave to return with Ellen to Lancaster. After his departure, Halleck wrote to McClellan that in Sedalia, Sherman's orders had had the effect of "stampeding" the troops. Halleck was convinced that Sherman's "physical and mental system is so completely broken down by labor and care as to render him for the present entirely unfit for duty. Perhaps a few days rest may restore him," he concluded with considerable skepticism.[25]

Ellen was deeply grateful for the "consideration" Halleck had shown her husband, in contrast to the "shabby" treatment accorded him by the authorities in Washington and Kentucky. She took Sherman home with hopes of nursing him back into fitness for the command Halleck assured her would be awaiting him.

For the first ten days in Lancaster, Sherman began to eat, sleep, and relax. Ellen read aloud to him from Scott and Shakespeare, and tried to provide a kind and embracing atmosphere. Then, on December 12, the *Cincinnati Commercial* of the day before arrived, with a scabrous account of Sherman's mental health, a sensationalized story that was immediately picked up by the wire services, and widely reprinted. GENERAL WM. T. SHERMAN INSANE screamed the headlines, and the story asserted that while commanding in Kentucky, Sherman had become "stark mad." The press report insisted that three times in one day Sherman had telegraphed the War Department for permission to evacuate Kentucky and retreat into Indiana, and that he had frightened the citizens of Louisville by insisting, as "one of his mad freaks," that their city could not be defended if the Confederates attacked. At Sedalia, he had also acted the "madman," issuing "preposterous" orders that his subordinates refused to obey. It was "providential," the article concluded, that this mad general had not lost an army or the state of Kentucky.

Sherman's immediate response to this fulfillment of his worst nightmares, withdrawal rather than denial, was typical of clinical depression. To Thomas Ewing he wrote concerning his "disgrace" that "in these times it is hard to say who are sane and who insane." Ellen wrote both Thomas Ewing, Jr., and John that Sherman's greatest fear was that the family would be "overwhelmed with mortification on his account." Ellen's immediate instinct was to begin to fight back. She assured John that Sherman had never telegraphed the War Department advising evacuation (and all available evidence concurs with her on this), and that officers in the War Department or reporters had concocted these lies. She failed to convince her husband to go to Washington to fight for his reputation, as he felt too "terribly" to do so, but she charged John with an effort to refute this libel.[26]

Ellen also wrote immediately to Halleck, telling him that her husband had been regaining strength until receiving the blow of this newspaper lie. Halleck responded with a generous letter to the effect that the Shermans ought not to fret much over such attacks, exactly of the sort made on him all the time, and to which he had grown inured. "Tell the General I will make a Yankee trade with him—I will take all that is said against him, if he will take all that is said against me. I am certain to make 50 per cent profit by the exchange." Halleck left Sherman's return date to the army entirely up to Ellen. Halleck also wrote to Sherman's stepbrother, Phil Ewing, assuring him that "squibs" in the press meant nothing and "can do him no serious injury," that he personally thought nothing "was the matter with him except a want of rest." And in response to Sherman's own letter asking reassurance that Halleck had not countermanded Sherman's orders at Sedalia because he took them "as evidence of want of mind," Halleck replied that he had simply not been ready to make an attack at the time, nor had he apprehended an attack by the enemy. Halleck did add, however, "in all frankness and kindness," that Sherman's careless comments about the "defenseless condition" of the Union cause in Missouri had "led to unfair and harsh accounts by those who did not know you. . . . I say this," he quickly added, "only to put you on your guard in future." After these gentle admonitions about Sherman's tendency to oververbalize his fears, Halleck concluded that he hoped to see his old comrade "well enough for duty soon."[27]

Evidently Sherman felt that remaining in passive disgrace in Ohio would be even more painful than renewing his combat with the Fates, and so, despite Ellen's misgivings, he did not extend his leave but entrained for St. Louis on December 19. During the ensuing three months, two people rescued him: In the army Halleck nurtured him back into active service with great tact and affection, while on the political front, Ellen organized and led a major campaign to reclaim his public honor, in Washington and against the press.

On December 23, Halleck assigned Sherman to the command of the huge Union base at Benton Barracks, St. Louis, placing him in charge of recruitment, training, and logistics. Halleck kept Sherman close by him, frequently discussing strategy with him, one of Sherman's areas of intellectual clarity. Sherman gathered strength in this position and began to calm down. Given the episodic nature of most major depressions, he might have turned the emotional corner at about this time in any event, but Halleck reemployed Sherman in a way that would help rather than hinder his recovery.

Sherman also struck up a friendship at this time with U. S. Grant— someone Sherman knew to be a fellow long-term peacetime failure, and a notorious drunk to boot—on the eve of Grant's smashing victories in Tennessee, at Fort Henry on February 6 and Fort Donelson ten days later. These first Union victories in the West buoyed Sherman enormously, and he let Grant know that despite being Grant's senior, he would be delighted to waive rank and support him in any way possible. "I . . . have faith in you. Command me in any way," he wrote Grant, who replied warmly to the "kind tone" Sherman had taken, and added that he would support Sherman's promotion to major general at the propitious moment. Sherman soon had a chance to begin proving his loyalty to Grant, for on February 14, Halleck assigned Sherman to an independent command at Cairo, Illinois, serving under Grant. After a month of observing his energetic logistical support of Grant from this staging area, Halleck gave Sherman a division in the field in Grant's army. Halleck, who could have ruined Sherman's career, instead had nursed him thoughtfully and steadily. Sherman was back in action.[28]

While Halleck revived Sherman from St. Louis, Ellen went on a two-pronged offensive on his behalf. In her letters, she reassured him of her love and of his worth. At the same time she organized a political counterattack for him, energizing and directing the powerful Ewing/ Sherman forces in Washington, and personally taking on the job of getting right to the top—to Abraham Lincoln.

When Sherman first left for St. Louis on the morning of December 19, Ellen was nearly defeatist on his behalf. "I feel desolate in my room now, without you, dearest Cump. . . . I may perhaps never see you again." She urged, "after this thing has passed by & the public have another victim to gloat over," he should either "resign or have some quiet place assigned," far from the gibes and stares of the "wicked." And it would also be so much the better for him if he could then gain religious faith in this monastic backwater.[29]

Her negativity lasted only a morning, however. That afternoon, Ellen wrote a powerful letter to the president on her husband's part. "Being of a nervous temperament," she wrote Lincoln, Sherman had shrunk from "the responsibility of his position [in Kentucky], which supplied no adequate means of defense." His perfectly reasonable requests for men and material had been ignored in Washington, and he had been relieved all too "readily" and "cooly." A week after he had left St. Louis for his furlough in Lancaster, "conspirators" in the military and the press, of whom she named Adjutant General Lorenzo Thomas, had "had time to arrange their plans" for the simultaneous publication across the Union that Sherman was insane. "No official contradiction has yet appeared and no official act has reinstated him. Will you not defend him from the enemies who have combined against him?" she implored Lincoln. She asked him to send for the general, or make "some mark of confidence" to relieve Sherman from "the suspicions now resting on him." His lowly position at Benton Barracks "seems an endorsement of the slander."[30]

Thomas Ewing agreed with his daughter, he told John, that there was an "extensive conspiracy" against Sherman. Conspiracy theory was the chief explanatory device of eighteenth- and nineteenth-century American politics, and all the Ewings and Shermans readily believed that there was such a cabal in this instance. Fleshed out by the family, this was a plot by fellow generals, using newspapermen as their "mere tools." In specific, Halleck and his associates in the West—"What care they!" for Sherman—and McClellan in the East were designing to "annihilate Cump and kick him back into obscurity." Ellen even convinced herself that McClellan, who was naturally "selfish and conceited," was an active traitor, a leader of the Knights of the Golden Circle, the much advertised Confederate fifth column organization in the North.[31] The most striking single element of this theory was its denunciation of Halleck at the same moment when Ellen was exchanging concerned letters about Sherman with him. Assuming hypocrisy on Halleck's part, and maligning him behind his back when all he was evidencing was real care, was duplicitous on her part.

Although highly unlikely, and to our ears hysterical, such accusations had the effect of galvanizing the Ewing/Sherman clan. Ellen had constructed a publicly defensible version of Sherman's recent military behavior—that he had been only normally anxious, that he had not been supported by superiors, but instead had been attacked by fellow generals for ulterior purposes. This public, external, political version contrasted with the domestic family version, which had been based on a psychologically realistic assessment of Sherman's mental depression. Ellen took the lead both in constructing the public conspiracy theory and in protecting the family secret; these dual stories exemplify the Victorian tendency to create double lives—with the grand public figure at odds with the private, wounded, human self.

On December 22, Hugh Ewing, by then a brigadier general stationed in Washington, wrote Sherman that he had been making the rounds of the army brass in Washington, who had assured him of Sherman's high standing with them, due in large part to a recent presidential visit, when Lincoln had praised Sherman's "talent & conduct" at considerable length to a large group of officers. Hugh added that "in a short time *your superiority will be demonstrated and publicly understood.*" Lincoln's word would carry enormous weight with the toadies on the army staff and their subsequent decisions would radiate out into the field. Ellen could also assure Sherman that subsequent to her correspondence with Lincoln, "John Sherman will attend to your interests in Washington," as would Thomas Ewing, Jr., "who has got great influence," and Thomas Ewing, Sr., who was "great friends just now" with the president.[32]

After having been delayed by the illness of two of her children, she set off for Washington. It took her and her father several days to get a preliminary appointment with Secretary of War Edwin M. Stanton, and a meeting with the president himself. By the time of this lengthy interview of January 29, Lincoln was well prepared. He had every practical reason to assuage this powerful Ohio (and Kansas) Republican clan, and he knew just how to talk to the aggrieved Ellen Ewing Sherman. As she wrote Sherman the evening after the meeting, Lincoln had greeted her with the "highest praise" for Sherman. Lincoln said he and Seward had been "strongly impressed" with Sherman when they had shared that carriage in Washington right after Bull Run, that he personally had promoted Sherman to brigadier general because of this positive impression, even before the Ohio congressional delegation had forwarded Sherman's name for promotion, and that he had felt *"safer"* after Sherman had taken command in Kentucky "than *before.*" "He said he wanted *you* to know," Ellen wrote, that he had the "highest & most generous feelings towards you," and that "recent reports"—a delicate phrase for Lincoln to have used—"were unfounded [and] that your abilities would soon merit promotion."

Ellen wrote that she then had placed her personal arguments before the president—that she had known her husband since he was ten years old, "and that you were the same [mentally] that you had always been." The problem was not in Sherman but in his "enemies among . . . fellow Generals," who employed journalists as their "tools." Lincoln repeated his "kindly" feelings for Sherman, chatted amiably with Thomas Ewing, and added that John Sherman "'turns up his nose at me, & won't ask me for anything,'" a gentle but pointed admonition he wanted conveyed to the chilly John, which also indicated that he, Lincoln, would have been glad to have responded positively to John had John called on his embattled brother's behalf.

Although Ellen Ewing Sherman was far from the only general's wife to campaign on behalf of her husband, she surely was one of the most effective. Perhaps her intercession was effective in part because Lincoln really did understand and sympathize with a fellow sufferer. After all, Lincoln experienced clinical depression too—which he called the "hypo," and described as a helpless, desperate condition—and if he had made it back from the abyss, he could encourage the Shermans.

Ellen and her father were delighted with this "most satisfactory interview," which she then followed with social calls on the wives of several generals, including Mrs. McClellan, as well as Mrs. Seward and Salmon P. Chase, the secretary of the treasury who was also the most powerful Ohio Republican. She felt well received everywhere. "A little time will wear away this slander and then you shall stand higher than ever," she closed her report of her assault on Washington, with elation.[33]

While she was acting so decisively and reporting vividly on her activities to her husband, Ellen was also doing her best to reassure him, in frequent letters, not only of her love but of her admiration. Shortly before her interview with Lincoln she wrote, "be patient, my dearest. . . . Keep cheerful and calm as possible . . . and in a *very short time* you will look back upon these dark days as a troubled dream—a nightmare." She rejected his repeated expressions of self-loathing. "Why will you say that you have brought disgrace on anyone? You in whom we all feel so much pride," you who are incapable of any "dishonorable action," you whose "talents are of the highest order." She urged him to "banish the spirit of self-distrust." He was fully worthy of the love and respect of the person who knew him best: He was a paragon, a man who was "the soul of honor & full of truest courage & withal so kind and forgiving. You only want Christianity to make you perfect."³⁴

Although he was deeply grateful for the efforts of Ellen and Halleck, Sherman found it nearly impossible to dig himself completely out of his depression. He wanted to believe Ellen's official version of an external conspiracy against him as the author of his problems, but fundamentally he stayed within the interior space of failure and despair. On his return to St. Louis on December 17, he wrote Ellen, "I see no hope at all. You can trust in Providence," while in his own heart, "why he has visited me with this terrible judgment is incomprehensible." He repeatedly wrote Ellen and John about the "disgrace" he had "brought on all associated" with him, which had left him with feelings "too horrible to contemplate [so that] I cannot rally under it."³⁵

As opposed to the conspiracy theory his family was weaving, Sherman accepted the fact that he had wildly "exaggerated the force of our enemy in Kentucky," a misconception that had "almost paralyzed my energy of action." In one letter to Ellen he suggested that his "former associations with the South" had been the underlying factor, which had "rendered me almost crazy as one by one all links of hope now parted." Poorly articulated, this confession suggests that he had not been able to reconceptualize the all-too-human and loving people with whom he had lived so recently as external enemies deserving of his punishment and destructiveness: He could not kill them in good conscience. Both this reservation and his "want of ability & nerve for . . . command" had in his own estimation rendered him unfit as a potentially major military figure. His disgrace and removal from command in Kentucky had been "deserved. . . . I confess I have not the confidence of a leader," he wrote John. In the same mode of self-contempt, he wrote Ellen that he would be content "to slide into any obscure place."[36]

Ellen's continual and fulsome reassurances to the contrary notwithstanding, Sherman obsessively insisted that he had failed her and their children. As he had been a bad husband in the past, he had proven by his collapse in Kentucky that he was unworthy of all the private love and public effort she was expending on his behalf. "I will try and be more punctual in future in writing you my dearest wife who has been true and noble and gracious and comforting always. That she should thus be repaid is too bad." Dishonoring himself, he had disgraced himself to her. "I have given you pain when it should have been pride, honor and pleasure." As he loathed himself so he abased himself before Ellen who was so good: "I ought to get on my knees and implore your pardon for the anxiety and shame I have caused you." On and on he went in a litany of guilt, quite typical for someone in the throes of depression.[37]

Disgracing his wife, he had also debased his patrimony to his children, Sherman insisted repeatedly and in great shame. "May God in his mercy keep them in his mind, and not let them suffer for my faults," he prayed. Only his knowledge that killing himself would have sealed his disgraceful legacy to them had stayed his hand. Sherman had not admitted his suicidal impulses to Ellen while he had collapsed in Louisville and Missouri, but now, on January 2, 1862, he admitted to John that "I should have committed suicide were it not for my children," and, more ambiguously, to Ellen a week later, "when the figures of Minnie & Lizzie & Willy stand before me I feel as though I should cast myself into the Mississippi."[38] His suicide, as he tried to pull himself out of his (to him) shameful depression, was a near-run thing.

Most often, Sherman presented a more abstract and passive version of his suicidal impulses, as he had during earlier depressions, through declaring a desire to "slide into any obscure place," an oblivion perhaps possible in this world, though more likely in the next, as he could not escape sufficiently into unconsciousness while living among men and events without sacrificing every shred of honor. Still, the desire to escape into oblivion was there all the time, as he wrote to Ellen: "How I envy the howling crowd that passes by that care not for the morrow."[39]

At his most morbid, Sherman united these themes of dishonor, suicide, and passively slipping away, when he twice told Ellen about his feelings for "Poor Lizzie," his nine-year-old second daughter, whom he found so "quiet and sensitive." He wrote to Ellen on January 19, 1862, "I almost wish she would quietly slumber in eternal rest and escape the sad events in store for us." Ten days later he returned to this macabre vision, making explicit the vicarious identification he felt with his most fragile child, the death wish he projected onto her. "Poor Lizzie. How I would like to lie us down together in that common grave and sleep the long sleep of eternity." All the other children in their brood "seem more of the world," and they did not worry him, Sherman told his wife. But as for Lizzie, "I feel toward her different." Were she to die, "I shall grieve but little," for then she would be safe from the world, "only I hope my time will be measured by hers. . . . I would feel safe with her gentle spirit."[40]

Her father did not consult Lizzie about this prospective death, nor visit her at this time save in his mind's eye. She was fine and safe enough in Lancaster. But it was as if the imagined dying innocent, poor Lizzie, were also a fragment of his archaic self-image: The grievously wounded child, unlike all other Sherman children, was also the nine-year-old Tecumseh who had been so suddenly abandoned, who never could become adult enough to cope with the clamor and chaos of this world, who would be better off dead in heaven, joined to the loving spirits of departed loved ones, with mother and father too, the other lost Sherman souls. He could join his long-lost parents, and be in spiritual union with his delicate daughter, and they would be waiting there when Ellen and the other, sturdier children would join them later on. In his despair at his failure to build an honorable career, to be a loving husband and father and family leader, he sometimes longed for worldly death and spiritual reunification, in that timeless place where all would be perfect, as it was not and could not ever be on earth. In his fearfulness he longed to reject the public world for the private, to resolve Victorian dualism in the direction of the inward, the childlike, the feminine. In his despair he urgently subscribed to Ellen's belief in divine domesticity—a family unification unreachable by the flesh-bound on earth, obtainable only by spirits in heaven.

After Grant's great victories at Fort Henry and Fort Donelson, after Sherman was given a new and more active command in Cairo—which also lent concrete evidence that the work and love of Ellen and Halleck were making an impact on his mind—he began to turn from despair and self-loathing to a somewhat more positive direction. By the beginning of March, his handwriting had recovered most of its usual coherence as well. "I think of you and our children all the time," he wrote to Ellen in a clear hand the day he reached Cairo, but this time he continued in a less morbid direction, "and wonder and dream if I can possibly erase the past and be to you a subject of pride and respect." On the eve of taking his division into the field in Tennessee to join Grant, Sherman's new resolve was more positive. "If it should so happen that I can regain my position and self-respect and should . . . ever be restored [in a public way], I will labor hard for you and the children." While he was arriving in Tennessee, Ellen was passing on to John the good news that by all the reports she was receiving, "Cump is in *first-rate* health." John had long urged his brother to push through his depression—"Above all be hopeful and push onward. Action, bold action, rigorous action is now demanded"—and Sherman was now asserting to John that he felt "perfectly easy and shall do my best."[41]

Yet there remained something tentative in Sherman's renewed resolve. In his letters he most often portrayed himself as the passive object, still more of a result of events than a maker of them. "I don't pretend to look ahead far and do not wish to guide events," he wrote Ellen from Pittsburg Landing, Tennessee, on April 3. "They are too momentous to be a subject of personal ambition." He was barely prepared for a new test of his leadership abilities; he remained on tenterhooks about his likely military performance and its meanings for his life in his world. He also retained a suicidal streak—yes, he should try to act bravely, but perhaps his death in battle would be the best proof of honor redeemed. As he had written to Ellen a few weeks earlier, "I should stand up to [events] like a brave man and perish if need be."[42]

Part II

TRANSFORMATION

7

Ecstatic
Resurrection
at Shiloh

SHORTLY AFTER 7:00 A.M. on the morning of April 6, 1862, near
the Shiloh Church on the banks of the Tennessee River, Brigadier
General William T. Sherman was riding with his staff in front of his
camp. Sherman's orderly, the handsome young Illinois cavalryman
Thomas D. Holliday, was riding beside the general. Suddenly, and to-
tally unexpectedly, a hidden group of Confederate pickets opened fire
on the Union party, shooting Holliday right off his horse, killing him
instantly. Massed enemy infantry then poured out of the woods,
throwing themselves in a desperate assault first against Sherman's division, and then against the whole Union army encamped around Shiloh.

Despite their later protestations to the contrary, both Grant and his
subordinate Sherman were unprepared for this attack. Grant, who always thought far more offensively than defensively, had assumed that
the Confederates, who were well entrenched twenty miles to the south,
at Corinth, Mississippi, would stay within their lines awaiting his attack. Partly for this reason, and partly out of concern lest his untested
troops lose their fighting nerve, Grant did not instruct his army to dig
defensive trenches around their camps. He also left his forces divided
by the Tennessee River, ignoring another obvious practice of battlefield organization. Sherman, encamped on the most exposed flank of
the Union army, compounded Grant's poor judgment by failing to

post defensive pickets or to patrol with sufficient energy in the direction from which the enemy might come. He also ignored the evidence brought to him several times of increasing numbers of Confederate cavalrymen and pickets in the woods to the south, in part out of overcompensation for his panic five months earlier in Kentucky, when he had so vastly overestimated the enemy. On April 3, three days before the battle, he had written to Ellen, echoing Grant's assumptions, "We are constantly in the presence of enemy pickets, but I am satisfied that they will wait our coming at Corinth." The next day, he wrote to Grant that he expected nothing more than continued picket firing. "The enemy is saucy [but] I do not apprehend anything like an attack on our position."[1]

Though he had been surprised, Sherman had a great battle, as did Grant. His division helped blunt the Confederate attack, and on the next day contributed to the victorious counteroffensive that drove the badly mauled Confederates from the field. He rallied his troops with coolness and determination, riding everywhere among his eight thousand men, despite having three horses shot dead under him, and suffering a grazing wound to his shoulder, and another more serious buckshot wound to his right hand, which he wrapped with a handkerchief, without ceasing to observe the battle and to give clear orders. So frequently did he expose himself to enemy fire that there seems to have been a suicidal element in his behavior. He knew that he could redeem himself from the charge of insanity and implied cowardice that had followed him from Kentucky only by heroic performance in battle. Being ready to die is often synonymous with being brave, even unreasonably brave, in the face of the enemy. An intelligent commander does not expose himself heedlessly to enemy fire. A heroic commander places himself in harm's way, often deliberately, thereby blurring the distinction between heroism and stupidity, in the name of honor. Civil War soldiers extended the chivalric tradition into the age of modern, mass warfare, which they helped to inaugurate. Men like Sherman reinforced the code of personal honor despite its increasing military counterproductiveness.

When he wrote his report on the battle, only three days after it had ended, Sherman discussed the behavior of the Union cohort in the heroic mode. On the second day of the battle, Sherman was marshaling his division for a movement into a Confederate-infested forest. He paused to watch some Kentucky Union troops attack. "Here I saw

Willich's regiment advance upon a point of water-oaks and thicket, behind which I know the enemy was in great strength, and enter it in beautiful style. Then arose the severest musketry fire I ever heard, which lasted some twenty minutes, when this splendid regiment had to fall back." Later that afternoon, a brigade of another "splendid division" from Kentucky "advanced beautifully, deployed, and entered this dreaded woods"; while yet another Kentucky brigade, Colonel Rousseau's, moved "in splendid order steadily to the front." In his report, Sherman then commended the colonels who had led several regiments as "cool, judicious, intelligent," as "brave and gallant," as behaving with "great gallantry . . . leading handsomely," showing "quick perception [and] great personal courage."[2]

Coming from the warrior who is perhaps best remembered for his 1880 statement that "Boys . . . War is all hell," such heroic romanticism seems out of place. But at Shiloh, Sherman grabbed at the chance to regain his honor, in full public view and in his own heart. In such romantic language, war remained an individual experience, a personal test for Sherman and for his fellow soldiers. Amid the carnage, Shiloh became, immediately on the retelling, a sublime experience for him— "beautiful and dreadful," as he soon told John—a test of brave men who had stood the greatest trial of manhood. Sherman wrote that way of others and they perceived him likewise.

On the second day of battle, the soldiers of Rousseau's brigade, who had despised Sherman when he was their commander in Kentucky, put their hats on their bayonets and cheered him as he rode by, with his wounded hand and powder-blackened face. "They recognized me and such shouting you never heard," he wrote Ellen on April 11. "I have since visited their camps and never before received such marks of favor."

If the men in the ranks cheered, so did Sherman's superiors, noting in particular his personal bravery while under heavy fire. On April 9, in his report of the battle, Grant, who was Sherman's immediate superior, wrote, "I feel it a duty . . . to a gallant and able officer, Brigadier General W. T. Sherman, to make a special mention. [Sherman] displayed great judgment and skill . . . although severely wounded in the hand the first day, his place was never vacant. He was again wounded and had three horses killed under him." On April 13, Henry W. Halleck, overall Union commander in the West, wrote to Secretary of War Edwin M. Stanton, "It is the unanimous opinion here that . . . Sherman saved the fortune of the day on the 6th . . . and contributed largely to the glorious victory on the 7th. He was in the thickest of the fighting on both days, having three horses killed under him and being wounded twice." Halleck then requested Sherman's immediate promotion to major general, to date back to April 6, the first day of his glory.[3] Clearly impressed by Sherman's recovery, as witnessed by his brave performance, Halleck also gathered reflected glory to himself for having rescued the depressed failure from Kentucky and having eased him back into active command.

Grant's praise meant the most to Sherman, who so much admired his cool and victorious leader. Grant returned the admiration on a human as much as on a military plane. He wrote his wife, Julia, three weeks after Shiloh, "In General Sherman the country has an able and gallant defender, and your husband a true friend." Sherman earned Grant's growing esteem not merely in battle but from his timely and heartfelt intervention when Grant's career was in jeopardy. In mid-April, partly in response to public outcry over the defensive unpreparedness of the Union army at Shiloh, Halleck came to the field from St. Louis and took over active command, placing Grant on the shelf as his unused second in command. When Sherman heard that in response to this demotion Grant had asked to be relieved from command—in effect, to quit the war—he immediately rode over to Grant's camp to talk him out of it. Essentially he told Grant to follow his own example. Before Shiloh, "I had been cast down by a mere newspaper assertion of 'crazy,' but that single battle had given me new life, and that now I was in high feather." Having moved through adversity, he now used his own difficult experience to give Grant solace. Sherman argued that Grant too should stick it out through bad days, because soon "some happy accident" would "restore him . . . to his true place." Luck would reward he who persevered. Grant took Sherman's advice, and five weeks later indeed was restored to his command, when Lincoln called Halleck to Washington to serve as general in chief. Grant was understandably grateful to Sherman for this act of friendship. He assured Ellen Ewing Sherman on July 7 that "there is nothing he, or his friends for him, could do that I would not do if it were in my power. It is to him and some other brave men like himself that I have gained the little credit awarded me, and that our cause has triumphed to the extent it has."[4]

Reinforcement from his brightest and most experienced subordinate was just the boost Grant had needed, and this augured well for their future relationship. Grant, who was not as politically obtuse as he often appeared, was fully aware that he was writing, through Ellen, to the powerful Ewing/Sherman political alliance. They might help him one day, and he, his star again on the rapid ascendancy, intended to help them. This was not cynicism on Grant's part, but higher politics, grounded in genuine, battle-tested friendship. The two men would trust, like, and admire each other until the end of the war. In a real sense, Sherman had cemented their alliance, accepting his subordinate role, and using his own previous history of mental distress in a creative and generous fashion.

Sherman shared his abrupt spiritual rebirth most fully with Ellen. Four days after Shiloh, in his letter of April 11, which can best be characterized as ecstatic, he first reassured Ellen that he was safe, despite his wounds, and briefly sketched his role in the battle. He then told Ellen that "they say that I accomplished some important results, and General Grant makes special mention of me in his report which he showed me." Three days later he would add that "I noticed that when we were enveloped and death stared us all in the face my seniors in rank leaned on me." In his first letter, written in the same oddly passive voice, he notified Ellen of his spiritual reversal. Whereas for months, and as recently as two days before the battle, he had proclaimed his desire to slip away (in his half-acknowledged dishonor) into some obscure corner, now he wrote, "I have worked hard to keep down, but somehow I am forced into prominence and might as well submit." The first and most profound demonstration of the new esteem of others had been the huzzahs of those Kentucky troops on the second day of the battle. Not just his conduct, but their recognition of it, and then Grant's, allowed him to feel that indeed he had reclaimed his honor and self-esteem. In a somewhat ironic manner, Sherman told his wife that he knew she would now commence reconstructing his personal history for their progeny, based on his reversal of fortune at Shiloh, through applying scissors and paste to the heretofore dreaded newspapers. "I know you will read all accounts, cut out paragraphs with my name for Willy's future study, all slurs you will hide away, and gradually convince yourself that I am a soldier as famous as General [Nathanael] Greene," of Revolutionary War renown. He added, three days later, that he was "not in search of honor or fame" on his own account, "and only court it for yours and childrens sake . . . and I know your father will be pleased." And ten days after that he sent a box of cannonballs and bullets he had gathered from the field at Shiloh to his two boys. "I would like to see Willy's eyes when he sees the dread missiles," he told Ellen. These were relics of his triumphant battle for his boys to heft, markers of a reputation reversed in the maelstrom of battle.[5]

Sherman was somewhat disingenuous in projecting his desire for fame onto his loved ones. His performance at Shiloh had led to immediate rewards that had validated his own bruised ego; he felt vindicated. However, a gentleman refrains from bragging, and so, after receiving word of the promotion to major general, for example, which Halleck had offered him, and which he and his family had sought so avidly as the imprimatur of his redemption, he wrote to Ellen, "I don't feel very solicitous on the point of promotion except they are making so many Brigadiers that the rank confers no honor."[6] In plain fact, he wanted his head higher than that of others, and well noticed. At the same time he wanted to pay back Ellen, his children, and his clan for all the grief he had caused them. As they had rallied behind him, so now should they share in his reward. Sherman's urgent vanity was quite apparent; his attempts at dissembling his egotism were transparent.

Sherman had closed his account of Shiloh to Ellen with a brief acknowledgment of the "horrid nature of war," but the single greatest impression his letter left was of an enormous mood swing, an emotional reversal. He did not mention that two thousand of his eight thousand men had been killed, wounded, or lost in the battle, nor did he make their suffering central to his account. The most vivid writing concerned his newly heroic self, barely concealed in the retelling. Pride replaced self-laceration. He would remain in this state of elation for the rest of the war. He had "seen the elephant" as the Civil War saying went—faced a death he almost courted in battle. Never again during the war would he return to depression. In the future he would confront personal reversals and attacks on him through explosions of rage rather than by swallowing them as had been his wont for the first forty-two years of his life. Verbally and in writing, he would attack, not retreat. His life would remain full of difficulties, but aggression would replace self-reproach when he met new conflicts.[7]

Ellen Sherman flowed with pride at her husband's reversal of fortune. Of course, she told him, Shiloh only confirmed for others what she already knew. "I felt as certain before that you would display those qualities as I feel now you have shown them but it is nevertheless a gratification to know that others are disposed to do you justice." The newspapers immediately published Grant's and Halleck's letters of commendation, which produced a response that had "astonished" Ellen, she told her husband, "a general interest" now was "felt by men, women & children of the town & the country." After Sherman's promotion Ellen wrote to John, noting that Stanton and Halleck—the very general whom a few weeks before she had named as an arch conspirator against her husband—"have certainly treated Cump nobly." Ellen told John of her "relief." "He is in fine spirits and has completely thrown aside those slanders now but he never did before." She was "perfectly satisfied, since he feels that he is vindicated from the charge of insanity & has made his brother officers feel his worth & most of them, his superiority." She then thanked John for having fought alongside her in Sherman's dark days. The Shermans and the Ewings had truly joined forces. "I now feel more than I ever have before that his people are my people." Thomas Ewing too was "exceedingly gratified," she wrote John. So not merely Sherman, but Ellen and all the Ewings felt vindicated.[8]

At the end of his April 11 letter, Sherman had added, almost as an afterthought, "the piles of dead and wounded and maimed make me more anxious than ever for some hope of an end, but I know such a thing cannot be for a long, long time. Indeed I never expect . . . to survive it." With this statement, Sherman entered the Civil War intellectually and emotionally, where before he had hesitated to commit himself. At the same time that he had to generalize from all those deaths to his own probable death, he had to gird himself for the long haul, for many possible future Shilohs, and so he had to deaden himself to the suffering around him in order to go on committing more men to battle, where many were sure to die in a war with no end in sight. Without a turning off to the suffering of his men in battle, necessary as part of turning on to responsible, fully engaged generalship, the emotional problems of military leadership would otherwise have been overwhelming. Perhaps an intuitive understanding of this necessity for extreme detachment had been one of the reasons Sherman had balked at his role prior to Shiloh. On the other hand, nine months earlier, after Bull Run, Sherman had already written Ellen that "the carnage of battle, men lying in every conceivable shape, and mangled in a horrible way . . . did not make a particle of impression on me, but horses run-

ning about riderless with blood streaming from their nostrils, lying on
the ground hitched to guns, gnawing their sides in death" had given
him a feeling of distinct horror. In this depiction of his first battle,
Sherman had transferred horror suffered by fellow humans onto
horses. Bull Run had been a much smaller battle, out of sync with
Sherman's continuing career. Shiloh was huge, and it came at the com-
mencement of what Sherman realized would be his possibly endless
participation in the war-long campaign in the West. Now, writing to
Ellen, he focused his horror at Shiloh, which marked the beginning of
his true military vocation, on one soldier's death—Holliday's—the
young, handsome orderly "who carried his carbine ever ready to defend me. . . . The shot that killed him was meant for me. After the battle
was over I had him brought to my camp and buried by a tree scarred
with balls and its top carried off by a cannon ball." Youth, whom Holliday represented, was killed, not age; the old tree had its greenest
branches lopped off; and the older man felt survivor's guilt.[9]

When she received this letter, Ellen immediately joined in her husband's grieving for Holliday, deepening it further by taking it into the
women's sphere of ritualized mourning. "Poor young Holliday," she
wrote by return post, "Where do his friends live? Tell me that I may
write to them: his parents, his wife or his sisters." In addition to ex-
tending condolences, she would pray for him: "Poor young Holliday. I
hope God has had mercy on his soul." Ellen also instantly participated
in her husband's fantasy that Holliday had replaced Sherman in the
grave, which had given Sherman his vicarious emotional interpretation
of the meaning of his orderly's death from the volley that ought to have
killed him instead. "Truly your escape from death seems miraculous,"
she wrote him. Then, as might be expected from this fervent Christian
wife writing to her unbelieving husband, she reminded Sherman of her
deepest fears for him. "Do not go into the battle as a heathen would
with no prayer for another world to which you may be hurried." For
Ellen, the underlying vicarious moral meaning of Holliday's death was
that her husband's final spiritual ascendency to heaven was at risk.[10]

Sherman, the deist, could not join his wife in this interpretation of
Holliday's death, and of Shiloh in general, as a personal victory that
would lead directly to spiritual redemption. In replying to her analysis,
he wrote that, even if she did, he did not feel "charitable" with himself,
because he had for so long "felt anxious . . . held back" in the war.
Because he had refused "to attempt to lead when all appeared so

dark," he was somehow disqualified both from his own charity and, implicitly, that of God. Despite his sense of worldly and emotional resurrection at Shiloh, he did not feel the need to press on into a spiritual, Christian rebirth. Where she had such enviable faith, he continued to experience only spiritual blankness. "[I] confess my only hope is in a Providence that is inscrutable to me."[11]

Although Ellen had been unable to obtain spiritual closure with her husband as the final reward of Shiloh, she could still rejoice in his success. She also allowed herself to express pride in the way she had pulled him up from destruction, thereby setting him on the path to glory. Two months after Shiloh, she wrote her husband with manifest pride at having acted, really acted, where she had always been passive. In her letter she went right back to her first memories of bold nine-year-old Cump and shy four-year-old Ellen, when he first moved into the Ewing home on Main Street in Lancaster. "Willy is on the tops of the trees after cherries. . . . How well I remember seeing *you* climbing the cherry trees when not much larger than him. Little did I think when I looked at you there, timid thinking and wondering at your boldness that in later years *my courage* would be called up to enable you to bear the bitter trials of life. But so it has been." Ellen did not suggest that this role reversal be made permanent. She had acted forcefully and publicly in response to the emergency situation created by his depressive passivity. Now he was whole and could once again act strenuously in the world, while she would return home and do honor to him. Indeed, she suggested that her activities on his behalf had always remained a form of tribute, albeit by unusual means. "I thank God that in our day of trouble my heart did homage to your peerless virtue. . . . You have nobly weathered the storm & you are thrice dear to me on account of the troubles you have had & the danger you have braved."[12]

If Shiloh had turned Sherman, in the eyes of others and in his own eyes, into a heroic general marching forward through war, it left Ellen, after her hugely successful foray into public life, back at home in Lancaster, tending house, servants, and children as always, fretful and passive as ever. On his next birthday, ten months after Shiloh, Ellen wrote Sherman that "sadly but secretly do I ponder . . . your every act of virtue & heroism." She wrote that in her state of inactive and melancholy pridefulness he was dear to her, but she also wrote that it was hard to be the quiescent woman, the wife of a man in the distant and noisy world of action, even if he was now a hero. "Could you know how I long to have you with us . . . you would feel what the trial of staying at home and *quietly* enduring is. As it is you know only the boisterous & stormy side of heroism, whilst I often have a dreary monotony, with nothing to divert me from the inevitable heartaches & pangs, fear dread regret and longing."[13] He could act, while she could only stay and brood. Memories of her assault on Washington and the reflected glory of Shiloh could only go so far; beneath her rather too-grand admiration for her hero lurked the old resentments about her daily life, her actual husband.

There is no doubt, however, that for the Union public Shiloh transformed Sherman the crazy alarmist into Sherman the hero. Even in certain reaches of the press, this image of the renewed Sherman flew up from the ashes of the old. Franc Wilkie, war correspondent for the *Chicago Times,* recalled meeting both Grant and Sherman soon after the battle. In an extended literary conceit, he compared the two newly minted heroes, mainly to Sherman's advantage. Where Grant was "broad and deep in the chest," Sherman was "narrow and almost effeminate"; where Grant was "taciturn," Sherman was "voluble, smiling"; where Grant's eyes were "almost fishy in their immobility," Sherman's were "light gray and penetrating, flashing incessantly in every direction"; where Grant moved rigidly as a "piece of marble," Sherman, "whether walking, talking or laughing, walked, talked and laughed all over . . . perspiring thought from every pore, and every agitation of the inner man produced a corresponding agitation of his outer one." Wilkie found the sum total of this soaring personality to be enormously attractive. Sherman was "pleasant and affable to his inferiors and engaging to his equals, with a mood that shifted like a barometer in a tropic sea. With an utterance so rapid at times to be almost incoherent, he at one instance related some laughable incident, and the next criticized the plans of one of Napoleon's campaigns, and a moment later occupied himself in hurling imprecations on some officers."[14]

The repellent and morbid loser in Kentucky of November 1861 had been transformed both in self-conception and in appearance, into the attractive and witty, energetic and explosive hero of April 1862. This sweeping mood change unleashed an enormous creativity and an equally enormous destructive rage. Formerly, Sherman had turned that rage against himself in terribly damaging self-reproach, and had fallen into ever-deepening depression. Now he would sublimate those extreme self-doubts into a fatalistic, almost transcendent commitment to battle. He would assault, verbally and militarily, all his enemies, one after the other, with mounting ferocity. His first target was the press, against whom he felt an enormous grudge that he intended to settle on his own punishing terms.

8

Purging the Devil: Sherman Assaults the Press

A FTER THE VICTORY AT SHILOH, the praise of Grant and Halleck, and the huzzahs of the Kentucky troops, Sherman had been flush with pride and self-congratulation, and thus it came as a shock to him when the newspaper reports soon began to filter back to the army, expressing a consensus that, due to the failure of Grant and Sherman to take sufficient precautions, the Union army had been surprised the first morning of the battle, and many Union troops had been killed in their tents. Rather than merely admitting the errors they had made at the onset of the battle and then stressing the undoubted strength of their holding action later in the day and the vigor of their counterattack the second day of the battle, Sherman and Grant sought to deny categorically that they had left their troops unprepared and unprotected. They insisted that excellent generals like themselves could do no wrong.

It was as if the press were not merely the hated messenger of defeat and failure, but the sum of all evils to Sherman. For him, they did not merely broadcast bad news, they also originated it. Their abuses of freedom incorporated, represented, and amplified the long-term rot of the American republic that had eventuated in the Civil War, and they threatened to destroy the army and the war effort in the name of the same licentious freedom that had produced the war. Bolstered by his suddenly heroic stature after Shiloh, Sherman now turned furiously on these antagonists in a different war.

Even before the battle, encouraged by Ellen's analysis of a conspiracy against him that was being orchestrated by the press, Sherman began to work up his rage toward newspapermen. They were "spies," flooding his camp, he wrote to Thomas Ewing, Jr. They were "fawning sycophants, and when your back is turned they become libelous or flattering according to the demands" of the moment. "I feel a loathing toward them."[1]

Interestingly enough, Sherman's first instinct was to blame not the press but those infantrymen who had broken and run from the shock of the first Confederate attack. On April 22, two weeks after the battle, Sherman wrote John, "The newspapers came back to us with accounts of our battle . . . as usual made by people who ran away and to excuse their cowardice by charging bad management on the part of leaders. I see [in the newspapers] that we were surprised, that our men were bayoneted in their tents . . . etc. This is all simply false." The two infantry regiments that had fled the field, the Fifty-third and Fifty-seventh Ohio, had run after taking only light casualties, Sherman asserted, and the regiments that stood their ground and fought well lost many more, none from bayonet, sword, or knife wounds, but all from musket and cannonballs, thus demonstrating that the Confederates had never breached the Union lines in a surprise assault. So the newspaper reports of "butchery" had been "gotten up by cowards to cover their shame. . . . [T]he common soldiers and subordinates ran away and now want to blame their commanders. This democracy won't go down with me."[2]

Yet Sherman had no choice but to be a commander of a thoroughly democratic army. Therefore, one of the benefits for Sherman of attacking newspapermen, beyond shoring up his embattled ego, beyond the pleasures of venting his anger, was in fact to increase his sense of solidarity with his own troops—nothing cements military cohesion so much as a big and available external enemy, like newspapermen, who do not fight, but merely hang about and scribble. His men could share in the resentment of such "slackers" quite readily, and thereby draw nearer their commander when he battled their mutual belittlers. Thus they cheered him when he insisted that rather than their having been surprised or alarmed even for an instant at Shiloh, such false news about them had come from the false "new master," the newspapers. "Their representatives the reporters are to me the most contemptible race of men that exist, cowardly, cringing, hanging round and gathering their material out of the most polluted sources."[3]

As Sherman reconstructed his version of Shiloh, he broke any link between "his" army and his enemies the reporters, the better to externalize and objectify what he would henceforth construe as the subversive enemy, the press. By June 6, he was writing Ellen that newspapermen "are the chief cause of this unhappy war. They fan the flames of local hatred and keep alive those prejudices which have forced friends into opposing hostile ranks." In other words, evil sayers of the press rather than genuine sectional issues, growing from deep economic and social divisions, had caused the war and remained the chief enemy within to the Union war effort.[4]

Newspapermen remained an obsession with Sherman for the remainder of the war, indeed for the rest of his life. His most common attack against them during the war was that they gave away valuable intelligence to the Confederacy. Hence he would often make statements such as, "I regard all these newspaper harpies as spies and think they should be punished as such." At different times, with his gift for invective, he called them "damned mongrels," "toadies," "sycophants and hirelings," "a set of sneaking, croaking scoundrels." But beneath the epithets, and the insistence that newspapermen were passing military information to the enemy, and even the contempt for the more freewheeling aspects of democracy, was Sherman's deeper anger about being criticized personally. As he wrote to one editor in Union-occupied Memphis, which he commanded in 1862, "personalities in newspapers are wrong and criminal." Samuel Sawyer of the *Union Appeal* had written a complimentary sketch of Sherman, which offended the general, ostensibly because the writer had made innocuous factual errors, but really because he had written about his personality at all. "I mention these facts in kindness, to show you how wrong it is to speak of persons." By way of extension, Sherman promised to be the "best friend" of the press in Memphis, if "I find them actuated by high principle and a sole devotion to their country," but if "I find them personal, abusive, dealing in innuendoes . . . selfish aggrandizement and praise, then they had better look out, for I regard such as greater enemies to the country" than Confederate armies. "As soon as any man rises above mediocrity he is made the butt for all the arrows of the envious or disappointed," he wrote concerning the Cincinnati press—the city where his Kentucky madness had been announced to the world. "Military men are chained to a rock, whilst the vultures are turned loose. We must be silent, whilst our defamers are allowed the widest liberty and license. . . . Reputations are not made by honest soldiers who stand by their colors, but by the crowd that flies back to their homes and employ the press." Sherman fancied himself the modern Prometheus, the vulture-tortured embodiment of truthful duty. "We dare not speak the truth unless that truth be palatable to the crowd. . . . I am not dependent on the press in any manner, never having sought popularity. In fact, I despise popularity obtained by the usual process of flattery and pusillanimity. I could easily win the applause of the masses by stooping to practices that would degrade me in my own estimation and that of posterity." All this Sherman wrote in a letter he sent to a newspaper for publication, to the very same press he was attacking in his letter in order to prove that he was above the press and the masses. Prior to this his ranting had been in private letters; now he fulminated in public in even more grandiose ways.[5]

In the months following Shiloh, this rage by the newly arisen hero against his traducers was not a trivial or secondary matter, but at the core of his concerns. John Sherman tried several times to calm him down, to urge him to be realistic about the inevitable presence of the press, and to win over reporters. "You cannot keep these fellows out of your lines. You ought to *use them,* not only for your own good and quiet, but for the good of the service." But Ellen encouraged Sherman in his campaign. As she told John, she too was "perfectly satisfied" that her general was "vindicated from the charge of insanity" and that he had "made his brother officers feel his wrath & most of them his superiority." From this new position of strength, with her support, Sherman "has opened a regular warfare upon the correspondents whom he detests."[6]

As the months passed in 1862, and well into 1863, the Union war effort in the West stalled, while in the East the Army of the Potomac suffered several major defeats. Public opinion in the North grew restive, fed by newspaper descriptions of army reverses. The Confederate bastion at Vicksburg, on the Mississippi, was the great problem confronting the frustrated Grant. In late December 1862, he sent Sherman to take the city, but the expedition failed. His forces were insufficient in manpower and firepower to dislodge the powerful Confederate forces from even their outer defenses at Chicasaw Bluffs, and he also lacked resources to lay a long siege. No general could have succeeded under such circumstances. Sherman did capture a lesser fort at the Arkansas Post, but Vicksburg proved impregnable until Grant took it in his daring campaign from mid-April to July 4, 1863.

Failure at Vicksburg distressed Sherman deeply, and he brooded about it in the months that followed. Already upset, he began to read reports about the campaign in the newspapers that criticized his generalship: His ever-present rage at the press boiled over. Telling a fellow general that "the war against us by the newspaper press has assumed large proportions," and John that criticism of him "was a conspiracy of the newspaper correspondents against me as their supposed inveterate enemy," Sherman set out to level his insolent foes once and for all.

Although he could have chosen any one of the half dozen or so reporters who had attached themselves to his army, Sherman singled out Thomas W. Knox of the *New York Herald* for a report he had published on January 18, 1863. In the story Knox rounded on Sherman quite unfairly for failing to produce a coordinated assault on the Confederate batteries at Vicksburg, thus committing the troops to confusion and piecemeal defeat. "Finding that his own plan of attack had failed, General Sherman now gave attention to the suggestions of his subordinates," Knox wrote in a contemptuous slur at Sherman's competence and leadership. In addition, Knox charged, "by some criminal oversight, there had been little preparation for the battle" by Sherman's medical corps, causing further suffering and death. Knox's nastiness triggered Sherman's. He accused Knox in writing of being a spy and a conscious character assassin, and ordered him to leave Sherman's army. Knox remained, and then Sherman took a highly unusual step, unprecedented in American military history before or since: He court-martialed a civilian newspaperman, not only to punish Knox, though that would have been sufficient reason for Sherman to act, but to intimidate all other reporters into putting down their damn pens.

Hearing of Sherman's charges and of his impending arrest, and realizing that Sherman was quite capable of carrying out such an astonishing innovation in military authority, on February 1, 1863, Knox wrote an apologetic letter to Sherman. "I find to my regret that I labored under repeated errors, and made in consequence several misstatements, which I now take pleasure in correcting. . . . I am now satisfied that neither to yourself nor any officer of your command can be attributed the failure to accomplish" the conquest of Vicksburg. After reading this letter, Sherman called Knox before him. At this point the issue might have been resolved. However, the interview was a disaster. As Sherman recounted the story later, Knox was provocative instead of contrite. Rather than accepting Knox's apology as the basis of this interview, Sherman demanded Knox's "motive" for writing the offensive story. He reported that Knox had replied, "Of course, General Sherman, I had no feeling against you personally, but you are regarded as the enemy of our set [the press], and we must in self-defense write you down." Reaffirmed in his righteous wrath by what he heard the man say, Sherman proceeded in his court-martial against Knox, ignoring warnings from his staff that such a trial would be illegal.

Despite being embarrassed by his project, several of Sherman's officers formed a court-martial panel and sat for nearly three weeks. The main witness for the prosecution was Sherman, their commander. Despite the obvious conflicts of interest, and the strangeness of court-martialing a civilian reporter, on February 19 Sherman's court found Knox guilty on the charge of disobeying Sherman's direct order that he leave the army, not guilty of the charge of being a spy leaking intelligence on the Union forces to the enemy, and not guilty of the charge of lying about Sherman and other officers. He was sentenced to banishment from the Union army in the West. At first Sherman was furious with this limited conviction because it did not completely vindicate his personal honor against Knox's smears. He wrote to John and Ellen, threatening to resign. Ellen replied forcefully that his resignation would cause her perfect "mortification," as it would be "dishonor. . . . You would be abandoning your country in her hour of peril. . . . You would be giving your enemies—the correspondents—the thing they wish—*They will have written you down.*"

Following the court-martial, several important reporters, all of whom (or whose editors) held back defending Knox during the court-martial, approached Abraham Lincoln on Knox's behalf. Realizing that Sherman had violated the First Amendment and had angered newspapermen, whose powers he recognized, but desiring to support his generals at war, Lincoln dashed off a wily "to whom it may concern" letter, saying that Knox's offense had been "technical rather than willfully wrong," and revoked the sentence of banishment "if Grant gives his express assent." His fellow journalists forwarded Lincoln's ambiguous message to Knox, who presented it to Grant. Grant, annoyed with the press for his own reasons, told Knox that because he had attempted to undermine Sherman's authority, and "blast his reputation . . . made insinuations against the sanity . . . of one of the ablest soldiers and purest men in the country," he would decline to readmit Knox to the army lines unless Sherman himself first gave his consent. Sherman then wrote Knox with scarcely concealed glee that he would readmit Knox only as a fellow soldier, "musket in your hand," sharing the soldier's fate "in sunshine and storm." But if Knox were to return, pen in hand, "which you yourself say makes so slight a difference between truth and falsehood . . . my answer is, Never." Knox remained banished.[7]

Sherman now not only felt exonerated and fully justified in the Knox case, but in the future, when and where he had the power to do so, he bluntly attacked the press, telling them that they had better behave in a manner to please him. Late in 1863, in charge of the military department that included Memphis, he twice warned J. B. Bingham, editor of the *Memphis Bulletin,* "You must print nothing that prejudices government or excites envy, hatred and malice in a community. Persons in office . . . must not be flattered or abused." Commanders such as he were above criticism: "I don't think you can conceive the mortification a soldier feels at the nauseating account given to the public as history." Lest the editor miss his drift, Sherman made their relative levels of power clear. Sherman claimed that he believed in "free thought, free speech and a free press," but he insisted that these freedoms be limited, lest they "generate discord, confusion and war." Of course that, along with anarchy, was precisely the effect newspapers had, in Sherman's opinion. Therefore, the *Memphis Bulletin*s of the reconquered American South were in permanent jeopardy. "If a man disturbs the peace, I will kill or remove him. . . . I have the right to use every means . . . within my limits to restore quiet, order, peace. . . . [T]hese ideas are very general and not very specific, but they give you the key to my conduct."[8]

These threats, as well as their rhetorical fury, demonstrated Sherman's willingness to issue repressive orders and his authoritarian bent. He would be the censor, acting on whatever were his responses to newspaper writing. Writers and editors had to try to discern the general's pleasure and act accordingly, lest he swoop down on them for whatever they wrote that aroused this angry man. Several newspapermen later admitted that Sherman had badly intimidated them. Thomas

Knox shifted to the eastern theater after his banishment, rather than attempting to reenter Sherman and Grant's lines. Henry Villard of the *New York Tribune* later recalled the fear he had felt when nightfall had compelled him to spend one night near Sherman. On that occasion, which he had tried to avoid and which he never repeated, he had received only "gruffness" and "very scant hospitality" from the general, surely understatements. Albert Richardson, another *Tribune* man, reported that when Sherman learned to whom he was talking after the two men were introduced, Sherman's manner "changed from Indian Summer to a Texas norther, and he asked, in freezing tone, 'Have you not come to the wrong place, sir?'" Sherman then shared a cigar with Richardson, taking the occasion to castigate the press as irresponsible falsehood peddlers, in a manner Richardson characterized as "often irritable and sometimes rude."[9]

There was a clear connection between Sherman the arbitrary censor and Sherman the principled antidemocrat. After the final conquest of Vicksburg, in which he had supported Grant ably, when he was again in fine feather, Sherman wrote another theoretical discourse to his brother. "A government resting immediately on the caprice of a people is too unstable to last. . . . [A]ll *must* obey. Government, that is, the executive, having no discretion but to execute the law must be to that extent despotic." As the nation had been drifting ever closer to anarchy, the more absolute the governmental authority grew, the better. "We have for years been drifting towards an unadulterated democracy or demagogism. Therefore our Government should become a machine, self-regulating, independent of the man." And the first target of the totalitarian machine, which ought to replace the "old school" politicians (implicitly including Abraham Lincoln), should be that very embodiment of democracy and demagogism, the newspapers. "As to the press of America, it is a shame and a reproach to a civilized people." Sherman made clear in a later letter to John, "If Congress don't provide, the Army will," by which he meant provide a dictatorship.[10]

Several other historians have tended to underanalyze or dismiss this authoritarian streak in Sherman as mere private venting of frustration and anger. Although it is true that Sherman expressed his flirtation with the principle of military dictatorship in private, he often acted on these same impulses. As head of an army of occupation, he bluntly censored the press at hand. As he gained larger commands he imposed his authority with increasing energy. During the Atlanta campaign, of which he was in charge, Grant having departed for the East on March 20, 1864, Sherman barred all newspapermen from his front in a famous circular in which he sought to "discourage the maintenance of that class of men who will not take up a musket and fight but . . . pick up news for sale . . . dangerous to the army and to our cause, and . . . bolster up idle and worthless officers" at the expense of the "hardworking and meritorious . . . who scorn to seek cheap flattery." Almost no one, Phil Ewing and John Sherman included, supported this *dictat,* but where he could Sherman gave it teeth. In June 1864, a month after he issued the circular, Sherman arrested and banished DeB. Randolf Keim for publishing a story in the *New York Herald* that disclosed that the Union army had deciphered the Confederate system of signals. During the long march to the sea and then up through the Carolinas, out of contact with the rest of the Union, no reporter could file a story, which suited Sherman perfectly. The more autonomous he became, the more dictatorially he controlled the news.[11]

Sherman was nearly as hard on those "political generals" (that is to say non–West Point men who obtained appointment through political clout rather than by dint of military training) who fed the newspapermen. Frank Blair was an able divisional commander and leading Missouri Republican from a family that rivaled the Ewing/Sherman clan for political influence, but Sherman raked him over the coals for supposedly feeding Thomas Knox false information. Blair responded to Sherman's charges point by detailed point, though under protest. "I confess myself greatly mortified and annoyed to be called on" in such a manner, he wrote Sherman, and asserted that he would respond this one time in good "spirit," but that never again would he allow Sherman to cross-examine him so rudely. Sherman replied that "I do not expect there will be a next time," and that Blair's "friendly spirit" ought to remain in place toward him. Sherman could not resist heaping new blame on Knox's head—"I could hardly believe that a white man could be so false as that fellow"—but he did not apologize to Blair. Later in the war, Sherman was even blunter with General Brayman, after reading an article in an Evansville, Indiana, paper "that looks as though you had communicated my instruction to private parties for publication. . . . If my dispatches to you reach the public . . . again, you will regret it to the ends of your days."[12]

Sherman even sought to apply the same angry censorship to the secretary of war, his superior, who was one of the chiefs of the despised political caste. While pounding on the gates of Atlanta in July 1864, Sherman wrote Henry Halleck, army coordinator in Washington, to "ask Mr. Stanton not to publish the substance of my dispatches, for they reach Richmond in a day, and are telegraphed at once to Atlanta." Politicians like Stanton ought to shut up as their part in the discipline necessary to educate the American people to proper order. "Absolute silence in military matters is the only safe rule. Let our public learn patience and common sense."

In reply to continuing complaints from Sherman and Grant that he was loose-lipped about Union plans, Stanton finally wrote Grant that the leaks all "came from Sherman's own army, and generally from his own officers, and there is reason to believe that he has not been very guarded in his own talk." Stanton certainly had a point. Sherman had a problem when others talked to the press, and with newspapermen whom he construed to be hostile to him. Others were demagogic when they went to the press, while he was correct and therefore undemagogic when he used the same means with newspapermen he trusted. During the Knox affair, Sherman used his cousin, Murat Halstead, eminent publisher and editor of the *Cincinnati Commercial,* to put his own spin on the story. Ironically, Halstead had been the very man who had published the story of Sherman going insane in 1861, but he was deeply contrite for the errors of his past ways, and Sherman was willing in this instance first to forgive him and then to use him. Sherman also used G. D. Prentice of the *Louisville Journal* to place information. Even more frequently he employed John Sherman in Washington, and Phil Ewing in Ohio, to plant stories with the press through their surrogates, and he urged Charles A. Dana, an influential newspaper editor now serving as assistant secretary of war, to leak military disinformation to Dana's many old colleagues in the press.[13]

Sherman never betrayed any awareness of the startling contradiction—or hypocrisy—between his condemnation of the press and the use made of the press by other Union military men, and his own similar manipulation. To his own satisfaction he was authoritative, part of that machinelike force for order of which he dreamed, and was inherently superior to the demagogic, democratic mass he opposed. Issuing his rude proclamations against the press, which he then visited through the back door, his ego seemed boundless.

By the time he presented Savannah as a Christmas present to Lincoln at the end of 1864, Sherman was being lionized in the hated press.

Stuck in the trenches at Petersburg, Grant was the goat of the season, while the conquering Sherman was the great Union hero. He admitted to Ellen concerning the new press consensus about him, "I dread the elevation to which they have got me. A simple mistake or accident [and down I] would tumble." Even at the height of his fame, he feared both military reversal and a renewed mental collapse, which he knew the press would report with their customary eagerness. When Ellen was set to go to Chicago right after the war ended, the ever-insecure Sherman warned her, "don't go near those *Tribune* men. . . . They would report your conversations and pick your pockets of my letters and publish them if it would contribute to their temporary advantage."[14] Of course Sherman's fears were not entirely unreasonable; the press did dump heroes at a turn of their fortunes. This knowledge fed his ever-active inner demons.

Sherman's complex of attitudes toward the press remained a fixed set of prejudices until the end of his life. He would plant stories, use surrogate writers, feed selected historians, and all the while condemn the press in particular and democracy in general. "Gossiping newspapers" fill the popular hunger for the "clamors of the hour or the day," he wrote a magazine editor in 1875, while gravely important issues such as much-needed long-term military planning go nowhere. "In peace we will tear down what is not needed at the moment—and when war comes, the people cry aloud for an army to come to their rescue, certain to pull it down the moment the scare is over." As late as 1880, when he was sixty, Sherman bragged to an acquaintance that right after the war he had bumped into one newspaperman at his brother's home in Washington and had "told him . . . that if he dared to report private conversations I would kill him." As a general proposition, he insisted, rather than truckling to newspapermen out of fear, "men of public station . . . *should kick them and treat them as curs.*"[15]

9

Turning Friends into Enemies

THE PRESS was the first external target to which Sherman applied his rage released by success in war. He could legitimate this attack on the press, with all its ramifications, well before he could allow himself to express such open anger toward the South and the Southern people. For a considerable period of time, he cordoned off this sector of rage, as it were, pouring hatred on the press while remaining ambivalent and even positive in his feeling toward the people of the Confederacy. His shift to a more brutal war against Southern civilians began hesitatingly. In part this was political reserve. In common with many Unionists early in the war, he at first sought only a limited victory, one that would win Southerners back to the Union with slavery intact. In part this was personal hesitation. He did not wish to be hated by Southerners, whom he saw as errant Americans, nor did he desire to hate them with the kind of hate he felt for the press.

Sherman's early attitudes toward Southern people were demonstrated clearly after he became commander of Memphis, Tennessee, on July 21, 1862, a Confederate city that had fallen to the Union on June 6 without a battle. Sherman remained in charge in Memphis until he left on December 20, to mount his unsuccessful attack on Vicksburg. He had enormous authority over a sizable civilian population during this period. Where the press had been essentially out of his control, and in his opinion, out of control altogether, he was the nearly absolute ruler of Memphis and therefore could choose to exercise his dominion over the population nearly to the degree and in the manner he might wish.

Sherman wanted to show to the people of Memphis, and to the people of the South generally, that renewed Union rule would be both lawful and benevolent, and that he was an upright and honest military governor. Observing his fair rule, Sherman assumed, the Confederate people would willingly abandon their cause, lay down their arms, and rejoin the land of their fathers.

Sherman insisted, for instance, that Union soldiers restrain their attacks on the property of enemy civilians. While his army moved from town to town on the road through Tennessee to Memphis in 1862, Sherman issued orders to his troops that "too much looseness exists on the subject of foraging. The articles of war make it almost a capital offense for an officer or soldier to pillage, which means taking property for his own use. It makes no difference if that property be of friend or enemy. Pillaging demoralizes the soldier, allows him to straggle from his ranks and neglect his duty." To reinforce this discipline, Sherman drafted rules concerning issuance of clearly written receipts for property taken, which would allow for future government repayment. Sherman was pleased with the immediate effect of this order. On the next day he told Halleck that "the quiet of a New England Sabbath prevails at La Grange, and our men are pretty well behaved."

But the good behavior seems not to have lasted, for three weeks later, now at Moscow, Sherman issued a renewed order on pillaging that indicated that his officers had continued to lose control over their men. "Stealing, robbery and pillage has become so common in the army that it is a disgrace to any civilized army," he insisted. "This demoralizing and disgraceful practice of pillage must cease, else the country will rise on us and justly shoot us down like dogs and wild beasts." At this time U. S. Grant also tried to restrain what he referred to as the "gross vandalism" practiced by his troops.[1]

When establishing his garrison in Memphis, Sherman ordered that his junior officers educate themselves about the rules of civilized warfare, and discipline the men in their charge. "All officers of this command must now study their books; ignorance of duty must no longer be pleaded." Sherman warned that he might make his officers take a pop exam. He sought to have them learn the precepts of military discipline, the better to present his rule over civilians in as virtuous a light as possible.

Sherman sought to establish a model military government. He would deal harshly only with avowed enemies—and few civilians in a Union garrison town would be so foolish as to declare their enmity—and deal with all others as not merely neutral but as potential allies, giving them the benefit of the doubt. On July 25, he wrote to Halleck that "all in Memphis who are hostile to us should be compelled to leave. . . . But if all who are not our friends are expelled from Memphis but few will be left. I will do nothing hastily, only if any persons manifest any active hostility will I deal with them summarily." He intended to rule in the spirit of not merely forbearance but of active magnanimity, as befit an officer who was a gentleman. On October 30, he issued a circular to his officers in which he asserted that "generosity and benevolence to the poor and distressed are characteristics of good soldiers." He then recommended that all units organize themselves to distribute their surplus food allowances to the needy. Sherman soon reported success in his charitable project. His men had placed the homeless in vacant buildings, cut them cord wood, distributed confiscated Confederate medicine and food to them, and enlisted local merchants and well-off families in voluntary aid campaigns for the poor.

Toward all citizens, rich and poor, Sherman acted as charitably as he could within the confines of his legal obligations as garrison commander. When he had to remove Memphis families from inside the expanded fortress he was building within their city, for example, he both issued them full receipts for future compensation and sought to find equivalent vacant houses for them elsewhere in the city. More generally, he declared that he "presumed to be loyal" all those in his town, that "so long as they remain quiet and conform to . . . law they are entitled to protection in their property and lives," and most significantly, that "we have nothing to do with confiscation. We only deal with possession, and therefore [enforce] the necessity of strict accountability."

To reinforce due process of the law against the abuses of his own troops in Memphis, Sherman regulated modes of honest dealing. He prefaced one such order, which dealt with the issuance of travel passes to civilians into the Confederate states, with the statement that "the general commanding announces with shame and mortification that he has discovered a case of bribery . . . the payment of $100 to a clerk in the office of the provost-marshal-general for a pass to Helena [Arkansas]." Sherman also issued careful instructions to centralize and systematize the registration of all confiscated goods in the office of the quartermaster.

In addition to acting forcefully against army corruption, Sherman paid special attention to policing Memphis. He promulgated stringent guidelines for his provost marshal, in effect the chief constable of the city, on the practices of his own troops, and he tried to reinforce the role of the local police at the same time. When the Memphis constabulary failed to reorganize well enough to control civilians, Sherman placed them under the authority of the provost marshal, D. C. Anthony, whom he later complimented for the "firmness, courtesy, and decision of character" that had enabled Anthony to achieve the "quiet and good order" of the city "with as little interference with the people as possible." Through such measures, Sherman emphasized his own probity and that of the occupying army and the government he represented.[2]

Sherman was quite pleased with his benevolence and with the results he obtained in Memphis. After being in charge for two months, he wrote Ellen that he believed he had gained the "unlimited confidence," not only of his own troops and local Unionists, but also of "most of the secesh. . . . All know that I stick to the law." As he was preparing to pull out of Memphis in December, he declared with satisfaction to an old friend that his policy had reconciled most enemy civilians to the Union, not through coercion but through moral suasion. "In Memphis and the district round for sixty miles I know I have done immense good. Thousands of people who hated us with the deep hate of secessionists now respect our authority and obey the laws of the United States from a sense of respect." And to John, Sherman insisted that Memphis was now in "good shape," and that "I have a strong hold on the people here who admit that I am just and strictly legal in all my acts."

But public opinion in the North had shifted quite rapidly toward the position that the South ought to be suppressed far more harshly, and Sherman's policy was widely viewed with suspicion as being soft on the implacable enemy. John wrote to his brother that the general criticism of him in the Union was in "your leniency to the rebels. . . . [T]he energy and bitterness which they have injected into the contest must be met with energy and determination. *La Vendee* presents the historical parallel." John informed him that popular opinion, which he thought was right nine times out of ten, now favored a reign of revolutionary terror over the Southern counterrevolutionaries, such as the one that had led to the slaughter of thousands during the French Revolution. "These rebels are bitter enemies to be . . . conquered by confiscation . . . by terror, energy, audacity, rather than by conciliation." To John, the general was insufficiently radical, too soft on the enemy, and well behind the current of Union sentiment, which was moving swiftly toward supporting a much more brutal war effort. John was all for the punishment of those civilians his brother was taking such pains to treat kindly.

Underlying the increasingly anachronistic conciliatory policy he was pursuing was Sherman's continued empathy for Southern civilians. To him, these were still essentially fellow Americans. He expressed this continuity of sympathy most openly in letters he wrote from Memphis to his eldest daughter, Minnie, who was now eleven years old. In one he simply declared, "I feel that we are fighting our own people, many of whom I knew in earlier years, and with many of whom I was once very intimate." In a more elaborate pronouncement, he wrote Minnie that though the people of Memphis looked on his army as "invaders," and on him as a "brutal wretch," he was always at pains to reassure them of his peaceful and constructive intentions. "We tell them we want nothing they have . . . their houses, their farms, their niggers . . . but they don't believe us, and I fear that this universal feeling will cause the very result they profess to dread." Sherman then recounted his sad feelings when military necessity had forced him to turn families out of their houses, and had forced him to send many women to join their husbands in Confederate camps. "Think of this, and how cruel men become in war when even your Papa has to do such acts." Sherman resisted the coarsening effects of war, feared converting Southerners in his own mind from fellow humans into the faceless enemy, the Other. "Your Mama and Grandpa think it is a great thing to be a high General," he wrote Minnie. "I would in any war but this, but I cannot but look at these people as my old friends."[3] In the city of Memphis, well governed by his Union garrison, Sherman could continue to see Southerners as resembling his comrades of old. Not merely were they not shooting at him, they were giving him daily evidence of their subordination to him, whether with friendliness or suppressed hostility. He could look into their faces and talk with them.

But the Tennessee countryside outside the garrison of Memphis was a different matter. There, Confederate guerrillas roamed, picking off

Union stragglers, attacking supply columns, firing on Union steamboats, killing passengers indiscriminately, looting supplies intended
for civilians as well as military stores. These guerrilla bands were not
enlisted Confederate troops subject to regular military control, but
self-constituted groups of young male civilians and deserters, indistin-
guishable from the farmers and village residents from whom they originated, back into whom they melted after raids, and who aided and
abetted them. As elsewhere when Union troops occupied hostile
Southern lands (or where Confederate troops occupied hostile Unionist areas, such as in the mountains of east Tennessee), these guerrillas
broke all the conventions of honorable war and led the occupying
forces into a deepening cycle of attack and counterattack, revenge and
retaliation, in a war that blurred all distinctions between the civilian
and the military, thus deepening war and brutalizing the combatants.[4]

As a result, even while he maintained a benevolent stance within
Memphis, Sherman began to revise his opinion of Confederate civilians and not just Confederate soldiers, from fellow Americans into
"the Enemy," when he confronted them as guerrillas. As early as July
1862, following the killing of a Union soldier during a foraging expedition by guerrillas, Sherman declared that "we have no other remedy
for their ambush firing than to hold the neighborhood fully responsible, though the punishment may fall on the wrong parties." There was
some hesitation in that final clause of Sherman's report to his higher-
ups. Two months later, after guerrilla sniping on Union supply boats
had intensified, Sherman had begun to lose his inhibitions against attacking civilians in retaliatory raids. On September 24, he ordered Colonel C. C. Walcutt to take two companies of infantry on a dawn
assault against the riverside town of Randolph, from which concealed
guerrillas had fired on Union troopships, commanding Walcutt, "you
will destroy the place, leaving one house to mark the place." After the
raid, Sherman reported to his superiors that "the regiment has returned and Randolph is gone. It is no use tolerating such acts as firing
on steamboats. Punishment must be speedy, sure and exemplary. . . .
The town was of no importance, but the example should be followed
up on all similar occasions." This casually brutal report was evidence
that Sherman was turning an emotional corner in his conception of the
war against the South. Unlike the still-real persons of Memphis, these
civilians were individually invisible to Sherman, and their homes were

insignificant. They were just markers in a nasty war of attack and reprisal.

What remained was for Sherman to up the stakes of guerrilla war, and then to generalize from counterinsurgency into a policy of carrying the war more and more against the civilian portion of the Confederate rebellion. Shortly after destroying Randolph, Sherman wrote Grant that he intended to expel ten secession families for every boat fired upon by guerrillas. "[I] will visit on the neighborhood summary punishment." Acting officially, Sherman drove several families from river towns, and in informal ways small Union units under his command expelled many more and killed others. When they did so they were only following the spirit of their commander's intentions. On October 18, Sherman wrote his superiors in St. Louis, from which the Union army was conducting an even more intense antiguerrilla war in the Missouri countryside, "I will expel every secession family from Memphis if [guerrilla] war is to be continued, and will moreover land troops on unexpected points and devastate the country."

Encouraging his men to campaign boldly against guerrillas and their civilian supporters, Sherman learned to justify their excesses, in effect covering up Union wrongdoing, a key element of the corrupting quality of counterinsurgent warfare. In one notable instance, on November 17, after finding one of their lieutenants shot, stripped, and mutilated, a Union company attacked the nearest house, that of the White family, beat to death the twenty-three-year-old boy living there, and burned down the home. His complicity in guerrilla activities was uncertain; indeed the family may have been Unionists. After the event, Sherman suggested to Grant that the Union act with "magnanimity" to the White family, and insisted that "of course I cannot approve the killing of any citizen on mere suspicion." He added immediately, however, that "the firing from ambush near the White's home, and the fact that Lieutenant Cunningham was mutilated and stripped of money," and the fact that the neighborhood was infamous "for supplying guerrillas," all had been "circumstances calculated to inflame the minds of soldiers." Sherman did not punish his soldiers; indeed, he exonerated them.

Fighting against guerrillas had led Sherman step-by-step toward the conclusion that, as he put it to Grant on October 4, "we know that all the South is in arms and deep in enmity. . . . We cannot change the hearts of those people of the South, but we can make war so terrible that they will [put down arms]." Although Sherman did not simply turn a mental page from conciliation to brutal war against civilians, although he remained conciliatory and ambivalent and aggressive by turns, he was moving toward a fundamental revision of his attitudes. Later on in the war he would return to that phrase about making war so terrible to Southerners, and amplify it ten thousandfold.

When Confederate generals wrote Sherman protesting as acts of barbarity the summary killing of guerrillas and the banishment of civilians, Sherman in turn blamed the Confederates for lowering the threshold of violence. "Ununiformed bands . . . when dispersed, mingle with the people and draw on them the consequences of their individual acts," he wrote Confederate Major General T. C. Hindman, in an overtly threatening letter. "You initiate the game, and my word for it your people will regret it long after you pass from the earth." When Confederate Lieutenant General J. C. Pemberton picked by lot four Union prisoners to shoot in retaliation for the death of the twenty-three-year-old White, Sherman threatened in return to end all prisoner exchanges. In each instance Sherman reiterated that he would rein in his reprisals should the South stop using guerrilla warfare—if they did not stop, he would "accept the issue" and act accordingly. Union troops would retaliate for guerrilla actions automatically. "You know full well that on your side guerrillas . . . commit acts which you would not sanction," Sherman wrote Hindman, "and that small detachments of our men commit acts of individual revenge leaving no evidence . . . whereby we can fix the responsibility." But in admitting that his troops committed illegal and brutal acts, he argued that they did so only in response to Confederate attacks. He did not take into the equation the probability that the guerrillas too had acted outside of Confederate military control. For him the burden of guilt was on the South. He instructed Hindman, "instead of yielding to this tendency we ought gradually to impose discipline so that each General in command can trace all acts and then assume full responsibility. If we allow the passions of our men to get full command then indeed will the war become a reproach to the names of liberty and civilization."

Sherman began to apply this logic of counterinsurgency back in his Memphis command. Thus when several women in Memphis petitioned Sherman protesting the expulsion of a number of women and children from the city, Sherman wrote one, "let the Confederate authorities

. . . not employ [guerrillas] in such deeds of blood and darkness," and let them say that they would not sanction future guerrilla atrocities, and then would he relent. He replied to another petitioner by demanding to know from him, "how would [you] like it if we would fire through the houses of their wives and families as they do through the boats carrying our wives and families?" Anyone "who feels for our people" would perceive that banishment to the Confederate lines is a "mild . . . measure of retaliation, and I do not promise that in future cases I will be so mild."

These citizens of Memphis were part of a larger regime that had crossed the line of legality and morality, in Sherman's opinion. Therefore, he would banish them from his benignly ruled Memphis, into the wilderness of the guerrilla terrain. They would then be enemies to "*our people*," swept into oblivion by the actions of guerrillas, abetted by the Confederate military. And next time around he promised to treat them even more harshly. If he still referred to a measure of traditional legality—regular soldiers ought to fight one another and leave civilians alone—there was an escalating retaliatory threat built into his manner of dealing with Confederate guerrillas. As had the guerrillas in fighting them, Sherman had blurred the lines between civilians and soldiers. He had begun to cross over into a ground he described so vividly as one of blood and darkness, from which it would be progressively harder to step back, and into which, in tandem with the increasingly wrathful enemy, this self-justifying and easily infuriated commander would move quite readily.[5]

On December 20, 1862, Sherman left his duties as the governor of Memphis and guerrilla fighter to take charge of the forces gathered to assault Vicksburg. On December 29, the undermanned attack on the powerful fortress failed. His troops, "disappointed . . . but by no means discouraged," reembarked on their transport ships on January 2, 1863, and Sherman was reduced to the command of a corps, his larger command turned over to John A. McClernand. Although McClernand was just the sort of political general Sherman despised, he was relieved to give up his command. McClernand "being now charged with fashioning and planning events," Sherman told Grant at this juncture, "I can subside quietly into the more agreeable office of corps commander, and shall endeavor to make it a good one."

This was Sherman's familiar tone of self-abasement in the face of failures, but this time his mind did not have time to deepen his depression. With excellent cooperation from the navy, Sherman's corps proceeded up the Mississippi River and up the White River, and stormed the Confederate fortress at Arkansas Post, which fell to him, with five thousand Confederate prisoners, on January 11, 1863. This victory evened Sherman's emotional keel somewhat, though in his general letter of thanks to Admiral David Dixon Porter, who had commanded the naval squadron during the attack, Sherman added, "As having failed I must play the modest part and mind my own business in the future plans designed for the reduction of Vicksburg." Still, Sherman continued in his letter to Porter with determination rather than despair, as if he were girding his loins, Vicksburg must be taken, and there was "no better time to begin than now." Sherman's doubting and tentative self-image should be contrasted with the pen picture taken of him at this moment by Thomas Kilby Smith, a Ewing family friend who wrote Ellen Ewing Sherman on January 17, after having shared a cigar with the general on the steamship *Sunny South.* "He is in fine health and first rate spirits. I never saw him look better." Sherman was full of plans for future campaigns. "His ego fairly blazes. . . . When his ego snaps and sparkles, you may be sure that the rest is all right."[6]

In this uncertain frame of mind, Sherman was delighted to serve in a subordinate role to a commander he unreservedly admired, during U. S. Grant's long, tenacious, discouraging, and ultimately brilliantly successful reduction of Vicksburg. Sherman much doubted Grant's daring strategy of running his troops down the Mississippi and past the Confederate guns, to the south of Vicksburg, cutting loose from his lines of supply and moving on a long raid around to the back door of the fortress city. Still, he offered Grant his full support, his chief role being to provide a diversionary mock assault from the north of the sort that he had failed to carry six months earlier. When Vicksburg fell, Sherman telegraphed Grant immediately, praising this great victory, which, he told Grant, was a result of Grant's honesty, modesty, and purity of character. Sherman was glad to share in Grant's reflected glory. "Though in the background, as I ever wish to be in civil war, I feel I have labored some to secure this glorious result." Somewhat self-deprecating in tone, this was not an envious response. This was Grant's splendid victory and Sherman was genuinely glad for him.[7]

Immediately after Vicksburg fell, Sherman marched three corps of Grant's army inland to attack the rail center at Jackson, Mississippi, with its ragtag Confederate garrison under the command of Joseph

Johnston. After a short but brutal Union siege, Johnston evacuated the town on July 17. During this brief and successful assault, which amounted to something like a speedy recapitulation of the victory at Vicksburg, Sherman experienced a surge of self-worth as a commander. With a special ferocity he had never so unhesitatingly expressed before, he now turned against Southerners as a whole, soldiers and civilians alike, not in the abstract, but face-to-face.

On July 14, Sherman had been knocking at the gates of Jackson, shelling the city and sending out detachments that threatened to cut off Johnston's lines of retreat to his rear. At this point Sherman had reported to Grant with unconcealed pride that, in addition to investing and turning Jackson, his foraging parties were savaging the countryside. "We are absolutely stripping the country of corn, cattle, hogs, sheep, poultry, everything, and the new-growing corn is being thrown open as pasture fields or hauled for the use of our animals. The wholesale destruction to which the country is now being subjected is terrible to contemplate, but it is the scourge of war, to which ambitious men have appealed, rather than the judgment of the learned and pure tribunals which our forefathers had provided for supposed wrongs and injuries."

This political justification for the havoc he was wreaking was an argument Sherman found morally enabling. Sherman's subsequent reports to Grant were less political and even more self-congratulatory on the destructive force he was unleashing, in the iron hand he had tightened around the Southern throat. In two telegrams sent on July 18, the day he marched into Jackson, Sherman wired Grant that "the inhabitants are subjugated. They cry aloud for mercy. The land is devastated for 30 miles around"; and later that day that "the enemy burned great parts of Jackson, and we have done some in that line. The place is ruined." With great satisfaction, Sherman reported that his army had annihilated the city.

Having reduced their city and the surrounding countryside to ruins with great force and happiness, Sherman could then listen to the pleas of the citizens for quarter. On July 20, he wired Grant, "The people are subdued, and ask for reconstruction. They admit the loss of the southern cause." Now the sole authority, this destroyer could dispense mercy at his whim. When the leading men of the city came to him, admitting that they were "beaten and subdued," as well as homeless and hungry, Sherman wrote to Grant, "Of course, I make no promise or pledges, but merely state that I believe that [my request for food] would be received with favor." Sherman stayed on for a few days to distribute the two hundred barrels of flour and one hundred of salt pork he had requisitioned. From his Olympian height of power, he could distribute mercy with as much satisfaction as he earlier had meted out destruction. He later reported, "The condition of the inhabitants . . . appeals to the human feelings of all who have beheld the utter ruin and destruction which has befallen their country." He had been the chief befaller.[8]

At Jackson, Sherman had let loose a ferocity from within himself toward Southern civilians that he had formerly reserved for newspapermen and then had extended to guerrillas. Subsequently, he began to instruct his subordinates and associates, when they were off on independent military errands, to unleash the furies of war without reserve. On October 24, to the garrison commander back in Memphis, he urged, "Notify the people of Paducah if any enemy of good government or manners insult or offend any of the Union people, the whole town will be held responsible, and the chief men banished and their property destroyed." To the leader of an expedition into the northern Mississippi countryside, Sherman urged, "now is a good time to clear out the country. Let it be done without gloves."

As the war lengthened, Sherman's attitude toward fighting guerrillas, always strident, became more and more direct and harsh. He had begun to reconceptualize all Southern civilians, who shielded guerrillas in their ranks, as the Other while conducting counterinsurgency from Memphis in 1862. Now, a year later, on November 12, 1863, he wrote to one of his brigade commanders that, "whilst at Pulaski let your mounted men hunt out the pests that infest the country. Show them no mercy, and if the people don't suppress guerrillas, tell them your orders are to treat the community as enemies." The next month, Sherman wrote John A. Logan suggesting that each sniper's bullet shot at a passing Union steamboat be returned by a thousand thirty-pound Parrott shells into "even helpless towns on every southern river, on which a boat can float." This was rough talk, and not every river town was leveled by Union gunboats. Nevertheless, destruction rather than conciliation was certainly the new order of the day: Sherman was becoming quite keen on taking the fight into the homes and hearts of Confederate civilians.[9]

In his relationships with Southern civilians he met along the way, in his expanded destructive role, Sherman upped the rhetorical stakes. He began taking on the role of "the reaper of these hostile districts," as he put it in one letter written on September 4, 1863, to Frederick A. P. Barnard, a fellow Northerner who had been president of the University of Mississippi when Sherman had founded LSU. He reserved special energy, he bragged to Barnard, for burning out old acquaintances of the gentry class, the very men who had built universities but had also led the secession movement. They had really asked for it, and while he had them in his grasp in Mississippi, he would deliver it. James Buchanan's secretary of the interior, Jacob Thompson, was "one of the political criminals" Sherman's men had burned out, a man "endowed with intellect, wealth, power and experience—He chose war, and for him I have no mercy. He should drink the cup of poisoned venom to its bitterest dregs." Sherman wrote Barnard that his troops had made a blockhouse out of Bishop Green's home, and that therefore "library, pictures, furniture & barrels of sermons all fell a pray to our 'Barbarian Host,' and before we left the flames finished the destruction." In mock pity, Sherman continued, "this last was done without orders and wrongfully, but I don't know but it was better that the flames should obliterate the traces of desecration to the sanctum of a learned and pious gentleman." Having soiled the bishop's study and his books, Sherman burned them to purify the remains. While he had been in Jackson, Sherman had said to a captured Confederate officer, he reported proudly to Barnard, while they were looking at "a burning block of buildings set fire to by one of our unruly soldiers—'Sir—we are not responsible for that work—you and your associates applied the torch to the only earthly power that would restrain the wicked and you are clearly responsible for the natural and necessary consequences of your own acts. I disdain all responsibility & say that Jeff Davis & adherents set fire to that building.' " Sherman insisted that in the "secession, anarchy and discord" that they had "foolishly and wickedly let loose," Southerners were the most extreme masters of the falsely democratic practices of "our hitherto *too* free and *too* ungoverned land." He, Sherman, would put a torch to all that as a step toward creating a properly disciplined, properly governed nation from the ashes of the Civil War.[10]

So expansive was Sherman becoming in his newly unleashed powers that he could even begin, for the first time, to make black jokes about his reputation for mental instability. "To secure the safety of the navigation of the Mississippi River I would slay millions," Sherman wrote

10

Niggers and Other Vagabonds

A S TO FREEING THE NEGROES, I don't think the time has yet come," Sherman wrote his wife on July 31, 1862. "When negroes are liberated either they or their masters must perish. They cannot exist together except in their present relation, and to expect negroes to change from slaves to masters without one of those horrible convulsions which at times startle the world is absurd."[1] In his profound racism, this Union general was in step with most of his fellow white Americans; in his defense of the institution of slavery, as were those Democrats who shared his views, he was increasingly out of step with Northern politics and public opinion; in his fear of a bloody slave revolt—used as an argument to exonerate slavery as a caste system—he was not only out of step with Northern opinion, but aligned to Confederate opinion. In sum, Sherman's still thoroughly proslavery ideology was becoming increasingly anachronistic fourteen months into a bloody civil war in which the abolition of slavery and not merely the restoration of the Union was well on the way to becoming the chief Union war goal.

While his division was marching through rural Tennessee early in the summer of 1862, Sherman acted on his opinions when issuing orders concerning the duties of his subordinate officers and men toward those many slaves who, as did Negroes all over the South, ran to join his columns in self-emancipation when Union troops advanced. "The well-settled policy of the whole army now is to have nothing to do with the negro," Sherman said, using as his authority Henry W. Halleck, his superior. "Exclude them from camp . . . is the reiterated order. We cannot have our trains encumbered by them, nor can we afford to feed them, and it is deceiving the poor fellow to allow him to start and have him forcibly driven away afterward." Using this kindly paternal interpretation of his actions, Sherman ordered his subordinates to "remove all such now in camp, and to prevent any more from following our . . . columns of march."[2] Presumably the slaves would then wander the countryside in privation, often to be recaptured into slavery by their masters. But that was none of this Union general's concern (though others made special provisions for caring for such fugitive slaves, several doing so earlier in the war). Sherman was at war with the master class, but not for the benefit of their bondsmen and bondswomen. He preferred to exclude the issue from his view by barring the fugitives from his camp.

After he took charge of Memphis on July 21, Sherman was confronted with the fact that thousands of slaves had escaped to this Union garrison town. He had to accept their reality and deal with them. He also realized that here in a land of hostile whites, he suddenly had a huge labor pool consisting of enemies of his enemies who were on his side, even if he was not on theirs. The day after his arrival in Memphis, he had begun to set large numbers of freedmen, eight hundred within a week, on the construction of the massive fort he was building, and employed hundreds more on other public works and as teamsters and servants.[3]

As an expedient, Sherman ordered that these laborers be fed and housed by the army and paid one pound of chewing tobacco per month in lieu of wages. He understood intuitively that these were not slaves but employees, who had a right to a wage, however minimal, for their labor. Given the ever-increasing numbers of slaves showing up in Memphis, and congressional passage of a law authorizing the army to receive and employ fugitives from slavery, on August 8 Sherman issued his own regulations, including a provision to account in writing for hours of work, and for payment from this account in clothing and tobacco but not in cash. "No wages will be paid until the court determines whether the negro be slave or free." In general, this order was narrowly concerned with army employment of fugitive labor, and was extremely reluctant in broaching the possibility of future emancipation. "It is neither [my] duty nor pleasure to disturb the relation of master and slave, that is for the courts," Sherman insisted, playing for Unionist sentiment among slaveholders. Should civil law be reestablished in Memphis, Sherman presumed, "the loyal masters will recover their slaves and the wages they have earned during their temporary use by military authorities." This suggested that Sherman was just leasing the slaves of loyal masters, while disloyal masters would lose theirs. This unlikely distinction was the conservative spin men like Sherman were trying to place on the reality of thousands of slaves who had in fact already freed themselves. Again in deference to Southern sensibilities, and in reference to his own values, Sherman declared that "no influence be used to entice slaves from their masters," nor to prevent their voluntary return to them, adding for the benefit of the throngs of masters who were knocking on his door demanding the return of their slaves, "no force or undue persuasion" would be allowed masters seeking to "recover such fugitive property." Fugitive property was less than human as a formulation, but it was property fugitive from his enemy and thus was of value to the Union, and therefore to be guarded, however reluctantly.[4]

In comparison to other Union officers operating in his own theater of war at this time, Sherman was narrow in his construction of the ambiguous status of fugitive slaves. Civil courts were closed, general military rules were nonexistent, and legislation could not catch up to the rapidly evolving situation on the ground, and so officers had rather a large range of practical options. For example, Sherman was at pains to reassure Confederate General Gideon Pillow that his General Orders Number 67 were simply his regulation of the "present labor of the slaves," with ultimate payment "to the master or to the slave, according to the case," to be decided after the war by reconvened state tribunals. In contrast, Union General Samuel R. Curtis had begun to issue letters of manumission to fugitive slaves who had "satisfied him they had been used as property to carry on the war," but where Curtis had given the benefit of the doubt to the fugitive slaves, whose humanity he thus acknowledged, Sherman reassured Pillow that he would "grant no such papers, as my opinion is it is in the provision of the court to pass on the title to all kinds of property"—fugitive slaves were still chattel property until judges might rule otherwise. Sherman's presumptive judgment was that in the present he would preserve slavery to the best of his abilities. In 1862, when a group of fugitives captured some riverboats flying a white flag and used them to escape to Union lines, Sherman ordered them delivered back across Confederate lines to their owners, because, he wrote, "the law is that negroes escaping from their masters into our military lines cannot be delivered back by me, but these boats . . . carrying our flag of truce were not actually or even theoretically in our military lines."[5]

After seeing a copy of Sherman's General Orders Number 67, his brother John wrote him that he thought they were acceptable except for the proviso holding back cash wage payments. "You ought to presume their freedom until the contrary is shown & pay them accordingly," John urged, demonstrating that he was certain that Unionists in authority ought to lean toward the fugitive slaves and away from reinforcing the institution of slavery. John believed that to defeat the South "we must make friends of the blacks. If we repel them in the future as in the past, we will check their disposition to aid us." This political realism, perhaps tinged with idealism, was spreading rapidly, John informed his brother. "You can form no conception at the change of opinion here [in Ohio, and in the North generally], as to the Negro Question." Men of all political persuasions, overcoming "both party divisions and our natural prejudice of caste," now "agree that we must seek the aid and make it the interests of the negroes to help us." John had understood the logic of the rapid flow of Northern opinion, and had concluded, as had nearly every Republican in Congress, "I am prepared for one to meet the broad issue of universal emancipation."[6]

This letter of John Sherman's, particularly the part about overcoming caste prejudice, was an admonition to the general to stop being recalcitrant to the point of reactionism on the "Negro question." Unlike Senator Sherman, General Sherman thought public opinion misguided and foolish. Also arguing from realism rather than from an overtly restated racism, he replied to his brother that the guiding principle of his orders had been to "appropriate the labor of negroes as far as will benefit the army," that "not one nigger in ten wants to run off" in any event, that the army could not possibly feed, clothe, and house all of them, and that they made a "horrible impediment" to an advancing army. In sum, "you cannot solve this negro question in a day." In his remaining months in Memphis, Sherman employed more and more fugitive laborers in practice, while fearing he would become overloaded with them, and he never abandoned the general principle that he opposed emancipation. "I do not think it to our interest to set loose negroes too fast," he wrote Grant in September. On November 12, in a letter to a Southern judge in recaptured Memphis he continued to plan to "reserve this question of slavery," while Northern and Southern armies fought out the real and "dire conflict between National and State authority."[7] Sherman remained a proslavery Unionist even three months after Abraham Lincoln issued the preliminary Emancipation Proclamation, on September 22, 1862.

Underlying the argument Sherman was making about the impracticability of emancipation lay, of course, his assumptions about the inferiority of the whole race of blacks that fitted them for slavery. This racialism was in large part replicated, during this same period, in Sherman's opinions of the Jews. He blamed the war on blacks as he blamed it on Jews. As he made the linkage in a letter to Ellen on August 20, 1862, "The cause of the war is not alone in the nigger, but in the mercenary spirit of our countrymen." For Sherman, the personification of this evil mercenary spirit was the speculator, and the speculator was the Jew. In Memphis, Sherman observed a lively trade in Southern cotton, and reasoned in a letter to Grant, "I found so many Jews & Speculators here trading in cotton and secessionists had become open in refusing anything but gold that I have found myself bound to stop it. This gold has but one use, the purchase of arms & ammunition" in Northern cities for smuggling south into the Confederacy. As for issuing new trading passes to "swarms of Jews, I have stopped it." Trading with the enemy, including illicit arms sales, was a problem for the Union army, and there were speculators eager to trade, a small minority of whom were Jewish, but for Sherman, as for many other Union generals, "Jews and speculators" was the offending category from which *and speculators* was often dropped. When he heard that the government had decided to encourage the trade in cotton rather than end it, Sherman fumed to Washington that "the country will soon swarm with dishonest Jews." In this categorization of traders, Sherman was in concert with Grant. On July 26, Grant ordered a subordinate at the cotton trading river port of Columbus, Kentucky, to "examine the baggage of all speculators coming South, and, when they have [gold] specie, turn them back. . . . Jews should receive special attention." On December 17, 1862, Grant went even further. Like a medieval monarch, he expelled "The Jews, as a class" from his department. Lincoln rescinded the order, pointing out that though he agreed with expelling crooked speculators, he could not agree to the exclusion of Jews "as a class, some of whom are fighting in our ranks."[8]

Jews like niggers, niggers like greasers (Mexicans) or Indians, were for Sherman, in common with many of his contemporaries, "classes" or "races" permanently inferior to his own. Lincoln in his way, and John Sherman in his, had an understanding that when it came to defining races, Americans employed customary hierarchical categories rather than natural absolutes—even if these two leaders often agreed with the customs—and thus Lincoln and John Sherman were open to change over time. Men like William T. Sherman did not share this cultural definition of race, taking their prejudices as fixed truths about natural and immutable racial categories. Thus for him Jews were Jews were Jews and "everyone" knew what that meant. Even after Lincoln's order rescinded Grant's expulsion of the Jews, Sherman continued expressing his unchanging opinion of them to his colleagues, if he now slightly disguised it. "Merchants as a class are governed by the law of self-interest," he wrote both Secretary of the Treasury Salmon P. Chase and Admiral David Porter on October 25, 1863. The high profits of contraband trade will call many to engage in it, "but this is confined to a class of men you and I know well." Porter certainly knew just whom Sherman meant. "The real merchant—that man who loves his country," the merchants who were not the you-know-who's—would not "endanger our lives" with illegal trade in arms.[9]

By the same form of racialist generalization, heightened by his habit of endemic contempt, for Sherman niggers were niggers were niggers, the mudsill of the society that had enslaved them and them alone. After the Emancipation Proclamation went into effect on January 1, 1863, freeing the slaves of the Confederacy, Sherman did not continue to reinforce the institution of slavery as he marched through the South, but neither did he change his opinion of blacks. Rather, he took emancipation as a further means of punishing his enemies. "The masters by rebelling have freed the negro, and have taken from themselves the courts and machinery by which any real law could be enforced in this country," he wrote General James B. McPherson on November 18, 1863. "They must bear the terrible infliction which has overtaken them, and blame the authors of the rebellion and not us." Concomitantly, Sherman now encouraged slaves to flee their masters and come to Union garrison towns, not to help blacks but to demonstrate to whites that they "must take the consequences" of their rebellion. Whatever the eventual fate of the Negroes, he told a group of Mississippi planters, "*ex necessitate,* the United States succeeds by act of war to the former lost title of master." For Sherman, emancipation had ended Southern white mastership as part of their ongoing destruction in war. He was not much concerned with its meanings for former slaves, of whom he, as a Union agent, was a new master.[10]

In Union war policy, emancipation had led directly to the active recruitment of black Union troops. This next giant step was taken by the Union leadership, from Abraham Lincoln on down. In his attempt to sell this dramatic new policy to the more conservative members of the public and his own army, Lincoln frequently employed arguments that were practical in nature, as he thought these might be more effective than more ideologically based modes of persuasion. As he wrote to one conservative Northern politician on August 26, 1863, "I thought that whatever negroes can be got to do as soldiers, leaves just so much less for white soldiers to do, in saving the Union," an opinion he anticipated most of his commanders could share, even archconservatives like Sherman. In his own beliefs, which he did not hesitate to express publicly, Lincoln went beyond such practicality to the moral meanings of emancipation tied to the use of black troops. Thus in this same letter he linked the practical with the ideal when he argued that "negroes, like other people act upon motives. . . . If they stake their lives for us, they must be prompted by the strongest motive—even the promise of freedom. And the promise being made, must be kept." Lincoln thus related *white* honor to the use of black troops. He also comprehended *black* honor, for he understood the liberation of the spirit that military participation would bring the freedmen. "There will be some black men who can remember that, with silent tongue, and clenched teeth, and steady eye, and well-poised bayonet, they have helped mankind on to this great consummation [of freedom]." Lincoln also insisted that white men who opposed the use of black troops, "with malignant heart, and deceitful speech," would be acting out of a spiritual dishonor they would be ashamed of in future years.[11]

"I have given the subject of arming the negro my hearty support," U. S. Grant wrote Lincoln on August 23, 1863. "This, with the emancipation of the negro, is the heaviest blow yet given the Confederacy. . . . By arming the negro we have added a powerful ally. They will make good soldiers, and taking them from the enemy weakens him in the same proportion they strengthen us."[12] In striking contrast to the opinion of his commander and closest military friend, of all the leading Union generals Sherman was the most outspoken in his resistance to this policy innovation, the most overtly racist in his opposition, and the most openly insubordinate to civilian dictates, from those issued by the president on down.

When Lorenzo Thomas began the active recruitment of black troops in Mississippi in April 1863 during the campaign against Vicksburg, Sherman made his feelings perfectly clear. In a letter to Ellen he asserted, "I would prefer to have this a white man's war and provide for the negroes after the time has passed. . . . With my opinion of negroes and my experience, yea prejudice, I cannot trust them yet. Time may change this but I cannot bring myself to trust negroes with arms in positions of danger and trust." Time and the spread of Union recruitment among blacks only served to deepen Sherman's prejudices. He insisted to Henry Halleck late in 1863 that as an abstract principle the Confederates would only "finally submit" to fellow white men who displayed courage and skill equal to theirs, superior resources and "tenacity of purpose," and a clear and single purpose—"to sustain a government capable of vindicating its just and rightful authority, independent of niggers, cotton, money, or any earthly interest." Unionism through war would have to be a kind of purification ritual, in which, to achieve victory, the whitest of white men would have to purge themselves of all forms of pollution, the two chief forms being filthy lucre and filthy niggers.[13]

In common with the prejudices of most of his soldiers, Sherman wanted to keep his troops free from the contamination they believed Negroes would bring. When Lorenzo Thomas addressed his men, telling them they would have to adjust to the presence of black troops, Sherman followed, telling his men—"who look to me more than anybody on earth"—that he hoped that if the government did make use of black troops, "they should be used for some side purpose & not be brigaded with white men." Reporting this speech to his brother, John, Sherman added that his experience with Negroes even in limited roles as teamsters and cooks had proven to be a disaster. "They desert the moment danger threatens. . . . At Shiloh all our nigger servants fled, and some of them were picked up by boats 40 miles down the River. I won't trust niggers to fight yet." He did not oppose taking them from the enemy, however, and finding other uses for them than fighting.[14]

He was perfectly willing to use Negroes as laborers and in "pioneer brigades," to dig the trenches, build the forts, chop the wood, and haul the water, all in aid to the real, white soldiers.

The more actively the government pursued its recruitment of black troops, the more urgently and angrily Sherman resisted the policy. In the spring of 1864, as Sherman was organizing his campaign against Atlanta, Lorenzo Thomas traveled west again to coordinate the use of agents from Northern states to come south to recruit Southerners, primarily blacks, into the army as one means of filling up draft calls made on those Northern states. "My special duties here are to organize colored troops, and I expect full cooperation on the part of all military commanders to enable me to execute these special orders of the Secretary of War [in which] the President has taken an interest," Thomas wrote to Sherman very pointedly from Natchez. Instead of cooperating, Sherman issued special orders that recruiting officers would not be allowed "to enlist as soldiers any negroes who are profitably employed" by the army, that his staff officers "will refuse to release him from his employment by virtue of a supposed enlistment as a soldier, and that any recruitment officer . . . who interferes with the necessary gangs of hired negroes" be arrested and if necessary imprisoned.[15]

This was insubordination. On the other hand, Sherman was coordinating a most promising campaign against Joseph Johnston's army on the way to Atlanta, and so rather than punish him, the authorities in Washington, without quite conceding that he had the authorization to override their clear orders, tried to sweet-talk Sherman. Lorenzo Thomas wrote Sherman that the secretary of war wished "to express his strong desire" (rather than ordering him) that Sherman cooperate in the recruitment of black troops at least by sending them on to Thomas, now in Nashville. "I have seen your recent order respecting the enlistment of negroes," Thomas continued, "the practical working of which, it seems to me, will stop almost altogether recruiting in your army. I know not under what circumstances it was issued, but the imprisonment of officers for disobedience seems to me a harsh measure." Reading this rather plaintive letter where he might have anticipated an angry rebuke accompanied by a renewed order, Sherman knew he had the upper hand. At first he replied to Thomas with a letter that contained an element of conciliation amid the reassertion of his authority in *his* military sector to imprison Union recruiters who disobeyed him. "I believe that negroes better serve the army as teamsters, pioneers and servants," he reiterated, "and have no objection to the surplus, if any, being enlisted as soldiers." But, he added immediately, "I must have labor and a large quantity of it. I confess I would prefer 300 negroes armed with spades and axes than 1000 as soldiers. Still I have no objection to the enlistment of negroes if my working parties are not interfered with." And then, defiantly reasserting his authority over Union recruiting agents on his turf by reaffirming rather than rescinding his offensive order, Sherman concluded that if his Negro working parties "are interfered with I must put a summary stop to it."

Sherman was not retreating but stonewalling. Indeed, in the guise of cooperation he soon wrote again to Thomas proposing the regularization of pioneer brigades as an alternative to the Union policy of black troops. After all, he concluded, "the great mass of our soldiers must be of the white race, and the black troops should . . . for some years be used with caution and with due regard to the prejudice of the races." Pressing forward to Atlanta, Sherman continued to protest black recruitment with increasing anger. "I must express my opinion that [such recruitment] is the height of folly," he wrote to Henry Halleck on July 14, in a letter he must have intended to reach Stanton and Lincoln. And as for the recruiting officers, "I will not have a set of fellows here hanging about on any such pretenses." Sherman was having his way.[16]

Four days later, the president himself replied to Sherman's string of insubordinate dispatches. As was his wont, Lincoln wrapped firmness in the cloth of tact. He was unwilling "to restrain, or modify the law" on black recruitment "further than actual necessity may require," he wrote Sherman, adding that, "to be candid, I was for the passage of the law." He had not apprehended that the law would prove so inconvenient to armies in the field, "as you now cause me to fear." Despite his acknowledgment of Sherman's sensibilities, Lincoln got to the point quite clearly, if with civility, reminding Sherman of the constitutional subordination of the military to the president as commander in chief. "I still hope advantage from the law; and being a law, it must be treated as such by all of us. We here, will do what we consistently can to save you from difficulties arising out of it. May I ask therefore that you will give your hearty cooperation?"

Writing to others who opposed his policy at about this time, Lincoln was far more direct and forceful about the utility of black troops. To a conservative politician in Buffalo, New York, Lincoln wrote on September 12, 1864, "Any different policy in regard to the colored man

[than black recruitment] deprives us of his help, and this is more than we can bear. . . . This is not a question of sentiment or taste, but one of physical force which can be measured and estimated as [can] horse-power and Steam-power. . . . Keep it and you can save the Union. Throw it away, and the Union goes with it." But Lincoln addressed his most recalcitrant general not on the moral or even the practical merits of the issue, but by appealing to Sherman's most general belief in law and constitutionalism, order, and authority. He had not asked for a conversion of belief, for he knew Sherman would not accept black troops with inward conviction, but for mere acceptance of a policy set by the commander in chief of the armed forces.[17]

In reply to Lincoln, Sherman telegraphed that of course he was a great believer in the due subordination of the military to civilian control, in principle: "I have the highest veneration for the law," he told Lincoln, "and will respect it always, however it conflicts with my opinion of its propriety." Conceding the principle, Sherman did not even address enforcement of the law at hand, instead reminding Lincoln, under a rather thin veneer of politeness, exactly who was going to win the battle that would save whose political skin. Grant was bogged down and suffering frightful losses in Virginia; Lincoln's political stock was never lower; only Sherman was advancing in a way that could reverse Union fortunes in general and Lincoln's in particular. Lincoln knew all that and Sherman knew it too. "When I have taken Atlanta and can sit down in some peace I will convey by letter a fuller expression of my views," Sherman instructed Lincoln. At this level, war was politics by other means, and Sherman fully understood that his hand was stronger than Lincoln's, at least for the foreseeable future. He had thrown Lincoln's request for cooperation right back in his face.[18]

Sherman had every intention of continuing his independent policy forbidding recruitment of black troops. Although he claimed he lacked the time and peace to respond fully to Lincoln's order phrased as a request, Sherman did have time the following week to write a lengthy reaffirmation of his independent political policy to John A. Spooner, the recruitment agent for Massachusetts, even while offering Spooner a pass within his lines to allow his pursuit of black recruits in the South, an apparent concession to Lincoln's request. Among the reasons he opposed Spooner's project, he wrote him quite candidly, were that "the negro is in a transition state, and not the equal of the white man." While claiming that he had conducted far more Negroes to safety behind Union lines than had any other Union general, he asserted that "I prefer some negroes as pioneers, teamsters, cooks and servants; others gradually to experiment in the art of the soldier, beginning with the duties of local garrison," and inferentially, none at all serving with his fighting forces. Sherman wrote Spooner that he might share this letter with other state agents, and sent several copies himself to other generals.[19]

When it leaked into the press a few weeks later, as Sherman surely must have realized it would when he circulated it, this defiant letter made a sensation all over the North. "I never thought my nigger letter would get into the press," Sherman pretended to a St. Louis friend, but since it had made a splash, Sherman continued, "I lay low. I like niggers well enough as niggers, but when fools and idiots"—those professing "nigger sympathy," as he put it in another letter—"try and make niggers better than ourselves, I have an opinion."[20]

Writing to his family at this time, Sherman was apoplectic about black recruitment and wholeheartedly loathing in his characterization of blacks. "I see the Government has settled down on the policy of . . . gathering up niggers and vagabonds," Sherman wrote Ellen. He liked that phrase, *niggers and vagabonds,* repeating it to Ellen, and transmuting it into "niggers and bought recruits" in yet another letter to her, and to "niggers and the refuse of the south" in a letter to Thomas Ewing. "This kind of trash will merely fill our hospitals and keep well to the rear," Sherman went on to Ellen. "I suppose I am to fight till this army is used and then wait for a new revolution." Sherman believed that he had "remonstrated to Mr. Lincoln in the strongest terms," but had been told by Lincoln that "it was the law and I have to submit." Sherman wrote Ellen that he feared racial role-reversal in his army. "Niggers wont work now," and half his white army was doing the kind of labor "which the very niggers we have captured might do, whilst those same niggers are soldiers on paper." This reversal of customary racial subordination was "an insult to our Race," Sherman fumed. "Modern philanthropy will convert our oldest and best soldiers into laborers whilst the nigger parades & reclines in some remote & soft place." Under such a regime, his army would soon shrink away.[21]

Sherman used only a slightly less strident tone when, after the fall of Atlanta, as he said he would, he wrote Henry Halleck a letter intended for the president, replying in full to Lincoln's abjuration to change on the issue of black recruitment. "I hope anything I have said or done will not be construed unfriendly to Mr. Lincoln or Stanton," Sherman began, perhaps with irony intended, or perhaps without. "That negro letter of mine I never designed for publication," he again protested, without disowning one whit of its contents, thus indicating that the semiofficial "nigger letter" indeed had been his reply to Lincoln's request for cooperation. "I am honest in my belief that it is not fair to our men to count negroes as equals. Cannot we at this day drop theories and be reasonable men?" Sherman asked, meaning that innovative assertions of Negro equality be dropped for the customs of racism. " 'Is not a negro as good as a white man to stop a bullet?' " was a question, Sherman wrote, he often had been asked. "Yes," he now answered, "and a sand bag is better; but can a negro do our skirmishing and picket duty? Can they improvise roads, bridges, sorties, flank movements, etc., like a white man? I say no. . . . Soldiers must do many things without orders from their own sense. . . . Negroes are not equal to this." Sherman told Halleck that he intended to march in the future as in the past at the head of a lily-white army. "I have gone steadily, firmly, and confidently along, and I could not have done it with black troops, but with my old troops I have never a waver of doubt, and that very confidence begets success."[22]

Given his continued insubordination on the use of black troops, it is ironic that Sherman's capture of Atlanta in September 1864 made the political impact Lincoln had hoped it would, for that victory immediately reversed public opinion about the progress of the war, and led directly to Lincoln's substantial electoral triumph two months later. Sherman had served in absolutely indispensable ways both Lincoln's immediate political needs and his larger war aims, even though he disagreed vociferously with those socially revolutionary goals.

After the fall of Atlanta, and perhaps in response to the ruckus his "nigger letter" had aroused, Sherman wrote a slightly more conciliatory letter on October 25 to Edwin Stanton, stating that he much preferred to keep black troops "for some time to come in a subordinate state, for our prejudices, yours as well as mine, are not schooled for absolute equality," but added that if the government had "determined to push the policy to the end, it is both my duty and pleasure to assist," and asked for the assignment of an officer to organize such black regiments in his sector. By this time, however, Sherman was well along in his plans to cut loose from his lines on his giant raid through Georgia.

Any black troops organized to his rear would not join him on his march, which he knew full well when he wrote to Stanton in the spirit of apparent compliance. His army would remain racially pure.[23]

Only after he had captured Savannah did the Union government succeed by fiat in attaching a black infantry regiment to Sherman's command, by shipping one in by sea from the East. What he was forced to accept, Sherman subverted. He stripped these trained troops of their arms, and converted them into laborers, teamsters, and servants. Picking up on the spirit of racial contempt that Sherman expressed in these actions and in his racial policy pronouncements, Sherman's soldiers brutally harassed these black recruits, rioting against them, killing two or three, and wounding many more. As one Ohio soldier wrote home, these few hundred black soldiers "were taught to know their place & behave civilly."[24]

In Savannah, Sherman began to receive admonitions from his friends and allies that he was increasingly out of step with political change not merely on the enlistment of black troops but on race relations in general. Lincoln, and most especially the more radical among the congressional Republicans, had won a triumphant reelection, and were beginning to push for civil and voting rights for the freedmen. As they moved with astonishing speed toward radical solutions to the American racial dilemma, they were no longer willing to tolerate every racial whim of the reactionary author of the "nigger letter," even if he was winning victories. "While almost everyone is praising your march through Georgia," the conservative Henry Halleck forewarned Sherman, "a certain class having now great influence with the President"—meaning the Radical Republicans—"are decidedly disposed to make a point against you . . . in regard to the 'inevitable Sambo.' They say that you have manifested an almost *criminal* dislike to the negro, and that you are not willing to carry out the wishes of the government in regard to him, but repulse him with contempt!" Sherman's reputation for racial contempt had been aggravated, Halleck wrote Sherman, by his policy of driving fugitive slaves away from his line of march during his march through Georgia. Especially damaging were the actions of one of his division commanders, Jeff C. Davis, who had crossed over one Georgia river on December 9, and then had pulled up his pontoon bridge immediately after his troops had crossed over, abandoning the large band of fugitive slaves trailing his division to the pistols and swords of Joe Wheeler's approaching Confederate cavalry, or as an alternative fate, to drowning in the swift river in panicked attempts to flee. Halleck urged Sherman to do something constructive and welcoming for the fugitive slaves in order "to silence your opponents."[25]

Salmon P. Chase, the secretary of the treasury and a powerful Radical leader who had always been a strong supporter of Sherman, was even blunter with Sherman, concerning the "apparent harshness of your actions towards the blacks. You are understood," he warned Sherman, "to be opposed to their employment as soldiers and to regard them as a sort of pariahs, almost without rights." As had Halleck, Chase urged Sherman to do something to counteract this reputation for "harshness & severity," and to set a military standard that "for good or evil, will be followed by officers of lower character and less discretion."[26]

As might have been predicted, given his history on this subject, Sherman's initial response to such criticism was anger and denial. "I deeply regret that I am threatened with that curse to all peace and comfort—popularity," Sherman replied to Halleck in fulsome sarcasm. "Thank God I am not running for office." As a general proposition he asked in exasperation, "But the nigger? Why in god's name, can't sensible men let him alone?" As to the specific charge against Jeff Davis, Sherman dismissed as "cock-and-bull" and as "humbug" the report that fugitive slaves were turned back so that Wheeler might kill them. Davis had told Sherman that he had forbidden certain slaves, old men, women, and children, from following him, "but they would come along and he took up his pontoon bridges, not because he wanted to leave them, but because he wanted his bridge." Davis also told Sherman that he did not believe that Wheeler's cavalry had killed "a single one of them," although Sherman had not pressed Davis for any evidence for this assertion. Sherman reported this callous and internally inconsistent tale as the truth and as morally unexceptionable. He took Davis's word as an officer and a gentleman. He was untroubled about those abandoned blacks, and thought Halleck need not concern himself either. In any event, Sherman insisted, far from being their enemy, "I profess to be the best kind of friend to Sambo." Just look at how the "darkies" of Savannah had greeted him. "They gather around me in crowds, and I cant find out whether I am Moses or Aaron, or which of the prophets; but surely I am rated as one of the congregation." (This greeting really tickled Sherman; to Ellen he commented, "It would amuse you to see the negroes, they flock to me old & young, they pray and shout—and mix up my name with that of Moses and Simon . . . as well as Abraham Lincoln, the Great Messiah of 'Dis Jubilee.' ") All the false, pseudohumanitarian infatuation with the blacks—"Poor negro—Lo, the poor Indian"—was nothing but a "humbug" of current fashion in the tradition of the parlor charity to Indians expressed by reformers in the East. Nevertheless, Sherman thanked Halleck for his "kind hint," and promised, "I do and will do the best I can for negroes."[27]

The administration effort to bring around the insubordinate hero of Atlanta and the march to the sea reached its unexpected denouement on the morning of January 11, 1865, when no less than the secretary of war disembarked from a federal revenue cutter at the port of Savannah. Edwin Stanton's ostensible mission was to supervise the reestablishment of Union rule and marketing procedures for cotton in the recaptured city, but his deeper purpose was to redirect toward administration goals Sherman's efforts in the field of race relations. Sitting down with Stanton, Sherman vigorously defended his practices, including those of Jeff Davis, and insisted that he was charmed by the simple character of the Negroes and by their faith in the Union war effort.

At Stanton's urging, Sherman organized a meeting with twenty of the leading freedmen of Savannah, mainly Methodist and Baptist preachers. In the racial context of the South in 1865, this was an unprecedented gathering, where blacks, so recently slaves, were treated as humans whose opinions were important. Just by calling this meeting, Stanton, who was something of a racial progressive, was making an emphatic point to Sherman about the essential humanity of the freedmen. Stanton also had a Union officer make an official transcript of the meeting, further elevating the occasion. After quizzing the black leaders about their understanding of the meanings of the Emancipation Proclamation, their relationship to the national government, and their opinion of the system of recruitment of black troops, Stanton had Sherman leave the room, and then asked the blacks what they thought of him. They told Stanton what they thought he wanted to hear, that Sherman was to them an agent of Providence. "Some of us called upon him immediately upon his arrival," they told Stanton, "and it is probable he did not meet [Stanton] with more courtesy than he did us. His conduct and deportment toward us characterized him as a friend and gentleman."

Despite the favorable publicity he received, Sherman was greatly affronted by Stanton's upending of racial protocol. This deep resentment still rankled ten years later when Sherman depicted this event in his *Memoirs.* "It certainly was a strange fact that the great War Secretary should have catechized negroes concerning the character of a general who had commanded a hundred thousand men in battle, had captured cities, conducted sixty-five thousand men across four hundred miles of territory, and had just brought tens of thousands of freedmen to a place of security; but because I had not loaded down my army by other hundreds of thousands of poor negroes, I was construed by others as hostile to the black race."[28] Sherman could not abide Stanton's demonstration of a tentative new racial order.

Following this meeting, which he hoped would motivate Sherman to consider a more charitable disposition toward blacks, Stanton urged him to devise some plan that would "meet the pressing necessities of the case"—namely, the existence of vast numbers of freed slaves in the South. At least that is the way Sherman reconstructed in his *Memoirs* what had followed this meeting. Sherman recalled that he had then sat down and drafted his Special Field Orders Number 15, which he issued after Stanton had edited them carefully. Other historians have stressed Stanton's role in the authorship, as well as that of the Joint Congressional Committee on the Conduct of the War. Whatever their exact genesis, these orders were an extremely radical proposal for redistribution of land confiscated from slaveholders to the newly freed slaves. In the Sea Islands of South Carolina, and for thirty miles up the rivers from the sea in South Carolina and parts of Florida and Georgia, "abandoned" plantations (from which the owners had fled on the approach of Union troops) were to be distributed in plots of "not more than forty acres of tillable ground" to black heads of families, each of whom was to be given "a possessory title in writing." Sherman and Stanton then appointed Brigadier General Rufus Saxton, a Radical Republican Sherman despised, as Union inspector in charge of this project.[29]

Beyond emancipation itself, this was the single most revolutionary act in race relations during the Civil War. It seemed to initiate a system of land redistribution, including the specific notion of forty acres to each black man, which only the most advanced minority of Radicals and freedmen would carry into the post–Civil War era, with even the majority of congressional Republicans balking at this invasion of the right to secure title in private property, a principle that might be extended into other governmental activities. How extraordinarily ironic it appears that a reactionary racist would father this extreme measure. Many historians have even insisted in disbelief that Sherman went along, not comprehending where Stanton was leading him. Stanton's presence undeniably forced Sherman to act, but Sherman wanted to do something dramatic to solve his problems with the administration once and for all.

In fact, the politics of the event and Sherman's reasoning were, though complex, not unfathomable and not really inconsistent with his earlier beliefs and with his desire to manage his current problems. Neither did he believe he had been gulled. In fact, he thought he had won the argument. He wrote to his wife while drafting the orders, "Mr. Stanton has been here and has been cured of that negro nonsense." He had proposed, he told Ellen, an alternative to the use of blacks as soldiers and a solution to the problem, which would be presented by those throngs of fugitive camp-followers he otherwise anticipated as he blasted up through the Carolinas: He would get them off his trail and onto the land. "I want soldiers made of the best bone and muscle in the land, and won't attempt military feats with doubtful materials. I want [the Negro] treated as free and not hunted and badgered to [be] made a soldier of, when his family is left back on the plantation. I am right and won't change."[30]

Sherman also believed that he had created a system that would put the administration of the freedmen of the deep South he was reconquering permanently into the hands of others, allowing him to walk away from those problems and look beneficent in the process. As he wrote to Major General J. G. Foster, commander of those parts of South Carolina already in Union hands, which was most of the territory covered by the Special Orders, "I think the impression at Washington is that both you and I are inimical to the policy of rearming negroes, and all know that [Saxton] is not, and his appointment reconciles that difficulty." Sherman cynically urged Foster to let the Radical political general Saxton take on the problem and make the inevitable mistakes, and then to pounce on him and punish him for those errors. To Stanton, Sherman wrote soon after he left Savannah that in his Special Field Orders he had been "unable to offer a complete solution" to the problem of the freedmen. However, "we have given an initiative and can afford to await the working of the experiment," he wrote Stanton in apparent sympathy for the project.

With his order, Sherman had washed his hands of his "Negro problem," rid his army of any serious potential black content, purged his columns of large numbers of black camp followers, passed the unwanted blacks on to a man he despised, Saxton, and at the same time neutralized Republican criticism of his racial motives and practices. While he had claimed to despise popularity and to loathe blacks, Sherman was sensitive of his reputation and defensive about his motives. Like most Southern racists of the time, he claimed paternal feelings toward blacks, and he was quite willing to help them out if he could construe such help as aiding rather than retarding his larger military project. After all, he was a Union general and wanted to be a helpful part of the conquest of the Confederacy, if he could bend the desires of other Unionists around his plans and square them with his own opinions.[31]

Neither was it the case that this was a radical project of Stanton's, seized opportunistically by Sherman. Land confiscation as one means of displacing the Confederate leadership had been discussed widely during the war. As early as August 24, 1862, John Sherman had written his brother, "If we can't depend upon the loyalty of the white men of the South, I would give the land to the blacks or colonize a new set [of northern whites]." The general too had, since 1862, threatened Southerners with dispossession, their land to be redistributed to Northern white colonists. On January 31, 1864, for example, he had written a full analysis on the subject to a military lawyer in Tennessee, in a letter clearly intended for publication. "When the inhabitants persist too long in hostility it may be both politic and right that we should banish them and appropriate their lands to a more loyal and useful population. . . . If they want eternal war, well and good; we will dispossess them and put our friends in their place. . . . Many people with less pertinacity have been wiped out of national existence." On April 11, enclosing a copy of this letter, Sherman had written even more directly to John, "The whole people of Iowa & Wisconsin should be transported at once to West Kentucky, Tennessee & Mississippi, and a few hundred thousand settlers should be pushed into South Tennessee." Sherman was talking about Northern white resettlement. Clearly his main goal was punishing disunionists rather than helping blacks. The next day, however, Sherman had made a racial shift in his thinking when he had written Lorenzo Thomas, his opponent on the issue of black recruitment, "I would prefer much to colonize the negroes on lands clearly forfeited to us by treason," proposing specifically the "rich alluvial region" on the Mississippi River ten miles below Vicksburg, prime cotton plantation land, "as the very country in which we might collect the negroes, and where they will find more good land already cleared" than anywhere else. "It would enable the negro at once to be useful." As an added fillip, this particular proposition, which was in fact enacted, stripped Confederate president Jefferson Davis himself of his land and gave it to his former slaves.

Thus Sherman had considered this project in land redistribution to blacks fully ten months before he issued Special Field Orders Number 15. He wanted to show Southerners that they had sacrificed all their property rights by rebelling against the Union and the Constitution. In addition, while on the verge of taking Savannah, Sherman had written Stanton that when he arrived there, "my first duty will be to clear the army of surplus negroes, mules and horses."[32]

If Stanton had also read and recalled Sherman's letter to Lorenzo Thomas of April 12, 1864, a not unlikely proposition, it would have been Sherman who had given the embryo of Special Field Orders Number 15 to Stanton rather than the other way around. Even if Stanton had not read the letter, it is clear that Sherman had been giving considerable thought, over a significant span of time, to a scheme of land redistribution. Both men might well have arrived at a similar policy conclusion, coincidentally and by different routes. Although such a project had beneficial implications for blacks, that had not been Sherman's initial goal. If, however, his orders were pleasing to blacks and Radical Republicans, that came as a bonus that would make the orders even more useful to him than they otherwise would have been, as they would get both these sets of antagonists off his back. He would be rid of the niggers, divesting himself of them as he would his excess mules and horses. At the same time, and of primary importance to him, he would, through this measure, keep young black males out of his army. If others took that as kindness, so much the better, as he could thus enact his self-proclaimed paternalist motives more credibly, and lay more claim to the title of friend of the freedmen. And in addition, land confiscation would be a major blow to the planter aristocracy that was running the war for the enemy. He wanted to smite his enemies in every possible way, and land confiscation would grievously injure the morale and material fortunes of his enemies, demonstrating their powerlessness before their conqueror, and humiliating them publicly with the insulting image of social pollution contained in the very thought that their ex-slaves would own their land. They would further be reduced toward nullities, having sacrificed their rights to their own property. In absentia, the Southern gentry would be able only to shriek in fury, thus deepening Sherman's greater psychological project of driving the war into the very hearts of Confederates.

With this highly ironic act of legerdemain, Sherman concluded his history of reactionary insubordination to Lincoln's policy on black troops by reaching to Lincoln's left to form an improbable political alliance on this one issue with the most ultra of the Radical Republicans. He had maintained an independent racial policy throughout his period of major command, continuously acting opposite Lincoln's wishes. In the end he served the war against slavery by his military success, which demonstrated that Lincoln understood the political implications of Sherman's successes better than did Sherman himself. To achieve victory, Lincoln had taken enormous guff from Sherman, and had coolly focused on the grand strategy of the war, letting go significant elements of his racial policy in the pursuit of that final victory that would achieve the revolution. With his guns and deeds, Sherman had furthered racial justice, despite the fact that he had consciously intended to serve his own racist political agenda while he was at war at the head of a punishing and purifying white army.

After the war, Sherman would claim that he intended his Special Field Orders Number 15 only as an emergency war measure, and he did not protest when Andrew Johnson revoked it in 1866. One doubts whether Sherman, or Stanton for that matter, was thinking that far into the future in January 1865 when the two authored their plan. Blacks and some Radical Republicans seized eagerly on the idea, seeing in it a pilot project for a revolutionary change, which would be to their great advantage. This was probably the origin of the slogan of "forty acres and a mule" around which blacks would rally during Reconstruction. For Sherman, this had been almost exclusively an expe-

11

Rage at the South: Psychological Warrior

WITH HIS COMMANDS rapidly enlarged from division to corps, to an army, and finally, in March 1864, to independent command of the main theater of war in the West, with his autonomy growing and his victories multiplying, as the war lengthened and deepened in intensity, Sherman increasingly released his anger against all of the people of the South. He applied his destructive energy not merely in a physical sense but in a psychological one as well. While setting his cannons to roaring, he focused the powerful outpourings of his tongue and pen against his enemy, thereby finding his most significant military vocation—chief terrorizer of the South. Unlike the taciturn Grant and the outwardly compassionate (if inwardly tough) Lincoln, Sherman was the one major Union leader not merely willing but eager to shake the South to its roots with his clearly expressed verbal violence. Later he would say in his *Memoirs* concerning his year of maximum power, from the spring of 1864 until the end of the war a year later, "my aim then was to whip the rebels, to humble their pride, to follow them to their inmost recesses, and make them fear and dread us." This was no pose; indeed, Sherman convincingly heightened the impact he made with his psychological warfare. Southerners certainly came to believe in the authenticity of his rage, and so did he. Coupled with his ability to move an army swiftly, Sherman's war against the "inmost recesses" of the South was his greatest contribution to the Union victory. He was the most creative destroyer.[1]

This confidence, this release of anger, this clarity of purpose came not all at once, but in stages, albeit in increasing stages. He had been in the process of developing his independence of vision during the first three years of the war. In keeping with his lifelong style, there was nothing that was other than highly self-dramatized in this growth. When he had been low he plunged all the way into clinical depression. Now, when he was high, he was manic in his intensity, sleeping little, perhaps three or four hours a night, and then catnapping during the day, writing, talking, smoking endless cigars, talking, talking. His ego inflated to tremendous size, but he was able to *use* that inflation and his manic energy to create a multimedia juggernaut that went bulldozing through the South. He made himself into a force of nature.

The war was an intimate event for Sherman—his person, his honor were in a death struggle with the person and honor of the South, in a grand personalization of warfare. In the midst of the Vicksburg campaign, for example, on June 13, 1863, Sherman asked of Ellen, concerning the hatred Southerners expressed for the Union army, "Why cannot they look back to the day and the hour when I, a stranger in Louisiana, begged and implored them to pause in their career, that secession was death, was everything fatal, and that their seizure of the public arsenals was an insult that the most abject nation must resent or pass down to future ages an object of pity and scorn?" That Sherman should believe that anyone in rural Mississippi, where he was fighting when he wrote this, should recall his prewar sojourn in Louisiana was an absurdity, and perhaps his question should be considered but a rhetorical device. However, in retrospect at least, he had taken the insult of the Louisiana secessionists to the Union personally—they ought to have listened to him and desisted. But as they had not listened to he who was the Union, he would punish them.

In another rhetorical formulation, early in 1864, Sherman asserted to an audience of Southerners now living in Union-occupied territory that Southerners had always "prided themselves on high grounds of honor," and that he was "willing to take issue . . . adopting their own rules." He compared their rules to those of the "most fashionable" city men's clubs. "If a member goes into an election he must abide by the result or be blackballed or put in Coventry." The South had lost the election of 1860, but instead of behaving as "honorable men" abiding the results, they had seized the arsenal at Baton Rouge and fired on army riverboats "from behind a cottonwood tree." Writing to Ellen, Sherman reported the effect this literary conceit had had on his Southern auditors. "I know what I said will be gall and wormwood to some, but it will make others think." Behind this elaborate formula was a deep threat—the man who broke the rules of conduct had removed himself from the cover of the rules of civilized warfare. Sherman believed himself to be just the person to judge this fundamental breach of honor and to provide the well-merited punishment.[2]

At least indirectly, Sherman was aware of the dangers of his own self-inflation, and sought to place bounds on it. Until the end of 1863, for example, he refused all requests for his autograph or biography, or for his photographic likeness. He instructed his brother John to give only "the most brief and general items" to anyone requesting information about him, "and leave the results to the close of the war or my career." As exponentially as his fame was growing, Sherman was worried that some "slip or accident" would send his reputation plunging, and of course he hated the messengers of the press for all sorts of additional reasons. But at a deeper level, Sherman feared not merely being exposed by others, but exposing himself entirely to himself. He feared a total *self*-revelation of personality because there were energies and conflicts inside of him that were frightening even to himself. Therefore, it was reassuring to fit himself in as a subordinate in a larger organization, to serve under the calm and steady Grant, for, as he wrote his brother on December 30, "with him I am as a second self." Inside the army, as Grant's right hand, his ego would have its bounds. Still, he was full of pride in his accomplishments, a pride he felt most comfortable expressing to family members, as though it would give them rather than him pleasure—a subtle but significant form of self-censorship. As he wrote John in January 1864, "You who attach more importance to popular fame would be delighted to see in what estimation I am held by the people of Memphis . . . and all along this mighty river." His fame was not for himself but for his family. This seems a rather transparent device through which to disguise egoism, but it kept Sherman at one remove from his pride and on an even keel.[3]

Sherman asserted himself most comfortably through leading his men into action. Thus in mid-February 1864 he could write in his official report of his raid, at the head of ten thousand men, on the railroad center of Meridian, Mississippi, that his "movement was successful in an eminent degree," and brag further to a colleague back in Memphis that "everything with my command was successful to the highest degree." As he had when he had burned Jackson, Sherman described his destructive task at Meridian with a vivid relish. "For five days 10,000 men worked hard and with a will in that work of destruction, with axes, crowbars, sledges, clawbars, and with fire, and I have no hesitation in pronouncing the work as well done. Meridian, with its depots, store-houses, arsenal, hospitals, offices, hotels and cantonment no longer exists." Although toward the end of this raid Sherman attempted to set some limits to the pillaging and burning his troops carried out, in fact he had signaled them none too subtly at the onset of the campaign to burn first and ask questions later. "In war we have a perfect right to produce results in our own way," he wrote to a naval officer on the nearby Mississippi, in a fashion that, judging by the results, must have been similar to his verbal instructions to his subordinates, "and [we] should not scruple too much at the means, provided they are effectual." Work well done in war, especially a prolonged one, comes to mean efficient destructiveness.[4]

As long as he served under Grant's direct command, Sherman willingly accepted certain constraints both on his expressions of military ferocity and on his inflation of self. Indeed, in terms of deference, Sherman remained Grant's subordinate, both in strategic thinking and emotionally, until about October 1864, well after Grant moved to take over the eastern campaign against the army of Robert E. Lee.

When he had prepared to move East and to cede personal command of the West to his most trusted subordinate, Grant had expressed his deep gratitude to Sherman for "putting forth of energy and skill" while serving under him. "How far your advice and suggestions have been of assistance, you know," Grant wrote generously. "How far your execution of whatever has been given you to do entitles you to the reward I am receiving, you cannot know as well as me." In return, Sherman heaped praise on Grant. Grant was, Sherman wrote him upon his departure, so "brave, patriotic and honest" and with such a "simple faith in success" as to make him "Washington's legitimate successor." Sherman added, about Grant's reserved and intuitive approach to the art of war, "My only points of doubt were in your knowledge of grand strategy, and of books of science and history, but I confess your common sense have supplied all these." Although he found Grant less intellectually acute and well versed than he was himself, Sherman nearly idolized this calm and clear leader and friend, whom he knew would always have come to his rescue if he had needed it. "I know wherever I was that you thought of me, and if I got in a tight place you would come if alive."[5]

On March 18, 1864, Sherman went up to Nashville to relieve Grant of command of the major Union armies in the West, and rode with him on the train as far east as Cincinnati. During this journey the two men discussed the grand strategy of the remainder of the war—analyzing it in the coordinated manner that they, for the first time, would impose successfully on the Union war effort. A transcript of that train conversation would probably reveal that the two generals discussed a protracted war of attrition in a ruthless way they could not share with anyone else, even the president. Such a transcript does not exist, of course, and one can only surmise what was said from later correspondence between the two men. It was clear, however, that Grant remained the dominant figure, with Sherman the willing subordinate, and that, even in the thinking of these two leaders from the West, the campaign against Lee in the East would take precedence over that against Joseph Johnston in the West.

From Washington Grant wrote back to Sherman, laying out Sherman's grand strategy for him, along the lines they doubtless had discussed during that train ride together. "You I propose to move against Johnston's army, to break it up and to get into the interior of the enemy's country as far as you can, inflicting all the damage you can against their war resources." Sherman was to feel "free to execute it in your own way," but, Grant added, "Submit to me, however as early as you can, your plans of operation." Even if he trusted Sherman to make plans and to execute them, Grant expected as a matter of course, as Sherman's superior, to pass on his approval, disapproval, or modification. In a later letter, Grant reassured Sherman that he was confident that Sherman would make a powerful enough attack in the West to keep the enemy from moving a substantial number of troops eastward to reinforce Lee's army. He expected Sherman to travel light in a war of rapid maneuver. "I hope my experience has not been thrown away," the master strategist of the Vicksburg campaign reminded his ablest student.[6]

Far from taking umbrage at Grant's continued assumption of military preeminence over him, Sherman quite willingly continued to subordinate himself to him. He promised Henry Halleck, who was now serving as something of a chief clerk to Grant in Washington, "I will try and hold my tongue and pen and give my undivided thoughts and attention to [my] military duties." Sherman was eager to do his best to fulfill Grant's grand strategy. "Like yourself to take the biggest load, and from me you shall have thorough and hearty co-operation," he promised Grant. "I will not let side issues draw me off from your main plan, in which I am to knock Joe Johnston, and . . . the resources of the enemy. . . . I would ever bear in mind that Johnston is at all times to be kept so busy that he cannot send any part of his command" to the East or elsewhere. Sherman's willing strategic subordination to Grant may have inhibited his aggressiveness to a degree. However, his military hesitancy, his self-silencing promise about stilling tongue and pen, and even his sense of subservience to Grant soon would begin to wear off.[7]

Sherman fought the six-month-long Atlanta campaign using indirection and movement. With one notable exception, he refused Confederate invitations to assault their entrenched lines, instead sliding his army repeatedly around to the right and toward the rear of Johnston's army, threatening his lines of communication and compelling him into a series of tactical retreats and reentrenchments until, after about four months, he had forced Johnston all the way back into the fortifications around the key rail and manufacturing center of Atlanta. With a great deal of territory at his disposal, and with a cautious enemy, Sherman gained ground without pulverizing his own army, or engaging in any major battles.

For his part, Johnston slowed Sherman's advance and minimized his own losses in a skillful exercise in Fabianism, but Southern popular opinion and Jefferson Davis lost confidence in Johnston during this long, slow retreat. Finally, Davis replaced Johnston with the impetuous and overly aggressive John Bell Hood, who did Sherman the immense favor of attacking the Union army outside Atlanta, causing a major Confederate defeat. Now, admitting that he was too impatient for a long siege, Sherman again swung his army to the right below Atlanta, threatening to cut off the Southern army from its lines of supply, and so on September 1, Hood blew up his own ammunition magazines and abandoned the city to the Union army.

In small ways as in large, Sherman conducted this campaign with pleasurable destructiveness, sometimes casually expressed. For example, he mentioned in passing that the best form of temporary housing, the *tent d'abris,* was easily built "when boards can be ripped off our neighbor's houses" or from their fences, and shakes from their roofs. This was normal destructiveness that would weaken the enemy while serving to the temporary advantage of his army. Sherman instructed his corps commanders in the art of destroying railroads in detail. "Let the destruction be so thorough that not a rail or tie can be used again." Sherman's method, in which he was an innovator, was to use the ties to fire the rails, and then to twist the rails with a grapple hook his engineers had designed, which made them impossible to straighten without milling machinery, and then often to bury them. A variation was to wrap the twisted rails around trees—the legendary Sherman Neckties. When one wing of his army seized Roswell, Georgia, Sherman insisted that all the serviceable shops and factories be burned, and that all the workers, male and female, be deported. "The poor women will make a howl" he knew, but that was insignificant. Indeed, when Abraham Lincoln himself had protested to Sherman his order deporting other Confederate civilians earlier in the campaign, Sherman had replied to the president, "I will not change my order," the "clamor" against which was nothing but "a humbug & for effect."[8]

As his guns bombarded Atlanta, Sherman took considerable relish in all the destruction. To Halleck, he wrote on August 7, "one thing is certain, whether we get inside of Atlanta or not, it will be a used up community by the time we are done with it." George Thomas noted to his commander that the Union shells "burst beautifully" on Atlanta. To another subordinate, Sherman then wrote contentedly that their army was on the right path "to destroy Atlanta and make it a desolation."

On the larger and even more brutal plane of grand strategy, in early August 1864, before Atlanta, Sherman wired encouragement to Grant, who was mired in his trenches outside Richmond, "Let us give these Southern fellows all the fighting they want, and when they are tired we can tell them we are just warming up to the task." Sherman was being kind to Grant, whose troops, unlike Sherman's, had taken fearful casualties during the summer campaigning, earning their commander the title of "Butcher" in the Northern press. Grant replied with determination and gratitude, "Your views about showing no despondence, but keeping the enemy with his last man now in the field, constantly employed are the same I have often expressed. We must win if not defeated at home. Every day exhausts the enemy at least a regiment, without any further population to draw from." By this point in the war the two leaders could acknowledge readily to one another that they were fighting a war of attrition, which they would lose only if public opinion turned in revulsion against such a war, and threw out the Republican Party in the fall elections, for a Democratic Party that was far more likely to sue for peace. The virulently anti-Republican Sherman now wished to save that party, which was persecuting the war vigorously, and to defeat the Democrats, whose views on race and social conservatism he shared. In August 1864, with Northern morale at an all-time low, Republican defeat was a distinct possibility. Grant was stuck and could not deliver any good news. Therefore, on September 3, when Sherman wired to the world that "Atlanta is ours and fairly won," it was his victory that saved both the Republican Party and the Union war effort.[9]

On MAY DAY 1864, a beautiful day, just prior to launching his long and difficult campaign against Atlanta, Sherman took a solitary horseback ride over his old battlefield at Lookout Mountain. That evening he wrote to Minnie, "The leaves are now coming out and the young flowers have begun to bloom. I have gathered a few, which I send in token of my love and to tell you that I gathered them on the very spot where many a brave man died for you and such as you." He also sent a second bouquet to Lizzie, "to commemorate this bright opening of Spring. You can keep this bouquet in some of your books and though it may fade away entirely, it will in after years remind you of this year, whose history for good or evil . . . may either raise our country's fame to the highest standard, or sink it to that of Mexico." This touching gesture in celebration of renewed life was in part a symbolic compensation for all the young men of his command who had died and would soon die (which proved to be 4,423 from then until September); it was also a protest that he had a heart that could beat with love, an affirmation of his continuing role as nurturing father even when he was far away and had to play the rough general, and a token of beauty plucked from his fear of renewed failure.[10]

Yet even Sherman's strongly aesthetic, romantic streak could turn from peaceful, familial images to martial ones. Terror as well as beauty resided in the sublime. In his September 15 report of the Atlanta campaign, Sherman drew word pictures of battlefields that were every bit as beautiful in their way as had been his description of the flower-strewn May Day memorial grounds. On June 9, his army moved forward, and Kenesaw, "the bold and striking twin mountains lay before us, with a high range of chestnut hills trailing off to the northeast," this continuous range of hills presenting a "sharp, conical appearance, prominent in the vast landscapes." To Sherman, the war works of man only improved the stunning natural landscape. "On each of these peaks the enemy had his signal station, the summits were crowned with batteries, and the spurs were alive with men busy in felling trees, digging pits, and preparing for the grand struggle impending. The scene was enchanting; too beautiful to be disturbed by the harsh clamor of war," but his army had to break the beautiful scene, for "The Chattahooche lay beyond and I had to reach it." When he saw the beauties of Kenesaw Mountain, of course he did not desist, but crossed over the river in roaring battle—into the bloodiest Union defeat of the campaign.[11]

Sherman, who responded openly to intense beauty and love as well as to anger and wrath, was also unlike many commanders in his compulsion to worry publicly about morality in warfare. He never merely acted, nor did he act only from tactical and strategic considerations: He needed to persuade himself that, even when he was at his most brutal, he was acting for the greater good. Something in him stood back from the furious warrior he also so much relished becoming. Still, his direction in 1864–65, during his great year as an independent war chieftain, was away from remnants of forbearance and toward *moral totalism* in his attack on the Southern people. His actions stopped well short of "total war" in the twentieth-century Nazi sense, but his rhetoric came to imply more and more that in potential at least he could make total war if he chose to, and his attacks on civilians grew increasingly blatant.

In his always personal conception of this war of honor, Sherman often recapitulated and revised his past in explaining and justifying his movement in the Civil War toward moral totalism. For example, in a letter written on August 14, 1864, to the mayor of Louisville, who was protesting Union military treatment of leading Southern sympathizers, Sherman described what he had done in Louisiana in 1860, his old abode, and worked forward through recent history in order to show how he, Sherman, had ever been the reluctant warrior, compelled into escalating armed struggle by the aggressive South. At the start of war, Governor Thomas O. Moore and Braxton Bragg, his old Louisiana friends, had made prisoners of war out of the Union garrison in Baton Rouge, which they had requested be sent there in the first place. Later, when he had been in charge of Memphis, it had been the secessionist guerrillas who had burned bridges and the houses of Unionists, while "I would not let our men burn fence rails for fire or gather fruit or vegetables when hungry, and these were the property of outspoken rebels." Not they, but "we at that time were restrained, tied by a deep-seated reverence for law and property." It was the rebels who had "first introduced terror." Then and only then were the Unionists "forced in self-defense to imitate their example." Our adversary appealed to war, tauntingly "dared us to war." Then did our rage explode in full justification. "We have accepted the issue and it must be fought out. You might as well reason with a thunder-storm." All such issues as "niggers, state rights, conciliation . . . etc., are all idle and nonsensical. The only principle in this war is which party can whip. It is as simple as a schoolboy's fight, and when one or the other party gives in, we will be the better friends."

In this argument, Sherman deflected moral responsibility for his actions onto his opponents. In his own mind he was only acting in self-defense against Southern aggression. Furthermore, war once entered was a complete and natural event in itself. It was destructive without need of the agency of human will, like a thunderstorm. It was an elemental and morally blind zero sum game—whip or be whipped. As far as he was concerned, in adopting this argument and thereby joining fully in the war, moral considerations of means had in theory ended for the formerly reluctant Sherman. There was no moral reservation contained within a war once truly entered. For the wartime interim this moralist would take a moralistically amoral stance. After victory by the one side and capitulation by the other, which was the only possible outcome, that empathy and generosity that had been the basis of normal moral peacetime relationships could once more be expressed.[12]

Immediately after Atlanta fell to his army, Sherman initiated a plan to expel all civilians from the city, something he had done on a much smaller scale before but that, at this level, amounted to perhaps the most extreme action yet taken against civilians by any general in the war. Anticipating Southern reactions, Sherman declared to Halleck, "If the people raise a howl against my barbarity and cruelty, I will answer that war is war and not popularity seeking. If they want peace they and their relatives must stop war." Writing this letter, on September 4, 1864, was the moment in which Sherman attained his most fully conscious and self-acknowledged role as psychological warrior. Though he had a military argument for getting civilians out of the way of his army—in order to use Atlanta as one big military rail depot—his greater purpose was to strike terror into Southern hearts. He would not remain a personality with human feelings, but would incorporate war itself. Having chosen transformation into the totalist warrior, he would offer Southerners a big puzzle—what would this particular general not do? In purpose and self-conception he would be barbarous and cruel, not from his peacetime person, but from his personal rededication in war, a war into which he had finally and fully entered.[13]

Three days after girding himself in this letter to Halleck, Sherman wrote John Bell Hood, the Confederate commander, offering a ten-day truce, during which he would ship every Atlanta civilian through Union lines to the Confederacy. Hood agreed to the truce, realizing that Sherman really had not given him any alternative. But, Hood added in a letter he wrote to Sherman but intended for the Southern press, "the unprecedented measure you propose transcends, in studied and ingenious cruelty, all acts . . . in the dark history of war. In the name of God and humanity I protest." Sherman replied in a letter he intended for the Northern press and not just for Hood, "If we must be enemies, let us be men and fight it out . . . and not deal in such hypocritical appeals to God and Humanity. God will judge us in due time," but military men, real men, will act out of pure force rather than hiding in effeminate appeals to higher moral powers. In any event, Hood's appeal to a "just God" was "sacrilegious," for it was the South that had "plunged a nation into war, dark and cruel war, who dared and badgered us to battle." Having created the war, the South would now experience it.

When the mayor and two city councilmen of Atlanta wrote Sherman, also protesting the expulsion order, which, they were certain, would lead to unimaginable "woe, horrors and suffering" on the part of the expelled civilians, Sherman replied in grim righteousness and with his previously rehearsed phrase, "You might as well appeal against the thunder-storm as against these terrible hardships of war. They are inevitable, and the only way the people of Atlanta can hope once more to live in peace and quiet at home is to stop the war, which can alone be done by admitting that it began in error and is perpetuated in pride." War had now visited them—as by extension it would visit all Southerners, that nation of sinners. They had to cry out in defeat before the war could cease. "You cannot qualify war in harsher terms than I will. War is cruelty and you cannot refine it," thundered Sherman in King James biblical cadences, which all Americans understood, "and those who brought war into our country deserve all the curses and maledictions a people can pour out." At this point Sherman the cool deist had become Jeremiah, the Old Testament judge, and an ancient war god emerged from his prophecy, the god of the terrible swift sword.

But there could be an end to this catastrophe and redemption from it. "I want peace, and believe it can now only be reached through union and war. . . . But my dear Sirs," Sherman promised, "when peace does come, you may call on me for anything. Then will I share with you the last cracker, and watch with you to shield your homes and families against danger from every quarter." This assertion of recrudescent postwar morality was intended to demonstrate to Southerners, and perhaps even more urgently to himself, that he was making morally purposeful war, not in the war measures he might take, but in purely peaceful ends radically split from whatever might prove to be necessary wartime means. This moral and temporal dualism served to heighten Sherman's fearsomeness, as morally disengaged means could lead potentially to any form or depth of destruction. Later kindness, as a reward for capitulation, used as a moral justification that reinforced Sherman in his promised wartime excesses, heightened rather than reduced the terrors of what he and the still-deepening war might bring to the South.

Only Sherman, of all Union leaders, had this level of insight linked to this degree of rage, frankness, and articulateness, only he had such conscious abilities to make psychological war against the Southern people. He presented Americans, North as well as South, as he still presents us, with a great moral problem about the uses of war. War unvarnished is brutality itself, as Sherman argued. He did shake Southerners with the prospect of their own destruction, which more restrained pronouncements—such as those made frequently by Lincoln—did not. Hearing them, and witnessing Sherman's ever-advancing, seemingly unstoppable, increasingly destructive army, undoubtedly was a major factor that caused the Southerners to lose heart, thus leading toward the end of the war. This furious man, with his considerable terrorist capacities, may thus have been effective in ending the war in a way more forgiving or at least more limited approaches to fighting the war had not achieved. Certainly Sherman's vision was the most explicit as well as the most inhumane about the meanings of war. He had come into personal focus, marshaled his anger, and expressed his rage against an enemy he saw as the culminating enemy to him and to his people.

Sherman's ferocity was tied to one sole issue: obedience to the authority of the Union. He continued in his conservative social and political opinions. He disclaimed any interest in taking, he wrote to the Atlanta leaders, "your negroes or your horses or your houses, or your lands or anything you have." When Hood wrote a long racist letter denouncing Sherman's supposed attempt to "make negroes your allies and . . . place over us an inferior race," Sherman denied he had any "negro allies in this army," denied that this was other than a white man's war. And as for Hood's assertion that he had broken the laws of war in shelling Atlanta without due notice, Sherman noted that it was the Confederates who had turned Atlanta into a fortress without removing innocent civilians, and dismissed Hood scoffingly for his ignorance about military history—"see the books" about shelling such fortified towns, he told Hood, and broke off the correspondence.

Sherman was delighted with the propaganda impact of this public exchange. Hood had "appealed to the public as a demagogue," Sherman wrote Halleck, and this had been a welcome event, "for the more he arouses the indignation of the Southern masses the bigger will be the pill of bitterness they have to swallow." Halleck too was pleased, and Sherman was widely praised in the Northern press for really taking the war to the enemy. In Southern newspapers, he now became Sherman the Beast, a denunciation the general quite enjoyed. As he wrote contemptuously to an old California friend, "This is somewhat on the order of the school bully who if he cannot whip you can call you hard names or make insults at your sister." Sherman had whipped Hood in the elemental schoolboy struggle. He had also just made what would prove to be the most famous martial pronouncement of the war, promising, with moral totalism, a war without implicit limits. The shelling of Atlanta and the subsequent expulsion of Atlanta's civilians gave proof to the language. These were not just words, but brutal actions justified by an unforgiving rhetoric. The combination was carefully thought through, consciously applied terror, containing a promise of ever-escalating future destructiveness if that proved necessary.[14]

On further reflection, many Unionists had reservations about what Sherman was saying and doing. Although he had thrilled them with his avenging fury, he had also attempted to erase all moral problems implicit in the means used by the Union army, and in the cooler light of dawn, this made many Unionists uneasy. For example, O. M. Poe, Sherman's bright young chief engineer, was deeply troubled by the fact that women and children had been killed during the shelling of Atlanta while rebel soldiers had been safely stored away, as the Union army knew they had been, in thick-walled forts. "You know I was opposed to shelling the place, for it did no good at all, and only brought harm to unoffending people," Poe wrote his wife shortly after Atlanta fell. "Shelling did not get us into town a *single second* sooner than we would have got in anyhow." It was the movement of the army to the enemy's rear that had driven out the rebel army. In Poe's analysis, the shelling of civilians, which George Thomas and Sherman had looked upon as a beautiful sight, had been pointless militarily. Poe could support the later expulsion of Atlanta's civilians on humanitarian grounds—it would save them further suffering—but he was not prepared, as was Sherman, for an escalating war of terror against Southern civilians. Where others, even loyal subordinates, continued to be uneasy with the argument that the end of the war justified every means, Sherman would continue to up the stakes, deriving real pleasure from doing so.[15]

In his denunciation of Hood, Sherman also reiterated his opinion that the defeated South must be ruled with bullets, not ballots. Unlike Grant and Lincoln, who were quite willing to encourage at least embryonic civilian government in recaptured regions of the South, Sherman argued for "simple military rule till long after all the organized armies of the South are dispersed, conquered or subjugated," as he had written to Halleck a year prior to the fall of Atlanta. "The only government now needed or deserved" in retaken territories "now exists in Grant's army." For Sherman, immersed in war, power grew out of the end of a gun. "This section of 30-pounder Parrott rifles now drilling before my tent is a more convincing argument" to Southerners than any political convention, he wrote Grant. To a Republican politician, he made his antidemocratic point about those same cannons even more clearly. "I am no voter, but I have some 20 lb rifles that have more sense than [thousands] of the voters of Ohio. . . . They can throw 20 pounds of metal right on the mark, and all the time for the honor & glory of Uncle Sam." War had at long last stripped away democratic electoral pretenses, and demonstrated what was the true basis of political domination. Not democratic restoration but the iron hand of the military should rule the conquered South.

Sherman was reluctant to have Halleck publish this letter, as so often happened during the war, on the grounds that it might "impair my usefulness with the South." However, one should not dismiss its contents as merely rhetorical. Sherman often acted upon his coarsest and most impolitic opinions, sometimes overtly—as he had at Atlanta—though sometimes in more camouflaged ways. A policy of harsh postwar military rule was quite consistent with his urge to follow the logic of his moral totalism. Such logic in part was what would lead him, for example, to his policy of land confiscation and redistribution to the freedmen. This tendency contradicted, however, his proclaimed self-image as potentially the most beneficent victor, and at the end of the war he would change his mind about repressive military reconstruction.[16]

In spite of his hard pronouncements and brutal acts, Sherman could never quite admit to himself that he had become an utterly inhumane warrior. In October 1864 he wrote to a Yale clergyman that he was aware that he was "represented" to be a "heartless Boor," but he protested this was untrue, using a fantasy of his relationship with his own children. "I rarely see my children, but were you to behold them watching for my expected coming, and rushing to me with eyes all love you would not say I was heartless." Beyond that image, Sherman insisted that he would "wish a comparison with more professing men." While making war he continued to do many "acts of charity when the left hand knoweth not what the right hand gives," even though he admitted that during campaigns his mind was "jealous of all delays and obstacles." Sherman sought to deny to this man of the cloth, and to himself, that he had become the completely heartless beast. Yet even this awareness had an obverse side: It indicated that Sherman knew how he was regarded, and that this representation lent him great ongoing power. He had tapped into elemental force, and he knew it.[17]

The last serious official restraint Sherman felt to the liberation of his warrior's ego was his sense of deference to Grant. The last expression of this subservience came on September 9, 1864, shortly after the fall of Atlanta, when Sherman wired Halleck concerning the replenishment of his cavalry with a fresh supply of horses. "As soon as General Grant determines for me his next move on the chessboard, I will estimate the number I want," Sherman wrote. By October 9, having realized that if he embarked on a large-scale raid through Georgia his lines of communications would be threatened, Sherman had quite independently formulated the march that he would indeed carry out. In a now-legendary wire to Grant, Sherman wrote, "I propose we break up the railroad from Chattanooga, and strike out with wagons for . . . Savannah. Until we can repopulate Georgia, it is useless to occupy it, but the utter destruction of its roads, houses and people will cripple their military resources. By attempting to hold the roads we will lose 1000 men monthly, and will gain no result. I can make the march, and make Georgia howl." Sherman also intended to send George Thomas northward with a blocking force of a third of the army to counter any advance by Hood.

Grant's immediate reaction, as well as those of Stanton and Lincoln, was quite hesitant. Both the objective and the method of dividing an army and marching such an immense distance after cutting loose from communications unnerved the leadership in the East. Grant wired Sherman on October 12, "If there is any way of getting at Hood's army, I would prefer that, but I trust to your own judgment." Lincoln let Grant know that he shared these doubts and "that a misstep by General Sherman might be fatal to his army." Sherman's reply, almost a lecture to Grant, was that he would infinitely prefer moving through Georgia, "smashing things to the sea," over chasing Hood. "Instead of being on the defensive, I would be on the offensive; instead of guessing what he means to do, he would have to guess on my plans. The difference in war is full 25 per cent."

After mulling things over another day, Grant was willing to give Sherman his lead. "On mature reflection," he wrote to Stanton on October 13, "I believe Sherman's proposition is the best that can be adopted," and Stanton wired Sherman that same day, "Your plans are approved by [Grant]," and Stanton promised full cooperation. However, on November 1, noting that Hood was campaigning with considerable energy, Grant renewed his misgivings. He asked Sherman, "Do you not think it advisable . . . to entirely settle with Hood before starting on your proposed campaign? With Hood destroyed you can go where you please with impunity." In response, Sherman restated his project, with reassuring specificity about the strength of the force he had created for Thomas. Mollified by this message, Grant acquiesced once again. "I say, then, go as you propose," he wired Sherman on November 2.

This exchange marked Sherman's attainment of independence from Grant. He, not Grant, had forged his own daring plans, and he would implement them despite Grant's reservations. He remained in some ways Grant's best student, for he was applying the lessons of breaking from one's own lines of communication in a war of rapid movement, the lessons of the Vicksburg campaign, which Grant had initiated against Sherman's reservations in 1863. Now Sherman was breaking loose from his master, and initiating an even bigger and seemingly more risky campaign, and Grant could but give him his blessing, still tinged with doubts. "Great good fortune attend you," he telegraphed Sherman on November 7. "I believe you will be eminently successful, and at worst can only make a march less fruitful of results than is hoped for."

In later years, Sherman altered this story somewhat, telling others that Lincoln and Grant had been stalling him until he simply cut the telegraph wires and marched off in implicit near-insubordination. Sherman had in fact received approval from Grant prior to cutting the wires, but he may have feared Grant would reverse himself, and even more significantly, he remembered the episode as the moment of his definitive assertion of will over Grant's. In the West, their grand strategic roles had been reversed during the planning of the march to the sea. Cutting the telegraph wires, breaking his ties to the Union and its authority structure as he had cut the cord from Grant, Sherman and his army set out through Georgia without any external constraints. As he made clear before he started, this march against essentially undefended enemy territory would be far less a military campaign than an exercise in symbolic, psychological warfare of the most telling kind he could achieve.[18]

Sherman had calculated, with cold and intelligently measured anger, the likely impact of his march on Southern morale. "This movement is not purely military or strategic, but it will illustrate the vulnerability of the South," Sherman lectured Halleck on October 19. The "rich planters . . . don't know what war means, [but] when they see their fences and corn and hogs and sheep vanish before their eyes they will gain something more than a mean opinion of the 'Yanks.' " His army would inflict not military defeat on a Confederate army, but intention-

ally humiliating destruction on the peaceful, cultivated Southern landscape and her people. "Even now our poor mules laugh at the fine
corn-fields, and our soldiers riot on chestnuts, sweet potatoes, pigs,
chickens, etc." He intended to be as thorough as possible, not merely
raking the surface of the Southern spirit. On October 19, the same day
he wrote to Halleck, he wrote to the Union commander back at Nashville, "I am going into the very bowels of the Confederacy, and propose to leave a trail that will be recognized fifty years hence." As Hood
moved north, Sherman noted with pleasure to Thomas, "already the
papers in Georgia begin to howl at being abandoned, and will howl
still more before they are done," howl like mortally eviscerated animals, victims of the sort of abandonment he knew in his bones.

While he continued planning the expedition, Sherman often repeated and sharpened his sense of sadistic purpose. To George
Thomas he wrote on October 29, "I propose to demonstrate the vulnerability of the South, and make its inhabitants feel that war and individual ruin are synonymous terms." On November 8, in a letter to
Grant that is now legend, Sherman wrote, "If we can march a well-
appointed army right through [Jefferson Davis's] territory, it is a demonstration to the world, foreign and domestic, that we have a power
which Davis cannot resist. This may not be war, but rather statesman-
ship," Sherman argued. It would be the most explicit public demonstration of the most elemental political logic. "If the North can march
an army right through the South it is proof positive that the North can
prevail in this contest, leaving only open the question of its willingness
to use that power." Only in that last phrase was Sherman disingenuous
or modest or misguided: Without any doubt he intended to demonstrate quite clearly that he was not merely willing but eager to use that
power, for just as long as it took.[19]

This was war as politics stripped bare, war as "whipping," war as
moral totalism. He was now in a position to do as he willed, which did
not mean that he would do everything in practice. Indeed, even in his
rage, he calculated and recalculated the effects of his means during his
march to the sea and its sequel through the Carolinas. But he planned
to chop with a ruthless ax, and to broadcast his purpose as loudly as he
could. It was not just the march and the destruction, but the creation of
the broadest possible public awareness of these actions that was his
purpose. He was shouting his triumph and his enemies' utter defeat in a
way that would be unmistakably clear to himself, to them, and to the

whole world, which indeed was listening. No one else in the Union had taken on this leading role as Grim Reaper. During the war, especially during his time in independent command, Sherman had transformed himself into an implacable warrior. This enormous terrorist had come to understand both his enemy and the inner meaning of war as has no other American soldier.

WHEN SAVANNAH fell to his army on December 22, Sherman, ever the phrasemaker, wrote in triumph to Lincoln, "I beg to present you as a Christmas gift, the city of Savannah, with 150 heavy guns and plenty of ammunition, and also about 25,000 bales of cotton." Sherman was delighted by Lincoln's reply. "When you were about leaving Atlanta for the Atlantic Coast, I was anxious if not fearful," Lincoln admitted, "but feeling that you were the better judge, and remembering that 'nothing risked, nothing gained,' I did not interfere. Now, the undertaking being a success, the honor is all yours; for I believe none of us went further than to acquiesce." This was vindication indeed, for the risk, for the self-asserted independence, and for the conquest.[20]

There had been a second front to Sherman's grand strategy, sending Thomas north to check Hood's advance. By the time he had linked up with the Union fleet prior to taking Savannah, Sherman began to receive worried letters from Grant concerning Thomas. Already nicknamed "Slowtrot," Thomas had been hesitant to move out of Nashville after the approaching enemy, claiming needs to equip more fully, remount his cavalry, and so forth. Grant grew so impatient that he sent a peremptory order to Thomas to attack Hood at once, and even started west to relieve him in person. Sherman too was concerned, knowing that Thomas was "slow in mind and action," but he also continued to believe he was "judicious and brave." Finally Thomas moved, lured the enemy into attacking, and on December 15 and 16, in the Battle of Nashville, destroyed Hood's army with a totality achieved in no other single Civil War battle.

Lingering concerns over Thomas had detracted from Grant's pleasure in Sherman's victory, but when Thomas smashed Hood, in Grant's words, "magnificently," both he and Sherman were relieved. Sherman now felt doubly vindicated, for his own triumph, despite all the doubters, and for that of Thomas, whom he had placed at risk. After the Battle of Nashville, Sherman wrote Thomas in paternal pride, "I do not believe your own wife was more happy at the result than was I. Had any misfortune befallen you I should have reproached myself for taking away so large a proportion of the army and leaving you too weak to cope with Hood. But as events have turned out my judgment has been sustained." Sherman crowed in delight for his own sagacity. "But I am none the less grateful to you . . . and to all for the very complete manner with which you have used up Hood."[21]

By the time he reached the sea, Sherman had already matured his plans for the next phase of the war. He visualized a second and even more destructive march through the Carolinas—with special visitation plans for the South Carolinian nabobs who had started the rebellion— and up to the rear of Lee's army in Richmond. He simply brushed aside Grant's request to bring his army to the Virginia front by water. This time, neither Grant nor Lincoln questioned even for a moment what Sherman wanted to do. By now, Sherman believed his army and his strategic capacities were invincible. On December 31, 1864, he bragged to John that "I saw my way from Atlanta to the Sea before starting as I do now after it is over. I have a singular capacity for knowledge of roads, the resources of the country and the capacity of my command." In an only slightly more modest vein, sharing a bit more of the glory with his men, Sherman had written Grant a week earlier, "I don't like to boast, but I believe this army has the confidence in itself that makes it almost irresistible."[22]

After ensconcing himself in the most handsome mansion in Savannah, and reviewing his equally cocky troops, Sherman took the time to read the outpouring of newspaper stories and letters written in fulsome praise of him. He realized in a burst of pleasure that he had been elevated to the position of the leading military hero of the Union. "I am told that were I to go North I would be feted and petted," he told Ellen on January 5, 1865, relishing his new status as icon, and wrote to her only weeks later with pride—"Step by step have I been led deeper and deeper in the game till I find myself a leader to whom not only my soldiers look to but the President and the People. Not only our own, but foreigners and the South now accord me one of the Great Leaders of armies, endowed with extraordinary qualities." Though he still claimed to be "mistrustful" of such honors, and said he preferred slipping quietly away with his peaceful little family, he could not disguise his great pleasure. By now he had become a kind of grand war duke. He had reached an apotheosis of energy, independence, and power.[23]

While in this buoyant frame of mind, Sherman outlined to Grant his next campaign. "I wish you would run down and see us: it would have a good effect, and would show to both [your and my] armies that they are acting on a common plan." It would also show the world that Grant acknowledged Sherman's equality to himself as a general, and that his was the second jaw of the enormous Union vise crushing the rebels.[24] Through travail and triumph, Sherman had merged his identity with that of his army. He was their head and they were his body. Together they had marched to glory and would now march to even greater glory. Though many of their comrades had died, Sherman's men fully returned their commander's admiration. To them, their victory was his as well, and his was theirs.

12

Facing Death: The Loss of Willy

L ooking at himself in the mirror of his bedroom in the sump-
tuous Savannah mansion where he was spending his Christmas
holiday at the end of 1864, Sherman could be proud of the face staring
intensely back at him; walking to the window, he could look down and
admire his hearty men as they noisily enjoyed their period of rest and
recreation, storing up new energy with which to savage the Carolinas
during the coming spring. The newspapers and his mailbag assured
Sherman of his glory. And the bluebloods of the town, some of them
friends from the old days when he was a junior officer of no special
account, came calling, fearful admiration in their eyes. "There are
some very elegant people here, whom I knew in better days and who do
not seem ashamed to call on the 'Vandal Chief,' " Sherman wrote Ellen
on January 5, 1865, quite enjoying his role of barbarian warlord.
"They regard us just as the Romans did the Goths and the parallel is
not unjust. Many of my stalwart men with red beards and huge frames
look like giants," wrote the red-bearded if slender Sherman, "and it is
wonderful how smoothly all things move, for they all seem to feel implicit faith in me not because I am strong or bold, but because they
think I know everything."[1]

Hostility without; love within. There is no doubt that the morale of
armies, contingent of course on military success, feeds on the bonds of
admiration and love among the soldiers who share a process of over-

coming mortal risk in the face of the enemy's murderous intent. This mutuality is shared most intensely within the company of approximately one hundred men whom the fighter sees daily, whose lives he can help save, and upon whom he can call when in direst trouble. The more distant officers, the brass, if insensitive, stupid, or brutal toward their own men, often become part of the enemy rather than part of the band of brothers. It is the rare army where the most intrinsically distant officers are felt to be part of that brotherhood, even as elder brothers. Sherman was not wrong when he told his wife in his abundant egotism that his men had come to love him as he loved them. His feelings of fraternity, tied to paternalistic feelings both he and they found appropriate, gave Sherman, the antidemocrat, his nearest and dearest approach to a democratic experience of life. And his observation that his troops were perceived as the Vandal hordes by Southerners was also quite accurate, as was the general's correlation between the great hostility of the civilian populace and the strong bonds within his army. "I hear the soldiers talk as I ride by, 'There goes the old man. All's right,' " Sherman wrote John from Savannah. "Not a waver, doubt, or hesitation when I order, and men march to certain death without a murmur when I call on them, because they know I value their lives as much as my own."[2]

By this point in the war, Sherman's men had transformed their leader in their own eyes into "Uncle Billy," the all-knowing but plain leader, a man who shared their hardships while guiding them toward victory. "His customary appearance was to walk along the roadside with his hands in his trouser pockets . . . and talk good earnest common-sense with some person nearest him, regardless of rank," one soldier later recalled. "This was delightful for a subordinate, knowing his exalted position and feeling at ease." Sherman's slovenliness added to his casual allure, for his authority and strength were in his real merit and not in some aloof and off-putting spit and polish. "It is an honor to enny man to have ben on . . . campaign with Sherman," an inelegant private wrote home. "You see him a riding a long you would think he was somb oald plow jogger, his head bent a little to one wide with an old stub of a sigar in his mouth." However reassuringly homey the old man appeared, such soldiers took their hats off and cheered whenever he rode by. As always, while on march, Sherman talked and chewed cigars obsessively, but victory in war had transformed these habits into endearing elements of his successful personality rather than suggestions of a wacky failure. His soldiers even converted his reputation for madness into part of his triumphant mystique. "Although he was pronounced crazy at one time, I wish all Generals were as afflicted as he is," wrote one soldier. Many of the men wrote home of the faith Sherman engendered in them. "It is wonderful what confidence this army has in Sherman," said one. "The idea of these rebels being able to do us any permanent harm is perfectly preposterous." His men so trusted him, so adored him, that they felt that as long as he was there at their head, they would march ever onward, overcoming their own personal weaknesses in the process of serving him. Wrote one private, "I am an awful Cow hart you know But I shall Die before I will leave as true a Solger as Billie Sherman."[3]

Victories they had won doubtless cemented this powerful bond within the army. But another important reason for the admiration and affection Sherman's men felt for him was their knowledge that, in comparison to the Army of the Potomac, so many fewer of them were being killed or wounded in battle. As Sherman marched them on Atlanta in a war of movement and maneuver, his men were reading in the papers and in letters from back home about the incredible slaughter of Grant's men. In one week of the Wilderness campaign, May 5–12, Grant's army took thirty-two thousand casualties, and in the following six weeks it would take thirty-three thousand more, before running out of offensive energy and bogging down in the protracted and bloody trench warfare before Petersburg, a stalemate that would last until the following April. In contrast, Sherman's whole Atlanta campaign, which took over four months, cost thirty-two thousand casualties, and the triumphant, ensuing march to the sea cost only 1,338 more.[4] Where Grant, tagged as the Butcher by the Northern press during his bloody advance southward during May and June of 1864, was still stuck in the mud outside Richmond, Sherman's army had gained fame as the victors of Atlanta and Savannah, at about a third of the price in human lives and limbs. Uncle Billy not only charmed his men, he seemed to them to spare their lives, and they loved him for that at least as much as for the glory.

There were, to be sure, considerable casualties in Sherman's army—particularly during the Atlanta campaign, where they faced a resourceful enemy in Joseph Johnston and his still-strong army. On the whole Sherman avoided tactical attacks on enemy trenches, preferring to slide his army around the enemy flank, compelling him to retreat. "I think everything here progresses and is progressing as favorably as we could expect," Sherman wrote to Halleck on May 17, "but I know that we must have one or more bloody battles such as have characterized Grant's terrific struggles."[5] Using his past successes as his surest predictor of future strategy, Sherman should not have felt the necessity of advancing this theory. That he did so may have been an indicator of his feeling of solidarity with Grant—what he suffers so should I suffer—or it may have been an assumption that somehow proving true honor required a bloody battle, or it may have been his disbelief that he could carry out an entire long campaign through such indirect attacks. Whatever were the complexities of his reasoning, on June 27, 1864, in the one bloody battle of the whole campaign, Sherman hurled his forces disastrously on Johnston's trenches at Kenesaw Mountain, losing three thousand men in a short morning attack, before calling it off in utter defeat. Grant had lost 17,500 men in the two days of May 5–6, in the Wilderness, and seven thousand on June 3 at Cold Harbor, over half during the first hour of battle, but by Sherman's standards, the frontal assault at Kenesaw Mountain had been both a major failure and an unnecessary departure from a winning and far less costly strategy.

As his army had approached Kenesaw Mountain on June 5, Sherman had written Halleck that he expected the Confederates to make a stand there, and stated unequivocally, "I will not run head on into his fortifications." Two days later he wrote that if Johnston offered battle at that place, "I will turn it," and five days later, on June 13, that he would develop yet another movement "to dislodge him or draw him out" of his entrenched position, as "we cannot risk the heavy losses of an assault." But by June 16, Sherman had suddenly abandoned his plans for another flanking movement, writing Halleck that he was "now inclined to fight on both flanks and assault the center. It may cost me dear but in results would surpass an attempt to pass around. . . . If, by assaulting, I can break his line, I see no reason why it could not produce a decisive effect."[6]

On the morning of June 27, Sherman sounded the bugles, and his men attacked the enemy fortifications, falling in swarms. Sherman had lost his patience, exercised his hubris, and led his men to slaughter on the basis of the fantasy of the decisive frontal assault. Sherman was a keen student of military history, and he had seemed prior to Kenesaw Mountain to have learned the bitterest lesson of the Civil War, that given the firepower of the contemporary rifle, frontal assaults on a well-entrenched enemy would fail nearly every time. In this attack he did not even attend to the deadly precedent of Grant's massive defeat at Cold Harbor only three weeks earlier. Never again would he abandon his indirect strategy.

It is not possible to know exactly why Sherman had lost the normal equipoise of his strategic thinking when ordering that attack, as all his comments after the battle were defensive rationalizations rather than reassessments. At the end of the day of battle, he wrote to George Thomas, whose corps had taken the worst beating, "Had we broken the line today it would have been most decisive, but as it is our loss is small, compared with some of those in the East. It should not in the least discourage us. At times assaults are inevitable." Inevitability—fate—as an argument served to diminish Sherman's moral responsibility, as did his invidious comparison with Grant's casualty rates. Two days later, Sherman defensively misrepresented the level of casualties: "Our losses . . . will not exceed 1,500. As usual, the first reports were overstated." By July 9, Sherman had constructed the rationalizations to which he would hold. "The assault I made was no mistake; I had to do it," he wrote Halleck. "The enemy and our own army and officers had settled down into the conviction that the assault of lines formed no part of my game," and that whenever the enemy entrenched, his troops would "take it easy, leaving it to the 'old man' to turn the position." In other words, Sherman blamed his men for relying too much on him, losing their independence and their fighting edge, turning soft; the assault had been a lesson in combat discipline. Sherman went on to blame George Thomas for lethargy, a criticism of Thomas that would become habitual with him and with Grant. "Had [Thomas's] assault been made with one-fourth more vigor, mathematically, I would have put the head of the army right through Johnston's deployed lines." His plans were faultless, really; Thomas had been a precisely fatal 25 percent slow in carrying them out. Additionally, had two brave brigadiers, Harker and McCook, "not been struck down so early the assault would have succeeded." In any event, the attack had shaken Johnston's ability to predict Sherman's strategy; he "has been much more cautious since, and gives ground more freely." Sherman closed this lengthy self-exculpation by asking Halleck to "write me a note occasionally and suggest anything that may occur to you," a curious and uncharacteristic plea for Halleck's strategic and moral support, which demonstrated Sherman's internal struggle over this defeat. In reply

Halleck first snapped that he had never written "encouragement or advice . . . mainly because you have not wanted either," but closed by reassuring Sherman that he had heard none of the usual "growling and fault-finding" of Washington applied to the Atlanta campaign. Five days after the battle, Sherman had resumed his flanking movements and the enemy abandoned Kenesaw Mountain. Sherman of course attributed this result to the previous battle, when it seems far more plausible that he could have achieved the same result with no battle at all.[7]

Even more chilling than this elaborate and unconvincing set of attacks and moral deflections was Sherman's comment in a letter to Ellen three days after the battle that "I begin to regard the death and mangling of a couple of thousand men as a small affair, a kind of morning dash—and it may be well that we become so hardened."[8] Rather than assuming that the Sherman who could write such a letter was a hypocrite when he professed affection for his troops, or that he was both Jekyll and Hyde, it is more helpful to conclude that all those defenses and that hardening grew from his very real affection for his troops, and from his awareness that as a general he indeed would have to commit some of them to death and then carry on as a commander, leading his men ever onward despite the death of some. He simply could not admit their deaths into his heart if he were to continue to function well. He also could not admit that he had made a major blunder, lest he lose his self-confidence as a leader. (This second point is also in part a matter of the psychological style and public self-presentation of all Civil War generals, with the exception of Robert E. Lee immediately after Pickett's disastrous charge at Gettysburg: None of them ever admitted making a mistake. In the late twentieth century, generals can make admissions of error as long as they are not of a whole campaign or war.) Sherman's ghastly gallows flippancy in his letter to Ellen was a demonstration that he could not afford to acknowledge fully the loss he really did feel. His was a gargantuan effort at repression.

Even when his favorite subordinate, James B. McPherson, was killed on July 23, 1864, at the height of the Atlanta campaign, Sherman could only pause briefly in grief. At age thirty-four, ten years Sherman's junior, McPherson was the golden boy of both Sherman and Grant. At the time of his death he was a major general in charge of the Army of the Tennessee, one of the three wings of Sherman's army. He was tall, handsome, bright, and magnetic. In Sherman's words, "He was a noble youth, of striking personal appearance, of the highest professional capacity, and a heart abounding in kindness that drew to him the affections of all men." The day after McPherson had been shot dead off his horse by a Confederate patrol while riding from Sherman's command post back to his own camp, Sherman officially reported his death to Lorenzo Thomas in Washington. "He had quitted me in haste but a few minutes before and was on his way to see in person to the execution of my orders," Sherman wrote, still in disbelief and with a kind of guilt that he had somehow sent McPherson off to his death. "General McPherson fell in battle, booted and spurred, as the gallant knight and gentleman should wish." Sherman then went on to list the attributes of the great fallen hero. "History tells us of but few who so blended the grace and gentleness of the friend with the dignity, courage, faith and manliness of the soldier. His public enemies ne'er spoke of him without expressions of marked respect; those whom he commanded loved him even to idolatry, and I, his associate and commander, fail in words adequate to express my opinion of his great worth." All American patriots would feel this loss, Sherman insisted. He assigned three officers of McPherson's staff to bear his body, on his shield, back home to Clyde, Ohio, for burial. Thus had passed a hero, a *man*.

These highly ritualized expressions of loss were all the emotion Sherman allowed himself to release at McPherson's death. As he wrote on September 15, in his report of the Atlanta campaign, "The suddenness of this terrible calamity would have overwhelmed me with grief, but the living demanded my whole thoughts." Even ten years later, when recording the story of this death in his *Memoirs,* Sherman barely paused to mention it in his onrushing narrative of the Atlanta campaign, although in many postwar letters and speeches he did mourn the death of McPherson retrospectively and ritualistically, as did Grant. In letters to Ellen shortly after the event, he discussed the risks of such an instant death that might take him, and the loss McPherson would be to the army, rather than expressing his personal sense of loss or grief. Consciously, Sherman vented his fatalism about the random nature of death in war and the concomitant necessity of therefore living in the present moment. Nine days after McPherson's death he wrote Ellen, "I don't pretend to see a week ahead," and reminded his wife that he well could be the next to die, "which is not improbable at any moment." Compounding this effect of McPherson's death on him, Sherman told Ellen that while writing this letter, "a solid canister shot passed me close and killed an orderly's horse . . . close behind me. . . . In fact I daily pass death in the most familiar shape and you should base your calculations on that event." Sherman rarely alluded to his frequent brushes with death, which would not have been the most thoughtful subject to write to a wife waiting in perpetual fear back home, but McPherson's death made him bring the feeling of that possibility nearer the surface of his consciousness more than was usual for him. In his irreligiosity, he interpreted such a death, or its absence, as the throw of some unseen and unknowable dice, rather than in any way stemming from the hand of God.[9]

At the end of august 1863, during a lull following the victory at Vicksburg, Sherman had sent for Ellen, Minnie, and Willy to join him at his camp by the Big Black River, twenty miles below Vicksburg. As he wrote Thomas Ewing reassuringly about this invitation, the camp "is in reality one of the best possible. It combines comfort, retirement, safety and beauty. . . . I have no apprehensions on the score of health . . . it is no hotter here than with you [in Ohio]." Sherman also admitted to Ewing that he wished in effect to bring down his family in order to have them share in his new fame—his claim to immortality—before his troops. "My children and children's children will now associate my name with their Country's History."[10]

The reunion with Ellen must have been joyful, for she became pregnant during the visit. And, most happily for Sherman, his favorite boy, nine-year-old Willy, his firstborn son and namesake, made a great splash as he rode out with his father to review the troops in a little sergeant's uniform sewn for him by one of Sherman's retinue of guards.

And then quite suddenly, Willy took sick at the camp with typhoid fever, suffered terribly during the trip back up the Mississippi on the *Atlantic,* and, at 5:00 P.M. on October 4, died at the Gayoso House in Memphis. Sherman described this terrible voyage in a private letter he wrote to Grant the day after the death of "Willy my oldest and healthiest boy." Still in shock, Sherman confessed that "this is the only death I have ever had in my family, and falling as it has so suddenly and unexpectedly on the one I most prised on earth has affected me more than any other misfortune could. I can hardly compose myself enough for work but must and will do so at once." In the next paragraph, Sherman abruptly broke off his grief and passed on to an analysis of his current problems in logistics and troop movements. Sherman also composed, and had printed and distributed, a letter to his guard battalion, beginning, "I cannot sleep tonight till I record an expression of the deep feelings of my heart to you . . . for [your] kind behavior to my poor child. I realize that you all feel for my family the attachment of kindred; and I assure you all of full reciprocity." It was his sense of duty that kept Sherman at his post, he declared, and that had led him to call his family to him "in that fatal climate . . . and behold the result." Tragedy had befallen his family. "The child who bore my name, and in whose future I reposed with more confidence than I did in my own plans of life, now floats a mere corpse, seeking a grave in a distant land, with a weeping mother, brother, and sisters clustered about him. . . . For myself I can ask no sympathy. On, on, I must go till I meet a soldier's fate, or see my country rise . . . till its flag is adored by ourselves and all the powers of the earth." This reiterated split of the personal from the military was an incantatory effort for instant repression of the impact of his son's death, for sublimation of domestic grief in martial service to the great national family.[11]

Willy's death would prove to be, however, the great exception to Sherman's rule of stoic repression. In tandem with Ellen, he mourned the death of his blessed son deeply and at extraordinary length. Indeed, throughout the year to follow, during the campaign against Atlanta and on down to the sea, his long letters to Ellen and hers to him would be filled with grieving for Willy. Far more than Sherman's complex and deadly military situation, far more than his bouts of self-inflation, which never ceased, and his eager seizing of victories, Willy would remain the obsessive subject of his correspondence with his wife.

Willy had always been his father's brightest star. He and Lizzie had been the children to remain behind with him in California when Ellen had gone back to Lancaster to stay with her eldest daughter, Minnie, and her parents. Willy was then his special pet. Of his year-old toddler, Sherman had written to Ellen in 1855, "Willy is as heavy a load as I want to carry, and he tyrannizes over me completely, making me carry him all round the yard an hour after each meal." The father had always been willing to spoil his pet boy. Over the years, Willy's eagerness for life grew and grew, bursting out in a letter he wrote his papa on June 3, 1862. "We have kept the pony about a week while grand pa was away. Cant me and Tommy go bare footed whenever we want to." And so on, through comments about the third-grade reader, the new chickens, and the stabbing by Jim Bulgar of John Anglum's hand—"they had a trial it was against Jim Bulgar was put in the Penitentiary old Mr Bulgar put him up to it." This was the sort of sweetly aggressive and curious child his father thought he had been, and Ellen had the same feeling when she saw Willy at the top of that cherry tree on June 1, 1863. When at war, the father gathered minié balls from the battlefield at Shiloh for his boy and, later, twelve canes for fishing poles from the battlefield at Vicksburg, asking eagerly for Willy's news in return. "You must continue to write me and tell me everything—how tall in feet and inches—how heavy—can you ride and swim—how many feet and inches can you jump. Everything." Such news, from the core of normal peacetime life, of his buoyant boy's everyday growth toward manhood, made for a private reserve of life affirmation amid the chaos of war. Willy was also the repository of his honor and the one expected to surpass him, as every American father thought his prize son ought to do. "Of me you will always hear much that is bad and much that is good . . . but you and my other children will feel and know that I am always good to them for they are growing up to fill stations higher and better than any I now fill and must be prepared."[12]

And now, as suddenly as if he had been shot in battle, the precious son and heir was dead. This loss, among all the terrible deaths he had been witnessing, even in comparison to that of his protégé, McPherson, tore at Sherman's heart in a way he could not so simply expunge through renewed action. Two days after the death, he wrote to Ellen in a letter she would receive when she got back to Lancaster with the body, "sleeping, waking, everywhere I see poor Willy. His face and form are as deeply imprinted on my memory as were deep-seated the hopes I had in his future." Sherman then blamed himself for Willy's death: He had been the one who had insisted on Willy's visit, denying explicitly that there were any health risks involved. "Why, oh why, should that child be taken from us, leaving us full of trembling and reproaches? Though I know we did all human beings could do to arrest the ebbing tide of life, still I will always deplore my want of judgment in taking my family to so fatal a climate at so critical a period of life." Sherman then indicated that he would need to put the memory of this death, too, out of his mind, taking from it the lesson of moral purity that Willy's life and death offered him. "But I must not dwell so much on [the death.] I will try and make poor Willy's memory the cure for the defects which have sullied my character."[13]

The same inner dialectic of trying to carry Willy with him, and needing to put Willy in some perspective, accompanied by self-reproach, characterized the next two letters he sent Ellen on October 8 and 10. The death was so terribly confusing for him that he was having trouble sorting out his feelings. "I hardly know how to feel. At times I cannot realize the truth so dreamlike, and yet I know we can never see his bright . . . face again." Life did not stop to let him sort out the meanings of this death, on which he would dwell: "But the world booms on." When he passed mentally from his continuing duties into his grief, time collapsed backward into dreamlike recollections. "The moment I begin to think of you and the children poor Willy appears to me as plain as life." Scenes of Willy's childhood flashed up from his memory: as a toddler, "stumbling over the sand hills" in the yard in San Francisco, "running to meet me with open arms" at the camp on Black River, "and last, moaning in death at this hotel." Sherman felt renewed guilt for having taken Willy into "that dread climate," which now he explicitly tied to survivor's guilt. "Why was I not killed at Vicksburg, and left Willy to grow up to care for you?" That guilt also included, though less directly, Sherman's sense of mourning for all the young soldiers who had died at Vicksburg while he, the older man who had sent them to death, as he had sent Willy, had survived. In a confused passage, Sherman seemed simultaneously to want to retain the memory of Willy's suffering and to place it in the past. "Though I can never efface from memory, nor do I wish to, the scene of afflictions through which we have passed—no that is so. I feel satisfied that it is past." If the death could not be put in the past, Sherman would have to dwell on his guilt for having caused it, and thus, through perpetual remorse, deprive himself of the authenticity of the feelings of loving care that he needed to emphasize he had offered Willy. "God knows I exhausted human foresight and human love for that boy, and [he] will pardon any error of judgment that carried him to death." Besides, the earthly life was full of terrors—Sherman surely knew that—and now Willy would be spared all those in going to that better home. "We did all we could for poor Willy—in life and in death, and it may be that he has escaped a long life of anxiety and pain mentally and bodily."[14]

Unlike her agnostic husband, the devout Ellen had a framework ready for understanding the meaning of Willy's death. His had not been just a beautiful death, but The Beautiful Death. In her first letter to her husband after her return to Lancaster, she wrote that when the priest had given Willy extreme unction while he lay on his deathbed, she had been absolutely sure of "the efficacy of the same sacraments which sanctified his soul." Though she too felt real pain, she also drew strength from her memories of the primal death scene she had just witnessed. "Father Carrier said when he told Willy he might die," Willy had said "that he was willing to die if it was the Will of God but that it pained him to have to leave his Father and Mother. . . . I feel as if my heart would break so vividly does this recall his patient suffering. Let us prepare for heaven & be ready when God calls to follow him." After his burial she wrote, "the body of our little Saint rests in the grave," and later she asserted, "he is not lonely and I know he is blest," for his soul was to live forever in heaven. He was the whole family's spiritual predecessor and their beacon of hope. He reminded all the Shermans that their true abode would be in heaven. "I would be glad if we could all be together with him," she wrote, in a thought that would only intensify as she realized the appeal of his spiritual call, "Oh, that we could only join him now." She too felt guilt about her role in his worldly demise, less from any act of bringing him to his place of death than because of what that death instructed her of her own generally sinful nature. "But I must submit to the will of God who suffered me to be thus blinded in punishment for my sins and bear the painful remorse as a penance for them." Concerning Willy, her grievous sin meriting punishment had been worldly pride: "My pride in him was too great and I treated him too much like a man." However, she continued, "Thank God he has no sins of a man to atone for now." In her obsessive moral lexicon lust was the supreme sin. She conflated her overweening pride in the manliness of her elder son with something in the carnality of her own nature. But he, unlike she, had not committed the sins of a sexually mature adult. Therefore, he certainly was now a saint in heaven, saved from the snares of sin set for adult men on earth by the original sin central to their very natures.[15]

It was as if all of Ellen's spiritualized life had been a preparation for this event. She had a deep belief in the existence of a fixed and permanent spiritual progression that would follow such a death, and she knew by heart the steps in the process of sanctification. Thus she could gather her feelings together and objectify them in a ritualized process, one that shaped her grief, giving her great solace. This was the main event and the teleological purpose behind her belief in divine domesticity. This was very much women's territory, this ritual process was women's work, but her husband, who had a deep hunger for solace, was willing, even eager, to overcome his own irreligiosity and his religious antagonism to her, and to follow her lead here as Ellen entered the Victorian fetish of deep mourning. Together, through this prolonged process, the Shermans would reach toward their second and final state, where the so manifestly imperfect Sherman family on this earth would be transformed into the imagined family sharing perfect love forever in heaven.[16]

This mourning ritual was both obsessive and extremely protracted. It formed the center of the correspondence between the Shermans until the end of the war, and was the explanatory device around which other experiences were arranged and interpreted. Both of them would also continue to memorialize Willy's death until their own deaths decades later.

Willy would remain his father's beau ideal, his image of perpetual perfection. Over five months after his death, Sherman wrote Ellen that "Willy lived more in my thoughts than [a] real person that I can yet dream of him as alive . . . brave and manly." This idealized personage could compensate for all the far-from-ideal persons with whom he was struggling in the terrible game of war. Sherman knew that he too could be sinful—impatient, rough, callous to those around him, not to mention being a lethal, intentional destroyer of his enemies—so how reassuring it was for him to be able to idealize his recollected role as loving father to that sainted boy. On November 14, 1863, Sherman wrote Ellen, "He knew how we loved him and if he sees us now, he knows how we mourn his absence." In that singular heavenly realm, cut off from the conflicts of this life, and from his limits as a parent of living children, Sherman could be the ideal father. Embattled here and now, in that imagined fatherhood he was calm and good and perfectly loving.[17]

Willy was also an idealized fragment of himself: "He was my alter ego," he wrote Ellen six weeks after Willy's death. During the remainder of the war, Sherman expanded and elaborated on this sensibility concerning Willy/William as the appropriate container of pride—the one with whom he could have ties of perfect loyalty. While Sherman was designing brutality into his proposed march to the sea, on October 29, 1864, he paused to write Ellen that to "see [Willy's] full eyes dilate and brighten when he learned that his Papa was a great general would be to me now more grateful than the clamor of the millions." He could not trust the adulation of the masses, who could always turn on him in disloyalty, accursed democrats that they were. But he could trust Willy who loved him perfectly, and whom he loved to equal perfection. "He seemed to know me better than anybody else, and realized the truth that if I labored it was his. He knew . . . that all I had was for him, whether of money or property or fame. I may be in error but with him died in me all such ambition and what has come to me since is unsought, unsolicited." Sherman was in error. As well as being embattled, his ego was enormously inflated, and growing more so with each victory and each word of praise. Sherman could displace that inflation by pouring it into Willy's cup—worldly success was all in service to this idealized alter ego. Everything that was good happened for Willy rather than for William. On the eve of his final victory, the surrender of his enemy at the end of the war, Sherman would write Ellen, "Oh that Willy could hear and see! His heart would swell to overflowing." In a glimmer of realization that his heart rather than Willy's might be the one that was swelling to overflowing, Sherman added that "it may be that 'tis better that he should not be agitated with such thoughts." That addendum came from his conscience, or from the voice of Ellen in his conscience, reminding him that the point of Willy's canonization was not for Sherman to glory in his own ego but was meant to remind him to seek to renounce his ego's overweening place of pride; not that Willy should descend to him in pleasure for his father's deeds, but that Sherman should strive spiritually to reach Willy's heavenly home. As often as he reminded himself of this ladder of spirituality, Sherman forgot it, using Willy for a boost of absolute loyalty in the here and now.[18]

Willy's beachhead in heaven for the Sherman family was enlarged, Ellen was certain, when her mother died. She wrote her husband on February 26, 1864, that her mother "has joined our darling Willy now, and together, I trust, they watch over us." In heaven they were secure from the trials of the world and yet still close to their loved ones, and the loved ones were still connected with them and therefore somehow safer. It was but a short distance in Ellen's heart from the reassurance these redeemed dead ones offered to the living to a morbid desire to reject this life, with all its contradictions and vicissitudes, for that perfect one after death. On January 4, 1865, Ellen wrote Sherman in a letter that also celebrated his triumph at Savannah, "Were that our journey were over we could be sure of joining . . . Willy in [his] home of endless joy." Ellen felt that her husband misinterpreted her "willingness that the children should be taken to heaven young" as an indication that this belief meant that Willy's death had other than left her "lonely" and in "anguish which the recollections of my boy's sufferings inflict upon my soul," but in fact she often did emphasize Willy's sufferings rather than his pleasures when he had been on earth as part of her larger tendency to turn firmly against this world for the next. Not merely did she do this for herself; she did it vicariously for her husband, whose soul, she believed, remained in great peril despite the home Willy's sainthood was preparing. Time after time she pressed Sherman for his conversion into the bosom of the Roman Catholic Church. She always had, but now his constant risk and Willy's death led her to redouble her demands, usually phrased as requests. On December 31, 1864, for example, she pleaded, "Were you to die without the faith you leave us miserable." Not merely was Sherman's soul in mortal peril because of his failure to convert to the true faith, his life work was spiritually misdirected, because it centered on worldly striving and earthly rewards rather than on cleansing renunciation of this world as preparation for the next and true one. Even while she praised her husband and relished his achievements, she also sought to reject reflected pride within herself, and urged the general to see past the transient for the permanent—that was the lesson of Willy. "God no doubt took Willy in mercy to us that we might realize what we before well knew, the vanity of human fame compared with the immortal life of one child." Such admonitions doubtless proceeded from the deepest motives of concern for her husband, but they were at the same time oblique attacks on his character, a continuation of the unending struggle in their marriage. Presumably, once safely in heaven, the Shermans would live in bliss, if only he took this offer from her outstretched hand, and Willy's. Willy's death lent strength to her interpretation of values; by heightening the meaning of the divine, deep mourning strengthened the feminized qualities of domesticity.[19]

Turning inward, turning upward, turning away from the world of action into such a religious conversion were not within Sherman's realm of meaningful choices. He would mourn Willy, but he would have to carry on. He therefore had to interpret Willy's death in less ethereal ways. One way of witnessing Willy's death would be for him to strive to be a better father and husband. "I feel I must try and act the comforter," Sherman promised Ellen on November 8, 1863. To begin that task, for Christmas that year he took leave, "for a few days to comfort my family, almost heartbroken at the death of [Willy]," Sherman informed Henry Halleck. And after Christmas, before returning to the front, he took his eldest daughter, Minnie, now nearly fourteen and a budding young woman, to a Catholic convent at Notre Dame, Indiana, telling Ellen afterwards that "Minnie will make a splendid woman, and for the next few years we must give her all she needs," and then soon reassuring Minnie herself that "there is nothing that I have or can obtain that you shall not have by asking, if for your good, and in return you must tell me everything that happens to you or interests you, no matter what, tell me and you need not fear." Sherman was striving to be the very best, most generous, most supportive, and most nonjudgmental father he could be to his eldest daughter, Minnie, the girl whose childhood he had missed when she had remained back in Lancaster with the Ewings while he was in San Francisco, the girl whom he wanted to remind that she was not now being abandoned far from home, as he had been abandoned as a child, the girl in whom he placed renewed outpourings of his heart now that Willy was gone. Sherman felt confident that Minnie returned his love and that he could give his heart to her, much as he had to Willy. "If I should be killed or wounded, I know that my sweet Minnie will think of me always," he wrote her. Although he never rejected explicitly the possibility that he might really have expected to join Willy in heaven, in this formulation to Minnie he seemed to indicate that wherever his soul might go should he be killed (which he thus acknowledged as a very real possibility that gave him concern), his memory would stay alive in the heart of his sweet daughter. Where the mourning led by Ellen was based on training for heaven while on earth, this was a modernized, inverted formula for approaching a kind of earthly heaven.[20]

Toward his remaining son, Tom, Sherman expressed demands rather than offering the kind of nurture he gave Minnie. One of Sherman's first impulses, less than a week after Willy's death, had been to write Ellen to "tell Tom for me that he must remember that he is our only boy and that he too must be good and learn so as to take care of you and all the rest, a heavy burden for so young a boy." Tom, the man of the house, had just turned seven. This placing of an enormous burden when one might have expected sympathy stemmed in part from the difference in the feelings and expectations Victorian fathers had for their sons as opposed to their daughters. In this case it also grew from Sherman's fears for this particular son, for where Willy, a happily extroverted and popular lad, had been his favorite, Tom, who was often aloof and irritable, was not so prized, perhaps in part, one suspects, because his personality contained certain traits of little Cump that the mature father disliked in himself. Ellen had often admonished Sherman to be kinder to Tom, and to refrain from playing favorites with Willy so obviously. Thus the weight Sherman now placed on the black sheep Tom was quite other than the affirmative warmth he showered on Minnie. Not surprisingly, Sherman was disappointed in Tom, with whom he had never established the kind of bond he had with Willy. On January 5, 1865, he wrote Ellen, after expressing mourning thoughts for Willy, "I don't think Tommy so identifies himself in my fortunes. He is a fine manly boy, and it may be as he develops he will realize our fondest expectations, but I cannot but think that he will show less interest in me than Willy showed from the time of his birth." After blaming Tom for failing to worship his father with enough ardor, Sherman turned to some failures for which he might have been responsible. "It may be that I gave [Willy] more attention when the mind began to develop." Where Sherman had been the primary rearer of the toddler Willy in San Francisco, when Ellen had been back in Lancaster, he had been away from home during most of Tom's young life. If now he wished to make from the moral lesson of Willy's death an improvement in his fatherly qualities, he failed to renew his paternal vows with Tom, and failed to give Tom the reassurance that he could ever become the alter ego Willy had been. Perhaps this omission stemmed in part from Sherman's own unresolved childhood-father-mother problems. In any event, the tension between Sherman and his second son would never really go away.

On April 28, 1864, just before setting out on the Atlanta campaign, Sherman wrote Ellen that he had just written Tom, and then added, "Oh . . . poor Willy . . . others may fill his place but not in our hearts that can never again be as sensitive as before." This was an indirect but clear reference to his relative lack of feeling for Tom. It also indicated his fears that his callousness toward the death of his men was threatening to overtake his whole heart, cutting off his ability to love Tom in particular, and, by extension, anyone at all. "Death and war scar our hearts & minds till nought is left but a callow mass that is hardly worth dying." If he could not feel love, how could he know he was alive? He feared that he had died inwardly with Willy.[21]

And then on June 11, 1864, Ellen telegraphed Sherman that they had a new son, born nine months after that visit to the Big Black, where Willy had become mortally ill. Sherman agreed with his wife that they should avoid the fairly widespread custom of naming the new boy after the one who had passed away. "I agree with you that we should leave Willy's name vacant . . . though dead to the world he yet lives fresh in our memories." Nevertheless, the new boy might prove a blessed replacement for the old. "I am pleased to know the sex of the child, as he must succeed to that place left by Willy, though I fear we will never again be able to lavish on anyone the love we bore for him." There was guilt in the implicit blasphemy of somehow forgetting the sainted Willy for a new earthly soul. At the same time there was hope: "Still we hardly know ourselves what is in store for us." Perhaps the new boy, named Charles, would be as splendid in his way as Willy had been in his. Sherman repeated this double anticipation of hope and fear to Minnie. "When you get home you will find a new brother to take Willy's place but I fear we all loved Willy too much to let another take his place."[22]

Ellen was delighted with her baby boy. When he was five weeks old she told her husband that "his head, face, forehead & form resembles you. His eyes are hazel, fine & large. . . . He seems the quickest most intelligent of all my babies." Unhappily, when he was five months old, Charles took sick with pneumonia and died. In her diary, Ellen grieved for her "little Saint," who had gone on up the same path as had her mother and Willy, the path prepared by Christ's atonement. "At 8 o'clock my darling baby passed from the sufferings of the earth to the joys of heaven. Thanks, forever thanks my Saviour for the sufferings and death which secured heaven for him."[23]

Down in Savannah, Sherman could scarcely feel loss over one more death, for the death of an infant son he had never seen. "It seems he too is lost to us, and gone to join Willy," Sherman wrote to Ellen, repeating a formula he knew his wife believed. "I cannot say that I grieve for him as I did Willy, for he was but a mere ideal where as Willy was incorporated with us and seemed to be designed to perpetuate our memories." Sherman then repeated his sense that in the face of so much death, an inner deadness was overtaking his whole heart. That toughness that was morally dangerous also seemed necessary. "Amid the scenes of death and desolation through which I daily pass I cannot but become callous to death. It is so common, so familiar, that it no longer impresses me as of old." He realized that as she was "surrounded by [the] life and youth" of the family, Ellen could not take things "so philosophically," by which he meant with his stoic detachment, which in this context he saw as a merit. He also realized, however, as he composed his letter, that her greater grief was assuaged by her "religious faith of a better and higher life elsewhere," a faith that, in the final analysis, he lacked. He felt "doomed" to be compelled to live his military life, "so that even my children will be strangers." His lack of faith compounded the impact of his distance from his loved ones and that made by all his experience with carnage and death. He felt at times like a heartless hero walking through the war.[24]

On the first anniversary of Willy's death Ellen put up a new portrait of him in her room as a shrine, "to keep him fresh in the minds and hearts of all the children," she wrote her husband, and annually, on the subsequent anniversaries of his death, she would enter a ritual lamentation of his memory into her diary. In another ritual, Ellen wrote Sherman on April 6, 1869, to commemorate the seventh anniversary of the battle of Shiloh, where he had "had the opportunity to vindicate your name." That triumph had made her realize that his life was to be one of "continued success & good fortune," she reassured him. In this letter and in her mind, Ellen had collapsed this ritual memory of the son's death backward in time into the father's victory. "Willy is more keenly appreciated in my mind with this day, than with any other of the war. His death took the fullness of joy from even later victory." Worldly fame was as nothing, Ellen told herself, and Willy's death was given her to check her pridefulness in her husband. She also reminded him to use the recollection of that death to check his pride.

Ellen's elaborate mourning climaxed in a memorial recollection she composed about Willy in 1868, primarily for the edification of her other children. At the moment of birth he had indicated his saintliness, for at that first moment, "a placid smile of peace and contentment . . . o'erspread his countenance." He had been the perfectly mannered son. "Never was he guilty of an act of disobedience and never did an improper word sully his pure lips." Even while engaged in sports "he remained gentle, courteous and noble," though Ellen hastened to add that he was no Goody Two-shoes, but always acted with "a proper spirit of self-defense & independence." He was a "fearless rider." As well as living such an exemplary life, Willy had died a beautiful death, "sorrowing" for leaving his parents but offering his soul to God "with loving abandon." In sum, he would always remain her "Christian hero." This image of the perfect son was the fitting abode for Ellen's longing for pure love. Such idolatry also allowed her to detach herself from her real husband and real children in the name of the saint.[25]

In the end, Sherman could not enter a competition for such purity of renunciation, for reasons of belief and temperament, and because he was busy fighting the Civil War. After his return to Memphis in January 1864, following his Christmas visit home, Sherman mulled over the relationship his ties to the strenuous life might have with his desire to reach a peaceful place like Willy's heavenly one. He wrote Ellen that he would love to rest, to simply leave the war and take off for California, but he knew that if he did so "my motives would be misconstrued." Instead, he had come back down the river to Memphis, where "I am now on the wave of popularity and the next plunge is away down. I know it well and would avoid it, but how is the question." He felt on the edge of failure, an old feeling for him, on the brink of depression, and at risk of death. Ellen was bearing, he told her that he knew, the "full load of care and anxiety . . . mourning for Willy" within the Sherman family, while he could simply not maintain that level of mourning. He had to come back out of his little family, back into the big war. "Just think of me with fifty thousand lives in my hand, with all the anxieties of their families. This load is heavier than even you imagine." His soldiers and their families were his family by extension. Such a quantity of mourning as all of them might demand was impossible if the general were to stay in active command, and so he felt he had to move on, even in the instance of his own Willy. Perhaps in renewed combat he could find some way to contribute to the spiritual purification not just of his own family, or of the greater family of his soldiers, but of the entire American family. As he wrote to Ellen another time while in the grip of this mood, "It may yet be that I may yet realize my dream that I may be a partial instrument in adjusting this fearful family quarrel."[26]

Yet so inured was Sherman growing from seeing the deaths of so many thousands of soldiers that the numbness threatened to overwhelm all his capacity for remaining empathetic in life. He might even lose his ability to grieve for Willy, he feared. Therefore, he kept alive that mourning process throughout the war as a tiny spark, in order to keep some part of himself open to human suffering. This was especially urgent for this harsh commander, who was visiting so much destruction upon so many enemies with such special energy. This inner region

13

The Selective Destroyer

O N NOVEMBER 12, 1864, Sherman's army cut all its links by wire and rail to the North, and three days later set off through Georgia. Free of any external restraints from Washington, opposed only by weak cavalry forces that could not challenge his march, Sherman could disperse his sixty-five thousand men over a sixty-mile-wide front and sweep southward, his troops stealing and burning as much as they could. Intent on inflicting the greatest possible destruction on the Confederate countryside, and spread so thinly and thus so far from effective command control, they became an "antilaw" unto themselves.

This freedom to destroy everything did not necessarily connote that everything was to be destroyed. There were not, however, many implicit inbuilt limits on that destructiveness, and so the tendency for Sherman's men, who well understood his rage against the South and shared in it, was to escalate continually their level of destruction until they reached some undefined and often personal limit beyond which they could not go. The point, after all, was to make Georgia howl.

Before departing, Sherman dictated his Special Field Orders Number 120 as guidelines to his army's task. Having severed communications, this giant raiding party would also be cut off from all lines of supply; therefore, Sherman ordered that "the army will forage liberally on the country during the march." This foraging was to be accomplished, Sherman ordered, by designated parties, "under the command of one or more discreet officers." Such regularity in foraging was especially important for control of those units who moved the greatest distance off from the roads traveled by the columns. Soldiers were forbidden to "enter the dwellings of the inhabitants, or commit any trespass," but they were encouraged at the same time "to gather turnips, potatoes, and other vegetables, and to drive in stock in sight of their camp." Artillery and cavalry units were admonished to "appropriate freely and without limit" all the "horses, mules, etc." they would find. Sherman also cautioned them, however, to be "discriminating . . . between the rich, who are usually hostile, and the poor or industrious, usually neutral or friendly."[1]

Eight days into the march, Sherman supplemented these orders with specific restrictions. He was learning that his foraging parties were frequently turning into self-formed groups of soldiers, either free of the discipline of officers or led by officers who savaged civilians with their men in ways even more insidious to discipline, as then the men felt sanctioned to move past the bounds of Sherman's orders. Therefore, Sherman reiterated that "more attention must be paid to the subject of foraging," that "none but the regular organized foraging parties be allowed to depart" far from the line of march, and that wagons captured "to bring their plunder to camp" be burned, as they tended to slow up the march and open up gaps in the columns (and although he did not say it, encourage plunder of household goods of no military use). In contrast to this attempt to reimpose limits on destructiveness, Sherman also ordered that wherever the enemy obstructed the march by burning crops or bridges or by other means, "the commanding officer of the troops present on the spot will deal harshly with the inhabitants nearby, to show them that it is to their interest not to impede our movements. Should the enemy burn forage and corn on our route, houses, barns, and cotton gins must also be burned to keep them company."[2]

Sherman's ever-increasing keenness to destroy shone through even his field orders, which were official documents almost certain to be more law-affirming than any practical limits he or his subordinates might set on actual behavior while in the heat of action. Certainly his men acted on their general's covert intentions rather than on his published orders. As one form of limit, Sherman's men were urged to make class distinctions: Sparing the poor and industrious translated as spare those civilians who resemble ourselves, people who might be split by such tactics away from what Unionists wished to believe was their weak loyalty to the Confederacy. It also meant, make a special effort to destroy the grand homes of those rich and therefore especially resented traitors who had made the secession. On balance, Sherman encouraged more rather than less destruction, with dwellings excepted if the enemy did not resist his army at all. Even then, unit commanders were given the widest possible discretion in interpreting which acts of the enemy merited destruction even of dwellings. The behavior of Sherman's men demonstrated their understanding of Sherman's basic desire. As Illinois private Ira Van Deusen observed to his wife, "You have no idea how the women & children suffer here whear we run there husbands & fathers from there houses & sometimes kill them at their [own] dorse & then our men take everything in the house & tair up the gardens & [pastures], there wheat fields & burn their fences. . . . Any whear near we pass everything is destroyed."

Earlier, during the Atlanta campaign, Sherman's officers of course knew of such behavior, which they considered to be an activity of only a minority of their men, and which many attempted to limit. Sharing the concerns of his officers, on June 4, 1864, Sherman had issued field orders instructing his commanders "at once [to] organize guards and patrols" to arrest and punish stragglers and "skulkers," and if necessary to shoot them on the spot, for he considered such men to be "common enemies of their profession and country." To give teeth to these orders, Sherman told his officers that when they would lay claim to promotion, "no officer having a loose, straggling command need expect any favor." At this time, Sherman was still jealous of his reputation for forbearance toward civilians. Indeed, after Atlanta fell, he had taken the time to write a Louisville newspaper, defending what he considered to be his kind treatment of those 1,572 civilians he had banished from that city. He enclosed a letter from a major in Hood's command who thanked Sherman for his "uniform courtesy" during the expulsion. Sherman added that the people of the North, who were "liable to be misled" by the falsehoods spread by a "desperate enemy," should be reassured that he had extended not only care but kindness to those Southern civilians.[3]

But after November 15, reflecting Sherman's deepening understanding of a psychological war of moral totalism, he issued no more orders to shoot "skulkers," nor did he reprimand misbehavior in any systematic way, as he had done on the road to Atlanta. Neither did he seek to justify himself any longer to the outside world (with which he had broken contact in any event) as a basically humane general. Sherman now rather celebrated the destruction his army brought. At the conclusion of the campaign, he noted pridefully in his official report that, having destroyed over one hundred miles of Georgia railroads, "we have also consumed the corn and fodder [for] thirty miles on either side of a line from Atlanta to Savannah, as also the sweet potatoes, cattle, hogs, sheep and poultry, and . . . more than 10,000 horses and mules, as well as countless . . . slaves. I estimate the damage done at $100,000,000, of which $20,000,000 has inured to our advantage, and the remainder in simple waste and destruction." Sherman recognized that to many in the North, even at this late date in the war, "this may seem a hard species of warfare," but insisted that only by behaving in this way could the Union "bring the sad realities of war home" to the Southern people, and not merely to the Confederate soldiers. Sherman acknowledged that at times his men had been "a little loose in foraging," and that they "did some things they ought not to have done," yet on the whole "they have supplied the wants of the army with as little violence as could be expected, and as little loss [to ourselves] as I calculated."[4] Sherman's men had minimized their own losses while maximizing those of their enemy. That was a standard rule of war, except for the point that these enemy losses were nearly all suffered by civilians rather than by Confederate soldiers. Sherman was gratified by this outcome. He did not disguise that he had shifted his military intentions toward civilians after beginning the march to the sea, but, rather, advertised it.

The war against an essentially undefended enemy civilian population ripe for the plucking turned into a giant party. After they had reestablished contact with the Union fleet when nearing Savannah, many soldiers wrote home in a joyful spirit about where they had been. "We had a long trip down here, and a very pleasant one," wrote one Indiana private, "except that we had to shoot a few times at the rebs." If risks had been low, rewards had been plenteous. "We always had plenty of fresh meat and ham, and honey and butter . . . and sweet potatoes without end and chickens much the same. It has been the richest time in the service to me." Privates such as this man gained what Georgia lost. "We burned cotton enough to nearly buy the state of Indiana." The marching boys even had a subservient black chorus singing them on their way. "It was rich to see the negros flock to the road to see the boys

make them pull off there hats and coats and dance while we were passing." Soldiers who had hitherto been shocked or at least disturbed by
the foraging practices of some of their comrades now dropped their
inhibitions and joined in looting, gaining increasing pleasure as they
did so. "Before we started this raid I had herd the boys tell about going
for things when they were out foraging. I thought I wouldnt be much
of a hand for such things," wrote James Greenalch, a formerly ruly
Michigan private, while nearing the end of the march, "but if I remember right I had my share of what the rebles raised through Ga and let
me tell you there was any amount of it but they havent got as much
now." Greenalch confessed that farms stripped bare and women crying "looked rather hard to see," but given Confederate raids into
Pennsylvania that summer, he believed that turnabout made for fair
play. Southerners now believed that they were devils, Greenalch continued to his wife. "I am satisfied . . . that some of the women . . . have
been convinced that the Yankees have hornes but not hornes on the
top of the head." Exploiting Southern women sexually was beyond the
pale for this private; at least when he wrote to his wife about his activities, he expressed shock "that men or those who pretend to be men
would become so demoralized and void of all deacency or respect."
Other soldiers expressed a similar dismay that their comrades would
take advantage of starving women by trading food for sex, which suggests that the practice was fairly widespread.

Nevertheless, the aura of free plunder of all goods, sex included,
characterized these young conquerors. In a letter written on December
18, 1864, Sergeant Rufus Mead of Connecticut summarized the festive
atmosphere, the glad destruction of a Southern cornucopia, and the
deeper psychological purpose of the raid, in language even more direct
than Sherman himself used. "We had a glorious tramp right through
the heart of the state, rioted and feasted on the contry, destroyed all the
RR. In short found a rich and overflowing contry filled with cattle hogs
sheep & fowls, corn sweet potatoes & syrup, but left a barren waste for
miles on either side of the road, burnt millions of dollars worth of
property, wasted & destroyed all the eatables we couldnt carry off and
brought the war to the doors of central Georgians so effectually I guess
they will long remember the Yankees raid. I enjoyed it all the time."
Mead was confident that even in their excesses the boys were doing
Sherman's real bidding. They would butcher a beef for the liver and
leave the rest to rot, ignore chickens for the best cuts of pork. This

might "seem wasteful to you [homefolks] but not to us." For, in sum, "the boys wasted as much as they used, in fact I think Genl Sherman didn't intend to leave anything for the Rebs." This served them right, for their own "wickedness & who can sympathize very much with them. I only hope experience will prove a good schoolmaster to them."[5] If Sherman did not command his boys to destroy innovatively, he winked when they did so, and they knew he winked.

One private who got a close-up reading of the general's intentions was Vett Noble of Ypsilanti, Michigan, one of Sherman's clerks. "When the General feels good he is real funny," Noble wrote his parents on December 15, 1864. On such a day, Sherman would invite his clerk to join him in a glass of plundered Madeira. "Bully for 'Uncle Billy.' He's cute," was the way Noble reacted to such invitations. The day before Noble shared this cocktail, another private, serving as Sherman's orderly, had asked his commander for a leave of a couple of hours. "The genl just for fun asked him what mischief he was up to now, said he knew the pranks of these boys." The orderly said he was going to take a carriage, that is to say steal it, and go for a ride. Sherman "then asked him if he had his lady engaged, if not would he take him?" They went out for a ride, parading the carriage in front of some rebel fortifications. Thinking they were civilians, the Confederate soldiers withheld their fire, "and Sherman and his orderly had a good laugh." Here, "Uncle Billy" was an indulgent uncle who encouraged his enlisted men to play youthful tricks on Southerners, which transformed them into the dehumanized butt of nasty jokes. His destructive energy fed theirs; theirs fueled his; destructiveness flowed both from the top down and from the bottom up.[6]

In a sense, Sherman's officers were trapped between the general and the men. Many simply joined their men, or led them on their rampages. Others tried to limit the bad behavior of the troops, whether out of moral revulsion for assaults on civilians, or out of concern for military discipline, or both. Although all wished to prosecute the war with vigor, many feared that their army was turning into an increasingly violent mob, and that their disciplinary role as officers was more and more being ignored and subverted.

Even during the earlier Atlanta campaign, some officers had been concerned that the men were getting out of control. On June 4, Colonel O. M. Poe, Sherman's chief engineer and one of his favored protégés, expressed his deep embarrassment in a letter to his wife, Nellie: "it al-

most makes me blush" that his duties brought him in contact with some of the "thieves & pillagers of this Army whose ideas do not rise above a henroost, and whose notions of the proper way to subdue the rebellion are exemplified in the maltreatment of women & children." At this time, Poe believed that such behavior did not characterize most units—"Thank God this class of ruffians are largely in a minority." However, Poe also felt he could not act on his natural desire to suppress the bad actors; indeed, he was certain that the ethos of this army directed him to cover up news of such excesses. Thus he wrote Nellie that even discussing the bad news with her amounted to "rampant treason," and warned her that she had better keep his letter to herself.

Returning to this subject three months later, Poe's distress had increased. He was no longer certain that the ruffians were in the minority or that such rascality could be assumed to be the exception to the rule. "A great many of the soldiers are acting very badly—robbing and plundering," he now wrote Nellie. He still took direct action against such men when he personally observed them at their nasty tasks. "I lose my temper . . . and make pretty free use of my physical strength with which Providence has blessed me, as more than one 'bunged up' face in our army can testify." Yet Poe was certain that he was fighting a losing battle against ever-spreading pillaging. "My attempts to stop this thing are but a small & feeble effort, when we regard the great number of those who either wink at it, or openly encourage it." Although he did not name Sherman explicitly among the winkers and encouragers, Poe believed that by not doing anything serious to curtail bad behavior, Sherman and his army were lending "additional cruelty to a war already . . . sanguinary without parallel."[7]

Such frustration of officers who wished to enforce discipline increased dramatically on the march to the sea. Nevertheless, many did try. If it was their own regiment, and that regiment maintained cohesion, such officers had a reasonable likelihood of being successful. Greater problems arose when officers encountered undisciplined troops from other, "bad" regiments. A clear case in point was two contacts between Colonel Oscar Jackson, of the Sixty-third Ohio Infantry, and members of the First Alabama Cavalry, a new, and even for Sherman's army, infamously undisciplined unit of vengeance-minded Unionists of Southern origin. On November 24, Colonel Jackson found one Alabama cavalryman ransacking a bureau in a house filled with frightened and crying women and children. Jackson knew the rules:

Sherman's orders forbade the soldiers to enter dwelling houses and to pillage anything not needed for the army. When he reminded the cavalryman of these orders, he "answered me a little short," Jackson wrote in his diary, "and I helped him out the door with my boot. Oh but he was mad." As Jackson then retreated to the doorway and tried to reassure the womenfolk, the cavalryman returned with several of his comrades, bent on revenge. Just then, the colonel spied a company of his own men marching down the road and waved them over, at which point the Alabama troopers fled. A few days later, Jackson came upon another group of the First Alabama while they were threatening to shoot an old man unless he told them where he had hidden his silver and gold. When the leader of the men "drew his pistol and cocked it, I rushed on him, disarmed and arrested him, and had the satisfaction of having him ordered into irons," Jackson wrote in his diary. The whole First Alabama was a "disgrace to the army," Jackson concluded, made up of "professed Union men [who] behave like robbers and marauders, besides there is no fight in them, not a bit." And yet even soldiers from "good" regiments, like Private Lake of the Thirty-second Wisconsin, also could be among the plunderers of inhabited houses. Jackson sat on the December 6 court-martial that sentenced Lake to death for stealing a pillowcase and some meal, a sentence intended in part to encourage discipline among other would-be looters. After this point had been made so strongly, and broadcast to the men, Lake's commanding general commuted the sentence to imprisonment for the duration of the war.[8]

It is difficult to know precisely how Sherman understood the effect of his own role in unleashing hyperdestructiveness. Perhaps the closest one can approach Sherman's position is through the diary of his old St. Louis friend and "legal officer," Major Henry Hitchcock, who was in close daily contact with Sherman, riding with him as a member of his immediate staff. Hitchcock admired and loved Sherman as "a man of genius," a "live man" who made for "capital company." Sherman had dictated his Special Field Orders Number 120 to Hitchcock, who was convinced on the eve of the march to the sea that the orders were perfectly clear. "General Sherman will hereafter be charged with indiscriminate burning, which is not true. His orders are to destroy only such buildings as are used for war purposes . . . all others are to be spared and *no dwelling* touched. . . . All private soldiers are expressly forbidden *to enter any* house, even to forage." By November 17, two days into the march, Hitchcock had seen plenty of evidence of foraging, but "no violence so far as I saw or heard." Soon enough, even though he was relatively isolated in Sherman's small retinue, Hitchcock began to hear plenty. On November 23, he began to discuss "straggling and burning, etc." with corps and division commanders. General Jeff Davis told him bluntly that "the belief in the army is that General Sherman favors and desires it, and one man when arrested told his officer so." By this point Hitchcock became convinced that such soldiers had not misapprehended Sherman's actual desire. "I am bound to say," he told his diary, "I think Sherman lacking in enforcing discipline. Brilliant and daring, fertile, rapid and terrible, he does not seem to me *to carry out things* in this respect." After finding fault with Sherman, Hitchcock immediately began blaming others. "Staff organization not systematic or thorough as [it] ought to be"; Sherman "has not [the] best staff." When Hitchcock brought up the issue of straggling with Sherman, the general replied, "I have been three years fighting stragglers, and they are harder to conquer than the enemy," a statement Hitchcock failed to analyze as indifferent, cynical, or irresponsible. Hitchcock also told himself, "the real fault lies with regimental and company officers," though whether Sherman had voiced this opinion or Hitchcock had drawn his own conclusion is unclear.

During the long march, Hitchcock seemed to take every opportunity to record acts of kindness by Sherman to the Southern civilians they met personally. After a frank but civil exchange with an elderly lady in Sandersville, Sherman emerged from her home, chased away some would-be plunderers, posted a guard, and the next day, after hearing about "much trouble about that old lady . . . had some coffee and other supplies sent her." Several days later, Sherman sent some food to J. B. Jones, after hearing that stragglers had stripped him bare. Such acts proved to Hitchcock's satisfaction that the widespread belief that stragglers acted as they did under Sherman's orders was a "damnable lie."[9]

Hitchcock's rationalizations—that Sherman never directly ordered plundering or burning of homes, that he was personally kind, that he was powerless to stop stragglers who were a naturally occurring and unavoidable event, that he was poorly served by his staff and by regimental and company officers—did not explain away his commander's de facto policy of omission to reinforce discipline, which amounted at the very least to turning a blind eye on the excesses of his men. The men did not misunderstand Sherman.

Many individual officers at least attempted to prevent the burning of inhabited houses in Georgia, but such efforts to enforce this limit melted away when Sherman's army entered South Carolina. Even prior to that campaign there was a nearly universal and quite explicitly stated consensus that South Carolinians above all others should pay the full price of all their property for their sins as the chief initiators both of secession and of civil war. Before Savannah fell, Sherman's army was already awaiting their next march with heady anticipation. Sherman led the way, but he was certain that he spoke for his men. "The whole army is crazy to be turned loose in Carolina," he wrote Halleck on December 11; "I judge that a months sojourn in South Carolina would make her less bellicose." On December 18, he added to Grant that thousands in Georgia, like the "whole United States, North & South, would rejoice to have the army turned loose on South Carolina to devastate that state." On Christmas Eve in his Savannah mansion, Sherman felt his pulse race when he thought about the incendiary campaign to come. "The truth is the whole army is burning with an insatiable desire to wreak vengeance on South Carolina. I almost tremble at her fate but feel that she deserves all that seems in store for her."[10]

As had been the case during the march to the sea, Sherman accurately read, reflected, amplified, and affirmed the sentiments of the men in the ranks. An Iowa infantryman wrote his father on December 22 about South Carolina, "she sowed the wind. She soon shall reap the whirlwind. She will yet weep tears of blood for her folly. . . . Well may she tremble." Another Union soldier wrote on December 18 that "we have laid a heavy hand on Georgia, but that is light compared to what South Carolina will catch." He reported that Georgia civilians egged him on. "Very often when we have been destroying property, the women would say, 'Well, I don't care, if you will serve South Carolina the same way, for they got us into this scrape,' and [our] men would say, 'Never mind, we won't leave anything there. We will make it a desert.'" By December 29, tired of his vacation in Savannah, this soldier was ready for another one of "Sherman's crazy spells" in South Carolina. The lust for destruction had become nearly universal, many soldiers reported. "Nearly every man in Sherman's army say they are for destroying everything in South Carolina," one private wrote home. Others contemplated joining in a level of destructiveness that they had merely observed while in Georgia. One soldier wrote his sister, "I have never burnt a house down yet, but if we go to South Carolina I will burn some down if I get the chance."[11]

Even many of the officers who had attempted to prevent the burning of civilian homes in Georgia now at least acquiesced to the greater destructiveness they knew was to be the fate of South Carolina. If they did not sign on to the more wanton policy, they did sign off their previous opposition to such destruction. "Now on to South Carolina," the formerly strict disciplinarian, O. M. Poe, wrote his wife on December 26, after having heard a rousing Christmas speech by Sherman. "We are on her borders, ready to carry fire and sword into every part of that state." General Henry Slocum, commander of one of the three wings of Sherman's army, who had opposed the army's excesses in Georgia, now had to admit that at the very least, "it would have been a sin to have the war brought to a close without bringing upon the original aggressors some of the pains."[12]

Unified as never before in a destructive policy, Sherman's army kept its word about ravaging South Carolina. Only the rare house now escaped the torches of Sherman's men, who also continued to strip the land and then burn it. Some soldiers continued to discriminate in favor of ordinary people. "The poor people are respected by the soldiers and their property protected," wrote one Indiana private to his sister, "while the rich are persecuted when caught and their barns, gins & houses fall victims to the invader's match." Many acted on their special resentments against the self-proclaimed aristocrats of South Carolina. "Their cant about aristocracy is perfectly sickening," wrote one Ohio lieutenant to his brother. One chaplain gave his blessing to this focus of anger among the men: "The wealthy people of the South were the very ones to plunge the country into secession, now let them suffer."

General Sherman shared this special fury against the South Carolina upper crust, just the sort of Confederate snobs who had proclaimed Northern whites such as Sherman's men to be lowly and ignorant plebeians. Near the end of the war, he asked Grant to tell Phil Sheridan, concerning the blue-blooded South Carolina cavalry commander he had come to despise thoroughly, "I make him a free gift of all the blooded stock of South Carolina, including Wade Hampton," commander of the ragtag cavalry that attempted without success to impede Sherman's march, "whose pedigree and stud are of high repute." In South Carolina, Sherman's army fought the nearest thing to a class war during the American Civil War, such social resentments adding a fillip to acts of destruction.[13]

It was not generally true, however, that the solid yeomen and numerous poor people of South Carolina were spared much of what was visited on aristocrats. Sherman's men burned far more than they passed over. Afterwards, several spoke quite openly about this new threshold of violence over which they had crossed. James Greenalch, a Michigan private, told his wife, Fidelia, after the march, "it was a general understanding throughout the entire army when it left Savannah that [South Carolina] would be made an example of and I can say it has been carried out to the letter." Some felt bad that ordinary folk had been swept into the firestorm along with the rich, but rationalized it as a necessary if unfortunate outcome of the war against the aristocrats. Wrote one corporal, "I commiserate [with] the destitution of the poor, but I can shed no tears for the rich. Great distress must prevail where we have been." This avenging army had been a force of nature guided by a shared mission. Another Michigan soldier confirmed to his uncle, "In South Carolina, there was no restraint whatever in pillaging and foraging. Men were allowed to do as they liked, *burn and destroy.*"[14]

Withdrawing disapprobation and sharing malice with their troops united commander, officers, and men against the people of South Carolina in the most violent and prolonged anticivilian campaign of the war. Colonel Oscar Jackson entered in his diary that, "We have given South Carolina a terrible scourging." Mercy and forbearance had been the rare exception, Jackson believed. "We have destroyed all factories, cotton mills, gins, presses and cotton, burnt one city, the capital, and most of the villages on our route, as well as most of the barns, outbuildings and dwelling houses, and every house that escaped fire has been pillaged." General Alpheus S. Williams, a division commander, replicated Jackson's images in a letter to his daughter about Sherman's campaign through the innermost heart of Dixie. "Our people, impressed with the idea that every South Carolinian was an arrant rebel, spared nothing but the old men, women and children. All materials, all vacant houses, factories, cotton gins and presses, everything that makes the wealth of a people, everything edible and wearable, was swept away." Williams claimed he did not personally order such destruction, but that neither could he nor would he have limited it. "The soldiers quietly took matters into their own hands. Orders to respect houses and private property not necessary for subsistence for the army were not greatly heeded . . . indeed not heeded at all. Our 'bummers,' the dare-devils and reckless of the army put the flames to everything," concluded Williams with awe and something approaching admiration. "We marched with thousands of columns of smoke marking the line of each corps. The sights at times, as seen from elevated grounds, were often terribly sublime." Williams confessed, however, that the same sights that had appealed to his romantic sensibility were "often intensely painful [judging] from the distressed and frightened condition of the old men and women and children left behind."[15]

Finding an acceptable way to justify such a level of warfare troubled thoughtful men like Williams, who split the colossal destruction they observed from the high ground as a terribly beautiful visitation on errant rebels, from the misery and privation they were inflicting on the old men and women and children in their wake. Colonel Jackson understood immediately after the army passed out of South Carolina that they had been behaving worse than ever before and that this was morally problematic, to say the least. Sherman's army exhibited "a recklessness by the soldiery [while] in South Carolina that they never exhibited before and a sort of general 'don't care' on the part of the officers."

Even the kind and devout O. M. Poe concluded that inflicting such calamities must have been the working out, not merely of the rage of Sherman and his men, but of some greater design of which that army was but the instrument—a holy war. "If the Southern soil must still run with blood, so be it.—That shed by us I believe to be in God's cause, and therefore for the benefit of man."[16]

In South Carolina, Sherman's army had merged, through unstated but programmatic destruction, with their commander's moral totalism in the war against the South. Even in South Carolina, however, Sherman's war did not become total war as have others, both before and after, and it is important to underline the limits this army, one that was essentially unopposed and could destroy what it wanted, placed on itself. Most of these limits were more implicit than explicit, which means that they grew from a set of moral understandings within the men and their culture, which even these ferocious warriors wished to observe, lest they lose their moral manhood altogether and become savages in their own eyes.

Sherman and all of the soldiers who discussed this issue agreed that almost no white women were raped. Colonel Oscar Jackson, for one, in the midst of entering into his diary his encyclopedia of the fire and pillage wrought by his men, while acknowledging that his soldiers exploited prostitutes, insisted that "the persons of women, it is my belief, have very seldom been violated, and I have been in a position to know." Sherman himself, indulgent in concern to most forms of destruction, believed that his men had observed these limits toward women. Jackson also added in his diary, "I here record my opinion that few of our soldiers had connection with blacks, very few," although this statement seems to be less concerned with rape than with voluntary sexual self-soiling by white soldiers with black women, which he would have abhorred more on racist principles rather than on grounds of humanity.[17]

Beyond refraining to rape, which they certainly had the power to do, and which many armies in other civil wars have done, casually, concertedly, or, in some cases, as a matter of policy, Sherman's army did not murder civilians in South Carolina. In addition, they did not even contemplate committing genocide. Neither did they force the evacuation of large numbers of civilians: Sherman never repeated his earlier expulsion of the peaceful citizens of Atlanta. Of course, many South Carolinians fled before his army, and Sherman had sanctioned redistribution of deserted coastal territories in South Carolina from masters to slaves before commencing his march, but he did not extend this policy to the interior. He also did not return to the theme of recolonization from the North while his men pillaged South Carolina. Even when Sherman took the Civil War to its outermost organized extremes in South Carolina, in these ways he did not anticipate, nor did he practice, total war. Even in their furious desire to destroy sinful rebels, he and his army never entirely submerged their sense that they were fighting white Americans quite like themselves.[18]

These limits to total war-making, of course, provided scant comfort to the ill-nourished, ill-clad, and homeless civilians Sherman's army left behind. Neither do they excuse him or his army for what they did do, although it also remains morally significant what acts they refrained from committing. What they did, they did gladly, and this was true of Sherman himself. Although he liked to emphasize his personal reluctance to destroy property by his own hand—he later claimed in his *Memoirs* that his one act of vandalism was to burn an old clock and an already broken bedstead for fuel one night—and his personal acts of kindness to some of the citizens he met, on the larger plane of the campaign he was second to none in ferocity.[19] This was especially true of the physical and moral climax of the campaign against South Carolina, the burning of her capital city of Columbia.

Columbia went up in flames on the night of February 17, 1865, more as a result of drunken chaos than from conscious intent. Withdrawing from the city that day, Wade Hampton's Confederate troops plundered many homes and businesses, and tore open stacks of bales of cotton in the main street of the city and set fire to them. Before Sherman's army crossed the Congaree River and entered the city, two or three hundred escaped Union prisoners and gangs of both white and black civilian toughs began a rampage. The first Union brigade to enter the city, ostensibly to guard it, got into the whiskey dispensed by the street gangs and joined in the pillaging. Their numbers in turn were swollen by many stragglers from other units of the army, and by the early morning of February 18, a full-scale riot, including considerable arson, was well under way. A sudden gale also spread flaming tufts of cotton alarmingly. At dawn, General O. O. Howard called in fresh troops first to extinguish the fire and then to put down the riot. Howard's own men arrested thirty-five hundred civilians and soldiers, and succeeded in putting out the flames only after at least a third of the city had burned, including most of the business district. At that time and later, South Carolinians charged Sherman with deliberately ordering that the fire be set, charges he always refuted.

In his official report of the incident, written six weeks after the event, when the outcry all over the South, led by Wade Hampton, was already very large, Sherman categorically denied "on the part of my army any agency in this fire, but, on the contrary, claim that we saved what of Columbia remains unconsumed." He had issued clear written orders to destroy public buildings of military value, but to spare all private dwellings and nonmilitary public buildings. The entire fault lay with Wade Hampton, not because of any "malicious intent" on Hampton's part, but from his "folly and want of sense in filling [Columbia] with lint, cotton and tinder." In the face of undying postwar criticism of his actions that night, and in defense against acknowledging responsibility for a level of destruction and riotous behavior that had gotten out of hand even by his standards, Sherman would stick to this basic analysis for the rest of his life. As late as 1888 he commissioned a reiteration of this very argument in the *North American Review* in reply to an attack on him by an aging Wade Hampton.[20]

Relatively few soldiers wrote eyewitness accounts of that night of whiskey and fire and, perhaps not surprisingly, few bragged directly that they had been active firebrands. One exception, Wisconsin private Ed Levings, wrote his parents four weeks later in a spirit that nearly affirms he had been a keen participant: "fire and soldiery had full swing, or sweep if you like that better, and vied with each other in the mischief. Never in modern time did soldiers have such fun." In his diary entry for February 17, Lieutenant Allan Morgan Geer wrote the single most plausible record of the event. Before he went to sleep in his tent outside the city, he recorded the events of the day in his diary in the present voice. "The troops go into camp, break ranks and make for the city, some for whiskey and excitement, a few to burn and destroy and I and Captain King for curiosity. As the flames spread from street to street, soldiers running wild noisy and intoxicated, citizens hurrying to and fro, women and children frightened and often weeping, the crash of falling buildings all present a grand but sad scene of devastating ruin." The following day, Geer returned to this scene of "terrible calamity." It was "the worst destruction to befall to any city since Napoleon burned Moscow," Geer wrote, adding in disgust, "plunder is very plenty with our army now." Geer observed not organized and planned mayhem, but that brought on by wild disorganization and indiscipline. He did not claim to have observed the whole pattern of pillage and arson, but what he saw struck him as awesome and terrible on a scale even his army had not previously reached.[21]

A third eyewitness, who had more likely than Geer been an active participant as well as an observer, or who at least approved of what he saw, was Lieutenant George M. Wise, of the Forty-third Wisconsin Infantry. He wrote his brother four weeks after the event, "many of our men had become intoxicated, and with firebrands in their hands were rushing from house to house burning as they went. Sober men were engaged in the same work, yelling, 'Here is the place where it all began and we will burn it.' " Summing up what he had seen, Wise believed that "it was plain that the city was given up to pillage and destruction."[22]

Although the widespread events of that night were intrinsically confusing, most of the soldiers who had not been in the city drew the immediate conclusion from what rioters and soldier observers told them
back in camp later on, that many of their comrades had been involved
deeply. "It is generally understood that our drunken soldiery fired it in
numerous places," Colonel Oscar Jackson recorded the next day in his
diary. A surgeon in an Illinois regiment added, with a clearer sense of
conviction as to culpability, "The soldiers had a terrible drunk [and]
run riot all night. They not only fired houses but robbed and pillaged
both houses and citizens indiscriminately." Sergeant Rufus Mead
wrote more vaguely in his diary, "We learned that the right wing went
into the city and burned it down," but he acknowledged that he had
not been able to determine whether it had been soldiers or civilians
who had done the deed. However, Mead added that regardless of who
did the actual burning, on the larger moral issue raised by such destruction, "I can't say I lament it either. A just judgment has overtaken
it whoever the avenging hand was." In a somewhat more impersonal
and less righteous mode, Colonel Oscar Jackson concluded that their
shared underlying and long-term desire to destroy Columbia had motivated the soldiers that night. "I do not believe it was done by order, but
there seems to be a general acquiescence in the work as a fit example to
be made of the capital of the state that boasts of being the cradle of
secession and started the war." Such a consensus would have led to a
tacit understanding that a drunken riot of arson and plundering would
have been the punishment to fit South Carolina's great crime.[23]

Sherman and his men had wished to burn into the very heart of
South Carolina, and in a not-very-abstract symbolic construction, the
capital city of Columbia easily became that heart. "The boys had long
desired to see that city burned to ashes," wrote one young soldier after
the event, while another added that "our men had such a spite against
the place they swore they would burn it, if they should enter it, and
they did." On December 24, 1864, writing from Savannah in response
to a broad hint from Henry Halleck that "some accident" might destroy Charleston, home of the most ultra of South Carolinian snobs,
Sherman had responded that Charleston was off his path, but that Columbia would be a perfectly suitable substitute: He promised to use his
Fifteenth Corps as his vanguard unit, "and if you have watched the
history of that corps you will have remarked that they do their work
pretty well." It was at this point that Sherman had added that his army

was "burning with an insatiable desire" to get at South Carolina, a fiery metaphor that expressed some of the energy that led his men into Columbia that night six weeks later, where they achieved an apotheosis of sorts.[24]

Seven years after the event, Sherman was cross-examined on the burning of Columbia before the joint British-American "Alabama Claims" commission, struck to assess reparations for war damages. Sherman, who came into the room in an irascible mood, lost his temper under questioning and revealed in his internally contradictory recollections the sort of anger and contempt he must have been feeling that remarkable night so many years earlier. He began and ended his testimony with a flat denial that either he or his officers had ever ordered arson. However, his responses to the issue of *moral* responsibility were far more complex. As he had written in his April 1865 report of his campaign, he once again assigned all the blame for starting the fire to "an imprudent act of Wade Hampton," ripping open and firing cotton bales in the street, "and then going away." Nature had done most of the rest of the work, for "God Almighty started wind sufficiently strong to carry that cotton [fire] wherever He would." Sherman was willing to concede that some of his soldiers, "after the fire originated may have been concerned in spreading it," in a tertiary sense, but he flatly denied that they had been "concerned at all in starting it."

Rather than simply sticking to this sufficient and efficient defense, Sherman, with very little prodding by his inquisitors, got mad and shot off his mouth protractedly. Not only was Wade Hampton responsible directly for the fire, he had done enough indirectly to provoke Sherman's men to burn Columbia. The night before the attack, even though it was "manifest" to Hampton that he could not hold the city, he had opened up with two cannons on some of Sherman's men, in a "cowardly way," knowing that he could not thus slow Sherman's advance, and that such a tactic "would only kill a few miserable soldiers, rolled up in their blankets asleep." Sherman said that this had given him sufficient moral reason to burn Columbia and that not only his men but he himself had "expressed . . . bitterness of feeling [very] intensely after the shelling," but that he had refrained from changing his orders, which were to burn only militarily valuable public buildings and infrastructure.

Why, given such bitterness of feeling, Sherman was asked, had he not forbidden his men to break ranks and enter the town in disorganized fashion? He replied that his men had done nothing to merit the punishment of confinement of camp. "I could have had them stay in the ranks, but I would not have done it . . . to save Columbia." That would have been a "harshness to my soldiers . . . and I was not going to treat them like slaves. . . . [T]hey were free to come and go." Thus had Sherman re-created before the commission that aura of implicit freedom to destroy, underpinned by burning contempt, that had characterized him and his men while they were in South Carolina. He refused moral culpability for his army's acts in part by denying that any such act would have morally amounted to anything, so contemptible were the enemy. If they were morally debased, as had been exemplified by Wade Hampton's stupidities, any action of his would have been trivial. Not only had this been true where Columbia had been concerned, but it was also true of other South Carolina towns his men had burned. Thus, of the burning of Orangeburg, he denied his men had done it, adding offhandedly, "I was told by a citizen that it was burned by some Jew." As for Blacksville, "I don't think it was destroyed; it was not destroyed when I was there; [my men] may have destroyed it when they left it, but it was a dirty little hole anyhow." The same remorselessness applied to Columbia. "If I made up my mind to burn Columbia I would have burnt it with no more feeling than I would a common prairie dog village." Nevertheless, having asserted that he could have done the deed with moral ease, Sherman added immediately, "but I did not do it, and I therefore want that truth to be manifest."

Sherman believed he had neither ordered nor sanctioned the burning of Columbia. He was retrospectively blind to his creation, in tandem with his men, of a pattern of destruction, nor did he feel that failing to impose special discipline that night had been sanctioning the fire by omission. And he remained proud of his toughness. He wanted Southerners to know in 1872, when it was unnecessary and even counterproductive to so declare himself, that he had been utterly sincere in his desire to drive dread into their hearts during his last campaigns of the Civil War. As late as 1888, writing to an old army comrade who had been a prisoner in Columbia freed that terrible February day in 1865, Sherman commented that, as opposed to the people of Georgia, who "bore their afflictions with some manliness," in South Carolina "the people whined like curs." No regrets. No apologies. Defiance and pride. And yet, of course, he did protest so very much.[25]

As his army crossed over the border into North Carolina two weeks after the burning of Columbia, Sherman and his leading generals clearly and explicitly reeled in their arsonist-plunderers, reestablishing far stricter controls over foraging behavior, and insisting that entering or burning private dwelling houses be forbidden once more. On March 6, Sherman wrote to H. W. Slocum, commander of the left wing of his army, that if the enemy offered no resistance, Fayetteville, the first sizable North Carolina town they would enter, ought to be spared. "I wish the town to be dealt with generously. Of course we will dispose of all public stores and property but will spare private houses. . . . [T]ry and keep the foragers from insulting families by word or rudeness." A few days later, as Slocum's troops were poised to enter Fayetteville, Sherman added instructions to "destroy nothing till I meet you, unless there be special reason that you know I will approve." Sherman had consciously tipped the balance back from wantonness toward forbearance: When in doubt, preserve, he now recommended. Do not freelance, but destroy only under orders to do so.

As the main reason for this major shift in policy, Sherman made a political analysis of the difference between the two Carolinas. To Slocum, Sherman wrote on March 6, "It might be well to instruct your brigade commanders that we are now out of South Carolina and that a little moderation may be of political consequence to us in North Carolina." Sherman expanded this reasoning the next day in a letter to Judson Kilpatrick, his cavalry commander, whose men had been the most wide-ranging of foragers. "Deal as moderately and fairly by the North Carolinians as possible, and fan the flame of discord . . . between them and their proud cousins of South Carolina. There never was much love between them. Touch upon the chivalry of running away, always leaving their families for us to feed and protect, and then on purpose accusing us of all sorts of rudeness." Sherman intended Kilpatrick and Slocum to use these arguments as much with their own men as with North Carolina civilians. Indeed, Slocum passed on Sherman's advice immediately through a direct order to his men. These were political arguments for the men, ones that would help persuade them to calm down and behave somewhat more sympathetically to North Carolinians. Sherman assumed that, like the Georgians who had urged Sherman to level South Carolina, North Carolinians shared that yeoman class resentment against the nabobs of South Carolina, and that they could be induced to believe that Sherman's army had attacked the aristocratic, secessionist principle rather than the common people of South

Carolina. He was suggesting a kind of class alliance between the plain men of his army and the plain folk of North Carolina, in order both to rein in his army and to lower resistance to its march. For the first time since November 15, 1864, when he had led his army off for the sea through Georgia, Sherman had developed a form of military and political analysis, persuasive to himself and to his men, which was intended to heighten rather than lower the threshold of violence.[26]

By indicating that renewed discipline was imperative, Sherman could acknowledge by implication that his troops had gone too far in South Carolina, without actually apologizing or expressing regrets. South Carolina had been different, and that chapter should now close. In this context, it also is significant that Sherman was anticipating an imminent renewal of contact with the rest of the Union. His army would link up with the Union-controlled North Carolina coast and the rest of the nation on March 11, placing him back under constitutional controls and public scrutiny. Therefore, cleaning up his army's act and its image for fear of repercussions must have contributed to his major shift in policy.

In addition, some of his senior subordinates had almost certainly leaned on him to reimpose discipline and decrease wild destruction. Certainly, several of Sherman's major commanders, notably Slocum and the politically astute Frank Blair, and Blair's superior, the Christian gentleman, O. O. Howard, whose troops were the leading Columbia rioters, leaped at the opportunity of issuing orders to restrain the men in their commands. They had long tried to curtail plundering, without success, but now, at long last, they felt free to crack down hard on their men's excesses. Their alacrity, and the thoroughness of their orders, suggests how disturbed they had become while watching their men rampage through South Carolina.

On March 7, still on the South Carolina side of the border, using as his pretext the statement that "General Sherman said that when we reached North Carolina he would . . . forbid foraging," Blair wrote Howard, insisting that the foraging system "is vicious and its results utterly deplorable," and that "there is no cure except . . . entire cessation." This angry argument for an even more restrained policy than Sherman had in fact suggested was an indirect rebuke of Sherman. Howard, disturbed by Blair's report to him, instructed John A. Logan, commander of the Fifteenth Corps, the chief arsonists of Columbia and the most notorious corps in general, to prevent all "outrages" by

foraging parties, promising a formal policy the next day, and concluding, "unless these outrages are stopped, an order will have to be issued
discontinuing foraging entirely." At the same time, Howard ordered
that all parties of foragers be dismounted immediately.

Continuing to act forcefully and swiftly, Howard produced his orders the next day, allowing but one mounted foraging party per division, and organizing beefed-up provost guards, "to consist of as many
picked and resolute men as the division commanders may deem sufficient [to] establish guards at every house on the line of march." Two
days later, Blair issued even stricter orders for his unruly corps. "Nothing should be taken . . . except what is absolutely necessary for the use
of the army." He also ordered that no man would "be permitted to
enter any dwelling house under any circumstances." To enforce this
new standard, he ordered that every foraging party be under the charge
of a commissioned officer, that no man forage without a written pass to
do so, that all other men be dismounted, and that officers arrest all men
breaking these dramatic new rules. Blair was convinced that these orders, which incidentally demonstrated quite precisely many of the ways
in which matters had gotten out of hand in South Carolina, could and
would stop excesses in foraging. He and Howard had reasserted discipline and had limited foraging with an urgency that demonstrated their
frustration when they had believed themselves compelled to acquiesce
to Sherman's intentions in South Carolina to accelerate foraging toward a level of destruction that had appalled them.[27]

Many lesser officers implemented this new policy with pleasure. Colonel Oscar Jackson, while still in South Carolina, had entered into his
diary on March 5 his deep regrets over the unparalleled recklessness of
the men and the indifference of the officers in South Carolina. On
March 18, after crossing into North Carolina, Jackson wrote how
much things had improved and how much better he felt. That afternoon he had done "myself the pleasure of giving . . . from my own
bread and meat" to a substantial farmer and father of a large family
named Barbry, whose lands had been stripped bare by Union foragers
that morning. Now at least he felt free to repair damage caused by
other Union units, and more generally he believed the army was behaving with greater generosity. "There must be suffering for food in the
rear of the army, although we are not destroying property in this state
like we did in South Carolina." Writing his first letter home in months,
on March 13, after Sherman's army reconnected with Union lines of

communication, Lieutenant George M. Wise made a similar observation. "We are now in North Carolina & we will burn nothing save what is rebel government property." Wise then went on to express other elements of the new policy, demonstrating how astutely Sherman had read the emotional and ideological sensibilities of his army. "Many who hate us & our cause will probably say that Sherman could not control his men. If they do it is a slander against this army." The new policy was an indirect denial of what had happened in South Carolina. Now, officers like Wise and Jackson felt sanctioned from above, through a coherent and forceful policy, to discipline their men, to return to the commissioned officer's job, which in effect had been suspended for so long. The genie of nihilism was being put back in its bottle, which proved in a way such officers wanted to believe that it had never been completely out.[28]

If the dismounted, redisciplined foot soldiers objected to the new limits, they failed to record it in their diaries and letters. Plunder and arson no longer dominated discussion, which suggests a real diminution of such activities, but morale remained high, and there was enough remaining burning and foraging of a sort still officially sanctioned to make for a certain continuity of pleasures. Rufus Mead noted while marching well up into North Carolina that a "few log houses & poor ignorant inhabitants" were all they saw, besides turpentine mills, "which certainly made the handsomest fire I ever saw, especially the smoke as it rolled up in huge black volumes was splendid. We blazed our way through." Dexter Horton, a hedonistic Michigan soldier, who had reported several times having had "heaps of fun" in South Carolina, wrote in his diary on March 12 from North Carolina, "made the acquaintance of several ladies. Certainly we are enjoying ourselves hugely." In Horton's opinion, the virtue of these ladies was as easy as that of their South Carolina sisters. He often recorded pleasure alongside misery, as he did on March 14, when he wrote, "had heaps of fun all day long, and saw many, many sad sights. Weeping mothers with babes in their arms begging for their meal and all such scenes." Horton reported the happiness it had given him that day to give tea, coffee, and meal to the folks in one house. If they refrained from burning out civilians, and aided more than they had in South Carolina, however, the men still stripped the countryside of food and livestock and burned public facilities. Some soldiers noted little difference between the overall results in the two Carolinas. An Indiana soldier wrote to his wife from Fayetteville, North Carolina, on March 14, "our march over the country has been like the blighting pestilence, for we have taken or turned upside down everything before us. I have a great many things in store to tell you."[29]

Even after ordering strict new limits on pillaging, Sherman himself maintained his essential hardness when he considered North Carolinians. On March 12, from Fayetteville, he reminded one of his major subordinates about the need to continue energetic foraging. "We can live where the people do, and if anybody has to suffer let them suffer." On April 9, as the war was nearing its end, Sherman told Ellen, "Poor North Carolina will have a hard time for we sweep the country like a swarm of locusts. Thousands . . . may perish but they now realize that war means something else than vainglory and boasting." North Carolinians, even if not as bad as the original sinners of South Carolina, were still Confederates after all, and Sherman would punish them to the last moment of their secession.[30]

Jointly with his men, with whom he had developed a direct and tight bond, often to the resentment of his officers, Sherman had pursued a prolonged war of purposeful terror. He had calibrated the effects of his policy depending on where he was marching, limiting arson and pillage in Georgia, increasing them dramatically in South Carolina, pulling them back in North Carolina. This last phase in North Carolina demonstrated that his had been an intentional policy and not just a lack of control. It also indicated that should the South not quit, he could do even more than he already had. The overall impact of this campaign was devastating for the South, both in material ways and in morale. This madman and his swarming bummers seemed to have no implicit limits, and Southerners could do nothing to stop him short of surrendering. Sherman's march had a great deal to do with the Southern defeat. His specially attuned sensibility, his ability to deflect his real sensitivity and to orchestrate his equally authentic rage, gave him great insight into a war of mass terror, a war that proved effective. Inside the hearts of Southerners, he was, as he remains in folk memory, the most feared and hated conqueror of the American Civil War.

THROUGH HIS TRANSFORMATION in war, Sherman had sublimated his terribly destructive self-doubts into a fatalistic, almost transcendent commitment to battle. He had evolved from the protec-

14

Sherman
the Forgiver:
A Separate Peace

O N APRIL 17, 1865, and the following day, William T. Sherman sat down convivially with his longtime Confederate opponent, Joseph Johnston, at the Bennett farm in the North Carolina hills near Durham, and drafted a peace treaty that would have traded Southern military surrender for a blanket amnesty, both military and civil. At the surrender of the symbolic sword, Sherman welcomed the Confederacy back into the Union. Three days later his treaty would be rejected out of hand in Washington, amid a thunderous clamor, which plunged Sherman into the midst of another huge public storm when he should have been enjoying his days of triumph.

The most extraordinary element in this highly charged episode was the apparent reversal, even revolution of character, whereby the harshest Union scourger of the South became with one pen stroke Sherman the forgiver, the maker of the softest and kindest peace. In fact this act was no internal revolution, but an expression of elements of Sherman's complex mentality elicited by a new and different issue from war making—that of what ought to be the composition of postwar American society. In the confused endgame of the Civil War, Sherman took enormous latitude—not for the first time—in attempting to impose his own political opinions on war and peace, what he believed ought to be the basic values and structures of American society. Strange things came to pass from Sherman's bold impatience to reconstitute the nation.

Grant's peace treaty at Appomattox with Robert E. Lee, which he had dictated eight days before Sherman met with Johnston, provided a clear model for what ought to have been the process of surrender of other Confederate armies. Grant had Lee's men give up their arms, except for the pistols of the officers, swear an oath not to take up arms against the United States, and return home peacefully, the officers with their horses and personal baggage. In the treaty Grant remained silent on all other issues, purposefully avoiding the introduction of political questions; Lee surrendered to a sovereign United States, which would then fix whatever terms for reconstruction they saw fit, unencumbered by anything Grant had offered in the treaty. This was not a draconian surrender such as many in the North were urging. Grant took great pains to write with a generous rather than a vengeful tone. Neither, however, was it a conditional peace. Though Grant used kind language, Lee had capitulated.

On April 12, Sherman received news of Lee's surrender with great joy. In reply to Grant's telegram announcing the peace and including its terms, which had taken two days to arrive at his command in North Carolina, Sherman wired back, "I hardly know how to express my feelings, but you can imagine them. The terms you have given Lee are magnanimous and liberal. Should Johnston follow Lee's example [and surrender unconditionally], I shall of course grant the same." Sherman also wired Edwin Stanton to assure him that when his turn came, "I will accept the same terms as General Grant gave Lee and be careful not to complicate any points of civil policy." Nothing should have been more straightforward than his next project.[1]

On April 14, with the Confederacy collapsing around him, its main army disbanded, its political leadership in flight, and his own men deserting in droves, Johnston wrote Sherman asking for a truce in order to allow the negotiation of a cessation of hostilities. The generals met on April 17, signing their treaty the next day.

In contradiction to his telegrams of April 12, to Grant, and April 15, to Stanton, Sherman did not even attempt to impose Grant's terms on Johnston, which the Confederate general most likely expected him to do. Rather than forcing a politically unconditional surrender as had Grant on Lee, Sherman made a treaty with Johnston that granted the South generous military and political terms. In exchange for an agreement to "cease acts of war," Sherman offered a "general amnesty" to all remaining Confederate armies and not just Johnston's, and an amnesty as well to all Confederate civilians. The officers and their men were allowed to keep their arms, in order to take them to their several state arsenals for deposit. Sherman also extended recognition by the executive branch of the Union to all the existing Confederate legislatures, as reformed Union state governments, contingent merely upon their taking an oath of allegiance to the Constitution of the United States, and he guaranteed to all Southerners "their political rights and franchises, as well as all their rights of persons and property." Sherman was silent on the issue of the complete abolition of slavery, although he assumed that both he and Johnston knew the institution was dead.

After the Johnson administration rejected it, one of Sherman's earliest defenses of this treaty, which went so far beyond his mandate, was that he had really offered Grant's terms to Johnston with the addition of some trivial "glittering generalities." What he thus dismissed rather lightly in fact amounted to blanket forgiveness and the promise of an instant return to the Union for a bitter enemy who was not even disarmed. . . . To say the very least, his expression of heart toward the South under these terms differed greatly from the one Sherman had offered to Columbia, South Carolina, for example, just two months earlier.[2]

Yet in a very real sense, Sherman's rage and his moral totalism in war making had always implicitly contained their opposite, of total forgiveness upon surrender. When on August 14, 1864, he had reduced war to the single, and otherwise apolitical, issue of win or lose—"the only principle of this war is which party can whip"—he had immediately added that this fundamental simplicity at the heart of war, like a "schoolboy's fight," meant that once one side gave in, both could make up immediately, as it were, with a handshake, and be "the better friends for it," a promise he frequently reiterated.[3]

For Sherman total forgiveness was the ultimate purpose of his promise of total destruction, at least when he cooled down the next day or the next week after having issued one of his ferocious proclamations. Like a war god, Sherman could dispense mercy after he had dispensed savage justice: Both were equally self-inflating notions. This attitude was also one way for him to convince himself that he was a man made in God's image, even while he had acted as a devilish destroyer.

When Sherman and Johnston met to talk peace on April 17, they took an instant liking to one another. At their meeting the next day,

Sherman pulled out a bottle of whiskey from his saddlebag and the men drank together. John C. Breckinridge—a wily and thirsty lawyer and politician who was the Confederate secretary of war and former vice president of the United States—was there, ostensibly in his military capacity as a major general. Johnston and Sherman found that they not only agreed both that the war and the institution of slavery were over but that real social as well as military peace ought to be easy to achieve. As Sherman wrote Johnston soon after the event, summarizing the hopeful concord they had drafted, "I believe, if the South would simply and publicly declare what we all feel, that slavery is dead, that you would inaugurate an era of peace and prosperity that would soon efface the ravages of the past four years of war." Such fellow feeling, rather a novelty for a man who knew full well how detested he was all over the Confederacy, relieved Sherman. He could allow himself to express his mercy to a defeated gentleman who returned his esteem to his former adversary, the man of honor to whom he was surrendering. After all, as the code of honor went, one offered a hand up to a gentleman one had bested in combat, and that hand was taken. To Grant, Sherman put this codified notion of the appropriate behavior of victors: "the South is broken and ruined, and appeals to our pity. To ride the people down with persecution and military exactions would be like slashing away at the crew of a sinking ship." Knowing his evil reputation, Sherman had every personal as well as professional reason not to continue to act the slasher. "I would blush for shame if I had ever insulted or struck a fallen foe," he later declared, reinforcing the gentleman's word he had offered Johnston at the peace table.[4]

In later years Sherman would insist that during these negotiations he had been guided by the express wishes of Abraham Lincoln to make a peace with generous political terms. Sherman claimed to have gained this affirmation when he, Grant, and Admiral David Dixon Porter had met on March 27 and 28, aboard the *River Queen,* off City Point, Virginia. Sherman's later reconstructions of this conversation, particularly the one in his *Memoirs,* are self-serving and untrustworthy, especially when he concludes that Lincoln had "distinctly authorized me" to guarantee the civil rights and governments of the former Confederate states "as soon as the rebel armies laid down their arms." In a private letter written in 1872, three years before the *Memoirs* version was published, Sherman's recollections read less like a laying on of political hands, and more like an account of the sort of rambling conversation Lincoln held many times with other leaders. "He said that he contemplated no revenge, no harsh measures, but quite the contrary," Sherman wrote in this version. As for the actual words Lincoln used, Sherman admitted he had only hazy memories of them. "I cannot say that Mr Lincoln or anybody used this [exact] language [to me] at the time." Indeed his chief impression, which he stressed to Ellen when he reported to her soon after the event, had been that Lincoln "was lavish in his good wishes" to Sherman. Lincoln was probably not very concerned in spelling out detailed conditions of peace at this occasion. After all, Lincoln could not have anticipated his assassination on April 15 and the political storms over Reconstruction that were to follow. Rather than a portentous postwar planning session, this meeting had seemed at the time more of a social visit and celebration. Therefore, in reconstructing the event years later Sherman exaggerated the political implications of the meeting by rendering explicit what he had inferred to have been Lincoln's drift. "I know I left his presence with the conviction that he had in mind, or that his cabinet had, some plan of settlement, ready for application the moment Lee & Johnston were defeated," he recalled in 1873. As the war ended, back in Washington Lincoln in fact had been engaged in an intense series of discussions over Reconstruction with Congress and his cabinet, and although he was playing his cards close to his chest, as was habitual with him, he was beginning to move toward accommodation with the Radicals, with whom he maintained constructive ties, and who had the clearest policy. The Radicals were demanding as yet unspecified punishment and political change as conditions of Southern civil and political restoration. Under the stress of significant political negotiations, it would have been characteristic of Lincoln to have remained vague and general to his military leadership, if kindly in tone, for they were not really political players in Washington. It is highly unlikely that Lincoln gave Sherman any clear instructions about the political contents of a peace treaty. Nevertheless, it is reasonable to suppose that Sherman took into his discussions with Johnston a general sensibility that the martyred Lincoln would have favored generous terms.[5]

In addition to his desire to be the honorable gentleman peacemaker, supported by what he construed to have been Lincoln's wishes, Sherman shared a profound political conservatism and Negrophobia with his negotiation partners. This was simply understood between them. Sherman had been nothing if not consistent in his endemic racial hatred for blacks during the war, and peace did not alter those prejudices. Therefore, it was natural for him to align himself with those who would seek to maintain the racial caste system even after the death of slavery. Breckinridge and Johnston certainly appreciated and shared Sherman's basic racial values, about which they would have known even before they met in North Carolina. When, on May 9, Sherman explained his position to his Radical Ohio ally, Salmon P. Chase, he aired opinions consistent with those he had been expressing for two years, which he likely had shared with the Confederates three weeks earlier: "I am not yet prepared to receive the negro on terms of political equality for the reasons that it will arouse passions and prejudices at the north . . . our own armed soldiers have prejudices that, right or wrong, should be consulted . . . which superadded to the causes yet dormant at the South, might rekindle the war whose fires are dying out now." Sherman then made his own position on Reconstruction crystal clear to Chase. Surrender should produce immediate political forgiveness as "war has ceased, and the question is, to adapt legal governments to constitutional communities which fully admit their subordination to the national authority." The North will never successfully impose racial change by fiat; "we can control the local state capitals, and it may slowly shape political thoughts, but we cannot combat existing ideas with force." Fundamental ideas and beliefs would change, but slowly, and therefore, "I prefer to work with known facts than to reason ahead to remote conclusions that by slower and natural laws may be reached without shock." In this argument Sherman seemed to have ignored the fact that he had been a prime instrument for the revolutionary elimination of slavery, which had been achieved only by the enormous shock of civil war! He repeated much the same argument to General O. O. Howard, his most racially progressive subordinate who would soon become head of the new Freedman's Bureau established to protect the rights of emancipated blacks, concluding that "I fear that parties will agitate for the negro's right of suffrage and equal political status, not that he asks for it or wants it, but merely to manufacture . . . votes for politicians." Americans would reject such innovation, for "there is a strong prejudice of race which over the whole country exists."[6]

Once more as so often in the past, Sherman made no real distinction between his military functions and his political opinions. He failed to discern where his beliefs and his ego ought to have stopped and where his constitutional subordination to civil government began. He had swept all before him, he was an undoubted hero, and he was used to being the fount of all law wherever he marched, cut off as he had been from any authority over him in Washington. Now, at the moment he entered negotiations with his foe, all was fluid politically, which increased his sense of latitude. Lincoln had been shot dead, Andrew Johnson was ill-informed and uncertain, and the Radicals in Congress and the various forces in the cabinet were confused and divided. Lincoln left behind him no clear policy, and without his masterful hand guiding through the chaos of political energies released by the end of the war, the government was in shambles. There were no authoritative political brakes on Sherman, who just bulled ahead on his own.

When he had met Joseph Johnston on April 17, Sherman had not been certain which peace terms he wanted; he had brought with him his eagerness to be loved, to forgive and be forgiven, to honor Lincoln's memory, to establish as quickly as feasible the most conservative possible political reconstruction including the suppression of blacks. Johnston must have read Sherman, who was never opaque, with relief and mounting anticipation. Indeed, years later, in a moment of candor, Sherman admitted that under this set of circumstances, during the peace negotiations he had allowed himself to be, in his word, "hustled."[7]

For the second day of the negotiations, Johnston brought along, in addition to the clever lawyer Breckinridge, a memorandum written by another lawyer, John H. Reagan, the postmaster general of the Confederacy. In his *Memoirs,* Sherman claimed that he simply set aside this memorandum when he drafted his treaty, but it is obvious that he incorporated the substance and much of the wording of Reagan's proposals. These included the disbanding of all Confederate military forces and the recognition of the authority of the United States government, but only with these conditions: "the preservation and continuance of the state governments . . . the preservation to the people of all political rights of persons and property, [and] freedom from further prosecution or penalties for their participation in the . . . war." This was the shrewdest possible deal for these Confederates. In exchange for admitting that they had been whipped—Sherman's only personal condition—they were returned to the Union, immediately and unpunished, there to stay and fight by other means.

Sherman was pleased with himself about the treaty he had drafted.

As he wrote to Ellen on April 19, he believed that the peace terms were "all on our side." He also informed Grant and Halleck, when he forwarded the treaty to Washington, that he thought he had obtained the surrender of all the remaining Confederate armies and not just Johnston's, that he had secured "absolute submission of the enemy" to American authority, to which they were now "perfectly subordinate," and that he had prevented the Confederate army from breaking up into guerrilla bands, indeed leaving them their arms as a means of repressing guerrillas, something Sherman had added to the Reagan memorandum. He told Halleck and Grant that both Johnston and Breckinridge had admitted to him that slavery was dead, which he found a sufficient guarantee on that issue.

In this letter, Sherman gave no indication that he realized he had stepped into political matters, either because he was dissembling, which was not his usual way, or, as seems more likely, because he had not noticed how he had been carried away. Such was his hubris, based on his smashing military victories and his long-term independence in command, that the appearance of submissiveness from his enemy was all he required. He never noted, then or later, that he had abandoned Grant's simple terms, nor that when acting the diplomat he was out of his depth and out of his proper role. At the very least he did not realize he had been foolish for not bringing along equivalent legal officers, whom he did have on his staff. Johnston and Breckinridge had manipulated the vanity and peacetime politics of their erstwhile enemy, trapping him rather easily.[8]

After the treaty arrived in Washington on April 21, the same day Lincoln's funeral train departed Washington for its painfully slow voyage to Illinois, President Johnson and his cabinet rejected it unanimously and immediately, and then all hell broke loose. It would perhaps be more accurate to say that the unexpectedly swift Southern military capitulation and Lincoln's assassination had created chaos in Washington, into which Sherman mailed his separate peace treaty. Just then, forgiveness was in short supply in the North, and in Washington, Edwin Stanton, the strongest political figure of the moment, was in full panic. No one knew how widespread the assassination plot had been—Secretary of State William Seward was nearly knifed to death by another member of the same conspiracy—nor how it had originated. In addition, Jefferson Davis was in flight southward, through North Carolina, reputedly with millions in gold specie, and there were rumors that he was bribing himself through Union lines in Sherman's military sector. Under these circumstances, given Sherman's treaty terms, as well as his Negrophobic and antidemocratic reputation, his insubordinate record with Stanton himself concerning black troops, and his flirtation earlier in the war with the ideal of military dictatorship, the wildly alarmed Stanton doubted Sherman's motives. How many of these fears he may have expressed at the April 21 cabinet meeting is unclear, but on the issues raised by the treaty, all were convinced that Sherman had gone well beyond his mandate when he offered an unconditional amnesty and immediate political reconstruction, and apparently affirmed for the slaveholders their property rights to own slaves. After the cabinet meeting, Stanton ordered Grant to notify Sherman that the treaty had been disapproved, that he was to resume hostilities, and that in effect he was to serve under Grant, who would relieve him of command.

Exercising the extraordinary tact of which he was capable, Grant, who wished to clear what he knew were very roiled waters, left Washington immediately to take word of this rejection personally to Sherman, along with his own cover letter in which he told Sherman that he had read the treaty "carefully myself before submitting it . . . and felt satisfied that it could not possibly be approved." Perhaps Grant believed he had failed his old comrade even by submitting the treaty to the president. In any event, he reserved his explanations for their meeting, where he softened the blow through personal contact.

When he slipped secretly into Sherman's camp on April 24—in order to prevent any rumors that he had come to displace or embarrass him—Grant succeeded in mollifying his old comrade. Clearly he said nothing of Stanton's attacks on Sherman's loyalty and motives. Grant wrote Stanton that, in fact, Sherman "was not surprised but rather expected . . . rejection" of the treaty. Grant then defended Sherman's motives. He had acted, Grant insisted to Stanton, "entirely [on] what he thought was precedent authorized by the President." The treaty may have been misguided, Grant implied, but it was neither disloyal nor insubordinate.

Grant then remained discreetly sequestered in Sherman's camp while Sherman returned to negotiations on April 26, and concluded a second treaty with Johnston, who, after a little hesitancy and an attempt to breathe new life into the previous agreement, accepted the new one, which was closely based on Grant's terms with Lee. And so the war ended with an anticlimactic whimper.

Sherman was grateful to Grant for the gentleness of his handling of the rejection of the treaty, but still felt that what he had done was proper. In a letter written on April 25, the day after Grant's arrival in Raleigh, Sherman argued for the record that his first treaty still made sense to him as a direct road to permanent peace and social harmony, but that he could accept its rejection. Here he inserted a face-saving argument that Grant helped him construct—he had been operating on his earlier understanding, never rescinded in Washington as far as he had been notified, that Lincoln had intended to restore civil powers to the existing state legislature of Virginia immediately after the cessation of hostilities. Sherman said he had taken this as his model in negotiating with Johnston. "I have not the least desire to interfere in the civil policy of our government, but would shun it as something not to my liking; but occasions do arise when a prompt seizure of results is forced on military commanders not in immediate communication with the proper authority."

Sherman could have rested comfortably on this formulation. It allowed him to write quite calmly to Stanton, on the same day, April 25, that "I admit my folly in embracing in a military convention any civil matters," but that the military and civil issues in this case had seemed to him "inextricably united." He also mentioned that when he and Stanton had met face-to-face in Savannah in January, he had understood Stanton as saying that the success of the Union cause would "warrant a little bending [of] policy" from time to time. Sherman confessed that he had been a bit upset by the curt tone of Stanton's directive rejecting the treaty, suggesting gently that Stanton ought to have afforded him the benefit of the doubt, given his record of "four year's patient, unremitting, and successful labor."

Having fully succeeded in his delicate mission, Grant returned to Washington on April 27, carrying the second, acceptable version of Johnston's surrender, and leaving behind a gratefully reassured friend. In his pocket was a telegram he had just received from a hysterical Stanton, telling Grant that as word had spread of Sherman's terms, his first treaty had met with "universal disapprobation. No one of any shade of opinion approves it. I have not known as much surprise and discontent of anything that has happened during the war." He also wrote that John Wilkes Booth was still at large, and urged Grant to keep in close contact, for "the hope of the country is that you may repair the misfortune occasioned by Sherman's negotiations." Grant did not share this telegram with Sherman, but kept it to himself as he hurried back to Washington, doubtless hoping to calm Stanton as he had Sherman.

What Grant did not yet know was that the "universal disapprobation" across the nation over Sherman's treaty making had been stirred up by Stanton himself. On April 22 Stanton had mailed to *The New York Times* a distorted version of the events at the cabinet meeting of April 21, which had rejected Sherman's draft treaty. The *Times* published the story on April 24. As well as emphasizing the unanimity of the rejection in cabinet, Stanton included a letter he sent to Grant on March 3, which had relayed Lincoln's instructions that any negotiation with Lee concern only Southern capitulation. By inference this had been Union policy, and Sherman therefore had been willfully insubordinate in the range of issues he had covered in his April 18 treaty. Stanton omitted to mention that Sherman had never been sent a copy of this letter. Stanton then charged that someone had probably opened the way "for the escape of Jefferson Davis to Mexico with his gold bars," quoting an unnamed intelligence source from Richmond that Davis hoped "to make terms with General Sherman or some other . . . Commander." Here Stanton implied that Sherman had already taken a bribe or at least that he had been offered one to let Davis pass through his lines. Stanton also revealed to the *Times* that he had sent Grant to North Carolina to take over Sherman's army, in effect, if not explicitly, relieving Sherman of his command, another insult Grant had concealed from Sherman during his visit. Stanton was a deeply suspicious and viciously short-tempered man who was always prepared to disparage the motives and loyalty of others in the most public of ways. In this giant slander, he retailed highly unlikely rumors as fact, and convicted Sherman by innuendo, in the press, and without a hearing, of insubordination, bribery, and, in effect, treason.

Stanton's calumny was only half the attack, for on April 26, Henry Halleck, who shared Stanton's panic, wrote Stanton from Richmond that he had ordered the other Union generals in the South "to pay no regard to any truce or orders of General Sherman suspending hostilities," and urged Stanton to telegraph them that they "obey no orders of Sherman, and . . . to take measures to intercept the rebel chiefs and their plunder." Even more openly than had Stanton, Halleck gave every appearance of accepting the rumors that Sherman had taken a bribe from Davis, and that his treaty with Johnston was part of this treason to the Union. As had Stanton's outburst, Halleck's telegram embodied the panic that had infected the Union leadership at the end of the war. Whether simultaneously or mutually, Halleck and Stanton had worked up to an extraordinary level of anxiety. This was a clear example of the tendency in nineteenth-century American political culture in times of stress to personalize fears into conspiracy theories, whereby a hero on one's own side could instantly be converted, without any hearing or benefit of the doubt, into a traitor, and be proclaimed so not by normal military or bureaucratic channels, but to the entire nation through the press.[9]

When he first read Stanton's attack in *The New York Times*, which arrived in North Carolina on April 28, Sherman was stunned and terribly hurt. Grant had just left him the day before with the feeling that the treaty-making mistake had been the result of comprehensible misunderstandings between trusted comrades that had now been cleared up with no great or lasting damage. A new treaty was in hand that would end the war, and Sherman had even admitted to Stanton and to himself that he had gone too far the first time, but that now all was well. But just when everything appeared amicably adjusted, he read a brutal attack on his motives and loyalty by Stanton in the public press he so detested. Up to that moment, Sherman had considered himself a close colleague of Stanton's. They had had their problems, but ever since working out Special Field Orders Number 15 together in January 1865, to place the freedmen on confiscated plantations, Sherman thought they were well in harness. As he had written as recently as April 5 to Ellen, "since Mr Stanton visited me at Savannah he . . . has become the warmest possible friend." He and Halleck, whose calumny he would soon read, had had an even longer and more intimate history together, and Sherman had felt great admiration and affection for the man who had been so instrumental in saving his career early in the war. Only seven months earlier, right after he had taken Atlanta to great acclaim, Sherman had written to Halleck, "I confess I owe you all I now enjoy of fame, for I had allowed myself in 1861 to fall into a perfect 'slough of despond,' [and] you alone seemed to be confident, and you gradually put me in the way of recovering from what might have proved an ignoble end." Even if Halleck had been kicked upstairs in

Washington, and was not widely admired in the army by 1865, still he had remained a helpful ally and source of inside Washington gossip, in Sherman's estimation. Therefore, part of Sherman's reaction of great hurt stemmed from his sense of abandonment and personal betrayal by two men he had considered close friends up to the moment he opened the April 24 issue of the *Times*.

Sherman immediately wrote to Grant in a shocked and defensive tone, telling him that, concerning the issue of the first treaty, only time would allow judgment of its merits. What hurt him most and made him feel ashamed was that he believed that his "rank" and his "past services, entitled me at least to the respect of keeping secret what was known to none but the cabinet until further inquiry could have been made, instead of giving publicity to documents I never saw [Lincoln's March 3 letter to Grant], and drawing inferences wide of the truth. . . . It is not fair to withhold from me plans and policy . . . and expect me to guess at them. . . . I have never in my life questioned or disobeyed an order, though many and many a time have I risked my life, my health and my reputation in obeying orders, or even hints, to execute plans and purposes not to my liking." (Here Sherman ignored his behavior on blacks in the army.) As to participating in further political contests, "I envy not the task of reconstruction, and am delighted the Secretary has relieved me of it." As for Grant having been sent South to take over command of his army, "I infer that on personal inspection your mind arrived at a different conclusion."[10]

Sherman's initial shock and hurt almost immediately turned to towering rage. As he would put it rather dryly in his *Memoirs,* "To say that I was merely angry at the tone and substance of these published bulletins . . . would hardly express the state of my feelings. I was outraged beyond measure, and was resolved to resent the insult, cost what it might." Sherman felt a direct attack on everything that made up his honor, his most essential public and private self, just at the moment of what ought to have been his triumph, which was the nation's as well. If this insult had occurred fifty years earlier, he would have challenged Stanton and Halleck to duels. Now the duel would be fought in the press. And he did not intend to be the first to leave the field of honor, but the last. At 3:00 A.M. on April 29, before dawn of the day after he had written his letter of hurt feelings to Grant, he followed it with another, far angrier one, in which he promised Grant, "I have no hesitation in pronouncing Mr Stanton's compilation of April 22, a gross outrage on me which I will resent in time." *Resent* meant avenge. He would embark on one last Sherman-style campaign.

By May 10, Sherman had attained his full splenetic literary form when he wrote to Ellen in the imperial third person, "Sherman, who was not scared by the crags of Lookout Mountain, the barriers of Kenesaw, and long and trackless forests of the South, is not to be intimidated by the howlings of a set of sneaks who were hid away to brag as danger was rampant, but now shriek with very courage. I will take a regiment . . . and clear them out."[11]

Sherman shared his fury not only with his family but with his whole army, who seconded his outrage. They did not agree with the terms of the now-infamous treaty, but they joined in Sherman's deep resentment for the public insults hurled by Halleck and Stanton. On April 26, even before she heard from him, Ellen, realizing how he would respond to the story she had just read in the press back in Ohio, was quick to reassure him. "I think you have made a great mistake. . . . You know me well enough to know that I never would agree in any policy as that towards perjured traitors [and] deserters." But as to the aspersions on his character, "I know your motives are pure. . . . I honor and respect you for the heart that could prompt such terms." She was aware he was no politician, she wrote, but insisted that she was certain he was "incapable of a mean selfish sordid motive." On May 2, John told his brother that in Washington and in public opinion, "it is fair to say [your treaty] was generally disapproved," for seeming to secure unadulterated political powers for the Confederates back in the Union and apparently continuing Southern property rights in slaves. However, in their "gross and damnable perversions" of his motives, John assured the general, Halleck and Stanton were "more severely condemned than your arrangement. . . . For a time you lost all popularity gained by your achievements," but now the ground was shifting rapidly, and opinion was denouncing "the base and malicious conduct of a gang of envious scamps." John preferred to think that Stanton had acted from "passion" rather than from "envy or malice," hinting at a possible reconciliation, but like Ellen, he was at his brother's side, not on the treaty but on the issue of honor.

Both Ellen and John believed, in common with Samuel Mahon, a lowly Iowa private in Sherman's army, that "his error if any has been of the head and not the heart." Many, probably most in his army, disagreed, as did Mahon, with Sherman's first treaty, but when they read the attacks in the press on their beloved leader at the same time he did, they rallied unequivocally to his side. "Sherman's army are with him to a man and his reputation is their reputation," Mahon wrote home, quite accurately reflecting the opinion of both men and officers. As before, the arrows of the external enemy united them, even if now they were being shot at from Washington rather than from Richmond, which they were nearing on their march north. "The army here is justly indignant at the way the northern papers are 'coming down' on Genl Sherman. ¾ of it all is a dirty political trick practiced by some Washington politicians to injure his reputation because they are afraid of his splendid record." Under the circumstances the army had regained much of its fighting anger.[12]

For his part, Sherman did not just get mad, he got even. He began with the smaller enemy, Henry Halleck. Doubtless having gotten wind of Sherman's rage at him, on May 8 Halleck invited Sherman to stay with him in Richmond when he arrived with his army the next day. "After your dispatch to the Secretary of War of April 26," Sherman replied immediately, "I cannot have any friendly intercourse with you. I will . . . march with my troops, and I prefer we should not meet." Smelling a strong whiff of Sherman's powder, Halleck wrote back defensively, "You have not had during this war nor have you now a warmer friend and admirer than myself. If in carrying out what I knew to be the wishes of the War Department in regard to your armistice I used language which has given you offence it was unintentional, and I deeply regret it. [I] wish to . . . receive you as a personal friend." But Sherman was certainly not about to let Halleck off the hook privately and easily after such a public insult. In his next letter, his rage mounted. Comparing the tone of Halleck's more recent missive to his message to Stanton back on April 26, which had as good as called him traitor, Sherman wrote Halleck, "I cannot possibly reconcile the friendly expressions of the former with the deadly malignity of the latter, and cannot consent to the renewal of a friendship I had prized so highly till I can see deeper into the diabolical plot." In a letter he read out at the top of his lungs to his army, who "received [it] with shouts," as he told Ellen, he then instructed his adversary not only that Halleck could not review the army as it passed through Richmond, as Halleck wished, but that if he even showed his face during the march, Sherman's men might kill him. In the history of military invective, Sherman's probably takes first prize. "I will march my army through

Richmond quietly and in good order . . . and I beg you to keep slightly *perdu,* for if noticed by some of my old command I cannot undertake to maintain a model behavior, for their feelings have become aroused by what the world adjudges an insult. . . . If loss of life or violence result from this you must attribute it to the true cause—a public insult to a brother officer when he was far away in public service, perfectly innocent of the malignant purpose and design." Whatever Halleck may have done, this letter from one general to another in the same army was simply outrageous.

Halleck remained out of sight, as Sherman told him to, thus not only being forced to receive a public insult, but placing him in a cowardly and dishonorable light before the sixty-five thousand men of Sherman's army who marched past his curtained windows in Richmond. Subsequently, Sherman publicized this counterinsult relentlessly, and neither his men nor he ever forgave Halleck. Reading in the press of his public attack on Halleck, Ellen assured her husband that she and all the Ewings were "truly charmed . . . that [you] have had so good an opportunity of returning the insult of that base man Halleck. . . . We have not felt so pleased . . . since . . . 'Sherman marched down to the Sea.' "[13]

Having humiliated Halleck, Sherman turned his sights on Stanton. That same evening, camped near Richmond, he wrote confidentially to Grant that he was planning to treat Stanton with "scorn & contempt," that he would obey orders only from Grant and not from the secretary of war, and that "no amount of retraction or pusillanimous excusing will do. Mr Stanton must publicly confess himself a common libeler or—but I won't threaten." In comparison to his open threats against Halleck, here Sherman kept his homicidal fury somewhat under wraps when writing to Grant about Stanton, but his anger was increasing rather than receding. On May 17, immediately after he arrived in his camp at Alexandria, across the river from Washington, Sherman announced to Grant, "the vandal Sherman is [here]. Though in disgrace he is untamed and unconquered." Grant sent for him immediately. "I want to talk with you on matters about which you feel sore. I think justly so, but which bear some explanation in behalf of those who you feel have inflicted the injury." As had Sherman's brother, John, and as would several others, Grant tried to place Stanton's undoubted insult in the context of the assassination panic, and to initiate a reconciliation. Sherman, who was interested only in Stanton's full and groveling public apology, rejected Grant's efforts. And then on May 24, when his army marched in grand review through Washington, Sherman, at the head of his army, mounted the reviewing stand, shook hands with President Johnson and others, and publicly refused to take Stanton's outstretched hand. This universally commented upon snub, the nastiest insult of which Sherman could conceive, remained a subject of pride for him until his death.[14]

Sherman's men joined him in returning insult for insult. Both before and after the grand review, in their Alexandria camp and in the streets and barrooms of Washington, Sherman's men got into frequent fistfights with eastern soldiers and with local citizens. Finally, on May 27, Grant wrote Sherman about the "deep feeling" of the westerners, "especially when a little in liquor, on account of the difficulties between yourself and Secretary Stanton." Grant was fearful of an escalation of violence that might arise from such incidents as that of the previous evening when many of Sherman's officers had been at Willard's Hotel, across from the White House, "drinking and discussing [Stanton] violently, and occasionally would jump up on the counter and give three groans for Mr. Stanton, then get down and take another drink." In reply, Sherman rejoiced in the way his men shared his own barely suppressed fury at Stanton, while promising Grant to calm them down. "I could not maintain my authority over troops if I tamely submitted to personal insult, but it is none the less wrong for officers to adopt the quarrel, and I will take strong measures to prevent it." No riot ensued, and by May 30, Sherman and his men broke camp and dispersed, taking to the railroads headed back west.*[15]

Sherman was seeking more than to return a personal insult to Stanton as he had to Halleck; in the process, he repoliticized his anger, attacking not just the man but his ideological position—the nascent policy of Radical Reconstruction. The day after passing through Richmond in his prolonged public insult to the cloistered Halleck, Sherman wrote to his wife, "Stanton wants to kill me because I do not favor the

---

*On March 16, 1876, Sherman wrote to Grant's biographer about his participation in the explosive endgame of the Civil War in a spirit of ironic detachment mixed with continued pride. "Today I might act with more silence, with more caution and prudence, because I am twelve years older. But these things did occur, these feelings were felt, and inspired acts which go to make up history; and the question now is not, was I right or wrong? but, did it happen? and is the record of it worth anything as an historic example?"

scheme of declaring the negroes of the South, now free, to be legal voters, whereby politicians may manufacture just so much more pliable electioneering material." As he had begun to establish during his negotiations with Joseph Johnston, Sherman was moving tactically to take up the next conservative political standard, one that comported as nearly as possible, given emancipation, with his old racial prejudices and social values. If there had been a dash of innocent credulity or at least thoughtlessness during his meeting with Johnston on April 18, by May 10, in his letter to Ellen, he was staking out his reactionary policy on Reconstruction, one that would seek to restore ex-Confederates to political power and allow them to suppress blacks systematically, a position he would hold to until the end of his official career. "The negroes don't want to vote," he wrote Ellen on May 10, "they want to work and enjoy property, and they are no friends of the negro who seek to complicate him with new prejudices."[16]

Talking and writing to others outside his family, especially fellow army commanders, Sherman soon got his old political wind back in his angry sails. As he had noted to Ellen, so did he to others, that once again he had picked himself up from a blow to return heroically to the fray against an enemy whom he saw with great clarity. On May 21, he wrote a fellow general, "I have been down before in public favor as well as on the battle-field, but am blessed with a vitality that only yields to absolute death." Now he would enter his next fight with full force. "I prefer to give votes to rebel whites, now humbled, subdued and obedient, rather than to the ignorant blacks that are not yet capable of self-government." On May 28, he wrote another general that he had "narrowed down" the "howl" (that word yet again) against himself to Halleck and Stanton, and that he had good reason to believe that Andrew Johnson would oppose Negro suffrage, the position with which he was aligning himself. "I never heard a negro ask for [the vote] and I think it would be his ruin. I believe it would result in riots and violence at all the polls, North and South."

Sherman insisted on the subordination of blacks, and not merely on their nonenfranchisement. In July he wrote to an old friend that in January, when he had taken power for the Union in Savannah, "I began a system of segregation . . . that began to work well." In common with many of those in the emerging Northern opposition to an active Reconstruction policy, Sherman feared the dilution of white blood—mongrelization, or as it was beginning to be called, miscegenation—

which in their opinions had brought down such nations as Brazil, Chile, and Mexico, and, in Sherman's words, might "yet issue" in bringing down the United States if Negroes were to gain equal political rights. As he would soon observe of Mexicans, "a mixture of Indians, Negroes & Spanish," such people were to him "as unable as children to appreciate the value of time, [and] can never be tortured into good citizens." In Mexico, bad blood-mixing had produced an essentially worthless race of perpetual, undisciplined children who could never be persuaded nor even compelled into moral adulthood. No, the ex-Confederates of the South would have to be returned to power, and the sooner the better. As he insisted to John on August 11, "We cannot keep the South out long, [nor] can we change opinions by force." Negroes cannot govern, nor can ignorant poor whites. "For some time . . . state governments must be controlled by the same class of whites as went into the rebellion against us."[17]

At the end of the war Sherman could not stop for reflection or happiness, nor to search for peace. Because of what Halleck and Stanton had made of his peacemaking credulity, he had plunged into yet another major struggle. But he had never been a happy man in repose, and he had come to enjoy his glorious and absorbing war career enormously. Therefore, he relished the renewal of hostilities. He noted no irony in the quick and almost preternatural energy with which he rushed to rehabilitate and restore to power those whom he had just done so much to debase and destroy. In making a separate peace with the South that he had attacked with guns and torches, words of rage, and terrorist calculation, Sherman reopened his separate war with a democratic nation that had never suited him. As he had transformed himself, so would he remain, the roaring warrior.

Part III

FAME

15

Indian Killer

WITH THE SOUTH at last subdued, American public energies could return to the long-term project of economic development and westward expansion. Vast new territories remained to be settled by white people and linked with the marketplaces of the East, and beyond the sea, with Europe. The dream of convenient links to the West Coast and Asia beyond, and the creation of a truly settled and interconnected nation, from Atlantic to Pacific, America's long-proclaimed Manifest Destiny, seemed within reach. The key to the realization of this great national and international project, which was the American version of the shared expansionist dream of the Western world, was the transcontinental railroad. The chief impediment to this objective was the nomadic, buffalo-hunting, warlike Indians of the Great Plains, with whom white Americans were convinced they never could cohabit. They would have to be dealt with while the railroads were abuilding. And they would be combatted only by a small army, as Congress reduced it to fifty thousand, then to thirty-five thousand, and finally to twenty-five thousand in the first few postwar years.

Although private corporations built the railroads, in the wider sense this was a vast public project. Financing came in great measure from land grants to the roads and from direct construction funding. The federal army offered security. In terms of personnel, Grenville Dodge, the head builder, had been one of Sherman's trusted generals, most of

Dodge's engineers were old West Pointers, and many of the laborers were Civil War veterans, many of these from Sherman's western army. And the military understood that its primary function in the West was to work hand in glove with the railroad builders and against the Indians. To achieve this project, Ulysses S. Grant went to Washington, with his immense prestige, to serve as commanding general while William T. Sherman was sent to St. Louis to serve as leader in the field and direct liaison with the railroad. Charged by Grant to "give the best protection to the overland lines of travel, and frontier and mountain settlements," Sherman replied that he well understood what his central focus was to be. "I regard the [rail]road as the most important element now in progress to facilitate the military interests of our Frontier." Central to this project, the army had to gain "absolute and unqualified control of the Indians."

For many years, Grant, who was in agreement with Sherman as to the means and ends of army Indian policy, would give Sherman complete support on carrying out the project. In 1868, when Grant went to the White House, Sherman came to Washington as commanding general and gave his full authorization to Phil Sheridan, his replacement on the ground in the West, to continue along the same lines. Thus the great triumvirate of the Union Civil War effort formulated and enacted military Indian policy until reaching, by the 1880s, what Sherman sometimes referred to as the "final solution of the Indian problem," which he defined as killing hostile Indians and segregating their pauperized survivors in remote places where they would not threaten white settlers. These men applied their shared ruthlessness, born of their Civil War experiences, against a people all three despised, in the name of Civilization and Progress.[1]

These warriors wrote to few others as candidly as they did to each other concerning the handling of Indians, but among themselves and through the army they acted in close concert. Of them, Sherman was by far the brightest and most articulate, and it was he who developed most of the long-term grand strategy. The structure and evolution of his thinking was central to what in fact transpired. Without any doubt Sherman's overall policy was never accommodation and compromise, but vigorous war against the Indians. They were a less-than-human and savage race, uncivilized to white standards, and probably uncivilizable. They were obstacles to the upward sweep of history, progress, wealth, and white destiny. Early on, Sherman anticipated that the war against them, which would be ugly and long, would necessitate what military analysts would now call a protracted low-intensity counterinsurgency, with temporary setbacks inflicted by the guerrilla foe, but that the war could be won at a politically acceptable level of human and monetary costs. In August 1866, he wrote Grant, "I do not apprehend a Genl Indian War, but for years we will have a kind of unpleasant state of hostilities that can only be terminated with the destruction of hostile bands . . . by putting our troops near where the Indians live." The Indians presented what to Sherman was an annoying and unpleasant prospect, but one a great deal less alarming than that the Confederate rebellion had created.[2]

This displacement would be a war of extermination if necessary but not necessarily a war of extermination if the "threats" Indians imposed could be removed by other means. As public opinion was divided between exterminationism, mainly in the West, and pacification by other means, mainly in the East, Sherman would contest both the Indians and elements of the white public, the government, and even the military, who would have preferred a less martial solution. Sherman never doubted that time was on his side, that he could neutralize white opposition while he exploited the weaknesses endemic to the Indians' precarious position to effect their elimination. And underneath his strategy was a great self-certainty that he was the agent of Progress, an overarching faith served by his equally deep and callous contempt for his enemy, one of those other, lesser races bound to lose in the harsh competition of History.

IN SOME RESPECTS, Sherman resented the inconvenience of premature settlement, that is to say, of settlers who straggled westward in advance of the army and the railroad. They went west, plows and guns in hand, as paramilitary farmers, ever ready to raid Indians as the Indians raided them. They demanded that the army wipe out the Indians, thereby presenting one of the political realities with which Sherman had to deal. They also put ceaseless pressure on the army to act like policemen, defending individual farmers from attacks by small groups of Indian warriors. "I will have enough troops to maintain a general state of quiet on the Plains," Sherman wrote Grant in 1865, "but if our emigrants and wanderers will go in small parties through the Indian Reservations and hunting grounds we must not be astonished if some of them lose their horses, cattle and scalps."

Military scattering was necessitated by widespread, thin settlement. Small army posts, often containing as few as one hundred men, were intrinsically inefficient. Settlers in trouble would rush to them, and they would tend to respond as policemen to the small-scale attacks at which the Indians were gifted, rather than as soldiers acting offensively and strategically. Although Sherman recognized the difference between "friendly" and hostile Indians, settlers rarely did. "No matter what these [friendly] Indians do," he told Grant in 1866, "they will be charged with all sorts of wrongs, and complicity with the hostile Sioux," and therefore settlers would demand instantaneous reprisals. The postwar shrinking of the army and the return of Congress to its usual penny-pinching of the military budget led Sherman to conclude to Grant as early as 1866, "I know that economy is now the order of the day"—Sherman knew he would have relatively few soldiers to police the huge expanse of the West.

In any event, policing was not an appropriate task for the army, Sherman was certain. "It was never contemplated that our soldiers should be employed in hunting down sniper murderers and thiefs, but this seems to [be] their habitual use," he complained to Grant in 1868. "When a citizen loses a horse, or some cattle or sheep, instead of calling on his neighbors to go and help find them, he rides some fifty or a hundred miles . . . to report the fact." Then the troops had to go off on a wild-goose chase lest the ungrateful citizen complain to the hated press, which "forthwith publishes some paragraph to the effect that the regular troops are no good."

Moreover, the posts on the Plains were dreadfully hard on soldiers. "Some . . . are really enough to make men desert, built years ago, of upright cottonwood poles, daubed with mud and covered with mounds of earth," Sherman wrote Grant in 1866. "We cannot expect troops to be worth anything, if we wish to winter them in holes, and force them to fight with rats, bed bugs and fleas for existence."[3]

Rather than sit in dozens of little hellholes waiting around to respond to sporadic crimes, Sherman, jointly with Grant and Sheridan, proposed a far more aggressive policy in the war against the Plains Indians. Perhaps he could separate out friendly Indians far more rigorously than had been the case: This was the most sympathetic and least bloody alternative. Sherman explained to Grant in 1867, "If we the military are to provide for these Indians we should know it, for if they wander about at pleasure no matter however peacefully disposed they will be charged with the acts of others and be embroiled with the whites. They should be located, and an agent should be with them all the time." But the active and straightforward and therefore more plausible general military policy would be to pursue the hostile Indians with maximum vigor, even if the friendly ones got caught up in the dragnet. In another 1867 letter to Grant, in which he discussed the need to protect "peaceable & dependent" reservation Indians, with an agent "right among them," and annuities paid "with the greatest regularity," conceding that "I have no doubt our people have committed grievous wrong to the Indians," Sherman went on to dismiss the possibility either of evenhanded justice or of peaceful coexistence on the Plains. "This conflict . . . will exist as long as the Indians exist, for their ways are different from our ways, and either they or we must be masters on the Plains." It would be "impracticable" to punish bad-acting whites, and therefore, "both races cannot use this country in common, and one or the other must withdraw. We cannot withdraw without checking the natural progress of Civilization."

It was to be our warriors versus theirs, and both Sherman and his enemies on the Plains were undoubtedly warriors. The most active men among them shared Sherman's belief that war was central and that it meant kill or die. Sherman believed that "we" were servants of the right side, that it was we who were ahead on the naturally upward incline of Civilization and that the Indians were on the downward side. That might be regrettable as a moral abstraction, but it was Natural Law. "It is an inevitable conflict of races, one that must occur when a stronger is gradually displacing a weaker." Each race would be true to its needs, and would struggle according to its own lights. "The Indians are poor & proud. They are tempted . . . to steal. . . . To steal they sometimes must kill. We in our turn cannot discriminate—all look alike talk and under the same pressure act alike, and to get the rascals, we are forced to include all." Therefore, Sherman assumed that he would lead not an all-out war but perpetual hostilities, "till the Indians are all killed or taken to a country where they can be watched."[4]

Even in the midst of this impersonalizing natural law description of the inevitable progress and regress of the races, Sherman planted a racist tautology. Some Indians are thieving, killing rascals fit for death; all

Indians look alike; therefore, to get some we must eliminate all. On the Plains, deduced from this racist tautology and this belief in natural progress, the less destructive policy would be racial cleansing of the land, while the more destructive one would be *extermination*—the key genocidal code word that had been entirely missing even in Sherman's most infuriated denunciations of Confederates.

When pushed by this or that incident, Sherman's racial contempt would emerge through his more distancing natural law justifications. "We are not going to let a few thieving, ragged Indians check and stop the progress of [the railroads], a work of national and world-wide importance," he insisted to Grant in 1867. In the simple conflict between the civilized strong and the savage weak, whether one put this dualism in anger or in calmness, the end result would be the same. Thus, to Ellen Ewing Sherman, a supporter of Catholic missionaries to the Indians, who was on the antimilitary side of the public debate, Sherman wrote on August 30, 1866, in his calmer tone as a consciously Social Darwinian servant of Progress, first admitting that good Indians got the blame for the deeds of bad, and that whites too committed bad acts, and then reasoning, "It is one of those irreconcilable conflicts that will end only in one way, one or the other must be exterminated and as Grant says our tail is largest and the poor Indians in the end must go under."

The harsher solution of extermination frequently appeared in Sherman's writing, most often qualified in some formulation such as, "I would not hesitate to approve the extermination of a camp . . . from which they send out thieving murdering parties to kill and steal . . . but I would not sanction the extermination of [peaceful bands]." Under duress, Sherman's self-censorship would break down, his never very subdued rage would break out, and his genocidal urges would pour forth. The clearest single example followed the December 1866 slaughter of Captain William J. Fetterman's company of eighty-one officers and men, near Fort Kearney, Nebraska. In response, Sherman wrote to Grant, "We must act with vindictive earnestness against the Sioux, even to their extermination, men, women and children." Writing two days later to his brother John, Sherman receded somewhat from his personal urge to sponsor genocide. "I suppose [the Sioux] must be exterminated for they cannot and will not settle down, and our people will force us to it." Once more, Sherman seemed the reluctant exterminator, where two days earlier he had bared a more active desire to lead the slaughter. Yet however mutely or overtly he might express it, genocide was one of the poles of his agenda, one he would never entirely adopt nor entirely reject. Extermination if need be; displacement for certain.[5]

In the spring of 1867, following the Fetterman disaster, and urged on by Grant, Sherman sent expeditionary forces right into the heartland of the most hostile Indians, fishing for a fight. This occurred at the same time the army was participating in the formation of a Peace Commission to parley with the Plains Indians, a commission on which Sherman would serve. "Make no change in your plans against the Indians," Grant wrote Sherman on April 10, "do not delay on account of the Commission." Sherman hardly needed encouragement on this score, for it was he who had pressed for aggressiveness. On February 18, he had written Grant, "Now is the time for action. For if we wait for grass their ponies will get fat & an Indian with a fat pony is very different from him with a starved one." By marching large units provocatively right into their hunting grounds, Sherman hoped to lure the Indians into a concentrated attack. If in response they scattered and fought guerrilla war, Sherman felt he might not be able to whip them. "I doubt much that we can accomplish anything positive by following these Sioux," he wrote Grant on April 20, "but now they are boastful and insolent and it is possible they will accept battle, which will be the best thing to hope for."

The Indians did not scatter, and this pleased Sherman, for he could regard their cohesion in itself as an act of aggression justifying attack on them, an act that improved the possibilities for inflicting a major defeat on them. On May 24, he wrote Grant, "If we assume the pure defensive . . . the Sioux will be free to roam at will, and attack any point of our defensive line—we have now five or six months of good weather, during which the camps that have been so insultingly placed almost in sight [of our forts] can be attacked and the war carried into their country." On April 19, General Winfield S. Hancock burned down a big Cheyenne and Sioux encampment, and in response, the Indians mounted an unusually large-scale raid against American forts. Although there was no general war that summer, in which the Indians would have offered themselves up to total defeat, Sherman took the lesson of that season as a need to redouble aggressive campaigning in the years to come, against Indians whose resistance he interpreted as insolent aggression. And the notion of actively taking war to the enemy and attacking their camps meant that women and children would be killed along with warriors. Sherman could accept this possible consequence without reluctance, even if he never openly ordered a genocidal campaign.⁶

Even if they had simply wanted to slaughter all the Plains Indians, which they did not, Sherman and Grant and the army were constrained further by divisions in public opinion and in governmental bureaucracy to which they had to relate politically. Many in the East, particularly Quakers, but other missionary groups as well as writers and artists entranced with the Noble Savage, vigorously opposed what they assumed was a simple policy of military extermination, favoring kindness, reservations, and the conversion of the Indians to farming and Christianity—into red replicas of their white selves and culture. To modern eyes, the contest almost appears to have been between genocide and "culturecide," with the Indians destroyed by either means, but in the later nineteenth century, the benevolent would-be whiteners of the Indians entered an earnest contest against the military and its supporters. Such people tended to dominate the Indian Bureau of the Interior Department as well as to serve as Indian agents in the West for the bureau. Thus bureaucratic jurisdiction over the Indians, which was divided murkily between the War and Interior Departments, was heavily politicized. Sherman, who privately despised the "Indian Lovers," nevertheless understood, as did Grant, that these forces could not simply be dismissed out of hand. Therefore, both men cooperated with the formation of the Commission to the Plains Indians, established in 1867 to attempt to make a general treaty, which, following a variety of internal wranglings and negotiations with Indians, resulted in a report, issued in October 1868. Sherman was the dominant figure from the military side.

Grant and Sherman did not really believe in the goals of a peaceful settlement, nor did they think this was likely to be a permanent outcome of the negotiations. Even before he was appointed, Sherman was champing at the bit, fearful of military inactivity and of further loss of control to the Indian Bureau. But he was also politically realistic. To one of his leading commanders in the field, he wrote on March 12, 1867, that despite Grant's recent suggestion that the army need not delay, "I would like to have those [hostile] Sioux taken down a good many notches, but I suppose we are forced to defer action until those Commissioners report & Congress has just made the appropriation for their expenses," until the peace process had dissipated its energy. On April 2, he told Grant that, "We can only destroy the hostile Indians in detail as opportunity affords. As soon as the Commissioners report we will be ready to take these Indians in hand." Sherman also shared his fear with Grant that the army might lose its power struggle on the commission to the Indian Bureau, and then become hamstrung militarily. "I have no hope we can do much of anything as long as our action must be kept subordinate to the opinions and interests of Indian Agents." Grant agreed that the Indian Bureau might win the internal power struggle, therefore tying down the army. It was about this infighting with which he was concerned when he mentioned in September to Sherman, who was already negotiating with the Sioux, "I hope your commission will prove successful; but my faith is not strong."[7]

Once he was immersed in negotiations, Sherman quickly discovered how he could manipulate the commission to the advantage of the army. To him, the Indians were inevitable losers, and he could fob off on the do-gooders the problems of dealing with them on a day-to-day level. He shared this analysis with Grant, as he did with Ellen on September 14: "I don't care about interesting myself too far in the fate of the poor . . . Indians, who are doomed from the causes inherent in their natures, or from the natural & persistent hostility of the White Race. All I aim to accomplish is to so clearly define the duties of civil and military agents of government so that we wont be quarrelling all the time as to whose business it is to look after them."

In Sherman's eyes, the Indians were incapable of negotiating in an adult and responsible manner. On September 19, he told Ellen that the Indian leaders had gone on a "big drunk last night." This loss of self-control at a crucial moment demonstrated to Sherman's satisfaction their racial inferiority. "Indians are funny things to do business with, and the more I see of them the more satisfied I am that no amount of sentimentality will save them the doom in store for them." Sherman believed that the pacifiers on the commission had projected false versions of competence on these Indians. Therefore, he thought they would be unable to persuade the Indians to become pseudo-white Christian farmers. He also understood that the enemy culture did not produce leadership or consensus in the prescribed fashion of white statehood, that they would be unlikely to maintain sufficient discipline to enforce a treaty on their own people as would a European government, and that, above all, they would not cease being warlike nomadic hunters. In 1870, he would explain political process among the Plains Indians to General C. C. Augur: Indian leaders would come to Washington, be impressed with the thick population, wealth, and modern industry among the whites, and would return to their people to urge peace with this overwhelming foe, "but when they get back to their people they lose their influence & popularity by reason of this fact of having tasted the white man's medicine, and are deposed to be replaced by young men who represent the feelings and habits of the enterprising bucks." Sherman appreciated, as eastern friends of the Indians did not, that he was up against a hunter-warrior culture rather than a potential Christian pastoralist culture, and that power would always flow to the young and fearless fighter in that society.[8]

Nevertheless, the Peace Commission did negotiate an agreement. Treaty in hand, Grant and Sherman waxed cynically pleased with its results. Grant dissembled slightly when he wrote to Sherman about some side effects that interested him. "Your peace commission may accomplish a great deal of good, beside that of collecting the Indians on reservations, by attracting the attention of Indians during the season practicable for making war, and also of our white people, who never seem to be satisfied without hostilities with them. It is much better to support a Peace Commission than a campaign against the Indians." Grant then caught himself being insincere, and pretended to subscribe to the manifest content of the treaty—a system of reservations. "I do not mean to insinuate that real and lasting good may not also result from your labors. On the contrary I believe it will; but the incidental good is a compensation." In reply, Sherman ignored Grant's euphemisms for his actual, hard-nosed conclusion. "I agree with you that the chief use of the Peace Commission is to kill time, which will do more to settle Indians than anything we can do." The commission was a harmless display that amounted to very little, in Sherman's opinion. The war against the Plains Indians would go on to its inevitably successful conclusion.[9]

Sherman had tried to keep on civil terms with the commissioners who opposed a military solution to the "Indian problem." He had begged to differ as a gentleman, and had insisted that he hoped for peace, but that as a military man he had to prepare for war. On August 13, 1868, as the commission was finishing its work, he insisted to Samuel Foster Tappan, a Boston philanthropist on the commission whose position he rejected, "as to your enthusiasm in the cause of the Indians

I assure you of my hearty sympathy and respect. I never [unlike you, Sherman was implying] expect to make of Indians good citizens. At best we can give them a chance and to so prepare things that our people may progress in their legitimate routes, and yet not come into violent collision with Indians." Displacement was the softest outcome, in which Sherman pretended little faith. Pressed by Tappan, on September 6 Sherman lectured him that he had "no hope of civilizing the Plains Indians," that those few likely to be "rescued from destruction" would simply not "work the soil," and that they would become a pauper race that Congress would soon tire of supporting and would then abandon. When Tappan refused to accept Sherman's pessimism about the character of the Indians, Sherman's contempt for his opponent surfaced. "I do not question the sincerity of your convictions, which in my judgment amounts to monomania," he told Tappan on September 20. Still trying to keep a civil pen, Sherman insisted that the commission had been "liberal, even to extravagance" in providing excellent reservations for "those savages," and that to this policy he had concurred "heartily."

Nevertheless, some bands of hostile Sioux had already resumed their raids, and the response to them, which was not covered by policies peace commissions could write, had to be military. "I have stretched my power and authority to help them go [onto the reserves]—but when they laugh at our credulity, rape women, murder men, burn whole trains with their drivers to cinders, and send word that they never intended to keep their treaties, then we must submit or we must fight them. When we come to fighting I will take my code from soldiers." He was, he reminded Tappan, a "man of action," who in the end could not "represent two opposing views"—pacification and aggression—at the same time, but needed "positive plans." His policy now would be to attack with vigor, while promising to use "extraordinary pains" to avoid attacking noncombatants, adding, however, that it was "almost impossible to distinguish" peaceful from hostile Indians.[10]

Sherman could say he had tried to make peace. There were the reserves—now the Indians had better move to them immediately. When the treaty-signing Indians proved unable to deliver all their bands to peace and to the reservations, which Sherman had been certain they never could, he seized on the first raids committed by the most energetic Indian rejectionists in order to resume the military attack. He had bent the commission experience to his advantage, for he could claim to have been spurned as a peacemaker. Then he could return to action, which was his actual desire. To John he outlined the future of "the Indian war on the plains," on September 23. The army had established out-of-the-way reservations for all. "All who cling to their old hunting grounds are hostile and will remain so till killed off." Given the size of the country and the mobility of the Indians, the lengthy, low-level "predatory war" would continue to produce shocking murders of whites for years, and therefore the army would have to take its "chances and clean out the Indians as we encounter them." Eventually all the Indians will "have to be killed or be maintained as a species of paupers," because their "attempts at cultivation are simply ridiculous." Two days later, having heard of more Indian attacks, Sherman concluded more simply to John, "We must not let up this time but keep it going till they are killed or humbled."[11]

After holding back to play the peacemaker game, Sherman felt a great release in breaking out into renewed warfare. To a subordinate on the Plains he urged "the utter destruction and subjugation" of hostile Indians, whom he defined as all those who remained off the new reservations. Sherman promised to "prosecute the war with vindictive earnestness . . . till they are obliterated or beg for mercy." Far from being a lonely or extreme voice, Sherman was articulating what many in the military were telling him at this time. For them too, violent action made more sense than what they considered to have been merely sentimental talk. Grant was pushing him. "I hope you will be able to squelch the Indians this time effectually." Grant urged Sherman to attack Indian villages, in effect telling him to disregard nice distinctions of the sort Indian lovers like Tappan cared about, between guilty warriors and innocent families. "Is it not advisable to push after their villages and families? The possession of them would bring them to terms." Even Admiral David Dixon Porter, Sherman's old Civil War comrade, wrote from Annapolis in support of the aggressive Sherman, "I hope you will have wiped out all the Indians before you have done with them."[12]

In the fall of 1868, Sherman hardly needed outside encouragement. In October, he charged Phil Sheridan, who was running the war on the southern Plains, to act with all the vigor he had shown in the Shenandoah Valley during the final months of the Civil War. The Peace Commission had held out both "the olive branch . . . and the sword," but this was not intended to create a "refuge from a just punishment" for past or future acts, Sherman admonished Sheridan. Our side was without guilt in the initiation of this war. "It was begun and has been carried on by the Indians, in spite of our entreaties . . . and warnings, and the only question to us is whether we shall allow the progress of . . . settlement to be checked and leave the Indians free to pursue their bloody careers." Exhaustive peace efforts had been rejected by the enemy. As "brave men and soldiers," the army now had to accept its "most unpleasant duty," and prepare to fight an "inglorious war," a necessary struggle, though one "not apt to add much to our fame." This duty could well lead to "extermination—the utter annihilation of these Indians." Sherman assured Sheridan that he intended to ignore any false humanitarian pleadings from Samuel Foster Tappan and his ilk. "I will say nothing and do nothing to restrain our troops from doing what they deem proper on the spot, and will allow no mere vague general charge of cruelty or inhumanity to tie their hands, but will use all the power confided in me to the end that these Indians, the enemies of our race and of our civilization, shall not . . . carry on their barbarous warfare." Sherman thus instructed Sheridan to attack without restraint, and promised to run interference against any complaints about atrocities from the East. "You may now go ahead in your own way, and I will back you with my whole authority, and stand between you and any efforts that may be attempted in your rear to restrain your purpose or check your troops."[13]

Although Sherman had not ordered an extermination campaign in so many words, he had given Sheridan prior authorization to slaughter as many women and children as well as men Sheridan or his subordinates felt was necessary when they attacked Indian villages. However many they killed, Sherman would cover the political and media front. They were freed to do anything. At the same time, Sherman maintained personal deniability—he could assert in any public forum that he had not ordered any atrocities that might occur. Soon Grant would go to the White House, Sherman to Washington as Grant's successor, and Sheridan to Chicago to take over Sherman's role as commander of the war against the Plains Indians. All three would work in perfect concord on this issue. In fact, after 1868, Sherman rather lost interest in this wretched little war. He had implicit trust in Sheridan, he was not very alarmed by the military threat the Indians might present, and although he anticipated some nasty temporary reverses, he was certain that his army was marching as a force of Progress, on to total victory in the not-too-distant future.

Rather than ending with a climactic battle, the war against the Plains Indians ground toward victory, as Sherman had predicted it would. On April 30, 1870, for example, he wrote Sheridan about the "annual swarming of the Sioux" with the level of perturbation that one might accord a swarming of some other pest, such as rats or hornets. "I look for the usual Spring & Summer scalpings & stealings, but somehow don't fear a combined attack on the settlements or the Pacific Railroad." Still the Sioux were a nuisance and, as he wrote Sheridan in 1874, "sooner or later these Sioux have to be wiped out, or made to stay just where they are put." If truth were known, "everybody . . . would be made happy if the troops should kill a goodly proportion," though given antimilitary opinion in the East, army commanders in the field, rather than being forthright and manly about their desire to slaughter, seemed to spend a lot of energy in covering up what slaughters the troops under their command in fact made. "They want to keep the record to prove that they didn't do it," Sherman wrote Sheridan, failing to note, however, that he kept his record the same way and for the same reasons. Sherman demonstrated his contempt both for the pestilential Indian and for their absurdly sentimental white defenders, who sought to limit army aggressiveness, when he wrote Sheridan in 1874, after one army attack he found insufficiently bloody, "I wish the troops had managed to kill more bucks—but when they are disarmed & unhorsed—and collected on Reservations under military surveillance, they will likely behave themselves for a time, at least until the Quakers manipulate them a while longer." Sherman wanted Sheridan to know, however, that within the inner sanctums of the army, strong attacks were still in favor, whichever Indians were killed. The more Indians killed, the more quickly would the protracted and squalid war against them be finished. Therefore, Sherman was delighted with news of any bold army attack on the savages. Thinking of the old days, as well as of more recent news, Sherman wrote Sheridan in 1874, "I am charmed at the handsome conduct of our troops in the field. They go in with the relish that used to make our hearts *glad* in 1864–5."[14]

Sherman's sense of assurance grew steadily during the 1870s. By 1875, he wrote in his annual report that the danger to white life and property by Indians was smaller than it had been in any former year, and that as for the future, "the prospect is that as the country settles up it will be less and less each year, till all the Indians are established on small reservations." The major remaining problem would be the expense to the government of feeding the remnant, for they were not learning to be farmers. Even the wiping out of General Custer and a large part of his regiment in July 1876 did not exercise Sherman greatly. Although certainly regrettable, it had been a temporary reversal, and the army responded with a relentless and successful series of attacks. Sherman endorsed Sheridan's public reassurance, after a vigorous fall and winter campaign that year, when Sheridan wrote, "I do not doubt the Sioux war, and all other Indian wars in this country, of any magnitude, will be over forever." As soon as March 1877, Sheridan's promise was fulfilled, and Sherman could congratulate him, "of course in common with all I am pleased to know that the hostile Sioux are steadily breaking up, coming in, and surrendering their arms, ponies, etc." Custer's last stand had proven to be the last stand of the Sioux warrior culture.[15]

Even while engaged in attacking the Indians militarily, Sherman was reassured by his observation of all the ways in which his favorite adage—time is on our side—was working out as he had long anticipated. One major factor working to the advantage of white settlers, as it had done ever since Columbus sighted the "New World," was disease. In June 1867, Sherman observed to his brother John, "Time is helping us & killing the Indians fast, so that every year the task is less."

In addition, as the railroads pushed westward, professional hunters and "sportsmen" were slaughtering the buffalo herds. Thus, despite the fact that the peace commissioners had ceded the Indians the right to hunt buffalo as long as they lasted, Sherman was pleased to inform John as early as 1868 that this apparent concession meant little, because "it will not be long before all the buffalo are extinct near and between the railroads, after which the Indians will have no reason to approach them." By 1873, Sherman had noted that areas much farther north were denuded of buffalo, and that very soon, in fact if not in principle, "these rights to hunt would be ended." By 1882, the buffalo were, for all intents and purposes, extinct. They had been the source of food, shelter, clothing, and even fuel, as well as of spirituality and cultural cohesion for the nomadic Indians. Stripped of their hunting livelihood, they could no longer travel widely and flourish as they had for so long. Further displacing the Sioux was the quickening pace of white settlement in western Nebraska. As early as 1867, Sherman noted to Grant that "increased population . . . will divide the northern and southern Indians permanently, when [the army] can take them in detail."[16]

Disease, slaughter of the buffalo, their economic base, and intrusion of white settlement, together with the extermination of the most warlike younger men, all were serving to eliminate the Indians. The capstone, literally uniting the white surge, was, as Sherman had always believed it would be, the railroad. Railroads began to move settlers west, and goods, like wheat and buffalo hides, to market. They also made the small army far more mobile and capable of concentration in their attacks on the shrinking bands of "hostile" Indians. The army was able to guard the railroads so effectively that raiding Indians failed to slow construction. In January 1867, Sherman had written to his old subordinate, Grenville Dodge, who was in charge of running the first railroad through the West, "I regard this road of yours as the solution of the Indian problem." On May 11, 1869, Sherman telegraphed Dodge of his enthrallment with the news of the driving of the last spike in Utah, which completed the first transcontinental railroad. In his telegram, Sherman noted that he had backed such a project ever since his California days in 1854, and wrote how delighted he was to have contributed to its completion. "All honor to . . . you brave fellows, who have done the deed," Sherman wired Dodge, "spite of danger, storms . . . and all the obstacles you have now happily surmounted." Sherman did not even mention the Indians as a major obstacle, subsuming them under the broader rubric of dangers. With the Union Pacific through, and three more lines to follow in swift succession, with all their attendant social, economic, and racial ramifications, Sherman could shove the Indians out of his mind while he and Progress were in the process of finishing them off on the ground.[17]

The remaining Indians were nearing starvation. "I think the Sioux are now so dependent on us that they will have to do whatever they are required to do," Sherman told Sheridan triumphantly and only slightly prematurely, on November 20, 1875. After a bit more mopping up he could believe he had achieved the final solution to the Indian problem as he had defined it a decade earlier—extermination for the hostile; reduction to dependency in out-of-the-way reservations for the rest. And it really had been cheap in white soldiers' lives: From 1867 to 1884, 565 officers and men were killed and 691 wounded, far less than in an average Civil War battle. Financially as well, the war had proved no great drain on the treasury: "It is all moonshine about the great cost of the war," Sherman bragged to a friend in 1875.[18]

For that remnant of a people he had ushered to their fate, Sherman felt little compassion and great contempt. He shared the resentments of settlers that, even on reservations, Indians were "non-producers, beggars and robbers, if not worse," as Sherman insisted to an acquaintance in 1873. No one was preventing them from working, but they would not work. If they utilized the "beautiful pastoral land assigned them" to raise cattle, they would soon become rich, but it seemed unlikely to Sherman that they would take this course. And then, "how long must the Government continue to clothe and feed them without any assurance of self-support?" Sherman asked rhetorically, especially when white settlers were pressing in on their reserves, eager to make productive use of the land. Sherman envisioned no further means of aiding the Indians. He was indifferent to them, and one infers that he would not have minded if they had been expelled from the reservations and left to starve off in the wilderness, although he did not articulate such a policy, but merely hinted at it. Even if, as some historians have emphasized, other army officers, such as George Crook, O. O. Howard, John Pope, and Nelson Miles, felt greater compassion for the Indians after fighting them for years, Sherman, the grand strategist of their demise, did not.[19]

On the other hand, Sherman was eager to clear from his memory, lest it be corroded, some of the venom he had used during the war against the Plains Indians. In 1875, he even resumed a friendly correspondence with his old adversary, Samuel Foster Tappan. "That Indian question over which we sometimes quarrel has passed out of our hands," he assured Tappan, "and we can look on and criticize those who pretend to know and do better. After all, Old Time is the Great Healer," he suggested, holding out an olive branch to a man toward whom he well could afford to feel magnanimous, as he had won their long quarrel. Time was on the side of cleansing his own conscience, and healing an old friendship, just as Time had been on the side of killing off the Indians. Indeed, in 1876, Sherman enlisted Tappan, whom he now addressed as "My Dear Friend," in a dispute with the venerable radical, Wendell Phillips, who had accused Sherman in an open letter to the press of having followed a policy of "universal extinction" of the Indians. To Tappan, Sherman insisted that "I did not 'exterminate' an

Indian, or think of such a thing," that he and all the army had always treated peaceful Indians "with the utmost kindness," and that he had "never advocated the killing of anybody . . . except as punishment for crime or to save the lives and property of our own people." Sherman requested that Tappan correct his friend Wendell Phillips in his misconstructions of Sherman's motives and actions.[20]

So positively glowing was Sherman feeling about the conquest of the West by the mid-1870s that not only could he make friends of old but now harmless foes; he could even regard Indian outbursts as almost quaint throwbacks. When he wrote in his 1877 annual report of Chief Joseph's brilliant long march in the small and not-very-bloody Nez Percés war, Sherman treated it as something of a travelogue, filled "with such varied and interesting incidents, covering a vast surface of the country." By July 25, 1879, during what had been for so many years previously the Indian "swarming season," and the time of year for aggressive army attacks, Sherman assured his old St. Louis friend, Henry Turner, with great pride, "time is working so beautifully in our favor that it is folly to precipitate trouble with the Indians." Order and peace covered the West as never before. "People are fast filling up the Western Plains, and soon we shall have no Buffalo, no Elk or Bear, and it may be no Indians. I think in our new National Museum"—the Smithsonian Institution in Washington of which he was an active patron—"we will have to collect samples of them for preservation to show our children."[21]

16

Officeholder

SUPPORT OF THE RAILROADS in particular and westward expansion in general, with its corollary, the elimination of the Plains Indians, was the most important public work Sherman accomplished after the Civil War. He had put in place the broad ideological and practical components of this policy by the time he moved to Washington late in 1868, to take over Grant's post of commanding general upon Grant's elevation—if that was what it was—to the White House. Sherman remained in this office for fifteen years, until his retirement in 1883, following his sixty-second birthday. It is true that this had never been a powerful post, with most of the power over the army focused in the hands of the secretary of war. But considering his close wartime relationship with Grant, his lengthy term in office, and his immense personal prestige, it is striking how little he was able to accomplish.

Some of Sherman's ineffectiveness can be attributed to his alienation from the political process and politicians. Temperamentally a saber slasher, he lacked the fine quick hand with which politicians applied the rapier to one another. He also tended to fall into lassitude or simply to flee Washington when conflicts grew too heated. And he was out of sympathy with both political parties on many of the major public issues of the day, although it must be added that in the later nineteenth century the national political establishment confronted very few real issues, particularly after the end of Reconstruction, preferring to fight highly personalized partisan battles instead.

One of the few important issues on which there was a general consensus after the Civil War was opposition to a large peacetime standing army. The volunteer force of the Spanish-American "war," and the great expeditionary force of 1917–18, were disbanded just as rapidly as their Civil War predecessor, and it was not until 1945 that Americans in general and Congress in particular were prepared to accept the notion of permanently powerful armed forces. In part this antimilitarism was traditional—as ever since the Revolution, Americans had feared a military establishment such as the British had employed to suppress them, preferring to use voluntary local militias when armed force was needed on a temporary basis. Partly this was a matter of economy, as Americans, then and now, have always believed that they were overtaxed and that the government was inherently corrupt. But it was also due to an abhorrence of peacetime conscription, which most Americans saw as involuntary servitude, and indeed of the very notion of the use of national armed forces either to quell internal disturbances or to venture into imperialist ventures abroad. Standing armies, conscription, military participation in government, imperialism—all were to be left to the corrupt Europeans: America was designed to be better than decadent foreign lands.

Therefore, when Sherman came to Washington in 1868 it was not the limits to his political capacities or the nature of this or that rapier fight among the politicians that undercut his effectiveness so much as it was widespread objections to a strong army. Only the Indians presented a military threat, and Sherman was able to accomplish their subjugation with relative ease. A small Indian-fighting army had been the norm prior to the Civil War. Thus it was inevitable, whatever Sherman's skills might have been, that the postwar army would have shrunk drastically. Indeed, it had already been reduced from its peak of a million men at the end of the war to about forty thousand when Sherman moved to Washington, and it subsided to its longtime level of twenty-five thousand by the mid-1870s, during his first few years in Washington. As the American economy boomed, the army was shoved back into its traditionally marginal place. Sherman and his comrades, so recently the heroic rescuers of the Republic, naturally resented their diminution in size and prestige, but most American movers and shakers considered the army to be trivial, and wondered how men like Sherman could paddle in a backwater when the current of action had moved elsewhere, into speculative capitalism.

When he came to Washington, Sherman expected that Grant would remain his staunch ally. Grant most likely intended to stand by his old lieutenant, but once in office he was quickly outmaneuvered by his nimble (and as time proved, corrupt) cabinet officers and personal staff, among them William W. Belknap, secretary of war for most of the two Grant administrations. Belknap moved to reconsolidate the power of his office over the military, which necessarily consisted in part of cutting the ground from under Sherman, whom he resented and envied. As before the Civil War, the post of commanding general had again become largely honorific. The heads of the army bureaus—adjutant general, corps of engineers, ordnance, quartermaster, signal corps, subsistence, and surgeon general—functioned independently, reporting not to the commanding general but to the secretary of war. They would order supplies, transfer men, and inspect their posts without even informing Sherman of their activities. The secretary of war had complete fiscal control of the army. He even wrested the power to appoint sutlers away from the army command. Increasingly, Belknap also took over line functions such as granting leaves of absence, transfers, and discharges to officers.

Congress also attacked the powers of the commanding general and the army as a whole. By 1870, Congressman John A. Logan of Illinois was in full charge of the House Military Affairs Committee, and he bore a great grudge. Logan, Sherman's old corps commander, remained embittered that Sherman had passed him over for an army command in favor of O. O. Howard, a West Pointer Sherman had imported from the East, when James B. McPherson had been killed during the Atlanta campaign. Logan despised West Point elitism and the whole notion of a professional army. He favored a reconstructed militia, to be led by gifted volunteers like John A. Logan, and he made Sherman's life miserable. As well as slashing at the size of the army and at appropriations for it, Logan introduced legislation to cut Sherman's personal pay in 1871, and even to forbid the commanding general from acting in the stead of the secretary of war when that official went on leave. In 1878, when the Democrats regained control of the House of Representatives, Logan and the Republicans were replaced by a party that had much of its power base in the South, and Sherman found that congressional oversight of his army was now controlled in large part by ex-Confederates. Thus both Congress and cabinet gained back their traditional powers over a greatly weakened military, with the commanding general a particular, though by no means exclusive, victim.[1]

His increasing powerlessness told on Sherman. In his first report to Congress on the army, after a full year back in Washington, one can sense Sherman seeking essentially to please the legislative branch by rationalizing the shrinkage of the military they had imposed, while pleading with them to pass new regulations that would strengthen rather than further weaken his authority over the army bureaus. Yet his tone toward Congress was defensive, almost plaintive. He urged improvement of the working conditions of his officers. "The great mass of them are banished to distant sections and kept there with indifferent shelter, without any of the facilities and associations of civilized life; [with] families that they scarcely have the means to educate and provide for. In my whole army experience I have never known the army officers so poor, and yet I believe they will continue cheerfully to endure . . . if they can see in the future any hope of improvement." Sherman did not even demand an increase in pay for his officers, which he believed to be a utopian desire, but merely asked that army pay not be diminished further.[2]

Over the next two years, Sherman sank into a kind of sullen resignation. "I find my office here more & more each day becoming a sinecure, the very thing Congress aims to produce," Sherman complained to General Edward O. C. Ord in August 1870. He realized that Belknap was slowly but steadily consolidating his power at Sherman's expense. "Little by little the Secretary of War has regained the actual control of the Army," Sherman wrote Phil Sheridan in 1871. *Sinecure* was the description of his post to which Sherman recurred frequently over the years. His subordinates looked to him for a protection he could not provide, and this frustrated him terribly. "I occupy a most unenviable post, for the law gives me no power at all," he admitted to Ord, "& yet all the officers suppose I will control the weather."

Feelings of impotence only increased. By 1873, Sherman was writing his old St. Louis banking colleague, Henry Turner, that in Congress, as among the public, "it is now the fashion to abuse the Army and Navy," and to attack the service academies. Sherman told Turner that he almost wished "they would try the experiment of disbanding the Army and trusting to the Militia only," which would "more than bankrupt the Treasury by claims for volunteers" to suppress the Indian wars that would break out all over the country. A year later, Sherman complained to Ord that when it came to appointments, the secretary of war disposed of them, in direct communication with post or bureau commanders, "and I often read of the orders in the newspapers for the first time. To pretend to comprehend any of this is a farce." Once in a while, the secretary of war or a bureau chief would ask his opinion, as if on a whim. "I am habitually neglected, and spasmodically consulted," Sherman wrote Irvin McDowell in 1875. "Where the line is drawn passes my comprehension."[3]

It got to the point where Sherman could not even defend his best friends, much less the army as a whole. Active officers with sufficient gall could run around their ostensible commander and appeal to civilian politicians in order to advance their careers in the service. To take one notable example, in 1880, Colonel Nelson A. Miles used his influence with the territorial legislature of Montana, the governor of Massachusetts, and even the secretary of the treasury, John Sherman (who was the uncle of Miles's wife, Mary), to appeal past the recalcitrant Sherman directly to the president. Rutherford B. Hayes compelled Sherman's old comrade, Edward O. C. Ord, to retire, and then appointed Miles to the vacant brigadier generalship, while the bypassed Sherman stood in powerless fury.[4]

Sherman held on to his sinecure in part because of its high salary, in part because he loved the adulation the public attached to him as officeholder and Civil War hero, innocent as they were of the political eunuch he had become, and in part because he believed that through his presence and his lobbying efforts he could limit the harm done to the army to some extent. But he squirmed and fretted and fumed in his powerlessness. When he finally retired in 1883, he confessed to his successor, Phil Sheridan, "the command of the Army at Washington never sat easy on my conscience, because it was not command, but simple acquiescence in the system which has grown up . . . where the President commands, the Secretary of War commands, each Head of Bureau commands, and the real general is a mere figurehead. If you change that you will be more successful than I was." No serious reform, giving more power to the military heads of the army, took place in the nineteenth century.[5]

A major and terrible aspect of Sherman's disappointing postwar career in Washington was the loss of his close bond with U. S. Grant. Their mutual admiration, affection, and support had grown in the maelstrom of civil war and lasted through the trying political fire-storms of the Johnson administration and the war against the Plains Indians. When the number one and number two figures in the army, they maintained a nearly perfect political consortium. As Sherman told John late in 1866, "both Grant and I desire to keep plainly and strictly to our duty in the Army, and not to be construed as partisans." When a Republican boom pushed the rather unwitting Grant toward the White House in 1868, realizing that Grant's election would bring him to Washington to fill Grant's position as head of the army, Sherman believed, rather naïvely, that their personal relationship would survive Grant's move into the overtly political sphere. "If Grant intends to run for President I should be willing to come on" to Washington, Sherman told John at this juncture, "because my duties would then be so clearly defined that I think I could steer clear of the breakers."[6]

It would have been impossible for Grant to have been other than political as president, or for Sherman to have been able to keep out of political issues. If Grant had been a man of great political skills, he might have been able to balance the needs of Sherman and the army with his other political tasks, but he proved both inept and inert. The leading figures of the Republican Party, especially those men serving in Grant's cabinet, praised him to his face and picked his pocket when he turned his back. Poor Grant seemed not to fathom his difficulties with his supposed allies, and he simply lacked the time and energy to deal with Sherman, who was not a major player, or with the army, which was no longer of obvious concern. William W. Belknap, the secretary of war, took a management problem off the president's hands, and Grant gave Belknap his lead, though this victimized Grant's old comrade, Sherman.

Sherman was aghast at Belknap's methods and his influence over his old friend, and hurt by Grant's aloofness and indifference, which allowed Belknap's diminishment of Sherman's office to prevail, but for once in his life he kept a lid on his fury. Even to trusted colleagues in the army, Sherman expressed a kind of sympathy for his old friend even while experiencing Grant's neglect. In this spirit Sherman wrote Sheridan in 1871, "I did hope that General Grant would, as he personally promised me, correct all this" arrogation of power by Belknap, "but he has his load of troubles, and I do not feel disposed to add to its weight."[7]

Along with genuine personal sympathy for Grant, Sherman felt relief as well as anger when he was denied entrée into the inner circles of Washingtonian political power. He did not approve of the political goals nor of the uses of the military during the later stages of Reconstruction, he hated conniving partisanship, and more generally, his Washington experience did not endear contemptible democracy for him. If he had been shoved aside for political and bureaucratic reasons, and stabbed with a thousand rapier thrusts of insults to his honor, there was also a certain payoff for him in remaining "above" politics while staying in office. "General Grant is so absorbed in his politics that he seems to forget his old associations and obligations," Sherman wrote Ord in 1870. "I will do nothing to complicate him, but I must look out for myself. The War is over, and all its lessons lost & swallowed up in present political necessities." Sherman would remain commanding general but he would never move toward the center of power, in part because he was disinvited rudely, but also in part because in his heart of hearts he did not want to play the politician or the democrat. Self-protection and fame became his chief goals.[8]

Nevertheless, Grant's ongoing indifference irritated Sherman, and, because he continued to swallow his anger, he grew depressed over the years. This depression remained relatively shallow and did not lead to another major episode, in part because Sherman took other paths to self-fulfillment, but even though he managed to stay afloat emotionally and professionally, he was very unhappy. "General Grant has gone back on me and I fear on the Army itself," Sherman told General Christopher C. Augur during the heat and torpor of the Washington summer in 1871. "His reasons [for doing so] I am unable to fathom, unless toadies are trying to step between us."

Grant's uncommunicativeness to Sherman hit a new low late in 1871, when Sherman recommended that the military base at Omaha be enlarged, and Grant instead issued orders through the secretary of war to close it. After the civic leaders of Omaha protested, compelling Grant to change his mind, Grant did not make it known that it was he who had countermanded Sherman's earlier suggestion, thus making it appear that it had been Sherman who had offended Omaha. This was "one of the meanest acts ever done by persons professing friendship," Sherman fumed to Sheridan, but he did not break with Grant, nor denounce him in any way, continuing to express to his associates and family his sympathy for the overburdened and troubled president.[9]

Sherman suffered on with Grant. The election of 1872 presented Sherman with the alternative of Horace Greeley as president, just the kind of reformer, and newspaperman to boot, whom he detested with a premium detestation. He insisted to Ellen Ewing Sherman that if Greeley were elected, "both the Army & Navy would be abolished and we would have to begin anew, for Greeley believes in the peaceful reign of editors and preachers that would have the whole world ablaze in five years." One can sense the backhanded quality of his support for Grant in a letter he wrote to one of his former officers, Willard Warner. "I do not feel that General Grant is as true to his friends as they have been to him; yet I see no alternative—for there is no better man who is willing to be in his place." One can sense the way in which Sherman was forced to endorse his own impotence in a letter his brother the senator wrote to him, that Grant would be reelected as would he, and that this would be best for the country even if he were unable to help his brother regain any authority. "It is better for the country that, in our relative positions, we are independent of each other," Senator Sherman instructed General Sherman. "I hope you and [Grant] will preserve your ancient cordiality; for though he seems willing to strip your office of its power, yet I have no doubt he feels as warm an attachment for you as, from his temperament, he can to any one. You have been forbearing with him, but lose nothing by it." This was a cheerless prediction of what the subsequent four years would offer Sherman, who would have to grin and bear it, just as John had understood he would.[10]

Sherman stood and watched as Grant's second administration spun out of control in scandal after scandal. At least his powerlessness meant that none of the messes would mar his reputation. "I am above Party and am not bound in honor or fact to toady to anybody," he wrote John in 1874. He intended to keep the one clean office in Washington, thus preserving his honor and that of the army. Therefore, "I shall never resign, and shall never court any other office, so they may reserve their advice to men who seek it." Sherman warned his friends both in and out of the army that he had little remaining political influence, and that he would not seek a more powerful position, but under the current political conditions he converted the very weakness of his official role into something of a virtue. "Grant and the cabinet think me less enthusiastic in their political management than I ought to be," he confided to a trusted friend in 1875, "and they may be right. . . . They are selfish and arrogant and are fast losing that hold in public respect they used to enjoy." He might not be rising but they were sinking, which might redound to his benefit one day. Or at least he would look good, relatively speaking.[11]

On March 8, 1876, the *New York Herald* disclosed the massive corruption of the "Army Ring," which brought down Belknap. Sherman felt a kind of grim satisfaction. He realized immediately that Grant's reputation would be badly tarnished by the scandal. If only he had listened to me, Sherman believed, more in sadness than in anger, he would have received real aid and comfort. On March 10, he told John with a certain satisfaction, "Gen'l Grant made me repeated promises to bring Belknap and me together to arrange amicably our respective fields of duty, but he *never* did." On the same day, Sherman fumed to his banker, in greater anger, "I do not think that General Grant is personally dishonest—but he does repay personal favors by official acts—I see no difference between selling an office publicly for money, or for votes, and our whole system of government is based on the principle of paying off political debts." This was not a radical or a reformer speaking, but rather a man who wanted desperately both to remain in public office and to remain above the democratic morass. He may have lost power and influence, even over his dearest comrade, Grant, but at least he had kept himself pure. "I have plenty of faults, and have made plenty of mistakes in my life, but I thank God I am not and never was a Courtier. The Court at Washington is as debasing as at Constantinople." Sherman would ever after regard Grant's presidency as a personal disaster for his admired wartime leader. He was appalled when Grant yet again entertained flatterers who sought to return him to a third term as president in 1880, when he "could so easily rest on his laurels." Grant's fall from grace was the price of the presidency, a lesson that Sherman took fully to heart.[12]

From the moment he had arrived in 1868, Sherman had been utterly revolted by politicians, the democratic political practice and even the city of Washington. "The moment a person is established in Washington friends begin to cool off and fall away, slander is let loose and is paraded in capital letters, and meanness is set to work to effect change," he wrote Grenville Dodge in 1868. The whole capital city reeked of Levantine decadence and of the barely concealed blood lusts of the barbarians. Even the magnificent home that several wealthy New York merchants purchased for him from Grant for $65,000, in 1868, proved to be a white elephant—with huge taxes and high costs of upkeep. He could not really afford to live like a Roman proconsul, and the costly imperial style seemed to mock his powerlessness. "I think Washington is doomed," he declared to Willard Warner in 1874. "It is in the hands of the Philistines, and nothing can extricate it."[13]

If he could not affect Washington, he could at least symbolically protest against its corruption by removing himself to the relatively pristine West from whence he sprang. Therefore, in 1874, rather than resigning his post he sold his grand house, and moved his skeleton staff and family to St. Louis, where he stayed for nineteen months. As he lamented to Ord shortly after Grant had given him permission to move, "to remain here as a kind of apologist for the [officers] of the army is beneath the dignity of my office and character, and though willing to make as much sacrifice as anybody, I cannot endure this longer. I will go to St. Louis . . . and if I pass into a nobody I will at least maintain my own self-respect." One of the final straws had been Grant's effort to force Sherman to "play the courtier" by taking Grant's son, Fred, onto his tiny staff. "I won't," Sherman told Ord. "Fred is good enough but three officers on my staff are of more merit & claims on my personal kindness." In this act, Sherman lowered himself in a rather petty and indirect insult to Grant, but it is clear that the move to St. Louis was a grander gesture aimed at Grant. There is no evidence that Sherman confronted Grant any more directly than this, or that the insensible Grant registered much of a reaction.

Many army officers were alarmed by this act of pique by Sherman. They protested to him that he ought to stand his ground in Washington and fight the good fight on their behalf, and they implied that he was being selfish. Sherman did not attempt to answer these charges directly. He had kept his job, however meaningless it might be, which was for him the chief point. In the first annual report that he wrote from St. Louis, he put the boldest possible face on his withdrawal to his Western tent. "I am . . . prepared to execute any duties which may be devolved on me by proper authority. Here I am centrally located, and should occasion arise, I can personally proceed to any point . . . where my services are needed." Neither Belknap nor Grant consulted him about anything; but at least their continued snubbing could not take place daily as it had when he had been hanging around Washington.

After five months in St. Louis, Sherman wrote back to his old friend, Admiral David Dixon Porter, that he felt nothing but "pity [for] you fellows in Washington from the bottom of my heart." He was well off out of all that. "St. Louis with all its smoke & dirt is far preferable. Like the oyster we are ugly outside, but inside cozy and comfortable defying the storms that agitate the surface." This was a revealing simile—in St. Louis the thin-skinned Sherman had been able to survive by escaping the political storms of the democratic surface of American life. He had acted out his often-stated desire to slip off into some obscure and tranquil place.

The chief product of Sherman's essentially idle St. Louis sojourn was the writing of his *Memoirs*. Other than that, "we made ourselves very comfortable, made many pleasant excursions into the interior [and] had a large correspondence." Sherman later admitted that all in all, even at the time, "I realized that it was a farce."

The St. Louis comedy ended shortly after the Belknap scandal broke in March 1876. Among other peculations, Belknap had demanded systematic kickbacks for those sutlerships he had wrested from Sherman's control. Ironically, the scandal made Sherman's earlier decampment look more like an act of principle than it had been—he had inadvertently freed himself from any taint of Belknap's corruption, the revelation of which had come as a surprise to him. Grant, and Belknap's successor, Judge Alphonso Taft, begged him to return to Washington as part of an effort to present a cleansing view of the War Department to the public. They promised to place two bureaus, the Adjutant General and the Inspector General, under his control. This token, and the respectful way Grant and Taft addressed him, were sufficient to cause his return. Although he regained little actual power, at least Taft and his four successors who served as secretary of war until Sherman's retirement in 1883 maintained, Sherman later stated, "the most intimate and friendly relations" with him. He was satisfied with civil treatment and did not demand any fundamental reflation of the powers of his office.[14]

Sherman's final years in public office remained as routine and dry as ever. All the big decisions were still made by the secretary of war, although he now took the courtesy to pass them down through Sherman's office to the adjutant general, who promulgated them. Sherman could do little, for example, to help the veterans who flooded his office. Indeed, at one point he wrote his brother the senator, as he wrote so many others, "Please don't send any old soldiers to me. I have not the patronage of a grocery clerk. . . . [M]y whole disposable force is 2 porters . . . and I am daily & hourly importuned." He asked John to tell such down-on-their-luck men to apply to the detestable Ben Butler, who was in charge of the Old Soldier's Homes in Milwaukee, Dayton, and Augusta, Maine. Year after year, Sherman's only real functions concerned bureaucratic minutiae. In 1878, he admitted to his son, Tom, "I am employed in official routine matters of no earthly interest save to the officers and soldiers concerned; but these things have to be done, transfers, movements of troops, leaves of absence, reports, returns, etc etc—an army like a family has an infinite variety of wants, which can only be reconciled by minute attention to details." With Belknap's monumental rudeness added to the pile, Sherman's position had been insufferable; with polite bosses, his job was merely drearily monotonous. It was a strange after-war award for the heroic man of action.

Even the ceremonial portions of the job grew gray and empty for this naturally gregarious man. Anticipating the start of his final year in office, Sherman wrote to his old comrade, John Schofield, who would become commanding general following Phil Sheridan's death while serving in that office in 1888, "tomorrow will be New Year's day—we will make the usual calls of Etiquette on the President, Chief Justice, etc etc, and then subside into the old routine until Congress adjourns."[15]

The one part of his job that contained the most authentic meaning for Sherman over the years was his role as what one might call first father of the army. He quite consciously saw himself that way, and he was so considered by others. For example, when, in April 1879, Lieutenant J. C. Scantling informed Sherman from Fort McHenry in Baltimore of his forthcoming marriage, Sherman replied, asking Scantling to tell the bride, "that I the Father welcome her into the Great Army family, and hope she will aid as well in making it what it should be—a charmed circle." In this vein, Sherman frequently wrote prospective mothers-in-law of his young officers to assure them their daughters were marrying into a most respectable, genteel, and comfortable profession. He would also provide letters of introduction for young ladies, such as the one he wrote for Miss Miriam Brairie of Lancaster, who was going to San Antonio for the winter. "I knew Miss Brairie's mother & grandmother, and doubt not she is a beautiful and accomplished young lady—and will be pleased if your younger officers will show her special attention," Sherman advised the army post commander in that town. Sherman wanted all his ladies and gentlemen to enjoy themselves together, and to marry in a way that would sustain the army family.

Sometimes the paternalist would take pity on the down-and-out veterans who flooded his outer office. For example, on November 22, 1878, L. D. Ingersoll left a note for Sherman, "Pity the sorrows of a poor man, who is sick and *dead broke,* and can't wait to get his pay, and lend him $20—till after Thanksgiving. I don't have but 25 cts., and 100 men are waiting their turn [to see you]. I can't." On the reverse side of this plaintive appeal, Sherman noted that he had loaned the man $20 by check, drawn from his personal account. Sherman was always a soft touch for the veterans of his western army who had fallen on hard times.

Sherman also spent a great deal of time attempting to mediate disputes between brother officers; he tried to be scrupulously fair in the posts to which he was assigning them; and he was generous in his praise of them to their new widows when it came time for that. He had very little to distribute, but he always tried to be as open as he could be in what he would offer, and when he could not confer position he could and would proffer kind words.

On formal occasions, as well as in smaller and more personal ways, Sherman always kept alive his fatherly role. Of no occasion was this more true than it was of the annual graduation exercise at West Point. For 1883, his last year as general of the army, Sherman passed the main address on to General Alfred H. Terry. When he did so, however, he instructed Terry closely about the ritualized contents that such a speech always had to include. "You speak of the noble profession of arms, its influence on History, its grandeur, and benevolence when argument and the pen have failed, the need of thought, of reason and an open heart, of preparation, toil, self-abnegation and all the noble qualities that dignify nature etc etc." Sherman's formula, honed over the years of giving such addresses, amounted to almost a medieval conception of joining the noble guild of arms. Sherman instructed Terry, "your address is to *them,* of welcome into the *fraternity of Knights,* brothers, gentlemen and *comradeship.*" This chivalric ceremony, as filtered through the novels of Sir Walter Scott, which Sherman probably read as a boy, was the formal *rite de passage* into full martial brotherhood, with the touch of the blessed sword provided by the first father at arms.

Not all paternal dispensations were positive ones, however, as Sherman frequently had to deal with disobedient or dishonest military sons. Then he could be quite stern. For example, in 1878, George Schneider of rural Buda, Illinois, who had been one of Lieutenant Sherman's men in Florida in the late 1830s, sent Sherman an affidavit for his signature, requesting a pension on account of his having lost his health from eating diseased pork way back then. That was a stretcher! "I have always been willing to stretch my conscience to the utmost to befriend an old soldier," Sherman replied with considerable heat, "but this is more than I can stand. . . . It is idle at this late date to trace your infirmity to pork in Florida. At all events you must get proof from some one else but me."

A more serious example of Sherman as punishing father concerned his nephew, Major Henry P. Reese, who was arrested in 1871 for mishandling army funds in his role as paymaster. Reese wrote his uncle complaining of General Benjamin Alvord, the paymaster general, who had turned Reese's case over to the judge advocate. Sherman replied in anger, "don't look to me or to [Senator] John Sherman to favor you in the least" on account of our relationship. "As head of the Army, I would be the first to prosecute the case, were it not already in process." He forbade Reese from writing him again before the result of the case was made public, and told him he was "deeply mortified" by Reese's besmirching of both the reputation of the family and the army. Sherman also reassured Alvord, a comrade of thirty-seven years' standing, that he and John did not "wish [Reese] to receive any favor because he is the son of our beloved sister . . . but on the contrary hold that this relationship to us by blood should subject himself to even a higher test of responsibility than otherwise."[16]

One of the most important roles of the father of the army ought to have been the nurturing of the talented younger officers, who were to become the future leaders of the family. In the most general sense, Sherman, who was quite interested in ideas and in intellectual play, did foster improvements in the educational level of the army. His two biggest accomplishments in office were the establishment of an advanced school for infantry and cavalry officers at Fort Leavenworth, Kansas, in 1881, and his support of reform-minded younger army intellectuals, most notably Emory Upton. After the Civil War, Upton wrote the new book on infantry tactics, and taught it at West Point. Following the smashing German triumph over the French in 1870, which Phil Sheridan and William B. Hazen had observed firsthand, Upton drafted and circulated a manuscript, "The Military Policy of the United States," which urged a fundamental reform of the American army based on the German model of a strong core regular army, which if adopted in the United States would dispense with the local militias and amateur voluntary regiments that had always been central to American military policy.

Such a basic change was unlikely to have been adopted in late nineteenth-century America, where antimilitarism reigned supreme, and indeed most of the young army reformers gathered around Upton were highly pessimistic about their chances, given the insufficiencies of American democracy as opposed to the discipline and organization available to monarchies like the admired German one. Upton in fact deepened the alienation of the elitist army officer cadre from the mainstream of American democratic life.

In their alienation, the Young Turks were as one with Sherman. Sherman's incapacity for political engagement reached its low point in 1878, when Congress at last considered a serious army reform. Amidst the violent national railroad strike of 1877, and fears of anarchist rebellion, a drive for reform was led by two Civil War generals, James A. Garfield in the House and Ambrose Burnside in the Senate, urged on by Sherman. Burnside's Senate Military Affairs Committee seriously considered a whole string of Upton-based reforms, including a proper General Staff, of the European type. Just when the bill was in greatest flux, Sherman left on one of his prolonged vacations, showing his usual contempt for politicians by withdrawing his support at the crucial moment. The bill was probably doomed by division in Congress and in the army itself, but in this his most likely opportunity to effect a major reform, Sherman did not stand his ground and fight. Indeed, considering that he served fifteen years as general of the army, Sherman accomplished very little in the way of positive change. Other historians have emphasized that he was open-minded and supportive of change within the force, and while this may have been true in the abstract, on concrete issues Sherman was a rather narrow and inflexible conservator of a tiny military elite.[17]

Not merely on military policy, but on the most important public issues of the day, Sherman was generally uninfluential. His weak official role contributed to his lack of influence, but he was also out of step with governmental policy on many issues. On no question was his weakness more evident than it was from 1868 to 1876, on Military Reconstruction, the one major postwar intervention by the national government on a major social issue—race relations in the South. The Grant administration did not run a consistently articulated or applied policy, but they did attempt, however haphazardly, to foster a new social and political order in the South, supporting it at times with military force.

As he had made clear at the end of the war, in his negotiations with Joseph Johnston and afterwards, Sherman deeply opposed, on racist grounds, the fundamental purpose of Reconstruction. In 1866, he argued to Willard Warner, "Of course I know there are bad men [in the South] as elsewhere, but legislation should aim to increase the good & law-abiding instead of forcing all classes into antagonism." Ever after, he interpreted this or that Reconstruction measure to aid blacks and repress the old leadership cadre of the South as fundamentally wrongheaded. He continuously opposed Grant's use of troops in the South, as ineffective in the practical sense as well as misguided in general. "[As] the small number of troops cannot be everywhere, the Ku Klux have it all their own way," Sherman told Christopher C. Augur in 1871. "It is notorious that no Southern man can be punished for murder and violence"—to black and white Unionists. Sending the army after night riders was thus as pointless as "locking the barn door after the horse is stolen." Sherman then argued that Congress would never give the president the power to declare and exercise systematic martial law, and that all lesser uses of the military were only serving to make the Grant administration look "simply ridiculous." Sherman seemed to be arguing that either abandoning the current limited policy or adopting something like military dictatorship were the only plausible alternatives to the chaos of Reconstruction as it was. He also feared that being "hauled about" under orders from sheriffs and treasury agents demoralized his troops, "until I fear they have become anything else than soldiers." It was beliefs such as these, which Sherman did not keep to himself, that were the primary political cause for Grant when he bypassed Sherman altogether and supported Belknap's policy of making direct commands to the army. Sherman was not "sound" on Military Reconstruction of the Grant variety. His political alienation led him out of the loop of power on this issue, and consequently on many others.

As the Republicans were pushed toward abandoning Reconstruction, blacks, and Southern white Unionists to the so-called Redeemers—the old ruling elite now come back to office—Sherman nearly crowed with the pleasure of the vindicated prophet. "My own official predictions as to the Reconstruction of the South have now been proven by actual events," Sherman told his son, Tom, in 1875, one year before the formal ending of Military Reconstruction, "so that hundreds and thousands who thought me in error in 1865, now realize I was right." It was only natural that politicians "colonized" on the South would sooner or later be replaced by "our native peoples," by which he meant the old white leadership, the natural heads of the South.

Soon enough this ending would have an ironic meaning for Sherman, which he realized as early as 1877. The Democratic Party had first captured the House of Representatives in the 1864 election, and "the southern element is so strong" among these Democrats, Sherman complained to Willard Warner, "that we find ourselves governed by the very men whom we fought as enemies." He had "always favored the recognition" of these men as "co-citizens," but now Sherman admitted that he had "hardly foreseen" that they would control Congress so soon. He was bracing himself for the next assault on the army, worse than Logan's, which indeed did come. Any Grant Republican would have warned him of this impact of the end of Reconstruction. Nevertheless, Sherman felt more comfortable with the South as it became than he had been with Reconstruction. No subsequent issue would divide him so greatly from the administration in power. This was one important reason for the greater civility of his relations with them after 1876, but he was not able to recapture for himself or the army much of the ground he and they had lost.

Oddly enough, Sherman's estrangement from politics gave him a real usefulness during the endgame of Reconstruction, the disputed election of 1876. When it seemed that Congress would not be able to resolve which presidential candidate would be victorious, as the Democrats were so heavily Southern in their orientation, so allied to the old Confederate elite, there was an undercurrent of fear that the Civil War might recommence. In this situation, Sherman was proud that he was keeping himself and the army "perfectly aloof" from the fray, and that he was making it clear to all concerned that the army would support the legitimate presidential victor. "I will try to do that which will result in national safety and honor," he told a New York journalist, adding cryptically that "I must be a man of action or nothing." To Phil Sheridan, Sherman promised to say nothing "except that the Army will obey the legitimate authority," but asserted that "if Revolution is inevitable then we must act when the time comes, as the occasion demands." Sherman then requested that Sheridan consolidate his scattered western forces in Chicago, "convenient for moving," if called. In the event, because leaders of both political parties wished to avoid open conflict, and because the Republicans were willing to abandon the blacks, both parties could use Congress to create a special commission that resolved the dispute, placing the Republican, Hayes, in the White House, with an implicit pledge to end Military Reconstruction, the Democrats' essential demand.[18]

Sherman's aloofness helped keep things cool during the crisis of 1876. It is quite significant that he suppressed so deeply at this juncture his belief about the necessity of a military dictatorship. If he had wished to have gone on an authoritarian, militaristic fishing trip, this would have been the occasion. But his hints were so vague at this point that they demonstrated that his antidemocratic fantasy life had receded after the Civil War.

It is perhaps even more curious, given his long-term fear of anarchy, that Sherman also remained aloof from all military actions, taken by the federal government in 1877 and afterwards, against violently striking workers, many of whose leaders were self-proclaimed anarchists. Rhetorically, Sherman was on the side of Law and Order. Commenting on the Haymarket Riot of 1886, in Chicago, Sherman told a group of veterans, "as to these red Republicans, though I am past fighting age, I am not afraid of the red flag." Therefore, "I would turn them over to the guard-house in charge of a corporal's guard," who, implicitly, would give them a good thrashing, "and if that would not settle it I would hang them and have done with it."

Tough talk notwithstanding, back in the summer of 1877, when President Hayes had called out the army to put down the first, bloody national railroad strike, Sherman played no role at all. He was off on one of his long excursions through the West, part army inspection and part camping trip, and not only did he fail to return voluntarily, he refused to comply with a direct presidential order to return to Washington at the height of the explosive strike. "I am hastily summoned to Washington," Sherman wired Sheridan. "I do hate to give up this trip, for I have a good start, and my heart is set on it. Surely these riots do not amount to civil war." In exasperation with Sherman, Hayes turned over the military operation to Winfield Scott Hancock, the commander of the Division of the Atlantic (who parlayed this prominent role into the presidential nomination of the Democratic party in 1880), and Sherman did not return to Washington until well after the violence had subsided. He never explained this insubordination. Perhaps he felt that if his office had no power it also should have no responsibility. Perhaps he also feared losing favor with all those men of his old army of the West who were numerous among the railroad workers on strike. Perhaps he felt that the damned politicians ought to sort out their own messes. Or perhaps Sherman believed, as he implied to Sheridan, that short of putting down a major rebellion, the army ought to stay out of domestic unrest.

In the aftermath, many in the military believed they could use this violent strike to reform and enlarge the army, the campaign that fizzled in Congress in 1878, at a time when Sherman yet again took off from Washington at an inopportune moment. When queried by one of the leading citizens of St. Louis about how new labor outbreaks might be quelled, Sherman advised that local elites build and stock strong armories in the centers of their towns as a means to focus resistance and launch counterattacks, arguing that the national army was simply too small to do that job in several cities simultaneously while fighting the Indians and manning the Mexican border all at the same time. He may well have been ambivalent about using any form of military coercion by the federal government—toward strikers as toward the South. Though he loudly proclaimed himself on the side of the social order, he did not want to politicize the army by inserting it into social disputes, which remained to him essentially local or state concerns. Sherman's antipathy to politics and to democracy took him so far out of the chief political issues of the day that he would not get involved in anything short of a second civil war. In some senses he used his office to slip away from the whirligig of events into the detached and airy calmness of ceremonial chieftainship.[19]

As he was nearing the end of his fifteen-year-long tenure as commanding general, Sherman's detachment and self-protectionism spread even to issues within his own direct bailiwick. The most prominent case in point was his role in the Whittaker case, one of the great public causes célèbres of the early 1880s. In this case, both the army and West Point came under frontal attack, and Sherman's ambiguous public role amounted to only a weak defense of his most important trenches.

Johnson C. Whittaker was one of the very few black cadets to be admitted to West Point in the post–Civil War period. Ostracized and hounded by the other cadets, rather marginal academically, Whittaker soldiered on in brave, almost silent isolation. Then on the night of April 6, 1880, he was attacked in his bed by three men, bound, beaten, and knifed like a hog in both ears. Found the next morning, he was almost immediately accused of self-mutilation. General John Schofield, the commandant, quickly took out against Whittaker in the press, and dismissed an internal West Point hearing into the case. The matter did not rest here, however. Many in the press and a few politicians kept the issue alive, in part out of moral outrage at an apparent miscarriage of justice, and in part to bash the elitism of West Point and the army officer corps, always a popular target.

Sherman immediately believed Schofield and disbelieved Whittaker, responding as he did with his customary racial prejudices, which led him to blame the victim. Sherman wrote Schofield on April 15 that this incident was just like the thousands of cases of "self-maiming" young men used to dodge military service during the Civil War. Besides, even if Whittaker had been attacked, the story of "maiming was exaggerated," since his "ears were damaged but little more than any girl does for her earrings," a suggestion that implied that if he had been attacked, he ought to have taken it like a real man, rather than as a sissy. On May 2, Sherman insisted to his old St. Louis friend, Henry S. Turner, that West Point "is in superb order," adding that "the darkey is still in the wood-pile, and strange to say Congress joins in the howl started by a class of small newspaper reporters." Sherman repeated his position that even if Whittaker's story were true, he was unfit to fight battles or command men. He had failed to call out for help or to fight back, nor was he bruised, all of which made his "alleged" maiming "simply farcical." Sherman went on to subscribe wholeheartedly to the exclusion of all blacks from West Point. "Social equality is a question of fashion, of individual preference, of prejudice, beyond the reach of a statute of compulsion. . . . You can bring whites and blacks into the ranks, side by side, equal in the eyes of the law, but not in social life. West Point is the first place where this truth is demonstrated." Returning to the "boy" at issue, Sherman concluded that although he would never "sanction cruelty or inhumanity," neither was he "willing to be humbugged by a boy, be he white, black, or red." Besides that, one should never take the word of a black "boy" against that of a white gentleman and officer, particularly one so eminent as General Schofield. As he would later tell Turner, "I . . . object to believing Whittaker, and discrediting Schofield . . . and other officers of a proved patriotism."

As public uproar grew, Sherman construed it as an attack on West Point, framed by his old enemy, the press, who were once more braying "like a pack of hounds." He wrote Schofield several times advising that they ought to lie low, to "say or do as little as possible," to "go right along in the even tenor of our work" and in a "dignified silence." The furor would probably die down, but "if we must go down let it be with colors flying." Sherman appended as an afterthought, in a later letter to Schofield, "I suppose I too am compromised—but care not a feather's weight."

Sherman soon had the occasion to demonstrate his protested loyalty to Schofield and indifference to his own reputation, for on August 17, President Hayes called Schofield to Washington to sound him out on an immediate transfer from West Point, which Schofield interpreted, of course, as a major insult and defeat. During this election year, Hayes was under great pressure from the Republican Party, which still needed black votes, however diminished in number, to deal with the Whittaker case in an apparently evenhanded fashion, including a court-martial for Whittaker and Schofield's removal. Following Hayes's request, Schofield left the White House to dine with Sherman, who told him that he would not intervene with the president on Schofield's behalf. Sherman told Schofield he had in effect already removed himself from any active role in the case, by not protesting when Hayes had taken it over. Schofield realized immediately that Sherman had betrayed him. "Thus 'had vanished into thin air' all his promises and support," Schofield bitterly wrote in his diary. In Schofield's hour of need Sherman had allowed Hayes to cashier Schofield without protest. The Whittaker affair had brought the army into disrepute, and rather than sticking to Schofield, Sherman removed himself from the public disapprobation attaching to the case. When the chips were down he cared more for his reputation than he did for his old friend and comrade.

And Sherman had betrayed Schofield in such a way that he could deny to himself that he had done so. Thus, when in December 1880 the lame-duck Hayes brought in the racial liberal, General O. O. Howard, late head of the Freedmen's Bureau, to command West Point, and created a hollow command for Schofield in the Southwest, Sherman could still write in a friendly fashion to Schofield that "the President has soured on me," and that he too was offended by what Hayes had done to Schofield. "The President has worked out this scheme himself, without asking my help, and I am glad of it, for I would not like to burden my conscience with such a bungle." It was as if Sherman did not realize that it was Schofield, not he, who had been injured, and that he had contributed to Schofield's injury by withdrawing his support and leaving Schofield dangling in the breeze. Sherman did not seem to notice just how he had cut his own personal losses. Once more for him it was those politicians doing in Sherman and the army. "I don't know but there have been more underhand, dirty intrigues," Sherman wrote Schofield concerning his removal, "than I can recall in the same period of time, it may be excepting Belknap's . . . inglorious career." To Howard he offered his "earnest support," even while reminding him that he had not been consulted on Howard's appointment. Sherman reiterated his belief in Whittaker's guilt and his continued moral objection to "the experiment of social equality" at West Point, but he did not instruct Howard on the case or on his new command. Later, Whittaker would never be exonerated, and Schofield would recover most of his reputation, as in the long run, in accordance with the deepening racism of the 1880s, racial prejudice and discrimination were no detriment to a successful army career. Having removed himself at the propitious moment from the line of fire, Sherman rode out the Whittaker case quite comfortably.[20]

17

Vagabond
and Icon

A VOIDING THE DISCOMFORTS of office was one of the incidental benefits Sherman enjoyed from his curious postwar exile from
power politics, which was as much self-banishment as external imposi-
tion. Literally as well as spiritually, Sherman would remain a vagabond for the remainder of his life. In his postwar life he was still the
antelope, albeit in a grander context, now lured to Washington by office and ceremony, now fleeing those undoubted attractions for open
spaces, distant from his responsibilities to his wife and to the army. He
traveled for the sake of movement, but even more for contact and mutual admiration with his old soldiers and the vast American public he
loved as well as detested. Restless motion helped him shake off his
tendency to depression. Rootlessness lightened his life, taking him
away from problems he could not resolve, conflicts that always threatened to overwhelm him. Sherman often acknowledged the wanderlust
in his nature quite consciously. For example, when in November 1865
he contemplated his immediate postwar command in St. Louis, which
would require visits throughout the "vast West," he wrote to Admiral
David Dixon Porter, "Our plains resemble your seas, and it will take
some years of cruising for me to familiarize myself with all the interests
and localities. I do not regret this for I naturally get tired of any one
place."[1]

During all his years in the harness of his generalship, and afterwards in retirement, in a sense Sherman's primary purpose at home was to plan his next trip. He traveled widely to inspect his far-flung army, often for as long as four months at a time. He established Ellen and his children at summer resorts—now Madison, now Lake Geneva, Wisconsin, now the Adirondacks, now Oakland, now Atlantic City—and then traveled to see them during his vacations, after long working trips. He toured Europe grandly for ten months between November 1871 and September 1872. He attended college graduations to receive honorary degrees, and he always joined in the graduation week at West Point. He orated endlessly at dinners and in the open air, at war monument unveilings and on national holidays. He visited his vast circle of friends for weddings and, increasingly over the years, funerals. And most of all he attended reunions of veterans. Indeed, he took more pride in his presidency of the Society of the Army of the Tennessee than he did in his generalship of the army, and he presided over the society with a good-humored authoritarianism, trying to keep the endless speeches short. If he had not been placed on the formal speakers list, there and elsewhere, he would have a speech dragged out of him not all that unwillingly. He was probably the most sought-after public man of his time. And frequent protestations to the contrary notwithstanding, he loved to be loved, urgently needed to be loved. So unlike his official life in Washington, the star circuit made him feel alive and well. He charmed the crowds, as he was clearly a charismatic figure. Being famous was the central meaning of Sherman's postwar life, for others and for himself.

During the war Sherman had discovered and entered this role as icon with considerable hesitancy. On December 30, 1863, when he was back in Lancaster to console Ellen over Willy's death, his newly gathering fame came in on him through the mails. "I have been opportuned from many quarters for my likeness, autographs, and biography," he wrote John. He was fending off all such requests out of fear of the humiliation of a possible future failure and depression, as he had fallen in the past. "I don't want to rise or be notorious, for the reason that a mere slip or accident may let me fall." A month later, back in Memphis, Sherman was pressed into the local hero's stance. "The mayor and citizens offered me a dinner, and I had to accept," he told Grant, and he had given a patriotic address to good effect, he felt. He then warned Grant of the adulation awaiting him back home. "I pity you when you would have to go back [North], for you will not be allowed to eat or sleep for the curious intrusion of the dear people." Sherman was projecting onto Grant the ambivalent pleasure he had felt recently when he had been lionized back home in Lancaster. So used to failure was he, he did not quite know what to make of fame.

After he had ridden into Savannah as the vandal chieftain, had learned of Thomas smashing Hood's army, and had read his mail and the newspapers, Sherman felt a shock of awareness that his fame was now irreversible. Now he could allow himself to relish this monumental attention, which he believed he had earned, and he also felt relatively secure that it would not likely vanish in some great future mistake. On January 5, 1865, he asserted to Ellen that "I do think that in the several grand epochs of this war, my name will have a prominent part. . . . My success is already assured, so that I will be found to sustain the title. I am told that were I to go north I would be feted and petted, but," he continued in the appearance of modesty, "as I have no intention of going, you must sustain the honors of the family." Sherman swelled with pride in the realization that his fame transcended the boundaries of America. He was reading articles from the English press reprinted in American newspapers. "I don't know that you can comprehend the magnitude" of my military feats, he told Ellen, but "you can see the importance attached to it in England where the critics stand ready to turn against any American general. . . . In my case they had time to commit themselves to the conclusion that if I succeeded I would be a great general, but if I failed I would be set down a fool." He had succeeded, and now he was a great general in the English press—a laying on of hands from the ever-critical motherland dear to nineteenth-century Americans, who also resented English condescension. Not only would his fame "be more appreciated in Europe than America"— the Europeans had long had a history of great generalship nearly missing in the new world—he would be understood best in comparison to classical heroes, something only the truly discerning could ever come to appreciate. "I warrant your father will find parallel in the history of the Greeks and the Persians, but none on our continent," Sherman wrote Ellen. "For his sake I am glad of the success that has attended me." Sherman now believed so firmly in his new stating that he was certain even the powerful and dreaded Thomas Ewing would accept his heroic status.

Adulation turned Sherman's head—he thought he had earned it and that it was his due for the rest of his life. "You can safely trust the fame of our children," Sherman assured Ellen as the war neared its end, "ignoring the past & regardless of the Future. The country owes you & my children an honorable maintenance." At about this time, Sherman received word of an Ohio subscription on his behalf that had raised $100,000 in contributions of $10 and less.

But adulation also annoyed him. It invaded his privacy, took up his time, and tired him out in his efforts to respond to it. By the time he reached North Carolina and reestablished contact with the Union, Sherman got a full dose of what was to come forever after. "I know you will make due allowances for the newspapers tell such wonderful tales of 'Mr Sherman's Company,' " Sherman told Ellen on March 31, "that you can trace my whereabouts, and almost find out what I got for breakfast, but in the many biographical sketches you will hardly recognize me. I don't recognize myself." Sherman had begun to discover the curious distortion of self that accompanies media glorification, so that in the end the hero is dehumanized, even to himself. He also began to learn the tedium of never-ending demands. "I now get bushels of letters and don't read one in five but let them go to my aide." Even to keep up with his official correspondence, Sherman noted that "I write as usual very fast and can keep half a dozen clerks busy in copying." He now employed one of his clerks full-time in sending out his autograph and locks of his hair.

On the train ride back West right after the war, Sherman was nearly mobbed in every city and town along the way. "Ellen & I tried to get a glimpse of you at Syracuse," Sherman wrote Ellen Lynch, an old family friend, "but all through New York such crowds besieged our cars that we had to talk out of the windows. When the people subside," he promised Lynch a calmer visit, but they never did subside. Back in Lancaster, the city fathers threw a ball at the City Hall, commencing with a grand entrance by Sherman, marching to a tune played by a full orchestra entitled "Sherman's March to the Sea." Continued demands for money and jobs and just attention, by the ambitious and the down and out, also started up right at the end of the war. "You have no idea how I am pressed by personal applicants," Sherman mused to his cousin, Charley Hoyt, in 1867, "all of whom claim to have a line on me of a peculiar kind."[2]

Fame brought trials, to be sure, but more often it was like spiritual elixir to Sherman. If he felt stymied and humiliated in Washington, his travels and his speeches brought him instant and thunderous gratification. To take just one example of hundreds, in October 1875 Sherman escorted President Grant to St. Louis, to the annual reunion of the Society of the Army of the Tennessee—Sherman's own boys. He was using this ceremonial occasion in part to snub the hated William W. Belknap, who he feared was trying to wrest leadership of *his* society from him, and to bring the president *to him,* to *his* city, to *his* veteran's association. Not surprisingly, his boys responded in a way to please their leader. As he reported to Ellen, "If Belknap [sought] to displace me in the Society—his failure was absolute. We had a most enthusiastic meeting, and to me personally the demonstration was so open that even Grant noticed it. The crowd in the theater called for me before Grant," Sherman wrote, although it would have been improper for him to have spoken before the president, "and it was with difficulty I could still the call and explain as presiding officer I would close the exercises." In command of the event, with Grant rather at his mercy, Sherman could afford magnanimity. This sort of symbolic victory, this sort of elevation by the massed veterans, provided great salve to Sherman's ever-sensitive and bruised ego. Replacement of diminished political power by outpouring adulation kept him on the road.[3]

In return for public praise, Sherman served as icon and as the bearer of the message that American Progress was the chief outcome of the Civil War, which therefore had been well worth fighting. Repeated endlessly over the decades, Sherman's set speech was a remembrance speech, always moving rhetorically from war to reunion, destruction to rebuilding, problematic past to glorious future. Many, many orations furthered this patriotic message.

Rather typical was the speech he gave in New York City on Decoration Day, May 30, 1878. The grand parade and the laying of wreaths at soldier memorials—"The fragrance of these flowers rising to heaven from these alters"—demonstrated the gratitude of the survivors for the martyred heroes of the Civil War, Sherman began. He declared that although he "would not for the world revive the angry passions" of that war epoch, nor "question the personal motives" of our old "antagonists," now reunited with us, nevertheless, Sherman insisted, "there are such things as abstract right and abstract wrong [and] we claim [that] we of the national union were right and our adversaries were wrong, and no special pleading . . . can change the verdict of War." God marched with us. Our war "saved this nation from absolute humiliation." Politicians made the war and sent 500,000 warriors to their graves. As head of the army, "I publicly proclaim our profession's [task] to be to prevent war." Having secured peace, the military man will now rejoice in "this common effort to make this great land of ours blossom from Maine to Texas, from Florida to Puget's Sound." Now all Americans are "so safe to life and property" that they may engage in that individual striving, which, taken additively, amounts to national progress, whether in "farming, mining, ranching, in navigation internal and upon the high seas, in every variety of mercantile and mechanical pursuit, each one to repeat the full measure of his own industry and sagacity, without envy of his neighbor." Confident in the steady march of Progress, Americans ought to stay vigilant for liberty, but ought not to become "too hastily alarmed by current [labor] unrest, for the armies that were disbanded in 1865 still live in the spirit and these will never . . . permit the government to drift into anarchy."[4]

Although Sherman claimed that his was a national vision, he was unable or unwilling to let go of all his anger toward the South. His most bitter public dispute with ex-Confederates after the war was with Jefferson Davis, an angry man who exchanged insult for insult with Sherman over the decades. At various times Sherman called Davis a "monomaniac," "the impersonation of all that was wicked" during the war, a species that ought to be "wiped off the face of the earth," while for his part, Davis branded Sherman as a violator of "all the rules of war," and a savage general who would have been at home in the genocidal Thirty Years' War.[5]

Nevertheless, Sherman strove mightily for a fully national viewpoint that would include the South, and he was able to reach a civil accommodation with most of his own Confederate military foes, many of whom had regained political, social, and economic power. Toward the end of Southern reintegration into the nation, he corresponded with several former Confederate generals, most often with Braxton Bragg, Joseph Johnston, and John Bell Hood, whom he had fought against so bitterly. Such were the sort of men who invited Sherman down to attend the Atlanta Exposition on November 15, 1881, a date that, Sherman noted dryly, some newspaperman had incorrectly disclosed as the seventeenth anniversary of the burning of Atlanta. Ten thousand people came to see "Sherman the Vandal," he told an old friend, as he attended a commemoration ceremony for the Mexican War, listening to an ex-Confederate orate in a manner "a little flowery, *à la Carolina*," Sherman wrote. Then the crowd chanted, "Sherman! Sherman!!

William Tecumseh Sherman (1820–1891). His face was a map of an eventful life lived in passion and pain. *Ohio Historical Society*

RIDING THE TIGER OF CIVIL WAR

Sherman's victory at Atlanta in September 1864, which he is anticipating from Union fortifications, saved Abraham Lincoln's re-election and capped Sherman's personal and social transformation from defeat to heroic stature. *Ohio Historical Society*

Sherman's staff during the last year of the Civil War, when they laid waste to Georgia and the Carolinas. From left to right, O. O. Howard, John A. Logan, William B. Hazen, Sherman, Jefferson C. Davis, Henry W. Slocum, Joseph A. Mower, Frank Blair. When Sherman brought in Howard, the one-armed West Pointer, to fill a vacant command, rather than promoting the able volunteer Logan from within, Logan never forgave the slight. *Ohio Historical Society*

At the end of the war, lithographs of Sherman's triumphantly stern face illustrated the pages of many mass periodicals. *Ohio Historical Society*

Upward Mobility

Sherman was born in 1820, on Main Street, Lancaster, Ohio, in the modest frame structure seen at the rear in this photograph. The brick front was added by another family, probably after the Civil War. *Ohio Historical Society*

After the Civil War, when he took command of the war against the Plains Indians, Sherman purchased this solid, bourgeois dwelling at 912 Garrison Street, St. Louis, which he later remodeled for his retirement in 1883. *Ohio Historical Society*

In Washington from 1868 to 1883, Sherman dwelled in this enormous mansion that grateful New York City capitalists first gave to U. S. Grant in 1865. Sherman, who had been nearly broke during much of his life prior to the Civil War, relished living in grand style. However, he constantly feared the penury that might be brought on by the high cost of upkeeping of this house, and its property taxes, which reached five thousand dollars per year. *Ohio Historical Society*

WIFE AND LOVERS

The marriage of the ebullient and irreligious William Tecumseh Sherman and the private and intensely pious Roman Catholic Ellen Ewing Sherman (1824–1888), shown here in 1873, was difficult and frequently vituperative from its start in 1850. They spent as much of their marriage apart, writing angry letters to each other, as together. However, following his mental breakdown during the first year of the war, she actively campaigned to save his career. *Ohio Historical Society*

After the Civil War, Sherman found far more intimate pleasures with other women, most notably in the 1870s with the sculptor Vinnie Ream, shown here, and in the 1880s with Mary Audenreid, the young widow of his chief of staff. *State Historical Society of Wisconsin, WHi(X3) 9605*

BELOVED DAUGHTERS

Elly Sherman Thackara

Rachel Sherman Thorndike

Although Sherman's relationships with his two surviving sons, Tom (1856–1933) and Philemon ("Cumpy") (1867–1941), were often tensely authoritarian, he indulged his four daughters, Minnie (1851–1913), Lizzie (1852–1925), Elly (1859–1915), and Rachel (1861–1919), both materially and emotionally. When their mother entered deep reclusiveness after the Civil War, Rachel and Minnie served as Sherman's hostesses and homemakers. Rachel waited until she was thirty, eleven months after her father's death, to marry Paul Thorndike. *Ohio Historical Society*

FROM FATHER TO SON

At the conclusion of the war, the general passed on the moral lessons of the great marches through Georgia to the sea and then back up through the Carolinas, to his admiring nine-year-old son, Tom. Willy (1854–1863), Tom's older brother and the apple of his father's eye, had died while visiting his father's camp near Vicksburg. His parents mourned together, deeply, for a very long time. Tom seemed to know that he could never measure up to the ghost of the sainted Willy. *Ohio Historical Society*

In 1878, Tom's announcement that he would not go into law and take care of family business as his father had planned, but join the Jesuit order instead, shocked and infuriated his father. It was as if Tom had fled his father's world for his mother's. Tom slipped into a deep depression for most of the last thirty years of his life until his death in 1933. *Ohio Historical Society*

THE LION IN WINTER

Sherman sat for Augustus Saint-Gaudens in 1887, who in his bust was rather kind to the weathered veteran, who is more accurately captured as he stares at the camera in contemporaneous photographs. *The Pennsylvania Academy of the Fine Arts* (top), *Ohio Historical Society* (bottom)

LAST RITES

On February 22, 1891, the Sherman funeral cortege moved through solemn and thronged St. Louis streets to Calvary Cemetery where Sherman was buried beside Ellen and little Willy. *Ohio Historical Society*

But perhaps more representative of his life was the monument Sherman's men had helped to make, and a Union photographer had preserved, of Columbia, South Carolina, on the morning after the fires of February 17, 1865. This utter defeat of the South was his indelible accomplishment. *Henry E. Huntington Library and Art Gallery*

. . . a call no one could resist," and so he spoke for fifteen minutes, "earnestly and rationally." He was certain the "audience realized I was in earnest, that I apologized *not* for the past, but insisted that we were, and must continue to be an United People . . . that we had reason to be satisfied with the Past, and hopeful of the Future." All in all, the old scourge of the South felt that he, and by extension the outcome of the Civil War, had been accepted on his own terms, that he had been "as much at home as in St. Louis," and that "there is no reason why we may not safely rely in the future," as any current sectional tensions were but "trifling in comparison to what we had to face in 1861." This was a dignified, mutually respectful truce between Sherman and the South, although it remained tentative and even forced, rather than being a Methodist love feast.

Privately, Sherman condemned the South for what he perceived as its developmental backwardness and cultural slothfulness. In his Yankee consciousness, the highest compliment he could pay a Southerner was to say that some portions of the South resembled the North. To Willard Warner, an old Northern friend who had invested heavily in hilly northern Alabama, Sherman wrote concerning northern Georgia and eastern Tennessee as well: "Your country is not Southern but Northern—where water freezes, and wheat grows—where the hickory, oak and chestnut groves are Northern, and it is a misnomer to call it Southern. Because slavery ever existed there don't affect the laws of Nature." To right that historical affront to geography, Sherman proposed that these lands "be taken up in small farms by Germans or Yankees," and then "the social question and even the political question would soon be settled." In this recapitulation of an old fantasy about Northern colonization in the South, which he had shared with many political abolitionists before the war, Sherman indicated the degree to which his underlying contempt for Southern society remained unreconstructed. Yankee displacement, if it transpired, would soon set the South on the path to national progress.

Concomitantly, Sherman urged several younger Southern men of action among his acquaintanceship to leave the impoverished South for the progressive North and West. For example, in 1861, Sherman told his old protégé, David F. Boyd, now president of "our old college," Louisiana State University, that he ought simply to abandon the parsimonious Louisiana legislature and the backwater institution. "You have clung to the South for too long. You have allowed your heart [the Southern organ] to govern your head [the Northern organ]. The commonest of the common schools of Iowa outrank in public estimation your university—popular, prosperous, rich states have arisen since you have been struggling in Louisiana." If Boyd disbelieved Sherman, who Sherman agreed was perhaps not an impartial judge of the South, Sherman urged him to use his head to examine the 1880 census tables, "and see where flows the strongest currents of our new life—get into it and keep in it—and it may lead you into a better place. You can hardly get into a worse." Benighted Boyd followed Sherman's advice to an extent, leaving LSU for the headmastership of a series of military academies in Virginia and Kentucky, in the somewhat less decayed upper South. Sherman did not really fear that the impoverished South would rise again.[6]

In his heart, as in his orations, Sherman the prophet of progress was quite certain that as for the continental United States, the Civil War had been the war to end all wars. Although he cautioned perpetual vigilance, he did not look for the need to return to the militaristic moral totalism that had characterized his great public pronouncements during the last year of the war. He looked upon his prior militarism as only a necessary episode rather than as a general policy. Only the most dire of causes might lead him to reopen this position, not that he regretted it at all, but that he found it unnecessary as a permanent position to assume in peacetime, progressive America.

It was with this sensibility that, on August 11, 1880, Sherman addressed five thousand veterans at the Ohio State Fair, in what has become known as his "War Is Hell" speech. In this brief, impromptu address, which followed a speech by President Hayes, Sherman admonished the youths in the crowd, "there is many a boy here today who looks on war as all glory, but, boys, it is all hell. You can bear this warning voice to generations yet to come. I look upon war with horror, but if it has to come I am here." At this point the crowd broke into an ovation. Sherman and the veterans were bearing witness to the horrors of war, in part to inoculate their sons against the sort of war fever then on the rise in Europe. But Sherman did not disown force for pacifism. He opposed cheap militarism, but he stood ready for another bout of war fought his way if need be. War and peace remained absolute opposites for him, and in peace he was an ardent man of peace. Yet he did not disown, nor did he regret, the morally total warrior he had been, even when he celebrated peace. The iron fist remained inside his well-worn glove.[7]

In addition to his ceaseless patriotic procession across America, like many men of his generation and class, Sherman also traveled to Europe to see the Old World, and in his case, to show himself and his flag, to find much of interest, but even more important, to reaffirm that his America really was a superior civilization. Just as Sherman believed there was a natural progression of the races, with whites, of course, at the apex, so did he believe that there was a progression of nations, with the United States, of course, at the pinnacle. Naturally, he found his prejudices confirmed by his travels.

At the bottom were the Turks and the Egyptians, who were not exactly white in his opinion. He found Cairo "a hard-looking old adobe town," he wrote Ellen, somewhat akin to the Mexican, with a similarly mongrelized and debased population—"a conglomeration of men women and children of some twenty different breeds with camels, donkeys, horses, dogs & vermin." These really were savages, and pretentious ones to boot. "I would sooner undertake to move the pyramids than the prejudices of a race that claims to have given civilization" to the world, "yet who look to me and talk and act just like our Indians." Only slightly higher on the scale of peoples were the Spanish. Although Sherman was presented to the king, he was far more impressed in Madrid by the lack of "comforts that every house in the United States possesses," he informed John. Not only did Madrid lack good plumbing, but as he noted to Ellen, in the countryside all the farm implements "looked like the times of Moses, and such a thing as a McCormick reaper . . . would be an innovation that would cause a riot among the laborers."

Not surprisingly, as Sherman moved northward in Europe, he found more signs of progress, which is to say more similarity with the advanced qualities of the northern United States. "Switzerland seemed more like our own country," he told the historian George Bancroft, then United States minister to Berlin, "inasmuch as people there live more on their own farms, though small, and all the people seemed active, industrious and cheerful." But Switzerland was a small place, almost Ohio-like, as opposed to the grander nations of the continent. In Berlin, General von Moltke greeted him with a warmth that made Sherman see him as a kindly old duffer, but "the emperor and the two warrior princes" snubbed him, making him feel that Berlin had a "frigid atmosphere." Rather than meeting an authentic military hero, the German royals remained at Potsdam to entertain the distinctly second-rate "Royal Visitor Humbert from Italy." Sherman was damned if he would truckle to the emperor. "I will have seen but little of this Court," he sniffed to John Jay, the United States minister to Austria, "and confess that I do not feel disposed to ask the favor, unless some little sign of cordiality or welcome is volunteered." The official French of the highest stations stayed similarly aloof, and Sherman could not warm to their imperial hauteur. Interestingly enough, the Russian military princes welcomed him warmly, and Sherman was quite impressed with their professional élan and what he saw as the efficiency of their national government, road system, hotels, telegraph, and so forth. In later years he would urge that his junior officers mingle with the Russians and English, rather than the French or Germans.

If he found easier rapport with the English, which might have been expected, and with the Russians, which might not, Sherman understood that the most significant national collision on the continent remained between France, which he disliked, and Germany, which he also disliked. He judged France as decadent and somewhat frivolous, using as his main basis of analysis the superabundance of elegant Parisian fashion salons. His daughter Minnie, who accompanied Sherman on his trip, supplied him with his contact in that department, when she shopped at a vigorous pace. On his return, Sherman had to join his wife in "looking over the unpacked contents of many trunks . . . on which I make the usual sage commentary," Sherman wrote a friend. "No wonder the whole world is bankrupt—when Paris tempts our girls & men too with such useless articles of luxury." Sherman was convinced that "so long as Paris remains Paris," it would be "easy of conquest to so hardy a race as the Germans," as had proved to be the case eight years earlier during the Franco-Prussian War. Thus Sherman downgraded the effeminate and degenerate French while marking up the Germans in their next likely military contest, only to mark down the Germans at the same time as barbarians. Inferentially, America was vigorous but not barbarian, comfortable but not degenerate, just about right.[8]

Although he found his trip interesting, although he found ready reinforcement for his faith in American superiority wherever he traveled,

Sherman did not get deep pleasure from his grand tour. Nowhere did adoring crowds greet him to a surfeit; nowhere did the national elite rush to meet the conqueror of Georgia and the Carolinas. At times, Sherman felt slighted by his countrymen as well, particularly when he found out that the American man-of-war sent to take him on a cruise through the Mediterranean had been reassigned elsewhere, purposely redirected, Sherman believed, by Grant. Once more it was Washington, "that damned place," that had "deprived me of a pleasure dreamed of for a lifetime," Sherman raged to Admiral Porter. To John he wrote that he was embarrassed by this failure of tact, which made the nation rather than Sherman look abandoned "to drifting about, dependent on chance opportunities," to traveling from capital to capital with a small, unofficial party, rather than in a more regal procession as befit a major hero of a great nation. Nevertheless, he insisted to John five weeks later, that because of his own stature, "I am everywhere received with as much distinction as if in a Man of War." The American ministers greeted him and showed him about; the foreign princes smiled civilly, even if many must have been somewhat mystified by the importance their guest seemed to claim for himself from all who met him.[9]

Back home, ceaseless travel and endless lionization could lose the charms of immediacy over the decades—become elements of the problems attendant on the icon more than parts of an inspiriting escape from Washington dreariness. As he neared the end of his long postwar official life, Sherman came to feel that his level of success left him jaded. For example, he penned a lengthy string of complaints about the tediousness of it all in a February 28, 1882, letter to Christopher C. Augur, who at that point was in charge of the army post in San Antonio, which Sherman was about to visit. "Please don't load us with balls, parties or dinners—we are sick of them, and it is partly to escape such things that we leave Washington." But of course Augur, his wife, and his officers would have been terribly disappointed to hide their grand old man, and so Sherman was not granted his request for a little peace and quiet. In another sector of his public life, Sherman felt besieged by the unending piles of requests for his photograph and his autograph. This demand, which cost him $400 or $500 each year, he found "indelicate and hard" to refuse. Finally, in 1883, he figured out the expedient of placing an engraving of his likeness, done by J. C.

McCurdy, for sale in bookshops across the nation, a strategy that would both "relieve my conscience," he concluded, and save him a lot of money.

As far as Ellen Ewing Sherman was concerned, her husband's life had become completely public, and so had hers, and she hated the spotlight. She wrote him in 1882 that he was always out "travelling so desperately," away from Washington and from his family, and yet was ever present in the press, not as her husband, but as some heroic presence. The "newspaper fiends" were forever rooting about looking for anything to discuss about the Shermans. "Papers and telegrams leave us nothing to say. Even if we were dead . . . they would be obliging enough to notify you by public telegraph." To the angry Ellen, who craved her privacy increasingly over the years, and in many ways to himself as well, Sherman really had become a Great American Hero as opposed to a person. So public had he become that he had lost track of the private man. So much had he become transformed into a national persona, a changeover he really had pursued, that in the end he seemed curiously emptied of his soul, even to himself.[10]

THE MOST SIGNIFICANT and continuous way Sherman resisted his transformation into the complete icon, the greatest reassertion he made of his own humanity, was in his refusal to become president of the United States. In a sense, Sherman was denying the logical denouement of his iconicization—his story of glory ought to have culminated in the White House. Republicans, newspapers, and public opinion all agreed on this. But where Sherman performed his role as peripatetic prophet of American Progress, grudgingly when not willingly, he drew the line at the nation's highest position. In his stubborn refusal to complete his public legend, he was asserting some essential privacy of person, checking his own ego, pride, and vanity, and insisting on a little realism about himself and his place in American history. Yet it must be added that he was also seeking to preserve his fame untarnished by the nastiest of public offices.

In every single public election, from 1868 through 1888, many friends and Republican wheelhorses sought to draft him for the office, and in each instance Sherman declined with steadfastness and a complete lack of equivocation. The problem was never that he was ambiguous but that "they" never took no for an answer. The most famous episode of this continual refusal came in 1884, after he had retired from his generalship, when Sherman refused a certain Republican nomination by wiring to their convention, "I will not accept if nominated and will not serve if elected." He meant it and the Republicans finally realized he did.

Elements in the Republican Party had gone after Sherman in earnest for the first time in February 1868, though there were feelers of a sort in 1864. To one of his would-be backers, a newly elected senator from California, Sherman wrote from St. Louis, "the more I see of politicians the more averse I become to be one of them, and have long since resolved that in no event will I allow the use of my name as a candidate . . . for President." This of course was but a reiteration, at a somewhat higher plane, of Sherman's contempt for politicians, and behind that, for politics, American style, which had always been one of his most cherished prejudices. "I never was a democrat or republican or a politician in any manner, form or shape," he insisted to his would-be California backer. This theme would remain central in Sherman's great refusal. As a corollary to his antipolitical thesis, Sherman asserted in this letter that "I have too much regard for my own comfort and reputation to be drawn into a canvass." This was in part laziness and in larger part concern for his hard-won military fame, which he was quite certain could only be diminished by the presidency, as well as because of his feeling against politicians. Interestingly enough, at this point, Sherman was quite certain that his close comrade, Grant, would also brush aside the boom on his behalf publicly, as he had to Sherman in private. "I wish he were more outspoken" in his refusal, Sherman worried, for he had begun to fear that Grant would listen to popular clamor. "Grant don't want to be a candidate, and will only consent in my opinion if he judges that his acceptance is necessary to save the country."

Grant's disastrous experience as president certainly affirmed Sherman in his own stance. He had been stung personally by Grant's weakness and incompetence as president, but Sherman was even more deeply impressed by the slaughter of Grant's reputation for honor and glory, which he had won through so much duress on the battlefields of the Civil War. To the historian John W. Draper, a prominent backer of Sherman's candidacy in 1875, Sherman wrote that Grant had thought at the start of his administration that he would "consolidate all that was good & great" in the nation, but that he was "hardly seated" in office when the Republican harpies convinced him that "he must make a Strict Party Government." Then Grant had begun to go "square back on his old tried and trusted friends," like Sherman, and instead had "put his destiny in the hands of . . . strangers of supposed fidelity & experience," who had proved to be a pack of crooks. And after the presidency, "the remainder of his days hold out little prospect of honor or ease. When he leaves the White House he will slip out of sight and it may be worse." Sherman feared that Grant might even be indicted for the crimes of his false friends.

In 1879, turning aside the appeal to run by the Reverend W. G. Eliot, an old friend who was president of Washington University in St. Louis and a prominent Missouri Republican, Sherman refused vividly to become an entrapped man as had Grant. "[I saw Grant] who never swerved in War, bend and twist and writhe under the appeals and intrigues from which there was no escape." This was a claustrophobic image, deeply telling for the vagabond who had by this point come to hate the trappings of his far lesser Washington office.

Not for me Grant's fate—no, no, no! Sherman reiterated over the years. "I see the *Herald* is out in full for me as President," Sherman had written to John in 1871. "You may say for me, and publish it too, that in no event will I ever be a candidate for President." No, he insisted yet again to John in 1874, "I would rather revert to my old [1861] station of President of the 5th Street Railroad than be President of the United States."

Not merely Grant, but nineteenth-century generals as a class had made unfortunate presidents, in Sherman's opinion. Generals got themselves flattered into running on the grounds that they could be above partisanship and politics, only to discover when they took office that they were controlled by the same wicked politicians who had flattered them into their bad choice. Sherman often used this argument as a larger case against running to reinforce the specific one provided by his pathetic comrade, Grant. "I recall too well the personal experiences of Generals Jackson, Harrison, Taylor, Grant, Hayes and Garfield," all of whom had been tempted by the siren voice of flattery, Sherman told an old Iowa military comrade who now had strong ties to his state's Republican machine. "It is too like the case of a girl who marries a drunken lover in the hope to reform him. It never has succeeded and never will."

There was no reason to believe that military men had any special qualifications for the presidency, Sherman believed. In this case he was quite capable of taking a clear and realistic view not only of other generals but of General William T. Sherman as well. He rather liked and admired Rutherford B. Hayes, for example, but by 1879 it was clear that Hayes too had failed, and would be a forgettable one-term president. "In Hayes position I would likely do pretty much as he does," Sherman admitted to a trusted St. Louis friend, "certainly no better. The country is full of his equals, and I propose to leave the office to them."

Sherman also believed that the office in itself was overrated. He had had a long-term, clear-eyed, and up-close view of the presidency, and he understood how powerless it was in comparison to Congress, cabinet, and political appointees. "The President is a mere executor of laws made by others, over which he exercises a doubtful control. He must take things as he finds them, and cannot purify Congress or the public administration, though the world holds him responsible for both, and the chances are that at the end of his four years, instead of acquiring fame or fortune, he loses both." This was an accurate assessment of the nineteenth-century, pre–Teddy Roosevelt, pre–imperial presidency. The president was only a queen bee. Once elevated by his friends to his supposedly "exalted position," Sherman argued, they "cease all honest work and turn to you for honors and support. You may grant the 99, but refusing the hundredth, you become a monster of ingratitude." All is trial and betrayal—and abandonment, that deepest-seated fear of Sherman's, and former presidents were kicked out from their hive and left to buzz about the country with only their tattered reputations.

The most serious attempt to make Sherman president was in 1884, when the Republicans were running especially scared, and would finally lose the presidency after they nominated their first nongeneral since 1864, the somewhat unsavory James G. Blaine, against Grover Cleveland. In responding to this push for him, Sherman added to his earlier and sufficient reasons for refusing the office new ones that came from even deeper in the core of his identity. To John, on November 28, 1883, he asserted the significance of "my family complications on the Catholic question. . . . The ruling class of our country is Anglo-Saxon and ought to remain so. They abhor the dogmas of that Church," and the way the Church "substitutes its authority on earth as above that of Kings." Sherman agreed with that set of judgments. Neither, however, did he wish to humiliate Ellen or himself by answering the questions newspapermen undoubtedly would pose concerning his loyalties. "I have had enough troubles on that score and want no more." As in his reading of the powers of the presidency, his assessment of American anti-Catholicism as it was practiced in 1883 was quite accurate. At long last, and in great irony, Sherman could make some use of his wife's religious obsessions in a way to help rather than injure his personal desires.

Even more telling was Sherman's heartfelt declaration, in the same letter to his brother, the Republican insider, that he hated the Republican Party. "When the Republicans were in a vast majority they attacked & insulted the very army which rescued them from destruction. . . . I owe the Republican Party nothing, and shall not sacrifice myself for it." Among the other benefits of his great refusal, here Sherman had expressed his real resentments at how the Republicans had abused him and his army. Therefore, his denial offered him a measure of revenge.

Knowing the general's extremely low opinion of the Republican Party, John Sherman used patriotism as his final appeal to reel in his brother to a presidential candidacy. If the country calls, he argued, one is not at liberty to decline. But the general rejected that inducement as absurd. To John Schofield, he insisted that "the country cannot call—a party by its convention may call, but that is not the country and I would be a fool to respond to such a call." Nor was it just the Republican Party that was evil: "Both parties are alike." Political parties and the political process were corrupt, not just this or that party. If he believed that the American people loved him now—"I have abundant faith in the honesty and gratitude of the whole nation"—he told Schofield, he had no faith whatsoever in the political system, "not a particle in that of any political party. They sacrificed you . . . at West Point," during the Whittaker affair, "they would do the same to me today if by doing so they could make 50 votes."

Sherman did not think that he could reach over the heads of the parties and of Congress directly to the American people. Neither did he believe that he could reform the democratic process where so many good men had failed before him. All he could do would be to refuse to allow himself to be the next sacrificial general to those nasty parties and that distasteful system. He would refuse to become a politician, he would remain a military hero—that would be sufficient unto his honor—and he would remain a beloved, superpolitical icon. He wrote to his cousin, James G. Blaine, who had first supported Sherman before going after the losing 1884 nomination for himself, that during the Civil War, "I simply did a man's fair share of work to perfectly accomplish peace," and therefore had won "an absolute right to rest." Let politicians like Blaine, who had been "schooled in the arts and practices" of their craft, "now do their work equally well." Enough. Sherman had proved everything he needed to prove to his own satisfaction. In 1884 he made his declaration of self against his previously ever-inflating role as icon. He would go off into retirement free of the demands of the political world, a world in which he had been neither happy nor successful. He would avoid becoming another hapless and joyless one-term Republican puppet president. He would remain the eternal vagabond, but to a certain extent, he reclaimed plain citizen William T. Sherman from General of the Army and Maximum Hero Sherman.[11]

18

Feuds:
The Tests of
Honor

DREARY OFFICEHOLDING and wandering iconicization hardly
exhausted William T. Sherman's postwar energies: As did many
old soldiers, he found a great outlet in conducting feuds—peacetime
equivalents to combat. So recently leaders of the epic national struggle,
when they had been lionized by the public, now aging generals were
rusticated in their occupational backwater while Americans passed
from wartime to peacetime concerns, such as making money and having fun, and while entrepreneurs and entertainers captured popular attention. One means for military men to regain visibility as well as to
shore up their egos was to slander one another as loudly as possible,
particularly in the press. In this activity, given his gifts for invective
and phrasemaking, Sherman shone.

Sherman and his military cohorts did not refight old battles as ends
in themselves; rather, in addition to gaining publicity, they sought
through their feuding to reinforce the boundaries of their own honor at
the expense of those who impugned it. Honor was served most vividly
through expression of its obverse—dishonor—which was always projected onto others. This led to a cycle of attack and self-defense
through attack—always phrased, of course, as repelling an attack. In
this process, one had bands of supporters and circles of enemies, which
in the end tended to include almost every major player in the war, as
well as the masses of veterans who served under them. Most often, one

feuded with fellow officers of one's own army. Indeed, one of the curiosities of post–Civil War feuds is the frequency with which officers praised their former enemies, even while attacking former colleagues.

There was a rather elaborate formalism to this feuding—rules of combat, so to speak. And these feuds had political as well as personal meanings so long as the feudists remained in public life. The competition of invective often ended only after the death of one of the combatants, at which time the survivors, in their eulogies, could at last positively reaffirm in the now safely dead soldier the ideal of the gentleman of honor. Yet even this posthumous honor could be withheld.

One hundred years earlier, these feuds would have proceeded from the insult to the dueling field. Although dueling had been organized in the same sort of elaborately ritualized manner as post–Civil War feuding would be, its results so often had proved mortal that the life-affirming qualities of romantic, evangelical culture had led to its dismissal as a form of murder. Combat remained, even the language of the duel remained, but now the weapon of choice was the pen rather than the sword. As befit a democracy, American late-nineteenth-century military feuding was fought out in the mass-circulation newspapers and magazines. Given his opinion of the press and of democracy in general, William T. Sherman's employment of the press seems ironic, but he had already used it effectively many times during the war, when it had suited his purposes, even while professing to despise it.

In Sherman's case, among the haunting wartime issues that returned after peace were the supposed lack of Union preparedness to receive the Confederate attack at Shiloh, and the military significance that Don Carlos Buell's reinforcements made later that day. On another major Civil War issue, Sherman's 1864 appointment of West Pointer O. O. Howard from the Army of the Potomac to replace the fallen James B. McPherson also returned in various feuds. Disclosures of more private Civil War opinions, such as those Sherman aired (for Grant as well as for himself) in his *Memoirs,* concerning the slowness of General George Thomas to offer battle against Hood before Nashville late in 1864, also led to major public feuds. Sherman clearly was the aggressor in all these instances, although in other cases he was more of a victim. Never taking an insult passively, however, he was always quite eager for a fight. Sherman rarely let bad feelings go without exercising them.

When Elizabeth Halleck, Henry's widow, set about compiling her late husband's memoirs in 1873, she wrote Sherman concerning the long personal history the men had shared—dating back to the late 1830s, at West Point. Sherman replied, professing at the onset of his letter his perfect willingness to explain any event as fairly and warmly as he could. "We both lived in turbulent times, and were both strong natures, and that we should have collided was to be expected," Sherman admitted to the widow, though insisting that he would honor Halleck in death and put a finish to any feuding, as a gentlemanly officer ought to do. "I always endeavored to do him in life all possible honor, and in death to cherish in memory his better qualities, and of myself will not now raise a controversy unless it is forced upon me." Sherman then attempted to relate his version of the endgame of the Civil War in a detached manner, but when he recalled—even eight years later—Halleck's instructions from Richmond that other officers disregard Sherman's orders, at the time when Edwin M. Stanton was denouncing Sherman in the press as a traitor, Sherman's blood boiled over once more. Your husband was "treating me as an open rebel [and] I was filled with indignation, and my army openly clamored at the insult." Sherman then insisted to Elizabeth Halleck that his famous letter advising Halleck to remain indoors—perdu—when Sherman's troops had marched through Richmond, had been for Halleck's own good, as "I actually feared that . . . my men would publicly insult" him, perhaps even "using their fire-arms." Thus Sherman was able to pretend to express pacific posthumous feelings for his enemy of 1865, while at the same time justifying his position concerning the great insult Halleck had done him.

Despite this promise to Elizabeth Halleck in 1873 to avoid future raising of the ghosts of this wartime controversy, Sherman laid it out pretty thoroughly and publicly three years later in his *Memoirs*. Indeed, as late as 1886, in the *North American Review,* after paying tribute to their long friendship—"I had in him the most unbounded confidence in 1862"—and to Halleck's intellectual and legal acumen, as the "best-informed scholar of the military," Sherman went on dismissively, "but war is a terrible test. Halleck did not stand this test, whereas General Grant did. Halleck was a theoretical soldier [who had] dwindled into a mere Chief of Staff [by 1864]. Grant was a practical soldier [who] had earned such renown that he was enabled to dictate his own terms to the President and the Secretary of War." This assessment of Halleck's steep wartime decline was accurate, but it was nevertheless an ungracious and rather gratuitous reopening of an old assault on a man who was not alive to defend his honor.[1]

Such wartime victories over military rivals gave Sherman a distinct advantage in postwar feuds. In such cases he could bolster his own reputation by blasting another at little risk. For example, in June 1863, while a corps commander serving under Grant during the Vicksburg campaign, Sherman, with the partnership of James B. McPherson, another corps commander, combined with Grant to rid the western army of John A. McClernand, an Illinois political associate of Lincoln's, who was serving as major general in charge of yet another of Grant's corps. All three of these professional military men had deeply resented the way Lincoln had issued provisional instructions for McClernand to lead a strike against Vicksburg in November 1862, and then, in January 1863, had appointed him as a corps commander when Grant took charge of McClernand's overall operation.

McClernand proved to be a boastful, incompetent publicity-seeker, ever with an eye to his political future. After champing at the bit for months—while McClernand boosted himself at the expense of others, particularly Sherman—McPherson, Sherman, and Grant finally moved in concert following the publication, unauthorized by Grant, of a "Congratulatory Order" to his troops that McClernand had published at the height of the Vicksburg campaign in the June 13 issue of the Memphis *Evening Bulletin*. McClernand had bad-mouthed the corps of Sherman and McPherson, contrasting their actions with those of his own brilliantly generaled corps. Encouraged by their officers and men to strike back at the hated McClernand, first Sherman and then McPherson wrote Grant blistering defenses of their honor and that of their two corps against McClernand's debasing order.

The so-called order was a "catalogue of nonsense . . . an effusion of vainglory and hypocrisy," Sherman blustered. Rather than an order it was a "monstrous falsehood," ostensibly addressed to his soldiers, but "manifestly designed for publication for ulterior political purposes [and] the ends of flattery & self-glorification." Sherman called Grant's attention to an army regulation forbidding the publication of unauthorized official reports, the punishment for which would be dismissal by the president.

McPherson then weighed in, reflecting, he wrote Grant, the protests of every one of his division and brigade commanders, to McClernand's "vainglorious" attempt to "impress the public mind with the magnificent strategy, superior tactics and brilliant deeds" of himself while demeaning others. "Though 'born a warrior,' as he himself stated, he had evidently forgotten one of the most essential qualities, viz: that elevated refined sense of honor, which, while guarding his own rights with jealous care, at all times renders justice to others." Sherman, like McPherson, sought to defend their honor through demonstrating McClernand's violation of that very code: He was no warrior at all and must be eliminated if honor in principle, as well as their honor in particular, was to be served.

Grant then dismissed McClernand, subject to the approval of the president. He did this knowing that he was removing an old friend of Lincoln's, in fact arguing that he had long tolerated McClernand in his "earnest desire," as he put it delicately, to carry on "without interference with the assignments to command which the President alone was authorized to make." Grant thus, despite his own deep contempt for McClernand, used the pressure from Sherman and McPherson to demonstrate the spirit of reluctant necessity out of which he had dismissed McClernand. "It was only when almost the entire Army under my command moved to demand it, that he was relieved," Grant assured Lincoln.

Twelve years later, when Sherman's *Memoirs* attacked McClernand again, reminding a vast American readership of his disgrace, McClernand wrote another old general whom Sherman had disparaged during the war that this was just the sort of viciousness one ought to have expected from a man whose "abnormal ambition and egotism . . . have crazed and betrayed him. . . . Dignities, emoluments and homages are not sufficient to satisfy him." Rather, he turns on others "cynically" and with "malice" to make himself look better. "True greatness has a very different bent. It is always magnanimous and generous." McClernand used the same standard of honor and dishonor as had McPherson and Sherman against him in 1863, simply reversing the actors. The asymmetry in this feud was one of power. Sherman, McPherson, and Grant had been able to use the code of honor to destroy McClernand's army career, while, years later, with Sherman still disparaging him, McClernand could only fume in private to another similarly debased old soldier.[2]

When McPherson had been killed in battle on July 22, 1864, Sherman brought in O. O. Howard to replace him as commander of the Army of the Tennessee, thereby creating two lifelong enemies, with whom he would feud for decades: Joseph Hooker and John A. Logan. After failing signally as commander of the Army of the Potomac, where he was Howard's superior, Hooker had been moved west as a corps commander under Grant. Therefore, when Sherman replaced McPherson with his former subordinate in a job Hooker believed should be his by virtue of senior rank and service in the army, he requested to be relieved of command. "Justice and self-respect alike require my removal from an army in which rank and service are ignored." Sherman was extremely pleased that Howard's appointment had had this secondary effect. "I must be honest and say he is not qualified or suited" to lead the Army of the Tennessee, Sherman wrote Halleck. "He is not indispensable to our success." Six weeks later, in another letter to Halleck, Sherman called Hooker "a fool."

After publication of Sherman's *Memoirs,* Hooker, by then a stroke victim living quietly in Garden City, Long Island, managed to gain a certain public satisfaction for this old insult when he told an enterprising reporter who visited him that he was disgusted by Sherman's "slanders." The retired general professed to "feel indignant at the desecration of the honored names" of others Sherman had defamed, presenting himself as the stoic, taking abuse and staying above the fray of Sherman's creation, thus displaying his continuing honor and Sherman's dishonor. He then got in his own digs. Sherman had "made war like a brigand, while many other generals never forgot that they were making war on their own countrymen." Sherman had left a "black streak in his rear" in Georgia and the Carolinas, which in some future time would "be considered disgraceful by the Christian world." He could not resist adding that "if Sherman is now ignored by the administration he has only himself to thank for it." Hooker's conclusion was that Sherman had been forced to the political periphery by Grant, who had discovered "the character of his lieutenant long before the war had ended."[3]

Sherman's decision to choose Howard to replace McPherson offended John A. Logan as well, and this evolved into a far more serious matter. Unlike Hooker, Logan was a popular and an extremely energetic and capable corps commander, one who had a powerful political career after the war, which armed him to feud right back far more effectively than Halleck, McClernand, or Hooker. Moreover, Logan had been McPherson's temporary replacement as commander of the Army of the Tennessee, a role he had assumed in the middle of a battle and had handled with excellence. Thus his reduction to command of his old corps had appeared to be a rebuke. At the time Sherman sang Logan's praises, even while bringing in Howard over him. Logan had "managed" the army "well," Sherman wrote Halleck, "and it may be that an unfair inference might be drawn to his prejudice, because he did not succeed to the permanent command." Yet Sherman could not resist adding that the choice of a permanent successor to McPherson had been a "delicate and difficult task," and that "instead of giving reasons I prefer that the wisdom of that choice be left to the test of time." He had meant no "disrespect" to Logan, who had "submitted with the grace and dignity of a soldier, gentleman, and patriot" to the return to his corps, all of whom continued to "love and respect" him.

Logan had first heard of his demotion not from Sherman himself but from the War Department in a formal letter. He tried to rationalize this at first. "I suppose this was all right as Howard is from the Potomac army, etc.," he told his wife, apparently accepting Howard's superior professional credentials. Soon afterwards, however, he began to burn with indignation, believing that, despite his record in the western army, Sherman had displaced him with an outsider, merely because Howard was, like Sherman, one of the West Point clique while Logan was a civilian volunteer.

Sherman did feel some guilt or at least regret, both then and after, over this decision. He did believe Logan to be a capable general, and to some degree he acknowledged that he had downgraded Logan in his mind as another politician and military opportunist.

To try to make amends, at the close of the war Sherman brought Howard to his side for the grand review in Washington, and placed Logan in command of the Army of the Tennessee. When he heard rumors of this, a bruised and wary Logan wrote his wife, "God only knows" if it would be done, and added, "I am sure I shall not ask it, as I have been so treated once before. I have nothing to expect at the hands of these men." When he got out of the service, he expected "to live a more quiet life than formerly."

In this case, however, what went around came around, for Logan became a political powerhouse as an Illinois congressman, capable of redressing old grievances in material ways. By 1870, he had risen to the chairmanship of the House Military Affairs Committee, and launched a reform bill that not only chopped ruthlessly at the budget and size of the army but attacked the pay and privileges of senior officers, and even threatened the future existence of West Point. Logan got only part of what he wanted, but that was a great deal—and it amounted to a substantial measure of revenge as well.

Sherman had absolutely no doubt, as he told his brother, that much of this attack was personal. "Logan will never forgive me for putting Howard in McPherson's place." He still insisted that Logan had not been qualified. "Logan was always full of prejudice & always removing to the rear to make speeches & political capital." Thus Sherman indirectly affirmed to his brother that he had demoted Logan on caste grounds—West Point versus citizen soldier—just as Logan had believed.

Logan stayed on the offensive, chipping away at army appropriations whenever he could. In retirement he wrote an obsessively long and angry book entitled *The Volunteer Soldier of America,* praising the militia and the naturally risen officer and damning the professional military as elitist, self-serving, and dangerous to a democracy. Logan's attack was principled as well as personal, and Sherman recognized this. He also continued to recall Logan's considerable military talents, and on some level the aging feudists remained capable of words of generosity to and about one another. Nevertheless, their feud damaged not only Sherman's sense of honor, but the army, which was caught in the cross fire.[4]

Another feud that carried long-term political ramifications occurred between Sherman and George Thomas, commander of the third of Sherman's army that Sherman detached from his main force while he marched to the sea, to go north and block Hood's advance into Tennessee. Sherman, like Grant, had maintained ambivalent rather than openly hostile feelings about Thomas during the war. Both admired his bravery and intelligence while being annoyed with his ponderous and tentative approach to combat. In his turn, Thomas was aware of the feelings of his superiors, and he was dubious of Sherman's talents, for he considered the man both flighty and impetuous. More implicit than explicit, this feud never broke wide open during the war, but there was a long-term clash of temperaments where there might have been more fellow feeling and empathy.

While marching on Atlanta, Sherman wrote with impatience to the departed Grant that his "chief source of trouble is [Thomas's] Army of the Cumberland, which is dreadfully slow. A fresh furrow in a plowed field will stop the whole column, and all begin to intrench." Thomas was also hindered by an enormous personal baggage train, the sort used by old-fashioned commanders. "I have again and again tried to impress on Thomas that we must assail and not defend; we are the offensive," and yet, "from its commander down to the lowest private," Thomas's army is "habituated to the defensive." Sherman was convinced that this posture had already deprived his army of at least two decisive victories. On the other hand, at times, particularly in victory, Sherman could acknowledge that he was impatient by nature and that the more deliberate Thomas had virtues. After Atlanta fell, Sherman wrote to Halleck that "George Thomas, you know, is slow, but as true as steel," which was greater praise than he had for his other major lieutenants. And as he approached Savannah, aware that Thomas was near a major battle with Hood, he wrote Grant, "I know full well that General Thomas is slow in mind and in action, but he is judicious and brave and the troops feel full confidence in him."

Thomas also irritated Grant. As Hood marched north, Grant agonized at Thomas's failure to move out of Nashville, and prodded him with increasing exasperation. On December 1, 1864, Grant wrote Sherman, "I have said all I could to force him to attack," and later he wrote in understatement that "it has been very hard work to get Thomas to attack Hood. I gave him the most peremptory order, and had started to go there myself before he got off."

When he did get off, Thomas smashed Hood's army to pieces on December 15 and 16, and both Grant and Sherman were quick to commend Thomas for his magnificent victory. Neither man had ever sought to destroy Thomas as they had McClernand, for example, and, when departing for Nashville immediately before the battle, Grant probably had not intended to replace him but merely to prod him. Indeed, from internal evidence it seems unlikely that Thomas even knew at the time that Grant was on his way. Victory stilled criticism and dampened an incipient quarrel. Despite Thomas's victory at Nashville, however, much of the implicit negative judgment of him remained, as evidenced by Grant as late as March 1865, when he wrote Sherman that "knowing Thomas to be slow beyond excuse," he had "depleted" Thomas's army to reinforce other, more active generals, for the final campaigns of the war.

Several months earlier, Sherman had attempted, during times of severe martial peril, to put this sort of negative judgment-making and bickering between commanders in some sort of perspective. He wrote that when he had taken over the western army in the spring of 1864, it had been "full of complaints, which I have labored hard to silence & think I have succeeded—though ready to break out at a flash. These little jealousies and mistrust where we have a common cause are terrible to me, and the more so because they are so difficult to break." In the end the grand strategy of splitting the western army worked perfectly, with glory enough to go around.

After the war, however, both Sherman and Thomas had their own veterans organizations, each of which believed its own general to have been the more heroic. Thus all the smoldering animosities broke into flames in 1875, five years after Thomas's death, when Sherman included long passages in his *Memoirs* disclosing publicly for the first time the negative feelings both Sherman and Grant had held of Thomas as well as their admiration of him. This quite accurate and full representation of what had been the complex feelings of Grant and Sherman for Thomas nevertheless seemed to Thomas's partisans ungenerous to their now-dead hero. They would admit no criticism, however evenhanded, of their favorite.[5]

Thomas's partisans were the most offended, but Buell, Hooker, Logan, Blair, and others had theirs, and even some of Grant's admirers believed that Sherman had taken retrospective glory at their hero's expense in his *Memoirs*. A former volunteer general and veteran Cincinnati journalist, Henry Van Ness Boynton, weighed into the *Memoirs* with his nasty attack, *Sherman's Historical Raid: The Memoirs in Light of the Record*. Sherman had attempted systematically to "claim the merit which belongs to others, and steps still beyond and attempts to belittle the deeds of men in no respect his inferior as Generals." Sherman's book was "the gigantic wrong of the false historian." Boynton then rummaged through military archives—to which he somehow had gained access—to prove, shotgun style, what a nasty fellow Sherman had been to Thomas and the others.[6]

Sherman, of course, was infuriated by Boynton's attack, not in the least because it was clear that someone with major governmental authority had given Boynton the run of unpublished and still-confidential official war records. Sherman was certain that it was Belknap, but it turned out to be Orville Babcock, Grant's private secretary. Many agendas were at work here, and it seems likely that Babcock's initial purpose had been to protect Grant's reputation. But as an ally of Belknap, Babcock might have also sought to help drive a wedge between

Grant and Sherman to aid Belknap. Ironically, Grant himself did not object in the least to Sherman's *Memoirs,* but by using Boynton, Babcock did succeed in alienating Sherman from Grant.

Assuming that it was his veteran enemy behind Boynton, Sherman wrote one of his circle of friends, "If Belknap wants to be noticed he must write on his own signature, and that he will not do. It is simply contemptible in him to use such a tool." This analysis went right to the core of the rituals of the feuds conducted by persons still in public life. Principals used surrogates to publish attacks on the character of others. This was the means by which principals could avoid appearing to dirty their own hands, while covertly sponsoring attacks on rivals.

In response to this "circle of fools," Sherman employed a surrogate of his own, Charles W. Moulton, a lawyer and journalist in Cincinnati, who was also his brother-in-law. Belknap had not written his own attack but had used a tool, Sherman wrote to Moulton; therefore he would "not notice such an adversary" as Boynton, which would be beneath his dignity. Moulton wrote back to Sherman, understanding Sherman's implicit request, that "no impartial person can read [his book] without a sentiment of disgust, and you must not descend to an altercation with him. . . . *You must not appear in this matter.*" Moulton did not propose that Boynton go unchallenged, however, and then gave words to Sherman's unarticulated desire. "You must imitate your assailants in that you must strike in the dark. Now who can you rely upon to come to the Front in this fight?" Moulton asked in the rhetorical voice of one of Sherman's loyal old soldiers. "*On me for one.* If you will undertake to furnish the facts, I will undertake to set them forth, but all of this must be profoundly confidential."

Answering conspiracy with conspiracy, Sherman bombarded his agent, Moulton, with instructions for specific forms of argumentation and texts to use. Sherman, his old legal friend Henry Hitchcock, Samuel M. Bowman, and General Jacob D. Cox, one of his corps commanders (who also wrote a long two-part defense of Sherman in the *Nation*), read and approved proofs of Moulton's lengthy counterattack, and Sherman sent them back "with a thousand thanks for your kind instrumentality." Moulton's effort, *The Review of General Sherman's Memoirs Examined, Chiefly in the Light of the Evidence,* implied at the outset that Boynton's attack had created "the impression that the book is an indirect production of the War Department," an impression strengthened by the "*ex cathedra style . . .* which indicates that the ideas were inspired by that office." Much of Moulton's response was an ad hominem attack on Boynton, though on the merits of Boynton's critique, Moulton argued that some controversial positions Sherman had taken were in fact true if a bit unpleasant. Thomas, for example, "was a little slow in executing military movements," but Sherman had given Thomas his positive due as well. "Slow or active, [Thomas's] fame is fixed and will continue to endure while the history of war shall last."[7]

Belknap's public disgrace over his bribe-taking the next year quite pleased Sherman, in part because Belknap took Boynton down too. *"I am glad that the* [scandal] *has come out,"* Sherman wrote his son, Tom, "for Belknap behaved shamefully [to me], finally employing that man Boynton to search in the war records for small extracts to combat my open declarations in the *Memoirs.* Now Belknap has fallen so hard that his acts will never give me any more trouble." To historian John W. Draper Sherman concluded happily that Belknap's "fall" had carried Boynton along with him, admitting however that he intended to write a second edition of his book that would "tone down some expressions which though literally true are impolitic."[8]

Indeed Sherman did feel regret over the long run for his more indelicate statements in his *Memoirs,* particularly those toward Thomas, even if the *Memoirs* had been accurate about the man's military ponderousness. To John Schofield, an admired associate of Thomas as well as of Grant and himself, Sherman wrote in November 1879, "we three knew Thomas better than any three men now living—we knew him inside and outside—We loved his great qualities and were charitable to his weaknesses—and what man has not such?" Privately, Sherman felt on the defensive, in part because of the continuing protests of Thomas's old soldiers. "I rejoice in his great popularity," Sherman told Schofield, referring to the veterans association for the Army of the Cumberland, which carried their hero, Thomas's, banner on high. Sherman was even preparing himself to sing Thomas's praises at the unveiling of Thomas's statue in Washington later that month.

As part of his attempt to make amends, Sherman wrote Grant to enlist him in filling out his picture of Thomas at the unveiling. He knew that Grant too bore Thomas the "most exalted respect," even though Grant had had to push Thomas very hard for the larger wartime good, because of what had "seemed slowness and deliberation when vehement and prompt action was called for." Thus, Sherman in effect handed Grant a script containing the correct posthumous line—to praise Thomas without denying Thomas's failings—as Sherman had done in his *Memoirs*. Sherman argued that this position would refute Boynton and "other pure mischiefmakers" who had suggested that Sherman and Grant had become "envious, jealous of [Thomas's] great fame and his deserved popularity."[9]

Thus, at the unveiling of the Thomas monument in 1879 Sherman recemented his ties to Grant, upheld his own reputation for veracity and honor, and smoothed out his memorializing of Thomas in a way to give less offense to Thomas admirers, while not retreating from his criticism of Thomas. Toward Boynton, however, he sustained his feud, for there was continuing emotional and propaganda capital in having such an unsavory and debased enemy—the sort of low fellow who would make one look good when carried as a public foe. Sherman felt more alive, more the man of action, when he could maintain a good hate than when he lacked one. Thus, it was with a keen eagerness—heightened by his hatred for newspapermen—that Sherman assaulted Boynton anew in 1880. This was the moment when he wrote an old acquaintance that the time had come to kick reporters and *"treat them as curs."* As for Boynton in particular, "like the whelp he is, he has gone crying to his Mama—I am not done with him yet."

In the war against the unforgivable Boynton, which was five years old by this time, Sherman had just given an interview to the *Cleveland Leader,* in which, either by design or, as seems more likely, by the inspiration of the moment, he opened up another phase of the feud. Moulton had torn Boynton's "pretentious criticisms to shreds," Sherman told the Cleveland reporter. "Everybody knows him to be a notorious slanderer. You could hire him to do anything for money." The reporter was rather struck by Sherman's vitriol and his candor—evidently Sherman did not ask the reporter to place this statement off the record. "Is he so bad as that?" the reporter asked, adding that many papers across the country praised Boynton as the "most truthful man on Newspaper Row and a Christian gentleman." Sherman replied, "A man of character and a Christian, bah! he is entirely without character. Why for a thousand dollars he would slander his own mother." Far from feeling he had gone too far with this reporter, a few days later, after the story had appeared, Sherman asserted to one of his old Civil War subordinates, "I conclude that I overestimated his price by setting it at a thousand dollars." Sherman was feeling grand about the emotional release this offensive brought him. He wanted Boynton to take the next step by suing him, for then he believed he could take Boynton apart in court, getting out into the open what he was certain had been a War Department conspiracy against him in 1875. Through this ritual he intended to gain a measure of public vengeance for all his years of humiliation in office.

Boynton rose to the bait, but only part of the way. He demanded in a letter that Sherman retract his statement in the Cleveland paper, but Sherman categorically refused to do so. Boynton, who had been a general of volunteers during the war, then tried to persuade the War Department to court-martial Sherman for conduct unbecoming an officer, but the secretary of war refused to oblige Boynton, judging such newspaper feuds to be outside his jurisdiction. At this point, Boynton threatened to sue in a civil court, which was just what Sherman desired. An astonishing number of men offered to testify on Sherman's behalf, and Sherman wanted Boynton in court and on the stand under oath—then out would come the truth. Sherman wrote an old ally that Boynton "had been paid by the war Department to write me down and to cause a break between Grant and myself." Boynton backed off, appearing the dishonorable coward, which in itself provided some reaffirmation of honor for Sherman.[10]

The tensions between Thomas's Army of the Ohio and Sherman's Army of the Tennessee, which reasserted themselves as post–Civil War feuds, had preceded Thomas's command of that army. On April 6, 1862, the Army of the Ohio, under the command of Don Carlos Buell, the selfsame general who had relieved the clinically depressed Sherman of his command in Louisville less than six months earlier, had reached Shiloh at the end of the first day of battle. Forever after, Buell's partisans liked to argue that Buell had saved the Union army, which had been rolled back in defeat before his arrival. Grant and Sherman always insisted they had stopped the Confederate advance themselves; indeed, they countercharged that Buell's men had taken unforgivably long to arrive at Shiloh, by which time any reinforcement they provided was a secondary matter.

A large part of the persistence behind Buell's self-aggrandizement over Shiloh stemmed from his later military passivity in Tennessee, which led to his removal in October 1862. After he was relieved he demanded a court-martial, which cleared his record of major wrongdoing but did not result in a new command. During and after the period of the court-martial, his closest associates, eager to repair his reputation, reopened the Shiloh issue. When one of them, J. C. Wright, without consulting Buell, attempted to act as Buell's surrogate to enlist Sherman in Buell's restoration, Sherman tried to warn him off, from pique rather than kindness. In any "personal controversies," which would surely arise if Shiloh were refought yet again in the press, Sherman wrote Wright on September 13, 1863, "Buell would get the worst of it." Rather, Buell and his supporters ought to seek active service "in the field in any capacity. . . . There should be no idlers now." Sherman warned Wright, the surrogate, that if he persisted in newspaper attacks on Sherman concerning Shiloh, "you are bound to advise Buell, and if he assents, he will repent it forever." Sherman threatened Buell, admonishing him to reclaim his reputation by taking a division in the command of someone whom he outranked. "When the war is over we may have a century in which to complain," Sherman added with considerable prescience. In April 1864, Sherman offered Buell his choice of two commands, both of which Buell refused. At that time, Sherman wrote to Colonel James B. Fry, formerly of Buell's staff and then in Washington, that there seemed to be a great deal of rumormongering coming from Buell's staff, which was being fed to "the damned newspaper scoundrels." Sherman was suggesting that he thought Fry himself might be that source. At about this time, Sherman wrote the editor of the *United States Service Magazine* that his soldiers still maintained memories of the "slow approach" of the Army of the Ohio to Shiloh on April 6, 1862.[11]

These festering wounds of honor burst open in 1884, when Fry published the old Shiloh rescue story in his hagiographical book, *Operations of the Army Under General Buell.* After reading it, Sherman exploded, and wrote a long denunciatory letter to Fry. "We, Grant's Army of the Tennessee, fought the first day of Shiloh without a particle of assistance from Buell." Indeed, Buell had been "derelict" in coming to the battle so "slowly and deliberately," Sherman insisted to Fry, and he had "not [been] over anxious to share our danger. . . . *And You know it.*" The second day of Union triumph had been a "walkover," for which Buell had not been needed. Fry responded by demanding a retraction of these charges, "which if true should consign Buell, me and others to infamy." Sherman had made, Fry countercharged, "deliberate, positive and specific statements injurious to the reputation of many esteemed soldiers." Fry threatened to turn Sherman's letter over to Buell and others, which meant publication as well. That was the protocol whereby private feuds between men of honor were made public and extensive. Realizing that he had impugned the motives of Buell beyond whatever might have been the disputed facts of the arrival of his army, Sherman wrote back to Fry withdrawing his charges and begging the return of the offending letter. Fry then mailed back Sherman's letter, and the feud did not go public but died down to its smoldering *status quo ante.* Coincidentally, as this heated exchange was occurring, Grant published in a periodical article his analysis of Shiloh, which, though written before Fry's book appeared, assessed the Battle of Shiloh much in the same manner as had Sherman.[12]

Privately aggrieved, Fry lay in wait, and a year later seized on an opportunity to go after Sherman's reputation in the most public and embarrassing way he could. Unbeknownst to Sherman, who dashed off dozens of letters weekly, Fry had gotten hold of one Sherman had written on September 5, 1885, during the angry Fry-Sherman exchange over Fry's book, to Captain R. M. Scott, the head archivist of the army's Civil War records. In an article in the prestigious *North American Review,* Fry quoted an apparently critical comment Sherman had made of Grant: "Had C. F. Smith lived, Grant would have disappeared to history after Donelson." In March 1862, Henry Halleck had placed Charles F. Smith in charge of Grant's army when he had temporarily removed Grant, partly on charges of drunkenness, but Smith had died the following month from accidental injuries just after Grant had been restored to command. Grant had just died when the *North American Review* published this article, and Fry could eulogize Grant while damning Sherman implicitly but clearly as Grant's dishonorably false friend. "Grant was one of the singular few who possessed qualities which probably would have gained for him a high place in history, no matter who had lived to compete with him in our great war," Fry wrote.

In the subsequent issue of the *North American Review,* the editor, Allen Thorndike Rice, wrote an editorial defending Sherman's honor vis-à-vis Grant, quoting another of Sherman's letters to Grant, written just before Grant's death, which had attested to his feelings of esteem for Grant's great qualities. Rice then editorialized on Sherman's behalf that Sherman had never inferred that Grant might not have come to the fore due to any lack of great qualities in himself. "It is proper to add," Rice concluded his editorial, "that General Sherman has called

on General Fry for his authority, and upon me to say that he repudi-
ates the sentiment attributed to him." With an eye to controversy and
sales as well as to the rules of honorable feuding, Rice also notified his
readers that Sherman and Fry were involved in an exchange of views
that would soon grace the pages of the *North American Review.*

In the following three monthly issues, and more widely in the newspapers, Fry and Sherman played out their feud before the public. Fry
stood by his position. Noting the "wide difference between repudiating
a position and denying the expression of it," Fry refused to furnish his
source until and unless Sherman should deny that "he used the language I have said he used." Sherman demanded the source; Fry refused
it. Sherman then wrote to Rice denying the "literal truth" of Fry's quotation. "Notify Fry that I believe he purposely and maliciously misrepresented me, and that the end is not yet," Sherman blustered. The
following day, December 17, 1886, Sherman wrote to the army adjutant general, requesting that the secretary of war demand that Fry, as
an officer of the army, disclose the source. "I surely take direct issue
with . . . the modern newspaper doctrine that a reporter may publish
any falsehood . . . leaving the victim to follow it up with a denial or
qualification." The secretary of war replied that although Fry might be
guilty of bad manners and discourtesy, his conduct did not make him
guilty of a breach of military law. Sherman was of course trying the
same route through the secretary of war that Boynton had attempted
against him in 1880, a maneuver Sherman had denounced at the time
as unmanly.

Sherman resumed his letters to the *North American Review,* increasing his personal invective against Fry. "Grant always regarded Fry as
one of the men most active in spreading the lies about us about Shiloh," Sherman wrote Rice, for publication. Fry was a seeker of "notoriety . . . he is Buell's mouth-piece," and the would-be champion of the
Army of the Cumberland. Sherman wrote that he and Grant "did not
know we had been surprised and slaughtered" at Shiloh; "we believed
that we had heroically defended our positions till reinforcements, *near*
and *long* expected, did arrive." Fry, "a man of words, not deeds," had
"invented" the quotation in question, falsely attempting to show
"friendship after death for the man in life he attempted to malign."
During the Civil War, Sherman and Grant had been "as brothers,"
Sherman concluded, insisting that it was "utterly impossible" that he
had written the phrases Fry had invented.

Sherman had fallen into Fry's rather obvious trap by denying that he had made the offending statement. In the following issue of the *North American Review* Fry disclosed his source and provided a facsimile copy of the letter Sherman had indeed written. Fry had damaged Sherman's honor by teasing Sherman's always barely suppressed anger out of him and into print. The following month, Sherman published a long essay in his defense. He admitted his authorship of the letter in question, but insisted that he had written it "hastily, *carelessly,*" and that Fry had quoted him so far out of context that his text amounted to a "*forgery.* . . . Can it be wondered that Sherman should be a little surprised that the habitual libeler of Grant," Sherman wrote of himself in the third person, "should attempt to assume the character of Grant's panegyrist at his expense?" If Fry thinks "he has achieved a cheap newspaper victory over Sherman he is welcome. The man who got off with my overcoat may keep it, for I have bought a new one." By declaring Fry a cheap purloiner of letters, Sherman attempted to maintain his dignity, though by allowing Fry to get his goat, he in fact had compromised his reputation.

Curiously enough, Sherman did not respond to Fry by pointing out that his observation on Smith's bad luck and Grant's good luck was a comment on the ironic importance of contingency in history—even Grant had needed fortune as well as ability in order to succeed. If Sherman had used his pen as a rapier rather than a saber, he could have won the argument even after admitting his authorship of the letter in question. But as in politics, blunt anger rather than subtle wit marked Sherman's feuding style.[13]

Throughout this controversy, in a more private way, Sherman felt the sting of Fry's contention that he had been disloyal to Grant. For example, to a friendly St. Louis acquaintance he protested that he had been "Grant's best friend from Shiloh till [he was] deposited in his tomb." To recapture this spirit, he employed one of his most trusted surrogates, S. H. M. Byers, to publish lengthy extracts in the *North American Review* from Sherman's letters to Grant during Reconstruction, which would demonstrate his deep loyalty to a man he so admired. During his feud with Fry, Sherman was especially at pains to write to Grant's son, Fred, and through Fred to Grant's widow, Julia, stressing that "from the day I reached Paducah [in 1862] till his death I was loyal to Gen'l Grant."

This earnest protest of uniform loyalty could not, however, cover every element of a long public as well as private relationship, which had had its downs as well as its ups. Thus in all honesty, Sherman felt compelled to remind Fred Grant of such bad times as when, in 1874, Grant "allowed Belknap to drive me out of Washington," and the following year, when he "permitted Babcock to employ Boynton with government clerks to gather garbled extracts of official reports" to use in his libelous book. On these same points, Sherman conceded to his brother, John, that "Belknap, Babcock & Boynton conspired to make a break between me and Grant—they partially succeeded." But when Grant had neared his death, Sherman wrote Fred Grant, he had told Sherman "that he himself felt that he had done me a wrong, which he nobly and generously rescinded." In turn, Sherman insisted that, however sorely tried had he been, he had never written or spoken of Grant in any manner other than "highly eulogistic."[14]

On a more private level, one less combative and sadder, Sherman often voiced the complexities and vicissitudes of his dramatic life and his intense relationships with other warriors. None of them, not even Grant, were the models of perfection their equestrian monuments made them out to be, and Sherman often had a rich and subtle ability to show the darker as well as the brighter sides of his closest allies, and was almost able to admit to his own mistakes and weaknesses of personality. But Sherman lost this complexity of consideration when he went public. Charging into the feuds in which he quite enjoyed debasing his foes, he tried to secure a reputation for loyalty and honor such as only angels might claim. All these moves and countermoves, attacks and defenses, which Sherman and his adversaries never questioned, dehumanized them. They were constructing and smashing idols rather than re-creating the hopes and fears, successes and failures of real generals in the chaos of actual battle. As do countless historians when they write their books about them, Sherman and his comrade-enemies were reaching for symbolic immortality, not historical understanding, when they fought their feuds.

Not in every instance did Sherman rush from a perceived insult into a full-scale feud; at times, particularly when the insult came from someone he had respected during the war, he was capable of playing the peacemaker. One example was Sherman's postwar treatment of Frank Blair, the political general from Missouri who served as the rather gifted commander of Sherman's own Fifteenth Corps after Sherman was elevated to the head of the army. In his *Memoirs,* Sherman praised quite highly Blair's skills in his military avocation, while criticizing him for his political vocation. Blair's elder brother, Montgomery, who had been Lincoln's postmaster general, immediately wrote a letter to the St. Louis newspapers denouncing Sherman for his "envious nature," his inability ever to express magnanimity, his wartime "timidity" in supporting Frank Blair's military efforts, and his numerous "slights" to Blair during the war. Rather than denouncing Montgomery Blair in print, thus escalating insults into a feud, Sherman wrote him personally, challenging him to point out what in the *Memoirs* was offensive to him. Montgomery Blair backed down by return post, admitting that at the time he had written his letter to the press, he had not actually seen the *Memoirs,* and had only reacted from the initial reviews of the book. Sherman followed this exchange with a letter to Frank Blair's wife, assuring her that, as in his *Memoirs,* "I have borne public and willing testimony to the Patriotism, Manliness and Courage of General Frank Blair, and throughout his most brilliant military career." Sherman then repeated to Mrs. Blair that "many and many a time, yea a hundred times" during the war did he "remonstrate with him in persisting in clinging to his political ambition," when he ought to have stuck to the army, for which he had a greater gift—"his true and congenial sphere." And yet Sherman had come to accept that Frank Blair "could not help" his political nature, for he was bred in politics "in his nature and youth, and with him, politics and patriotism were synonymous terms. I did not and could not see it in that light." In this case of a man he truly did admire in many ways, Sherman defused a potential feud with tact, patience, and a fair-minded spirit, and yet without truckling.[15]

After having been deserted by Sherman during the Whittaker affair, John Schofield carried around considerable anger and resentment for his old chief, to which, however, he did not give expression. Four years later, however, coincidentally with Sherman's retirement, Schofield did write him an irate letter. This letter was provoked by a paper given on October 17, 1883, by Captain J. Barber, at the Sixteenth Annual Convention of the Society of the Army of the Tennessee, over which Sherman had presided. Barber had been highly critical of Schofield, who was not at the convention and who had never been in the Army of the Tennessee during the war. Sherman replied to Schofield's letter with an angry one of his own. This exchange could have escalated into yet another feud.

To an even greater extent than had been true with Frank Blair, Sherman had truly admired Schofield during the war, and he continued to like him personally, and perhaps to bear a certain guilt for having abandoned him during the Whittaker affair. Therefore, he took a deep breath and wrote a second letter to Schofield a week after his angry one, in effect suing for peace. As president of the society, he had never censored speeches in advance, he wrote Schofield, and he insisted that the offending Captain Barber had to answer for himself. But he believed that he had been a "real friend" to Schofield ever since Schofield had first reported to him in 1862, and that ever after he had done "many, very many acts of personal and official kindness and respect to you." Therefore, he offered to "withdraw" his offensive letter if Schofield would withdraw his, "and matters between us will be *status quo ante-bellum* . . . mutual relations of affection and respect." Schofield wrote back a friendly letter including Sherman's earlier angry one, and Sherman reciprocated. "My original letter . . . shall be destroyed and the record thereof expunged. So I see no reason why our friendship should not be even more firmly established than before." Sherman then assured Schofield a prominent place on the program of the subsequent convention of the society in order to exercise his right of reply. Sherman had pulled Schofield and himself back from the brink.[16]

If only to a far lesser extent than in the negative rituals of the feud, Sherman and his cohort could reinforce their honor through a more affirmative view of one another and through an amplification of the beau ideal of the honorable gentleman-soldier. They needed heroes as well as enemies.

The man Sherman most nearly hero-worshipped was Grant. Even during the war, Sherman's admiration of Grant far surpassed the bounds of esteem he felt for any other soldier. He went so far as to place Grant on par with the father of the nation. "I believe you are as brave, patriotic, and just as the great prototype, Washington," he wrote Grant on March 10, 1864, as Grant was setting out to take overall charge of the Union war effort, "as unselfish, kind-hearted and honest as a man should be," and capped with "the simple faith in success [like] the faith a Christian has in his Savior." If Grant continued to be true to himself—"simple, honest and unpretending"—he would never fall from this "almost dangerous elevation" to the status of national cofounder, which he had reached. "You will enjoy through life the respect and love of friends, and the homage of millions [for] securing to them and their descendants a government of law and stability."

Although Sherman believed, when vexed with Grant during his presidency, that Grant had sacrificed much of his claim to untarnished, Washington-like national fatherhood, he never lost his admiration for him. The two had a mutually heartfelt reconciliation when Grant had neared death from cancer. "General Grant says my visits to him have done him more good than all the doctors," he reported in a touchingly childlike tone to Ellen. After Grant's death, Fred Grant assured Sherman that his dying father had been increasingly "recognizant of the truth that I had been his most loyal friend," Sherman told his wife. Returning affection for affection, the dying Grant had released Sherman from the alienating ambivalence both men had come to feel during the latter stages of their colliding careers. In death as during the Civil War, Grant was Sherman's great and shining hero.[17]

Second only to his elevation of Grant—the one Union general who he thought surpassed him in the art of war—was Sherman's admiration for William T. Sherman, a hero to whom he quite often referred in the third person. Throughout his later life as icon, he thought of himself as the eternally plucky warrior. He often revealed his self-love, as in an offhand comment he made in 1881, to the historian John W. Draper: "I myself continue vigorous—fighting yet for what I believe to be right. . . . I am not an advocate of war and its maxims—but I contend for the manly qualities in common life, which war needs when it does come." The martial feudist, fighting for the right, was the very personification of the manly ideal.[18]

Though Sherman had relatively few heroes on earth, he had more in heaven. In his frequent military eulogies, he was able to reattach the ideal to the actual man, or perhaps just to overlook his feelings for the actual man once departed. Its object safely dead, and thus out of the feud and other forms of combat, Sherman's final tribute would then ascribe timeless perfection to his fallen comrade-hero. This was a more public and male version of the rituals of mourning whereby Ellen Ewing Sherman and her husband had beatified little Willy in 1863, placing him in a beckoning heaven, where all the vicissitudes of life would be smoothed over eternally. Similarly could the Union comrades be reunited in perpetual peace in an enduring sphere far from their strife-filled worldly arena. Dying had, as it were, swept clean the contentions and contradictions of life. This was true in the highly formalized letters Sherman would write to grieving widows and children as well as in his public orations given at funerals and at the unveiling of monuments.

As head of the army until 1883 and, when major figures were concerned, even after his retirement, Sherman wrote literally hundreds of such letters, and he attended dozens of funerals. Although he personalized each occasion, the forms remained constant. Take, for example, Sherman's letter of March 12, 1880, to George and Marion Sykes, the children of George Sykes, whom Sherman had known since their cadet days at West Point, and who had been one of Meade's corps commanders at Gettysburg. Sherman wrote of the newly deceased Sykes as having contained all the basic elements of the ideal martial gentleman. "We always esteemed your father as a Model Soldier, handsome, prompt, and brave in action, generous and manly in sentiment, and magnanimous in victory." This model of the hero, so opposite to the picture of the enemy portrayed by feudists, would serve his descendants forever, as the very personification of all the heroic virtues for which any person ought to strive. "This should be to you a precious memory, and an incentive to be industrious and honest in your future lives." At the final hour, Sherman, as father of the army, could extend paternal protection as well as gratitude to the martial family. "You may always call on me at any and all times for any favor in my gift."

Sherman repeated himself in all his letters. In addition, when he had attended the funeral, Sherman would also note to the survivors how well the ceremony had honored the dead army comrade. To the widow of George Meade, the maximum hero of Gettysburg, Sherman wrote on November 12, 1872, that at the funeral, "we did all man could do to honor his memory during the august funeral. . . . May the virtue of his impetuous career of manhood enshrine [his grave site] and make it sacred to generations to come, whose homes he so bravely defended. May you and his children live long, to gather there at times to feel anew that love which governed his life." The ideal soldier had served his family and the national family in war; his family could take full pride in his honor, and could be assured of his American immortality.

It took heroes to conquer the West just as it had the South, and Sherman honored the soldiers of the wars against the Indians as he did Civil War veterans. In his letter to George Custer's widow, about a man he privately considered something of a fool, Sherman wrote on August

11, 1876, of the larger symbolic meaning of Custer's death. Custer had stood as a warrior "between civilization and barbarism . . . between the peaceful agriculturalist and the savage hunter." Thus, in future years when "the Yellowstone becomes the highway of travel between East & West," and when "peaceful farmers and graziers" fill Montana's valleys, they would point with veneration to the spot where Custer and his men had fallen, "that their children might live in peace in a land . . . rescued from the profanations of the bloody Sioux."[19]

If Sherman lacked a conventional Christian faith, he did believe fervently in the indispensable role played by the heroic soldier in the great morality play of national redemption, a belief that lent final, holy certainty of meaning to his own life as well as to those of his departed comrades at arms. This was immortality as a final goal, achieved through their lives of strife. The end was opposite to the means: The progression was through countless stormy passages up into a calm and cloudless pantheon.

Ironically, ceremonies of posthumous honoring emphasized the separation between the manly ideal and the feud, even as the feud had been fought to protect the manly ideal from its detractors. Feuds were dreadful, demeaning affairs for all concerned, no more so than for Sherman, whose venom poisoned himself as much as his enemies. But even though they strike us as a curious way of achieving immortality, feuds were fought with such tenacity because the reward would be entrée to a plush corner of heaven. The moral and personal stakes of these rituals were high—at risk was personal and familial honor, masculinity, historical reputation, and the inner meaning of the redemption of the nation.

Sherman even employed this ritual enshrinement of the manly ideal in his anthropomorphic memoir of "Old Sam," the war horse who had carried him from the battle for Vicksburg, in mid-1863, until the end of the war. Sherman wrote this eulogy on January 22, 1875, to the man from Chicago who had mailed Sherman the death notice of Old Sam from a Chicago newspaper. In part, Sherman was of course satirizing the eulogy as a literary genre, and himself in his all-too-familiar role as paternal eulogist; in part he really did desire to do tribute to Old Sam, who had stood the war like a manly fellow. "I can only hope that he now rests from his worldly labors in the place where good horses go," Sherman wrote. Old Sam always had a fine appetite for life and he never shirked duty. "He was always hungry and fat—never got lame and was never on the sick list." He was brave in battle. Once a musket ball passed through his neck, "but he didn't complain and went right along at his work as though he was used to it. As to artillery fire, he regarded it as a useless noise in which he had little concern." All irony aside, in the sentimental sector of Sherman's memory, Old Sam was linked to the most precious of immortal values. "What endeared the horse most to me and my family was that he was the favorite of my son Willy," during that fatal visit to his father's camp on the Big Black River in October 1863. "When the war was over Mrs Sherman . . . asked me to keep Old Sam in memory of our Willy." Surely Willy was mounted on Old Sam's broad back, up in heaven, where one day there would be room enough for him to sit behind his son, fury all dissipated.[20]

19

The Struggle of Marriage, and Other Women

A GOOD MARRIAGE was an indispensable component of the manly ideal for Sherman and his comrades. Both nature and society intended that the gentleman be a married man, a good husband and father. Then as now, actual marriage was another matter, of course, but men like Sherman had no doubt about what ought to be.

One of Sherman's more ritualized forms of correspondence was his letters of congratulations to those of his wide circle of acquaintances who were about to be married, though he made little fuss when the couples later brought babies into the world. He would write separately to the prospective bride and groom, praising each to the other in his best paternal manner. "I give you my best wishes for all the joys of married life that you have figured out in your dreary [single] state," Sherman wrote to the New York publisher William W. Appleton in 1881, "and will venture to congratulate the lady in having brought you to terms." Although Sherman expressed just a dash of resentful misogyny in that formulation, with the naturally wild man fearing taming by the *femme civilatrice,* he also conveyed an impression that a gentleman ought to submit to his taming by his partner, to become a proper husband and father, as this would fit him into the natural ordering of society. "The world must go on—must have people," Sherman continued to Appleton, "and no better plan has yet been invented than for man and woman to pair off."

Appleton was a younger man and a civilian. Sherman paid even more attention as the paternal spokesman for the marital ideal when he was addressing someone in the army family. This was true of his many letters to junior officers and their fiancées, and it was also true of those he wrote to his old comrades when they contemplated remarriage. Part of the delicacy of this latter formulation was to honor the memory of the first wife while affirming the joy the second ought to bring. When his good friend and old Civil War aide-de-camp Alexander McCook announced his intentions to remarry in 1884, Sherman broke into his crowded schedule to travel from St. Louis to Wisconsin for the marriage ceremony. Announcing his intentions to do so, Sherman told McCook, "our days on earth are numbered, and when death intervenes there is no good reason why man should be alone—therefore I hope that the woman you have chosen to succeed your . . . extraordinary beautiful and angelic . . . Kate may be all your fancy paints her." Sherman wrote to the bride, Miss Annie Cole, on the same day, praising the first Mrs. McCook—"a more lovable creature never existed on earth, too good for this world and called early to another & I hope better." Sherman then praised his old comrade as "the soul of kindness, hearty, jovial and cheery at all times." Such a lively, affirmative fellow would dispense much happiness, and he deserved it in return. "I cannot blame him for wishing another close companion to share his life [and] from his description I infer you have all the graces & accomplishments of womankind." However, he welcomed Annie Cole less for what she might be than as the wife of his old friend: "Whatever contributes to McCook's happiness and success will ever be precious to me, and [as] for yourself I shall ever honor the woman whom McCook has chosen for his wife." He would praise the woman who would make his friend a happy home. She would, he was certain, "make his house what he always wants it to be—a hospitable and pleasant place for his children . . . and his larger family of accomplished officers." For Miss Cole was marrying a man of "conspicuous . . . rank and position," and therefore she was joining an already established larger army family as well as becoming the stepmother to McCook's children. This definition of the ideal second marriage contained a rather cautionary subtext. Not only was the idealized Kate McCook still a presence of perfection in Sherman's mind, which might be a burden on Annie Cole rather than an encouragement, but in addition, Sherman assigned to Annie Cole McCook a complex and rather daunting task as peerless hostess.

She was to be the uncomplaining and cheerful helpmate to the dominant husband.

Both the more affirmative and the more shadowy qualities of this formal and conventional letter of congratulations were projections of Sherman's own marital situation. After the Civil War, the problems endemic to the Sherman marriage had deepened, and for many years he and Ellen barely continued as man and wife. In his letters to the McCooks one sees references to his own situation that contrasted with his idealized marital picture—his home was more closed than open to his friends; his wife was not affectionate; his wife did not even try to make him happy. When Sherman wrote to Annie Cole McCook, "I am jealous of you for taking his Katie's place," he was expressing a double jealousy toward McCook—both for his first genial marriage and for the prospect of a second one, when his own marriage, which promised to last forever, was so barren.[1]

After they fought the Civil War in tandem, with Ellen first rescuing and then admiring her increasingly famous and successful husband, the Shermans returned to combat. Not merely did their old disputes return, they intensified. Sherman now wrote angry letters not only to his wife, but about her to others; she in turn retreated even further from her husband into vituperation toward and seclusion from him. Generally her letters to him revealed more of their profound marital discord than his, but their hostilities clearly remained mutual.

Religion remained a huge barrier between them. When he was traveling in Europe in 1872–73, for example, Sherman agreed to visit Archbishop Manning on her behalf, though he hated calling on Roman Catholic clergymen. Along with her request, she had reminded him of his lack of proper spirituality. "I am sufficiently conscious of my weaknesses & faults, but don't like to have them rubbed in as salt on a fresh wound," he complained to her in return. He knew that the English Catholic Church would publicize his audience with the archbishop, "because they make use of [such visits] for their purposes, not mine." Sherman argued that although he did feel "respect for a man of true piety" of any faith, he hated piety being "used as a mere machine, sect, clique or church." If he were to make his visit, "it will be whispered and printed that the American General is a Catholic." And then the general made it clear to his Catholic wife how strongly he rejected her faith. He was "not a Catholic, and from the nature of my mental organization could not be." When he was getting ready to come home after his ten-month European tour, Sherman wrote again, to "earnestly beg a truce" in their war of religion. He did not doubt her sincerity, he said, but felt her "zeal for one cause" absorbed all the "better instincts in your nature." He did not object that their children had been raised Catholic, he claimed, only hoping that Tom would not "question the sincerity of others"—implicitly himself first and foremost—and that Elly and Rachel would not "follow their cousins into a convent," but would "grow up qualified to make good wives." Sherman feared losing his children altogether to his wife's sphere.

To his brother, John, in 1875, Sherman argued that one reason he had refused to be considered for the presidency was that his candidacy "should be complicated with the Catholic Question," during an extremely anti-Catholic period of American history. How bitterly ironic such a Papist tarring would be, for "I am not Catholic and could not be so because they exact a blind obedience & subordination that is utterly foreign to my nature." His wife's fundamental identity thus was also utterly foreign to him. "Ellen is [obedient and subordinate] by nature, and it is so deep-seated that it can never be eradicated, and she will work like a beaver to spread her Faith."

Ellen would not have disagreed with this assessment, though she would have evaluated it differently. She shored up her domestic religious camp, bringing her children's Catholic friends into it, associating with Catholic families herself; and her husband was excluded unless he became a convert. To Eliza Starr, a New England girlfriend of her daughter, Ellen wrote in 1886 that "Rachel . . . is very fond of you, as are we all; you are a very captivating little *Yankee*—The term is used in its highest & best sense, since I married a Yankee. . . . Yankees make the most strict Catholics. I love them for that." Eliza Starr was a paragon of New England conversion to her true faith whom Ellen could hold up to her unconverted Yankee husband. The battle lines could hardly have been drawn more clearly.[2]

Other issues grew between them like cancer. The general thought his wife a neurasthenic and a shirker, sitting in perpetual seclusion, smoldering and snapping at him. Shortly before her death of heart failure, he complained to an old Civil War army friend that "Mrs S begins to feel the force of age—and has all sorts of complaints—but in fact is only too inert and fat, with an indisposition to work it off." She ought to be up and about as was he, but she had retreated into hostile immobility, rejecting both his official life and more generally, the world of available pleasures.

Ellen Ewing Sherman would not entertain his friends and other public figures in good grace, and she categorically refused to accompany him when he went out into the social whirl he so much enjoyed. For example, when German General Schwinitz, with his wife and children, came to Washington in 1874, Sherman accepted an invitation to a dinner honoring the visitor, adding, "I . . . will come, but cannot answer for Mrs Sherman who dislikes beyond measure occasions of ceremony or etiquette."

The theater was one of the general's great postwar passions, but here again, his wife refused to accompany him. In 1875, he complained to his daughter, Elly, that "Your Mama wont go because she is afraid the theater will take fire and burn up—of this there is little or no danger—but when one gets that idea it takes away all pleasure and satisfaction."[3]

Crowded theaters, like sailing ships, caused Ellen Ewing Sherman to suffer panic attacks. There is no evidence that her husband ever sympathized with such mental distress; to the contrary, he assumed that she was merely stubbornly opposed to fulfilling his beliefs as to what a wife ought to be. His angry reproaches undoubtedly intensified her resistance, and he would go out into the world, nearly every day, slamming the door angrily behind him, while she stayed behind in fury.

In her constricted domestic sphere, Ellen brooded endlessly and frequently exploded in anger. She lacked such outlets as feuding with other generals and door-slamming, and instead turned against other members of her extended family. When Willy had died during the war, for example, she felt keenly that her younger brother, Thomas Ewing, Jr., had ignored mentioning the event in his letters to their parents in Lancaster where she was living with them. After five months of Tom's failure "to remember dear Willy or to name his poor mother in her sorrow," Ellen raged to her husband that Tom was a "supremely selfish man," made so by his corrupting wife, and that "I hope to see them but seldom again in my life and I wish my affairs kept from their observations & criticism." She urged her husband to "extend to him no confidence founded on the fact of his being my brother." Ellen then turned on her husband, accusing him of frequently betraying her by talking of her faults "freely before members of my family [and] before strangers," something he clearly did, judging by his letters.

In 1878, it was John Sherman's turn to feel her fury when she believed John had let her down on her request to find a job for one of her circle. "Should I ever be a widow I should not be left under his control or power in any way, nor compelled to exchange letters or views with him," she insisted to her husband: Again her rage spilled over to him, a member of the enemy camp. Clearly feeling her own relative powerlessness, she wrote how much she disliked "the immense patronage & power you & your brother have." She concluded that she would never trouble him or John—"I shall never again make any . . . application . . . of anyone or for anyone." She would withdraw entirely from public life—Elly could replace her, "always with due satisfaction to my authority." She would pull away from all her enemies, from her family as from the surrounding world.

Often Sherman would try to make peace between the enraged Ellen and his family or hers. For example, when Charles Ewing avoided visiting the Shermans after Ellen had rounded on him, Sherman wrote Charles, asking, "by the way, are you going to make a permanent break with us?" He then advised Charles to "drop in casually, forgetting and forgiving." Three days later, when Charles still demurred, Sherman wrote again that he did not "suppose [Ellen] will ever apologize—she is too stubborn for that—and she asserts that she disclaimed any purpose to offend, and that is sufficient apology." He once more suggested that Charles just drop in casually, "and let an opportunity arise for a subsidence of any feeling whatever." Evidently this pacifying strategy, one that placed Sherman in a more empathetic light than usual toward Ellen, succeeded in this case.[4]

Most of the time, however, Ellen appeared to have kept her grievances toward their families away from anyone but her husband and to have rarely complained about him to others in their families. One notable exception was a livid letter she wrote to her revered father on March 10, 1868, concerning her husband's lack of sympathy for her delicate health. "Cump says I have been complaining all my life and never was sick an hour, that it is pure imagination whenever I complain & if I chose I could always be well." It is also probable that Sherman expressed his sexual resentments at her loss of attractiveness and her lack of interest. The last Sherman child had been born in 1867, and at forty-four, Ellen's sex life with her husband may have declined or ended. Sherman was only forty-eight, highly energetic, and very magnetic to other women. Ellen complained to her father that her husband was a savage rather than a modern gentleman toward her. "I think he missed his calling when he took a civilized wife, as nature made him the spouse of a squaw; [and] when he retires to the tribe in which he may lose his identity, should they ever give him any power or he attempt to force his views into practice he will kill off by severity and want of kindness and comforts the remaining squaws of the unfortunate doomed tribe." In this remarkable portrait, Cump was essentially Tecumseh and not at all William. Ellen's package of resentments was perfectly clear—in his want of sympathy and affection and in his unceasing demands, which clearly were sexual in nature though far from exclusively so, he was not at all what a husband ought to be; in fact, he was her main emotional enemy.

When she aired this view of her husband to her father, she claimed that she had never confronted him with this, her true opinion of him—"I do not tell him so," she insisted. She also told her father that she knew how to get even with her husband, by pulling away all affection and sympathy from the savage Cump, staging a withdrawal into her more civilized and moral womanly heights. Her husband was a man who could not bear silence, and so when she put him in more or less permanent emotional Coventry, she indeed struck deeply, and intentionally, at his needs and fears. "Fortunately I know how to take care of myself and I look no longer for . . . comfort and sympathy in my multiplicity of small woes (such as most women have in this day and generation), but I endeavor to make the love of my children in heaven my guiding star . . . and I try to make a perfect offering to my dear Saviour, who suffered so much for me, of all the pains and sorrows I feel." The would-be martyr realized when she wrote this line that this letter of complaint was less than a perfect offering to Christ. "I have failed this time however insofar as I have gone to you with my complaint. But you are my Father."5

When Thomas Ewing died in 1873, Ellen edited, and the Catholic Publication Society printed, a 290-page memorial, including letters from lawyers and judges and public officials who had worked with Ewing. There was also a letter from Sherman, who praised his stepfather/father-in-law at a great emotional distance, as an Augustan hero, a man of "industry . . . logical order . . . and natural love for the good and the beautiful." Ellen herself wrote the conclusion to this book. It was a lengthy prayer to her father in heaven. "Dearest and best, ten-derest and truest of earthly fathers!" she began. She described his per-fect love for the sinful she who was Ellen, love he had given her every hour of her life. "No word or act of mine was ever deemed too weak for the kind, approving glance of thy sweet eye; no willful, wayward ex-pression e'er exhausted the fund of thy patient, loving forbearance." Even in life he had granted her a Holy Grace. "Thy hand rested upon my head in benediction, or was held forth to guide and support." Thomas Ewing had undergone a deathbed conversion to the true, Roman Catholic faith; this final loving act made certain that he had joined his wife and Ellen's children in heaven, and that Ellen would soon enough come to him in transcendent and perpetual reunification. "Thou wilt not return to me, but I shall go to Thee. . . . I shall again behold Thy face, whose glorified beauty cannot express more than has ever been for Thee the desire of the heart of Thy child."[6]

The conflation of her father with God the Father, the worship of this paragon of a father, could not have been more complete. Nor could the distance between the "sainted Father" and the dreaded husband have been greater. Ellen worshiped her father even more intensely in his death and resurrection, and held out this ideal as a cross to ward off her savage Cump. Their marriage worsened rather than improved after the death of Thomas Ewing.

Over the next four years, the Shermans carried out their bitterly dis-cordant marriage primarily in the privacy of their own home, and thus did not leave a full literary trail behind. However, the record becomes much clearer after January or February 1877, when Sherman moved to a hotel, and Ellen—with son Tom, daughter Rachel, and the ten-year-old Philemon, also nicknamed Cump—soon moved to St. Louis, leav-ing her daughter Elly behind with her father, who then returned to the Shermans' Washington house. Ostensibly, Ellen was accompanying Tom while he attended law school, but in fact she and her husband were also initiating what we would call a trial separation, one that would last for nearly two years.

From his hotel room, on February 27, Sherman wrote to Tom, now twenty-one, about the initiation of the separation. He rehearsed ele-ments of the old quarrel, but more in a tone of tired exasperation than in anger, almost as though it were the start of a reconciliation rather than a step toward a conclusive break. "We cannot change the charac-ter of Washington which from its political population must continue a place of hollow fashion and custom—Society here will have its own rules & will not be governed by our wishes," Sherman wrote, not that he liked Washington but that he accepted his role in it. "This seems peculiarly obnoxious to your Mama: who wants seclusion & exemption from the everlasting and ever changing stream of visitors, but at the same time wants [her daughters] to share in the society of the place." Sherman believed these to be irrational and mutually contradictory desires on Ellen's part, but he was tired of arguing and thus supported her going her own way for now. "It is hard to choose any course that fulfills all these conditions, but I am perfectly willing for your Mama to try."[7]

It is through Ellen Ewing Sherman's letters to her estranged husband that one can best reconstruct the ebbs and flows of the separation. Previously when they had been apart each wrote to the other at least every three days; now the letters came only once a month, and on a specific day. Indeed on July 17, 1877, Ellen wrote her husband, "the 20th is the date set for our letters but I like to anticipate a little so that I may not be hurried when the time comes." Ellen's spending habits had always provoked her husband, and so Sherman put the wife he considered a spendthrift on a fixed allowance. Although she must have negotiated her allowance before the separation, she continued to resent the amount he gave her as it included no cushion for her old age, should they remain separated. He also seemed to have held back the income her own funds were earning in Washington. "I do not like to deprive myself of the little interest I have belonging to me personally. It might be of some vital importance when I am older and even more disagreeable than ever." The children were another problem. Minnie and Lizzie were married, but Elly remained with him and the other three children were with her and missing their sister and father terribly. Rachel in particular pined for her father. Ellen wrote more as if she had been banished by her husband than as if she had chosen this separation or had agreed to it mutually and equally. One cannot know if her version of events explained the full dynamics of their parting.

To a certain degree the separation began to work as both parties hoped it might. Thoughtfulness began to replace instant anger. Ellen began to plan in terms of returning to Washington after a year had passed: She wrote to Sherman that "we would probably not leave you alone a great while, we can take a year to discuss a better plan in case you should not like this . . . and we will not have done anything abruptly or without due reflection." Sherman visited St. Louis first in May or June 1877, and then in October. After the second visit their correspondence became more frequent. At times the tone was still negative, such as on November 5, when Ellen complained, not long after a visit from her husband, "you have told me you do not like sentiment—nor many other things to which I am prone." But sometimes she was more upbeat, as when she told him a month later, on December 8, "we are beginning to feel impatient for the time for your return. . . . I hope you will enjoy your visit." He came for Christmas. Before his next visit in late March 1878, she indicated with similar warmth, "All are looking forward to your visit with great pleasure." Affection increased, if tentatively. For example, on March 4, 1878, when Congress threatened to cut Sherman's pay, Ellen wrote him that if they did so, "give me what you care to spare, & let me manage the best I can. I promise not to overstep the amount nor to disturb you with repinings." Ellen was now trying hard to be self-controlled and fair over money, acknowledging in this manner that she had been a contributing party to at least part of their quarrel and not merely a passive victim.

Yet considerable coolness characterized many letters, and the Shermans did not rush to reunite their family. In April 1878, Sherman accompanied Elly to Cleveland, where she stood up in a friend's wedding, but Ellen refused to join them. On May 2, Ellen noted, but only in passing, the news that "yesterday was the 28th anniversary of our marriage," something he neglected to mention. On May 13, Ellen Ewing Sherman attended Tom's graduation from law school, completing the cover story the Shermans had constructed for public consumption as to why she had moved to St. Louis. Still she did not return. Rachel went to Washington for a visit instead, filled with "the happiness of being with you," Ellen assured him. She instructed her husband how to attend to Rachel's monthly "calls of nature"—poultices, and if they were insufficient, hypodermic injections of one-sixth grain of morphine, tonic of iron or muriatic acid, and rest.

By August 1878, after eighteen months of separation, Ellen was readying herself to come home, but on explicit terms. "I will live my own life in Washington & Elly can represent the family." This trial return did not work, and after about a month, Ellen moved into a boardinghouse in Baltimore, where Rachel and little Cump enrolled in Catholic schools. On October 11, 1878, she told Sherman, with bare civility, "we are very comfortably settled here and hope you will come down sometime and spend an hour or two with us in the middle of the day." He was not invited to stay the night, which limited the contact to family gatherings in the parlor. Certainly there was to be no time alone, no meeting in their bedchamber, which would be the place for new arguments or for sex, neither of which she wanted. They did pay one another visits, and since Washington was near Baltimore, this was a less drastic phase of their separation. On January 10, 1879, Ellen informed her husband that her boarding contract was nearly up, to which he responded, "you had all better come over here," and she agreed to do so.

As a trial reconciliation Ellen now proposed she stay a month, so that the "girls could be together." As for herself as wife, she suggested that they have separate bedrooms, ostensibly for his peace of mind. "If I should take my trunks into your room & scatter my things about you would feel discontented & I would be greatly in your way." However, she did not wish for this room to be at the other end of the house either. "I intend to have a room very near." It is not implausible to conclude that she desired to resume sexual relations with her husband, while maintaining greater distance than that provided by a double bed shared all night. While planning this trial reunion, Ellen's reply to her husband's query, "what I thought we had better do next winter so as to all be together" was that they take a small house and live quietly, "and let the only entertainment be dinners to gentlemen given by yourself."

Judging by the long gaps between letters after March 9, 1879, and the occasional bursts of renewed affection after then, Ellen must have returned to the couple's home in Washington to stay some time between March and June 1879. While summering in Atlantic City in July, Ellen invited Sherman down, "as I am sure you will enjoy the bathing & driving," and later that summer, when she was in Oakland, California, Ellen wrote of "getting home" in early September and putting down new carpets.

The Shermans seemed to have managed to agree to some sort of general truce. They continued to travel separately, often for months at a time. Socially, Sherman remained the gadabout to Ellen's recluse. But they apparently dampened down their previous firestorms of hostility, and respected each other's individuality to a greater extent. At times, Ellen would admit quite openly that she missed him. In July 1882, after he paid his family a brief visit in Oakland where they were summering once more, she confessed to him, "I was very glad to receive a letter from you this morning for it has seemed lonesome without you & we all missed you very much." Three summers later, she wrote him from Columbus, Ohio, "I am by no means anxious to stay away from home a day longer than I find necessary." They had restored a livable equilibrium that, if not very affirmative, was no longer so terribly destructive.[8]

SOCIALLY, EMOTIONALLY, and erotically, after the Civil War, Sherman was quite occupied outside his home. Fame is an aphrodisiac, and Sherman was as famous an American man as ever lived. His circle of acquaintanceship was enormous, in part because he was so gregarious, and in part because everyone wanted to touch the great war hero. He was also charming, witty, energetic, and aggressive, and in his peregrinations around Washington, St. Louis, and the nation at large, many admiring women came to him with an eagerness of their own. In his biography of Sherman, John F. Marszalek recounts a legendary story, reprinted in the *New York World* shortly after Sherman's death, that when Grant told his friend that he was going to take up horses as his hobby after the war, Sherman had replied, "you may drive your fast horses, and I will kiss all the pretty girls . . . that shall be my fad."

Rumors of Sherman's womanizing reached the press, at least in humorous innuendo. Thus when Sherman retired from the army and left Washington for St. Louis, the semiofficial *Army and Navy Register* printed a spoof of a "very private letter" to "Dear Old Tecumseh," from "Eve's Daughters," pining for the newly absent social lion. "We miss you very much. . . . It is really awful to think of going through a whole season here in Washington without one jolly talk with you. We don't have such fun with anybody else. . . . Please come back and bring Mrs. Sherman and the girls if you can. But come anyway, and see how glad we shall all be to welcome you." This letter from Eve's Daughters closed with the postscript, "If you will come right soon you may kiss us just as often as you like."[9]

Evidently Sherman passed off his kissing habits as a kind of fatherly joke, but some women at least were quite offended by embraces they did not welcome. Marszalek quotes the unpublished memoir of Mildred Hazen Dewey, who when the young wife of General William B. Hazen, one of Sherman's former division commanders, found Sherman's advances "cunning" and quite aggressive. At one party the general backed her into a corner until she finally "called a halt."[10]

Sherman frequently referred to the allure of even younger, adolescent girls, nearly always phrasing this as the admiration of an old man who, when he saw such a young beauty, wished he were decades younger. To George Bancroft, the sixty-seven-year-old retired general, Sherman wrote how much he envied the aging historian for his granddaughter. "The beautiful face and exquisite manners of that sweet grandchild who now hovers near you must be a foretaste of what we are promised in the hereafter." This virginal apparition was angelic, but that did not answer the ancient question of whether or not there was sex in heaven. Sherman continued: "Say to her for me that she is lucky that I am not a young Lieutenant of Artillery for I should haunt her, but every Jill has her Jack, and if you don't keep a doubled barreled gun by your side she will some day be carried off to succeed her Great Grandmother Eve." There is no reply from the new Eve or her grandfather in the archives, but the erotic charge of Sherman's fantasy strikes modern ears quite loudly. Expressed in bantering irony, Sherman's desires were not so deeply buried.[11]

If the woman was grown and independent as well as alluring to him, Sherman would pursue her with the same intensity he brought to other aspects of his life. One does not know how many women he chased, or the number of his conquests—Victorian codes of seduction were deliberately cloaked with ambiguity, and the archival record is far from complete on such matters—but judging by the available evidence Sherman must have been a very energetic womanizer.

In 1882, Sherman wrote to Mrs. Blanche Roosevelt Machetta, whom he addressed as "My Dear Friend," to thank her for her little volume on the home life of the good gray poet, Henry W. Longfellow. "I knew you were handsome, that you had a cultivated sweet voice, but did not know that you were an authoress," he began, clearly envying and identifying with Longfellow. Sherman told her that it was a "lucky thing for him that you became acquainted." He also found it a charming conceit that Longfellow had called her "Pandora." He then blurred Pandora with the temptress Eve. "The box you opened to him was surely of blessings and pleasures and not of evil as is sometimes attributed to the first of your sex." That this metaphor was sexual rather than innocent was reinforced by Sherman's expressed desire that he "would like to hear from you what are your plans & prospects for the near future, and if I may hope to have the pleasure of meeting you soon again, face to face, to say much that cannot be written." That was a lightly coded proposition, probably a request for a repeat stand.[12]

The stage for many of Sherman's sexual meanderings was in fact the theater, which was his other major postwar hobby. Quite aware of being a performer himself in his role as leading general, he was attracted to the make-believe, the social outings, the actors, the "demimondeness" of the theater. Indeed, when he moved back to New York from St. Louis in 1886, later in his retirement, a major reason for this choice was increased proximity to his Bohemia, on and off Broadway. One pleasure was the respectable cover the theater offered him for taking out the young women of his own circle. To the actor Lawrence Barrett, he wrote in 1888, "Ellen (Mrs Sherman)—will not go to the theater, yearning for the grandchildren, not for our Old Relative Julius Caesar—my own girls will be away, but I have a large family who style me Father or 'Uncle' and even you and Booth may claim a place with them" in after-theater entertainments.

The actresses themselves often became great favorites of this playgoer. They were respectable enough to be seen with in polite company, but at the same time, many of them were independent, beautiful women, interested in famous and charming men, and sometimes sexually available, and Sherman clearly enjoyed seeking out their companionship. In 1876, Sherman advised his old comrade Phil Sheridan, who lived in Chicago, of the coming of Mary Anderson, one of his longtime favorites. "Should you drop in and see her, you would find her young, handsome and reasonably attractive." To his old San Francisco friend, Judge Ogden Hoffman, Sherman wrote of the imminent appearance of Adelaide Restoria, "a tragic actress of established fame," accompanied by her husband, the Marquis de Guillo, and her daughter, Bianca Capranica. It was the daughter, not the mother, whom Sherman was passing on. "If you were a younger man I would not trust you to see Bianca, but I know that you appreciate intellect, refinement, and culture, and it will need only a short visit to discover all these and more." It is barely possible that "all these and more" was not a reference to sexual availability.[13]

One of the general's great and good actress friends was Ada Rehan. From London she wrote him in June 1888 that "I have flattered myself . . . that you would be pleased to have a line from one to whom upon so many happy occasions you have been so much more than kind and friendly. . . . I hope we will meet soon with the same hearty feeling that we parted with." When she returned to New York that fall, hearing from her producer that Sherman was asking for her address, she wrote him with it immediately, adding, "If you are thinking of honoring me with a call, I am not going to let you forget it. . . . I will be at home any time you name. Please drop me a line when you are coming, for I would not be out *for worlds.*" Sherman wrote back the next day, promising to call at noon one day early in the next week. Of course this may have been just a warm, flirtatious friendship, which Ada Rehan pursued with as much suggestiveness as the general, but that does not seem the most likely meaning of her letters.[14] Such dalliances take on even more meaning when one places them in the context of far more intense correspondences Sherman had with two other women, which have survived in the archives.

ON VALENTINE'S DAY afternoon in 1873, four years before the trial separation with his wife, Sherman visited the Senate chamber in the Capitol to inspect the plaster models of Admiral David Farragut that several artists had prepared for the commission competition for a major statue. As he was passing through the rotunda, Sherman bumped into the sylphic Vinnie Ream, a singer as well as a sculptor, who had called at one of the Shermans' regular Friday night receptions the previous month. They must have chatted amiably, and something passed between them, for Vinnie invited the general over to her studio in her little house, and Sherman wrote her that evening, "I will with the greatest pleasure take the earliest opportunity to call as promised, preferably Sunday, unless that day be regarded as too sacred." The fifty-three-year-old general and the twenty-six-year-old artist became lovers almost immediately.

Sherman felt real admiration and affection as well as lust for Vinnie Ream. He immediately adopted the role of protector and sponsor as well as lover. "If you succeed I will rejoice with you: but even if you fail I will still be an ardent admirer as ever," wrote the gallant older man. Immediately he began to lobby the Committee on Public Buildings, which would choose the artist for the Farragut statue, on her behalf. He even enlisted John Sherman and Ellen Ewing Sherman in the effort, which was successful. He assured Vinnie, "I really believe you have made the best likeness of the Admiral," and he also identified with the struggle of her career—"Aim high, let nature be your guide, and success will crown your labors." With Vinnie, Sherman could combine nurturing paternalism with eroticism. "With each award the critics will be silenced of the charge that your success is due to your pretty face and childish grace. . . . If in your hard struggle for fame, you can keep a loving woman's breast you will have a double claim to the respect of true and brave men." In Vinnie Ream, Sherman could have both a charming and sexy little girl and a brave and independent woman. More multidimensional than a traditional kept woman, this Bohemian artist appealed to Sherman's love of the apparently respectable tied to the demimonde.

Sherman enjoyed a powerful erotic bond with Vinnie Ream, especially for the following twenty months, until he moved his office and home to St. Louis. He often wrote her to make assignations, and some of his letters were erotic in a way unusual to a man who was generally guarded in his written expressions of the sexual. On April 19, 1873, seven weeks into the affair, the deeply infatuated Sherman wrote to "my foolish little pet," who was off in New York, that "I miss you more than I thought possible, and your little foolish ways. A great deal can be compressed in a 'small space.' " Sherman encouraged Vinnie to write him as often as she pleased, as he opened his own letters; but also instructed her, "I destroy [your] letters—you must do the same of mine for in wrong hands suspicion would not stop short of wrong—which we must not even think of." Whatever fears of exposure and scandal she shared with Sherman, Vinnie guarded the letters of her famous swain closely rather than burning them.

A year later, Sherman's secret sexual ardor continued undiminished. On April 4, 1874, Sherman looked up a line from Sir Walter Scott's "Lady of the Lake," which Vinnie had bet him was by some other poet, and Sherman wrote, "So you see I was right and you can pay the bet, when we next meet, which I hope will be soon." A month later, Sherman offered to drive Vinnie out into the countryside one afternoon. He could hardly wait to get his hands on her, he confessed. If he brought the buggy, she would have to be on the "look out, as then I must drive myself and will have no arms to hold the horses." If he brought the closed victoria, there would be a driver, and they would have "the back seat all to ourselves." One hot July day he wrote Vinnie from work, sending back the handkerchief he had pocketed the night before in her studio. "The day is hot—business slack in this office. And I feel half tempted to come down & have you sing some of those songs which you say I have never heard." With Vinnie Ream, Sherman could be the hedonistic fantasist he could not be with his wife.

After his departure for St. Louis in the fall of 1874, Sherman continued to visit Vinnie when he came to Washington, though the long-distance lovers drifted apart. In July 1875, he wrote in great disappointment that he had not known she had been in New York when he had been, "else I should have made it a point to stop over and have a good look at you." Mrs. Sherman and the children were to go off to Lake Geneva for the summer, and Sherman sighed, "I wish you could find some excuse to come out West—for Washington seems . . . a long way off now."

If he was losing his lover by dint of great physical distance, Sherman would at least share with her by mail his memories of their relationship. On his birthday, February 8, 1875, two years after he first had made love to her, Sherman wrote, "I often think of your studio and my precious moments there and wonder if you miss me—and who now has the privilege of toying with your long tresses, and comforting your imaginary distresses." In later letters, Sherman referred to that "suspicious sanctuary," that nook in her studio holding the bed they had shared. And when she sent him her photo he wrote her, "I prefer to think of you in your artist's garb, plain and simple," the garment she had taken off when they had entered the suspicious sanctuary. Sherman also expressed his sense that in some ways their affair was inappropriate for him. "I must heed the progress of time, for [I am] 55 years old, and I must play the part of Old Man the rest of my career, but I hope still to pursue a fondness for the young and the favored." He was not ready to give up his love life among young women, even if, according to conventions he half accepted, he was supposed to act the restrained senior statesman. Eros was stronger than common sense.

Though wistful, and missing her body and her company, Sherman was not possessive toward Vinnie Ream. He expected her to pass on. "Who is your special friend now? Look out that some old fellow don't eat you up." Although he had not known it, Sherman had not been her only old soldier even during their affair. Albert Pike, an even older general, of the Confederate persuasion, had been there too, and he knew about Sherman. He wrote Vinnie in 1886, clearly in reply to a letter from her, "As to my loving 'some other woman' in 'those old days' I could say the same of you." Still, Pike assured Vinnie that he treasured her photograph, which pictured her as she had been back then, and the memory of "being loved by one whom we love in return as I love you."

After he returned to Washington in 1876, Sherman visited Vinnie occasionally of an afternoon, but the intensity was gone. On May 28, 1878, when she married Lieutenant Richard Hoxie of the Corps of Engineers, a man more her own age, the Shermans attended. The day before, Sherman had written Vinnie a heartfelt letter of congratulations, and he made every effort to help Hoxie's career when he could. Over the subsequent years, Vinnie, now an ex-sculptor living in Montgomery, Alabama, with her husband and two little boys, occasionally wrote to Sherman as her confidant. He encouraged this and assured her that he missed her, as one of the "few intimate friends whose flattery and caresses were extremely pleasant at the time & especially so in memory." As late as 1887, Sherman could write with real longing, "I sometimes think that Mormons are right and that a man should have the right to change—tell Hoxie I will swop with him. . . . I hope that some happy accident may bring us together again, for you are much younger than I and remember me in my better days."

Vinnie must have written back with considerable ardor and even expectation, for five weeks later, Sherman wrote her, "Dear Vinnie, the old times will *never* come back . . . *we* change." Telling her he would gladly exchange his "years, honors and privileges for the lusty youth of one of the newsboys who clamor on the street," Sherman went on, like Polonius, to instruct little Vinnie that "true philosophy consists in accepting the inevitable and enjoying what of life we may." With the passage of the years, he now considered both her and her husband "as Children," and asked her to remember him "as I was in my prime in Washington." This letter marked the end of Sherman's correspondence with Vinnie Ream, a woman with whom a piece of his heart had fit so well.[15]

EVEN MORE SIGNIFICANT than his quasi-Bohemian alliance with Vinnie Ream was Sherman's affair, which lasted from 1880 until 1888, two years before his death, with Mary Audenreid, a more substantial woman of his own social circle, with whom he had more in common. Mary Audenreid was in her mid- to late thirties when she began her affair with the sixty-year-old Sherman. She was the independently wealthy daughter of a rich and socially prominent Philadelphia merchant, the mother of a rebellious teenage daughter, Florence, and the widow of Sherman's aide, Major Joseph C. Audenreid, who had served with Sherman since 1863. When the major died suddenly in June 1880, the general took Mary and Florence under his wing as a semiofficial guardian; within six months she took him to her bed.

About six weeks after her husband's death, writing that "you are too young to settle down to a state of despondency," Sherman asked Mary to join the two-month-long West Coast tour he was going to take as part of the party of President Rutherford B. Hayes, to "maternalize" Sherman's nineteen-year-old daughter, Rachel. Several months later Mary sent a dozen embroidered handkerchiefs to the general for his birthday—"altogether too fine for such as me," he wrote her. "Rest assured that I am impressed by such a mark of your affection, that I fully reciprocate it." A month after that, on March 25, 1881, when there was no birthday, she sent him a pair of silk socks, a somewhat more intimate gift, and he promised to visit her the next day—"meantime believe me as always lovingly and affectionately yours." And on April 30, he invited her for a day-long drive in that closed victoria of his, out into the country, including a stop for dinner. This was the spring in which, bored with office and beginning to anticipate retirement, he was swept away with love for Mary Audenreid.

As a paternal figure, Sherman wanted what was right for Mary; as a lover he wanted to possess her. He frequently expressed this tension within his desires in his letters to her. For example, on August 14, 1881, he insisted, "you ought not to be alone—you must not be—for your nature demands a mate. . . . I value your attachment to me and hope to show you my appreciation by doing that which I would do for one of my own." Sherman thus held Mary to him in the present, while arguing (with himself) that the best token of that love would be to act toward her as if she were his daughter, and give her away to an eligible, younger man. "You are young, most loving and attractive—and must in due time marry one of your own age and circle—I shall be most happy to witness the event." When Mary answered immediately, evidently reiterating her passion for him, Sherman replied the next day that her "heart's thoughts . . . can soon be transferred to another and then we can smile at the dream of the past . . . you are a loving woman & must have some object on which to expend that love—all in good time."

In due time, all in good time, were clear enough indicators that Sherman was not yet ready to let go of Mary Audenreid, and for her part, she was unwilling to break with him and remarry. Sherman would rephrase this inner dialogue between the father and the lover many times to Mary, to both push her away and hold her to him. "Of course you must marry again," he wrote her in July 1882, when she was in France. "And it is the veriest nonsense to talk about an old man. You should marry a man your own age." He then listed the attributes that would make her some man's ideal wife—"You are naturally so calm, and yet so affectionate, and so genteel . . . and your house is so well-ordered— and so tasteful, and everything about you so sweet." Such qualities, of course, also made her his ideal lover, and so he continued, though "I really feel to you as I do to Elly and Rachel . . . caress and love you as a child rather than as a woman . . . you naturally yearn for sympathy and affection, and until you find some more worthy subject, waste it on me."

As had been the case the previous decade in his relationship with Vinnie Ream, once again feelings for a much younger woman, who made him feel young and virile, were fulfilled in his relationship with Mary Audenreid. More even than Vinnie, Mary gave Sherman deep and lasting pleasure, a pleasure reciprocated by these two women who adored their powerful old man. The father/lover/counselor/swain would write his letters of double meaning to Mary Audenreid for many years. Sherman brought his innermost fantasy to the surface on August 2, 1886, when he wrote Mary from the hotel room he now shared with his daughter Lizzie, the very room he had occupied when Mary had made that trip with Sherman, Rachel, and the Hayes presidential party back in 1880. "Last night I had the most vivid dream," he wrote Mary. "I thought you & Rachel were in bed in the next room, that I knocked at the door & was called in, that I kissed Rachel good night and passed round to you, that you throw your arms about my neck and lavish on me the most loving caresses, that you exclaimed that you were lonely & I must not leave you. Whilst assuring you of my protection I woke up and for some moments could not [believe] that you were not actually present." The older man was embracing his young lover who was in bed with his own daughter, thus blurring and redoubling his forbidden pleasures.

That summer of 1886, as he was traveling in the West, his passion for Mary was much on his mind. Six weeks prior to his California dream, he wrote her of his longing to see her once more. "I hope to see you in person—as we have so many thoughts in common that we must be dear to each other." He then cast his memory back to the first times he and Mary had met. "Even in the hey-day of your young married life you told me you liked me better than Audenreid—that was not exactly proper, but no man dislikes such a compliment." Part of the pleasure of conquest of this younger woman was that it included a triumph over a younger man—her husband and his rival.

Quite often, Sherman would dissemble guilt for his stolen pleasures by insisting that he was Mary's adoptive father. "Look to me as a Second Father, wishing you every happiness, and loving you as a favorite child," he wrote her in 1882. Often he identified the ideal man for her— "some young, handsome fellow in who you could feel a pride and satisfaction," went one iteration, while another advocated a man of her own age, "healthy, ambitious, and who will love you *hard.*" Really, she ought not to "waste her affection" on him—"an old soldier soon to be turned out"—or "the last of the Mohicans," as he put it in several letters he wrote her after burying one or another of his old Civil War coheroes. In the abstract he could conclude with conventional disgust, "the mating of a young woman and an old man is simply an outrage against humanity." That was Mary's second father writing, as opposed to the old man who loved this young woman *hard.*

In time Sherman diminished the energy with which he pushed Mary away. Late in 1883, writing of her role as mother, he told Mary that he realized she was in "no hurry" to remarry, and that "unless some transcendent man and genius comes to you I somehow want you to wait now till Florence is well married." As Florence was a willful little flirt, in his opinion, he did not anticipate that her marriage was imminent; thus he was telling Mary how delighted he was with her status quo, and inferentially, theirs. He was confident that no genius more transcendent than he was likely to come along to lay a bigger claim to her hand than he offered her, even if she only got part of him.

Indeed, by 1885, Sherman was reinforcing Mary Audenreid in her enviable position as a wealthy widow—she had $7,500 per year income from her father's estate alone—in control of her own life. Referring to a medieval model for the powerful widow rather than to any contemporary feminist model of the new woman, he wrote how lucky she was to be "acting as the 'femme sole'—free, independent—Millions of women envy you this condition of absolute independence." Sherman was encouraging Mary in her unmarried state of independence, which she was clearly telling him was her desire.

However, as he had prepared for his November 1, 1883, retirement and his family's move back to St. Louis, Sherman had also taken steps to break off with Mary Audenreid. On June 2, he wrote her that it was "really doubtful if I can see much more of you—for my career is near its end—and your duty is elsewhere." She continued to write him passionate letters, which he tried at first to deflate, assuring her of her "warm place in my affections" and memory, but instructing her that he knew "I must play the part of father, not that of lover."

Soon after his return to St. Louis, Sherman's resolve weakened. After writing her in a chatty letter all about his remodeled house in St. Louis, especially his private suite of study, bedroom, and bathroom, he told her that his family had expressed a "well-settled opinion" that she ought to come soon and visit, preferably "as the wife of some good man." But he could not resist adding, "I surely hope you will come in any capacity you choose."

The more he thought of bringing Mary to St. Louis, the more aroused Sherman became. On December 18, 1883, he wrote her in the role of the ancient Greek kidnapper that he was coming to Washington on January 16, "ready to carry you bodily (willingly if possible—violently if necessary) to St. Louis, Missouri, where your friends demand your presence." Though he disguised his desires lightly by suggesting that he was merely passing on the wishes of his wife and daughters, he slyly indicated that really he wanted her there for his private purpose. "You can have the guest room right over my office and though somewhat jealous of my rights, I think I will let you have pretty free range of my sanctum"—his private dayroom and bedroom. He planned to bring his mistress to his bed right under his despised wife's nose, passing her off as a friend of his wife and daughters.

Whatever transpired in the inner sanctum, Mary's visit did not go well: She got into a quarrel with Ellen Ewing Sherman and her daughter Lizzie on the subject of religion. The issue apparently came up when Mary made some reference to the Louisville convent in which, despite being a Protestant, she was placing her increasingly wayward daughter, Florence, a comment the Sherman women took as slighting to their faith. It is impossible to know whether Ellen and Lizzie also discovered or suspected Mary's sexual bond with their husband and father. In any event, Sherman soon wrote Mary Audenreid that Mrs.

Sherman had struck her off her list of friends and placed her on her enemies-of-the-Church list. Any negative reference to the Church was like "the red flag to the wild bull," Sherman wrote Mary, as Ellen felt a "bigoted devotion to the Church." Mary had crossed the line, and was excommunicated from the Sherman home. He would not fight this expulsion, "as I do honestly want to live out the balance of my days in peace." Sherman would no longer bring his lover inside his family.

In a way, though he had lost one form of adventure with Mary, this episode gave him a new tie to her, for it allowed him to vent his smoldering fury on the subject of his wife's religious oppression of him. "[Ellen] would be made supremely happy if I would give up fame, country, everything, for conversion to her faith," he wrote Mary. This was an endless insult to which he would return repeatedly in his letters to her. He related with special heat one especially invidious comparison his wife had used, one that evidently dated from long in the past. "Mrs Sherman is not a Roman Catholic, but an Irish Catholic and [prefers] an Irish drayman who gets drunk six times a week and belabors his wife and children—yet who has kept the true faith and goes to Church on Sunday—as a higher type of manhood than a patriot soldier at the head of a victorious army." This story, which Sherman repeated several times in different forms over the years to Mary, has the ring of an old fight, in which Ellen had unleashed her heaviest religious artillery, damning her husband in contrast to the most loathsome form of masculinity he might imagine. Because she had been attacked by Ellen on the same religious grounds Ellen used against him, Mary's role as his spiritual ally against his enemy of a wife had deepened their bond.

Concomitantly, Sherman shared with his young lover his equally long-term resentments over his wife's perpetual sickness. "Mrs S considers herself a hopeless invalid but is not as sick as she supposes, but demands full attention," he complained to Mary only weeks before Ellen's death. Ever restless and claustrophobic, in retirement as earlier, Sherman felt more trapped than peaceful. His traveling did not diminish, as it took him out into the world where his "boys" loved him, and where, at times, Mary Audenreid did too.

On June 21, 1884, five months after Mary's visit to St. Louis, Ellen Ewing Sherman opened and read one of Mary Audenreid's letters to Sherman, one that was less offensive for any affectionate content than for anti-Catholic sentiment. Either she then burned all of Mary's letters in Sherman's files, or, as seems more likely, he did so in self-defense. "All your letters are destroyed, and I do not think Mrs Sherman had read any except the last," he wrote Mary after describing the incident. In turn Sherman blew up at his wife for invading his privacy. This issue over Mary continued between the Shermans for months. On November 26, 1886, he told Mary that he understood why she had been so "chary" in writing recently, and instructed her that should she "ever have occasion to write what is meant for me & me alone" to send her letters by registered post. He added, reflecting the anger he had doubtless expressed repeatedly to his wife, "you need not hesitate to write at any time . . . as Mrs Sherman will not open my letters *more.*"

Sherman had compelled his wife to apologize for opening that letter on the grounds of the standard of women's honor. On April 21, 1885, he wrote Mary, "I have repeatedly told Mrs Sherman what she knows as well as any woman, that no lady is willing to have her letters read by another, and she assures me that she never opened but one of your letters, about a year ago, when she supposed it was for her." In any event, Sherman urged Mary to resume pouring out her feelings to him without fear of discovery by Mrs. Sherman. On May 5, 1885, he assured her, "you can always write me as free & full as you think and feel—it will be a relief to you and you may be sure that I will destroy each and every letter . . . as you specially requested of me."

This destruction of love letters was terribly important to publicly prominent lovers like Sherman and Mary Audenreid, for their exposure could cause a major scandal. The greatest concern was for the woman involved, if she were socially prominent, as was Mary. Conclusive evidence of an adulterous affair would mean the destruction of her reputation and social standing. All respectable doors would slam shut on her. Thus, relatively early in their affair, Sherman wrote Mary from the Fifth Avenue Hotel in New York, "your letter which was handed me . . . gave me pleasure and pain. I am very fond of you and want your love, affection and veneration, but nothing which can cast a shadow on your after life."

Sherman, who had crashed before in public scandal in 1861, feared for his own reputation as well as for that of his lover. Thus, he wrote Mary in June 1886, "I promise on my honor as a soldier that no letter will remain in my file from your indulging in an expression of love & affection, so you ought to be equal in this, and destroy all of mine [where] more ardor than will stand the test [remains]." But Mary Audenreid ignored this injunction, as had Vinnie Ream.

As had been the case with Vinnie, Sherman was not a jealous lover to Mary. Indeed, he sensed from several of her letters that she was trying to arouse his jealousy by telling him of other men she was seeing. "I don't scare worth a cent, and am glad to hear that you are branching out a good deal," he wrote her from St. Louis in 1883, not long after he had moved there. Two years later, he repeated that he was "pleased you are 'going out,' and there is no reason that you should not get out of life all the pleasures and satisfaction you can," while he was in St. Louis and she in Washington. When he learned from her of her interest in another old general, Stewart Van Vliet, he understood that she continued to want the kind of company he had provided her, and assured Mary that Van Vliet was "an honest, kind hearted good fellow" who, "if you need a special friend would be good to you." General Absalom Baird, the aging inspector general of the army, whom she was seeing in 1886, was a "fine gentleman" as well, but "too old for you" in the way of marriage.

Evidently Mary Audenreid preferred not only older men, but older married men. In the summer of 1884, she visited the home of John R. Reed in Philadelphia, creating rather the same situation she had entered in the Sherman household in St. Louis nine months earlier. "Your preference seems to be for men already married, such as Reed," Sherman wrote her while she was with the Reeds. "I of course cannot properly encourage you to displace another woman, for she would torture your life—there is not fiend on earth so vindictive as a Woman robbed of her husband." Clearly, Sherman was projecting here. This was the sort of horror the very thought of divorcing Ellen gave him. If she was as vengeful as she was while he was living with her, imagine her wrath should he leave her for another woman!

Mary Audenreid's choices in other men must have provided on some level reassurance for Sherman that he was not about to lose her altogether into that appropriate marriage he often urged on her. Neither did her wandering ways dim his ardor, for he affirmed her sexual and emotional appetites as much as he did his own. He did not believe in, nor did he practice, a sexual double standard. Although she acknowledged to him that she took other lovers while remaining his, she remained very desirable and admirable to him. Whenever he could he would visit her in her Washington home, which he found tasteful and relaxing, and he also arranged assignations with her in New York City.

Sherman visited Washington and Mary Audenreid several times during his St. Louis years of retirement, 1883–86. When the timing was propitious he would forewarn her not to "invite company to visit me" in her home: "I would much rather visit you alone—and by not accepting dinners or parties I can accomplish more." That left his days for business and his evenings and nights for pleasure with Mary. On July 4, 1885, Sherman celebrated Independence Day by writing Mary of his ardent desire to see her. "I cannot write you everything: but can tell you much which ought not be written—Therefore I hope you will be in position to come to the Fifth Avenue Hotel [in New York] about August 20." She came, after which he assured her that they would continue to "go down the stream of life together with arms around each others necks."

Such visits increased in 1886, after the Shermans moved from St. Louis to New York. Indeed, as he was anticipating this change, he wrote Mary that one of the joys this move would bring him would be closer proximity to her. "I hope to see you soon in person—as we have so many thoughts in common that we must be dear to each other." Going back West for some engagements in the fall of 1886, he promised her several times that he would not be gone long, and that "after that I will be quick." He suggested she write him at his office at the Army Building in New York, with her social schedule, that they might clear their calendars in order to be together.

Late in 1886, Sherman had come to Washington for a visit and had not managed to see Mary alone. Evidently she wrote him in some vexation about this omission, for he replied, saying that he had been at the dentist's office every morning, that he had been "forced to make" many official calls, and that when he had come round "daily" she always had been "surrounded by friends and guests. . . . Of course I should have preferred to see you alone," he wrote placatingly. He promised to make up for this omission when next he visited Washington, asking her to choose the date in a letter she was to send him at his brother's house in Washington.

Clearly frustrated with the limitations of their relationship, Mary Audenreid began to press her position. In this, she posed a potential danger for her lover that Vinnie Ream had not, for she moved in the same social circles as Sherman and could quite easily bring him down if she were angry enough to destroy her own reputation at the same time. In the fall of 1887, she had aroused Mrs. Sherman's "enmity," Sherman wrote her in alarm, because "you do not speak of her with respect to mutual friends and exhibit my letters to show that I still retain my correspondence with you." By bad-mouthing Ellen, news of which came back to Sherman, Mary was breaking the woman's code of honor, just as Ellen had broken it by opening another woman's letter to her husband. All Mary would have to do in addition to what she had already done to cause a huge scandal would be to read aloud some of those letters to mutual women friends of Audenreid and the Shermans. Although the vexed Sherman wrote that "I still retain my fondness [for you]," he warned Mary quite sharply to back away from the incipient scandal she was creating. "[I] wish as far as possible not to give Mrs S. good cause of complaint." Sherman was drawing a line beyond which Mary had better not go or he would drop her rather than leave his wife. In the same letter, Sherman promised, in response to Mary's rather peremptory order to do so, that he would come to her hotel to escort her and her daughter off on the ocean liner taking them to Europe for a tour, even though he did not approve of her abandoning her "pretty home" in Washington (where he might have continued to visit her) to "run about" on the Continent. In this manner did their relationship reach an impasse after seven years. Mary could not displace Ellen Ewing Sherman to a degree sufficient to please her; Sherman would not leave his wife to live openly with her. He simply would not participate in such a desperate game. She could then flee the scene to punish him, but this would punish her as well, because she really did love him.

Mary and Florence stayed in Europe for thirteen months. When Sherman went to greet her at the Victoria Hotel in New York immediately after her return, "at the hour appointed," he found that she was not there and that she had left no message for him. "I confess I was sadly disappointed and have waited for an explanation. I think you owe me one," he wrote her, quite upset. Happily for them both, the letter announcing her arrival on a later sailing arrived the next morning, and he met her at the Victoria a few days later. The lovers must have made up, for he reassured her, on November 15, 1888, that in his new home at 75 West Seventy-first Street, "you need not fear that your letters will be seen by any eyes but mine . . . no letter addressed to me goes upstairs" to Mrs. Sherman, who was bedridden most of the time. When Ellen Ewing Sherman died, two weeks later, on November 22,

1888, the general accompanied her body to St. Louis for burial. On December 7, he wrote Mary Audenreid that he had returned to New York City, "for good and all," though everyone had been kind to him in St. Louis. "Ellen was so strong intellectually and was so absolutely devoted to her children that we miss her very much." "But," he told Mary, "Lizzie is a better manager than her mother and we go right along." Thus did Sherman convey a very unaffectionate and limited admiration for his dead wife of thirty-eight years, and then, far more strongly, and with an offhand brutality, express his continuous and continuing resentment toward his spouse, and his considerable relief that she was dead. This ruthless letter to Mary, although it did not capture all his ambivalent feelings about Ellen, did serve as a revealing final demarcation of the immensity of conflict that had characterized his marriage.

However, rather than bringing them together, Ellen's death marked the start of a final drift apart for Sherman and Mary Audenreid. Where before he had acted the patient counselor, Sherman now began to focus on Mary Audenreid's faults. More and more he found her a complaining, spoiled, rich widow who indulged every whim of the truant daughter through whom she lived far too much. When Mary and Florence were about to go on another one of their European trips to husband-hunt for Florence, Sherman scolded Mary, writing that another such voyage would be "a sin and a shame—Put that little foot down and say what *you* mean to do, and let Florence conform. Otherwise you are lost." Mary really did complain too much. She was independently wealthy, and "with a single child to worry you," Sherman admonished her, whereas he was burdened with six children and eight grandchildren, "every one of whom has wants, cares and aspirations as high as those of your Florence." Sherman then protested that he still wanted to hear about her life, a life in which he would continue to "mourn" and "rejoice" on cue—a life that, he implied, was petty and foolish, and finally boring, compared to his.

Sherman thought Florence such a handful that he was clearly glad she was not one of his brood. To one old army aide he wrote that "she surely is pretty, but the man who chooses her for wife can hardly expect a peaceful home." For several years, Florence dragged her mother through Europe, making and breaking engagements with various impoverished European aristocrats in a sort of sub–Henry Jamesian fashion. One, an Italian count, was, Sherman wrote Mary, merely "in search of a *dot* unencumbered by a woman," a mighty nasty slap at Florence; with a thread-needle Austrian baron Florence had just met on a riverboat up the Nile, Sherman wrote with equal disparagement, Florence had made what was clearly "another fool engagement."

Florence finally settled on a French count, and when she passed through New York with him on her way to Washington to be married, neither of them had "the politeness to attempt to recognize" his call on them in their hotel with a return call or even a card, he wrote Mary in disgust. Florence later told him that she was angry with him for refusing to give her away at her wedding. He was now seventy, he protested to Mary, and felt he had earned the right to refuse such social obligations, especially for such a rude girl. Florence's marriage did not work, and soon she broke down and underwent a rest cure at the hands of the noted psychological therapist S. Weir Mitchell, in Philadelphia.

"I have my own flock to look after," Sherman admonished Mary in 1890, thus placing her and the mess that was Florence outside his tent. By this point, Sherman's disengagement with Mary Audenreid was quite complete. In the end, peace and calm meant more to him than the excitement provided by his wealthy, beautiful, and troublesome mistress. He certainly did not want to marry this flamboyant mother and daughter team at this late date. One marriage had been more than enough.

And yet he carried an erotic flame of memory for Mary even after he had deactivated their relationship. When she was in Egypt in 1890, he wrote her, recalling his trip there in 1872, and fantasizing about the sensuality the mysterious East aroused in him. "I will not be the least astonished if the mysterious cable announces that [you] Philadelphia girls have been abducted into the hareem of some rich merchant of Smyrna, squatting on the divan eating sweet meats and delighted when the little bell tinkles and tells his favorite that he wants her." Sherman broke into this reverie with a declaration that he understood she was a modern American woman, free and independent. "No! the world has changed. Woman is no longer the slave of man, but his equal." And then Sherman defined equality as being women's control of the domestic sphere. "The wife of an American is the family, on which all society is based—take away the mother and the world goes back to chaos."

Mary Audenreid had been Sherman's equal in philandering, but she had failed as a wife and mother, Sherman implied, ignoring in his judgment-making his rather spotty service as a husband. Outside the family, wandering in Europe, she was ripe for the plucking by some grossly sensual Eastern slaveholder. In fact, at home, she had practiced non-nuptial polyandry with several older men, some among them married. Sherman did not rebuke her directly for that, but he did demonstrate that it was Ellen after all who had run his family, and that without her mothering, of himself as well as their children, his world would have collapsed. He had hated her in many ways, but he did give her primacy of place in his social values, even if he had been unfaithful to her in matters of the heart.[16]

With his actresses, with Vinnie Ream, and especially with Mary Audenreid, Sherman found a source of pleasure and intimacy that he never established with Ellen Ewing Sherman. He cashed in on his Civil War fame, his power, and his presence to attract younger women, but he loved them romantically and they loved him. His affairs were voluntary and jointly pursued rather than one-sided or exploitative on his part. Perhaps these relationships allowed him to continue a mutually painful marriage, at times with better grace than if he had remained monogamous. Without private happiness of the sort he found with Vinnie Ream and Mary Audenreid, the limitations of those relationships notwithstanding, he might well have collapsed into renewed depression under the frustrating burden of his demanding public life and his marriage. Whatever release he found with other women, however, he also exacted a terrible price from his wife in the way he was her husband. Her retreat into bitter isolation bore witness to her deep unhappiness, a great deal of it due to her marriage. Unfortunately for them both, divorce was unthinkable in their time and social place, and so they tortured one another to the grave.

20

Crisis of Patrimony: The Loss of Tom

IN THE GENTLEMANLY IDEAL to which William T. Sherman subscribed, patrimony was the indispensable corollary to matrimony. One of the basic and essential purposes of life was to raise, nurture, and send successful children out into the world to carry forward the larger familial purposes. Unlike his matrimonial trial, in which Sherman was an incomplete, ambivalent, and often angry partner, and from which he derived little pleasure and much pain, in his fathering Sherman was generally quite accomplished and happy. Although he complained incessantly about the financial cost of it all, he indulged his children in their material wants as no one had indulged him when he was young. He could leave his grand public sense of himself behind and express his zest for living, his sense of fun when he was with his children, and they could love him with a directness he could not find elsewhere.

At Christmastime 1865, only months after the end of the war, Sherman expressed something of the tenor of his affectionate attention for his children when he wrote to an associate that his most pressing social obligations were "solely to keep a promise to my little children to take them during these holy days to the opera, to the play and to . . . the Negro minstrels." Often the Shermans would gather around the piano together to sing away the evening, or the children would sit hushed while their father read to them from Shakespeare or Dickens.

Though their extravagances, especially in dress, astonished him, Sherman spent a great deal of money on his four daughters and clucked his tongue approvingly when they modeled their purchases for him. After his eldest daughter, Minnie, married Thomas W. Fitch in 1874, and Elly married M. Alexander Thackara in 1880, Sherman settled considerable sums on both young women and purchased homes for them as well. Sherman also invested in a St. Louis wireworks of which Fitch became president, and in a plant manufacturing fancy gas fittings that Thackara began in Philadelphia, when he left the navy the year after his marriage. In 1884, the Fitch wireworks went bankrupt, and for several years Sherman provided a monthly allowance for Minnie while Fitch sought to reestablish himself as a manufacturer in Pittsburgh.

All of his daughters doted on their father. For example, when Sherman helped Thackara with his debts in 1882, Elly told him, "You are *too* good as usual, Papa," and in 1890, on his seventieth birthday, she wrote to reassure him that "Every child & grandchild is rejoicing in their rich possession of the best of fathers as well as the world's best general." His daughters' one complaint was that he could not spend more time with them.

Angela Ewing, one of Sherman's nieces, recalled for Lloyd Lewis, one of Sherman's biographers, a visit she had made to her uncle's family, probably in the early 1880s, in St. Louis, which revealed the closeness of Sherman and his youngest daughter, Rachel, then a teenager. One evening during her cousin's visit, Rachel said, "Oh Angela, I think it is so nice to hear you say 'Father' and 'Mother'; we always say 'Papa' and 'Mama.' I think I'll change after this." The next morning at breakfast Rachel tried this reform out by asking for something, starting with, "Oh, Father," with the immediate result, Angela Ewing told Lewis, that "the General laid down his knife and looked at her with hurt and pain on his face, and asked 'What have I done to make you call me "Father"?' " According to Ewing, Rachel never repeated this experiment in formal diction.[1]

Sherman was far more demanding on his sons. It was they who were to go out to establish careers while protecting the women of both their natal family and the families they would head one day. Sherman projected much of his masculine anxiety onto his sons, fretting over them, wishing both to abet and to control them. After the Civil War, he understood they would bear a special load as the sons of such a famous father, though he tended to focus more on the advantages he could give them in their problems rather than on what his great fame might cost them.

After Willy, the apple of his eye, died in 1863, and he joined his wife in beatifying him, Sherman immediately turned to Tom with enormous expectation and equally great apprehension. Charlie would die in infancy in 1864, and Philemon Tecumseh (Cumpy) was born in 1867, when Tom was already eleven, and remained a baby while Tom was passing through adolescence. Thus, Tom bore nearly the full weight of Sherman's hopes, fears, and filial demands, which were compounded by the extra burden of Willy's emotional ghost.

As a toddler Tom was the most stubborn and angry of the Sherman clan, the hardest to break of willfulness, a form of suppression that the Shermans, in common with most Victorian parents, considered their fundamental duty to accomplish. Ellen wrote her husband as Tom was turning three, "Tommy is a much better boy than when you left. He fondles me a great deal and I have had no occasion to whip him since you left but once or twice." This was the positive side of the coin. Later in his third year, however, his mother reported to his father that Tommy was the "outlaw" of the family, "pretty much given up" by his sisters and playmates. He had become the renegade to her as well, which she indicated when she wrote that "our children are healthy and, with one exception at least, they are good . . . bright and pretty," by which she clearly meant Tom. Tom was the black sheep for his father as well. In 1862, when Tom was six, Ellen wrote her husband, "You seem to think so much more of Willy than of Tommy that they all perceive it." All his siblings picked up on the cold shoulder his parents offered Tom.[2]

When Willy died, Sherman immediately placed a crushing burden as the only son and heir on little Tommy's shoulders, while at the same time expressing his fears that Tommy would never measure up. On the reverse side of a copy of that printed letter of gratitude he sent to his guard regiment right after Willy's death, Sherman wrote to Tommy, who was not yet seven, "You are now my only Boy, and must take poor Willy's place, to take care of your sisters, & to fill my Place when I too am gone." Sherman instructed his remaining son that he had promised his soldiers that wherever and whenever Tom would meet a soldier who had known Willy, Tom would give him "half you have." This compulsory gifting, whether it meant half of the money in his pocket or half his estate, would guarantee that, in return, when he was a grown man the veteran's charity would "insure all you need in this world." Thus, little Tommy was charged with an elaborate ritual, surely incomprehensible to him, that he was to fulfill for both his dead hero brother and his father, should the general be killed at war.

Time after time, Sherman would repeat to Tom, as he did during the march to the sea, on November 10, 1864, "always remember that on you now rests the care of our family. Minnie and Lizzie . . . will marry and change their names, but you will always be a Sherman and must represent the family." In this letter, Sherman informed eight-year-old Tom that he was now experiencing a "full measure of . . . what the People call fame & glory," which he would willingly give up to "come home quietly and have you and Willy meet me at the cars." Breaking into this reverie, Sherman then added to his remaining son, "Willy will never meet me again in this world and thus you and I must take care of the family as long as I live & then will be your turn, so you have a great deal to do." Sherman then instructed Tom that not only did he have much to learn in school, but "I want you also to learn to ride, so if I come home you can go along, when I want to ride on horseback. The girls can ride in carriages, but boys & men are better in a saddle." Willy had been a fearless rider, who had accompanied his father on inspections of his troops, decked out in his little sergeant's uniform, while Tommy had remained in the carriage with his sisters, like a little girl.

At times Sherman would quite consciously try to boost Tom's shaky self-esteem, as he did when he wrote in January 1865, "Mama always tells me what a fine manly boy you are growing to be and I am very proud of you." The father realized that there was something less than martial in the nature of this rather fragile boy, but that boys could grow up to be different from their fathers and still make good, competent men. Thus, he could forgive Tom the lack of rugged manliness he imagined had been his own characteristic when he had been a boy, a quality that had been true of Willy as well. "When I was a boy I was not as small as you and you can take your time learning as fast as you please, and when you get old enough can choose for yourself whether to be a soldier, a lawyer, doctor or farmer. . . . I don't want you to be a soldier or a Priest but a good useful man." Sherman indicated that he could accept the fact that Tom was not cut out to follow his father's martial career; neither did he want him to follow his mother's inner path to a churchly vocation. That left the useful professions of the law, medicine, or farming. The merchant alternative seems to have been unacceptable to this anxious parent, one who was loving as well, and who tried to recognize his son's potential, even while he was also quite didactic toward him.[3]

By the time Tom was fourteen, Sherman had settled on the law for him. Among other benefits, this choice would free his father from the burdens of looking after family business, enabling him to indulge that vagabondage that best suited his nature. From one of his jaunts to the wilds of Texas, Sherman wrote Tom in 1871, "this wild prairie life suits me so well that I expect to be at it for most of my days, and you will have to manage the family." While he was in Europe later that year, Sherman put a less self-serving face on this paternal proposal when he assured Ellen that "Tom has the industry and strength of purpose to make a lawyer worthy of his lineage." After all, his own father had been a lawyer and judge, one of a long Sherman line of lawyers and judges, and Thomas Ewing was a renowned lawyer as well. Perhaps his own martial career had been the aberration, he implied, and Tom would revert to the tradition of solid Sherman lawyers. Linked to this chain of reasoning was Sherman's own considerable disillusionment with the postwar army, which convinced him to advise Tom to decline President Grant's 1873 offer of a place in West Point, a refusal that would keep Tom independent of politics and government, that form of public service that Sherman felt was grinding him down into misery. Tom did decline. In his father's mind it was rather daring thinking to excuse his son from military service, but there were potential long-term benefits for himself as well as for his son in the choice.[4]

Sherman was authoritarian about the education he wanted for his son, which would prepare him for that useful, independent vocation he had chosen for him in the law. Such an education should be grounded in the most realistic, scientific forms of knowledge. "Logic, mathematics & the actual exact sciences embrace knowledge of things and of laws as they actually exist," Sherman instructed his son. Indeed, a personal career could be mapped out on a predictable, scientific trajectory. "Life is a problem in virtual velocity. The purpose . . . is the direction. The first resolution is the force—and if it be in the laws general direction, then the result shows a long successful career." The certitude of physics expressed the way the individual could tie into the scientistic progressivism true of the nation as a whole, Sherman believed, for "the next period will be suited to men who think and work

[on] the foundations [of] positive knowledge of natural law, of mechanics, of chemistry, metallurgy, etc." Sherman rejected out of hand the opposing and to him antiquated view of education as moral training. "The classics at best will only serve to show what existed under an old & past system. . . . Moral studies contemplate man & objects [only in] artificial relations . . . and ought to be left to the family and the home."

Sherman thus guided his teenage son—who was then a student at the Catholic academy attached to Georgetown University, which Sherman detested—away from what he considered the superstitious and toward what he believed to be the rational. "I am not satisfied that Georgetown [has] professors skilled in teaching modern science." This portion of Tom's education was only a narrow Catholic one, "but your Mama thinks religion so important that everything else must give place to it." Attempting to enlist Tom on his side of the marital quarrel, Sherman insisted that Tom was, at age eighteen, "big enough to think for yourself," which would lead him to choose a practical, scientific education over a merely religious one. He insisted that Tom freely choose to reject his mother's religious, superstitious, retreatist worldview for his father's rationalist, activist one. To this end he urged Tom to choose to attend the new Sheffield School of Science at Yale University. Eager to please his father, Tom did so, enrolling in 1874.[5]

During his three years at Yale, Tom was a hardworking and successful student. Though he was highly conscious of being a Sherman, he did not merely trade on his famous name and play at his student role, but applied himself seriously. Although he wrote his father that Yale "is a poor place to practice economy," especially "when a boy comes with a name and social position," nevertheless he refused to accept the "false standard . . . making dress and wealth more desirable . . . than scholarship or brains," and he scorned joining the deeply entrenched, elitist "little societies" at Yale, which, he believed, only "nourish a foppish feeling." Tom assured his father that he was fast becoming the progressive, useful, bourgeois sort of man his father intended him to be, and that instead of joining "cliques" he was trying to "encourage an open debating society" at Sheffield. He failed in this attempt, but such efforts demonstrated that Tom was attempting to be a self-made meritocrat rather than a parasitical loafer, that he was just the sort of eager beaver he knew his father wanted him to be.

Even as Tom was entering Sheffield, his father had mapped out his later career. After Yale he was to proceed to law school in St. Louis, where subsequently he was to join a practice that would doubtless flourish by the time of his father's retirement, thus providing a sure and comfortable transition of active work and wealth-creation from father to elder son. As early as the fall of 1874, when Tom had just entered Sheffield, his father wrote his old comrade, Phil Sheridan, "Tom is at Yale College, much complimented, and will in a few years be a lawyer, self-maintaining, when I can feel relieved of the dread of leaving [my family] unprovided for." He had already begun to approach several prominent St. Louis lawyers, each of whom expressed great interest in taking Tom into his firm, no doubt contemplating with interest the business such a famous connection might generate for them.

Sherman had designed his son's future; Tom merely had to work hard to fit the course his father had prepared. Telling Tom that he had a law office all picked out for him, Sherman added, "thus far you have had more advantages of travel and instruction than almost any young man of your day—I will continue to afford you the same advantages till you can feel independent." Sherman was doing all he could to provide for his elder son in ways his father had been unable to provide for him. However, this did not mean that Tom would necessarily perceive this road as the path to independence.

In early 1875, Tom did agree to a legal career in St. Louis, the future his father thought right for him, which gave his father a great deal of relief and satisfaction. To Ellen Ewing Sherman, who was living in St. Louis with Tom during her trial separation from her husband, Sherman asserted in 1877, while Tom was attending the law school at Washington University, "I am sure that if Tom goes on as now, he will in two years enter on a career not only brilliant but successful in a business sense—my business friends [in St. Louis] will be his, and they are among the best men in the West." Sherman then pointed out to his wife, in a needling way, "I know that you are more concerned as to his moral and religious station—but the other is equally important. Indeed no man can be himself unless he attain a position among men prominent for intellectual or business qualification." At the same time Sherman told Tom, "there is not a shadow of a doubt of your professional success in due time, and the acquaintances you already have of your own and of mine, will be to you a fortune some day." Sherman also reminded his son again that his own path to retirement was being eased by Tom's steady and certain upward path.

Tom was keen to begin repaying his father for all his father had done for him. When he moved to St. Louis to attend law school in the fall of 1876, Tom began to demonstrate his future service to his father by taking over direction of the general's considerable business affairs in that city. He handled numerous real estate and banking problems and reported on them in great detail to his father, with the same hunger to please through service that the youthful Sherman had shown to his demanding and distant stepfather, Thomas Ewing, before the Civil War. Indeed, as he reassured his father during his last year at Yale, "what ambition I have comes from the fact that I am known as General Sherman's son," to which he added on January 28, 1878, "I know that I should be very ungrateful to Providence and to you if I did not appreciate the many advantages I possess in having my time free for study, in having a charming home and abundance of everything that a man can want; and I assure you I am as happy & contented as I ever want to be."6

And then, four months later, on May 22, 1878, Sherman received a letter from Tom that declared, "I do not intend to become a lawyer [because] I have chosen another profession—in one word I desire to become a priest—a Catholic priest." He had wanted to become a priest ever since his adolescent years at the Georgetown preparatory school, he now told his father. He had never wished to become a lawyer, but had kept his vocation to himself for four years—"that have seemed to me like an eternity"—because he knew that his conviction would "wound and grieve the kindest and tenderest of fathers." He had waited until his twenty-first birthday, when he would "attain an age when every man feels that he must act for himself . . . that as a rational being he must follow the dictates of his own reason, and that nobody on earth can relieve him of doing so." He had told his mother of his decision only a week earlier. After recovering from her initial surprise, she had agreed with him, "completely and in principle," and had given her approval, he reported to his father.

Sometime after the event, the Sherman family destroyed the general's furious immediate response to Tom, a letter accusing him of dereliction of social duty, desertion of his family, and self-absorption. In response, Tom stood up to his father, man to man. "We stand on two sides of the shield," he wrote with considerable bravado on May 25, "and neither of us can see fully the other's side. Starting with different premises we reach different conclusions, and each of us feels that argument is vain and useless." Two days later, Tom wrote again, denying that he had the future of the family dependent on him as his father had insisted was to be the guiding star of his life, and arguing that, far from retreating from the world, after a few years of "study for the profession as a man does at West Point," he would be "actively employed among his fellow men" in an "honest calling." He would continue to emulate his father, who remained his "model of every manly virtue, spotless honor, unsullied purity, kindness, patience, and forbearance, forgiveness of injuries and every other virtue." Such a father would forgive such a son, Tom implied, even as he tried to mollify his father who was still expressing anger at what had happened. He intended as a priest to "reach the lower classes . . . and thus aid the government in suppressing Communism, etc.," Tom argued. After all, he was joining not a monastery but the Jesuits—the most militant, almost military branch of the Church. He was intending to carry on his father's war for America by other means, in a new age. He also announced to his father that he had booked passage for June 5 on the *Scythia* to sail for seminary in England. Such decisiveness would make his father "feel easier when the suspense and doubt are over," he insisted.

Receiving Tom's declaration of independence, the general panicked—it was a "thunder-clap" and a "great calamity," he wrote to several of his closest friends within days of hearing the news. The announcement came as a shock because, as he told his brother, John, Tom "has always been so good, so obedient," and, far from hinting at his vocation, had seemed so happily set on the lawyer's course his father had outlined for him. Rage quickly overtook stunned disbelief. Tom had taken as his purpose "to abandon—to desert me now," a fulfillment of Sherman's deepest fears throughout his lifetime. In addition to abandoning his father, Tom had deserted his whole family, and had shirked his life duty. "I have four daughters all dependent in a contingency not unlikely of my death or downfall, upon my oldest son—this duty he has no right to throw off, even to save his own soul, or the souls of others. His own peace of mind must be secondary to his duty to others." The father had created a perfect future for his family, with elder son Tom at the apex of the design, and now Tom had deserted and the whole plan had collapsed. "He was the keystone of my arch, and his going away lets down the whole structure with a crash."

Sherman immediately displaced much of the wrath he felt for Tom onto the Roman Catholic Church that had purloined him. To his close friend, Henry Turner, he argued on May 27, "I cannot turn against him, but I do against that Church, which has poisoned his young mind, wound its tendrils around his heart and weaned him from his Father who has never denied him anything, but has afforded him extraordinarily opportunities to travel, to study, and to mingle with the youth who must take the helm of this Government." Tom had deserted to the enemy camp, forcing Sherman into the "ranks" of those who regarded the Catholic Church as "our public enemies." He declared to an old associate on June 5, "my feelings are now fast crystallizing into deep damnable hatred of that Church, which teaches that parents have no rights, that the Church may . . . appropriate to its own uses the child, the moment he reaches manhood." It was the "call of that insidious whispering set of priests" that had seized Tom from him and "all my plans of life are . . . thus absolutely blown to the wind."

Prior to leaving for England, Tom came to pay his father a visit of leave-taking. In a rush of tumultuous feelings, Sherman tried every sort of approach to stop Tom's desertion. "I *never* consented," to Tom's going, Sherman wrote a close friend three weeks later. "I tried coaxing, persuasion, threats, demands—everything, almost abasing myself before my own son—and before the Catholic clergy to save him and myself from this dread consequence." When Tom had told him he had found a "vocation from Heaven," he had replied from "my heart it was a vocation from Hell." As a last resort, when Tom stood his ground, Sherman wrote to John Cardinal McClosky of New York, pleading with him to intercede on his behalf with Tom to stop his son's desertion. Whatever the cardinal might have said did not deter Tom. The night before he left, he wrote to his eldest sister, Minnie, "I felt overwhelmed and crushed by Papa's grief and much contrary advice. . . . My step seems rash and hasty to all who do not know what it is to watch & wail & hope & pray & long & dwell & despair until a young heart grows & can face anything to attain its object—especially where the object is God."

To gain his independence, Tom had felt compelled to launch a coup d'état. So obedient to his father had he always been, so dutiful and so enthralled, that he had been compelled to create a second, inner persona—the priest to be—to oppose the Tom his father was defining and controlling. His coup against his father and his father's version of him was utterly ruthless, and it drew an enormous response from his father, which must at some level have contained antiauthoritarian satisfaction for Tom, even as he fled across the Atlantic Ocean from an authoritar-

ian father to an authoritarian clerical order. Perhaps it took such a totalist counterauthority to shore Tom up sufficiently to go through with
his rebellion. He was very dramatic, as are all young men when they go
through their identity crises, but there was also unmistakable pride in
Tom's assertion of his own, or at least of an alternative, definition of
manhood. And by telling his father at the same time, as he did, that
General Sherman remained his manly ideal in his new priesthood, Tom
could deflect his own guilt for his actions and affirm to himself that he
would become a general in the army of the society of Jesus, *his* army,
not his father's, his *own* generalship, but a generalship all the same.

Sherman remained distraught. "I can hardly endure my thoughts,"
he wrote Henry Turner on May 27, adding to another St. Louis friend
the same day, "I am simply miserable, and it will embitter my whole
life." The next day Sherman told John Schofield that he felt "cruel and
humiliated in the extreme," a revisitation of dreaded emotions from his
antebellum past, and that his heart had turned "cold as lead." The following day he cried out to John in great anguish that he had cast Tom
out of his lead-cold heart and wished him dead. "I believe now I would
rather decorate his grave than to know that in a few days he will sail
from New York to a worse than grave." Though he denied that he had
denounced Tom to his face, or that their break had been final, after
Tom sailed, Sherman did insist to another close friend, "I regard Tom
as dead." The Tom he had imagined, the Tom who was an extension of
his own dreams, was indeed dead, and the newborn Father Thomas the
priest was a monster from a nightmare.[7]

In a very real family sense Tom had chosen to desert his father's field
for his mother's. Nevertheless, after reading Sherman's initial letter to
Tom bemoaning the "ruin" of the family, Ellen wrote her husband on
May 25 that Tom "never gave me even a hint" of his thinking until
May 12, and thus had been "uninfluenced" by her, an assertion her
husband evidently accepted at first. She insisted that she had "not
dared to meddle with anything so sacred as between his soul & his
God." Ellen did not, however, hide from her distraught husband her
intense pleasure at Tom's decision. Her faith made her believe, she told
him, that Tom's act was not "a disgrace but . . . an honor—not . . . a
defection but a heroic response to a call from the Lord." Indeed, far
from losing Tom she believed he would remain "less sequestered" from
the family than if he had chosen to marry. She knew her husband's
response was to feel "stunned and distracted," but she expected him to

return to his "normal condition of kindness and gentleness of heart and generosity and justice of sentiment," and to bear this reversal with the "natural heroism" and "glorious resignation" he had shown when he had given Willy up to God during the war. Indeed, she concluded rather matronizingly, "I look beyond the dark cloud which hangs over your spirits to the glorious sunshine which God will shed upon you in recompense for this trial well borne."

Ellen Ewing Sherman seized her opportunities like the powerful domestic politician she was, and extracted considerable rewards from them. She shared in Tom's excitement, and in the drama of the conflict he was acting out. She scarcely concealed her pleasure in a series of letters to her eldest daughter, Minnie. On May 17, five days after Tom had told her and three days before he wrote his father, Ellen wrote Minnie not to be "alarmed" by any "dispatches" she might receive, "when we hear from poor Papa next week." On May 21, the day after Tom had written, Ellen contentedly reported to Minnie, "he feels very happy, like a bird set free, and I feel the same for him," adding that the "sundering of ties is terrible," and, most significantly, that "your poor Papa cannot have the consolation we have and I feel great sympathy for him." In other words, she shared in Tom's feelings of victory over his father while professing sympathy for Sherman in his defeat, which was exactly what she knew he would consider Tom's act.

Three days later, Ellen wrote Minnie that she was waiting with Tom, "in dreadful suspense," for the explosion that was certain to come from Washington, a response that she anticipated would "burden" her "with a heavy load that may not be shaken off till long after I am safe within a monastery's walls, for whose protection, in view of his chagrin, disappointment and possible opposition, you may be sure I am now longing most heartily." She was prepared to follow Tom into the sanctuary of the Church as a means of final escape from her husband's wrath.

When the dreaded letter came, however, Ellen discerned immediately that her husband was more stunned than angry, and that despite his arguments to Tom, "he evidently does not hope to alter the determination," she assured Minnie on May 25. He lacked effective heavy artillery after all, and she would not have to retreat behind the walls of a convent. She concluded quite cooly, "I think he will feel better after awhile." She felt her enemy had been confounded and that she and Tom were in the stronger position. Indeed, Tom had written his father "most tenderly" that morning. Her subsequent letters to Minnie were calm and detached: She felt quite in control of Tom as well as of his father. Papa's second letter, of May 27, was "much less gloomy" than the first, and "poor Tom feels greatly relieved, as do we all." Three days later, "Papa writes rather bitterly. . . . He has evidently got to the second stage of the malady & will feel better when he becomes more familiar with the idea and talks it over with others," she judged, with almost clinical detachment. Preparing to send Tom off to Washington to say farewell to his father and thence to sail for England, Ellen was certain, she wrote Minnie, that he would "leave your poor Papa's heart soothed & reconciled." However unlikely the potential for such an immediate conversion of her husband's feelings might be, Ellen felt "very cheerful about it all," certain that for the remainder of his life Tom would be "anchored in port just outside of heaven."[8]

The other Sherman children were torn in their loyalties between their parents: They all loved their father, but they were devout Catholics whose lives focused around religious practices, and their mother held the stronger cards in any deep family division over religion. One can see some of their conflicting loyalties in the letters nineteen-year-old Elly wrote back to St. Louis after Ellen had dispatched her and seventeen-year-old Rachel to be with their father when Tom arrived. "He cries and cries—is absent-minded—looks old and does not take his nap, but reads or thinks," Elly reported to her mother on May 31, though by her description she actually may have been observing obsessive brooding. In considerable anguish because of her divided loyalties, she added that "I feel so like a spy when I write you this." She had a terrible headache from her confusion, she told her mother, noting that she was trying to distract her father by talking "brightly" about every issue, a tactic that would work for a time until her father would break into her sprightly conversation, asking her, "How about Tom?" The day after Tom left for England, Elly wrote her papa from West Point that she was so anxious about Tom she could "scarcely think of anything else."

Sherman wrote to Elly, to Lizzie, and to Minnie over the next few months, ceaselessly repeating his sense of Tom's desertion, of his betrayal, of his voluntary choice of death in life. The deceit had been so great, he felt. As he wrote to Elly a week after Tom's departure, "What wounds me to the quick is that Tom by no word look or sign gave me a hint" of his decision till he had "arranged with strangers for the means to enable him to carry into effect his purpose." All through the years he had planned Tom's life, Tom had consented without any apparent ill-feeling until he backed "square down" at the last moment, telling his father that he "had *never* intended to be a lawyer." This calling to the priesthood could not be a heavenly vocation—"God does not act in this way." Sherman then concluded rather wanly to Elly that she had "always been a good child & whilst life lasts I will try to be a good father to you." He was trying to reassure her that he would not take out on her the hurt paternal feelings Tom had caused him.

But his faith in his fatherhood was badly shaken: Which of those Catholic children could he really trust—which would not decamp as had Tom? He wrote quite angrily to Minnie on June 16 that he was now deeply suspicious of "you and all Catholics," and that he was furious with their Church, "which utterly ignores the claims of the father to his child, and absolutely robs him of the sympathy of his family in his duties." If he had always feared at some level that he was the odd man out in the family, Tom's rebellion, and the circling of Tom's Catholic siblings around his choice and around their mother, had confirmed his worst fears. Under such pressure he could not empathize with the stress Tom had visited on his sisters, seeing only their religion and not their torn daughterhoods.[9]

Thus Sherman's sense of betrayal and abandonment was deepened not only by Tom's flight but by his realization of how near his family was to disintegration. With Tom gone, Ellen was preparing to rent out the Shermans' St. Louis house, and he and she had not reconciled from their separation. Ellen was planning to go next with the children to Baltimore, where they would enroll in Catholic schools. Sherman did not know where Ellen and his children might land, and he was terribly afraid. In his mind his family was aligned with an all-encompassing Church from which he was excluded, which made him a monster in their eyes. Writing to his Iowa confidant, S. H. M. Byers, Sherman deepened this sense of the Church as having cleaved Tom and all his family away from him. "This terrible and entirely unexpected act has broken up my family circle completely." Mrs. Sherman had leased out the St. Louis house "to a stranger for a nominal sum," and had gone back to Lancaster, "her parental home," and thence to Baltimore and God only knew where else, "and I don't know if we will ever again have a home." Although Ellen wrote him that "I fear you are very lonely, dear Cump, without the girls," and invited him to visit them wherever they might go, Sherman did not know if he would remain a father in any meaningful sense of the word to any of his children, much less Tom.[10]

Sherman's friends tried to calm him down by helping place Tom's departure in context. Writing that "I deeply sympathize . . . with your disappointment," U. S. Grant reassured his old comrade that he ought to find "good consolation" that Tom had not gone, "as too many young men do, into a life of dissipation and general worthlessness." Both Grant and Sherman knew many fathers who had suffered that real moral loss, and to the contrary, Tom, "wherever he is and whatever he does . . . will be an ornament and a credit to his profession."

John Schofield wrote an equally sympathetic and more searching letter. While recognizing that for his friend Sherman it was impossible to regard Tom's choice as other than a "great calamity," in Schofield's experience, "young men of intellect and self-will rarely if ever follow blindly . . . what their fathers have marked out for them." Thus, Tom's rebellion was natural, and he had acted not from some selfish motive but from "the higher and nobler sense of duty," the same sort of sensibility felt by all great "churchmen, statesmen or soldiers who have given to the world all in it that is good and great." Schofield was certain, he wrote Sherman, that Tom would yet do his father proud by his actions in the world of public events. He was in effect telling Sherman that Tom had chosen a route in which he might be independent as well as socially responsible on his own terms, and that Sherman ought to take this choice not as a personal rejection but as a deeper affirmation of the heroic sense of duty in which Tom was carrying on his Sherman inheritance. To Schofield's sensitive analysis, Sherman replied, "my grief is now too poignant to be cured by philosophy."[11] He simply could not detach himself sufficiently from his sense of his loss to reenvision Tom as an independent but still worthy man.

Deriving little comfort from his friends' advice, deeply wounded by his elder son, quite suspicious of his other children, Sherman spent a miserable summer and fall in 1878 alone in Washington. The Army Bill then in Congress threatened to cut his pay by 40 percent, and he feared he might be forced from office. Even more significantly, news of Tom's grand departure and the continuing tensions within the Sherman family began making the gossip rounds in Washington and leaking into the press. Indeed, on October 27, Sherman felt compelled to write a letter to the *Chicago Tribune* in response to what he called widespread "untruth and gossip," insisting that Mrs. Sherman and his unmarried children were living with him in Washington, and that Mrs. Sherman was merely passing "much of her time" in Baltimore, where Rachel and little Cumpy were in school. In fact, Ellen was boarding full-time in Baltimore as Sherman wrote this letter, in her continuing separation from her husband, and visiting from time to time in Washington. The cover story that the Sherman family remained as a proper family should be was wearing thin.

This family crisis climaxed over the Christmas season in 1878. Refusing to be trapped into the endless round of Washington Christmas parties, Ellen entrained for the holiday to Baltimore, insisting that Lizzie and Elly join her and the two younger children for Christmas day, leaving Sherman alone. Rejecting his demands that she return to Washington and do her duty, Ellen wrote him a furious letter on December 21 from Baltimore, in which she threw down the gauntlet. "I fully intended and desired to spend Christmas with you & the girls in Washington although you did not signify the slightest wish to have us," she began. Feeling ill and fatigued, she had elected to stay in Baltimore instead. Besides, as a "poor plain old woman" (doubtless a direct quotation from her husband when he had barked at her recently), she believed she had no duty whatsoever to be in Washington. "I owe the public nothing & I am nothing to the public."

As for compelling the older girls to come to her, she denied that she had given orders " 'over your head'—to speak in military phrases," the phrases in which the general had accused her of misbehaving. But, she continued, throwing her husband's martial language back in his face, "they are under my 'immediate command' & to follow still further the military metaphor, you gave Elly orders & then acted on them over my head." Elly had told her that " 'Papa . . . told [me] to come,' " and at this point, Ellen told her husband, she had supervened with orders of her own. So the general would have to be alone for once on Christmas—"alone in your room"—she mocked, but after all, "you do not care anything particularly for Christmas." He always proclaimed his aversion to sentimentality, posing as a tough soldier. Rubbing in his isolation and his compulsive gregariousness even further, she repeated, "you cannot be alone in your room a day according to you." If it were that impossible for him to be alone, he could come to Baltimore if he wished. As for herself, she would be back for the Shermans' annual New Year's Eve reception, "to receive guests where you live," not to please or honor him but to the end of "the protection of my own name [and] the maintenance of my true position in the eyes of the world, which for the peace of my daughters I must somewhat regard." Beyond that one occasion, he had better not make any further family plans, "without seeing beforehand how far you can rely on keeping it up," on his own, for "I can do very little in the future."

In this brutal diplomatic note, Ellen Ewing Sherman laid down powerful conditions for the maintenance of the Sherman family. If the final break were to come, all the children would follow her orders, as she had just demonstrated in her successful pulling of the older girls to her for Christmas, and as Tom had demonstrated in his independent action on which she had capitalized. If separation were to become permanent the general would be left all alone, stripped of a respectable wife and family. He had better not try any further military-style ordering about of her—she was not his subaltern, but her own person—and if push came to shove, she would be the commander of the Sherman children.

Staring this near ultimatum in the face, the general backed down. As for commanding Lizzie and Elly, he stressed to his wife, by return post, after he had received her letter, "I gave no orders. On the other hand Lizzie told me that you had called for her & Elly to come over for Christmas . . . two days before you notified me of this." If he now complained about who was peremptory, he did not dispute Ellen's authority, nor her effectiveness. "I had declined several invitations because I understood you were to be here," he insisted, and then Ellen's orders to the girls had "simply left me out." As to Ellen's public duties, Sherman wrote, "you think you are old and owe nothing to the public. I think you do, and can *well* do it if you willed—but you don't will." But, rather than reiterating any demands, he just restated his feeling that *he* could not escape his social duty, whatever she might choose to do. As for his peremptory demands on her, as she put it, "I am not as bad as you claim, and I have never questioned your character or motives." In addition, Sherman reminded his wife of his fear of loss of pay and of his even greater fear of public exposure. "We cannot stop the tongues of scandal, and always the worst construction is put on human actions. [We are] surrounded by gossips who can wound and cannot heal." Sherman then promised to send Ellen $600 before Christmas, as a peace offering. She had won through *force majeure*. He had begun a retreat.

The next day, December 23, Sherman wrote a self-pitying letter to Minnie, in response to one of her infrequent letters, complaining that he rarely heard from her, but conceding, "I rarely think of writing a letter except on business," an expression of his feeling that he could not really trust intimacy with any of his children. Sherman emphasized that "Tom's course has embittered me more than I ought to write," and complained, "I did not know that your Mama wanted the girls with her on Christmas—a religious holiday [as Ellen would have it], as also a family holiday [as he would have it], till I declined several invitations so that I will be alone that day." Then Sherman summarized his saddest complaint: "I sometimes feel bad when I realize that the Church demands all my family, and drives me further and further into the society of strangers." He feared that scandal might "drive me out of the Army," at severely reduced pay, and that he did not have any safe place "to seek refuge" if worse came to worst.

On Christmas day, Sherman sat bleakly and humiliated in his study, writing to distant old friends. "All my people are over at Baltimore and I am alone," he wrote Henry Turner. At least on New Year's Eve, "the social day of Washington . . . Mrs Sherman and the children will all be here." But Christmas day "is a sort of Sunday, offices closed, streets abandoned and diners at home. I have no home and am therefore sort of vagabond." Vagabondage had generally suited Sherman, but only when he was the one doing the wandering, temporarily away from home base.[12]

Faced with the prospective loss of his wife and his other children, as he had recently lost Tom, fearing the loss of his office and 40 percent of his salary and his public reputation as well, Sherman experienced a long night of the troubled soul at Christmastime in 1878. Most telling was Ellen's threat to make a final rupture, taking their children with her. Though she cared for her public station and reputation as Mrs. General Sherman more than her husband may have realized, she drove him into a panic by demonstrating at the time of the traditional family festival just how far she was apparently willing to go to isolate and abandon him. She threatened to destroy his whole life, private and public. Most telling of all for Sherman was the potential loss of *all* his children and not just Tom.

Sherman began to back away from this impossible conclusion in his letter to Ellen of December 23, where he acquiesced to her sense of first place in the family. One cannot know conclusively what shouting

matches had preceded this letter, though Ellen had quoted quite liberally from his martial denunciations in her letter of December 21 to him.
More significantly, one cannot discover to what degree Sherman
openly blamed Ellen for Tom's decampment into the priesthood. Perhaps he simply maintained or heightened his earlier denunciations of
her religious retreatism and her numerous other shortcomings; perhaps he directly blamed Tom's choice on her, dealing with it as the logical outcome of her mothering of his son. Certainly his fury with her
reached some sort of climax because of Tom, whether or not he overtly
spelled it out that way.

Whatever the content of his verbal invective, Ellen drew an unmistakable line that Christmas, and he retreated to a degree at least minimally acceptable to her, for New Year's Day 1879 marked the real
beginning of the end of their separation. Although he had no way of
knowing it at this time, a year later he would begin his long affair with
Mary Audenreid, but this became a second, secret, compensatory emotional life; to the world and to Ellen and his children he renewed his
vows of respect and affirmation and the Sherman family remained repaired on the surface for the following decade, until the end.

Tom had presented a crisis of patrimony for his father. He broke his
father's belief that he could control him, and showed his mother the
ruthless and efficient path she also could use for breaking out toward a
kind of independence from her husband. At the same time, Tom first,
and Ellen subsequently, showed Sherman the yawning void beneath
the social construction of his heroic life, and pushed him into renewed
paternal efforts in order to reduce his fears of plunging into the chasm
of permanent disgrace.

Although he wrote Tom out of his will and refused to correspond
with him after he had gone to England to study, Sherman could not cut
off his concern for his son, which always remained alongside his rage.
Almost immediately, he supplied Adam Badeau, Grant's longtime
military associate, who now served in the United States consulate in
London, with Tom's address, and asked him to call on Tom. Badeau
understood the general's underlying desire, and sent back several glowing reports of Tom. Stressing Tom's dedication to his new vocation, he
also emphasized that Tom was forever his father's son. "He is wonderfully like you in looks and manner," Badeau wrote. "His eyes sparkled
as he called you a glorious man." As much as he could, Badeau was
preparing Sherman for an eventual reunion with Tom. "Time is a won-

derful solvent," he insisted. If he did not want to communicate with the deserter directly, neither did Sherman wish to lose track of him, and Badeau sensed this.

While in England, Tom wrote frequently to his mother and sisters, and they no doubt spoke of him before their father. Then, in August 1880, more than two years after his decampment, Tom returned to the United States to continue his studies. Years later, his sister Rachel described his reunion with his father. Rachel went to New York to meet Tom's ship, and then took the train with him down to Washington. "We were horribly agitated at not knowing how my father would receive him," Rachel wrote, and this suspense was heightened when the general was not at the depot in Washington, instead sending his valet, Pat, with the carriage to pick them up. "At the house, our old nurse Emily . . . motioned to the parlor door which was slightly open. Tom went in and with a cry my father threw his arms around him & I left them in each other's arms."

The next day, Tom reported to his eldest sister, Minnie, that "Papa has let his great heart get the best of past disappointment. . . . We are good friends again and that is a great happiness to us both." The general could admit to friends, if somewhat grudgingly, that he was glad to see Tom. To Henry Turner, Sherman wrote of this rapprochement, "I discussed nothing, treated him kindly, took him everywhere." Sherman went arm-in-arm with Tom on his regular Washington social rounds, thus demonstrating to the world in which he moved that whatever displeasure he had caused his father, Tom was still his son. Rachel characterized this behavior as the product of "the tenderest heart," the one in her father's breast. She and her siblings never really doubted that he "loved us devotedly," Rachel insisted. Along with his other emotions, including the particularly well-developed wrathful ones, Sherman clearly had a big heart, especially for his children, with whom he could not bear to break. Keeping his children near him emotionally was as important to him as was his fame; not coldly authoritarian paternalism, but *loving* authoritarian paternalism, was an indispensable element of his makeup.[13]

Nevertheless, the general continued to bear an unending grudge against Tom in another sector of his heart. After his son's second visit, for Christmas in 1880, Sherman confided to S. H. M. Byers of Tom's continuing priestly novitiate, that it remained "directly antagonistic to my idea of right—he ought to be in some career to assist us, and to take part in the Great Future of America—I feel as though his life was lost, and am simply amazed he does not see it as I do." This resentment remained with Sherman. For example, in 1885, a full seven years after Tom's rebellion, in a letter to Mary Audenreid, Sherman revealed that he always carried about inside him the terrible feelings produced "when Tom left me, his duties & all for the Church . . . an awful crime against nature, for I had a right to depend upon him in my old age to look after those dependent upon me." Both the father's love and his continuing anger remained true emotions at one and the same time. Sherman stayed loving, resentful, and unreconciled in his feelings for Tom—a conglomeration of wounded feelings from which he never fully recovered. In most, if not all, of his summings up, Tom was lost to him as Willy was, as had been his own father when he was only a boy.[14]

When Tom was ordained in 1889, Sherman simply could not bring himself to attend, and so he used a trip to Denver as his excuse, promising to visit Tom soon after the event: Thus did Sherman continue to love the son and reject the priest. For his part, Tom clung to every word of his father's infrequent letters, every tender moment during his visits home. He idolized his father, writing poems of praise to him, comparing him to Cincinnatus and other Old Roman heroes, and at other times almost begging for closer ties. In 1886, he wrote his father, both apologizing for disappointing him and asserting his scorn for money and fame, by this second means attempting to confront his father as an equal. "You and I can never argue because we start off from different principles. . . . As between men like ourselves it is certainly a pity even to hint at old sores." In one of his last letters to his father, from the Cunard liner *Umbria,* Tom wrote that the captain had seated him at his table, which made him feel "rather too much an object of notoriety to be both a Priest and the son of the General."[15]

Tom often trumpeted his own independent manliness, about which he clearly had great doubts and fears. In fact, the priesthood never provided an independent role sufficient to Tom's needs. He was an unsuccessful teacher at the Jesuit universities of Detroit and St. Louis, unable to focus on the subject he was teaching, rambling on in the classroom about himself and about current affairs, frequently absenting himself to travel about the country visiting his sisters and cousins. In the 1880s, he became a Jesuit missionary to the working classes, using his name to draw large audiences where he would present the Catholic Church as the only real alternative to Godless anarchy and communism. The vehement extremism of these talks finally so embarrassed the Jesuit order that they shunted him back to teaching.

Always irascible, high-strung, self-important, and quick to anger during this period, after his father's death Tom fell into periodic bouts of deep depression, accompanied by paranoid delusions that his fellow Jesuits were conspiring to destroy him. Father Joseph Hamilton, who knew him well, later wrote that Tom once said he was more insane than his father had ever been. More generally, Tom appeared obsessed with the memory of his father's fame. While visiting Hamilton's home, Hamilton later related, "he would get out my grandfather's Civil War uniform and sword, don them, and walk up and down for long periods before a full length mirror." In 1911, Tom begged to be released from the Jesuit order, which they pretended to do to mollify him. He then spent two decades in solitary depression in a tiny house in Santa Barbara, California, punctuated by bouts of renewed travel, at times ending up in rags on skid rows. His mortified brother and sisters finally arranged with the ever-tactful Jesuits to take the deeply melancholic Tom into a nursing home in New Orleans, where he died in 1933, after renewing his Jesuit vows.[16]

Though he dodged it through his career choice, Tom was never able to escape the emotional control of his father, with tragic results. If there is an endogenous genetic component in mental illness, Tom suffered from the deepest version of the depression that visited others in the Sherman family, his father included, to a lesser extent. Tom's steep decline, however, coming after his father's death, and perhaps being triggered by it in part, meant that his father never witnessed Tom's terrors, and thus was not forced to come to terms with them.

Sherman grieved for his own loss in Tom, and he continued to love a son he also resented. How much Tom understood of his father's complex feelings concerning him is unclear. Tom did not become the man his father tried to form, and his father instead experienced an unhealable wound to his patrimonial desire to pass on what he considered to be the best of his inheritance in some ideal form to the next generation. After his one desperate act of rebellion from that ideal type his father was making of him, Tom could not build a truly independent life for himself. Father and son became alienated in their struggle over defining Tom's career. Both men sought to create some new form in which to transmit the heroic fame of an aging general to his son, but unlike his father, Tom never found the war in which he might have been saved.

21

Celebration and Reconciliation

E ARLY IN 1884, soon after Sherman retired, little Mary Day of San Luis Obispo, California, wrote to the exalted general, begging for his autograph. In his high-grumpy fashion—"this autograph business sometimes is a nuisance"—Sherman instructed the girl that in the future she send a blank card and a stamped, self-addressed envelope when she requested autographs of great men. But then, with that spontaneity of heartsomeness that sometimes contradicted his quick-to-fire irascibility, Sherman shared with Mary Day the reaction the name of San Luis Obispo aroused in him. "It seems to me but yesterday when I was at the old mission" as a young lieutenant of artillery in 1848, "where a few natives were lounging in the sun, and the fleas so crowded that I went some six or seven miles off to camp in the open air." At that time San Francisco, still named Yerba Buena, Sherman recalled, was an equally flea-bitten "village of less than 400 souls. But now, less than four decades later," Sherman commented, "I have since seen California rise to a state of over a million people, and San Francisco grow to 300,000." Mary Day had reminded Sherman, as he interpreted these changes, of an ethnic revolution—from lazy, dirty Mexican to progressive white American—and of the astonishing speed with which progressive Americanization had taken hold.

It was not as if Sherman saw himself for a moment as a mere passive witness to this nationalizing revolution: Privately, he believed he had been the central actor in the elimination of the Confederate threat coupled to the "winning of the West." And during his retirement, in his more sanguine moods, he celebrated his achievements with great pride and satisfaction. As he had made his last tour of the West prior to his retirement, he had written to Ellen from Santa Fe, "the whole Western world recognizes the truth that since the closing of the Civil War I have so used my power and office to encourage the growth and development of the Great West, giving me a hold on their respect and affections worth more than gold." When he wrote these lines he was traveling in a special three-car train of opulent Pullman cars, supplied free of charge by grateful railroad magnates, riding in luxury around an internal empire, "every mile of which is free from the dangers of the savage and is being occupied by industrious families."

Sherman did not claim that he and the army had accomplished this massive conquest alone, but he did insist that they had "gone ahead and prepared the way," and that everything he now saw in the West "reminded [me] of little things" he had done that "have borne fruit." So fine did the adulation of railroad owners and western settlers make him feel, he wrote his wife, "in a fair contest I would beat John Sherman or Blaine at their own game" and be elected president. He hastened to reassure Ellen that he was steadfastly refusing the Republican push on him to run, and insisted that he would "prefer a tent on the banks of the Coeur d'Alene than the White House," but it did give him a not-so-secret pride that he was, in his own opinion, the most popular American hero. To his daughter Elly, he would soon write with unconcealed happiness, "no man ever closed a military career with more of the good will and respect of his comrades and compatriots than I." He believed he was leaving official life with unsurpassed fame and unchallenged honor, "so that I may not leave my children with wealth, I can surely leave with a name which will be a pass-word as long as they can hope to live."[1]

Whatever Tom had done with this patrimonial inheritance, Sherman felt extremely proud that for his own part he had created a heroic persona to pass on to the succeeding generations of Shermans. He suppressed recollections of the tensions in his marriage in his belief that he had provided a familial as well as career model on which not only his own children but American youth in general could nourish themselves. If he remained angry and quarrelsome until the end of his life, which he certainly did, he also began to feel increasing contentment within himself and reconciliation with those around him. This was true within his family as it was with his enormous circle of friendly acquaintances—with his intimate world and with the broad world. Thus the public and the private Sherman, while retaining tensions and contradictions, attained what taken unkindly might be considered ample smugness, but what taken kindly might be considered a measure of wisdom.

Despite his claims to Elly that he would leave her and her brothers and sisters an inheritance that would be measured in degree of fame rather than in accumulation of wealth, despite his personal financial conservatism and endless poor-mouthing, Sherman was in fact keenly interested in money and those more material things of the world, all the while claiming to be above the rapacious greed of the gilded age. There was no unsurpassable moral barrier to his gaining wealth and living well. After all, he, in common with most of his class and generation, regarded wealth as an outward reward demonstrating honor and hard work. Unlike many of them, Sherman was honest in his business dealings, if quite grasping for his public salary and for more private perquisites, such as lushly appointed Pullman cars.

When he retired, in addition to his pension of $15,000 per year—100 percent of his final pay—Sherman had accumulated $40,000 in what he called "good cash assets," and about $60,000 in "good productive property"—five or six rental houses in St. Louis and a farm across the Mississippi River in Illinois. He was also free from debt. As did many self-made men who had failed financially in their younger years, Sherman remained insecure about finances—with that set of fears also serving as a cover for deeper and more personal fears of reversal and loss. It was out of anxiety rather than any realistic analysis of his extremely secure finances that he wrote Elly from St. Louis in 1884, that though he would "try to keep up this house as a refuge for any of my children," she would have to understand that he would not do so if this required his taking on new debt, "for I will steal, rob, murder—anything rather than borrow—debt and credit are greater crimes than murder and robbery."

Five days before he wrote this letter to his daughter, Sherman had bragged to an old army chum that he kept four servants, four horses and three carriages, which with his house and $15,000 annual pension, put him in the "first class of citizens" in St. Louis. In the teeth of the protracted recession of the 1880s, and despite property taxes, which he considered confiscatory, far from pulling in his horns this first citizen

continued to accumulate possessions, by 1886 maintaining six servants, six horses, and, quite extraordinarily, seven carriages, about
which he was not hesitant to boast to others. Later that year, he sold
off some of these assets to move to New York, to a very large suite of
rooms in the swankiest hotel in town. For 1887, he calculated his family expenses at exactly $17,194.02, which was $2,194.02 more than his
pension. However, his income from property and bond interest
grossed $5,534 and netted $3,022.12, which left him with a surplus for
the year of $828.10. In his figuring, Sherman forgot to add another
$3,000 or so in income from royalties and for periodical articles, which
he would dash off for between $500 and $1,000 per piece. He also continued to receive considerable perquisites and gifts from a grateful public. In retirement he managed to do quite well by having done good.[2]

Plenty of speculative capitalists crossed Sherman's path during his
retirement years, offering him glittering opportunities to increase his
wealth rapidly and without work, but Sherman stoutly refused to cash
in on his fame that way. He often noted the bankruptcies of several of
his friends who tried speculation, with overt horror and covert pride in
his own morally superior conservatism. He explained to Elly in 1884
that he would leave her a house and his good name, better by far "than
if I had embarked on Wall Street, with its promise of millions and reality of bankruptcy and loss of honor."

U. S. Grant provided Sherman the clearest example of what to avoid
in the financial realm, as he had done earlier in the political sphere
when Grant had taken on the presidency to his ultimate dishonor. Already deeply ill with the cancer that would kill him in 1885, Grant saw
his personal fortune evaporate after taking a jolt in the stock market,
and Sherman was awestruck at his friend's collapse. Despite feeling
that the Grants "did not deal generously by me in Washington" for all
those years, as he wrote Elly, Sherman traveled to New York to see
what he could do toward restructuring Grant's debts, or at least ex-
empting Grant's personal goods from the auctioneer's gavel. Sherman
also drew out his personal moral from Grant's morass to present to his
progeny. "I hope you and all my children now realize why I have been
so mean in the past—We have lived on what we had." To William F.
Vilas, the fabulously wealthy Wisconsin lumber baron and politician,
Sherman indicated with horrified wonder and identification that despite having known poverty as a boy, and having learned "the value of
a single dollar earned by the sweat of his brow," Grant, when at the

"very pinnacle of his fame risked all to compete with Wall Street, filled with the sharpest & most unscrupulous set of 'boys' that ever gathered around the roulette table." For his own part, his "name," which included soundness on the subject of money, was worth far more to him than the pursuit of great wealth at all costs.[3]

Having chosen the path of comfort rather than ostentation, Sherman rested quite contentedly in the bed he had made for his family. Nearly a decade after Tom's defection, Sherman began to pass the business part of his patrimony on to his remaining son Philemon ("Cumpy"), who had been born in 1867. Cumpy stuttered, which worried his father, but otherwise he seemed an alert, bright boy, keen to please his father. Numbed by his experience with Tom, Sherman was frightened that Cumpy might repeat his older brother's "desertion," and thus he remained somewhat aloof from his last boy. Sherman's tentativeness about Cumpy is clear in his letters to his wife and daughter Elly just before his own retirement in 1883, when Cumpy was sixteen and a student at Georgetown Academy. "If Cumpy will only take a fancy to being a mechanic, merchant or farmer, and not a priest, I will be reasonably content," he told Ellen, "but if he like Tom runs off with the Church I will not answer for the consequences." Sherman's distrust of whatever role Ellen might have played with Tom, and might yet replay, was palpable. To Elly, writing the same day, Sherman was less threatening and more concerned with the manner in which Cumpy might confirm the version of the useful life he felt he had lived out. Repeating his pride in his role in the opening of the trans–Mississippi West, on which he would "rest content as much as if I had attended Church every day of my life," a customary swipe at Elly's mother, Sherman wrote that "I hope Cumpy will not follow in Tom's footsteps, but recognize the truth that this world has claims as well as the next." If Cumpy would only carry out what his father had first scheduled Tom to do, the general could retire in contentment, knowing a son of his had followed the footsteps appropriate to real men—men such as he had been. Rather than revising his beliefs about what a son ought to do for a father, he had transferred them intact from Tom to the still-adolescent Cumpy, and he awaited Cumpy's passage into manhood with at least as much trepidation as hope.

When Cumpy reached nineteen, Sherman sat down with him to plan his future. At this meeting, Sherman informed his brother, John, "I tell him as long as I live I will afford him every possible opportunity for education to enable him to compete in the next epoch, and he chooses Yale College, Scientific Dept., afterwards commercial law in New York." This was the same course Tom had "chosen" before deserting. In this case, Cumpy's father contributed a first job in a leading New York law firm, parallel to the way he had chosen a leading St. Louis law firm for Tom when the Sherman business interests had been concentrated there a decade earlier. Whatever his lingering private anxieties, Sherman acted the contented and upbeat papa to his younger son. In 1887, Sherman visited Cumpy at Yale, and though he was kept busy by college officials during the days, in the evenings, a delighted Cumpy wrote to his mother, the general was "very cheerful [and] ran away from everybody & sat up in his room & talked with me."

In 1888, Cumpy graduated from Yale. He looked "vigorous and strong," Sherman reported to an old friend, and ready to "pitch into the law." The aging father's hopes were soaring once more in the belief that a son of his was following the right route. "I hope in two years he will be self-maintaining, thus recovering the last ten years I lost by Tom going into the Church." Cumpy did fine, in the prescribed fashion. Two years later his father would repeat that Cumpy was steady, punctual, and attentive to detail as a young lawyer, and insisted that "I leave him perfectly free to make his own plans for the future." Cumpy exercised that liberty within the confines of the legal profession, which was what his father meant by freedom, and in 1891 set himself up in a legal partnership at 52 Wall Street. He took care of his father's real estate and of his sisters' business interests, both then and after his father's death, which Tom was to have done, and led a sound and safe if conventional and uneventful bachelor's life until his own death in 1941. Cumpy's budding career gave his father considerable affirmation during the last years of his life.[4]

If he continued to resent Ellen Ewing Sherman and she him until the end, if they still fought, and spent as much time separated as together, it was also true that there began to be an element of reconciliation in their relationship, almost a truce in hostilities, as each expressed something approaching admiration in the tenacity of the other, and tacitly recognized at least a little how stubborn each had always been. Writing from Elly's home in Philadelphia in 1887, for example, Ellen remarked to her husband that he had always been "very liberal & generous with me in money matters. . . . You like to growl a little but you have never questioned me or held me to a strict account." In such moments, Ellen could put her husband's irascibility in the context of his considerable generosity of spirit. As Sherman refurbished the new family home on 75 West Seventy-first Street, which would take them out of living, as they had for two years, in the Fifth Avenue Hotel, Ellen wrote in warm anticipation, "our minds and hearts are filled with thoughts of *our home* which you are fitting up for us." And on the eve of her arrival at the new house, she reassured her husband, "you can continue to be 'Boss' . . . as long as you choose so you need not dread our coming." If there was something mock-submissive and rather tentative in that remark, there was also something quite affectionate about it. She really did long for a comfortable last home with her growly bear of a mate.

Although Sherman's resentments remained nearer the surface than did hers, he was also capable of guarded, somewhat ironic bursts of affection. Writing Ellen in the summer of 1887, noting that his army associations and her church and children kept them dashing around the country and away from one another, Sherman concluded, "you will most likely fetch up at some monastery and I in the Rocky Mountains—Meantime you had better come to the Fifth Avenue Hotel and make yourself as comfortable as possible." In the final analysis, he was telling her, their innermost natures were indeed different: Hers was religious and reclusive, his was wandering and somewhat savage, and yet they could find a shared area of comfort and relaxation.[5]

Ellen reached the new Sherman home on West Seventy-first Street on September 24, 1888, and, much to her husband's annoyance, took to her room in what he considered to be a continuation of her wasteful career as neurasthenic, but her heart soon gave out. If he could write in his anger to Mary Audenreid that he was well shut of Ellen, shortly after she died on November 28, he was soon writing, as Christmas approached, out of the more generous portion of his nature that he was realizing just how much there had been to admire in her. To William F. Vilas he wrote of Ellen's bravery in the face of their pre–Civil War poverty, which she had been "the last to advertise to the world." The courage of men on the battlefield was as nothing compared to that of a woman, "young, contented, indulged in every way," when she had chosen to "surrender herself body & soul to a man who expected her to subsist on a Lieutenant's pay of $76.50 per month."

Similarly, he began to wonder at the intensity with which he had fought a war of religion with her all those years. She had been "by inheritance & nature a strong Irish Catholic," he acknowledged to his old army friend, Alexander McCook, while "in me remained some of the nature of the Puritan." Never for a moment had he doubted that she was "honest true and faithful," and he also realized retrospectively that in turn she realized his "fidelity to principle." Ellen had had her faith, while his beliefs had been "subject to mathematics." Still, looking at this religious gap between them, Sherman could only wonder, a month after Ellen's death, about the intensity of their arguments. "How absurd now seems those petty differences." Sherman moved away from the introspective conclusion that religion might have stood in for other emotional issues they had never dealt with, much less resolved. By choosing to focus on the literal meanings of their dispute, he could quite quickly narrow what had in fact been a far deeper incompatibility of temperaments, the better to cleanse his memories and find a path to honoring her in death as he had not in life. He was certain, he told McCook, that at the very end, Ellen had "a feeling of home & satisfaction," which made Sherman feel "perfectly compensated" for all those years of acrimonious struggle.[6]

Sherman did not seek to replace Ellen with a new wife. Quite to the contrary, he backed away from his established intimacy with Mary Audenreid, and did not enter another such love match. The woman with whom he spent the most time in the last four years of his life was Mary A. Draper, whom he met in 1887 when he was sixty-seven and she was forty-eight. She was the wealthy and socially prominent widow of the son of the historian John W. Draper, an old intellectual associate of Sherman's. Sherman often asked Mary Draper to the theater he so much loved, and to dine before or after the shows. From time to time he called on her in her Madison Avenue town house, and at least once visited her for a Sunday at her country home in Dobbs Ferry. For his seventieth birthday she sent him a silver calendar stand. But there was little that was flirtatious or suggestive in his letters to her.

Indeed, the only emotionally charged missive came in October 1890, when he wrote her that "like a ship carrying too much sail with old spars I am resolved to take in many a 'reef,' to lessen the chances of disaster." Perhaps Mary Draper had hinted at a desire for closer bonds, or perhaps he was fending off his own desires of that sort, or both. Perhaps their embraces had become too warm for his comfort, to whatever degree they had gone. In any event, he followed this distance-maintaining declaration with a somewhat compensatory promise that he would like to see her again, if only the following spring, in her "palatial home" on Madison Avenue, and "would be rejoiced to be summoned to the wedding feast where the mistress chooses her new mate," for the "long and happy remainder" of her life. That bestowal of prospective paternal blessing was a repetition of what he had told Vinnie Ream and Mary Audenreid quite frequently during their affairs, and one can assume that as with his grandest loves, this reiteration to Mary Draper also connoted erotic desire on his part, and his perception that the lady fancied him. Whether he was warning off Mary Draper, or warning himself against a potentially deeper relationship, this letter was clearly an avoidance strategy.[7]

Sherman was content with the company of Mary Draper as he was with his ever-flourishing social life. After his 1886 move to New York City, Sherman not only continued to see his old army and political friends and his actors and actresses, but branched upward into the emerging "high society," which was centered increasingly in New York. This was primarily a rough-hewn, if socially ambitious, set of capitalists, and although he steered clear of their speculations, Sherman was eager to respond when they sought out his company. He fit well into what was becoming the usual American elite of big money, beautiful women, and famous public figures, including entertainers and statesmen. Thus his calendar was jammed with dinners with the Astors, the Vanderbilts, and the Carnegies, often in honor of distinguished European visitors, such as the Comte de Paris (whom Sherman rather despised personally).

That Sherman was quite impressed by the powerful social circle into which he had moved was demonstrated by an uncharacteristically toadying letter he wrote thanking Mrs. Andrew Carnegie for the seventy white roses she sent him for his birthday in 1890. "Let the Astors, Vanderbilts and Goulds take a back seat for I am the richest man in New York," he gushed. "All the wealth of Wall Street has not the precious value of my seventy heart offerings. The flowers may fade . . . but the memory of a sweet thought is part of the Eternal and will never perish." This was just the sort of sentimentality that Sherman had refused to offer Ellen, indeed that he had frequently denigrated to her as female claptrap. In this instance, class awe overcame his reluctance to pander to the hyperfeminine.[8]

Sherman's ability to gain a modicum of happiness in his latter-day personal life was paralleled by his increasing comfort about the meanings of his career. He was able to some extent to grow reconciled to his public role and to his old enemies, even while he continued to be annoyed with the demands of iconicization as well as with those men whom he believed were attacking him. He took undiminished pride in his role in the Civil War and the war against the Plains Indians, although he softened somewhat his bitter Negrophobia. Ever the restless and angry man, he took increasing satisfaction out of his awareness that he had become a hero permanently affixed in the upper echelons of the American pantheon.

Although he continued his feuds with James B. Fry and Jefferson Davis, among others, as he aged Sherman became eager to reconcile when possible with old enemies. He had long since done so with many prominent Confederate generals, and these warm postwar relations fed his contentment. For example, on January 8, 1891, a month before his death, he affirmed with pleasure to Joseph E. Johnston that "you and I became reconciled in April, 1865; have remained so ever since with no apologies or concealments." Noting the reconnections of the South and the North into genuine nationality, Sherman felt a real release from his fears of renewed sectional disharmony. "The cause which made you and me enemies in 1861 is dead as the rule of King George in 1776, and like Humpty-Dumpty, 'all the King's horses and all the King's men cannot bring it to life again.' " There was no insuperable reason remaining for sectional or personal hatreds.

Three years before John A. Logan's death in 1886, he and Sherman made an emotional reconciliation, following their prolonged and bitter feud that had had such important political and institutional ramifications. Logan made the first move, an impromptu tribute at Sherman's retirement banquet in 1883. Declaring that Sherman's star had ever shone bright because of his "ability, integrity and true bravery as an officer," Logan proudly counted himself among Sherman's old veterans, each of whom pledged, he insisted, that "wherever he may go, wherever he may be, whatever may be his condition in life, there is no one who would not stretch out a helping hand to that brave commander who led them to glory."

Deeply moved by this affirmation, Sherman walked across the room and embraced Logan. Soon he wrote Logan how very touched he had been by Logan's public praise, as it had helped ease his route into retirement knowing the "kind and respectful feelings" Logan had offered so freely. In turn he reassured Logan that "your course was manly, patriotic and sublime throughout the war." Sherman then went through the long-ago bypassing of Logan for Howard with great regret for the hurt it had caused Logan, although without quite apologizing for having made the "best practicable" decision he could have made at the time. "My course is run, and for better or worse I cannot amend it," Sherman concluded fatalistically, though insisting that he would ever bear enthusiastic public witness to Logan's "heroic personal qualities" and his "intense zeal and patriotism." In return, Logan told Sherman that he understood that "as a rule" it was "probably correct" to choose professional officers over volunteers for major commands, but added that "the experience of the world has occasionally found exceptions to this rule." Thus he clung to his principle in reciprocity to Sherman's holding to his. He also insisted to Sherman that he did not "feel aggrieved as you think, but will ever remain your friend." With this highly formal but sincere exchange, these two old combatants, who had always been fond and admiring of one another at some level, made their peace.[9]

Sherman remained first father of the army until his death. For example, up to 1889, he continued to attend the graduation ceremonies at West Point, where he gave variants of the same patriotic speech. He loved the joy of the occasion as well as its ideological meanings, admonishing the graduates of 1889 to be true to the flag and also promising one, "My boy, if you have not yet picked out your girl, wait! They'll become all the prettier, next year!" When Sherman died in 1891, Superintendent John M. Wilson wrote Washington and asked permission for the entire corps to go to St. Louis to march behind his hearse to the graveyard. "They loved General Sherman as a father, and he loved them as his children," Wilson wrote.[10]

Sherman's paternal pride in the veterans of his Civil War army also deepened over the years as many of them gained public prominence. In 1888, he wrote a letter of profuse congratulations to C. N. Humphrey, who just had been voted governor of Kansas, making him the fourth of "my boys" to be elected to a governorship that year, not to mention his other old boy, Benjamin Harrison, one of his brigade commanders during the Atlanta campaign, who just had been elevated to the White House. Sherman insisted to Humphrey that he was just as proud of the privates as of the generals who had served with him, and that "as to my hold on the affections of my old comrades I have evidence enough to satisfy me. I can hardly venture to Columbus, Indianapolis, Chicago, Springfield or St. Louis without being torn to pieces for relics of 'Uncle

Billy.' " Beyond bearing witness to his continued thirst for fame, Sherman also concluded more generally that the Civil War veterans must always "be held aloft as examples to the lusty youth who must soon take the helm and guide our ship of state on her glorious voyage into the unknown future."

When captured by such an optimistic sense of the American future, which had been created and nurtured by the spontaneous and gargantuan wartime efforts of heroes such as his boys (led by such as he, it went without saying), Sherman could even be sanguine about the future of the American army: He could almost forgive American politicians and American democracy. Writing in 1883 to an American diplomat, who had noted with alarm the enormous advances of European armies in organization and in advanced weaponry that were leaving the United States army far behind, Sherman remained rather calm. He was certain that nothing would move Congress to a serious rearmament program "except absolute necessity." When the time came, America would profit from the technological advancement brought by the enormous expenditures on "big guns and iron clads" made by European militarists. But more important, when needed, the traditional American spirit of improvisational ingenuity under stress would come to the forefront. "I believe we have the men and the knowledge— and like in our Civil War—when the necessity is upon us we shall rise to the occasion."[11]

In retirement as in office, Sherman remained every inch the public man. He still needed to love and be loved by the vast public, to be seen and to pronounce on every subject of concern to him, which left out the tariff issue, civil service reform, and the question of money supply, but not much else. Yet he complained and complained of feeling he was being voraciously consumed by that popular demand he also sought. Soon after retiring he began grumbling to friends such as General Christopher Augur that he was trying to get out of those "special claims" that had made his life in Washington "a sort of hell or purgatory." If he were to accept even so much as one invitation in ten, "I would have to shut up house—abandon family & friends & take to the road as a Methodist preacher."

Veterans were the most strident demanders, and the hardest to turn down. In 1887, Sherman reckoned that about twenty invitations each week came in from the four thousand Grand Army of the Republic posts scattered across the nation. In the face of this deluge he sometimes threatened just to take off for solitude in the Rocky Mountains, but he did not mean it. Many of the "boys" also importuned him when he visited them, or through the mails. To a woman who had been a friend during his Ohio boyhood, he complained that he had "a family of 100,000 soldiers every one of whom has a boy named after me and who expects me to educate & provide for him."

On top of army demands were endless requests to send out his photo and autograph, to grant interviews, to write articles for newspapers and magazines, and to lecture. To the GAR post commander in Brooklyn, who requested a speech in 1884, Sherman replied in his most fulsome voice of exaggeration that "autograph fiends, book agents, lighting rod men and Missionaries" had long since been recognized as the "plagues of Egypt," to which he now proposed to add the "lecture fiend." Why was it that all these human plagues assumed he had nothing to do in his retirement? Sherman asked rhetorically. Though he felt great love in his "innermost heart" for his old army comrades, he did feel he had earned a "right to be occasionally at home." To S. H. M. Byers, his old Iowa friend, he wrote in 1887 that this unending public use of him had just reached something of a climax, for "*I am now advertised like Barnum's Circus* at Cincinnati May 4—at Philadelphia the same day."

Greeting the grasping public even contained physical dangers. In February 1886, Sherman broke a bone in his right hand while shaking hands with a vast throng in New York, and the following summer he lost two fingernails shaking hands in Providence, Rhode Island, which gave him several more weeks of pain. But it was the unrelenting quality of this torrent of public demands that bothered him the most. Yet he never withdrew for long from the public to whom he felt grateful, and to whom he felt attached by some mystic chord of memory and patriotic promise.[12]

One of the major tasks Sherman took on himself during retirement was to serve as historical publicist-in-chief for the Union cause. He quite consciously assumed this job in his speeches, articles, and interviews, and in his encouragement of other old Union men to join him in countering the rising tide of ex-Confederate polemicists who were busy writing about what they claimed to have been the superior nobility of their lost cause. Indeed, the Southerners in many respects were winning the postwar propaganda struggle over the moral dimensions of the Civil War. In this task they were aided by the collapse of Reconstruction, and by increasing Northern acquiescence and even sympathy for Southern white domination of blacks, which included segregation and as much antiblack violence as Southern whites deemed necessary, widespread lynching included. This drift in national public opinion troubled Sherman deeply, as he believed the Southerners had been morally wrong in their rebellion and that the North had been right. After all, if the moral basis of putting down the rebellion had been uncertain or wrong, then General Sherman's morally totalistic war measures would have been wrong. And this insidious propaganda attack, as Sherman viewed it, was cropping up everywhere during the 1880s.

When the English viscount General Wolseley adopted much of the ex-Confederate viewpoint in an essay he wrote in *McMillan's Magazine* in March 1887, arguing that General Robert E. Lee had towered far above all the Union generals during the Civil War, Sherman grabbed his pen. Writing in the *North American Review* two months later, Sherman attacked Wolseley and Lee, frontally. While not directly denying Lee's stature as a gentleman and capable soldier, Sherman insisted that he had acted incorrectly, from an anachronistic, narrow, and provincial perspective. "His sphere of action was . . . local. He never rose to the grand problem which involved a continent and future generations. His Virginia was to him the world." Had Lee taken the modern, nationalizing approach rather than his old-fashioned localist one, he would have been entitled to the moral preeminence his followers wished to accord him. "Many of us believe that, if he had stood firm in 1861, and used his personal influence, he could have stayed the Civil War." But he did not, thereby sacrificing his honor, and Sherman insisted that "we who fought on the right side" would continue the fight "with pen and speech" to keep the record straight.

Even on the narrower issue of military talent, Wolseley was wrong, Sherman argued, for "as an aggressive soldier Lee was not a success, and in war that is the true and proper test." In contrast to the false canonization of Lee, Sherman proposed as a corrective the emplacement of Grant as the greatest hero of the war. Grant's military stature was greater than Lee's, for he fought well offensively, and produced total victory. His power was "equal in strategy, in logistics, and in tactics to any of Napoleon, and grander than any ever contemplated by England," Sherman wrote, putting down the presumptuous Englishman, and placing Grant on par with the European military figure most impressive to all nineteenth-century Americans who thought about martial grandeur. Grant was in intelligence, in heart, in results, and in popularity the second George Washington, Sherman asserted. Not only was he a military victor to Lee's loser, but he had fought against a regressive particularism and for a morally progressive nationalization.[13]

Not merely did Sherman oppose the rise of the New South in the propaganda war over the higher meanings of the Civil War, he feared as well the political recrudescence of the ex-Confederate elite as it consolidated its influence inside the national Democratic Party. By 1878, when they recaptured the House of Representatives for the first time, and especially after 1884, when Grover Cleveland was elected as the first postwar Democratic president, Sherman began to tremble before the power of the former Confederates. This political revitalization, Sherman slowly grew to understand, was pinned to moral interpretations of the Civil War, of Reconstruction, and of white supremacy. This realization presented Sherman with his own moral quandary, for he had been an extremely vocal and well-known racist during the war and Reconstruction. Now he was beginning to comprehend some of the political payoff he had handed Southern Democrats as a staunch Union man who was at least as racist as they, and who had been so eager to make a generous peace with them in 1865. Additionally, if Sherman insisted, as he did on the level of cultural warfare, that the Union had been right morally and the Confederacy wrong, it was difficult for him to exclude the issue of slavery and racism from his moral measurements. More and more he discovered that his racism contradicted his nationalism, on moral as well as political terms. Without ever acknowledging, much less apologizing for his earlier racist polemics, he began to shift ground.

After the Democratic electoral victories of 1878, Sherman continued to write his confidants that, in having pushed "illiterate negroes" into the franchise and political office, Southern Republicans inevitably had "produced a reaction." However, Sherman now believed himself forced to "admit the reaction has gone further than is comfortable." He hoped the current exodus of "industrious negroes" to the North and West, tied to memory of the loyalty of the slaves during the war, when they had "guarded, protected and maintained" their masters' families, might push the "ostentatiously" self-proclaimed "chivalric race" of ex-Confederate leaders to "recognize the great [Civil War] proof of virtue in the black race, whom they claim to be inferior in social and political matters." It was Sherman who was growing "uncomfortable" with the white supremacy he used to declare to be true.

After Cleveland's election in 1884, Sherman was simply appalled by the appointment of so many famous Confederate luminaries to the cabinet, the American diplomatic corps, and most especially to the Supreme Court. This reassignment of national public office southward led Sherman to fear, as he wrote his brother, John, that history might someday record "that what the Union armies conquered in war . . . the South conquered in politics. The South (solid) which is the majority of the Democratic Party rules it, and consequently the United States." His desire for sectional reconciliation notwithstanding, this was more than one too many bitter pills for the old Union warrior to swallow. Therefore, he insisted to John that either "the Republican Party which gave the negro the vote, must make that vote good," or, conceding the decision of the Southern white electorate that the "white race must dominate forever in the South," pass legislation scaling down the number of Southern representatives in the House, and thus the electoral college as well, to reflect the true size of the lily-white Southern electorate, in order to diminish their power in national politics.

In his own public role as Unionist senior statesman, Sherman finally spoke out publicly, in 1888, for the former option, the reenfranchisement of blacks in the South. His argument in "Old Shady, With a Moral," which he published in the *North American Review,* was paternalistic and condescending, but his conclusion was unequivocal. Old Shady had been an escaped slave who had served as steward and cook to General James B. McPherson in Vicksburg during the war. After dinner, his singing ability had often "brought tears to our eyes," Sherman recalled, and in general Old Shady personified all blacks—"They are a kindly and inoffensive race." During the war they had "always answered our questions truthfully and honestly . . . and best of all they did *not* resort to the torch and dagger, as their race had done [earlier in the century in Haiti]." While still maintaining that slavery had not been "cruel and inhumane," while still honoring old slaveholding Confederates like Braxton Bragg for their "great integrity," Sherman urged these honorable Southern whites to acknowledge the value of blacks by granting them the vote. Blacks were "gaining in experience and intelligence every day." They were true Americans, unlike the swarms of newer immigrants—"I would far prefer Old Shady as a voter than any of the Bohemians who reach Castle Garden by the thousands every day of the year." Sherman then added as a threat his alternative political proposal. "The Northern people will not long permit the negro vote to be suppressed, and yet be counted in the political game *against* them." And yet he concluded not with a political argument but with an overt plea for racial justice. "Let us freely accord to the Negro his fair share of influence and power, trusting the perpetuity of our institutions to the everlasting principles of human nature which tolerate all races and all colors, leaving each human being to seek in his own sphere, the enjoyment of life, liberty and happiness."

Although Sherman grounded his argument for the black franchise in part on political considerations, it would be wrong to conclude that "Old Shady" was merely expedient. Even on political grounds, Sherman exhibited courage, as by the late 1880s the South was mired in the nadir period of race relations. Lynching was nearly epidemic, and virulent racism was on the steep ascent, as it was across the Western world. Particularly in this political climate, given Sherman's history on this question, he had little extrinsic need to speak out. Rather, he was expressing a change of heart, attempting to expiate himself of guilt for having been what he now realized he had been—an active racist.

When he had rebutted General Wolseley the year before, Sherman had included the statement, if rather in passing, that "I confess to a feeling of pride that at no period in our history has the idea of a military dictator found permanent lodging in the brain of an American soldier or statesman." Sherman had espoused just such an idea during the secession crisis and the opening phase of the Civil War, which he may have obliterated from his memory. If he had recalled this old and embarrassing belief, the remark in the Wolseley essay was the way he chose to purge that antidemocratic sin. In his eleventh-hour rejection of military dictatorship as an ideal, and his espousal of the need for racial justice, Sherman affirmed in his last major public pronouncements that democracy, for blacks as well as for whites, was a good idea rather than a bad one after all. He recognized at the end of his life that his long career as a warrior would leave far less of value to his nation if it were merely negative.[14]

If, in the celebration and reconciliation of his old age, Sherman felt morally compelled to reverse his racism and welcome blacks into fuller membership in the American family, he never expressed a similar set of compunctions when it came to the Indians. To his dying day he did not reconsider his leadership of what he frequently termed "the great battle of civilization with barbarism." Though mentioning the importance of railroads and of white farmers, he often stressed, as he did to George Custer's widow in 1889, the leading role of the regular army in "the picket line at the front of the great wave of civilization resulting in the peace which now happily prevails from the Atlantic to the Pacific."

In 1882, more than a decade before Frederick Jackson Turner's famous speech on the subject, Sherman in effect declared that the frontier period of American history was at an end. Where for decades, "we have been sweeping across the continent with a skirmish line . . . now we are across and have railroads everywhere, so that the whole problem has changed." While in 1865, the West had been occupied by "wild beasts . . . and by wilder Indians, now . . . this vast region has become reduced to a condition of comparative civilization." Sherman also believed that "the Indian-fighting pioneer is gone with the era of homespun clothing and log cabins," to be replaced by more refined classes. As for himself, though he had neglected "hundreds of opportunities" and done many things "I should not have done, and left undone still more" he should have done, he reminisced in 1887, still, "I am content; and feel sure that I can travel this broad country of ours and be each night the welcome guest in palace or cabin." Westerners all recognized him as the father of their section; of this he was certain.

Many other American expansionists dealt with the closing of the frontier by urging their nation to race against the European powers in colonial conquests across the oceans, but Sherman did not become an imperialist. He continued to hold traditional American racialist fears of presumably unassimilable "mongrel" Catholics south of the American border, and he also opposed expanding American military power to achieve geopolitical ends. "We want no more territory," he wrote John in 1887. To the north, "Ontario would make a good state," but most of Canada was "inchoate"—vast and empty and barren, and would cost more than it would produce. And southward, "I am dead opposed to any more of Mexico. All the northern part is desert. . . . Further south the population is mixed Spanish and Indian, who can never be harmonized with our race. Eight millions of such people would endanger our institutions. We have already enough disturbing influences."

Thus, with the notable exceptions of Mexicans, Indians, and to a degree the newer southern and eastern European immigrants, the aging William T. Sherman reached toward a more tolerant, affirmative, and liberal-minded vision of the America he had helped to foster. While still filled with fixed opinions, many prejudices, and considerable anger, he learned to balance these feelings with more compassion, and even with a touch of ironic self-awareness. He made a kind of truce with his old enemies. "As all the world's a stage and all the men and women are merely players," he concluded when remembering his part in the conquest of the Confederacy and of the West, "I claim the privilege to ring down the curtain."[15]

While, during his retirement, Sherman grew more affirmative toward his family and friends, and his nation as well, many of his fellow Americans in turn became increasingly fond of the aging but still salty hero. They never misunderstood him as a sweet and benign old chap, but took him as he was, anger and all, as one of the most important and at the same time most human heroes of American history.

One well-crafted retrospective appreciation of Sherman, published in 1888 in the *North American Review,* captured the lightly ironic but warm tone of the appreciations written about the old warrior late in his life. Although the essay ostensibly dealt with the prospect of Sherman's presidential candidacy that year, it really accepted his word that he would never run, and instead dealt with what a fine president he would have made had he ever consented to stand for office. The essay compared Sherman to the deceased Grant, who was characterized as "powerful, silent, immobile," in contrast with "the fiery Sherman [who] moves, his path a swift destruction." In assessing Sherman's Civil War career, the *Review* concluded that "the destroyer has his place . . . for the destruction of the old clears the ground for the sounder building of the new. It has been so for this nation." Now, decades later, Sherman remained "vigorous, plain spoken and original as ever." Though the *Review* did not seek to deemphasize the intentionally destructive role Sherman had played, it now saw that rage as mellowed with time and placed in appropriate channels to which he was entitled by his great career. "We see . . . 'Uncle Billy' . . . now, when his hair has turned white . . . taking his rest after the labor of an eventful life: cheery as a lark, flying about as restless as ever, kissing all the pretty girls, full of original sayings, and rich with quaint humor." Lest he be made to appear too harmlessly avuncular, the *Review* noted that in his frequent after-dinner speeches and in his letters to editors and other writings, "sometimes the old fighter gets uppermost in him," and he becomes "peppery." At such times, he continued to "tread on corns," and the "pigmies of the press" then complain, as they always had, "there's General Sherman again! He's always saying something dreadful. Why *will* he say such things!" Rising to his defense, the *Review* reproached the press on Sherman's behalf. "The old warrior has a right to [speak out]. He has earned it if any man has." Sherman had lived long enough to become the Senior Warrior as artifact.

Augustus Saint-Gaudens, the gifted sculptor, provided an aperçu of the private Sherman as he appeared in 1888, which rather confirmed the public version of Sherman as portrayed in the *North American Review*. In 1888, Saint-Gaudens made a bust of Sherman that required the general to sit for eighteen two-hour sittings. Saint-Gaudens found Sherman to be an excellent model, except when he passed to Sherman's side to study his profile, which aroused his suspicious uneasiness. "His eyes followed me alertly, and he turned his head too, as if to defend his 'communications from the rear,' " Saint-Gaudens later recalled. Other than that, Sherman rambled on about the Civil War and men and events with "delightful freedom."

At the same time that he was modeling Sherman, the sculptor was doing a bas-relief of Robert Louis Stevenson. Told of Saint-Gaudens's other sitter, Stevenson professed great admiration for Sherman and pressed the sculptor to introduce them. When he told the general of Stevenson's request, Sherman asked Saint-Gaudens who he was. "Is he one of my boys?" Sherman had not heard of Stevenson's famous novels that Saint-Gaudens mentioned, but when, recalling that the general loved the theater, Saint-Gaudens mentioned that Stevenson was the author of *Dr. Jekyll and Mr. Hyde,* then a smash hit on Broadway, Sherman said, "the man who wrote that is no fool," and told the sculptor he would be glad to meet Stevenson. Saint-Gaudens then invited Mrs. Stevenson to his studio to make arrangements for the meeting with her husband, who was dying of consumption. "Mr. Stevenson is a great admirer of yours," she told Sherman, to which he replied, "Ah is that so? Is he one of my boys?" At this point in his narrative of the meeting, Saint-Gaudens inserted dryly, "I must say here that we were approaching the end of the General's life." Mrs. Stevenson reminded the general of her husband's play, and memory thus refreshed of the importance of the author, Sherman agreed to plans for a meeting at his abode. On the appointed day, Stevenson and Saint-Gaudens were kept waiting in the anteroom of Sherman's apartment in the Fifth Avenue

Hotel, much to the famous writer's annoyance. After Sherman finally entered, Saint-Gaudens introduced them, and Sherman immediately asked him if he was one of his boys. "On being told that he was not," Saint-Gaudens wrote, Sherman "seemed to lose interest in the interview." The conversation flagged badly until Stevenson asked Sherman about some fine point in one of his campaigns. Sensing that Stevenson knew what he was talking about, "immediately the General brightened," and soon he had stretched out a map on the round table in the center of the parlor room and had begun to lecture the enraptured Stevenson about his military accomplishments.[16]

Sherman seemed to be losing contact with others at the end of his life; he became even more deeply absorbed in himself and his fame. But he did not pretend to be other than he was, and when he was engaged by others he remained bright and amusing. There he was to the end an authentic hero, made of dross and brass and gold.

On February 3, 1891, three days before his seventy-first birthday, Sherman wrote an affectionate and cheerful letter to his brother, John. "I am drifting along in the old bent—in good strength, attending about four dinners out per week at public or private homes, and generally wind up for gossip at the Union League Club." He asked his brother for a dozen copies of John's recent speech on the silver question to distribute to his Union League cronies. The next day Sherman attended the Casino Theater and enjoyed himself as always, but he woke up on the morning of February 5 with a bad cold that, partly because his lungs had been weakened by his lifelong asthmatic condition, quickly deepened into pneumonia.

As he lay dying on February 13, drifting out of consciousness into a final coma, Sherman's children sent for a Catholic priest, who administered extreme unction to the dying general, of which he was almost certainly unaware. A priest could give this final rite, for six decades earlier in Lancaster, at the behest of the Ewing family that had taken him in after his father's death, and without consulting the little boy, nine-year-old Cump had been converted and baptized by the Catholic priest who had added the good Christian name William to the too-savage Tecumseh. Sherman died on the afternoon of February 14, St. Valentine's Day. The day after his death, *The New York Times* reported that both the general and John Sherman, whom the children had called to New York on February 9, but who had been away from the house when the children had called the priest, had been hostile to the Catholic Church, and that the Sherman children had in effect spirited the priest into the death chamber against the will of the Sherman brothers.

Perhaps it was fitting that the general be embroiled in one last newspaper controversy as he died. It was also appropriate that the issue should have been the religious divide in the Ewing/Sherman household. Be that as it may, John immediately sent an indignant letter to the *Times,* denying that the priest had been insinuated into his brother's house against the will of either brother. Though not a Catholic, General Sherman had been "too good a Christian and too human a man to deny his children the consolations of their religion," John insisted. If he had been present, or if his brother had been conscious, neither of them would have denied this wish of his children, nor the prayers offered by any other Christian minister, be he priest or preacher. John accepted extreme unction in a tolerant light, bowing to the fervent desires of his brother's children. Sherman's children urgently wanted their father to be prepared in the only true faith to join Willy and Charlie and Ellen Ewing Sherman, and when their time came, all of them too, in heaven.

John was probably right. The general had grown somewhat reconciled to the Catholic profession of his family, and over the years he had frequently expressed his longing to join little Willy after his final day on earth. Both to this end and to please his children, as well as to honor the memory of Ellen, Sherman most likely would have capitulated in the final hour to what had been his wife's most fervent demand throughout their unrelenting war of religion.

Or so his children and his brother chose to believe. Increasing mellowness notwithstanding, the general's anger blazed out until the end, as his children all knew, and they did not dare to confront him before he lapsed into his final coma. He might have flown into one final, obstinate and destructive rage, denying their deepest wish. To the end this was William *Tecumseh* Sherman.

As he lay dying, Sherman called out that he wanted to see Tom. The other children had cabled their brother, who was studying at a Jesuit seminary on the Island of Jersey, and Tom boarded a Cunard liner in England. He arrived five days after his father's death. The family had kept all funeral plans on hold until Tom arrived. When he did, there was an enormous procession, including thirty thousand soldiers, accompanying Sherman's coffin to the train station for the slow trip west to St. Louis. There, on February 23, following a high mass performed by Tom, and after the biggest funeral procession in the history of St. Louis, Sherman was laid to rest in Calvary Cemetery, beside Ellen and Willy after all.[17]

Abbreviations

Grant Papers	John Y. Simon, ed., *Papers of Ulysses S. Grant,* 19 vols. to date (Carbondale: University of Southern Illinois, 1967).
HL	Mark DeWolfe Howe, ed., *Home Letters of General Sherman* (New York: C. Scribner's Sons, 1909).
Huntington	Huntington Library, San Marino, California
LC	Library of Congress
Lewis	Lloyd Lewis, *Sherman, Fighting Prophet* (New York: Harcourt, Brace, 1932).
Marszalek	John F. Marszalek, *Sherman: A Soldier's Passion for Order* (New York: Free Press, 1993).
Memoirs	William T. Sherman, *Memoirs of General Sherman,* 1st ed., 2 vols. (New York: D. Appleton, 1875).
Merrill	James M. Merrill, *William Tecumseh Sherman* (Chicago: Rand McNally, 1971).
ND	Sherman Family Papers, University of Notre Dame Archives, South Bend
Ohio	Ohio Historical Society, Columbus
OR	*The War of the Rebellion: A Compilation of the Official Records of the Union and the Confederate Armies,* 127 vols., index and atlas (Washington, D.C.: Government Printing Office, 1880–1901).

SL   Rachel Sherman Thorndike, ed., *The Sherman Letters* (New York: C. Scribner's Sons, 1894).

(Other manuscript collections, archives, and book titles are cited fully in the notes.)

Notes

1 Rosebud: A Truncated Patrimony

[1] Memoirs, I, 9–12.

[2] Sherman, Memoirs, 2nd ed. (New York: D. Appleton, 1887), I, 12–15. Many years later, Ellen Ewing Sherman would recall that his mother had been "alone with him in the parlor of our [Ewing] house for a long time before he started" for West Point, and that when he visited Ohio during the 1840s, he stayed with his mother rather than with the Ewings, "because he had money to help her." Significantly, Sherman never mentioned this level of personal contact and intimacy, either in his Memoirs or in his correspondence. Ellen Ewing Sherman, "Recollections for My Children," unpublished manuscript, Washington, D.C., 1880, ND.

[3] Thomas Ewing to Ellen Ewing Sherman, February 13, 1865, Ewing Family Papers, LC; recounted in Lewis, 32.

[4] Lewis recounts this story in his biography, p. 34. Lewis informs us, p. 66on, that the main sources for this story were five of Sherman's grandchildren, whom he interviewed in the 1920s. Later in life, Sherman was confused on this issue, insisting that his natural father had named him William Tecumseh. Judging from internal evidence, Lewis considers this highly unlikely. On the posthumous white settler admiration for Tecumseh (who was killed in 1813), see Bil Gilbert, *God Gave Us This Country: Tekamthi* [Tecumseh] *and the First American Civil War* (New York: Atheneum, 1989), 325–41.

[5] Thomas Ewing to Maria Ewing, December 9, 1831, Ewing Family Papers, LC, quoted in Lewis, 39–40.

[6] William T. Sherman to Thomas Ewing, Lancaster, April 22, 182[8 or 9], Ewing Family Papers, LC.

[7] William T. Sherman to Thomas Ewing, Lancaster, May 5, 1836, Ewing Family Papers, LC.

[8] William T. Sherman to Maria Ewing, West Point, October 15, 1836, Ewing Family Papers, LC.

[9] William T. Sherman to Ellen Ewing, West Point, August 31, 1839, Sherman Papers, ND, reprinted in part in HL, 10. Italics added.

[10] William T. Sherman to Thomas Ewing, Fort Moultrie, South Carolina, January 20, 1844, Ewing Family Papers, LC. Italics added.

[11] William T. Sherman to Hugh Ewing, Marietta, Georgia, March 10, 1844, Hugh B. Ewing Papers, Ohio. Italics added.

[12] William T. Sherman to Dan McCook, New York, January 11, 1891, McCook Family Papers, LC; Sherman to Thomas Ewing, Fort Moultrie, May 17, 1845, Ewing Family Papers, LC. For more financial details of the same problem, see Sherman's letter to Ewing of June 17, 1844.

2   In the Army: A Dead-end Career

[1] On the history of West Point see Stephen E. Ambrose, *Duty, Honor, Country: A History of West Point* (Baltimore: The Johns Hopkins University Press, 1966); Sidney Forman, *West Point: A History of the United States Military Academy* (New York: Columbia University Press, 1950); and the relevant portions of Edward M. Coffman, *The Old Army: A Portrait of the American Army in Peacetime, 1784–1898* (Oxford University Press, 1986).

[2] Sherman to Phil Ewing, West Point, September 30, 1837, Philemon B. Ewing Papers, Ohio.

[3] Sherman, Memoirs, 2nd ed., I, 17.

[4] For Sherman's toothache see Sherman to Phil Ewing, West Point, April 15, 1838, Philemon B. Ewing Papers, Ohio; on the West Point diet, Ambrose, 148.

[5] Sherman to Phil Ewing, West Point, September 30, 1837, Philemon B. Ewing Papers, Ohio.

[6] Ambrose, Forman, and Coffman speak of Benny Havens as the standard site for a lark. On Sherman and his circle frequenting the tavern, see the comments of William P. Rosecrans, quoted in Lewis, 64. So few cadets were caught and expelled, however, that Benny Havens either had an excellent early warning system, or, as seems more likely, the officers turned a

blind eye to this practice, except on those occasions when cadets got too blatantly drunk and disorderly.

[7] William Ewing to Phil Ewing, West Point, January 27, 1838, Philemon B. Ewing Papers, Ohio. Also see the comments of William Rosecrans, quoted in Lewis, 63, for a fuller description of the contents of the secret meals and of "old Cump's" leading role in their creation.

[8] Sherman to Ellen Ewing, West Point, August 21, 1839, HL, 9.

[9] Sherman to Phil Ewing, West Point, January 27, 1838, Philemon B. Ewing Papers, Ohio.

[10] Sherman to Phil Ewing, West Point, July 11, 1837. Pitcher, who came from a well-established Lancaster mill-owning family, served irregularly as an auctioneer and a publican, but then, according to the 1898 local historian of Lancaster, "deserted his wife . . . went to New York and 'tis said got into trouble and finally went to the state prison." C. M. C. Wiseman, *Centennial History of Lancaster* (Lancaster: C. M. C. Wiseman, 1898), 374–75. Also see Charles R. Goslin, *Crossroads and Fence Corners: Historical Lore of Fairfield County* [Fairfield Historical Association, 1976], 61.

[11] Sherman to John Sherman, West Point, March 7, 1840, SL, 11–12. John would not only do well at the law, but would have a long and distinguished career in both houses of the United States Congress. Lieutenant Sherman was not advising John nearly so much as he was expressing his own hopes and fears.

[12] Sherman to John Sherman, Fort Pierce, March 30, 1841, SL, 14. On the Seminole War see John K. Mahon, *History of the Second Seminole War, 1835–1842* (Gainsville: University of Florida Press, 1967); Virginia B. Peters, *The Florida Wars* (Hamden, CT: Archon Books, 1979), and Henrietta Buckmaster, *The Seminole Wars* (New York: Collier, 1961).

[13] Sherman to Phil Ewing, Fort Pierce, March 19, 1841, Philemon B. Ewing Papers, Ohio.

[14] Sherman to Phil Ewing, Fort Pierce, June 2, 1841, Philemon B. Ewing Papers, Ohio.

[15] Sherman to John, Fort Pierce, January 16, 1841, SL, 17–18; Lewis, 68. Interestingly, the *Sherman Letters* silently omit the expression of regret about hunting these poor people, which Lewis included. I have not found the original of this letter. Sherman to Ellen, Fort Pierce, September 7, 1841, HL, 14.

[16] Sherman to John, Fort Pierce, January 16, 1841, SL.

[17] Lewis, 68.

[18] Sherman to Phil Ewing, Fort Pierce, June 22, 1841, Philemon B. Ewing papers, Ohio.

[19] Sherman, Memoirs, 2nd. ed., I, 27. It is for reasons such as this that I

treat memoirs as a separate genre, rather than as credible historical recon-
structions. For greater detail on this phase of Sherman's career see Jane F.
Lancaster, "William T. Sherman's Introduction to War, 1840–1846,"
Florida Historical Quarterly, LXXII (July 1993), 56–72.

[20] Sherman to John, Fort Moultrie, South Carolina, May 23, 1843, LC.

[21] Sherman to Hugh Ewing, Marietta, March 10, 1844, Hugh B. Ewing
Papers, Ohio.

[22] Sherman to John, Fort Moultrie, May 23, 1843, LC. This portion of this
letter is not reprinted in HL.

[23] Sherman to Ellen, Fort Moultrie, February 4, 1844, HL, 24–25.

[24] On the Mexican War, see K. Jack Bauer, *The Mexican War, 1846–1848*
(Lincoln: University of Nebraska Press, 1992); Otis A. Singletary, *The
Mexican War* (Chicago: University of Chicago Press, 1960); Robert W.
Johannsen, *To the Halls of the Montezumas* (New York: Oxford Univer-
sity Press, 1985); James M. McCaffrey, *Army of Manifest Destiny* (New
York: New York University Press, 1992).

[25] Sherman to Ellen, Monterey, November 10, 1847, HL, 108–109. It is
impossible to discover why Sherman was pulled from his regiment when it
was sent to Mexico.

[26] Sherman to Ellen, Monterey, February 3, 1848, ND.

[27] Sherman to Ellen, Monterey, August 28, 1848, ND, and quoted in
Lewis, 77.

[28] These parts of Sherman's August 28, 1848, letter to Ellen, in the Notre
Dame archives, are not quoted by Lewis.

[29] Grammatically, because the indirect object of the phrase "will have to
receive" is not explicit, agency is ambiguous.

[30] Sherman to Ellen, Monterey, April 10, 1848, HL, 114–15. Sherman's
use of racist stereotypes when discussing Mexicans was quite explicit. In
his June 1867 description of Santa Fe, New Mexico, he wrote to Ellen that
the people were "with a few exceptions *greasers* of the commonest sort,
and their houses, gardens, etc., are about as they were when Moses was a
baby." They shared their houses with "dogs, ants, bugs & fleas." All in all,
"as between the Mexicans & Indians it is an open question which is the
most or least civilized." HL, 376–77, emphasis in the original.

[31] Sherman to Ellen, Monterey, March 12, 1847, ND.

[32] Sherman to Ellen, Monterey, August 28, 1848, ND.

[33] Sherman to Hugh Ewing, Alexandria, Louisiana, April 15, 1860, Hugh
B. Ewing Papers, Ohio. On Sherman's erotic envy of the wild Hugh
Ewing, see chapter three.

[34] I am indebted to George Fredrickson for the definition of hypergamy.

[35] Sherman to Col. Jonathan D. Stevenson, Monterey, August 26, October 28, 1848, Rare Book 375180, Huntington.

[36] Sherman to Ellen, Monterey, August 28, 1848, HL, 117.

[37] Sherman to John, Monterey, August 7, 24, 1848, SL, 38–45; Sherman to General George Gibson, August 5, 1848, Document 375180, Huntington. On Sherman and vigilante law in California in 1856, see chapter four.

[38] Memoirs, I, 38–39, 58–59, 72–79; Sherman to Hugh Ewing, August 3, 1849, Hugh B. Ewing Papers, Ohio.

[39] Sherman to George Gibson, Monterey, April 29, 1849, Document 375180, Huntington. On his being bypassed for promotion, see Lewis, 80.

[40] Sherman to Col. R. B. Mason, Monterey, January 27, 1849; Sherman to Lt. H. W. Halleck, January 29, 1849, Sherman Papers, LC. On feuds and duels in the nineteenth-century army, see the prescient analysis by Coffman, in *The Old Army,* 66–70. Coffman concludes that "there was so much quarreling that it could be considered a major characteristic of the nineteenth-century army." On the special relationship of Halleck and Sherman during the Civil War, see chapters six and fourteen.

3 Marriage Triangle

[1] Sherman to Ellen, San Francisco, March 5, 1849, ND.

[2] See chapter nineteen for his sometimes erotic and more widely expressive letters to the "other women" during his postwar life.

[3] Sherman to Ellen, Fort Pierce, Florida, September 7, 1841, HL, 16.

[4] Karen Lystra has written a rich history of courtship correspondence among middle-class Americans in *Searching the Heart: Women, Men, and Romantic Love in Nineteenth-Century America* (New York: Oxford University Press, 1990). Although soul-searching and self-doubt characterized this literature, the Sherman/Ewing correspondence was far more doubting, and less positive emotionally than almost all of what Lystra describes.

[5] Sherman to Ellen, Fort Moultrie, November 19, 1845, ND.

[6] Sherman to Ellen, Fort Moultrie, January 31, 1846, ND.

[7] Sherman to Ellen, Fort Morgan, Alabama, April 7, 1842, HL, 17–20.

[8] Sherman to Ellen, Fort Moultrie, February 8, 1844, ND.

[9] Ellen to Sherman, Lancaster, July 2, 1844, ND. Emphasis in the original.

[10] Ellen to Sherman, Lancaster, January 19, 1849, ND.

[11] Ellen to Sherman, Lancaster, February 5, 1849, emphasis in the original; Sherman to Ellen, Fort Moultrie, June 14, 1844, ND.

[12] Anna McAllister, *Ellen Ewing: Wife of General Sherman* (New York: Benziger Brothers, 1936), 62. McAllister, in this authorized biography,

may have had access to some Ewing/Sherman papers in the possession of the Sherman family that I have not found in the archives. This story sounds, however, more like the sort of legend passed down from mother to children, especially daughters, and McAllister may have had conversations with Lizzie, before her death in 1925, with Philemon, who did not die until 1941, or with one or more of the Sherman grandchildren, several of whom knew their grandparents quite well. Still, given the hurried wedding date, set right after Sherman's return from a four-year absence, the story is not implausible in its romanticism. Despite their often unaffirmative tone to each other, there were patches of fondness between them, and Sherman was nothing if not impulsive, while Ellen was often swept up in his moods.

[13] Sherman to Ellen, Mansfield, Ohio, March 7, 1859, quoted in McAllister, 79.

[14] Sherman to James A. Hardie, New York City, April 12, 1850, James A. Hardie Papers, LC.

[15] Lewis, 83–85; Merrill, 81. This daughter's nickname would be Minnie.

[16] Sherman to Ellen, St. Louis, September 22, 1850, ND.

[17] Sherman to Ellen, St. Louis, September 25, October 23, 1850, ND.

[18] Sherman to Hugh Ewing, St. Louis, January 5, 1851, Hugh B. Ewing Papers, Ohio.

[19] Sherman to Hugh Ewing, Lancaster, March 8, 1851, Hugh B. Ewing Papers, Ohio.

[20] Sherman to Thomas Ewing, Lancaster, March 11, 1851, Thomas Ewing and Family Papers, LC.

[21] Sherman to Hugh Ewing, St. Louis, January 15, 1852, Hugh B. Ewing Papers, Ohio.

[22] Sherman to Hugh Ewing, St. Louis, May 6, December 8, 1851, Hugh B. Ewing Papers, Ohio. In the slang of the day, *seeing the elephant* meant experiencing the wildness of the frontier for yourself. During the Civil War, the same expression would mean experiencing the frightening reality of battle for the first time.

[23] Sherman to Ellen, St. Louis, September 30, 1852, HL, 128.

[24] Lewis, 87–89; Merrill, 92–95.

[25] Sherman to Thomas Ewing, St. Louis, August 22, 1853, Thomas Ewing and Family Papers, LC.

[26] Sherman to Thomas Ewing, St. Louis, September 29, 1853, Thomas Ewing and Family Papers, LC.

[27] Sherman to Thomas Ewing, San Francisco, February 19, 1857, Thomas Ewing and Family Papers, LC.

[28] Sherman to Thomas Ewing, Jr., Lancaster, August 7, 1857, Sherman Papers, LC. Sherman, in fact, frequently confessed his want of business

acumen to Thomas Ewing, Sr.—see for example his letter of March 3, 1858, from San Francisco, in which he wrote, "when I leave here I will be absolutely penniless. . . . I would not commit the mistake again . . . of beginning on a large scale before I have personally mastered the principle of the business." Thomas Ewing and Family Papers, LC.

[29] Sherman to Ewing, San Francisco, April 7, 1858, quoted in Lewis, 99.

[30] Ellen to My Dear Brother, San Francisco, May 3, 1854, Sherman Papers, Ohio.

[31] Sherman to Henry S. Turner, San Francisco, April 4, 1858, Sherman Papers, Ohio.

[32] Sherman to Ellen, [circa January 1860], ND.

[33] Sherman to Ellen, San Francisco, July 14, 1855, ND.

[34] Sherman to Henry S. Turner, San Francisco, May 16, 1855, Sherman Papers, Ohio.

[35] Sherman to Ellen, Alexandria, Louisiana, February 23, 1860, ND. This is a small but representative sample of Sherman's standardized complaint list, well matched to the subsequent list of her complaints.

[36] Ellen to Hugh Ewing, San Francisco, January 25, 1854, Sherman Papers, Ohio.

[37] Ellen to Sherman, Lancaster, June 1, 1859, ND.

[38] Ellen to Sherman, Lancaster, July 26, 1857, ND.

[39] Ellen to Sherman, Lancaster, June 6, 8, 20, 1859, ND. Emphasis in the original.

[40] Ellen to Sherman, Lancaster, June 1, 1859, November 3, 6, 29, 1860, ND.

[41] Ellen to Sherman, Lancaster, October 24, November 21, 1860, ND.

[42] Ellen to Sherman, Lancaster, April 29, 1855, June 3, 1859, May 1, 1860, ND. The notion that the domestic sphere was the training ground for heaven, and hence morally superior to the public sphere, was widespread among American Victorian women. See Jane Tompkins, *Sensational Designs* (New York: Oxford University Press, 1985), especially her chapter on Harriet Beecher Stowe, pp. 122–46. Though Tompkins is discussing Protestant women writers of sentimental fiction, much of this argument applies to the values of Ellen Ewing Sherman, who was a Catholic letter writer, but one who was deeply influenced by the predominantly Protestant culture in which she lived.

[43] Sherman to Ellen, St. Louis, August 14, 1852, ND.

[44] Sherman to Ellen, Alexandria, Louisiana, December 23, 1860, ND.

[45] Sherman to Henry S. Turner, San Francisco, May 16, 1855, Sherman Papers, Ohio.

[46] Ellen to Sherman, Onboard the *Golden Age,* April 29, 1855, ND. In her

most affirmative formulations, Ellen would always emphasize Sherman's devotion and his kind heart. See, for example, Ellen to Sherman, April 6, 1860, ND.

[47] Ellen to Sherman, Lancaster, October 11, 1858, ND.

[48] Ellen to Sherman, Lancaster, October 13, 1858, ND. Sherman scoffed at this offer, which he found phony, in his letter of April 7, 1858, to Thomas Ewing, quoted above on page 41 and in note 29.

[49] Ellen to Sherman, Lancaster, April 5, 1860, October 28, 1859, ND. Emphasis in the original.

[50] Ellen to Sherman, Lancaster, May 1, 1860, ND.

[51] Sherman to Ellen, Pittsburg Landing, Tennessee, May 1, 1862, ND.

[52] Sherman to Ellen, New Orleans, February 21, 1860, ND.

4 Failure as a Banker and Debts of Honor

[1] Sherman to John, St. Louis, March 4, 1853, Sherman Papers, LC. Also in the Sherman papers at this point is the sales slip for $504.35 from the auction house, A. M. Montgomery & Co., of St. Louis.

[2] John to Sherman, Washington, [circa March 10, 1853], quoted in Merrill, 94.

[3] Sherman to John, San Francisco, June 3, 1853, SL, 52–53.

[4] Sherman to John, San Francisco, June 3, 1854, Sherman Papers, LC.

[5] Sherman to John, San Francisco, September 29, 1854, Sherman Papers, LC. On his health also see Sherman's letter to Henry S. Turner, San Francisco, January 5, 1856, Sherman Papers, Ohio.

[6] Sherman to Minnie, San Francisco, October 19, 1856, Sherman Papers, Ohio.

[7] Sherman to Turner, San Francisco, April 17, 1856, Sherman Papers, Ohio.

[8] Sherman to Turner, San Francisco, October 15, 1854, Sherman Papers, Ohio.

[9] Merrill, 106; Lewis, 96; Sherman to John, San Francisco, November 30, 1854, Sherman to Braxton Bragg, June 3, 1855, Sherman to Turner, August 31, 1856, Sherman Papers, LC. In addition to Bragg, other army investors included John G. Barnard, Don Carlos Buell, Ethan Allen Hitchcock, William J. Hardee, and George Thomas.

[10] Sherman to Turner, San Francisco, January 15, 1855, Sherman Papers, Ohio.

[11] Sherman to Turner, San Francisco, February 25, 1855, Sherman Papers, Ohio.

[12] Sherman to Phil Ewing, San Francisco, August 30, 1856, Philemon B. Ewing Papers, Ohio.

[13] Sherman to Thomas Ewing, San Francisco, August 3, 1856, Thomas Ewing and Family Papers, LC.

[14] Sherman to Turner, San Francisco, May 18, 1856, Sherman Papers, Missouri Historical Society, St. Louis.

[15] Sherman to Turner, San Francisco, July 2, 1856, Sherman Papers, Ohio.

[16] Sherman to John, San Francisco, July 7, 1856, SL, 58–59.

[17] Sherman to John, San Francisco, August 3, 1856, SL, 59.

[18] Sherman to Turner, San Francisco, October 19, 1856, Sherman Papers, Ohio. On May 15, 1855, Sherman had written Turner of declining the city treasurer nomination, "I told them I was not a politician at all, [in any] event, not a Democrat. I never voted for President in my life, my family and relatives are nearly all Whigs, etc., etc." Sherman Papers, Ohio.

[19] In addition to the Sherman letter quoted here, see most especially his letter to Thomas Ewing of June 16, 1856, Sherman Papers, reprinted in Dwight L. Clarke, *William T. Sherman: Gold Rush Banker* (San Francisco: California Historical Society, 1969), 178–227; Sherman, "The Vigilance Committee of 1856," *The Overland Monthly,* XII (February 1874), reproduced in Doyce B. Nunnis, Jr., ed., *The San Francisco Vigilance Committee of 1856* (Los Angeles: The Los Angeles Westerners, 1971), 158–69; and Sherman's artfully self-serving account in his Memoirs, I, 118–32.

[20] Sherman to Turner, San Francisco, November 4, 1856, Sherman Papers, Ohio.

[21] Sherman to Turner, San Francisco, December 4, 1856, Sherman Papers, Ohio.

[22] Sherman to Turner, San Francisco, January 18, 1857, Sherman Papers, Ohio. Turner's announcement of the decision, which must have come a day or two earlier, and which provoked this response, is missing from the manuscript record.

[23] Sherman to Turner, San Francisco, March 4, April 2, 1857, Sherman Papers, Ohio.

[24] Sherman to Turner, April 2, 1857, Eleanor Sherman Fitch Collection, New York Public Library.

[25] Sherman to Ellen, New York, July 27, October 6, 1857, ND (the July 27 letter is reprinted, but only in part, in HL, 148–49); Sherman to John, New York, August 22, September 4, 1857, St. Louis, April 8, 1861, Sherman Papers, LC; Sherman to James A. Hardie, San Francisco, April 14, 1857, James A. Hardie Papers, LC; Lewis, 94–97, 106–107.

[26] Sherman to Turner, New York, October 6, 13, 1857, Sherman Papers, Ohio.

[27] Sherman to John, September 4, 1857, Sherman Papers, LC.

[28] Sherman to Turner, New York, August 10, 1857, Sherman Papers, Ohio.

[29] Sherman to Turner, New York, September 17, October 9, 1857, Sherman Papers, Ohio.

[30] Sherman to Turner, San Francisco, April 18, 1858, Sherman Papers, Ohio.

[31] Sherman to Hugh Ewing, St. Louis, November 26, 1857, Hugh B. Ewing Papers, Ohio; Sherman to Ellen, New York, July 29, 1857, ND.

[32] Sherman to Turner, February 18, 1858, Sherman Papers, Ohio.

[33] Sherman to Ellen, New York, July 29, 1857, ND.

[34] Sherman to John, February 4, 1858, Sherman Papers, LC; Sherman to Ellen, San Francisco, March 3, 1858, HL, 152–53.

[35] Sherman to John, New York, October 9, 1857, LC.

[36] Sherman to Ellen, Leavenworth, Kansas, September 18, 1858, Indian Creek, Kansas, April 15, 1859, HL, 155, 159.

[37] Sherman to Col. Samuel Cooper, Lancaster, December 16, 1857, Andre de Coppet Collection, Princeton University Library; Sherman to Ellen, Fort Riley, Kansas, September 25, 1858, ND; Sherman to John, Lancaster, December 27, 1857, Sherman Papers, LC.

[38] Sherman to Thomas Ewing, Jr., Lancaster, August 9, 1858, Sherman Papers, LC.

[39] Sherman to Ellen, Leavenworth, September 18, 1858, ND, reprinted, but only in part, in HL, 154.

[40] Sherman to John, Leavenworth, April 30, 1859, Sherman Papers, LC.

[41] Merrill, 131–32, has the best description of these business operations.

[42] Sherman to Ellen, San Francisco, June 20, 1858, Sherman Papers, LC; Sherman to Turner, San Francisco, March 4, 21, 1858, Sherman Papers, Ohio.

5 Going South and Leaving: The Ambivalent Unionist

[1] Lewis, 112.

[2] Sherman to John, November 30, 1854, March 20, 1856, Sherman Papers, LC; both letters are reprinted in SL, 53–55.

[3] Sherman to Turner, San Francisco, May 4, 1856, Sherman Papers, Ohio.

[4] Sherman to John, Leavenworth, April 30, 1859, reprinted in part in SL, 69–70.

[5] See Eric Foner, *Free Soil, Free Labor, Free Men: The Ideology of the Re-*

publican Party Before the Civil War (New York: Oxford University Press, 1970); on Democratic ideology, Jean H. Baker, *Affairs of Party: The Political Culture of Northern Democrats in the Mid-Nineteenth Century* (Ithaca: Cornell University Press, 1983), and Forrest G. Wood, *Black Scare: The Racist Response to Emancipation and Reconstruction* (Berkeley: University of California Press, 1968).

[6] Sherman to Ellen, Onboard the *L. M. Kennett,* October 29, 1859, HL, 162–63. He certainly thought Ellen lacked common sense on religious issues, but it is not clear that he was digging at her in this particular letter.

[7] Sherman to David F. Boyd, Lancaster, September 30, 1860, quoted in Walter L. Fleming, *General William T. Sherman as College President* (Cleveland: Arthur H. Clark, 1912), 291.

[8] Sherman to Hugh Ewing, Alexandria, January 21, 1860, Sherman to Thomas Ewing, Jr., Alexandria, December 23, 1859, both in Thomas Ewing and Family Papers, LC; Sherman to Ellen, Alexandria, November 29, 1860, HL, 185. In the last slur, Sherman was referring to an English actor he had seen performing the title role in *The Toodles,* a play about English rustics, by Richard John Raymond, performed in New York in 1853, after being rewritten to suit American tastes. Raymond, *The Toodles* (New York: William Taylor, 1853).

[9] Sherman to Thomas Ewing, Jr., Alexandria, June 21, 1860, Thomas Ewing and Family Papers, LC.

[10] Sherman to Thomas Ewing, Alexandria, June 8, 1860, Thomas Ewing and Family Papers, LC.

[11] Sherman to John, Alexandria, December 29, 1860, January 16, 1861, Sherman Papers, LC.

[12] Sherman to Minnie, Alexandria, December 15, 1860, Sherman Papers, Ohio.

[13] Sherman to Ellen, Alexandria, December 23, 1860, ND.

[14] Sherman to Ellen, Alexandria, February 3, 10, June 28, 1860, ND. Reprinted in part in HL, 174–75.

[15] Sherman to Thomas Ewing, Alexandria, January 8, 1861, Thomas Ewing and Family Papers, LC.

[16] Sherman to G. Mason Graham, Alexandria, Christmas 1860, quoted in Fleming, 318.

[17] Sherman to Ellen, Alexandria, January 5, 1861, HL, 189. Sherman's reference to Southern filibustering referred primarily to the illegal proslavery adventures of William Walker, especially to Nicaragua, which Walker ruled for a period in the mid-1850s. My use of the phrase, *an excess of democracy,* is taken from a celebrated conservative essay of that title in David Donald, *Lincoln Reconsidered* (New York: Vintage, n.d.), 209–35.

Sherman's argument is almost precisely Donald's. On this theme also see Sherman to G. Mason Graham, Alexandria, January 5, 1861, quoted in Fleming, 329.

[18] Sherman to Ellen, Onboard the *L. M. Kennett,* October 29, 1859; Alexandria, July 10, December 18, 1860, HL, 128–29, 162, 188; Sherman to John, Alexandria, February 3, 1860, Sherman Papers, LC.

[19] Sherman to Ellen, Alexandria, January 8, 1861, HL, 190. Sherman was far from alone in this notion of Northern moral degeneration and the need for radical regenerative measures. Such views were particularly widespread among Old Whigs, New England elites, and intellectuals, although most of them put the possibilities for regeneration in a more positive and reformist light than did Sherman. See George M. Fredrickson's recently reissued 1964 study, *The Inner Civil War* (Urbana: University of Illinois Press, 1993).

[20] Sherman to John, Alexandria, February 3, 1860, Sherman Papers, LC; Sherman to G. Mason Graham, Alexandria, January 5, 1861, Fleming, 329; Sherman to Ellen, Alexandria, January 27, 1861, HL, 193. During the first two years of the Civil War, conservative Unionists often discussed dispensing with Lincoln and setting up a military dictatorship for purposes of national salvation. George McClellan was most often the Louis Napoleon presumptive, talk that he, a bantam-cock egoist, did not always discourage, and that he even used.

[21] Sherman to David F. Boyd, St. Louis, May 13, 1861, quoted in Lewis, 161.

[22] Sherman to John, Alexandria, December 9, 18, 1860, Sherman Papers, LC; Sherman to Ellen, Alexandria, December 18, 1860, ND.

[23] Sherman to John, Alexandria, December 29, 1860, Sherman Papers, LC; Sherman to Hugh Ewing, December 18, 1860, January 12, 1861, Hugh B. Ewing Papers, Ohio.

[24] Sherman to John, Alexandria, December 9, 18, 1860, Sherman Papers, LC.

[25] Sherman to Ellen, Alexandria, December 16, 18, 1860, ND.

[26] Sherman to Ellen, Alexandria, December 23, 1860, ND.

[27] Sherman to Governor Thomas G. Moore, Alexandria, January 18, 1861, Sherman Papers, LC.

[28] Sherman to Ellen, Alexandria, December 18, 23, 1860, ND.

6   Into the Abyss: Collapse in War

[1] Ellen to John, January 30, 1861, Sherman Papers, LC. There is a good picture of Sherman's last days in Louisiana in Lewis, 146–47.

2 Memoirs, I, 168.

3 Sherman to John, Lancaster, March 9, Cincinnati, March 21, St. Louis, April 18, 22, 26, 1861, Sherman Papers, LC.

4 Sherman to Montgomery Blair, St. Louis, April 8, 1861, reprinted in Memoirs, I, 170–71.

5 Sherman to Thomas Ewing, Jr., St. Louis, April 26, 1861, Thomas Ewing and Family Papers, LC; Sherman to David Boyd, St. Louis, May 13, 1861, quoted in Lewis, 161.

6 Sherman to Thomas Ewing, Jr., St. Louis, May 23, 1861, Thomas Ewing and Family Papers, LC.

7 Sherman to Minnie, Alexandria, Virginia, July 14, 1861, Sherman Papers, Ohio.

8 Sherman, Report, Fort Corcoran, July 25, 1861, OR, ser. 1, vol. II, 367–71; Sherman to adjutant general, Fort Corcoran, July 22, 1861, OR, ser. 1, vol. II, 755.

9 Sherman to Ellen, Washington, August 3, 1861, HL, 212–13.

10 Sherman to Ellen, Washington, August 3, 1861, HL, 212–13. Sherman to John, Fort Gore, August 19, 1861, Sherman Papers, LC, reprinted in part in SL, 126–27.

11 Memoirs, I, 188–91.

12 Memoirs, I, 192–93; Sherman to Ellen, [circa August 20, 1861], ND.

13 Sherman to Oliver D. Greene, Muldraugh's Hill, Kentucky, September 27, 1861, OR, ser. 1, vol. IV, 279.

14 Sherman to Brigadier General Crittenden, Sherman to Garrett Davis, Sherman to Colonel Jackson, Sherman to General Ward, Louisville, October 8, 1861, all in OR, ser. 1, vol. IV, 297–99; Sherman to Abraham Lincoln, Louisville, October 10, 1861, OR, ser. 1, vol. IV, 300; Sherman to Adjutant General Lorenzo Thomas, Louisville, October 22, 1861, OR, ser. 1, vol. IV, 316.

15 Sherman to George H. Thomas, Louisville, November 5, 11, 12, 1861, OR, ser. 1, vol. IV, 335, 350–51, 353–54; Sherman to Lorenzo Thomas, Louisville, November 6, 1861, OR, ser. 1, vol. IV, 340–41.

16 Memoirs, I, 200–204; Lorenzo Thomas to Simon Cameron, Washington, October 21, 1861, OR, ser. 1, vol. III, 548–49; ser. 1, vol. IV, 313–14.

17 Brigadier General A. McD. McCook to Sherman, Camp Nevin, November 5, 1861, OR, ser. 1, vol. IV, 337; D. C. Buell to George B. McClellan, Louisville, November 22, 1861, OR, ser. 1, vol. VII, 443.

18 William F. G. Shanks, *Personal Recollections of Distinguished Generals* (New York: Harper & Brothers, 1866), 17–18, 22, 25–26, 52–59, emphasis in the original; Henry Villard, *Memoirs of Henry Villard: Journalist and Financier,* 2 vols. (Boston: Houghton Mifflin, 1904), I, 206–13. Of course

the same lack of self-censorship and his tendency to blurt out everything, a lifelong habit exacerbated in times of stress, also make Sherman an ideal subject for the historian. That Sherman was so unguarded to journalists makes his hatred of them as a species all the more complex.

[19] Sherman to Ellen, Louisville, October 3, 6, 12, 20, 23, 25, November 1, 1861, ND. Sherman revealed much of this pattern of fears, though in somewhat less interior ways, to John as well. See his letters of September 9 and October 5, 1861, Sherman Papers, LC. In addition to receiving his brother's letters, John was hearing a great deal from his political and military contacts in Washington and from Ellen, as for example in her letter of October 4, in which she urged John to do his all to secure regular troops and better supplies for the embattled general. Sherman Papers, LC.

[20] Ellen to Sherman, Lancaster, September 29, October 4, 10, 1861, ND. As the Shermans saved nearly every letter they wrote one another, one suspects that some time after the war either one of them, or one of their children who served as their literary executors, silently destroyed these letters. It is also possible that in his distraught condition, Sherman either mislaid or destroyed them at the time he received them.

[21] Ellen to John, Louisville, November 10, 1861, Sherman Papers, LC. At the start of this letter, Ellen copied for John the telegram that had been sent to Thomas Ewing.

[22] John to Sherman, Mansfield, Ohio, November 17, 1861, ND.

[23] Marszalek, 169; Marszalek, *Sherman's Other War: The General and the Civil War Press* (Memphis: Memphis State University Press, 1981), 67-68.

[24] J. C. Kelton, Special Orders Number 8, Department of the Missouri, St. Louis, November 23, 1861; Sherman to Halleck, Sedalia, November 27, 28, 1861; Schuyler Hamilton to Sherman, St. Louis, November 28, 1861, all in OR, ser. 1, vol. VIII, 374, 381-84, 391; and for the doctor's report, Marszalek, 164.

[25] Halleck to McClellan, St. Louis, [circa December 2], 1861, OR, ser. 1, vol. LII, pt. 1, 198.

[26] The *Cincinnati Commercial* article of December 11, widely reprinted, is available in full in Lewis, 201. Ellen to John, Lancaster, December 10, 12, 17, Ellen to Thomas Ewing, Jr., December 16, Sherman to Thomas Ewing, December 12, 1861, all in Sherman Papers, LC; McAllister, *Ellen Sherman*, 199-204.

[27] Halleck to Ellen, St. Louis, December 14, Sherman Papers, LC; Halleck to P. B. Ewing, St. Louis, December 17, Sherman to Halleck, Lancaster, December 12, Halleck to Sherman, St. Louis, December 18, 1861, OR, ser. 1, vol. VIII, 441-42, 445-46, 812.

[28] Special Orders Number 87, St. Louis, December 23, 1861, General Or-

ders Number 37, St. Louis, February 14, 1862, OR, ser. 1, vol. VIII, 459, 555; Sherman to John, February 23, 1862, Sherman Papers, LC; Sherman to Grant, Paducah, Kentucky, February 15, 1862; Grant to Sherman, Fort Donelson, Tennessee, February 19, 1861, Grant Papers, IV, 215–216, V, 249.

29 Ellen to Sherman, Lancaster, Thursday morning, December 19, 1861, ND.

30 Ellen to Abraham Lincoln, Lancaster, December 19, 1861, Sherman Papers, LC; also reprinted in part in McAllister, 203–204.

31 Ellen to Sherman, Washington, January 29, Lancaster, April 24, 1862, ND; Ellen to John, February 20, March 10, Sherman Papers, LC.

32 Thomas Ewing to John, Lancaster, December 22, Hugh Ewing to Sherman, Washington, December 23, 1861, Ellen to Sherman, Lancaster, January 11, February 4, Washington, January 29, 1862, all in ND. Emphasis in the original.

33 Ellen to Sherman, Washington, January 29, 1862, ND; McAllister, 208–210.

34 Ellen to Sherman, Washington, D.C., January 22, 1862, Lancaster, January 8, March 7, 14, 1862, all in ND. Emphasis in the original.

35 Sherman to Ellen, St. Louis, December 17, 1861, January 1, 1862, ND; Sherman to John, St. Louis, January 4, 1862, Sherman Papers, LC.

36 Sherman to Ellen, St. Louis, January 1, 19, ND; Sherman to John, St. Louis, January 4, 1862, Sherman Papers, LC.

37 Sherman to Ellen, St. Louis, January 1, 5, 1862, Paducah, February 21, 1862, ND.

38 Sherman to John, St. Louis, January 4, 1862, Sherman Papers, LC; Sherman to Ellen, St. Louis, January 1, 11, 1862, ND.

39 Sherman to Ellen, St. Louis, December 19, 1861, January 19, 1862, ND.

40 Sherman to Ellen, St. Louis, January 19, 29, 1862, ND. On depression and suicide in historical context see Howard I. Kushner, American Suicide: A Psychohistorical Exploration (New Brunswick: Rutgers University Press, 1989). Also see William Styron's haunting and illuminating essay, Darkness Visible: A Memoir of Madness (New York: Random House, 1990).

41 Sherman to Ellen, Cairo, March 3, March 12, 1862, ND; Ellen to John, Lancaster, March 9, John to Sherman, Washington, February 15, 1862, Sherman Papers, LC. Emphasis in the original.

42 Sherman to Ellen, St. Louis, January 11, Pittsburg Landing, Tennessee, April 3, 1862, ND.

7 Ecstatic Resurrection at Shiloh

[1] "Report of Brigadier General W. T. Sherman," Camp Shiloh, April 10, 1862, OR, ser. 1, vol. X, pt. 1, 249; James Lee McDonough, *Shiloh: In Hell Before Night* (Knoxville: University of Tennessee Press, 1977), 56–58 and passim; Sherman to Ellen, Pittsburg Landing, April 4, 1862, ND; Sherman to U. S. Grant, Pittsburg Landing, OR, ser. 1, vol. X, pt. 2, 93–94. In mutuality of recollection, both men, in their memoirs and elsewhere, would deny that they had been surprised at Shiloh, an assertion that contemporary journalists and later historians have rejected unanimously. See for example, Memoirs, I, 229–30; U. S. Grant, *Personal Memoirs of U. S. Grant,* 2 vols. (New York: C. L. Webster, 1885–86), I, 340–41. The question of surprise versus nonsurprise was just the kind of test of honor that all the rusticated Civil War generals would argue about in their advanced years, passionately, nastily and endlessly, as I discuss in chapter eighteen.

[2] "Report of . . . Sherman," 248–54.

[3] Sherman to Ellen, Shiloh, April 11, 1862, HL, 222; Lewis, 229; Sherman to John, near Corinth, May 7, 1862, SL, 145; Grant to Captain N. H. McLean, Pittsburg Landing, April 9, 1862, OR, ser. 1, vol. X, pt. 1, 110, and reprinted in Grant Papers, V, 32–37; H. W. Halleck to Hon. E. M. Stanton, Pittsburg Landing, April 13, 1862, OR, ser. 1, vol. X, pt. 1, 98. For a full discussion of the personalizing of the Civil War, see Gerald F. Linderman, *Embattled Courage: The Experience of Combat in the American Civil War* (New York: Free Press, 1987).

[4] U. S. Grant to Julia Dent Grant, Monterey, Tennessee, May 4, 1862, Grant Papers, V, 111; also see Grant's praise of Sherman to Julia on June 9, 1862, from Corinth, Mississippi, Grant Papers, V, 140–41; Memoirs, I, 255; Grant to Ellen, Memphis, July 7, 1862, Grant Papers, V, 200–201.

[5] Sherman to Ellen, Shiloh, April 11, 14, 24, ND. The letter of April 11 is reprinted in HL, 220–25.

[6] Sherman to Ellen, Pittsburg Landing, April 14, May 3, 1862, ND.

[7] In *Battle Cry of Freedom,* James McPherson writes that this experience "proved to be the turning point of [Sherman's] life. What he learned that day at Shiloh—about war and about himself—helped to make him one of the North's premier generals." (New York: Oxford University Press, 1988), 409. I agree with McPherson, and stress here that in very particular ways Shiloh was an *emotional* turning point for Sherman. This did not revolutionize his entire personality, but rather tilted him, as it were, outward from his clinging sense of failure and self-hatred and into a more engaged participation in the world.

[8] Ellen to Sherman, Lancaster, April 18, 1862, ND; Ellen to John, May 4, 1862, LC; also see Sherman to John, Shiloh, April 16, 1862, LC; John to Sherman, Washington, April 20, 1862, SL, 142–43.

[9] Sherman to Ellen, Shiloh, April 11, 1862, HL, 220–23; Sherman to Ellen, Fort Corcoran, Washington, D.C., July 25, 1861, HL, 208.

[10] Ellen to Sherman, Lancaster, April 19, 1862, ND. This discussion was on the final page of a letter begun the day before. Ellen appended this discussion immediately after opening Sherman's letter of April 11. The meaning of Holliday's death was the subject of her entire response to the news contained in her husband's triumphant first account.

[11] Sherman to Ellen, Camp [at Pittsburg Landing], May 2, 1862, ND.

[12] Ellen to Sherman, Lancaster, June 1, 1862, ND. Emphasis in the original.

[13] Ellen to Sherman, Lancaster, February 2, 1863, ND. Emphasis in the original.

[14] Franc B. Wilkie, *Pen and Powder* (Boston: Ticknor, 1888), 159–60.

8 Purging the Devil: Sherman Assaults the Press

[1] Sherman to Thomas Ewing, Jr., Camp Shiloh, April 4, 1862, ND.

[2] Sherman to John, Camp Shiloh, April 22, 1862, Sherman Papers, LC. Most of this letter is reprinted in SL, 143–45. However, the last sentence is omitted, and it is the last sentence that is most significant.

[3] Sherman to Thomas Ewing, Sr., Camp Shiloh, April 27, 1862, Thomas Ewing and Family Papers, LC.

[4] Sherman to Ellen, Camp at Chewalla, June 6, 1862, HL, 226–27.

[5] Sherman to Grant, Memphis, August 17, 1862, OR, ser. 1, vol. XVII, pt. 2, 178; Sherman to James B. Fry, Nashville, April 10, 1864, OR, ser. 1, vol. XXXII, pt. 3, 320; Sherman to John, Jackson, Mississippi, July 19, 1863, Sherman Papers, LC; Sherman to Grant, April 28, 1863, Grant Papers, VIII, 131; Sherman to Samuel Sawyer, Memphis, July 24, 1862, OR, ser. 1, vol. XVII, pt. 2, 116–17; Sherman to Colonel W. H. H. Taylor, Memphis, August 25, 1862, OR, ser. 1, vol. LII, pt. 1, 275.

[6] John to Sherman, Washington, March 20, 1862, Sherman Papers, LC, emphasis in the original. This was an admonition John would make frequently to his brother over the ensuing decades. Ellen to John, Mansfield, May 7, 1862, Sherman Papers, LC. Also see Sherman to Ellen, Camp at Chewalla, June 6, 1862, HL, 226–27.

[7] Sherman to Samuel R. Curtis, Camp before Vicksburg, February 7, 1863, OR, ser. 1, vol. XXIV, pt. 3, 38; Sherman to John, Camp before Vicksburg, February 7, 1863, Sherman Papers, LC; *New York Herald,*

January 8, 1863, quoted in the court-martial charges against Knox, Young's Point, Louisiana, February 19, 1863, Sherman to Murat Halstead, Camp near Vicksburg, April 8, 1863, Lincoln to Knox, Washington, March 20, 1863, Knox to Grant, Onboard the *Continental,* April 6, 1863, Grant to Knox, before Vicksburg, April 6, 1863, Sherman to Knox, before Vicksburg, April 7, 1863, all in OR, ser. 1, vol. XVII, pt. 2, 890, 893–94, 896; Ellen to Sherman, Mansfield, February 22, 1863, ND, emphasis in the original; and on the newspapermen calling on Lincoln, John F. Marszalek, *Sherman's Other War,* 142–43. The Knox affair is well documented in OR, ser. 1, vol. XVII, pt. 2, 580–91, 882–97. In addition, see the detailed and sensible discussion in Marszalek, *Sherman's Other War,* 126–47.

8 Sherman to Editors of *Memphis Bulletin,* Iuka, Mississippi, October 27, 1863, OR, ser. 1, vol. XXXI, pt. 1, 765; Sherman to J. D. Bingham, Fayetteville, Tennessee, November 9, 1863, OR, ser. 1, vol. XXXI, pt. 3, 97.

9 Henry Villard, *Memoirs of Henry Villard,* I, 271–72; Albert D. Richardson, *The Secret Service* (Hartford: American Publishing Company, 1965), 247–49.

10 Sherman to John, Camp on the Big Black, August 3, 1863, Nashville, April 4, 1864, Sherman Papers, LC. The first letter is also in SL, 211–213. Emphasis in the original.

11 Circular, Kingston, Georgia, May 30, 1864, Sherman to George H. Thomas, Thomas to Sherman, Sherman to James B. McPherson, Kenesaw, Georgia, June 29, 1864, OR, ser. 1, vol. XXXVIII, pt. 4, 272, 637; Marszalek, *Sherman's Other War,* 65–67.

12 Sherman to Frank Blair, Camp near Vicksburg, February 1, 2, 1863, Blair to Sherman, February 1, 1863, OR, ser. 1, vol. XVII, pt. 2, 581–88; Sherman to General Brayman, Nashville, April 2, 1864, OR, ser. 1, vol. XXXII, pt. 3, 230–31.

13 Sherman to Henry W. Halleck, near Chattahoochee, Georgia, July 7, 1864, OR, ser. 1, vol. XXXVIII, pt. 5, 73; Edwin M. Stanton to Grant, Washington, November 11, 1864, OR, ser. 1, vol. XXXIX, pt. 3, 740; Sherman to Murat Halstead, Camp near Vicksburg, April 8, 1863, OR, ser. 1, vol. XVII, pt. 2, 895–97; Sherman to G. D. Prentice, [Chattanooga, circa November 16, 1863], OR, ser. 1, vol. XXXI, pt. 3, 168; Sherman to C. A. Dana, Kingston, Georgia, November 10, 1864, OR, ser. 1, vol. XXXIX, pt. 3, 727.

14 Sherman to Ellen, Savannah, January 15, Raleigh, North Carolina, April 22, 1865, ND.

15 Sherman to William H. Appleton, Washington, June 10, 1875, William

H. Appleton Papers, Columbia University Library; Sherman to J. H. Sturgeon, Washington, February 14, 1880, ND.

9 Turning Friends into Enemies

[1] Orders Number 44, La Grange, Tennessee, June 18; Sherman to Halleck, La Grange, June 19; Orders Number 49, Moscow, Tennessee, July 7, 1862, OR, ser. 1, vol. XVII, pt. 2, 16–17, 81; Special Orders Number 1, La Grange, Grant Papers, VI, 266–67.

[2] General Orders Number 62, July 24; Sherman to John A. Rawlins, July 25, Sherman to Commanders of Regiments and Companies in the Service of the United States, Memphis, October 30, Sherman to Rawlins, November 1, Orders Number 58, July 22, Sherman to Captain Fitch, August 7, General Orders Number 66, August 7, General Orders Number 82, September 15, Sherman to John Park, Mayor of Memphis, July 27, General Orders Number 72, August 14, General Orders Number 90, October 25, Sherman to Colonel D. C. Anthony, October 25, 1862, all written from Memphis, and all in OR, ser. 1, vol. XVII, pt. 2, 112–13, 118–19, 121–23, 127, 156–58, 173–74, 219–20, 294–96, 853–54, 856–58. As late as January 12, 1863, while establishing Union control over the newly captured Port of Arkansas, Sherman issued orders that "ignorance of the rules of war as to pillage and plunder can no longer be pleaded"; and promised to clap in irons the officers of regiments who allowed their men to keep captured horses, mules, guns, saddles, or other property. General Orders Number 3, Port of Arkansas, in OR, ser. 1, vol. XVII, pt. 2, 556–57.

[3] Sherman to Ellen, September 25, ND; Sherman to Colonel E. D. Townsend, December 14, Alfred Wagstaff Collection, West Point; Sherman to John, December 14, John to Sherman, Mansfield, August 14, both in Sherman Papers, LC; Sherman to Minnie, October 4, 1862, Sherman Papers, Ohio.

[4] I have discussed these and other issues of guerrilla warfare during the American Civil War in Missouri, which saw the worst such fighting, in *Inside War: The Guerrilla Conflict in Missouri During the American Civil War* (New York: Oxford University Press, 1989).

[5] Report of a skirmish near Wolf River, Moscow, July 14, OR, ser. 1, vol. XVII, pt. 1, 23; Sherman to Colonel C. C. Walcutt, September 24, OR, ser. 1, vol. XVII, pt. 2, 235–36; Report of the burning of Randolph, September 26, OR, ser. 1, vol. XVII, pt. 1, 144–45; Sherman to John A. Rawlins, October 2, 18, November 19, OR, ser. 1, vol. XVII, pt. 2, 279–80, 285–86, 870–71; Sherman to Curtis, October 18, OR, ser. 2, vol. IV, 633; Sherman to Grant, October 4, OR, ser. 1, vol. XVII, pt. 2, 261; Sherman to Major

General T. C. Hindman, September 28, OR, ser. 1, vol. XIII, 682–83; Sherman to Hindman, October 17, OR, ser. 2, vol. IV, 631–32; Sherman to Lieutenant General J. C. Pemberton, November 18, Sherman to Miss P. A. Fraser, October 22, Sherman to Mrs. Valeria Hurlbut, November 7, 1862, all in OR, ser. 1, vol. XVII, pt. 2, 287–88, 860, 872–73.

⁶ Sherman to Rawlins, Milliken's Bend, Louisiana, January 3, Report from the Port of Arkansas, January 13, 1863, OR, ser. 1, vol. XVII, pt. 1, 605–12, 754–61; Sherman to Admiral David D. Porter, Onboard the *Forest Queen,* January 20, 1863, Haskell Collection, Clements Library, Ann Arbor; Thomas Kilby Smith to Ellen, January 17, 1863, Sherman Papers, LC.

⁷ Sherman to Grant, Camp on Bear Creek, July 4, 1863, OR, ser. 1, vol. XXIV, pt. 3, 477.

⁸ Sherman to Grant, Army before Jackson, July 14, Sherman to Grant, Jackson, July 18 (twice), 20, 21, Sherman to Rawlins, Camp on the Big Black, July 28, Sherman to C. H. Manslip, Mayor of Jackson, July 21, Manslip to Sherman, July 21, all in OR, ser. 1, vol. XXIV, pt. 2, 525–27, 529, 530–31, 532–38, 539. Also see Sherman to Admiral David D. Porter, Jackson, July 19, 1863, Bixby Collection, Missouri Historical Society, for a similar, pleasure-filled description of the conquest of Jackson.

⁹ Sherman to Major General S. A. Hurlbut, Iuka, Mississippi, October 24, 25, 1862, OR, ser. 1, vol. XXXI, pt. 1, 718–19, 734; Sherman to G. M. Dodge, Winchester, Tennessee, November 12, 1863, OR, ser. 1, vol. XXXI, pt. 3, 131; Sherman to John A. Logan, Nashville, December 21, 1863, Logan Papers, Yale University Library.

¹⁰ Sherman to Professor F. A. P. Barnard, Camp on the Big Black, September 4, 1863, Barnard Papers, Columbia University Library, emphasis in the original.

¹¹ Sherman to John A. Logan, Nashville, December 21, 1863, OR, ser. 1, vol. XXXI, pt. 3, 359–60; Sherman to Dearest Minnie, Onboard the *Silver Cloud,* January 19, 1864, Sherman Papers, Ohio.

10 Niggers and Other Vagabonds

¹ Sherman to Ellen, Memphis, July 31, 1862, HL, 229.

² Orders Number 43, La Grange, Tennessee, June 18, 1862, OR, ser. 1, vol. XVII, pt. 2, 15–16.

³ Orders Number 60, Memphis, July 21, 1862, Sherman to Colonel John A. Rawlins, Memphis, July 30, 1862, OR, ser. 1, vol. XVII, pt. 2, 113, 140–41.

⁴ Orders Number 60, Orders Number 67, Memphis, August 8, 1862, OR,

ser. 1, vol. XVII, pt. 2, 158–60. On the degree to which Sherman improvised these orders to create rules with which to handle the importuning of the masters, see Sherman to Rawlins, August 14, 1862, in OR, ser. 1, vol. XVII, pt. 2, 169–71.

[5] Sherman to General Gideon Pillow, Memphis, August 14, 1862, OR, ser. 1, vol. XVII, pt. 2, 172; Sherman to Captain H. M. Lazelle, Memphis, October 2, 1862, OR, ser. 2, vol. IV, 589–90.

[6] John to Sherman, Mansfield, Ohio, August 24, 1862, Sherman Papers, LC; quoted, but only in part, in SL, 156–57.

[7] Sherman to John, Memphis, September 3, 1862, Sherman Papers, LC, quoted, but only in part, in SL, 160–61; Sherman to Rawlins, Memphis, September 1, 1862, Sherman to Brigadier General Hovey, Memphis, October 29, 1862, Sherman to Judge Swayne, Memphis, November 12, 1862, all in OR, ser. 1, vol. XVII, pt. 2, 201, 856, 863–65.

[8] Sherman to Ellen, Memphis, July 31, August 20, 1862, HL, 229–32; Sherman to Rawlins, Memphis, July 30, 1862, OR, ser. 1, vol. XVII, pt. 2, 140–41; Sherman to Adjutant General of the Army, Memphis, August 11, 1862, OR, ser. 3, vol. II, 350; Grant to Brigadier General J. T. Quinby, Corinth, Mississippi, July 26, 1862, Grant Papers, V, 238. In general on this anti-Semitic expulsion see Grant Papers, V, 238–40; VII, 50–56; and McPherson, *Battle Cry of Freedom,* 441–42, 622–23.

[9] Sherman to Admiral David D. Porter, Iuka, Mississippi, October 25, 1863, OR, ser. 1, vol. XXXI, pt. 1, 736–38. Sherman also copied this letter to Chase.

[10] Sherman to James B. McPherson, Bridgeport, November 18, 1863, Sherman to General Buckland, Sherman's Headquarters, September 9, 1863, Sherman to H. W. Hill, Chairman of Meeting of Citizens, Warren County, Mississippi, Camp on the Big Black, September 7, 1863, OR, ser. 1, vol. XXX, pt. 3, 187–88, 401–404, 476.

[11] Lincoln to James C. Conkling, Washington, August 26, 1863, in Roy Basler, ed., *The Collected Works of Abraham Lincoln,* 9 vols. (New Brunswick: Rutgers University Press, 1953), VI, 409–410.

[12] U. S. Grant to Abraham Lincoln, Lincoln Papers, Library of Congress, quoted in James M. McPherson, *Ordeal by Fire: The Civil War and Reconstruction,* 2nd ed. (New York: McGraw-Hill, 1992), 359n.

[13] Sherman to Ellen, Camp opposite Vicksburg, April 17, 1863, HL, 252–52; Sherman to Halleck, Memphis, October 10, 1863, OR, ser. 1, vol. XXX, pt. 4, 234–35.

[14] Sherman to John, Camp before Vicksburg, April 26, 183–63, Sherman Papers, LC.

[15] Lorenzo Thomas to Sherman, Natchez, March 30, 1864, [Sherman]

Special Field Orders Number 16, In the Field near Dallas, Georgia, June 3, 1864, OR, ser. 3, vol. IV, 210–11, 432. It is worth noting that even while Sherman was impeding black recruitment, his stepbrother, Thomas Ewing, Jr., was organizing black regiments in Missouri. In OR, ser. 3, vol. IV, 433.

[16] Thomas to Sherman, Nashville, June 19, 1864, OR, ser. 3, vol. IV, 437; Sherman to Thomas, In the Field, Big Shanty, June 21, 1864, OR, ser. 1, vol. XXXIX, pt. 2, 132–33; Sherman to Thomas, Near Kenesaw Mountain, June 26, 1864, OR, ser. 3, vol. IV, 454–55; Sherman to Halleck, near Chattahoochee Creek, July 14, 1864, OR, ser. 1, vol. XXXVIII, pt. 5, 137.

[17] Lincoln to Sherman, Washington, July 18, 1864, Basler, VII, 449–50; Lincoln to Isaac M. Schermerhorn, Washington, September 12, 1864, Basler, VIII, 3.

[18] Sherman to Lincoln, near Atlanta, July 21, 1864, OR, ser. 1, vol. XXXVIII, pt. 5, 210.

[19] Sherman to John A. Spooner, In the Field near Atlanta, July 30, 1864, OR, ser. 1, vol. XXXVIII, pt. 5, 305–306.

[20] Sherman to William M. McPherson, [Atlanta, circa September 1864], Sherman Papers, Huntington.

[21] Sherman to Ellen, Near Atlanta, August 6, 1864, ND; Sherman to Thomas Ewing, Near Atlanta, August 11, 1864, Thomas Ewing and Family Papers, LC; Sherman to John, Nashville, April 5, 1864, Sherman Papers, LC. Also see Sherman to Ellen, Near Atlanta, August 2, 1864, HL, 304–305.

[22] Sherman to Halleck, South of Atlanta, September 4, 1864, OR, ser. 1, vol. XXXVIII, pt. 5, 791–95.

[23] Sherman to Stanton, Gaylesville, Mississippi, October 25, 1864, OR, ser. 1, vol. XXXIX, pt. 3, 428–29.

[24] Levi D. Bryant to his wife, March 28, 1865, Michael Winey Collection, United States Army Military History Institute, Carlisle Barracks, Pennsylvania, quoted in Joseph T. Glatthaar, *The March to the Sea and Beyond: Sherman's Troops in the Savannah and Carolinas Campaigns* (New York: New York University Press, 1985), 67. Glatthaar has an excellent discussion of the aversive and abusive reactions of Sherman's men to the introduction of black troops, at pages 66–67.

[25] Halleck to Sherman, Washington, December 30, 1864, reprinted in full in Memoirs, II, 247–48. Emphasis in the original.

[26] Salmon P. Chase to Sherman, January 2, 1865, Sherman Papers, LC.

[27] Sherman to Halleck, Savannah, January 12, 1865, OR, ser. 1, vol. XLVII, pt. 2, 36–37; Sherman to Ellen, Savannah, December 25, 1864, HL, 319.

²⁸ Minutes of an Interview between the Colored Ministers and Church Officers at Savannah with the Secretary of War and Major General Sherman, January 12, 1865, OR, ser. 1, vol. XLVII, pt. 2, 37–41; Memoirs, II, 244–47.

²⁹ Memoirs, II, 249–52.

³⁰ Sherman to Ellen, Savannah, January 19, 1865, HL, 327–28.

³¹ Sherman to Major General J. G. Foster, In the Field in South Carolina, February 1, 2, 1865, OR, ser. 1, vol. XLVII, pt. 2, 201, 210–11; Sherman to Stanton, Savannah, January 19, 1865, OR, ser. 1, vol. XLVII, pt. 2, 87–88.

³² John to Sherman, Washington, August 24, 1862, Sherman Papers, LC; Sherman to Major R. M. Sawyer, Vicksburg, January 31, 1864, OR, ser. 1, vol. XXXVII, pt. 2, 278–81; Sherman to John, Nashville, April 11, 1864, Sherman Papers, LC; Sherman to Lorenzo Thomas, Nashville, April 12, 1864, OR, ser. 3, vol. IV, 225; Sherman to Stanton, Onboard the *Dandelion,* December 13, 1864, OR, ser. 1, vol. XLIV, 700–701. For other interpretations of this episode, and for more information about it, see Memoirs, II, 242–52, Lewis, 477–85, Marszalek, 314–16.

11 Rage at the South: Psychological Warrior

¹ Memoirs, II, 249.

² Sherman to Ellen, Camp on Bear Creek [Mississippi], June 27, 1863, Onboard the *Juliet,* January 28, 1864, HL, 267–69, 280–82.

³ Sherman to John, Lancaster, December 30, 1863; Onboard the *Juliet,* January 28, 1864, SL, 220–21.

⁴ [Sherman] Report, Vicksburg, March 7, 1864, Sherman to Lieutenant Commander E. K. Owen, Vicksburg, January 30, 1864, OR, ser. 1, vol. XXXII, pt. 1, 173–85; Sherman to R. P. Buckland, Vicksburg, February 28, 1864, OR, ser. 1, vol. XXXII, pt. 2, 493; James B. McPherson, Orders Number 6, February 26, 1864, OR, ser. 1, vol. XXXII, pt. 1, 243. For the fullest description of this raid, see Margie Riddle Bearss, *Sherman's Forgotten Campaign: The Meridian Expedition* (Baltimore: Gateway Press, 1987).

⁵ Grant to Sherman, Nashville, March 4, Sherman to Grant, Near Memphis, March 10, 1864, OR, ser. 1, vol. XXXII, pt. 3, 18, 49.

⁶ Grant to Sherman, Washington, April 4; Culpepper Court House, April 19, 1864, OR, ser. 1, vol. XXXII, pt. 3, 244–45, 409.

⁷ Sherman to Halleck, Nashville, April 2; Sherman to Grant, Nashville, April 10; Sherman to James B. McPherson, Nashville, April 24, 1864, OR, ser. 1, vol. XXXII, pt. 3, 221–22, 312–14, 479–80. In his recent, prizewinning study of the Atlanta campaign, Albert Castel stresses the degree to

which Sherman's subordination to Grant undercut his forcefulness and effectiveness as a general. While this may have been true at the start of the Atlanta campaign, I believe it became less so over time. Indeed, on June 28, Grant explicitly instructed Sherman to ignore the issue of reinforcements moving eastward, as he believed that Lee could not feed additional troops. I shall argue below that Sherman's residual deference to Grant disappeared during the planning phase of the Savannah campaign in September and October 1864. Sherman also had sound military reasons of his own for using a war of maneuver rather than frontal assaults during the Atlanta campaign. For a thorough depiction of this campaign, see Castel, *Decision in the West: The Atlanta Campaign of 1864* (Lawrence: University Press of Kansas, 1992). Grant's June 28 letter to Sherman is in OR, ser. 1, vol. XXXVIII, pt. 4, 629.

[8] Sherman to M. C. Meigs, Chattanooga, May 3, 1864, OR, ser. 1, vol. XXXVIII, pt. 5, 20; Sherman to George Thomas, Red Oak, Georgia, August 28, Sherman to General Kenner Garrard, Near Chattahoochee, July 7, 1864, OR, ser. 1, vol. XXXVIII, pt. 5, 76–77, 688–89; Lincoln to Sherman, Washington, May 4, Sherman to Lincoln, Chattanooga, May 5, 1864, Basler, VII, 330–31.

[9] Sherman to Halleck, Near Atlanta, August 7, George Thomas to Sherman, August 10, Sherman to O. O. Howard, August 10, Sherman to Grant, August 7, Grant to Sherman, City Point, Virginia, August 9, Sherman to Halleck, 26 miles South of Atlanta, September 3, 1864, all in OR, ser. 1, vol. XXXVIII, pt. 5, 433–34, 439–40, 448–49, 776–77.

[10] Sherman to Minnie and Lizzie, Nashville, May 1, 1864, Sherman Papers, Ohio.

[11] Sherman, Report, September 15, 1864, OR, ser. 1, vol. XXXVIII, pt. 1, 67.

[12] Sherman to James Guthrie, Near Atlanta, August 14, 1864, OR, ser. 1, vol. XXXIX, pt. 2, 247–49.

[13] Sherman to Halleck, Near Lovejoy's, Georgia, September 4, 1864, OR, ser. 1, vol. XXXVIII, pt. 5, 794.

[14] Sherman to Hood, Atlanta, September 7, 10, 14, Special Field Orders Number 70, September 10, Hood to Sherman, September 9, 12, Sherman to Halleck, September 13, 20, Halleck to Sherman, Washington, September 28, James M. Calhoun, et al., to Sherman, September 12, Sherman to Calhoun, et al., September 12, all in OR, ser. 1, vol. XXXIX, pt. 2, 356–57, 370–71, 414–23, 503; Sherman to H. V. Casserly, n.p., [circa September 1864], Andre de Coppet Collection, Princeton University Library. Most of this exchange is reprinted and discussed in Memoirs, II, 110–29.

[15] O. M. Poe to Nellie, September 7, 1864, O. M. Poe Papers, LC.

[16] Sherman to Halleck, Vicksburg, September 19, 1863, OR, ser. 1, vol. XXX, pt. 3, 732; Sherman to Halleck, Memphis, October 19, 1863, OR, ser. 1, vol. XXX, pt. 4, 234–35; Sherman to Charles Andrews, Big Black [circa July 28, 1863], Document AND 1556, Huntington.

[17] Sherman to Rev. Joseph P. Thompson, Gaylesville, Alabama, October 21, 1864, William G. Thompson Autograph Collection, Yale University Library.

[18] Sherman to Halleck, Atlanta, September 12, Sherman to Grant, September 20, 1864, OR, ser. 1, vol. XXXIX, pt. 2, 365, 413; Sherman to Grant, Atlanta, October 9, 11, November 1, Grant to Sherman, City Point, October 11, 13, November 1, 2, 9, Edwin M. Stanton to Grant, Washington, October 12, Stanton to Sherman, October 13, Grant to Stanton, October 13, all in OR, ser. 1, vol. XXXIX, pt. 3, 162, 202, 222, 239–40, 576–77, 594, 697; Sherman to A. W. Plattenberg, New York, November 13, 1889, Sherman Collection, Chicago Historical Society.

[19] Sherman to Halleck, Summerville, Georgia, October 18, Sherman to James H. Wilson, October 19, Sherman to George Thomas, October 20, Rome, October 29, Sherman to Grant, Kingston, November 6, all in OR, ser. 1, vol. XXXIX, pt. 3, 358, 377–78, 498, 659–61.

[20] Sherman to Lincoln, Savannah, December 22, Lincoln to Sherman, Washington, December 26, 1864, OR, ser. 1, vol. XLIV, 783, 809.

[21] Grant to Sherman, City Point, December 6, 18, Sherman to Grant, Savannah, December 16, 1864, OR, ser. 1, vol. XLIV, 636–37, 726–29, 740–41; Grant to Thomas, December 6, 1864, OR, ser. 1, vol. XLV, pt. 2, 70; Sherman to Thomas, December 25, 1864, Sherman Papers, Huntington.

[22] Sherman to John, Savannah, December 31, 1864, Sherman Papers, LC; Sherman to Grant, December 24, 1864, OR, ser. 1, vol. XLIV, 797–98. On the campaign to Savannah see Burke Davis, *Sherman's March* (New York: Random House, 1980), and Lee Kennett, *Marching Through Georgia* (New York: HarperCollins, 1995).

[23] Sherman to Ellen, Savannah, January 5, 21, 1865, ND.

[24] Sherman to Grant, December 24, 1864, OR, ser. 1, vol. XLIV, 797–98.

12 Facing Death: The Loss of Willy

[1] Sherman to Ellen, Savannah, January 5, 1865, HL, 324–27.

[2] Sherman to John, December 31, 1864, SL, 241–42. The most searching single analysis of the bonds of men in combat remains J. Glenn Gray, *The Warriors* (New York: Harper & Row, 1967).

3 William Hamstreet, "Little Things About Big Generals," *Military Order of the Loyal Legion of the United States—New York,* III, 160–61; D. R. Lucas, *History of the 99th Indiana Infantry* (Lafayette: Rosser & Spring, 1865), 81; Robert Bence to his Wife, September 11, 1864, Robert F. Bence Papers, Indiana Historical Society, Indianapolis; Charles E. Wills, *Army Life of an Illinois Soldier: Letters and Diary of the Late Charles W. Wills* (Washington: Mary E. Kellogg, 1906), 307; George F. Shepard to Dear Wife, December 24, 1864, George F. Shepard Papers, State Historical Society of Wisconsin, Madison. All these quotations come from Joseph T. Glatthaar's pathbreaking analysis of the lives of ordinary soldiers, *The March to the Sea and Beyond,* 16–17.

4 These casualty figures are derived from McPherson, *Battle Cry of Freedom,* 732, 742, and Memoirs, II, 132, 221.

5 Sherman to Henry Halleck, Resaca, Georgia, May 17, 1864, OR, ser. 1, vol. XXXVIII, pt. 4, 219.

6 Sherman to Halleck, Allatoona Creek, June 5, Acworth, June 8, Big Shanty, June 13, 16, 1864, OR, ser. 1, vol. XXXVIII, pt. 4, 408–09, 433, 466, 492.

7 Sherman to George Thomas, near Kenesaw Mountain, June 27, Sherman to Halleck, near Kenesaw Mountain, June 29, 1864, OR, ser. 1, vol. XXXVIII, pt. 4, 611, 635; Sherman to Halleck, near Chattahoochee, July 9, Halleck to Sherman, Washington, July 16, 1864, OR, ser. 1, vol. XXXVIII, pt. 5, 91–92, 150–51; Sherman stuck to this argument in a later letter of July 12, to Grant, and in his report on the Atlanta campaign that he submitted on September 15: OR, ser. 1, vol. XXXVIII, pt. 1, 68–69, 123–24. For a full and vivid narrative of the battle of Kenesaw Mountain, see Charles Royster, *The Destructive War: William T. Sherman, Stonewall Jackson and the Americans* (New York: Knopf, 1991), 296–320.

8 Sherman to Ellen, In the Field, near Marietta, June 30, 1864, HL, 299–300.

9 Sherman, Report of the Atlanta Campaign, September 15, 1864, OR, ser. 1, vol. XXXVIII, pt. 1, 73, 75; Sherman to Lorenzo Thomas, near Atlanta, July 24, 1864, OR, ser. 1, vol. XXXVIII, pt. 5, 241; Memoirs, II, 76–78; Sherman to Ellen, near Atlanta, July 29, 1864, ND, reprinted in part in HL, 301–304.

10 Sherman to Thomas Ewing, Camp on the Big Black, August 13, 1863, Thomas Ewing and Family Papers, LC.

11 Sherman to Grant, Memphis, October 4, 1863, Grant Papers, IX, 274–75; Sherman to Captain C. C. Smith, Memphis, October 4, 1863, Manuscript KS6, Huntington. On the same day, Sherman reported Willy's death to Halleck with a similar effort to cut off his grief: "My eldest boy, Willy,

my California boy—nine years of age died here yesterday of fever and dysentery contracted at Vicksburg. His loss to me is more than words can express, but I would not let it divert my mind from the duty I owe my country." OR, ser. 1, vol. XXX, pt. 4, 73.

[12] Sherman to Ellen, San Francisco, May 31, 1855, HL, 140–42; Willy to Dear Papa, Lancaster, June 3, 1862, Sherman-Thackara Collection, Villanova University Library; Ellen to Sherman, Lancaster, June 1, 1863, Sherman to Willy, before Vicksburg, June 2, 1863, ND. Also see Sherman to Dear Little Minnie, Vicksburg, June 13, 1863, Sherman Papers, Ohio.

[13] Sherman to Ellen, Gayoso House, Memphis, October 6, 1863, HL, 275.

[14] Sherman to Ellen, Gayoso House, Memphis, October 8, 10, 1863, ND.

[15] Ellen to Sherman, Lancaster, October [8], 10, 16, 23, November 15, 1863, ND.

[16] My framework for understanding Victorian deep mourning owes a great deal to the as-yet-unpublished work of my friend John Gilles, a most creative historian of modern Britain. I heard a version of John's arguments in a paper he delivered in the spring of 1992, at the University of British Columbia.

[17] Sherman to Ellen, Onboard the *Westmorland*—approaching Memphis, March 10, 1864, Bridgeport, Tennessee, November 14, 1863 ND.

[18] Sherman to Ellen, Fayetteville, Tennessee, November 8, 1863, October 29, 1864, ND, Goldsborough, North Carolina, April 5, 1865, HL, 338–42.

[19] Ellen to Sherman, Lancaster, February 26, March 30, November 18, December 31, 1864, January 4, 1865, ND.

[20] Sherman to Ellen, Fayetteville, Tennessee, November 8, 1863, Onboard the *Juliet* en route to Paducah, January 5, 1864; Sherman to Minnie, Onboard the *Juliet* near Cairo, January 6, Onboard the *Juliet* near Vicksburg, January 28, 1864, ND; Sherman to Halleck, Lancaster, December 26, 1864, OR, ser. 1, vol. XXXI, pt. 3, 497–98.

[21] Sherman to Ellen, Corinth, Mississippi, October 14, 1863, Nashville, April 26, 1864, Onboard the *Juliet*—from Cairo to Paducah, January 5, 1864, ND.

[22] Sherman to Ellen, Big Shanty, Georgia, June 12, 1864, ND; Sherman to Minnie, near Marietta, June 30, 1864, Sherman Papers, Ohio.

[23] Ellen to Sherman, Lancaster, July 20, 1864, Entry for December 4, 7, 1864, Diary of Ellen Ewing Sherman, ND.

[24] Sherman to Ellen, Savannah, December 31, 1864, ND.

[25] Ellen to Sherman, November 8, 1864, April 6, 1869, "Recollections of Willy Sherman," [circa 1868], ND. Emphasis in the original.

[26] Sherman to Ellen, Memphis, January 15, Onboard the *Juliet,* January 25, 28, 1864, ND.

27 Sherman to Smith P. Gault, New York, February 9, 1890, Sherman Papers, LC. This was a printed letter, clearly intended for circulation among the St. Louis GAR members.

13 The Selective Destroyer

1 Special Field Orders Number 120, Kingston, Georgia, November 9, 1864, OR, ser. 1, vol. XXXIX, pt. 3, 713–14.

2 Special Field Orders Number 127, Milledgeville, Georgia, November 23, 1864, OR, ser. 1, vol. XLIV, 527.

3 Ira Van Deusen to his Wife, June 8, 1864, in Ron Bennett, ed., "Ira Van Deusen: A Federal Volunteer in North Alabama," *Alabama Historical Quarterly*, V (June 1943), 207; Special Orders Number 17, Kingston, June 4, 1864, OR, ser. 1, vol. XXXVIII, pt. 4, 405–406; Sherman to_____ Tyler, Atlanta, September 26, 1864, OR, ser. 1, vol. XXXIX, pt. 2, 481, enclosing a letter of William Clare of Hood's staff to Colonel Willard Warner of Sherman's staff, Rough and Ready, September 21, 1864.

4 Sherman, Report to Henry W. Halleck, Savannah, January 1, 1865, OR, ser. 1, vol. XLIV, 13–14.

5 Jacob W. Bartness to his wife, December 18, 1864, in Donald F. Carmony, ed., "Jacob W. Bartness Civil War Letters," *Indiana Magazine of History*, LII (June 1956), 157–86, at p. 177; James Greenalch to his wife, Savannah, December 26, 1864, in Knox Mellon, ed., "Letters of James Greenalch," *Michigan History*, XLIV (June 1960), 192–240, at p. 230; Entry for September 26, 1864, Robert G. Athearn, ed., "An Indiana Doctor Marches with Sherman: The Diary of James G. Patten," *Indiana Magazine of History*, XLIX (December 1953), 405–22, at p. 413; Rufus Mead, Jr., to Dear Folks at Home, near Savannah, December 18, 1864, Savannah, December 28, 1864, in James A. Padgett, ed., "With Sherman Through Georgia and the Carolinas: Letters of a Federal Soldier," *Georgia Historical Quarterly*, XXXIII (March 1949), 55–58. For many more examples of foraging, destruction, and pillaging by Sherman's men see Joseph Glatthaar, *The March to the Sea and Beyond*, 119–55. Also see, more generally, Linderman, *Embattled Courage*.

6 Vett Noble to his Mother, January 17, 1865, in Donald W. Disbrow, ed., "Vett Noble of Ypsilanti: A Clerk for General Sherman," *Civil War History*, XIV (March 1968), 15–39, at pp. 34–35.

7 O. M. Poe to Nellie Poe, North of Atlanta, June 4, August 30, 1864, O. M. Poe Papers, LC.

8 Entries for November 24, December 2, 6, 1864, Diary of Oscar L. Jack-

son, in David P. Jackson, *The Colonel's Diary* (Sharon, PA: Privately Published, 1922), 165, 168–69, 170, copy in Huntington.

[9] Entries for November 2, Rome, Georgia, November 17, near Yellow River, November 19, Newborn, November 23, Milledgeville, November 26, Sandersville, December 1, 1864, Herndon, January 6, 1865, Savannah, Diary of Henry M. Hitchcock, in Mark A. DeWolfe Howe, ed., *Marching with Sherman* (New Haven: Yale University Press, 1927), 23, 66, 75, 86–87, 96–97, 122. Emphasis in the original.

[10] Sherman to Halleck, Onboard the *Dandelion,* December 11; Sherman to Grant, near Savannah, December 18; Sherman to Halleck, Savannah, December 24, 1864, OR, ser. 1, vol. XLIV, 701–02, 741–43, 798–800.

[11] Samuel Mahon to his Father, Savannah, December 22, 1864, in John K. Mahon, ed., "The Civil War Letters of Samuel Mahon, Seventh Iowa Infantry," *Iowa Journal of History,* LI (July 1953), 233–66, at p. 258; Entry for December 18, 1864, James G. Patten Diary, in Athearn, 415; John Herr to his Sister, February 5, 1865, John Herr Papers, Duke University Library; Fred Marion to his Sister, January 24, 1865, Fred Marion Papers, Illinois State Historical Library, Springfield. Herr and Marion are quoted in Glatthaar, 79.

[12] O. M. Poe to Nellie, Savannah, December 26, 1864, O. M. Poe Papers, LC; Henry W. Slocum to My Dear Cal, January 6, 1865, J. Howland Papers, New York Historical Society. Slocum is quoted in Glatthaar, 79.

[13] Charles Cox to his Sister, Katie, Robertsville, South Carolina, February 1, 1865, in Lorna L. Sylvester, ed., " 'Gone for a Soldier': The Civil War Letters of Charles Harding Cox," *Indiana Magazine of History, LXVIII* (September 1972), 181–237, at p. 229; George M. Wise to his Brother, Fayetteville, North Carolina, March 13, 1865, in Wilfred M. Black, ed., "Marching Through South Carolina: Another Civil War Letter of Lt. George M. Wise," *Ohio Historical Quarterly,* LVI (April 1957), 187–95, at p. 193; Entry for February 3, 1865, Diary of George S. Bradley, in Bradley, *The Star Corps* (Milwaukee: Jermain & Brightness, 1865), 256; Sherman to Grant, Goldsborough, North Carolina, April 8, 1865, OR, ser. 1, vol. XLVII, pt. 3, 128–29.

[14] Eli S. Ricker to Dan Smith, Goldsborough, North Carolina, April 2, 1865, in Edward G. Longacre, ed., " 'We Left a Black Track in South Carolina': Letters of Corporal Eli S. Ricker, 1865," *South Carolina Historical Magazine,* LXXXII (July 1981), 210–24, at p. 223; James Greenalch to his Wife, North Carolina, March 21, 1865, Mellon, 233–34; ——— to My Dear Uncle, near Goldsborough, North Carolina, March 28, 1865, Sherman Papers, Haskell Collection, Clements Library, Ann Arbor.

15 Entry for March 7, 1865, Jackson, ed., *The Colonel's Diary*, 191; Alpheus S. Williams to his Daughters, Fayetteville, North Carolina, March 12, 1865, in Milo M. Quaife, ed., *From the Cannon's Mouth: the Civil War Letters of General Alpheus S. Williams* (Detroit: Wayne State University Press, 1959), 373–74.

16 Jackson, *The Colonel's Diary*, 191; O. M. Poe to Nellie, 23 miles West of Goldsborough, March 21, 1865, Poe Papers, LC.

17 Jackson, *The Colonel's Diary*, 191; Memoirs, II, 183.

18 I have discussed the ways in which, even during its worst phases, the American Civil War stopped short of becoming a total war, and placed total war in a wider historical context, in "At the Nihilist Edge: Reflections on Guerrilla Warfare During the American Civil War," in Stig Forster and Jorg Nagler, eds., *On the Road to Total War: The American Civil War and the German Wars of Unification, 1861–1871* (New York: Cambridge University Press, 1995).

19 On the burning of the clock and bedstead, see Memoirs, II, 256.

20 Sherman, Report on the Campaign in the Carolinas, Goldsborough, North Carolina, April 4, 1865, OR, ser. 1, vol. XLVII, pt. 1, 21–22; A. E. Wood, "The Burning of Columbia," *North American Review*, CXLVI (April 1888), 490–94. Also see Sherman to John, St. Louis, April 2, 1866, Sherman Papers, LC; Sherman to Willard Warner, Washington, D.C., August 3, 1881, Willard Warner Papers, Illinois State Historical Library; Memoirs, II, 279–88. Sherman's legal aide and friend, Henry Hitchcock, repeated the same explanation in a letter written to his wife from Fayetteville, North Carolina, March 12, 1865, *Marching with Sherman*, 268–70.

21 Edward D. Levinger to his Parents, Fayetteville, North Carolina, March 12, 1865, Edward D. Levinger Papers, Wisconsin State Historical Society, quoted in Glatthaar, 146; Entries for February 17, 18, Diary of Allan Morgan Geer, in Mary Ann Anderson, ed., *The Civil War Diary of Allan Morgan Geer* (Denver: Robert C. Appleman, 1977), 197.

22 George M. Wise to his Brother, Fayetteville, North Carolina, March 13, 1865, "Another Civil War Letter . . . ," 184.

23 Entry for February 18, 1865, Diary of Oscar Jackson, *The Colonel's Diary*, 184; entry for February 18, 1865, Diary of E. P. Burton, E. P. Burton, *Diary* (Des Moines: Historical Records Survey, 1939), 63; Diary entry for February 17, 1865, contained in the letter from Goldsborough, North Carolina, March 25, 1865, of Rufus Mead to his Dear Home Folks, Padgett, 71.

24 Jesse S. Bean, "Note on the Burning of Columbia," J. S. Bean Papers, University of North Carolina Archives; William Baugh to Father, [circa March 1865], William G. Baugh Papers, Emory University Archives, both

quoted in Glatthaar, 144; Sherman to Halleck, Savannah, December 28, 1864, OR, ser. I, vol. XLIV, 799.

[25] Deposition and Testimony of William T. Sherman, December 11, 1872, *Report Before the Mixed Commission on American and British Claims* (Washington, D.C.: Government Printing Office, 1873), 59–118, at pp. 72, 77, 90–91, 95–97, 102–103; Sherman to S. H. M. Byers, New York, February 10, 1888, S. H. M. Byers Papers, Iowa State Historical Society, Iowa City. In his careful and thoughtful examination of the evidence, Marion Brunson Lucas, the most thorough scholar of the fire at Columbia, argues that there was a great deal of merit in Sherman's claims that Wade Hampton had been responsible for the fire, and that it had not been set as an act of Union policy. I do not disagree with those conclusions in themselves, but find them somewhat too narrowly argued. Whatever Hampton's troops started, thousands of Sherman's men certainly did riot that night, torching widely, looting and pillaging with a level of intensity unusual even for them, and all this reflected a shared conviction of their implicit destructive task. Moral culpability is often broader than legal culpability. See Lucas, *Sherman and the Burning of Columbia* (College Station: Texas A & M University Press, 1976).

[26] Sherman to H. W. Slocum, Cheraw, South Carolina, March 6, 10, Sherman to Judson Kilpatrick, Camp on the Fayetteville Road, March 7, [Slocum], General Orders Number 8, Near Sneedsborough, North Carolina, March 7, 1865, all in OR, ser. I, vol. XLVII, pt. 2, 703–704, 719, 721, 763–64.

[27] Blair to Howard, Beaver Dam, South Carolina, March 7, A. M. Van Dyke [for Howard] to John A. Logan, Brightsville, South Carolina, March 7, Howard to Sherman, March 7, [Howard], Special Field Orders Number 56, Laurel Hill, North Carolina, March 8, [Blair], Special Orders Number 63, Near Rockfish Creek, North Carolina, March 10, Blair to Van Dyke, Fayetteville, North Carolina, March 11, 1865, all in OR, ser. I, vol. XLVII, pt. 2, 714–15, 717–19, 728, 760–61, 783.

[28] Entry for March 18, 1865, Diary of Oscar Jackson, *The Colonel's Diary,* 198; George Wise to his Brother, Fayetteville, North Carolina, March 13, 1865, "Marching Through South Carolina . . . ," 193.

[29] Diary entry for March 7, contained in Rufus Mead to Dear Folks Back Home, Goldsborough, March 25, 1865, in Padgett, ed., 74; Jacob Bartness to his Wife, Fayetteville, March 14, 1865, in Carmony, ed., 181; Entries for March 12, 14, 1865, Diary of Dexter Horton, in Clement Eaton, ed., "Diary of an Officer in Sherman's Army Marching Through the Carolinas," *Journal of Southern History,* IX (May 1943), 238–54, at p. 248.

[30] Sherman to John M. Schofield, Fayetteville, March 12, 1865, OR, ser. I,

vol. XLVII, pt. 2, 799–800; Sherman to Ellen, Goldsborough, April 9, 1865, ND.

14 Sherman the Forgiver: A Separate Peace

[1] Grant to Lee, Appomattox Court House, Virginia, April 9, 1865, OR, ser. 1, vol. XXXIV, pt. 1, 48–49; Sherman to Grant, Smithfield, North Carolina, April 12, Sherman to Edwin Stanton, Raleigh, North Carolina, April 15, 1865, OR, ser. 1, vol. XLVII, pt. 3, 177, 221. This sequence is reprinted in the Grant Papers, XIV, 372–76.

[2] Sherman and Johnston, Memorandum of Agreement, Near Durham's Station, North Carolina, April 18, 1865, OR, ser. 1, vol. XLVII, pt. 3, 243–45. Sherman first used the phrase "glittering generalities" on May 22, in testimony before Congress, and repeated it on May 25, in his report on his last campaign in the war. *Report of the Joint Committee on the Conduct of the War* (Washington: Government Printing Office, 1865), III, 5; Sherman, Report of May 25, 1865, OR, ser. 1, vol. XLVII, pt. 1, 35.

[3] Sherman to Hon. James Guthrie, Near Atlanta, August 14, 1864, OR, ser. 1, vol. XXXIX, pt. 2, 240–41; also see Sherman to General Leslie Coombs, August 11, 1864, OR, ser. 1, vol. XXXIX, pt. 2, 246–48; Sherman to James C. Calhoun, et al., Near Atlanta, September 12, 1864, Memoirs, II, 125–27; Sherman to N. W——, Savannah, January 8, 1865, John D. Nicholson Scrapbook, Huntington.

[4] Sherman to Johnston, Raleigh, April 21; Sherman to John A. Rawlins, Goldsborough, April 29, 1865, OR, ser. 1, vol. XLVII, pt. 3, 265–66, 345–46; Sherman, Report, May 25, 1865, OR, ser. 1, vol. XLVII, pt. 1, 65.

[5] Sherman, Memoirs, II, 327; Sherman to Hon. J. N. Arnold, Washington, November 28, 1872, Sherman Papers, Chicago Historical Society; Sherman to Ellen, Goldsborough, April 5, 1865, HL, 338–42. This is an absolutely central point, as both Sherman and his 1932 biographer, Lloyd Lewis, used the dead Lincoln to justify their own reactionary Reconstruction politics. Lincoln wanted to forgive the South and act against the Radicals, who were eager for punishment, the story goes, and Reconstruction proved terribly unfair to Southern whites, and demonstrated far too much concern with the undeserving freedmen. This was a projection of values onto Lincoln, who unlike his successor, Andrew Johnson, was a master of keeping political options open, and who had grown in the direction of the Radicals on racial and political issues throughout the war. To prove his thesis, in his memoirs, Sherman even had Admiral David Dixon Porter, who was there, back up his political interpretation of the March 27, 28, 1865, meeting. Memoirs, II, 324–32; Lewis, 518–80.

[6] Sherman to Salmon P. Chase, Onboard the *Russia*, Beaufort Harbor, May 6 (two letters), Sherman to O. O. Howard, Dumfries, Virginia, May 17, 1865, OR, ser. 1, vol. XLVII, pt. 3, 410–12, 515–16.

[7] The remark about being hustled was in a letter to John S. Wise, from *The End of an Era* (Boston: Houghton, Mifflin, 1899), quoted in Lewis, 542.

[8] Sherman to Ellen, Goldsboro, April 19, 1865, ND; Sherman to Grant or Halleck, Raleigh, April 18, 1865, OR, ser. 1, vol. XLVII, pt. 3, 243–45.

[9] Stanton to Grant, Washington, April 21, Stanton to John A. Dix [of *The New York Times*], April 22, Grant to Sherman, Washington, April 21, Grant to Stanton, Raleigh, April 24, Sherman to Grant, Raleigh, April 25, Sherman to Stanton, April 25, Stanton to Grant, April 25, Halleck to Stanton, Richmond, April 25, 1865, OR, ser. 1, vol. XLVII, pt. 3, 263–64, 285–86, 293, 301–303, 311–12.

[10] Sherman to Ellen, Goldsborough, April 5, 1865, HL, 338–42; Sherman to Halleck, In the Field, September 4, 1864, OR, ser. 1, vol. XXXVIII, pt. 5, 791; Sherman to Grant, Raleigh, April 28, 1865, OR, ser. 1, vol. XLVII, pt. 3, 334–35.

[11] Memoirs, II, 373; Sherman to Rawlins, April 29, 1865, OR, ser. 1, vol. XLVII, pt. 3, 345–46; Sherman to Ellen, Opposite Richmond, May 10, 1865, ND.

[12] Ellen to Sherman, Lancaster, April 26, 1865, ND; John to Sherman, Mansfield, May 2, 1865, SL, 248–49; Samuel Mahon to his Mother, Petersburg, Virginia, May 8, 1865, in John K. Mahon, ed., "The Civil War Letters of Samuel Mahon, Seventh Iowa Infantry," *Iowa Journal of History*, LI (July 1953), 233–66, at p. 262. Sherman's clerk, Vett Noble, and his legal attaché, Henry Hitchcock, also reflected this nearly unanimous set of feelings: Noble to his Mother, Hanover Court House, Virginia, May 12, 1865, in Donald W. Dishbrow, ed., "Vett Noble of Ypsilanti: A Clerk for General Sherman," *Civil War History*, XIV (March 1968), 15–39, at p. 38; Entry for May 26, 1865, Near Washington, Diary of Henry Hitchcock, in Howe, ed. *Marching With Sherman*, 318–20.

[13] Halleck to Sherman, Richmond, May 8, [9], Sherman to Halleck, Fort Monroe, Virginia, May 8, Manchester, Virginia, May 10, OR, ser. 1, vol. XLVII, pt. 3, 435, 454–55; Sherman to Ellen, Opposite Richmond, May 10, Ellen to Sherman, Lancaster, May 17, 1865, ND.

[14] Sherman to Grant, Camp Opposite Richmond, May 10, 1865, Grant Papers, XV, 74–75; Sherman to Rawlins, Camp near Alexandria, May 19; Grant to Sherman, Washington, May 19, 1865, OR, ser. 1, vol. XLVII, pt. 3, 531; Memoirs, II, 377.

[15] Grant to Sherman, Washington, May 27, Sherman to Grant, Washington, May 28, 1865, OR, ser. 1, vol. XLVII, pt. 3, 576, 581–82; Sherman to

Adam Badeau, Washington, March 16, 1876, in Badeau, *Military History of Ulysses S. Grant,* 3 vols. (New York: D. Appleton, 1868–81), III, 710, reprinted in Grant Papers, XV, 75.

16 Sherman to Ellen, Onboard the *Russia,* May 8, 1865, ND; Sherman to Ellen, Camp Opposite Richmond, May 10, 1865, HL, 352–54.

17 Sherman to Stewart Van Vliet, Camp near Alexandria, May 21, Sherman to John Schofield, Camp near Washington, May 28, 1865, OR, ser. 1, vol. XLVII, pt. 3, 546–47, 585–86; Sherman to Charles Anderson, Lancaster, July 28, 1865, Sherman Papers, Huntington; Sherman to John, August 11, 1865, SL, 254; Sherman to John Brazer, St. Louis, November 7, 1866, Sherman Papers, LC. Sherman's letter to Brazer followed his mission to Mexico right after the war, made as part of the American project of chasing the French out of their imperialist adventure there. Sherman also discussed the possibility of an American annexation of Mexico, which he opposed, because such a lazy and ungovernable mixed race "would have to be exterminated before the country could be made available to us." For another rendering of this view toward Mexico, see Sherman to General Edward Ord, Washington, June 26, 1875, Sherman Papers, LC.

15 Indian Killer

1 Grant to Sherman, Washington, October 31, Sherman to John A. Rawlins, St. Louis, October 23, Sherman to Grant, October 24, 1865, Grant Papers, XV, 377–83. For the phrase, "final solution of the Indian problem," see Sherman to Frederick T. Dent, St. Louis, December 27, 1875, Frederick Tracy Dent Papers, Southern Illinois University Library; and Sherman to Sheridan, Washington, September 26, 1872, Sheridan Papers, LC. There is a rich and varied historiography concerning the whole grand project of building the railroads and eliminating the Indian "threat." For an illuminating discussion of many issues of Sherman's policy toward Indians, see Robert G. Athearn, *William T. Sherman and the Settlement of the West* (Norman: University of Oklahoma Press, 1956). On broader issues of military policy, see in particular, Robert M. Utley, *Frontier Regulars: the United States Army and the Indians, 1866–1891* (New York: Macmillan, 1973). And for a general and insightful synthetic history of Indian-White relationships, much wider in scope than its title implies, see Frances Paul Prucha, *The Great Father: The United States Government and the American Indians,* 2 vols. (Lincoln: University of Nebraska Press, 1984).

2 Sherman to Grant, St. Louis, August 31, 1866, Grant Papers, XVI, 252–53.

[3] Sherman to Grant, St. Louis, November 6, 1865, June 22, 1866, Sherman to Grant, Santa Fe, June 7, 1868, Sherman to Rawlins, St. Louis, July 18, 1866, Sherman to G. K. Leete, St. Louis, July 3, 1866, all in Grant Papers, XV, 379, XVI, 162–63, XVII, 24–25, XVIII, 258.

[4] Sherman to Grant, St. Louis, March 7, June 10, 1867, Grant Papers, XVII, 57, 174–78.

[5] Sherman to Grant, May 28, 1867, Grant Papers, XVII, 162; Sherman to Ellen, Fort Laramie, August 30, 1866, ND; Sherman to Grant, St. Louis, December 28, 1866, quoted in Athearn, 99; Sherman to John, December 30, 1866, SL, 287.

[6] Grant to Sherman, Washington, April 10; Sherman to Grant, St. Louis, February 18, April 20, May 24, 1867, Grant Papers, XVII, 53–54, 110–13, 160.

[7] Sherman to General C. C. Augur, St. Louis, March 12, 1867, C. C. Augur Papers, Illinois State Historical Library; Sherman to Leete, St. Louis, April 2, Grant to Sherman, Washington, September 18, 1867, Grant Papers, XVII, 58–59, 343–44.

[8] Sherman to Ellen, September 14, 19, 1867, ND; Sherman to Grant, Onboard the *St. Johns,* September 7, 1867, Grant Papers, XVII, 257–59; Sherman to Augur, Washington, June 9, 1870, Augur Papers.

[9] Grant to Sherman, Washington, May 19; Sherman to Grant, Santa Fe, June 7, 1868, Grant Papers, XVII, 257–59.

[10] Sherman to Samuel Foster Tappan, Fort Leavenworth, August 13, St. Louis, September 6, 24, November 21, 1868, S. F. Tappan Papers, Colorado Historical Society.

[11] Sherman to John, St. Louis, September 23, 25, 1868. The September 23 letter is reprinted, but only in part, in SL, 321–22.

[12] Sherman to W. B. Hazen, St. Louis, October 17, 1868, quoted in Athearn, 229; Grant to Sherman, Galena, Illinois, September 25, 1868, David Dixon Porter to Sherman, Annapolis, October 22, 1868, Sherman Papers, LC.

[13] Sherman to Sheridan, St. Louis, October 15, 1868, Sheridan Papers, LC.

[14] Sherman to Sheridan, Washington, April 30, 1870, March 6, September 12, October 30, 1874, Sheridan Papers, LC, emphasis in the original.

[15] Sheridan to Sherman, n.d., n.p., in Sherman, *Annual Report* [for] *1876* (Washington, D.C.: Government Printing Office, 1877), 34; Sherman to Sheridan, Washington, March 2, 1877, Sheridan Papers, LC.

[16] Sherman to John, Fort Union, New Mexico, June 11, Denver, June 17, 1868, Sherman Papers, LC; Sherman to Sheridan, Washington, May 2, 1873, Sheridan Papers, LC; Sherman to Grant, St. Louis, May 27, 1867, Grant Papers, XVII, 150–60.

[17] Sherman to Grenville M. Dodge, St. Louis, January 16, 1867, Washington, May 11, 1869, in Grenville M. Dodge, "How We Built the Union Pacific Railway, and Other Railway Papers and Addresses" (Washington: Government Printing Office, 1910), 14, 25. On the relative ease of military protection of the railroad construction crews, see Sherman to Augur, November 23, 1868, Augur Papers. On October 7, 1872, Sherman suggested to Sheridan that he expected the Indians to oppose the building of the Northern Pacific, "because they look on it as their last stand." This statement indicates Sherman's reading of the desperation of the enemy rather than any concern on his part about their potential for serious resistance. Sheridan Papers, LC.

[18] Sherman to Sheridan, Washington, November 20, 1875, Sheridan Papers, LC; casualty figures from Paul A. Hutton, *Phil Sheridan and His Army* (Lincoln: University of Nebraska Press, 1985), 345; Sherman to William Scott, St. Louis, July 18, 1867, W. P. Palmer Collection, Western Reserve Historical Society, Cleveland.

[19] Sherman to Herbert A. Preston, Washington, April 17, 1873, Letterbooks, Sherman Papers, LC. Frances Paul Prucha stresses the degree of compassion for the Indians of Crook, Pope, Howard, Miles and others, in *The Great Father,* I, 544-49. This approach, while a useful corrective to an oversimplified historical emphasis of exterminationism, tends, in my opinion, to understate Sherman's powerful racial antipathy and his influence on policy, as well as the overall contempt for the Indians and the readiness to slaughter them that were widespread in the army.

[20] Sherman to Tappan, St. Louis, December 29, 1875, Tappan Papers; Washington, July 21, 1876, Letterbooks, Sherman Papers, LC.

[21] Sherman, *Annual Report* [for] *1877* (Washington, D.C.: Government Printing Office, 1878), 7-15; Sherman to Henry Turner, Washington, July 25, 1879, Sherman Papers, Ohio.

16   Officeholder

[1] The fullest analysis of the institutional and personal isolating of Sherman as commanding general, from which several of my examples are drawn, is Richard A. Andrews, "Years of Frustration: William T. Sherman, the Army, and Reform, 1869-1883," Ph.D. Dissertation, Northwestern University, 1968. Also see the relevant passages in Coffman, *The Old Army,* and Russell F. Weighley, *History of the United States Army* (New York: Macmillan, 1967).

[2] *Report of the General of the Army,* November 20, 1869, House of Representatives, 41st Congress, 2nd Session, Executive Document 1, Part 2

(Washington, D.C.: Government Printing Office, 1970), 252–54 and passim.

[3] Sherman to Phil Sheridan, Washington, April 1, 1871, Sheridan Papers, LC; Sherman to E. O. C. Ord, Washington, August 1, October 28, 1870, May 23, 1874, E. O. C. Ord Papers, LC; Sherman to Irwin McDowell, St. Louis, May 29, 1875, Sherman Papers, Missouri Historical Society; Sherman to Henry Turner, Washington, February 16, 1873, Sherman Papers, Ohio.

[4] Coffman, 269.

[5] Sherman to Sheridan, Washington, November 17, 1883, Sheridan Papers, LC.

[6] Sherman to John, Washington, October 31, 1866; St. Louis, February 14, 1868, SL, 279–82, 305.

[7] Sherman to Sheridan, Washington, April 1, 1871, Sheridan Papers, LC.

[8] Sherman to Ord, Washington, August 1, 1870, Sherman Papers, Missouri Historical Society.

[9] Sherman to C. C. Augur, Washington, July 8, 1871, Augur Papers, Illinois State Historical Library; Sherman to Sheridan, Washington, December 28, 1871, Sheridan Papers, LC. Richard Andrews makes an excellent analysis of this incident, 90–91.

[10] Sherman to Ellen, June 13, 1872, ND; Sherman to Willard Warner, Cairo, Egypt, March 26, 1872, Willard Warner Papers, Illinois State Historical Library; John to Sherman, Mansfield, July 16, 1872, SL, 332–33.

[11] Sherman to John, St. Louis, October 23, 1874, Sherman Papers, LC; Sherman to S. H. M. Byers, St. Louis, January 26, 1875, S. H. M. Byers Papers, State Historical Society of Iowa. Also see Sherman to Byers, April 7, 1875.

[12] Sherman to John, St. Louis, March 10, 1876, Sherman Papers, LC; Sherman to J. C. Williams, St. Louis, March 10, 1876, Diedrich Collection, Clements Library, Ann Arbor; Sherman to Byers, May 11, 1880, Byers Papers.

[13] Sherman to Grenville M. Dodge, June 22, 1868, Eldridge Collection, Huntington; Sherman to Ellen, Santa Fe, New Mexico Territory, June 7, 1868, HL, 376–77; Sherman to John, Washington, July 8, 1871, Sherman Papers, LC; Sherman to Willard Warner, Washington, July 29, 1874, Warner Papers.

[14] Sherman to Ord, Washington, May 23, 1874, Sherman Papers, Missouri Historical Society; *Report of the General of the Army* [for 1874], St. Louis, October 24, 1874 (Washington, D.C.: Government Printing Office, 1875), 5; Sherman to Admiral David Porter, St. Louis, February 6, 1875, David Dixon Porter Papers, LC; Sherman, Memoirs, 2nd ed., II, 453–55. For a

full and thoughtful discussion of the St. Louis months, see Andrews, 110–81. One should not understate the degree to which the move had been actuated by narrow financial concerns. On August 20, 1874, he wrote John, while still in Washington, "I can manage to live on my pay in St. Louis which . . . is impossible to do here—The acceptance of the Grant property has been fatal to me." Sherman Papers, LC. Such financial complaints are one of the continuing themes of Sherman's postwar correspondence.

[15] Sherman to John, Washington, December 18, 1872, Sherman Papers, LC; Sherman to Tom Sherman, Washington, January 18, 1878, ND; Sherman to John Schofield, Washington, December 31, 1882, Hiram Barney Collection, Huntington.

[16] Sherman to Lieutenant J. C. Scantling, Washington, April 15, 1879, Sherman Papers, Missouri Historical Society; Sherman to Augur, Washington, November 11, 1881, Augur Papers; L. C. Ingersoll to Sherman, Washington, [circa November 22], 1878, Sherman Papers, LC; Sherman to General Alfred H. Terry, Washington, March 23, 1883, Terry Family Papers, Yale University Library; Sherman to George Schneider, Washington, November 14, 1878; Sherman to Major Henry P. Reese, Sherman to General Benjamin Alvord, Washington, September 19, 1872, Sherman Letterbooks, Sherman Papers, LC, emphasis in the originals. For an example of Sherman trying to calm a dispute between his brother officers, see his letter of December 8, 1879, to John Schofield, in which he tried to remind Schofield that John Pope had his strong points as well as his weak ones, in Hiram Barney Papers, Huntington.

[17] On Sherman as an army reformer, see Weighley, 273–83; Coffman, 271–75; Andrews, 221, 245; and passim.

[18] Sherman to Willard Warner, St. Louis, February 11, 1866, Washington, December 6, 1877, Warner Papers; Sherman to C. C. Augur, Washington, March 18, 1871, Augur Papers; Sherman to Sheridan, Washington, September 7, 1872, December 11, 26, 1876, Sheridan Papers; Sherman to Tom Sherman, St. Louis, January 16, 1875, ND; Sherman to Henry S. Turner, Washington, December 5, 1876, Sherman Papers, Ohio; Sherman to Edward Lester, Washington, December 6, 1876, Sherman Papers, Haskell Collection, Clements Library, Ann Arbor.

[19] Sherman's undated speech to the veterans, which had to be from 1886 or later, is quoted by Horatio G. King, in *The Life of General William T. Sherman, by Distinguished Men of His Time* (Baltimore: R. H. Woodward, 1891), 259; Sherman to Sheridan, July 29, 1877, quoted in Andrews, 190; Sherman to Colonel T. T. Gantt, Washington, May 8, 1878, Letterbooks, Sherman Papers, LC. In general on political issues see Andrews, 188–92.

[20] Sherman to Schofield, Washington, April 15, May 2, 26, August 9, De-

cember 2, 13, 16, 1880, Hiram Barney Papers, Huntington; Sherman to Henry S. Turner, Washington, May 2, 1880, January 16, 1881, Sherman Papers, Ohio; Sherman to O. O. Howard, Washington, December 7, 1880, Sherman Letterbooks, Sherman Papers, LC. For the diary entry of August 17, 1880, in which Schofield wrote of his realization of Sherman's betrayal by withdrawal, see pp. 48 and 298, n. 21, in John F. Marszalek's monograph on the Whittaker case, *Court-Martial: A Black Man in America* (New York: Scribner's, 1972).

17 Vagabond and Icon

[1] Sherman to David Dixon Porter, St. Louis, November 24, 1865, David Dixon Porter Papers, LC.

[2] Sherman to John, December 30, 1863, SL, 220; Sherman to Grant, Memphis, January 24, 1864, Sherman to H. W. Halleck, Onboard the *Juliet,* Bound for Vicksburg, January 29, 1864, both in OR, ser. 1, vol. XXXII, pt. 2, 201–202, 259–61; Sherman to Ellen, Savannah, January 5, Goldsborough, North Carolina, March 31, April 5, 1865, ND, reprinted in part in HL, 324–27, 338–42; Testimonial Newspaper Clipping on a Subscription to Raise $100,000, February 22, 1865, VFM 4102, Ohio; Sherman to Mrs. Ellen Lynch, Lancaster, July 11, 1865, Andre de Coppet Collection, Princeton University Library; Grand Ball Program, VFM 386, Ohio; Sherman to Charley [Hoyt], St. Louis, March 20, 1867, de Coppet Collection.

[3] Sherman to Ellen, St. Louis, October 4, 1875, ND.

[4] "Address by General W. T. Sherman in New York City on Decoration Day, May 30, 1878," transcript in Letterbooks, Sherman Papers, LC.

[5] All the quotations on the Jefferson Davis–Sherman name-calling cartel are from Marszalek, 472–75.

[6] Sherman to Henry Turner, Washington, November 24, 1881, Sherman Papers, Ohio; Sherman to Willard Warner, St. Augustine, Florida, February 9, 1879, Willard Warner Papers, Illinois State Historical Library; Sherman to David F. Boyd, December 2, 1880, W. L. Fleming Papers, New York Public Library.

[7] *Ohio State Journal,* August 12, 1880, photostat in Lewis, 635.

[8] Sherman to Ellen, Madrid, January 6, Cairo, March 24, 1872, ND; Sherman to John, Madrid, December 21, 1871, Sherman Papers, LC; Sherman to John Jay, Berlin, June 5, 1872, Jay Family Papers, Columbia University Library; Sherman to George Bancroft, Paris, July 11, 1872, George Bancroft Papers, Massachusetts Historical Society; Sherman to George P. Healy, Washington, November 10, 1873, Sherman Papers, LC; Sherman

to Francis Vinton Greene, Washington, October 23, 1877, January 13, 1878, Francis Vinton Greene Papers, New York Public Library.

[9] Sherman to Porter, Malta, March 9, 1872, Porter Papers, LC; Sherman to John, Malta, March 9, 1872, Constantinople, April 16, 1872, Sherman Papers, LC.

[10] Sherman to C. C. Augur, Washington, February 28, 1882, Augur Papers, Illinois State Historical Library; Sherman to _____ Strong, Washington, May 30, 1883, Schoff Letters, Clements Library, Ann Arbor; Ellen to Sherman, Washington, March 21, 1882, ND.

[11] Tom Sherman, Speech to the Society of the Army of the Tennessee, 1892, in the *Reports* of the society, quoted in Lewis, 631; Sherman to E. Casserly, St. Louis, February 10, 1868, de Coppet Collection; Sherman to John, Fort Richardson, Texas, May 18, 1871, St. Louis, October 23, 1874, November 28, 1883, Sherman Papers, LC; Sherman to John W. Draper, John W. Draper Papers, LC; Sherman to Rev. W. G. Eliot, Washington, August 3, 1879, William G. Eliot Collection, Missouri Historical Society; Sherman to S. H. M. Byers, Washington, December 12, 1882, S. H. M. Byers Papers, State Historical Society of Iowa; Sherman to John Schofield, St. Louis, November 29, December 3, 1883, Hiram Barney Papers, Huntington; Sherman to James G. Blaine, St. Louis, May 28, June 7, 1884, James G. Blaine Papers, LC.

18   Feuds: The Tests of Honor

[1] Sherman to Mrs. Elizabeth Halleck, Washington, March 16, 1873, Letterbooks, Sherman Papers, LC; Memoirs, II, 372–74; Sherman, "An Unspoken Address to the Loyal Legion," *North American Review,* CXLII (April 1886), 293–308, at pp. 298–99.

[2] Sherman to Grant, June 17, McPherson to Grant, June 18, Grant to Lorenzo Thomas, June 26, 1863, OR, ser. 1, vol. XXIV, pt. 1, 158–59, 162–64; John A. McClernand to George W. Morgan, Springfield, Illinois, November 30, 1875, Sherman Letters, Western Reserve Historical Society, Cleveland.

[3] Sherman to Halleck, Hooker to William D. Whipple, near Atlanta, July 27, 1864; Sherman to Halleck, In the Field, September 4, 1864, OR, ser. 1, vol. XXXVIII, pt. 5, 272–75, 793.

[4] Sherman to Halleck, near Atlanta, August 16, 1864, OR, ser. 1, vol. XXXVIII, pt. 5, 522–23; Sherman to John, March 21, 1870, Sherman Papers, LC; Logan to his wife, July 31, 1864, May 20, 1865, Logan Papers, LC; Logan, *The Volunteer Soldier of America* (Chicago: R. S. Peale, 1887). On Sherman's analysis of Logan's 1870 attack on West Point as well as on

the army, see Sherman to Grenville Dodge, Washington, April 11, 1870, and Sherman to C. C. Augur, Washington, June 9, 1870, Sherman Letterbooks, Sherman Papers, LC.

⁵ Sherman to Grant, In the Field, June 18, 1864, OR, ser. 1, vol. XXXVIII, pt. 4, 504; Sherman to Halleck, South of Atlanta, September 4, 1864, OR, ser. 1, vol. XXXVIII, pt. 5; Sherman to Grant, Near Savannah, December 16, 1864, Grant to Sherman, City Point, December 6, 1864, Washington, December 18, 1864, OR, ser. 1, vol. XLIV, 636–37, 728, 740–41; Grant to Sherman, City Point, March 16, 1865, OR, ser. 1, vol. XLVII, pt. 2, 859–60; Sherman to Thomas, Near Atlanta, August 12, 1864, Sherman Papers, Huntington. The manner in which Thomas held Sherman in contempt is a major theme of Castel, *Decision in the West*. See Castel, p. 318, for some especially pointed barbs Thomas sent Sherman's way.

⁶ Henry Van Ness Boynton to George W. Morgan, August 1 [1875], MSV File, Western Reserve Historical Society, Cleveland; Boynton, *Sherman's Historical Raid: The Memoirs in Light of the Evidence* (Cincinnati: Wilstock, Baldwin, 1875).

⁷ On Babcock's role see Richard T. Andrews, "Years of Frustration: William T. Sherman, The Army and Reform, 1869–83," Ph.D. dissertation, Northwestern University, 1968, 140. Sherman to Charles W. Moulton, St. Louis, June 23, November 1, 9, December 4, 15, 18, 1875, Moulton to Sherman, Hastings-on-Hudson, November 24, 1875, Sherman Papers, New York Public Library; Moulton, *The Review of General Sherman's Memoirs Examined, Chiefly in the Light of the Evidence* (Cincinnati: Robert Clark, 1875). Emphasis in the originals.

⁸ Sherman to Tom, St. Louis, March 4, 1876, ND; Sherman to John W. Draper, St. Louis, March 9, 1876, John W. Draper Papers, LC.

⁹ Sherman to John Schofield, Washington, November 8, 1879, Hiram Barney Papers, Huntington; Sherman to Grant, Washington, October 18, 1879, Letterbooks, Sherman Papers, LC.

¹⁰ Sherman to J. H. Sturgeon, Washington, February 14, 1880, ND; Cleveland *Leader,* January 15, 1880, copy in the John P. Nicholson Scrapbook, Huntington; Sherman to Judson Kilpatrick, Washington, January 24, 1880, Letterbooks, Sherman Papers, LC; Boynton to Sherman, Washington, January 16, 1880; Sherman to Boynton, Washington, January 16, 1880; Sherman to William C. Church, Washington, January 25, February 25, 1880, William C. Church Papers, LC. In general on the Boynton affair, see Andrews, 137–45, Marszalek, 460–66.

¹¹ Sherman to J. M. Wright, Camp on the Big Black, September 2, 1863, OR, ser. 1, vol. XXX, pt. 3, 294–95; Corinth, October 14, 1863, OR, ser. 1, vol. XXX, pt. 4, 357–58; Sherman to James B. Fry, Nashville, April 10,

1864, OR, ser. 1, vol. XXXII, pt. 3, 319–20; Sherman to Professor Henry Coupee, Near Kenesaw, June 13, 1864, OR, ser. 1, vol. LII, pt. 12, 559–61.
[12] Sherman to Fry, St. Louis, September 3, 25, 1884; Fry to Sherman, New York, September 14, 22, 28, 1884; Grant to Sherman, October 19, 1884, Sherman Papers, LC; See Grant, "The Battle of Shiloh," *Century Magazine,* XXXIX (1885), 593–613.
[13] James B. Fry, "An Acquaintance with Grant"; [Allen Thorndike Rice], "Sherman on Grant"; "Sherman's Opinion of Grant"; Fry, "An Open Letter"; Sherman, "An Unspoken Address to the Loyal Legion," all in *North American Review,* CXLI (December 1885), 540–52, CXLII (January, February, March, April 1886), 111–13, 200–208, 292–93, 295–308.
[14] Sherman to William G. Eliot, St. Louis, February 7, 1886, William G. Eliot Collection, Missouri Historical Society; Sherman to S. H. M. Byers, St. Louis, February 3, 1886, Sherman Papers, LC; Byers, "Important Historical Letters; Reconstruction Days," *North American Review,* CXLIII (July, September 1886), 72–86, 219–24; Sherman to Colonel Fred Grant, St. Louis, January 8, 17, 1886, Grant Family Papers, Southern Illinois University Archives; Sherman to John, May 14, 1886, Sherman Papers, LC. Also see Sherman to Fred Grant, December 18, 1885, January 2, March 8, May 15, 1886, Grant Family Papers, and Sherman to John, January 23, 29, February 23, 1886, Sherman Papers, LC.
[15] Montgomery Blair to the Editor of *Southern Magazine,* May 21, 1875, clipping in the John B. Nicholson Scrapbook, Huntington; Sherman to Mrs. Frank Blair, St. Louis, July 15, 1875, Sherman Papers, LC. Sherman discussed his exchange of letters with Montgomery Blair in his letter to Mrs. Frank Blair.
[16] Sherman to John M. Schofield, St. Louis, January 31, February 6, 1884; Willard Warner to Sherman, Tecumseh, Alabama, February 23, 1884; Sherman to Warner, February 26, 1884; Captain John M. Bacon to Schofield, February 27, 1884, Hiram Barney Papers, Huntington. Bacon's letter to Schofield concerned Schofield's right of reply. Schofield's angry letter of January 14, and Sherman's reply of January 23, were destroyed.
[17] Sherman to Grant, Near Memphis, March 10, 1864, OR, ser. 1, vol. XXXII, pt. 3, 49; Sherman to Fred Grant, St. Louis, May 5, 1886, Grant Family Papers; Sherman to Ellen, St. Louis, November 22, 1884, New York, July 27, 1885, HL, 392–93.
[18] Sherman to John W. Draper, Washington, January 17, 1881, John William Draper Papers, LC. For three engaging studies of the manly ideal, see E. Anthony Rotundo, *American Manhood: Transformations in Masculinity from the Revolution to the Modern Era* (New York: Basic Books, 1993), James Walvin, *Manliness and Morality: Middle Class Masculinity in Brit-*

ain and America, 1800–1940 (New York: St. Martin's Press, 1987), and John Fraser, *America and the Patterns of Chivalry* (Cambridge: Cambridge University Press, 1989).
¹⁹ Sherman to George and Marion Sykes, Washington, March 12, 1880, ND; Sherman to Mrs. General G. G. Meade, Washington, November 12, 1872, Sherman to Major Francis U. Farquhar, Washington, December 22, 1878, Sherman to Mrs. General George A. Custer, Washington, August 11, 1876, all in Letterbooks, Sherman Papers, LC.
²⁰ Sherman to M. Landon, St. Louis, January 22, 1875, ND.

19 The Struggle of Marriage, and Other Women

¹ Sherman to William W. Appleton, Washington, April 14, 1881, W. W. Appleton Collection, Columbia University Library; Sherman to Alexander McDowell McCook, Sherman to Miss Annie Cole, Washington, August 23, 1884, McCook Family Papers, LC.
² Sherman to Ellen, Paris, July 7, Glasgow, August 25, 1872, ND; Sherman to John, St. Louis, December 29, 1875, Sherman Papers, LC; Ellen to Eliza A. Starr, Eliza A. Starr Papers, Smith College Archives.
³ Sherman to Willard Warner, New York, February 7, 1888, Willard Warner Papers, Illinois State Historical Library; Sherman to John Jay, Washington, May 23, 1874, Jay Family Papers, Columbia University Library; Sherman to Elly Sherman, St. Louis, January 29, 1875, ND.
⁴ Ellen to Sherman, Lancaster, February 22, 1864, August 27, 1878, ND; Sherman to Charles Ewing, Washington, January 4, 7, 1874, Thomas Ewing and Family Papers, LC.
⁵ Ellen to Thomas Ewing, St. Louis, March 10, 1868, ND.
⁶ [Ellen Ewing Sherman, ed.], *Memorial of Thomas Ewing of Ohio* (New York: Catholic Publication Society, 1873), 67, 290.
⁷ Sherman to Tom, Washington, February 27, 1877, ND.
⁸ Ellen to Sherman, St. Louis, March 13, May 11, July 17, November 5, December 8, 1877, March 4, 12, May 2, 17, August 27, 1878, Baltimore, October 11, 1878, March 8, 1879, Oakland, August 27, 1879, July 6, 1882, Columbus, Ohio, September 20, 1885, all in ND.
⁹ *New York World*, February 22, 1891, quoted in Marszalek, 416; *Army and Navy Register*, December 15, 1883, clipping in the John P. Nicholson Scrapbook, Huntington.
¹⁰ Mildred McLean Hazen Dewey, unpublished memoirs, Rutherford B. Hayes Presidential Center, quoted in Marszalek, 417.
¹¹ Sherman to George Bancroft, New York, January 8, 1887, George B. Bancroft Papers, Massachusetts Historical Society.

[12] Sherman to Madame Blanche Roosevelt Machetta, Washington, May 21, 1882, Sherman Papers, Huntington. On Victorian sexual and romantic codes more generally see Lystra, *Searching the Heart.*

[13] Sherman to Lawrence Barrett, January 3, 1888, Sherman Papers, West Point; Sherman to Judge Ogden Hoffman, St. Louis, March 9, 1885, Sherman Papers, Huntington.

[14] Ada Rehan to Sherman, June 11, October 11, 1888, Sherman Papers, LC; Sherman to Ada Rehan, October 12, 1888, Ada Rehan Collection, University of Pennsylvania Library. Emphasis in the original.

[15] Sherman to Vinnie Ream [Hoxie], Washington, February 14, 20, 25, March 22, April 3, 19, 1873, January 22, April 4, May 6, July 1, 1874, St. Louis, July 12, September 24, November 14, 1874, January 29, February 8, 25, May 10, June 30, August 26, 1876, Washington, December 5, 1877, May 27, June 16, 1878, St. Louis, March 9, 1885, New York, October 9, November 27, 1887, Sherman to Eli Perry, Washington, February 18, 1873, Sherman to Admiral S. H. Stringham, Washington, April 3, 1873, Ellen Ewing Sherman to Vinnie Ream, Washington, January 2, 1873, Albert Pike to Vinnie Ream Hoxie, Washington, December 13, 1886, all in the Vinnie Ream Hoxie Collection, LC; Sherman to George M. Robeson, St. Louis, December 22, 1874, Sherman Papers, LC; Sherman to Virginia Farragut, Washington, August 4, 1874, Sherman Papers, Huntington. I would like to thank Charles Royster for pointing out the Vinnie Ream Hoxie papers at the Library of Congress.

[16] Sherman to Mary Audenreid, Washington, July 31, August 4, 1880, February 8, March 25, April 30 (twice), July 30, August 14, 15, October 3, 1881, July 11, August 20, 30, 1882, February 8, 19, 23, March 4, April 27, June 2, 1883, New York, June 6, 1883, St. Louis, November 20, 21, December 4, 18, 1883, January 2, February 11, 17, March 12, April 21, May 25, June 9, 21, 1884, Lake Minnetonka, Minnesota, August 10, 1884, St. Louis, November 26, 1884, New York, December 22, 1884, St. Louis, February 8, April 21, May 12, 21, 27, June 2, July 4, September 13, November 19, December 4, 1885, April 11, May 27, June 20, 21, 1888, San Francisco, August 2, 1886, St. Louis, September 29, 1886, New York, October 4, 18, November 30, December 29, 1886, February 8, October 4, 1887, February 10, April 5, November 1, 6, 15, December 7, 15, 1888, February 9, 25, March 21, April 17, May 17, June 10, July 25, September 11, October 4, 1889, January 20, March 25, June 25, November 5, 1890, Washington, December 30, 1890, all in Sherman Papers, LC; also, Sherman to S. H. M. Byers, Washington, August 1, 1880, S. H. M. Byers Papers, State Historical Society of Iowa; Sherman to James G. Blaine, Washington, February

21, 1883, James G. Blaine Papers, LC; Sherman to John E. Tourtelotte, New York, November 6, 1889, Sherman Papers, West Point.

20 Crisis of Patrimony: The Loss of Tom

[1] Sherman to James H. Hatchett, St. Louis, December 29, 1865, Sherman Papers, Haskell Collection, Clements Library, Ann Arbor; Eleanor Sherman Thackara to her Dear Papa, Boston, June 21, December 4, 1880, Philadelphia, October 17, 1881, June 6, October 28, 1882, February 15, 1883, February 8, 1890, Sherman to Mr. Thackara, Sr., Washington, June 25, 1881, all in Sherman-Thackara Collection, Villanova University Library; Sherman to R. M. Scott, St. Louis, October 23, 1884, Sherman Papers, Missouri Historical Society; Angela Ewing interview with Lloyd Lewis, n.d., n.p., quoted in Lewis, 628.

[2] Ellen to Sherman, Lancaster, October 9, 1859, May 1, 1860, April 29, 1862, ND.

[3] Sherman to Tommy, Memphis, October 4, 1863, on the reverse side of a printed letter to Captain C. C. Smith, of the Thirteenth Regulars, Sherman to Tom, Kingston, Georgia, November 10, 1864, Savannah, January 21, 1865, Goldsborough, North Carolina, April 9, 1865, all in ND.

[4] Sherman to Tom, Fort McKaveth, Texas, May 8, 1871, ND; Sherman to Ellen, Glasgow, August 25, 1872, HL, 384. Sherman's discussion of Grant's offer to Tom of a West Point appointment, and his consequent advice to his son, are in Sherman to General _____, Washington, April 11, 1873, Benham-McNeil Family Papers, LC. Sherman thought little of Fred Grant, who had followed his father into the army, and resented the way his old comrade pushed Fred's career in preferential ways. This might have contributed to his opposition to Tom following him into the army.

[5] Sherman to Tom, Cairo, Egypt, March 29, 1872, Washington, September 13, November 17, 1873, ND.

[6] Tom to Sherman, New Haven, November 15, 1875, [circa spring 1876], St. Louis, January 28, 1878, Sherman to Tom, Washington, September 24, 1875, April 6, 1876, Sherman to Ellen, Washington, March 3, 1877, all in ND; Sherman to Sheridan, St. Louis, October 30, 1874, Sheridan Papers, LC; Sherman to John, Washington, October 30, 1874, Sherman Papers, LC.

[7] Tom to Sherman, St. Louis, May 20, 25, 27, 1878; Tom to Minnie, New York, June 4, 1878, ND; Sherman to John, Washington, May 29, 1878; Sherman to Cardinal McClosky, Washington, June 3, 1878, Sherman Papers, LC; Sherman to Henry S. Turner, May 27, June 5, 28, July 7, 24,

1878, Sherman Papers, Ohio; Sherman to Major Henry Hitchcock, May 27, 1878, Sherman Papers, Missouri Historical Society; Sherman to John Schofield, May 28, 1878, Hiram Barney Papers, Huntington; Sherman to S. H. M. Byers, June 30, 1878, S. H. M. Byers Papers, State Historical Society of Iowa.

8 Ellen to Sherman, St. Louis, May 25, 1878, Ellen to Minnie, May 17, 21, 24, 25, 27, 30, 31, 1878, ND.

9 Elly to her Dear Mama, Washington, May 31, New York, June 1, Elly to her Dear Papa, West Point, June 6, Sherman to Elly [June 10], 1878, Sherman-Thackara Collection; Sherman to Minnie, June 16, 1878, Sherman Papers, Ohio.

10 Sherman to Minnie, Washington, July 11, 1878, Sherman Papers, Ohio; Sherman to Byers, June 30, 1878, Byers Papers; Ellen to Sherman, Lancaster, July 2, 1878, ND. At another level it was almost as if, at age twenty-one, Tom had come out of the closet and declared himself a homosexual, such was his father's consternation about Tom's refusal to become a "real man." This might have been a subtext for both father and son; Tom might have been a homosexual who used the priesthood as a means to evade the implications of that orientation.

11 U. S. Grant to Sherman, Ragatz, Switzerland, September 21, 1878, John Schofield to Sherman, West Point, May 29, 1878, Sherman Papers, LC; Sherman to Schofield, June 5, 1878, Hiram Barney Papers, Huntington.

12 Ellen to Sherman, Baltimore, December 21, 1878, Sherman to Ellen, Washington, December 22, 1878, Sherman to the Editor of the *Chicago Tribune,* Washington, October 27, 1878, ND; Sherman to Minnie, Washington, December 23, 1878, Sherman to Henry S. Turner, Washington, December 25, 1878, Sherman Papers, Ohio.

13 Adam Badeau to Sherman, London, August 2, November 14, 1878, Sherman Papers, LC; Note written by Rachel Sherman Thorndike, n.d., n.p., appended to a letter of Sherman to Ellen, Washington, August 24, 1880, Tom to Minnie, Washington, August 26, 1880, ND; Sherman to Turner, Washington, August 25, 1880, Sherman Papers, Ohio.

14 Sherman to Byers, Washington, January 2, 1881, Byers Papers; Sherman to Mary Audenreid, St. Louis, April 2, 1885, Sherman Papers, LC.

15 Tom to Sherman, Detroit, January 6, October 30, 1886, from the *Umbria,* August 6, 1890, ND. Unfortunately Sherman's letters to Tom from this period were not preserved, so one cannot know how the father responded to the son.

16 "Notes on Father Sherman," collected by Rev. Joseph Hamilton, ND. For a full discussion of Tom Sherman's tragic life, see the aptly titled *General Sherman's Son: The Life of Thomas Ewing Sherman, SJ,* by Joseph T.

Durkin, SJ (New York: Farrar, Strauss and Cudahy, 1959). Durkin's book is marked by compassion for the terrible pain of Tom's long depression, a sensitivity that also characterized the way in which the Jesuits treated their mad brother. The book is marred, however, by its McCarthyite polemics: Durkin used Tom Sherman as an early anti-Communist crusader of the ilk Durkin admired explicitly.

21 Celebration and Reconciliation

[1] Sherman to Mary C. Day, St. Louis, February 23, 1884, Andre de Coppet Collection, Princeton University Library; Sherman to Ellen, Santa Fe, September 16, 1883, HL, 391–92; Sherman to Elly, St. Louis, February 12, 1884, Sherman Papers, Ohio.

[2] Sherman to John, Washington, June 7, 1883, New York, January 13, 1888, Sherman Papers, LC; Sherman to R. M. Scott, St. Louis, July 5, 1884, Sherman Papers, Missouri Historical Society; Sherman to Elly, St. Louis, July 10, 1884, Sherman Papers, Ohio; Sherman to Mrs. O. M. Poe, St. Louis, December 23, 1885, O. M. Poe Papers, LC.

[3] Sherman to Elly, St. Louis, May 25, December 24, 1884, Sherman Papers, Ohio; Sherman to William F. Vilas, New York, May 19, 1888, William F. Vilas Papers, State Historical Society of Wisconsin. Also see Sherman to Phil Sheridan, Philadelphia, December 29, 1884, Sheridan Papers, LC.

[4] Sherman to Ellen, Santa Fe, September 16, 1883, HL, 391; Sherman to Elly, Santa Fe, September 16, 1883, Sherman Papers, Ohio; Sherman to John, St. Louis, January 19, 1886, New York, August 7, 1888, Sherman Papers, LC; Sherman to J. C. Tourtelotte, New York, February 6, 1888, September 4, 1890; Philemon T. Sherman to his Mother, New Haven, June 22, 1887, ND; Philemon to his Father, New Haven, February 18, 1888, Philemon to Elly, May 29, 1891, June 15, 1892, Sherman-Thackara Papers, Villanova University Library.

[5] Ellen to Sherman, Philadelphia, April 4, 1887, Woodstock, New York, August 20, 1888, Rosemont, Pennsylvania, September 22, 1888; Sherman to Ellen, New York, June 19, 1887, ND.

[6] Sherman to Vilas, New York, December 5, 1888, Vilas Papers; Sherman to Alexander McDowell McCook, New York, December 10, 1888, McCook Family Papers, LC.

[7] Sherman to Mary A. Draper, New York, March 16, 1887, January 25, March 25, April 17, 21, July 21, December 6, 8, 1889, January 3, 28, February 11, 21, April 10, October 11, 21, November 19, 1890, January 3, 1891, Henry Draper Papers, New York Public Library.

[8] Sherman to Mrs. Andrew Carnegie, New York, February 9, 1890, Carnegie Autograph Collection, New York Public Library.

[9] Sherman to Joseph E. Johnston, New York, January 5, 1891, Sherman Papers, LC. Logan's speech of February 1883, his letter of February 18, and Sherman's letter to him of February 11, are all reprinted in Grenville M. Dodge, *Personal Recollections of President Abraham Lincoln, General U. S. Grant and General W. T. Sherman* (1914; Reprinted, Denver: Sage Books, 1965), 160–67.

[10] Charles Rhodes to his Mother, June 13, 1889, John M. Wilson to O. O. Howard, February 18, 1891, both quoted in Ambrose, *Duty, Honor, Country*, 200–201.

[11] Sherman to Governor Elect C. N. Humphrey, New York, December 26, 1888, Sherman Papers, LC; Sherman to John Jay, Washington, May 24, 1883, Jay Family Papers, Columbia University Library.

[12] Sherman to C. C. Augur, St. Louis, June 27, 1884, C. C. Augur Papers, Illinois State Historical Library; Sherman to Fred Cochran, St. Louis, September 27, 1884, Sherman Papers, Haskell Collection, Clements Library, Ann Arbor; Sherman to May _____, St. Louis, May 27, 1886, Diedrich Collection, Clements; Sherman to S. H. M. Byers, New York, May 1, 1887, S. H. M. Byers Papers, State Historical Society of Iowa; Sherman to Hiram Hitchcock, New York, July 27, 1887, Haskell Collection; Sherman to Ellen, New York, August 8, 1887, HL, 399.

[13] Sherman, "Grant, Thomas, Lee," *North American Review*, CXLIV (May 1887), 437–50. As early as August 11, 1873, Sherman had insisted, "we must contend historically that General Lee knew better but did worse; that his is not a safe model for the imitation of youth, save in his personal morals and courage." Letter to William T. Manford, Manford-Ellis Family Papers, Duke.

[14] Sherman to Murat Halstead, Washington, March 10, 1879, Sherman Papers, West Point; Sherman to Rev. W. G. Eliot, Washington, May 26, 1879, Sherman to John, St. Louis, September 15, October 14, December 22, 1885, New York, April 1, November 8, 1888, February 28, 1890, Sherman to James G. Blaine, St. Louis, September 28, 1885, Sherman to Allen T. Rice, New York, November 14, 1888, all in Sherman Papers, LC; Sherman, "Old Shady, With a Moral," *North American Review*, CXLVII (October 1888), 361–68; "Grant, Thomas and Lee," 439.

[15] Sherman, *Annual Report of the General of the Army* (1882) (Washington, D.C.: Government Printing Office, 1883), 32; Sherman, *Annual Report* (1883) (Washington, D.C.: Government Printing Office, 1884), 45–48; Sherman to Mrs. General Custer, New York, January 24, 1889, Sherman to John, Washington, February 28, 1882, New York, September 6, 1887,

Sherman Papers, LC; Sherman, *Memoirs*, 2nd ed., II, 457. Several of these quotes appear in the excellent summing-up chapter in Athearn, *William T. Sherman and the Settlement of the West*, 334–49.

[16] "Possible Presidents: General William T. Sherman," *North American Review*, CXLVI (April 1888), 416–23; Augustus Saint-Gaudens, *Reminiscences* (New York: Century, 1913), 378–83. Saint-Gaudens completed the bust in 1892, and went on to create the magnificent equestrian monument of Sherman in the Grand Army Plaza in New York. See John H. Dryfhout, *The Works of Augustus Saint-Gaudens* (Hanover, N.H.: University Press of New England, 1982), 168, 253–56. For another pen portrait of the elderly Sherman see Alexander K. McClure, *Recollections of Half a Century* (Salem, Mass.: Salem Publishing, 1902), 336–40. I would like to thank Wanda Corn for pointing out these references to Saint-Gaudens.

[17] Sherman to John, February 4, 1891, John to the Editor of *The New York Times*, New York, February 17, 1891, Sherman Papers, LC. John dictated this letter at his brother's house, on his brother's stationery, to James G. Burrett, his brother's secretary. On Sherman's death and funeral also see Lewis, 650–53, and Marszalek, 490–99.

Index